INTERNATIONAL MANAGEMENT AND ECONOMIC DEVELOPMENT

McGRAW-HILL SERIES IN MANAGEMENT

KEITH DAVIS   Consulting Editor

ALLEN   Management and Organization

ALLEN   The Management Profession

ARGYRIS   Management and Organizational Development: The Path from XA to YB

BECKETT   Management Dynamics: The New Synthesis

BENNIS   Changing Organizations

BENTON   Supervision and Management

BERGEN AND HANEY   Organizational Relations and Management Action

BLOUGH   International Business: Environment and Adaptation

BOWMAN   Management: Organization and Planning

BROWN   Judgment in Administration

CAMPBELL, DUNNETTE, LAWLER, AND WEICK   Managerial Behavior, Performance, and Effectiveness

CLELAND AND KING   Management: A Systems Approach

CLELAND AND KING   Systems Analysis and Project Management

CLELAND AND KING   Systems, Organizations, Analysis, Management: A Book of Readings

DALE   Management: Theory and Practice

DALE   Readings in Management: Landmarks and New Frontiers

DAVIS   Human Behavior at Work: Human Relations and Organizational Behavior

DAVIS AND BLOMSTROM   Business, Society, and Environment: Social Power and Social Response

DAVIS AND SCOTT   Human Relations and Organizational Behavior: Readings and Comments

DE GREENE   Systems Psychology

DUNN AND RACHEL   Wage and Salary Administration: Total Compensation Systems

DUNN AND STEPHENS   Management of Personnel: Manpower Management and Organizational Behavior

FIEDLER   A Theory of Leadership Effectiveness

FLIPPO   Principles of Personnel Management

GLUECK   Business Policy: Strategy Formation and Management Action

GOLEMBIEWSKI   Men, Management, and Morality

HICKS   The Management of Organizations: A Systems and Human Resources Approach

JOHNSON, KAST, AND ROSENZWEIG   The Theory and Management of Systems

KAST AND ROSENZWEIG   Organization and Management: A Systems Approach

KOONTZ   Toward a Unified Theory of Management

KOONTZ AND O'DONNELL   Principles of Management: An Analysis of Managerial Functions

KOONTZ AND O'DONNELL   Management: A Book of Readings

LEVIN, McLAUGHLIN, LAMONE, AND KOTTAS   Production/Operations Management: Contemporary Policy for Managing Operating Systems

LUTHANS   Contemporary Readings in Organizational Behavior

McDONOUGH   Information Economics and Management Systems

McNICHOLS   Policy Making and Executive Action

MAIER   Problem-solving Discussions and Conferences: Leadership Methods and Skills

MARGULIES AND RAIA   Organizational Development: Values, Process, and Technology

MAYER   Production Management

MUNDEL   A Conceptual Framework for the Management Sciences

PETIT   The Moral Crisis in Management

PETROF, CARUSONE, AND McDAVID   Small Business Management: Concepts and Techniques for Improving Decisions

PIGORS AND PIGORS   Case Method in Human Relations

PRASOW AND PETERS   Arbitration and Collective Bargaining: Conflict Resolution in Labor Relations

READY   The Administrator's Job

REDDIN   Managerial Effectiveness

RICHMAN AND COPEN   International Management and Economic Development

SALTONSTALL   Human Relations in Administration

SARTAIN AND BAKER   The Supervisor and His Job

SCHRIEBER, JOHNSON, MEIER, FISCHER, AND NEWELL   Cases in Manufacturing Management

SHULL, D'ELBECQ, AND CUMMINGS   Organizational Decision Making

STEINER   Managerial Long-range Planning

SUTERMEISTER   People and Productivity

TANNENBAUM   Control in Organizations

TANNENBAUM, WESCHLER, AND MASSARIK   Leadership and Organization

VANCE   Industrial Administration

VANCE   Management Decision Simulation

INTERNATIONAL MANAGEMENT AND ECONOMIC DEVELOPMENT

WITH PARTICULAR REFERENCE TO INDIA AND OTHER DEVELOPING COUNTRIES

BARRY M. RICHMAN
Professor of Management and
International Business
University of California
Los Angeles, California

MELVYN COPEN
Director of the Office of
Management Improvement
U.S. Department of Agriculture

McGRAW-HILL BOOK COMPANY

New York   St. Louis   San Francisco   Düsseldorf   Johannesburg
Kuala Lumpur   London   Mexico   Montreal   New Delhi
Panama   Rio de Janeiro   Singapore   Sydney   Toronto

**INTERNATIONAL MANAGEMENT
AND ECONOMIC DEVELOPMENT**

1234567890KPKP798765432

Library of Congress Cataloging in Publication Data

Richman, Barry M
  International management and economic development.

  (McGraw-Hill series in management)
  1. International business enterprises. 2. Technical
assistance. 3. Economic development. 4. Industrial management—India. I. Copen, Melvyn, joint author. II. Title.
HD69.17R53   658.1'8   72-631
ISBN 0-07-052341-X

This book was set in Univers by Allen Wayne Technical Corp.
The editor was Richard F. Dojny;
the designer was Allen Wayne Technical Corp.;
and the production supervisor was Alice Cohen.

The printer and binder was Kingsport Press, Inc.

CONTENTS

Preface   vii

PART 1   INTRODUCTION AND CONCEPTUAL FRAMEWORK

1   Introduction   3

2   Conceptual Framework   21

PART 2   ENVIRONMENT

3   Educational Environment   65

4   Sociological-Cultural Environment   98

5   Political-Legal Environment   181

6   Economic Environment   234

7   International Environment   302

v

PART 3   THE MULTINATIONAL CORPORATION

8   The Multinational Corporation: Bridge or Barrier to Development?   361

9   Management of Multinational Corporations   375

PART 4   ENTERPRISE MANAGEMENT, OPERATIONS AND PERFORMANCE ABROAD

10   Overview of Management and Performance   405

11   Planning and Innovation   431

12   Control   451

13   Organization   470

14   Staffing and Personnel   494

15   Direction, Leadership, and Motivation   519

16   Union-Management Relations   537

17   Government Relations   560

18   Production   565

19   Procurement and Imports   596

20   Research and Development   614

21   Marketing and Exports   620

22   Finance   641

23   Conclusion   650

Index   665

PREFACE

This has been a difficult and time-consuming book to write, not only because of its length, but also because of its scope and aims, its aspirations, and its depth. We have attempted to do a truly interdisciplinary study using a comprehensive systems approach which has both significant and broad theoretical and empirical relevance.

We have used a broad conceptual framework which focuses on critical and strategic factors of both a macro and micro nature. Within this framework we have tried to integrate the fields of comparative and international management, general management theory and policy, international business, and economic development. To do this we have had to deal with a wide range of environmental factors—educational, sociological-cultural, political, legal, economic, and international—in addition to the basic and universal managerial and enterprise (or productive) functions. In essence, the study attempts to consider in a relatively balanced and meaningful way both public and private policy issues of profound and widespread importance in the world.

In order to strengthen both the theoretical and applied contributions that this book hopefully offers, we have presented numerous examples, a great deal of concrete data, and many policy implications, suggestions, and recommendations. We have attempted to remedy some of the failings found in many books in this subject area by broadening the field of study, working within a strong conceptual framework, and offering practical suggestions for the application of our theories.

We have based this book on many years of research in the field, as well as countless secondary sources. Extensive firsthand research was undertaken in both the United States and India. We have also done research and other kinds of work in over two dozen other countries for more limited periods. These include nearly a dozen Latin American nations, Communist China, the Soviet Union, Czechoslovakia, Poland, Japan, Taiwan, Hong Kong, Israel, Lebanon, Canada, and several countries in Western Europe. Our colleague and good friend Professor Richard Farmer, of Indiana University, who was a principal collaborator in the development of the conceptual framework used here, has done firsthand research and/or worked in Saudi Arabia, Egypt, Lebanon, Syria, Kuwait, and several Latin American countries. His findings and experiences have contributed much to this book. The same is true of the ten or so doctoral dissertations, involving field research in a variety of foreign countries, completed by our former doctoral students.

We hope this book will be of interest and benefit to a wide variety of scholars, students, and practitioners, as well as many other people who are concerned about the major problems it treats. The book is likely to be of greatest interest to people in the areas of management, international business, economic development, government planning and policy formulation, and Indian studies. Because of its interdisciplinary and comparative emphasis, it may also be of value to many people in such fields as sociology, psychology, anthropology, education, law, political science, international organization, economics in general, various branches of business administration, and regional or area studies involving developing countries other than India. Since the study links and integrates macro-environmental factors with micro considerations involving firms and their managers, it may provide new insights for readers who have had only either a relatively strong micro or macro orientation.

For instructional purposes, this book can be used along with a wide range of case studies available through the Intercollegiate Case Clearing House administered by the Harvard Business School, or with case studies found in many case books. In particular, *Incidents in International Business*, written by Professor Richard Farmer, contains short cases built around the same basic conceptual framework we applied.

Because a very large number of people and organizations have contributed significantly to this book, it is impossible for us to thank them all individually. We do, however, greatly appreciate the time, cooperation, frankness—often involving sensitive and confidential matters—and hospitality extended to us by so many people at so many enterprises, government agencies, educational institutions, and other organizations in all of the countries in which we have conducted research.

We owe a special word of thanks to two former research assistants who helped us considerably and effectively in connection with this book. They are Surendra Mansinghka and Vinay Gupta. We would also like to thank Dr. Francis Masson of the U.S. Agency for International Development, Dr. Marshall Robinson of the Ford Foundation, and Professor Morton Grossman of Harvard University.

We would like to acknowledge the outstanding support provided in the preparation of this manuscript by Linda Copen and Vivian Richman (whose contributions extended far, far beyond just preparation), as well as Charlene Moore and Barbara Bray. Helen Schwartz of UCLA also deserves special mention for the wonderful job she has done in coordinating and participating in the typing and collating of the various drafts of our massive manuscript. We also appreciate the typing done by individuals at the Center for the Study of Democratic Institutions, as well as the other facilities provided by the Center.

Finally, we want to express our sincere gratitude to a number of institutions for their truly indispensable roles—financial and otherwise—in making most of our research and the emergence of this book possible. They are the Ford Foundation, the University of California at Los Angeles, the Massachusetts Institute of Technology, Harvard University, the University of Houston, the Institute for International Education, the United States Agency for International Development, and the Indian Institutes of Management at Calcutta and Ahmedabad.

Barry M. Richman
Melvyn Copen

PART 1
INTRODUCTION AND CONCEPTUAL FRAMEWORK

CHAPTER1
INTRODUCTION

I don't give a damn. We have a schedule to meet, and I am not going to postpone the start of a new piece of equipment just because the stars aren't right. If the workers want to honor the spirits of the machine, they'll have to do it on their own time. That machine represents a substantial investment and a great deal of effort, and I am not going to have it sit idle because of some religious superstition. Every hour we lose costs us money.

Sometimes you just can't figure things. When we started operations, we decided to give yearly increments to our workforce on the basis of merit. We did this for two years. A few people did not get increases, but most received substantial raises. Our supervisors liked the system, but the workers and union objected and finally, after a serious strike threat, we changed to the local custom of fixed increments for all hourly workers. While we used the merit system, the yearly increments averaged just under ten percent of our payroll. Now it averages six percent. Yet the workers seem happier with this method. It just doesn't make sense.

Our biggest problem is securing a steady supply of acceptable quality raw materials. Local suppliers are expensive and unreliable, and their quality leaves much to be desired. Imported materials require long lead times, and their availability is subject to the whims of the government import-licensing authorities. We are continually scrambling through fire-fighting techniques to keep our production operations going and to supply our marketing people with the merchandise they need, when they need it.

> Ours is primarily a marketing and distribution function. Our primary task is to encourage and assist with the establishment of local distributors. These distributors need a great deal of help and guidance, but my local staff cannot seem to handle this task effectively. They would rather socialize, or lecture, than work with the distributor and his problems. I have a lot of good men with high potential in my organization, but it never seems to develop. As a result, I'm having to bring two men in from the States to staff my number two and three positions. There are just no nationals to whom I can entrust the responsibility.

These statements were made by top managers of U.S. subsidiaries in developing nations in Asia, Africa and Latin America. They are representative of basic kinds of problems encountered in the transference of U.S. management know-how to less developed environments. Each of the difficulties described could have been alleviated or eliminated, had these managers been more adept in effecting the transfer. The walkout which ensued in the first case, and the less-than-cordial labor relations which evolved from the protracted dispute in the second were largely the results of transferences of managerial patterns which were incompatible with and unacceptable to the local environments. Both incidents relate attempts to graft U.S. values and practices to environments basically hostile and unprepared to accept them. Rejection was the result. The latter two examples are indicative of a second type of problem area — the failure to utilize managerial techniques (in these cases, relating to supplier and managerial development) which could have been transferred with relatively little effort but were not. These incidents along with numerous others will be examined in more depth during the course of the book.

The keystone of the research upon which much of this book is based is the hypothesis that much — but by no means all — of the management know-how developed and applied in U.S. industry can be effective and is needed in developing economics (in many cases, in somewhat modified form), and that there is a systematic method which can be used to identify and effect a successful transfer of these practices. Too often, the problems of operating in developing nations are created or augmented by the failure to apply managerial practices commonly used within U.S. domestic operations. On the other hand, in many other situations, problems are created by trying to force a "square" technique into a "round" hole in the environment. The first situation results in lower degrees of operational efficiencies within the firm, while the second amplifies conflicts between the firm and its host environment.

Corollary to the above hypothesis, the manager who is best prepared to blend U.S. practices with the needs and nature of the local foreign environment will be the most successful. This has broad implications for the selection and training of personnel at all levels in the subsidiary.

We use the term management "know-how" to mean the implementation of managerial skill, and not only the mere possession of such skill. It includes managerial processes, practices, concepts, policies, techniques, tools and methods. For the sake of brevity, we shall often use only one of these terms when referring to managerial know-how or skill. For example, we may refer only to managerial practices, processes or techniques when various other aspects of management are also involved or implied.

This book focuses largely on the applicability and transferability of U.S. management know-how to foreign environments, especially in developing countries such as India. While the study deals primarily with the Indian experience, it has broad applicability to other developing and underdeveloped nations. The methodology utilized also has relevance for developed countries.

There is a subtle difference in our use of the terms transferability and applicability. We generally use the term transferability when considering management process transferences by an international or multinational company to its foreign subsidiaries or affiliates. For example, a U.S. firm may desire that its subsidiaries abroad make use of contingency planning, greater decentralization of authority, or the discounted cash flow concept in investment decisions.

We use the term applicability in the following ways. First, in connection with whether such a desired or attempted transference is applicable in the foreign environment; that is, does it yield the desired results. We also use the term applicability when a management process transference per se is not involved, but where the indigenous organization — rather than a foreign affiliate — desires or attempts to manage in certain ways that are basically foreign and relatively uncommon in the local environment.

To analyze the transferability and applicability of management know-how, it is necessary to identify and analyze critical environmental constraints bearing on managerial performance and productive efficiency. The environment in this study is analyzed in terms of four broad categories or classes of factors: 1) educational, 2) sociological-cultural, 3) political-legal, and 4) economic. This takes us beyond the limited sphere usually ascribed to international business and comparative management and into the broader and related spheres of economic development and industrial progress which are also of major interest in this book.

There are many similarities between the managerial know-how transference process and the biological mechanisms at work in the area of medical organ transplants, and it is useful to think of the process in terms of the analogous biological system. The local environment can be considered as the host body and the U.S. managerial techniques and practices the organs to be transplanted. A successful transplant requires a thorough understanding of the nature of the two organisms involved; the host, and the donor.

Great care must be exercised in anticipating rejection mechanisms. The established traditions, institutions and environment of the host society represent the antibodies which fight the intruder. In some cases, a transplant should not be attempted because the metabolic life processes of the host have already made the best adaptation to the conditions which affect it. In other cases, the success of the transplant is dependent upon careful preparation of the host and the new organ to make them compatible. In still other cases, such as a blood transfusion, it is possible to find almost "universals" which, once identified, can be transplanted with a minimum of adjustment. The success of the operation will be highly dependent upon the careful research of the doctor and his understanding of the factors which affect the transfer. The more vital or sensitive the area, the more difficult this process is likely to be.

This same situation faces the U.S. company in a developing nation. The local environment is both alive and different from that of the United States. It will respond to virtually any new stimuli. Often, the tasks required for effective management of industrial enterprises are foreign to the environment almost by definition: the host is a less developed country because it lacks the resources, skills, attitudes, institutions and practices necessary to spawn and maintain an advanced industrial society. The introduction of such practices requires change and adaptation, and man, regardless of his geographic domicile, seems to be characterized by an inherent resistance to change. Only by obtaining a thorough understanding of the interacting environments can a manager successfully facilitate the transference. He requires this knowledge to select the appropriate practices and to adapt them to form an effective fit.

Since the local environment has such an important influence on the management of foreign subsidiaries, it follows that multinational management and control systems must provide enough flexibility for individual country operations to adjust their practices so that they achieve an adequate degree of harmony with the local environment. At the same time, this must be done without destroying the communications links, and some of the critical controls which the international parent must exercise as it views the totality of operations.

The degree of success or failure a company experiences, the respect its image receives in local eyes, and the satisfaction obtained by its employees will be directly related to the effectiveness of the blend between U.S. managerial practices and local environmental conditions. A successful adaptation (both in employing the techniques available and applicable — albeit often in modified form — and in adjusting practices to local customs where necessary) is requisite for the conduct of effective and efficient operations.

We are therefore concerned with an analysis of the environment, the goals which it is reasonable for a firm to seek, the managerial practices which appear to be necessary to reach the objectives, and the skills required of the executives who must achieve the blend. This is not an easy task, since the number of variables is almost endless, and combinations and permutations which are possible are so great that a haphazard approach will be both overly time-consuming and unwieldy. To facilitate such an analysis, much of the book is organized according to a conceptual framework developed by one of the authors and a colleague.[1] This provides a logical and structured approach to focus on strategic factors and determine priorities in a meaningful way. An outline of this framework is presented in the following chapter.

It should be apparent that a critical assumption underlies the entire study — that industrialization of less-developed nations is both necessary and desirable. The degree and areas of industrialization are debatable subjects, but the economic advancement of less developed countries does require marshalling of resources, both physical and intellectual, to promote industrial activity. We believe that many of the managerial values, techniques, practices, policies, and concepts developed in the more advanced industrial world are highly useful within developing nations for accelerating this process. Therefore, by facilitating this transference and enabling companies from developed nations to better adapt to local environments, those environments will be strengthened. Furthermore, the economic performance of industrial enterprises — indigenous as well as foreign — will be improved. It is primarily for these reasons that this book has been written.

BASIC AIMS OF THE BOOK

The basic aims of this study can best be stated in point form as follows:

1. To develop answers to key questions of transferability in the fields of international business, comparative management, and economic development. These questions are: to what extent and degree can managerial approaches which tend to be effective in one country, especially the United States, be transferred and applied successfully in another, particularly a developing nation such as India? To what degree does the environment in a given foreign country, such as India, seriously constrain or prevent such transferences and applications? What are the costs involved in management know-how transferences? (The point about costs is significant; many things may be transferable but the costs, including time, may be prohibitive vis-a-vis derived benefits.)

2. To identify, describe, explain, and predict the impact that critical environmental constraints (i.e. given conditions) which are largely beyond the control of individual enterprises, tend to have on managerial performance and productive efficiency in developing countries.

3. To help develop prescriptive guidelines that can serve as a basis for effective action by the managements of enterprises — both foreign and indigenous — in their attempts to reduce the impact of negative environmental constraints on performance.

4. To aid companies in making better foreign investment and foreign collaboration decisions by providing a comprehensive conceptual framework, related methodologies, and deeper insights into critical variables and their interrelationships.

5. To formulate prescriptive guidelines, for India in particular and developing countries in general, that indicate what priority actions might best be taken in dealing with environmental constraints which substantially hinder managerial effectiveness and productive efficiency.

6. To link managerial and firm performance to industrial progress and economic development on a macro-scale within a total system framework of analysis.

While not an aim of this book, our conceptual framework and related approaches can and are being applied to managerial problems within the United States in such areas as urban development, poverty, and minority business enterprise.

BASIC APPROACHES

Along with the above six broad aims, our book utilizes two basic research approaches or focuses; the macro approach and, the micro approach. The macro approach is concerned primarily with aims 1, 2, 5 and 6, as cited above. The micro approach is primarily concerned with aims 1, 2, 3 and 4. Both approaches utilize the same conceptual framework discussed in Chapter 2.

The macro approach deals with dominant or at least relatively widespread patterns of managerial and firm performance.[2] Empirically, analysis by industrial categories seems to be the most feasible focus for macro studies of this type, although generalizations which emerge about patterns found in a given country's overall industrial sector are often meaningful. With this macro emphasis, management philosophy, the personalities and skills of individual managers, and the management process itself are treated as dependent variables, and viewed chiefly as products of the country's environment. Here we deal with hypothetical, representative dominant types of managers and firms. The dominant macro-managerial personalities and management philosophies prevailing in a given country tend to be shaped largely by educational and sociological-cultural environmental forces.

With the micro approach, individual managers and firms are given personalities, and the management process is treated in a partially independent manner — i.e., not only determined by uncontrollable or given environmental forces, but also by independent managerial action. In fact, educational and sociological-cultural environmental factors are treated in a micro way as partially internal to individual firms, instead of constraints wholly beyond the control of firms. In this way it is possible to focus on problems of transferability and applicability, and to develop prescriptive guidelines for independent managerial action aimed at reducing the impact of negative environmental constraints. This is the major focus of this book.

POTENTIAL CONTRIBUTIONS OF THIS STUDY

A better understanding of the critical factors involved in transferring and successfully applying U.S. management know-how to developing countries has an impact on four major areas. The first relates to enhancing the performance of U.S. — and other foreign — subsidiaries and affiliates abroad; the second to improving operations of indigenous firms, especially in developing countries; the third for creating environments more conducive to economic development; and the fourth concerns U.S.

foreign policy and upgrading the U.S. image abroad. This book has been written in the hope of positively advancing all of the above areas.

ECONOMIC PERFORMANCE OF U.S. SUBSIDIARIES ABROAD

U.S. international companies have very substantial investments and earn substantial profits in developing countries.[3] They desire to nourish and protect both existing investments and the already large, but potentially vast, markets which many such countries afford. As of the early 1970s, total U.S. investment abroad is around $150 billion, nearly 500 percent greater than in 1950. The total value of U.S. direct private foreign investment now exceeds $70 billion, compared with less than $12 billion in 1950 and $33 billion in 1960. The growth of direct private foreign investment has been much greater than the growth of the American economy, and such investment now amounts to about 7 percent of U.S. GNP. The volume of such investment is, in fact, greater than the total GNP of all but a few of the most advanced countries in the world. The total annual sales of U.S. subsidiaries abroad are currently estimated at more than $225 billion, or the equivalent of more than 20 percent total United States GNP. This compares with total annual U.S. exports of only $35 to $40 billion.[4]

Although less developed countries still account for under 40% of the United States' direct private foreign investment, the rate of investment in such countries has been substantially higher than in advanced nations in recent times. An examination of net earnings figures of U.S. direct private foreign investment further accentuates the role of such investments in developing nations. In the last several years over 50 percent of total overseas earnings have been derived from these parts of the world — Asia, Africa, Latin America, the Mid-East, and the poorer countries in Europe. Moreover, the average return on U.S. investment for all developing areas has been two to three times greater than for the relatively advanced regions.

The above figures reflect the magnitude of the tremendous stake which U.S. business has abroad, and the increasing importance of developing countries in this regard. Any steps which improve the effectiveness of these operations will strengthen the positions of both individual firms and the American economy.

A final point relates to the stability of U.S. operations in developing nations vis-a-vis political and emotional reactions to foreign business operations. The spirit of nationalism which pervades many of the developing nations cannot be underestimated. The close ties between unions and political parties which exist in many of these countries bring the issues right into the hearts of companies. Often the issues are purely emotional in nature, and even though nationalistic sentiments may result in outcries for actions which are not in the best interests of the nation, they do represent the sentiments of large numbers of people at the time. Governments, often for reasons of self-preservation, are forced to react to these clamors. The short-run goal of survival becomes much more pressing than the long-run goals of economic development and progress.

Foreign companies can easily find themselves at the focal point of such reactions, solely because of their nationality. Actions taken by these firms which are abrasive to local customs can seriously influence the situation. Probably the only defense available to a foreign firm is good corporate citizenship, and this requires careful attention to living with the rules and values of local society. This does not mean that companies must be content to accept the environment, but that they must be sensitive enough to be able to introduce necessary changes with as little friction as possible.

OPERATIONS OF INDIGENOUS COMPANIES ABROAD

The value of U.S. know-how to indigenous firms is almost self-evident. These are companies which are already familiar with the environment, and therefore subject to fewer of the pressures and uncertainties experienced by foreign firms. However, they are products of the local environment, and as such, often lack the skills, talents, attitudes and motivation necessary to conduct efficient industrial activity. If they can secure information and knowledge about U.S. techniques and practices, and can break enough with past traditions to embrace some of the Western goals and values commonly associated with these practices, they can make extremely rapid gains for their country and themselves. The transfer process has a great deal to offer them, as can be witnessed by the strong desire of many firms in developing countries to establish collaborative ventures and to hire U.S.-trained nationals.

CREATION OF AN ENVIRONMENT MORE CONDUCIVE TO ECONOMIC DEVELOPMENT

Significant macro or national policy implications for industrial progress and overall economic development can emerge through identifying and analyzing those environmental factors or constraints which tend to have a negative impact on managerial and firm performance. All too often, relatively poor countries striving for rapid development gains go about this enormous task in haphazard, unstructured, and hence ineffective ways. They fail to properly identify and effectively deal with critical relationships between environmental constraints, the way that the management process is performed at the firm level, and operating results. We feel that our conceptual framework and approaches will enable developing nations to do a better job in these areas, particularly in creating more favorable conditions for the transferability and applicability of substantially more effective management know-how.

U.S. FOREIGN POLICY AND THE U.S. IMAGE

Finally, any improvement in the effectiveness of foreign subsidiaries and indigenous companies through the transfer of U.S. managerial know-how strengthens the position of the free enterprise system, or at least strengthens respect for the western way of life. To many people in developing countries, "free enterprise," "capitalism," "socialism" and "communism" are just words — but words which carry a high degree of emotional impact. Most of these people (the masses) have seen "exploitation" of the type Marx attributed to capitalism. Most have living standards so remote from those of the United States that the claims for U.S. capitalism seem clearly impossible. They cannot conceive of workers owning cars, television sets, and air conditioners. Many cannot even realistically aspire to living in houses with roofs over their heads. On the other hand, they have seen exploitive capitalism at work within their own countries. Many movies, their primary contact with the United States, either show cowboys riding the range or gangsters shooting it out in Chicago during prohibition days. The impression that the United States is only a dream and that capitalism means exploitation is not dispelled.

Many live in dire poverty under governments which profess to be moving ahead through free enterprise or socialistic systems, or a combination of both. Recent changes have awakened them to the potential the world has to offer. These people are ripe targets for agitators and opposition political movements, many of which, especially the communists, have been effective in using this opportunity. When people are discontent, promises of glowing futures, although perhaps incapable of fulfillment, are more desirable than the status quo.

The U.S. government, along with the governments of developing countries, at times attempts to counteract these activities by publicizing the "American or Western way of life." But these are vague words. The masses are living, and things actually happening around them leave a greater impression than words directed at them by some political entity. Here is where U.S. business and U.S. management know-how play a vital role, and anything which can be done to enhance this role assists in the process of development, and often in the creation of a better U.S. image as well.

U.S. foreign subsidiaries are living examples of the free enterprise system. Whether they desire to do so or not, they serve as ambassadors of this ideology. Their affect is not confined solely to their employees. Their every move is analyzed in detail by local government agencies, political and labor leaders, newspaper editors, and the public. Their actions are contrasted with the activities of indigenous and other foreign firms, and the examples they set are seen as representative of the methods, values and principles upon which the free enterprise system is built. Every time a charge of exploitation can be justified, that system is torn down a bit, and every time the activities of these subsidiaries further the cause of the host nation, that system is enhanced.

A company can go too far in trying to avoid conflict and end up by accomplishing little. The adage "you cannot have progress without friction" is probably more true in the international situation than anywhere else. It is not friction per se which is to be avoided. It is rather a question of the degree of friction and its ultimate ends which must be considered. A company may act with the best of motives, but unless these are understood and approved, difficulties result. Again, the process of transference and accommodation is important. The more effective U.S. companies are in identifying and applying useful managerial know-how to operations in developing nations and in effecting a smooth transfer, the more impressive an example of the free enterprise system they will present. U.S. industry can be a very effective tool, not of the U.S. State Department, but of the basic ideology which has led to the nation's industrial might.

Scope of the study and sources of information

The problems encountered in managing business enterprises in different developing nations have many similarities. Resources are scarce and often numerous government controls and regulations are imposed in an effort to promote uniform economic development. Communications, transportation and other elements of the infrastructure are in rudimentary stages and often human skills and attitudes required for the efficient conduct and dynamic expansion of industry are scarce or lacking. Developed markets are small and frequently ancillary industries are non-existent. Added to this, the low aspirational levels of the populace impede the process of development. Although each nation (and often each region or individual section of one country) is different from every other, many management problems are similar. Consequently, many managerial approaches and problems relate to all of these environments. Furthermore, uniform methods of analysis can be employed to ferret out key environmental variations which call for differences in treatment of problems.

The geographic focus of this book is India. The book examines salient features of the environment of this nation and the managerial problems faced by industry within it. References and examples will be used from other developing countries, but the primary focus is an in-depth probe of the Indian experience.

In many ways, India is an ideal subject for an examination of the transferability of managerial know-how. There, business enterprises are confronted with most of the problems encountered in developing nations, many in extreme form. These range from the imposition of strong governmental controls on industry to the fatalistic attitudes that pervade the fabric of India's predominantly Hindu society. They show up in extreme over-population and unbalanced income distribution. The dominant feelings and attitudes of the population, the political nature of local labor unions, the nonalignment policies of the government, the relatively huge government bureaucracy which has evolved, strong sellers' markets, critically scarce foreign exchange, and the lack of a strong federal system are but a few of the factors with which foreign as well as indigenous enterprises must deal. Consequently, India presents a wide and complex field in which to examine the problems of transferability and development, and contains broad implications for developing countries in general.

Moreover, even though India is one of the world's poorer countries in per capita terms, it is among the top ten or so countries in terms of total industrial output. It contains foreign subsidiaries from many countries, foreign collaboration agreements, even with communist countries, and a sizeable and growing public industrial sector.

One of the difficulties imposed by the choice of India as a subject relates to the fact that India does not have a highly uniform cultural base. Neither, for that matter, does the United States. But if one is examining each nation in relative terms, there are certain elements or dominant patterns of each culture which seem to run through most of its fabric and which distinctively differentiate the two. In other words, the internal variations diminish significantly in magnitude with respect to the dominant differences between the two cultures.

This book is based primarily on firsthand research conducted by the authors over the last decade. Nearly five years of this has been devoted to research in India. However, our more limited firsthand studies and projects in quite a few other countries have also contributed to this book. During the 1960s Professor Richman has done firsthand research and limited pilot studies in Communist China (he is a Canadian), the Soviet Union, Czechoslovakia, Poland, Taiwan, Hong Kong, Japan, Israel, and parts of Western Europe. Professor Copen has done the same in ten Latin American countries: Argentina, Brazil, Mexico, Peru, El Salvador, Nicaragua, Guatemala, Panama, Honduras, and Costa Rica.

Studies by colleagues such as Richard Farmer (Saudi Arabia, Lebanon, Kuwait, Egypt, Mexico) and Arvind Phatak (India) have also contributed to this book. Furthermore, we have studied the domestic operations of many of the U.S. parent companies whose subsidiaries were examined abroad.

In this book we have drawn on a number of doctoral dissertations which deal with firsthand field studies abroad. Countless secondary sources of many other types have also been perused — including books, journals, newspapers, magazines, government, United Nations and World Bank reports, confidential documents, and company reports.

Professor Copen was in India during the 1963-66 period when he was a visiting Harvard professor at the Indian Institute of Management at Ahmedabad. Professor Richman was an MIT visiting professor at the Indian Institute of Management at Calcutta during 1965-66. He has made two follow-up research trips to India, one in the spring and summer of 1968, and the second in the summer of 1969.

In India, we conducted hundreds of on-site interviews with managers and a wide range of other personnel (including workers) of U.S., Indian and some European firms located in that country. We have studied company operations in almost every Indian state, although most of them have been headquartered in major industrial cities such as Bombay, Calcutta, Madras, Delhi, Baroda, and Ahmedabad. Visits to many of the companies were frequent and were spread over many months, and in quite a few cases over several years. In addition to personal interviews, observation, and meetings attended, company records and documents of many types, often going back a decade or more, were obtained and analyzed wherever possible. Executives of many of the U.S. subsidiaries' international headquarters were also interviewed, both in India and the parent firm's home base.

The internal company studies were supplemented by numerous interviews with union leaders; government officials (ranging from top ranking cabinet ministers to local civil servants such as factory inspectors); suppliers and customers of firms studied; officials of business, industrial, and professional associations; executives of banks and other financial institutions; lawyers; scholars and educators. In such interviews and discussions we frequently focused on the environmental conditions which have such a significant bearing on industrial enterprises and their managements.

The primary focus of the field research has been an examination of managerial practices, behavior, performance and enterprise results in response to problems and opportunities presented by the environment. Areas examined within the firms included the basic managerial functions — planning and innovation, control, organization, staffing, direction, leadership and motivation, and union relations — as well as the key functions of production, procurement, marketing, finance, research and development, and public and external relations (especially government relations). The study is concerned not only with the companies' activities and the consequences of their actions, but also with the reasons they chose various courses of action, the uses made of available resources, the way they viewed and responded to the environment (both local and, where applicable, international), and the way they learned from their experiences and applied this knowledge to the future.

Portions of the research were designed to highlight direct comparisons between patterns of U.S. and Indian managerial practices and attitudes. These focused on particular industries and, within the industries, wherever possible, firms of comparable size and similar product lines, but of different nationalities (mainly Indian and U.S.) were examined. Answers to a number of problems were sought. Were the problems, as perceived by firms of differing nationalities and by the researchers, different or similar? How did their managerial methods differ? What could explain the differences? Did these differences lead to different operating results? Were there any patterns?

SAMPLES OF COMPANIES STUDIED

One of the industries studied extensively was the pharmaceutical sector, an industrial group under even greater pressure than the average due to government regulations, related and widely publicized social and moral issues, the need to maintain high quality standards, and the presence of a sizeable number of competing or at least partially competing firms. Although we have concentrated on the pharmaceutical industry we also have done in-depth studies of chemical and engineering firms and those producing batteries and flashlights. However, our findings have significant implications for the Indian economy as a whole, as well as for industry in developing countries, and even relatively advanced countries.

We have chosen to focus attention on samples of firms in these sectors for a number of reasons. They are relatively modern and technologically advanced sectors as compared to the major, more traditional industries in India such as textiles, clothing, tea, food-processing and handicrafts. They are basic to India's development and require a relatively high degree of managerial and technical skill if they are to function at even a moderate level of efficiency and effectiveness.

The more progressive firms in these sectors are also among the front-runners in Indian industry in terms of managerial know-how, and this can suggest much about the relatively low levels of managerial skill and performance in various other industries. Firms in the above sectors are also typically faced with more, or at least increasing, competition though varying degrees of sellers' markets still exist for some of their major products, as compared to enterprises in most other industries in India, and this forces them to focus their attention on managerial effectiveness and productive efficiency. They have also been under increasing pressure in recent years to engage in import substitution and to substantially increase their exports, and it is important to investigate whether pressure to make them more competitive in foreign markets and self-sufficient has also tended to lead to significant improvements in managerial performance and efficiency.

Moreover, a number of firms in the above sectors which have had adequate data for purposes of our India research project have been willing to participate candidly and patiently in it. In some cases, we have helped indigenous firms set up reporting systems and to generate the types of data we have desired — and they have needed anyway! Many of the firms studied, some indigenous as well as virtually all of the foreign companies in terms of majority ownership and control, have at least some Western-trained and educated managers and technicians working for them in key jobs. Many of the indigenous Indian firms have technical collaboration agreements with firms in advanced countries, and most of them which do not to date (the exceptions being mostly small companies) now wish to enter into such agreements.

In the drug industry, as well as the battery and flashlight sector, there are several indigenous and American firms and plants which are comparable in terms of products produced, and to a lesser extent technology and size. The industries also contain other foreign firms, especially pharmaceuticals. We have studied matched samples of indigenous and American, and in some cases British and other, companies in these sectors, and this has enabled us to focus on dominant managerial patterns, and to get to the heart of the transferability and applicability of the managerial know-how and practices issue. On a more limited scale, we have studied both purely indigenous companies (in terms of ownership) and firms with foreign equity participation (mostly involving foreign control, but in some cases with a minority equity interest) in the chemical and heavy engineering sectors. We have also studied some Indian public sector enterprises. More will be said about the comparative methodology involved to match samples of firms of differing nationalities and in different environments in the next chapter.

LIMITATIONS AND QUALIFICATIONS OF THE RESEARCHERS

While further references will be made to limitations of our research and findings in the later chapters, including the next one which deals with our conceptual framework, some comments are in order in this introductory chapter.

The data upon which this book is based are far removed from the precise, sterile numbers that can be obtained during a controlled experiment in a spotless laboratory. The environment in which the research was conducted contained so many closely interrelated and changing variables that it frequently became difficult to clearly isolate any one or even a few, and became even more difficult when attempts were made to quantify relationships. The dynamic nature of the interaction between industrial enterprises, their managements, and their environments often obscures many of the variable interdependencies. Problems involving comparability, the availability and accuracy of data (both micro and macro), concepts and measures of efficiency and effectiveness, the types of goals pursued by different firms and managers, sampling problems, and so forth, have been very real and often vexing.

Consequently, the selection of data and the analyses which have been undertaken, although done systematically, have been based in large part on the experiences of the authors buttressed by the perceptions and opinions of the various qualified experts who were interviewed. Our backgrounds have provided the knowledge and experience which led to the particular design of the research, the collection and analyses of data, and the findings and conclusions which have emerged. Wherever feasible, conclusions have been supported by quantitative data, but for many situations, such data has been unavailable.

In many situations, a considerable amount of judgement and interpretation has been required. An important limitation imposed by the intercultural nature of this research results from the cultural filters which any outsider brings to a new environment. In spite of the close contact we have had with India, we both spent most of our lives in countries which were much more economically advanced and very different from India. As a result, our values and perceptions have been imbued with those of advanced industrial societies. We have made every effort to eliminate these filters in the course of our work, but some must inevitably remain. We have further tried to weed these out by cross-cultural checking of impressions, data and conclusions with Indian and other colleagues and secondary sources, but it is difficult to completely eliminate one's own cultural biases.

Of course, the problems and limitations noted above could be largely avoided if one chose to undertake a less comprehensive or complex study involving a few relatively clear-cut and quantifiable variables. However, we feel strongly that in highly imperfect scientific fields like management, economic development and international business, indeed in the applied social sciences in general, there is much more to be gained from a broad, interdisciplinary, and comprehensive view of reality, than from a rigorous statistical analysis of a few variables in a neat model where numerous critical factors typically must be assumed away. Both kinds of studies, of course, may prove valuable; but we strongly feel that there have not been nearly enough investigations of the former type. And this type of study, in spite of the many problems and limitations involved, may in many respects be more important and valuable in terms of policy implications in the real world.

There clearly has been increasing disillusionment with traditional or conventional economic development theory because in a large number of cases the approaches used do not work well. Many developing countries have quite sophisticated national plans, prepared with considerable care and precision by economists trained in the modern, Western tradition. They often use sophisticated quantitative techniques; but rarely do such plans jibe very well with the realities of the situation.

Difficulties have arisen because, in an effort to simplify the detail, many critical variables have been neglected. This seems to be particularly true with regard to sociological-cultural variables and (happily to a lesser extent in recent years) educational variables as well. Often such parameters are by far the most important to economic development and industrial management problems. They tend to be difficult to quantify, but this does not mean that they can be ignored.

Another major problem is that, usually, no attempt is made to interrelate or integrate macro or environmental variables, micro-managerial or firm variables, and relative levels of effectiveness or efficiency in a systematic way. Much more analysis of the effects of macro environmental conditions, and of changes on the internal management, operations and performance of productive enterprises is needed.

DESIGN OF THE BOOK

The following chapter briefly presents the conceptual framework used in the remainder of this book. This framework is made up essentially of three broad components. The first is a classification scheme of the critical elements of the management process. Before one can consider the question of what aspects of management can or should be transferred or applied in different countries or environments, one needs to identify them.

The second broad component is a classification of critical environmental factors or constraints which have a significant impact on management and firm performance in any country. The overall environmental component is actually subdivided into domestic and international environmental factors in this study.

The third major component of our conceptual framework contains sets of effectiveness and efficiency indicators or measures (both macro and micro) used in this study. Significant differences in managerial effectiveness and productive efficiency are explained in large part by differences in the way critical elements of the management process are performed by different firms. In turn, differences in the management process are explained in large part by differences in environmental conditions, especially between the U.S. and Indian environments.

Part 1 of the book contains five chapters (3 through 7), each dealing with a key dimension of the environment of management and industry. There are chapters dealing with education, sociological-cultural factors, the political-legal environment, and economic factors. Chapter 4 contains an appendix with four short case studies which highlight the importance of the sociological-cultural dimension of the environment. One chapter examines the international environment, as it affects industrial enterprises and their managements.

Part 3 contains two chapters (8 and 9) which focus on the multinational corporation. Chapter 8 distinguishes between various kinds and degrees of international and multinational corporations, in terms of their philosophies, styles, policies and practices. It then examines common charges involving conflicts of interest between international companies and host countries. This is followed by an examination of the major potential benefits host countries and world development can derive from international business operations. The chapter concludes with a discussion of the kinds of competitive advantages that multinational corporations frequently have over purely indigenous or domestic companies, focusing on basic managerial and productive functions. Chapter 9 presents a general overview of the management of multinational corporations. It also examines the special environmental aspects and dimensions of international companies.

Part 4 deals with enterprise management, operations and performance in developing nations. It also presents comparisons between the domestic operations of U.S. parent companies and their foreign subsidiaries.

Twelve of the fourteen chapters in this part treat specific basic managerial or enterprise functions. Chapter 10 presents a concept we have called the "Adaptation Spectrum." It reflects degrees of traditional vs. Americanized (or Westernized) management and the relative economic success of firms studied. This approach can be used in a wide variety of situations and ways. This chapter provides an overview of the transferability of management know-how, the aggregate performance of foreign vs. indigenous companies, managerial change and adaptation, and stereotypes of the highly traditional Indian firm and the highly Americanized company.

Chapter 24 is the concluding chapter. Since this is such a large and comprehensive book, it is not feasible to present a very detailed summary in the concluding chapter. Many of the other chapters do contain their own summaries and conclusions, and therefore the final chapter presents only key highlights and policy implications.

CHAPTER 1   FOOTNOTES

1. See also R. Farmer and B. Richman, *Comparative Management and Economic Progress,* Richard D. Irwin, Inc., Homewood, Ill., 1965. R. Farmer, and B. Richman, *International Business: An Operational Theory,* Richard D. Irwin, Inc., Homewood, Ill., 1966.

2. See B. Richman, *Industrial Society in Communist China,* Random House, Inc., New York, 1969 for a comparative study which focuses primarily on the macro-approach.

3. Unless otherwise noted, figures in this section are from *Survey of Current Business and Overseas Business Reports* published monthly by the U.S. Department of Commerce.

4. See E. Mason, "The Corporation in the Post Industrial State at Home and Abroad," *California Management Review,* Summer 1970, pp. 16–17, and the sources cited therein; see also page 3 of Statement of Judd Polk, August 11, 1967, to the Subcommittee on Foreign

Economic Policy of the Joint Economic Committee of U.S. Congress, as published by the United States Council of the International Chamber of Commerce, Inc.

5.   A. Phatak, *External Environmental Constraints and Their Impact on the Internal Operations of Firms in the Pharmaceutical and Engineering Industries in India,* Doctoral Dissertation, University of California, Los Angeles, 1966 (completed under the guidance of Dr. Richman).

CHAPTER 2
CONCEPTUAL
FRAMEWORK

In discussions dealing with managerial activities, or the transferability and applicability of U.S. management know-how to other countries, it is often assumed that all parties or readers are aware of and agreed upon the implicit definitions of what managerial activities are and, in fact, what management is. Because of their education, experience, and insights, individuals often have quite different ideas about what management involves. Since it is the central theme of this book, it is necessary to indicate the nature of the management process clearly in order to undertake a comparative analysis of the things that different enterprises and their managements do. The classification scheme we have used for this purpose is presented in Table 2-1 of this chapter.

WHAT AND WHO IS MANAGEMENT?

Before we proceed with our operational classification scheme of the management process, it is best to define and elaborate on *what* and *who* management is in general.

In terms of *what*, we view management as administration plus entrepreneurship. Administration is basically an organizational process concerned with the implementation of objectives and plans and internal operating efficiency. It often connotes

bureaucratic structure and behavior, relatively routine decision making, and maintenance of the internal status quo. Entrepreneurship implies more creative external or
open systems orientation. It involves innovation, risk taking, and relatively dynamic
leadership. The true modern professional manager tends to be both an administrator
and an entrepreneur, although in varying degrees. Entrepreneurship tends to become
more important the higher one goes up the managerial hierarchy in a modern enterprise. However, even middle and lower level professional managers must often
innovate, take risks, and exert dynamic leadership if they, their units, and their firms
are to function effectively and efficiently.

Traditional firms in developing countries are likely to be deficient in the administrative and entrepreneurial dimensions of management. Internal operating efficiency
suffers greatly because of ineffective administration. These firms are slow to change in
response to changing conditions, are characterized by relatively little real innovation or
risk taking, and are lacking in dynamic leadership all because of the dearth of effective
entrepreneurship. Of course, such firms may survive and even reap substantial profits,
as long as they continue to function in a sellers' market and are protected from more
dynamic and effective competitive forces. Management may be able to get, through
various means, often illegal or at least unethical by American standards, lucrative
licenses and concessions from the government which enable the firm to produce items
in short supply, and even to expand and diversify. But this is not really entrepreneurship in the modern sense, since the firm is betting on a winner in advance. And
it may well "win" with little or no planning, with relatively little risk involved, and
with poor internal administration and management in general. This may be fine for
the firm, but it may not be very good for the economy or society at large in the long
run.

When significant pressures emerge which call for substantially improved internal
administrative efficiency and entrepreneurial effectiveness, such firms are likely to
find themselves in serious trouble; their viability may even be in jeopardy. This is, in
fact, what has been happening in India, during the last several years.

With respect to *who*, in this study management is perceived as the hierarchy of
individuals in a given organization who play a direct and major role in the performance
of basic universal managerial functions, in decision making and policy formulation,
and in the arrangement of the basic enterprise productive functions. In most cases a
manager will probably be a person having subordinates under him, but this may not
always be the case. A so-called staff man or specialist may also fit into our conception
of the managerial hierarchy, and we have for this reason carefully avoided differentiating between line and staff personnel in our definition of management.

Even in very poorly managed industrial firms in underdeveloped countries, or in
Soviet or Communist Chinese enterprises, managements engage in similar basic
functions, the firms perform similar productive functions, and they operate in accordance with a common framework of critical policy issues pertaining to these functions.[1]
In reality the managerial and enterprise functions are closely interrelated. How and

how well they are performed determine the economic results achieved not only by individual firms, but also by entire industries in a given country, and in the aggregate by the country itself. We shall now discuss each class of functions briefly in an introductory way.

KEY ENTERPRISE OR PRODUCTIVE FUNCTIONS

The basic productive unit in any economy is the firm or enterprise. The firm, or more specifically its management (which is itself a key factor input), takes other inputs comprising land (including natural resources and materials), labor, and capital (including real capital such as plant and equipment) and transforms them into usable and desired goods and services which are consumed by various parts of society. This general productive process is accomplished by the performance of certain key enterprise or productive functions.

An enterprise function is a process which necessarily must be performed by the firm in any country in order for the firm to function at all. The usual catalog of such functions contains production, procurement, marketing or distribution, finance, research and development, and public relations. In reality the enterprise functions tend to be closely interrelated. Note that every enterprise does not necessarily have to perform all of these key functions.

Production and procurement

Goods and services must be produced before any further economic activity can take place. As a part of production, raw materials and components must be purchased or otherwise obtained by the firm, and procurement is intimately related to the production function.

A typical problem in production is that there are many ways to produce the desired item, and management's task is to select the process which does the job most efficiently under given and known conditions. Trade-offs may be made between capital and labor, or between one type of material and another. The basic production processes used will depend, in addition to available technical knowledge and data, on the costs of various inputs, levels of production, availability of skilled labor, and capital equipment on hand, among other factors.

In international operations, such production problems may become very complex because in the different countries in which production of a certain product takes place the prices and availability of various inputs may differ greatly. Thus a manufacturer of electrical machinery may use aluminum wire in some of its American production, since this material is relatively cheaper than copper. But in its West German plant, copper will be used, because there, costs are lower than for aluminum. A motor vehicle manufacturer in the United States is likely to subcontract to other U.S.

firms certain parts because he can be confident that the subcontractors are able to produce his specifications without difficulty. But in India, where quality control standards are much less developed, the producer is likely to decide to manufacture most of these parts even though the cost may be higher. Or in some cases he has no choice, since there are no local sources of supply available and foreign exchange limitations prohibit import.

Production lines laid out with the implicit notion that certain kinds of skilled labor, as well as technical and management skills, are available, may have to be modified when the firm begins to operate in a country with different labor supply and human skill characteristics. The same is true regarding the availability of various kinds of natural resources and materials.

A common error in production planning and organization is made in the assumption that because much of production is technically and scientifically oriented, it can be performed in the same manner in any country. But it is often true that production activities have a direct connection with various environmental conditions external to the firm, and increasing complexity of this function occurs as the international firm expands from its home country to other nations.

Marketing

Products must not only be produced, they must be distributed and sold in order for them to fulfill the functional and end uses intended. Marketing is generally concerned with the creation of place and time utility, and included in this enterprise function are such problems as pricing and price policies to be pursued as well as channels for distribution of products. This function interlocks closely with production.

Environmental differences of many kinds become relevant in the sphere of international marketing. For example, problems of design can assume great importance, as supported by the fact that most American and European automobiles have special radiators for marketing in tropic countries, and heavy duty springs if they are to be sold in countries with poor roads. On occasion, even innocent local design features can cause trouble abroad, as one American firm discovered when a large shipment of its cleansing tissue was refused admittance to Saudi Arabia because its sales emblem, which contained a six-pointed star, was interpreted to be pro-Israel. Its entire marketing effort, and all other company plans involving Saudi Arabia, had to be discarded. Such problems rarely arise when a company operates solely within one country.

Research and development

In contemporary managerial terms, R and D is a systematic effort to improve performance through the extended use of scientific methodology. This can apply to both a process and product technology as well as managerial practices. Many companies have formal R and D programs, although the major number of them are located in the advanced countries of the world. A key constraint in less developed nations is an adequate supply of highly trained manpower to perform the R and D function effectively.

Note again how an international firm may have significant advantages in this area over purely domestic companies, particularly those in poorer countries. If Germany has a superior environment for conducting certain types of chemical research, the multinational firm can capitalize on the research facilities in Germany not only for itself, but also for operations in Japan, India, Chile, and elsewhere. The company can pick and choose the most favored research countries to its own advantage.

Finance

Firms never have unlimited resources at their command, and typically one of the most scarce resources is liquid funds. Management must decide how to obtain money, if more than one option is available; how funds are to be allocated among competing claimants within the enterprise; how to protect already invested capital; and how earnings are to be divided between ownership and new investments.

Firms in international business tend to have more financial options, as well as greater risks, than purely domestic companies. General Electric, for example, can tap money markets in Europe as well as the United States, although the terms of lending may be considerably different. A U.S. subsidiary in India may be able to obtain assistance from its U.S. parent if it finds itself in dire need of funds, especially scarce foreign exchange.

Public and external relations

An industrial firm deals with customers, suppliers, bankers, investors, representatives of governments, politically-based unions, possibly educational institutions, and others outside the enterprise. In general, relations the firm maintains with such outside interest groups is likely, in the long run, to greatly influence its performance. A firm noted for its efforts to destroy unions by force will probably have quite different labor productivity records than one reputed to be fair but firm in its dealings with employees. A company known to be a consistent tax evader, a cheater on safety regulations, an ignorer of standards of quality, is likely to have quite a different problem with governmental regulatory agencies than one known to be straightforward and honest in these areas. Or an enterprise which has a reputation among its customers for giving a high level of service, for being a good supplier of spare parts and technical advice, and for keeping its delivery promises, is likely to be in a considerably better position than one reputed to be sloppy or deficient in these areas. In short, the corporate image is important, not only to salve the egos of executives, but also because poor public and external relations have direct impacts on firm efficiency, and ultimately on survival.

Internationally oriented firms must please not one, but many national publics. What seems proper and desirable in one country may not be highly regarded in another. In many lands, being foreign is in itself a black mark against the company, and often a U.S. or European firm must go to considerable lengths to convince a suspicious local population that its intentions are honest, and that it is not some sort of "bloodsucking imperialistic exploiter" of the local population. Considerations of this sort, which may not be very relevant at home, can assume great importance in foreign countries in which the firm operates.

A note on certain other functions

We have chosen to deal with the personnel function, which is treated by some as an enterprise function, under the broad categories of staffing, direction, leadership and motivation. We have also chosen not to treat accounting, information systems, and data processing as separate enterprise functions or sets of policy issues, but as part of the managerial functions of planning and control.

CRITICAL POLICY ISSUES

Industrial enterprises everywhere operate within policy frameworks which correspond to the enterprise functions outlined above. Many formulate policies and perform functions in a basically intuitive rather than formal or planned manner. However, consciously or unconsciously, the firm must make policy decisions relating to its different enterprise (and managerial) functions. In some cases, this is done by default. In essence the lack of policy itself becomes policy. (For example, when a firm has no clear-cut policy regarding prices charged for its products, this in itself becomes a pricing policy involving the setting of prices on an order or individual basis.)

Hence, it is possible to establish a universal classification scheme involving critical policy issues and related enterprise functions in international business, comparative management, and even in general management studies.

MANAGERIAL FUNCTIONS

Managerial functions refer to the kinds of activities managers perform as managers per se, regardless of the specific types of managers they are. Managerial functions are performed in the course of coordinating and carrying out key enterprise functions. A useful and often used division of managerial functions is: planning and innovation, control, organization, staffing, direction, leadership and motivation.[2]

If an industrial enterprise is to continue operating, regardless of its nature, the above functions of management must be performed, in one fashion or another. Objectives and plans must be formulated, operations must be controlled, and organization structures of some kind must be established; at least some authority must be delegated and responsibility exacted if there is more than one level in the organization; and personnel must be recruited, selected, trained and appraised, as well as motivated, led, and supervised. Moreover, firm managers are generally expected to improve operations and results through innovation where feasible. Let us examine each basic managerial function in more detail.

Planning and innovation

The planning function determines organizational objectives and the policies, strategies, programs, schedules, procedures, and methods for achieving them. Planning is essentially decision making involving the future. It involves choosing among alternatives, and it encompasses innovation. There are major plans, including basic policies, from which stems a wide variety of subplans to be carried out as the result of the initial plan Thus, a decision to produce a new chemical would be followed by a series of subplans concerning the basic production processes entailed, acquisitions of new machinery, labor training, purchases of materials and components, the manner in which the general plan will be financed, detailed specifications for the new product, staffing involving new personnel, and so on.

Plans necessarily have time horizons. Managers may plan for twenty years or twenty minutes, depending on the problem and the way in which they view their planning function. Even virtually no planning is a plan of sorts, since implicitly the firm merely waits to see what happens and reacts, which *is* a plan or strategy. Plans also can be flexible or inflexible, highly scientific and sophisticated or sketched out on a matchbox, or simply carried around in the manager's head.

It is clear that variations in planning among different firms lead to striking differences in the efficiency with which the firm carries out its functions. Bad planning can lead to such problems as inadequate financing, inept marketing, frequent breakdowns of production lines and facilities, shortages of supplies, inadequately trained personnel, and poor public relations. No firm or manager can avoid completely the possible poor results of having to face future unanticipated problems, but good planning can dramatically improve the probabilities for success.

Planning in an international company must take into account various aspects of the international dimension of the firm. As a result it is likely to be more complex than for a purely local enterprise.

Control

The control function includes those activities designed to compel events to conform to plans or to recognize deviations therefrom. It is thus the measurement and corrective function. It involves the establishment of control standards and the gathering of information required for evaluating performance, and provides the inputs for subsequent planning.

A close link between planning and control exists in all parts of the firm and in all functions. For example, some of the most important controls are budgets, which are widely used by productive enterprises. Many, however, are never written down, but merely carried in managers' heads. But the budget is both a plan and a control. The control technique works only when actual performance is measured against planned performance.

It is likely that the more refined the control techniques the firm may have in its corporate accounting and other information systems, the better its control job will be performed, although there are dangers from over-control, as well as economic considerations in cases when the costs of control systems outweigh the benefits derived. In addition to the usual accounting tools and practices, firms may also use various statistical techniques, operations research methodologies, electronic computers and many other control (and planning) practices.

Organization

The organizing function involves the determination and enumeration of activities necessary to carry out plans, the grouping of these activities, the assignment of such groups of activities to units headed by managers, and the delegation of authority to carry them out. It is the totality of such activities and relationships that make up the function of organization. All enterprises have some form of organization, however simple or informal.

Internationally active firms may encounter problems in this function, due to more than just the fact that their organizations are large and geographically extensive. Whereas a rather highly decentralized pattern of organization may work very well at home, subsidiary personnel from other countries may have greatly different attitudes toward organization, motivation and direction. They may actually prefer authoritarian organizations, since they are accustomed to commands from the top. To them, consultative, decentralized management may appear as vacillating and weak. Difficulties may also arise when the kinds of manpower needed in a decentralized operation are not available in a foreign country, and efforts to force men into molds which do not fit their cultural, psychological or educational patterns may create serious organizational problems.

Staffing

The staffing function includes those activities essential to man, and keep manned, the positions required in the organization structure. It thus involves defining the human requirements for jobs to be done and the recruitment, appraisal, and selection of candidates for positions, as well as training and developing both candidates and incumbents to perform well. It also includes the provision of adequate basic inducements to attract and maintain needed personnel.

Staffing is intimately related to the skills and expectations of the individuals involved. Consequently, international firms generally have both additional problems and opportunities in this function as compared to purely local firms. Where a country has too few people with a particular type of key ability, the international firm usually has an easier task importing them. However, recruiting and selection techniques valid in one country may not be effective in another. Thus, if the firm is accustomed at home to obtaining certain types of technicians or workers by advertising in trade papers, and no such papers are available or many workers can't read overseas, it is clear that the technique will have to be changed.

Direction, leadership, and motivation

The managerial function of direction, leadership, and motivation embraces those activities related to supervising, leading, and motivating personnel so that they will perform their tasks in desired ways. This function entails human communication, man-to-man relationships, and the use of incentives or penalties to motivate people in desired directions.

As with other managerial and enterprise functions, the way in which this function is performed makes a considerable difference in the efficiency of the firm. However, what motivates men to better performance in some cultures may not work very well in other cultures. While leadership may prove quite difficult to define precisely, most perceptive observers can readily detect a situation characterized by weak, vacillating and ineffective leadership as compared to one in which the leader is competent, respected, and effective.

CRITICAL ELEMENTS OF THE MANAGEMENT PROCESS

The above enterprise and managerial functions in effect answer the question: What are the important kinds of things that firms and their management do? The overall management process in this study involves critical elements pertaining to both the managerial and the enterprise functions, including related critical policy issues. These functions can be broken down and sub-classified into descriptive elements, each one a variable, common to the management process virtually in any integrated industrial enterprise in any country.

The elements, a total of 76, that have been identified as being most critical are presented in Table 2-1 on the following page. They are referred to as B's. The selection and classification of these critical elements is based on firsthand research in several diverse countries, the study of secondary sources, the research of several close colleagues and doctoral students, as well as many interviews and questionnaire surveys involving experts in different areas of management and business administration. The list of elements in Table 2-1 is by no means exhaustive or conclusive, but it is adequate for our study.

Although we now have a universal classification scheme of the management process, it should be stressed again that each element is a variable, not a constant. Each element can show up or be performed in several ways.

The specific ways and degrees of efficiency in which the overall management process and its individual critical elements are performed often vary widely among firms not only in different countries, but even in the same country. However, there do appear to be various dominant, or at least widespread common patterns in the management process among firms in a given country, particularly when a specific type of industry is being studied and the nationalities of the firms and their managers are taken into account.

TABLE 2-1 Critical elements of the management process

B_1 *Planning and innovation*

1.1 Basic organizational objectives pursued and the form of their operational expression.
1.2 Types of plans utilized.
1.3 Time horizon of plans and planning.
1.4 Degree and extent to which enterprise operations are spelled out in plans (i.e., preprogrammed).
1.5 Flexibility of plans.
1.6 Methodologies, techniques and tools used in planning and decision making.
1.7 Extent and effectiveness of employee participation in planning.
1.8 Managerial behavior in the planning process.
1.9 Degree and extent of information distortion in planning.
1.10 Degree and extent to which scientific method is effectively applied by enterprise personnel — both managers and non-managers — in dealing with causation and futurity problems.
1.11 Nature, extent and rate of innovation and risk-taking in enterprise operations over a given period of time.
1.12 Ease or difficulty of introducing changes and innovations in enterprise operations.

B_2 *Control*

2.1 Types of strategic performance and control standards used in different areas; e.g., production, marketing, finance, personnel.
2.2 Types of control techniques used.
2.3 Nature and structure of information feedback systems used for control purposes.
2.4 Timing and procedures for corrective action.
2.5 Degree of looseness or tightness of control over personnel.
2.6 Extent and nature of unintended effects resulting from the overall control system employed.
2.7 Effectiveness of the control system in compelling events to conform to plans.

B_3 *Organization*

3.1 Size of representative enterprise and its major sub-units.
3.2 Degree of centralization or decentralization of authority.
3.3 Degree of work specialization (Division of labor).
3.4 Spans of control.
3.5 Basic departmentation and grouping of activities. Extent and uses of service departments.
3.6 Extent and uses of staff generalists and specialists.
3.7 Extent and uses of functional authority.
3.8 Extent and degree of organizational confusion and friction regarding authority and responsibility relationships.
3.9 Extent and uses of committee and group decision making.
3.10 Nature, extent, and uses of the informal organization.
3.11 Degree and extent to which the organization structure (i.e., the formal organization) is mechanical or flexible with regard to causing and/or adapting to changing conditions.

B_4 *Staffing*

4.1 Methods used in recruiting personnel.
4.2 Criteria used in selecting and promoting personnel.
4.3 Techniques and criteria used in appraising personnel.

TABLE 2-1 Critical elements of the management process (Cont.)

4.4 Nature and uses of job descriptions.

4.5 Levels of compensation.

4.6 Nature, extent, and time absorbed in enterprise training programs and activities.

4.7 Extent of informal individual development.

4.8 Policies and procedures regarding the layoff and dismissal of personnel.

4.9 Ease or difficulty in dismissing personnel no longer required or desired.

4.10 Ease or difficulty of obtaining and maintaining personnel of all types with desired skills and abilities.

B_5 *Direction, leadership and motivation*

5.1 Degree and extent of authoritarian vs. participative management. (This relates to autocrats vs. consultative direction.)

5.2 Techniques and methods used for motivating managerial personnel.

5.3 Techniques and methods used for motivating non-managerial personnel.

5.4 Supervisory techniques used.

5.5 Communication structure and techniques.

5.6 Degree and extent to which communication is ineffective among personnel of all types.

5.7 Ease or difficulty of motivating personnel to perform efficiently, and to improve their performance and abilities over time (irrespective of the types of incentives that may be utilized for this purpose).

5.8 Degree and extent of identification that exists between the interests and objectives of individuals, work groups, departments, and the enterprise as a whole.

5.9 Degree and extent of trust and cooperation or conflict and distrust among personnel of all types.

5.10 Degree and extent of frustration, absenteeism, and turnover among personnel.

5.11 Degree and extent of wasteful time and effort resulting from restrictive work practices, unproductive bargaining, conflicts, etc.

B_6 *Marketing (policies pursued)*

6.1 Product line (degree of diversification as specialization, rate of change, product quality).

6.2 Channels of distribution and types and location of customers.

6.3 Pricing (for key items, in relation to costs, profit margins, quantity and trade discount structure).

6.4 Sales promotion and key sales appeals (types used and degree of aggressiveness in sales promotion).

B_7 *Production and procurement*

7.1 Make or buy (components, supplies, facilities, services, extent to which subcontracting is used, etc.).

7.2 Number, types and locations of major suppliers.

7.3 Timing of procurement of major supplies.

7.4 Average inventory levels (major supplies, goods in process, completed output).

7.5 Minimum, maximum and average size of production runs.

7.6 Degree to which production operations are stabilized.

7.7 Combination of factor inputs used in major products produced.

7.8 Basic production processes used.

7.9 Extent of automation and mechanization in enterprise operations.

TABLE 2-1 Critical elements of the management process (Cont.)

B_8 *Research and development*

    8.1   Nature and extent of R & D activity (e.g., product development and improvement, new material usages, new production processes and technology, etc.).

B_9 *Finance*

    9.1   Types of financing (e.g., equity, debt, short term, long term, etc.).

    9.2

    9.3   Sources of capital

    9.4   Major uses of capital

    9.5   Protection of capital

    9.6   Distribution of earnings

B_{10} *Public and external relations*   (The relationships, attitudes and policies of enterprise management regarding major types of external agents and organizations.)

    10.1   Customers and consumer relations (e.g., does firm management regard consumer loyalty and satisfaction as being important, or is it chiefly interested in short run results, quick profits, etc.).

    10.2   Supplier relations.

    10.3   Investor and creditor relations.

    10.4   Union relations.

    10.5   Government relations.

    10.6   Community relations (e.g., educational institutions, chamber of commerce, business and professional associations, community welfare activities, etc.).

It is possible to measure, at least roughly, as well as identify, describe, analyze, explain and even predict, significant differences in the management process among different firms in the same and different countries. However, to arrive at meaningful explanations or predictions of significant differences in the management process among firms in different countries it is necessary to relate them to environmental conditions external to the enterprise. It is also possible to quantify, or at least rank, the specific elements deemed most important in general or with regard to specific problems faced by an individual firm or manager.[3]

ENVIRONMENTAL FACTORS OR CONSTRAINTS

The second major component of our overall conceptual framework consists of environmental factors or constraints largely, if not totally, external to and beyond the control of individual industrial enterprises and their managements. These are essentially the "givens" within which firms and their managements must operate in a specific country and they vary, often greatly, from country to country. Our chief interests in this study are with the Indian, and for comparative purposes, with some related aspects of the U.S. environments.

While much of the management process is concerned with internal enterprise operations, managerial and firm performance depends on responding to factors external to the firm. A productive enterprise necessarily forms a part of a complex educational-sociological-cultural-political-legal-economic whole. No industrial enterprise can exist separate from its environment. Firms both influence and are significantly influenced by the nature of their total environment.

In this study we use the terms environmental or external factors, constraints, characteristics, conditions, and variables synonymously unless otherwise noted; however, we prefer the term constraint. In essence, a constraint circumscribes the opportunities for managerial action — sometimes very narrowly but usually fairly broadly. We are specifically interested in how environmental conditions (or constraints) result in or produce dominant patterns of managerial and firm behavior in given countries, regions, or industries.

If it is true that the external environment directly and significantly influences managerial and firm performance, and if the critical environmental constraints can be identified and isolated, it should be possible to alter the environment in order to improve the efficiency of firms in a particular country or industry. Since it may be much easier in the national or political sense to alter broad environmental conditions rather than the internal affairs of numerous individual firms in order to obtain greater economic progress, such knowledge could be useful not only for enterprise managers but also political leaders, economic planners, and other kinds of macro technicians.

If it were known that in the United States or in India, changing a certain law would probably enable a substantial number of business firms to improve efficiency in certain key areas by roughly 5 or 10 percent, it might be relatively easy to change the law. If, on the other hand, this improvement could be made only by direct interference with the internal operations of the firms, such changes probably would prove more difficult, time consuming, and costly. This is not to imply that a specific enterprise is entirely a passive victim of its environment, on the contrary this is why we focus on the transferability and applicability of imported managerial know-how, but it is clear that macro environmental changes can frequently lead to substantially better economic performance on a widespread scale than reliance on improvements initiated and implemented by individual firms.

During the course of our research we have identified two broad spheres of environmental constraints: 1) national environmental constraints which involve domestic conditions in a given country[4]; and 2) international constraints[5] which primarily involve relationships and conditions between countries.

National environmental factors

Table 2-2 presents the essentially domestic or national, environmental constraints which have the most significant bearing on managerial performance and productive efficiency in general. They have been classified into four categories: education, sociological-cultural (which include personality and psychological factors), political-legal, and economic. In all, 29 strategic environmental factors have been identified. They are referred to as C's.

We have found that relating environmental constraints to the critical elements of the management process facilitates meaningful explanations, and in many cases prediction and prescription, of differences in managerial and firm performance.

The environmental variables presented are obviously complex, and a detailed study of even a limited number of them for even one country such as India could take a lifetime. However, if only the portion of each constraint directly and significantly bearing on industrial management is considered, the task becomes greatly simplified and more manageable. Hence, we are interested not in all laws or political conditions relevant to India, but only in those portions which influence the management process and productive efficiency in industrial enterprises. Similarly, our concern with education includes not all pedagogy but just the portion having direct relevance to industrial management.

It is evident from Table 2-2 that many of the environmental constraints are closely interrelated, and this makes analysis of them even more difficult. Attitude toward education may be closely connected with attitude toward achievement and work, attitude toward scientific method, attitude toward change and class structure; attitude toward achievement may be closely connected with class structure, attitudes toward risk taking and change, and various educational and political factors. The result is a very complex set of interrelationships which determine in large part how efficiently individual firms and an entire country perform economically.

All of the environmental factors can be quantified, at least conceptually. Because of their number, selectivity and sound judgment in focusing on the most strategic variables which explain the most significant differences in managerial and firm performance is essential for research.

Another problem is that the environment of a given country, or at least some portions of it, tends to be dynamic rather than static. Environmental conditions change with time, sometimes greatly within a relatively short time. In turn, relationships between environmental constraints, managerial elements and productive efficiency, change.

In spite of the serious conceptual and actual problems pertaining to research involving environmental constraints, we feel that our conceptual framework serves as a useful guide for generating pertinent data, and for analyzing significant implications for international business, comparative management, and economic development.

The international environment

The firm operating in two or more countries has two or more national environments to consider. However, there is also an added dimension resulting from the interaction between countries which should be considered in order to operate effectively and efficiently.

TABLE 2-2 National environmental constraints

C_1 *Education*

1.1 Literacy level: The percentage of the total population and those presently employed in industry who can read, write and do simple arithmetic calculations, and the average years of schooling of adults.

1.2 Specialized vocational and technical training and general secondary education: Extent, types and quality of education and training of this type not directly under the control or direction of industrial enterprises. The type, quantity and quality of persons obtaining such education or training and the proportion of those employed in industry with such education and training.

1.3 Higher education: The percentage of the total population and those employed in industry with post-high school education, plus the types and quality of such education. The types of persons obtaining higher education.

1.4 Special management development programs: The extent and quality of management development programs which are not run internally by productive enterprises, and which are aimed at improving the skills and abilities of managers and for potential managers. The quantity and quality of managers and potential managers of different types and levels attending or having completed such programs.

1.5 Attitude toward education: The general or dominant cultural attitudes towards education and the acquisition of knowledge, in terms of its presumed desirability. The general attitude toward different types of education.

1.6 Educational match with the requirements of industry and manpower utilization: The extent and degree to which the types of formal education and training in a given country fits the needs of productive enterprises and all levels of skill and achievement, and the degree to which manpower utilization is effective. This is essentially a summary category; depending on the type of job involved, different educational constraints indicated above would be more important.

C_2 *Sociological-cultural*

2.1 View toward industrial managers and management: The general or dominant social attitude toward industrial and business managers of all sorts, and the way that such managers tend to view their managerial jobs.

2.2 View of authority, responsibility and subordinates: The general or dominant cultural attitude toward authority, responsibility and persons in subordinate positions and the way that industrial managers tend to view their authority, responsibility and their subordinates.

2.3 Interorganizational and individual cooperation: Extent and degree to which business enterprises, government agencies, labor unions, educational institutions and other relevant organizations cooperate with each other in ways conducive to industrial efficiency and general economic progress. The degree to which individuals employed in productive enterprises cooperate with each other towards this end.

2.4 View toward achievement and work: The general or dominant cultural attitude toward individual or collective achievement and productive work in industry.

2.5 Class structure and individual mobility: The extent of opportunities for social class and individual mobility, both vertical and horizontal, in a given country, and the means by which it can be achieved.

TABLE 2-2 National environmental constraints (Cont.)

2.6 View toward wealth, material gain and self interest: Whether or not the acquisition of wealth from different sources is generally considered socially desirable, and the way that persons employed in industry tend to view material gain.

2.7 View toward scientific method: The general social and dominant individual attitude toward the use of rational, predictive techniques in solving various types of business, technical, economic and social problems.

2.8 View toward risk taking: Whether or not the taking of various types of personal collective or rational risks is generally considered acceptable, as well as the dominant view toward specific types of risk taking in business and industry. The degree and extent to which risk taking tends to be a rational process in a particular country.

2.9 View toward change: The general cultural attitude toward a social change of any type which bear directly on industrial performance in a given country, and the dominant attitude among persons employed in industry toward all types of significant changes in enterprises operations.

C_3 *Political-legal*

3.1 Relevant legal rules of the game: Quality, efficiency, and effectiveness of the legal structure in terms of general business law, labor law, tax law, and general law relevant to business. Degree of enforcement, reliability, etc.

3.2 Defense and military policy: Impact of defense policy in industrial enterprise in terms of trading with potential enemies, purchasing policies, strategic industry development, labor resources competition, and similar factors.

3.3 Foreign policy: Impact of policy on distrail enterprise in terms of trading restrictions, quotas, tarrifs, customs, unions, foreign exchange, etc.

3.4 Political stability: Influence on industrial enterprises of revolutions, changes in regime, stability or instability over protracted periods, etc.

3.5 Political organization: Type of organization in constitutional terms; degrees of centralization or decentralization; degree and extent of red tape, delays, uncertainty and confusion in industry-government dealings; pressure groups and their effectiveness; political parties and their philosophies, etc.

3.6 Flexibility of law and legal changes: Degree to which relevant barriers to the efficient management of industrial enterprises can be changed and the timeliness of such changes; predictability and certainty of legal actions, etc.

C_4 *Economic*

4.1 Basic economic system: Including such factors as the overall economic organization of the country (i.e., capitalistic, marxist, mixed), property rights, and similar factors.

4.2 Central banking system and monetary policy: The organization and operations of the central banking system, including the controls over commercial banks, the ability and willingness to control the money supply, the effectiveness of government, policies regarding price stability, commercial bank reserves, discounting credit controls, and similar factors.

TABLE 2-2 National environmental constraints (Cont.)

4.3   Fiscal policy and the state budget: General policies concerning government expenditures, their timing, and their impact; the general level of deficit, surplus, or balance; total share of government expenditures in gross national product.

4.4   Economic stability: The vulnerability of the economy to economic fluctuations of depression and boom, price stability, and over-all economic growth stability.

4.5   Organization of capital markets: The existence of such markets as stock and bond exchanges, their honesty, effectiveness, and total impact; the size and role of commercial banking, including loan policies and availability of credit to businessmen; the existence of other capital sources, such as savings and loan associations, government sponsored credit agencies, insurance company loan activities, etc.

4.6   Factor endowment: Relative supply of real capital and land (agricultural, minerals, and other raw materials) per capita; size and general health of the work force.

4.7   Market size: Total effective purchasing power within the country plus relevant export markets for different branches of industry making up the total industrial sector.

4.8   Social overhead capital: Availability and quality of power supplies, water, communications systems, transportation, public warehousing, physical transfer facilities, housing, etc.

Each country is sovereign, and each is able, within limits, to adjust its posture toward foreign countries, enterprises, and individuals. It is common for a nation to have special rules, laws, regulations, as well as attitudes, behavior patterns, and other conditions directed specifically at particular foreign countries, firms and individuals or at foreigners in general. International firms in a given country, and many indigenous companies as well, must factor this into their consideration of the environment.

These international constraints, referred to in this study as I's, often differ substantially between countries. They become especially important when we consider international companies and the transferability of managerial know-how from one country to another.

Since India and the United States are the prime countries of interest in this study, attention will be given to a number of international constraints operating in each of these two nations. The operations and performance of a U.S. subsidiary located in India are likely to be affected by various of India's international constraints, certain U.S. international constraints, domestic or local Indian environmental constraints, possibly some domestic U.S. environmental conditions, as well as constraints or conditions imposed by its parent company. (Constraints imposed by the parent company will be considered in Part 3.)

Table 2-3 presents a classification scheme of key international constraints which tend to have a significant bearing on firm operations and management in virtually any country involved with international business. Fourteen such constraints have been divided into three categories: sociological, political-legal, and economic. The educational category, found in our classification of national constraints, is omitted, since education in an international environment per se is relatively unknown today. Typically, education is tied to some country and can be considered as a local environmental constraint. If various citizens of a given country are educated abroad, and this has significant relevance for industrial management, this can be handled through other environmental factors (e.g., foreign policy, to name one). The other types of constraints may differ enough between domestic and international segments of a given country's environment to be considered and analyzed separately.

TABLE 2-3 International constraints

I_1 *Sociological constraints*

1.1 National ideology: The general collective ideology of a nation, as exemplified by their writing, speaking, and other manifestations of a national point of view.

1.2 View toward foreigners: The general attitude toward non-nationals, as evidenced by overt behavior.

1.3 Nature and extent of nationalism: The manifestation of the collective nationalistic feelings within the country, as evidenced by actions, writings, and behavior.

I_2 *Political-legal constraints*

2.1 Political ideology: The political viewpoints of existing governments, as demonstrated by the prevailing pattern of rule, philosophy of leading political parties, and similar factors.

2.2 Relevant legal rules for foreign business: The special rules of the game applied only to foreign owned firms, including special discriminatory labor and tax legislation.

2.3 International organization and treaty obligations: Formal obligations of the country in terms of military responsibilities, political obligations, copyright, postal, and patent obligations, and similar matters.

2.4 Power or economic bloc grouping: Membership in formal and informal political, military, and economic blocs, such as communist marxist, or neutralist groups; explicit and implicit obligations of such blocs.

2.5 Import-export restrictions: Formal legal rules controlling exports and imports, including tariffs, quotas, export duties, export restrictions, and similar matters.

2.6 International investment restrictions: Formal legal and administrative restrictions on investments by foreigners within the country.

2.7 Profit remission restrictions: Formal legal and administrative restrictions on remittance of profits of local operations to foreign countries.

2.8 Exchange control restrictions: Formal legal and administrative controls on the conversion of the local currency to any or all foreign currencies or gold.

TABLE 2-3 International constraints (Cont.)

I₃ *Economic constraints*

3.1 General balance of payments position: The general state of the balance of payments, including deficits or surplusses on current account, the flows of capital, both long and short term, new term international financial obligations, and tendencies for chronic deficits or surplusses in the balance of payments.

3.2 International trade patterns: The usual flows of exports and imports to and from the country. Patterns of commodities and services traded, by countries and regions.

3.3 Membership and obligations in international financial organizations: Obligations and responsibilities of the country toward international organizations such as the World Bank and the IMF; rights of the country as a member of such organizations.

Table 2-4 indicates how the international constraints are interlocked with national constraints. As might be expected, most I's are related directly to corresponding C's. Thus legal-political international constraints are related generally to corresponding political-legal C's. However, some of the legal-political I's may also be related to sociological and economic local constraints. A law appears as law to a foreign firm, but the reason for the law might be a sociological attitude or an economic problem in the given country.

For a given U.S. subsidiary in India, the Indian C's and I's and the U.S. C's and I's are interrelated to some extent. The firm may find that local educational constraints in India are such that an adequate supply of certain types of high talent manpower is unavailable. It may decide to overcome this shortage by importing men from the United States, where such skilled personnel can readily be found. That is, the educational constraints at home are better than those in the host country. But to bring such persons into India, visas must be obtained and legal rules regarding the importation of such personnel must be observed. Here an international legal constraint of the host country is important. It is also possible that a given home country (not necessarily the United States) or parent company may place constraints on allowing various kinds of personnel to be employed in certain foreign countries (e.g., Red China or Cuba).

In general, then, international firms typically operate within certain rules of the game and other environmental conditions which do not apply in the same way, or possibly at all, to indigenous enterprises. Such conditions can have either positive or negative impacts on performance, depending on the specific situation. At the same time, international companies, especially those from advanced countries, frequently are in a better position than local firms to improve their management and performance because they can more readily transfer know-how and resources to the host country, thus at least partially offsetting the negative impact of various local constraints.

TABLE 2-4 International-national constraint interrelationships

Int'l Constraints (I)	Educational C1. 1	2	3	4	5	6	Sociological C2. 1	2	3	4	5	6	7	8	9	Legal Political C3. 1	2	3	4	5	6	Economic C4. 1	2	3	4	5	6	7	8
I1. 1	x	x	x		x		x	x		x	x	x	x	x	x	x		x	x			x							
2	x	x	x		x	x	x	x		x	x	x	x	x	x	x		x	x			x							
3	x		x				x	x		x	x	x	x	x	x	x		x	x			x							
I2. 1	x		x		x		x			x	x	x	x	x	x	x		x	x	x	x	x							
2							x	x	x	x	x	x	x		x	x	x	x	x	x	x	x							
3									x			x		x	x	x	x		x	x		x							
4														x	x	x	x	x		x		x							
5																x	x	x		x		x	x	x	x	x	x	x	x
6												x		x		x	x	x				x	x	x	x	x			
7												x		x		x	x	x				x	x	x	x	x			
8																x	x	x				x	x	x	x	x	x		
9												x		x		x	x	x				x	x	x	x	x	x		
I3. 1																x	x	x	x	x	x	x	x	x	x	x	x	x	x
2																x	x	x				x	x	x	x	x	x	x	x
3																x	x	x				x							

For definitions of C's, see Table 2-2
For definitions of I's, see Table 2-3

CONSTRAINT-MANAGEMENT PROCESS RELATIONSHIPS

A central theme of our research involves an investigation of the significant relationships existing between environmental constraints, both domestic and international, and critical elements of the management process. For example, if there tends to be a significant relationship between C 2.4 and B 5.7 (see Tables 2-2 and 2-1), what tends to happen to B 5.7 in a specific enterprise, group of firms, or an industry when C 2.4 changes significantly in a certain direction? We are interested in explaining significant differences in the management of different firms and countries in terms of environmental constraints. We are interested in dominant patterns of management and firm behavior among firms which are of the same and different nationalities and which operate in the same and different countries.

Table 2-5 presents a constraint — management process (C-B) matrix which indicates suggestive relationships between national environmental constraints and the critical elements of the management process. The environmental factors or C's, following the notation in Table 2-2, are placed horizontally across the table, while the elements of the management process or B's, following the notation of Table 2-1, are listed vertically. The X's in Table 2-5 indicate which C's and B's tend to be related. It is possible to break off

TABLE 2-5 Critical managerial elements and external constraints

	C_1 Educational						C_2 Sociological									C_3 Political-Legal						C_4 Economic							
	1	2	3	4	5	6	1	2	3	4	5	6	7	8	9	1	2	3	4	5	6	1	2	3	4	5	6	7	8
B_1:																													
1		x					x		x	x	x	x	x	x	x	x	x	x	x	x	x	x	x	x	x	x	x	x	x
2	x	x	x	x		x	x	x	x				x	x	x	x	x	x	x	x	x	x	x	x	x	x	x	x	x
3		x	x	x				x	x				x	x	x	x	x	x	x	x	x		x	x	x	x	x		
4		x	x	x		x	x	x	x			x	x	x	x	x	x	x	x	x	x	x				x	x		
5		x	x	x					x				x	x	x	x	x	x	x		x	x	x	x	x	x			
6		x	x	x				x	x			x	x	x	x	x	x	x			x	x				x			
7	x	x	x	x	x	x	x	x	x	x	x	x	x	x	x	x						x					x		
8		x	x	x	x	x	x	x		x	x	x	x	x	x														
9	x	x	x	x	x	x	x	x	x	x	x	x	x	x	x					x	x								
10	x	x	x	x	x	x	x		x	x		x	x	x															
11	x	x	x	x	x	x	x	x		x	x	x	x	x	x	x	x	x	x	x	x	x	x	x	x	x	x	x	x
12	x	x	x	x	x	x	x	x	x	x	x	x	x	x	x	x	x	x	x	x	x	x	x	x	x	x	x	x	x
B_2: 1	x	x	x	x	x	x	x	x			x	x	x	x	x	x	x	x				x			x	x			
2	x	x	x	x		x	x	x		x			x	x	x	x	x	x				x			x	x			
3	x	x	x	x		x	x	x		x			x	x	x	x						x			x				
4	x	x	x	x		x	x		x				x	x	x	x						x			x				
5	x	x	x	x	x	x	x	x	x	x	x	x	x		x	x			x	x		x				x			
6	x	x	x	x	x	x	x	x		x	x	x	x	x	x	x			x	x	x	x							
7	x	x	x	x		x	x	x	x	x	x	x	x		x	x	x	x	x	x	x	x	x	x	x	x			
B_3: 1	x	x	x	x		x	x	x	x	x	x	x	x	x	x	x	x	x	x	x	x	x	x	x	x	x	x	x	x
2	x	x	x	x	x	x	x	x			x	x	x	x		x						x					x		x
3	x	x	x	x		x	x	x	x	x	x	x	x			x						x					x	x	x
4	x	x	x	x		x	x	x		x	x		x														x		
5	x	x	x	x		x	x	x	x	x	x		x																x
6		x	x	x		x	x	x	x	x	x		x			x						x					x		x
7	x	x	x	x		x	x	x		x	x		x			x													
8	x	x	x	x	x	x	x	x		x	x		x			x			x			x							x
9		x	x	x		x	x	x		x	x		x		x														
10	x	x	x	x		x	x	x		x	x																		
11		x	x	x	x	x	x	x		x	x		x	x	x	x						x							
B_4: 1	x	x	x	x	x	x	x	x		x	x	x	x			x	x											x	x
2	x			x	x	x	x	x		x	x	x	x			x												x	x
3	x	x	x	x	x	x	x	x		x	x	x	x			x													
4	x	x	x			x	x	x		x	x		x			x													
5							x	x		x	x	x	x			x						x			x	x	x		
6	x	x	x	x	x	x	x	x		x	x	x	x		x	x											x		
7	x	x	x	x	x	x	x	x		x	x	x		x		x											x		
8				x			x		x	x		x				x											x		x
9							x	x		x	x					x			x	x									
10	x	x	x	x	x	x	x	x		x	x	x	x			x	x					x	x	x	x		x		x

TABLE 2-5 Critical managerial elements and external constraints (Cont.)

	C_1 Educational						C_2 Sociological									C_3 Political-Legal						C_4 Economic							
	1	2	3	4	5	6	1	2	3	4	5	6	7	8	9	1	2	3	4	5	6	1	2	3	4	5	6	7	8
B_5: 1	x	x	x	x			x	x		x	x																		
2		x	x	x		x	x	x		x	x	x	x			x													
3	x	x			x	x	x	x		x	x	x	x			x													
4	x	x	x	x	x	x	x	x		x	x	x	x																
5	x	x	x	x		x	x	x		x		x	x			x													
6	x	x	x	x	x	x	x	x		x	x	x															x		
7	x	x	x	x	x	x	x	x		x	x	x	x														x		
8	x					x	x	x		x	x	x		x	x	x											x		
9							x	x	x	x	x	x				x													
10	x	x	x	x	x	x	x	x	x	x	x	x		x	x	x										x		x	
11							x	x	x	x	x	x				x			x	x		x				x		x	
B_6: 1								x					x	x	x	x	x	x				x	x	x	x	x	x	x	x
2								x					x	x	x	x	x	x				x	x	x	x	x	x	x	x
3								x				x				x	x	x				x	x	x	x	x	x	x	x
4	x										x	x	x	x		x						x			x			x	x
B_7: 1								x				x				x	x	x				x			x	x	x	x	x
2								x				x				x	x	x				x			x	x	x	x	x
3								x				x				x						x			x	x		x	x
4								x				x	x			x	x					x			x	x	x	x	x
5								x				x	x			x	x					x			x	x	x	x	x
6								x				x	x			x	x	x	x	x	x	x	x	x	x	x	x	x	x
7	x	x	x	x		x	x	x		x	x	x	x			x	x	x				x	x	x	x	x	x	x	x
8	x	x	x			x	x			x						x	x	x	x			x			x	x	x	x	x
9	x	x	x			x					x					x	x	x	x			x			x	x	x	x	x
B_8: 1	x	x	x	x	x	x					x	x	x			x	x	x				x			x	x	x	x	x
B_9: 1										x	x	x				x				x	x	x	x	x	x	x	x	x	
2																													
3							x				x	x	x			x			x	x		x	x	x	x	x	x		
4							x				x	x	x	x		x	x	x				x	x	x	x	x	x	x	x
5											x	x	x	x		x	x	x	x			x	x	x	x	x			
6							x			x	x	x	x	x	x	x						x				x	x		
B_{10}: 1											x	x	x	x	x	x			x	x		x				x			x
2									x	x	x	x	x	x	x	x	x	x	x			x			x	x	x		x
3								x	x	x	x	x	x	x	x	x			x	x		x	x	x	x	x	x		
4	x	x	x			x			x	x	x	x	x	x	x	x			x	x	x	x	x	x	x		x		
5							x	x	x	x	x	x	x	x	x	x	x	x	x	x	x	x							
6	x	x	x	x	x		x	x	x	x	x	x	x	x	x	x				x	x	x	x						

limited pieces of the matrix for empirical study, and this we have been doing and have done in this study, rather than attempting to deal with the whole matrix at once.

The relationships suggested in Table 2-5 can be presented in the form of equations. For example, following this table we have:

B 3.3 = f(C 1.1, C 1.2, C 1.3, C 1.4, C 1.6, C 2.1, C 2.2, C 2.3, C 2.4, C 2.5, C 2.6, C 2.7, C 3.1, C 4.1, C 4.6, C 4.7, C 4.8)

This equation says that the degree of work specialization (division of labor) depends significantly on all but one of the educational constraints; attitudes toward industrial managers and management, authority and subordinates, achievement and work, scientific method, wealth and material gain; interorganizational cooperation; class structure and individual mobility; legal rules; general economic framework; factor endowment; market size; and social overhead capital. Of these, the educational constraints, attitude toward achievement and work, class structure and individual mobility, legal rules, and economic framework might be most important in, say, India.

If nothing else, Table 2-5 provides a useful checklist for both researchers and practitioners, and it permits the statement of a large number of suggestive relationships in a very small space. What it does not indicate, however, is what quantitative relationships are indicated by the C to B relationships. It has not been possible to undertake a comprehensive or precise quantitative analysis in this study; nor has it been possible to consider nearly all of the relationships in this table. We have focused our efforts on what seem to be the most significant relationships, and where feasible we have attempted to arrive at, at least qualitative assessments of their relative quantitative importance under given conditions and situations.

In Table 2-5 no mention is made of the international constraints or I's. If three-dimensional charts could be drawn in a book, it would be possible to construct a C-I-B matrix showing interrelationships of all of these variables to each other. Lacking this ability it should be noted that Table 2-4, which deals with C-I relationships, relates directly to Table 2-5, which interrelates C's and B's. From these two tables I-B relationships can readily be determined.

MANAGERIAL EFFECTIVENESS AND PRODUCTIVE EFFICIENCY

The final major dimension of our conceptual framework and related research deals with the perennially intricate problem of effectiveness and efficiency.[6] If one wants to do really valuable research in the field of comparative management as a career, at some point he will undoubtedly smack head-on into the question "is Company A more efficient than B, and why or why not?" The practicing manager in particular, as well as many action-oriented scholars, is also concerned with the basic question of what can be done to become more efficient, or to make A as efficient as B. Here we are in the realm of both prediction and prescription, which we feel is the most important and complex realm for an applied field like management.

In our research we are concerned with the relationship between environmental and management process factors on the one hand, and managerial effectiveness and productive efficiency on the other. We attempt to explain differences in managerial effectiveness and productive efficiency for firms in the same industry in the same and different countries, and for the overall industrial sector and economy among different countries, by exploring the impact that key environmental and international constraints have on critical elements of the management process.

We define managerial effectiveness as the relative degree or level of efficiency with which the overall management process or specific critical elements of it are performed, with respect to external constraints confronting management. Each element of the management process (B) can be quantified in terms of its relative degree of efficiency, at least conceptually, by rank ordering or the assignment of points on a grading scale. Productive efficiency involves measures of performance or results in the conventional input-output (I/O) sense. It does not explain performance, it just measures and quantifies it.

Both managerial effectiveness and productive efficiency, as used here, are *relative* concepts involving comparisons of specific managers, firms, or entire industrial or economic systems. A relative approach is necessary since there are few absolute scales of effectiveness or efficiency in the fields of management or economics.

In analyzing efficiency indicators to arrive at a relative measure or index of managerial effectiveness one must constantly be aware of suboptimation problems. That is why we advocate, where possible, the use of a combination of efficiency indicators, preferably in a weighted formula, to overcome or substantially reduce the possibility of serious subsystem optimization distortions. However, to date the design of a precise weighted formula has been difficult if not impossible. We have attempted the next best thing, by maintaining constant vigilance with the suboptimization problem while collecting information analyzing and interpreting our findings.

We have been concerned with efficiency indicators and the concept of managerial effectiveness at several levels. Starting at the top, these focus on total national efficiency, branch of industry, aggregate firm and finally intrafirm efficiency measures. In this study, greatest attention is paid to the latter two types of measures for U.S. and Indian firms.

We have been seriously limited in using efficiency comparisons in monetary or financial terms, especially where the related product and factor input prices in various countries and industries have not been established primarily by the market forces of supply and demand. This is therefore a serious problem in Indian-United States comparisons, since India is an economy of this type. Hence, we have found it necessary to rely greatly on efficiency measures stated in physical, percentage, ratio, and time terms. This clearly makes our research task more difficult than if we could rely more on monetary efficiency measures, but it by no means makes it impossible or fruitless.

Let us briefly indicate some of the key efficiency measures useful at the various levels of analysis. Wherever possible it may be desirable to use some unit of measure other than money, or in addition to money, for each efficiency indicator. Where money is used in inter-country comparisons, great pains should be taken to convert it with as much accuracy as possible into a standard unit of value (usually U.S. dollars).

National efficiency measures

At the country or total economy level use can be made of the following measures as well as others.

1. Level and rate of growth of real GNP (Gross National Product).
2. Level and rate of growth of real per capita income.
3. Rate of utilization of key factor inputs (plant, material, power, etc.).
4. Useful output in relation to total output.
5. Level and rate of growth of total real industrial output.
6. Physical output and growth rates for specific major commodities.
7. Total industrial employment and rate of growth of same.
8. Level and rate of increase in industrial labor productivity (in terms of output per man hour or year).
9. Level and rate of increase of industrial output per capita and per gainfully employed citizen.
10. Value added contribution of overall industrial sector to GNP and trends over time (in percent).
11. Value added per industrial employee and trends over time.
12. Incremental capital-output ratios and trends.
13. Ratios of inventories to output produced and sold.

Branch of industrial efficiency indicators

The second level of efficiency and managerial effectiveness comparisons pertains to branch-of-industry indicators which enable inter-country comparisons involving the same industries in each case. These industry indicators take the same basic form as several of those at the national level, and most of those at the firm level within their respective industries. In fact most branch-of-industry efficiency measures are averages comprised of the results achieved by the firms in the industry. This level of analysis not only enables inter-country comparisons on a branch-of-industry basis, but also an analysis of relative performance among firms in the same industry in the same country.

A comparison of the performance of specific firms to related branch-of-industry averages often reveals whether a given firm is likely to be confronted with significant suboptimization problems in certain areas. An ideal firm would be one that ranks relatively high in the industry in relation to all of the branch-of-industry averages used. If a given firm ranks high on some indicators and quite or very low on others, this often suggests significant suboptimization problems.

One serious limitation in the use of branch-of-industry averages as efficiency indicators is that such data is not available in many countries for many specific industries. Good statistics of this kind are scarce in India. This is unfortunate, since we feel that data of this type is very important for valuable comparative research. Where average data for a whole industry in a given country cannot be obtained, it may be adequate to utilize efficiency indicator averages based on the performance of a sample of firms in the industry, as we do in several cases in this study.

Efficiency indicators at the firm level

In studying specific enterprises, which is the heart of our empirical research, we make use of both overall or aggregate firm efficiency indicators and intrafirm measures. The latter type are the most important. We do, of course, make use of such aggregate firm indicators as total profit, sales, output and/or costs; rate of return; market share; growth rates with regard to the above; and actual versus planned performance. But we have found that it is frequently not very meaningful to focus on such aggregate measures in comparative research, particularly when highly diverse countries are involved. More disaggregate measures seem to be more fruitful for analysis.

It is often extremely difficult to gauge or analyze the impact on firm efficiency in any country by moving right from a given environmental constraint to aggregate efficiency measures such as those mentioned above, or even by jumping from critical management process elements to such aggregate measures. It seems that one must look more deeply into the firm's operations and performance for fruitful analysis or problem solving.

An effective method involves tracing and analyzing the impact of critical environmental constraints (I's as well as C's, where applicable) on affected critical elements of the management process (B's), and relating the way that the B's are performed to mini-micro and quantifiable intrafirm efficiency indicators (referred to as e's). Then it is often possible to estimate, by inference and often qualitatively, the impact that a given e or set of e's has on the more aggregate firm efficiency measures.

For example, considerable non-productive time due to unanticipated equipment breakdowns probably shows up in the firm's aggregate profit, output, cost, productivity, and sales performance; similarly, relatively high rates of employee absenteeism, material wastage, quality rejects, and customer returns show up in aggregate results as well. If these are widespread problems among firms in a given industry or on a national scale, they will also be reflected in branch-of-industry and national efficiency performance and related indicators.

Below is presented a partial list of the intrafirm efficiency indicators or e's which we found useful in our empirical research. Rate of change over an extended period of time with regard to the following e's is also important in many cases.

1. Usable output per employee (this indicator may be broken down by specific types of employees, products, and/or productive sectors within the firm).

2. Sales and/or value added per employee (this too can be broken down by products, types of employees, departments, etc.).

3. Unanticipated equipment breakdowns in relation to total operating time (total and/or productive areas).

4. Degree of plant utilization (can be divided by productive sectors within the firm).

5. Product yields (reflects percentage of material wastage).

6. Rejects (defective output) and scrap as a percentage of total output of major products.

7. Absenteeism rates.

8. Personnel turnover rates.

9. Accident frequency rates and resulting lost time.

10. Sales, profits and output in relation to total payroll (or for certain parts of the firm).

11. Unit cost breakdowns and trends for major products.

12. Labor input per unit of output.

13. Incremental sales and output in relation to incremental investment in fixed and/or working capital.

14. Inventory levels for major commodities in relation to production and sales, and inventory turnover rates.

15. Fixed and working capital per employee (also for certain units of the firm).

16. Various other fixed and working capital ratios.

17. Uncompleted or unsatisfied customer orders and late delivery rates by major products, and as a percentage of sales and output.

18. Goods returned in relation to sales and output.

19. Marketing and distribution costs in relation to sales and profit margins of major products.

20. Debt equity (and asset) and current ratios (assets vs. liabilities).

21. Cash velocity or cash flow indicators.

22. Import substitution indicators and export trends.

23. Nature and timing of product prices changes and prices in relation to other similar firms.

24. Various innovational indicators relating to new products and processes developed and introduced.

25. Time taken to successfully implement changes in operations, practices, techniques, procedures, methods, etc. (this is meaningful when similar comparisons can be made with other firms).

26. Planned vs. actual performance with regard to many of the above e's.

Admittedly, many of the above intrafirm efficiency indicators are crude measures of performance. However, they are among the best measures a comparative management, international business or economic development researcher has to work with.

The above e's tend to be subject to suboptimization problems, in that one can often be improved at the expense of another within a given firm. Thus, a manager might improve his maintenance record by incurring excessive cost. One can often, and should where possible, recognize suboptimization dangers in both research endeavors and managerial decision making.

Control conditions for managerial and efficiency comparisons

Specific firms which are directly compared should generally be producing basically similar types of products or product lines. If this control condition does not exist, many of the intrafirm efficiency comparisons will not be particularly meaningful. For example, comparing clothing firms with steel mills in terms of productive efficiency and managerial effectiveness is not generally likely to yield useful results. On the other hand, comparisons at highly aggregate levels, involving entire countries, may be highly significant since, even by allowing for a substantial margin of error, the gaps may be relatively large.

We have found that it is not necessarily essential in obtaining efficiency comparisons to hold such things constant as the sizes of firms, the precise technology they employ, or even the markets they sell in, or from which they obtain personnel. Holding such factors constant makes it easier to isolate and explain various differences in the management process and productive efficiency. However, our conceptual framework enables us to explain, and at times predict, significant differences with regard to why the various firms under study are the size they are, use the technology that they do, sell in the markets they do, and obtain personnel where they do.

In the final analysis, the individual researcher in the comparative and international management field or the economic development field has considerable discretion as to what control conditions he chooses to establish. This should be determined largely by what he is attempting to describe, explain, and predict. Moreover, he should also keep in mind the important distinction between measurement, which is basically what efficiency indicators are all about, and explanation which deals with why there are differences in efficiency performance.

THE QUESTION OF MANAGERIAL AND FIRM OBJECTIVES

In the overall field of management, the question of managerial and firm objectives arises sooner or later, as it does in economics with regard to national economic goals. In our analysis of managerial effectiveness and productive efficiency, our major concern is not with the different specific objectives individual managers, firms, or countries may have, although our conceptual framework is useful in helping to explain why significant differences in such objectives might exist. We devote some attention to why different firms and managements pursue substantially different objectives, and to whether the objectives they pursue are realistic. However, we focus on an evaluation of objectives in terms of concepts and measures of efficiency usually applied to highly developed industrial activities, such as those indicated earlier in this chapter. We realize that by doing this we may be imputing Western motives to some firms and managers which are alien to their own values, and hence in conflict with various objectives they might pursue. Whether they desire to pursue objectives linked to economic efficiency and achievement is for them to decide. Our interest is in evaluating whether or not they do, and if not, to explain why.

We have found that in order to do fruitful comparative management research, a common or universal concept of ultimate objectives is essential in order to evaluate managerial effectiveness and productive efficiency. Without some universal criterion regarding objectives, efficiency comparisons tend to lose much of their meaning. We feel that a good selection for such an objective is the basic determination of most nations to become steadily more efficient as time goes on.

In basically capitalistic countries with relatively effective market price systems, improved efficiency generally means higher profits and greater rewards for firm owners, managers, and other employees and better utilization of scarce resources. At the same time society benefits from more useful goods and services. It is true that profits are often not a good measure of efficiency. But even in communist and "mixed" economies the planners stress productive efficiency, which implies improvements in managerial effectiveness, so that individual firms and the nation as a whole can produce more useful output with given inputs. Since a country's total output (and wealth) is the sum of the output of component productive enterprises, including farms, of course, the more efficient each productive unit is, the more efficient in the economic sense the country will be.

In most countries there are constraints on the basic economic efficiency goal because other goals are also highly valued. Such constraints may include a desire to reduce unemployment or a desire for more leisure time. However, the evidence seems to be overwhelming that economic progress through increased productive efficiency, and by implication increased managerial effectiveness, is desired by virtually all countries. To date, virtually no country, India and the United States included, has expressed a serious desire to reduce or even hold constant the total flow of goods or services, or to utilize its resources less efficiently, no matter what its various precise goals may be.

COMPARATIVE METHODOLOGY INVOLVING MATCHED SETS OF FIRMS

We have made use of a comparative case study approach which is similar to the classical "Latin Square" experimental design. As noted in Chapter 1, we have studied some samples or sets of sufficiently comparable U.S. subsidiaries, plants and affiliates in India, indigenous companies, and also some comparable U.S.-based divisions and plants of the parent corporations of U.S. subsidiaries. For further comparative purposes, we have also studied a few European subsidiaries and collaborations in India.

Most of the U.S.-based parent companies generally attempted to utilize and implement management processes in their Indian subsidiaries which were similar to those used in their domestic operations. This commitment was reflected in their staffing policies, training programs, and other practices and "rules of the game". Some relied more on intuition while others used more formalized cost-benefit types of analyses regarding the transferability and applicability of various elements of the management process to their subsidiaries. Several parent firms tended to be substantially over-Americanized (or "ethnocentric") with regard to their subsidiaries; while a few ("polycentric" types) made relatively little effort to transfer or apply more modern management concepts which would have been effective in their subsidiaries.

In general, we found some significant differences in the patterns of U.S. subsidiaries and their indigenous Indian counterparts, as well as between subsidiaries and the domestic operations of their parent companies. Figure 2-1 depicts our comparative research model involving matched sets of firms.

Looking at Figure 2-1, the degree to which various key environmental factors constrain or prevent the effective application of selected elements of the management process by a U.S. subsidiary committed to Americanizing or modernizing its management methods may be roughly estimated, or at least suggested, by analyzing the difference between BY and BX compared to the difference between BY and BZ.

If BY is substantially more similar to BX than to BZ, this would suggest that certain environmental factors are significant in constraining the way this specific element (or set of elements) is performed in India (assuming that companies are operating at efficient levels). If, on the other hand, BY is similar to BZ, this would suggest that environmental conditions are not greatly constraining with regard to the performance of these elements, and that a fairly high degree of applicability of foreign practices is likely to exist.

Efficiency measures in this type of research design indicate the extent to which given B's are performed well or poorly by the indigenous Indian firm (EX), the U.S. subsidiary in India (EY), and the U.S.-based firm (EZ). The bigger the differences in relative efficiency, the more desirable it would be for significantly lagging firms to shift their management processes in the direction of the leader, providing that they have some leeway to do so, and assuming that they want to improve performance in this area.

Although we have been using the above approach for some time and feel that we have generated some significant findings and implications, a few words of caution about limitations are warranted. In order to effectively use this approach and the implied line of reasoning, it is necessary that the critical Indian environmental conditions bearing on the specific B's under study are basically similar for both U.S. subsidiaries and indigenous firms involved in such comparisons. Generally speaking, this condition is reasonable. However, at times there are significant exceptions, where

FIGURE 2-1 Comparative research model

	Relevant Environmental Constraints	Selected Critical Elements of the Management process	Related Efficiency Measures
Indigenous Indian firm	CI's	BX's	EX's
U.S. subsidiary in India	CI's	BY's	EY's
U.S.-based operations of the parent company of the subsidiary in India	CA's	BZ's	EZ's

CI's — Environmental constraints in India

CA's — Environmental constraints in the United States.

BX's — Critical elements of the management process (how each is performed) in the indigenous Indian firm. (Especially a relatively representative indigenous firm in a given industry.)

BY's — Critical elements of the management process (how each is performed) in the U.S. subsidiary in India. (Especially a subsidiary committed to the "Americanization" of its management methods to the point where this is effective in terms of net results.)

BZ's — Critical elements of the management process (how each is performed) in the U.S.-based firm.

EX's — Resulting level of efficiency in a given area at the indigenous Indian firm.

EY's — Resulting level of efficiency in a given area at the U.S. subsidiary in India.

EZ's — Resulting level of efficiency in a given area at the U.S.-based firm.

constraints are markedly different for U.S. (or other foreign) firms in India and similar kinds of indigenous firms being compared.

Another caution pertains to the abnormally progressive — in terms of management — indigenous firm. Though there seem to be relatively few companies of this type in India, there have been cases where indigenous firms have performed various elements of the management process in ways closely resembling comparable and relatively progressive U.S. subsidiaries. In fact, we encountered a few cases where progressive indigenous firms were even more Americanized or modernized in various aspects of management than their U.S. counterparts, and in even rarer cases, more than some of the domestic operations of U.S. parent firms. Typically, such indigenous firms employ substantial numbers or proportions of Western (usually American) trained local nationals, and in some cases even foreigners, in key managerial, technical, and staff specialist jobs.

The best way to avoid faulty or inaccurate generalizations is to study an adequate sample of comparable firms or plants and depict any significant dominant patterns which exist. This also holds true for the samples of U.S.-based companies studied. Only in this way can valid generalizations and meaningful conceptions of the "representative firm" be developed. This we have tried to do in the selection of our samples of firms wherever possible.

Finally, we have not plunged into this kind of research assuming that the more Americanized a firm is in terms of all aspects of management, the more efficient and effective it will always be. (That is, the closer BY is to BZ in all cases the better the results.) Analyses of various efficiency indicators, and especially of other data of a more qualitative nature, indicate that this is not necessarily the case. We have come across a number of cases where over-Americanization of management methods has led to highly undesirable results.

Regarding efficiency, the U.S. domestic operations studied were generally substantially more efficient than their subsidiaries in India, although there were exceptions in certain areas. This shows up vividly in intrafirm efficiency indicators (e's), but not necessarily with regard to aggregate measures such as profitability or sales growth because of great differences in degrees of competition and the functioning of market forces.

The U.S. subsidiaries surveyed in India were, as a group, substantially more efficient than their indigenous counterparts, although there were a few notable individual exceptions. Superior management has been a major factor in this regard. Even the best managed and most progressive indigenous firms have not been as efficient or economically successful as the best managed U.S. subsidiaries, although some have typically been better than many U.S. and other foreign firms in the country.

It is interesting to note that differences in the relative levels of efficiency among the U.S. domestic companies studied were generally not nearly as great in magnitude as those found among firms studied in India. This is due chiefly to the substantially greater competition, market forces, and other environmental conditions which exist in the United States and tend to serve as equalizing factors. This kind of pattern probably holds true with regard to the United States compared to developing countries generally.

The larger differences found in the developing nations are also due to smaller and less uniform talent pools. Innovative managerial personnel tend to cluster around those companies which have established environments which nurture and reward effectiveness. These tend to be firms which are run either by foreign interests or by the rare local individuals who have been able to successfully break with indigenous patterns and traditions.

APPLICATION OF OUR CONCEPTUAL FRAMEWORK

In view of our research experiences to date, we have concluded that in our investigations we should try to obtain and focus on available efficiency measures, particularly those of the e type. This we have done in this study. An examination of the relative efficiency performance in a given area — say, for example, lost time due to equipment breakdowns, employee absenteeism, or average amount of material x used in manufacturing product y — for two or more firms in the same sector, a similar branch of industry in two or more countries, or even for the overall industrial sectors of two or more countries, will frequently reveal significant differences that are worth studying in depth. If we see that A, whether it is a firm, industry, or country, is significantly more efficient in a certain area than B, it seems important to describe and explain why this is so. Once this has been done adequately, we are in a better position to predict and prescribe what action should be taken which will lead to B moving in the direction of A in terms of efficiency.

Moreover, by focusing on significant relative differences in efficiency performance we can more easily identify and analyze the most strategic or critical elements of the management process, rather than randomly studying many or all elements in a general way. In turn, once the most critical management process elements are identified, there is a much better chance of identifying and then analyzing the most critical environmental constraints on managerial performance and productive efficiency in a given area.

If, through extensive empirical research at the enterprise level, the same kinds of B's and related C's show up constantly as being strategic in explaining relatively poor efficiency performance in a given area, we are clearly on the path of fruitful theory building. Eventually, it will be possible to prescribe what action macro planners as well as firm managers should take with regard to various C's (or I's) to improve efficiency in a given area, and predict the outcome with a reasonable degree of confidence.

Before presenting an actual example, let us elaborate and illustrate more clearly what we are trying to do. By focussing on intrafirm efficiency measures or e's, one may discover that in a given country, a given firm or industry's machines experience unanticipated breakdowns equivalent to 10 percent of their operating time, while in other countries or firms the downtime rate is only 2 percent. Or one may discover that absenteeism rates average 15 percent in one case, and only 5 percent in another case. In both of the above examples the differences are clearly significant in terms of productive efficiency and managerial effectiveness, and further investigation would probably be worth while.

Once the relevant e's warranting further study have been identified, it is usually possible to isolate the critical elements of the management process (B's) which directly affect the e's in a significant way. Thus for the equipment breakdown problem, it is typically true that planning of maintenance is critical. B1.4 (degree and extent to which enterprise operations are spelled out in plans or pre-programmed) tends to be important here. How well is the firm planning its maintenance work (i.e., how well is the management performing this critical element)? Also, B7.3 (timing and procurement of critical spare parts) is typically important in this type of problem. How well is management performing the function? One could go on to identify many, if not all, relevant B's which affect the performance of maintenance or otherwise relate to equipment breakdowns within the firm. If unanticipated equipment breakdown is a serious problem, then it is usually true that many relevant B's are being performed poorly.

A problem here is that close examination of the critical element B list may lead to most if not virtually every B being considered as relevant to the problem. But if one is considering the practical solution of problems, it is generally necessary to consider only a small number of the most critical B factors. It is typically true that a limited number, say five or six, of the most significant B factors will account for perhaps 50 to 90 percent of the problem. The variation here may result from the kind of e measure being considered and the complexity of the efficiency problem.

The B's can be rank ordered in terms of their importance to the problem. Thus in the maintenance question above, planning may be substantially more important than procurement problems, so this factor would be ranked higher and warrant more attention. One good way to supplement the researcher's judgement in ranking B's (or C's and I's) in terms of their significance is to call upon the managers or experts who deal with the problem to give their rank orders. If the problem is considered important enough, more refined methodology, such as the use of the Delphi Technique (developed at the Rand Corporation), can be used to get a more accurate rank ordering.[9] The Delphi Technique involves several rounds of expert opinion with controlled information feedback to the experts, with the aim of obtaining a voluntary convergence of relative rankings.[7]

In general then, really complicated efficiency problems may involve as many as 10, 15, or more B's, and several sets of B's ranked according to relative importance might be necessary. The purpose of limiting the first pass of the problem to a relatively few B's is to avoid formulating questions of too great complexity for meaningful analysis.

Once the most strategic B's have been identified and studied, the next step is to move to identification and analysis of the relevant environmental factors (C's and if applicable I's) bearing on the B's in the problem. A number of possible identification techniques or guidelines in addition to direct observation and subjective judgement exist here. One could use the hypotheses of C-I-B interrelationships (as presented in Tables 2-4 and 2-5) since these matrices do have some empirical basis. Or one could again use expert opinion, including the Delphi Technique, in identifying and ranking key environmental constraints, given the relevant B's. Here, the number of relevant C's or I's is also not an exhaustive list, since only those pertaining to the few critical B factors seen as most important need be listed. As with the selection of the B's, an effort should be made to analyze only those C's and I's which have the most impact on the B's in the problem.

At this point it is possible to construct a mini-C-I-B matrix, consisting only of the most relevant variables which bear on the specific efficiency problem at hand, and such a matrix will be presented shortly. The interrelationships between the B's and the C's and I's can be analyzed thus indicating what the manager might do about this problem, and just as important, what is causing it. The firm will be in a better position to cope with key environmental constraints, as well as B's, bearing on the problem, once they are identified.

If a given efficiency problem is fairly widespread in a given country or industry, and a common set of B's and C's are involved, macro planners and policy makers are in a better position to attempt effective environmental changes. Thus it may be found that equipment breakdowns are a serious and widespread problem in a given country, and that one major cause is the great scarcity of skilled technical personnel, particularly mechanics. Once a firm has identified this C factor as being crucial, it may find that it can reduce its impact by a special training program, higher pay to attract mechanics, and so on. But it cannot solve the country's problem in this manner. It can only minimize its own difficulties. However, a country's macro decision makers, seeing the sort of matrix analysis noted above, might be more inclined to launch a major national or regional program to reduce this C defficiency. The micro and macro analyses tend to converge on this sort of question. If the same C or group of C's show up time and time again in the analysis of different kinds of efficiency problems, the implications become clear for macro decision makers in a given country who are concerned with establishing priorities for environmental changes.

Let us now briefly capitulate the key steps with regard to our research approach. In reality, later steps may precede earlier ones in various instances.

1. Identify efficiency problems or areas that are causing trouble or where improvement is desired for a given firm, group of firms, industry, or country through comparative analysis.

2. Identify and analyze the B elements which are most important to a specific efficiency problem. Put them in rank order and focus on a limited number of the most important ones.

3. Identify and analyze the relevant C and I constraints which are most important for the B factors. Rank order them and focus on the most important.

4. Prepare a mini-C-I-B matrix and analyze the important interrelationships.

5. Isolate solutions — that is, which B's are done relatively poorly because of which C's and why? If the relevant interrelationships can be determined, the firm, the industry, and/or the country is likely to be in a much better position to do something effective in solving critical efficiency problems.

ILLUSTRATIVE CASE

The case involves unanticipated equipment breakdowns in relation to total planned operating time over a period of three years at three adequately comparable plants: a plant in the United States, a plant of the same parent firm's subsidiary in India, and an indigenous Indian plant. Figure 2-2 indicates the performance of each plant with regard to these.

FIGURE 2-2   Unanticipated equipment breakdowns in relation to total operating time

(A)	U.S. factory in the United States	Less than 1%
(B)	U.S. subsidiary plant in India	about 7%
(C)	Indigenous Indian plant	15 to 20%

All of these factories were in the same basic manufacturing sector, and produced essentially similar kinds of products. Even the basic technology employed was roughly comparable in all three cases. However, both the U.S.-based plant and the U.S. subsidiary were operating at higher rates of both planned and actual plant capacity than the Indian firm. So, if anything, the performance of the latter with regard to the *e* under study was relatively worse than reflected above. The problem is to explain why these significant differences in equipment performance existed by focusing on critical B's, C's and where applicable I's.

Examination of possible B's in the firms which might cause equipment breakdowns suggested immediately that the problem was a complex one. This case revealed, incidentally, why good maintenance is so difficult and why a relatively good equipment breakdown record is so hard to achieve in a developing country, such as India. Many kinds of decisions bear on the problem, and firms have to perform many activities with reasonable efficiency to get good performance in this area. It proved quite difficult to isolate the small number of B's which probably explain more than half the problem.

The nine most critical B's (see Table 2-1 for numbering) for the firms studied were the following:

B 1.4: *Degree and extent to which enterprise operations are spelled out in plans.* Firms which do not spell out maintenance plans clearly and integrate these with their production plans are likely to be in trouble on maintenance. Because maintenance tends to be effective when it is preventive rather than corrective, firms need to plan very carefully in this area. Quite often minor problems become very serious and lead to breakdowns because they are not corrected routinely through good preventive maintenance planning.

B 2.3: *Nature and structure of information systems used for control purposes.* Equipment maintenance calls for many kinds of feedback of performance, and interpretation of this feedback, in order for maintenance to be performed properly. This information ranges from good maintenance records on given pieces of equipment to monitoring of various gauges and instruments while equipment is in action for signs of trouble. An improperly prepared maintenance record, for example, might fail to indicate that certain lubrication procedures were not done. As a result, premature equipment failure is likely. Or an oil pressure gauge which shows low pressure, but which is not monitored, could cause premature bearing failure. These and many other examples of failure to design and properly utilize feedback of information about maintenance are common.

B 3.3: *Degree of work specialization.* Many kinds of in-plant maintenance call for specialized skills. Firms also find it expedient to organize special maintenance crews, staffed by specially trained men, to handle such maintenance. If these personnel are poorly trained, lacking in ambition, or otherwise unable to perform their tasks properly, equipment breakdown troubles are relatively common. Some firms which do not realize the importance of maintenance may also fail to organize any special work crews for this purpose, utilizing instead general workers from other departments. A subtle and often very complex organizational problem exists here which must be solved properly if the firm is to do its maintenance well and avoid equipment breakdowns.

B 4.10: *Ease or difficulty of obtaining and maintaining personnel with desired skills and abilities.* Many countries simply do not have men with the necessary training and skills to do complex maintenance work properly. If they have a few, these men are not enough to do nearly all maintenance work properly. Indeed, even in the United States it is likely that there is a general shortage of some types of maintenance personnel, such as electronics specialists. Failure to obtain the right kind of trained men can lead to many kinds of maintenance problems.

B 5.7: *Ease or difficulty of motivating personnel to perform efficiently and to improve their performance and abilities.* Unless personnel responsible for maintenance work and equipment breakdowns inherently want to do a good job and are inclined to worry about failures, performance in this area is likely to suffer. On the other hand, if they take equipment breakdowns seriously, and have a basic desire to improve the situation, performance is likely to be better. Anyone who has worked with maintenance problems anywhere is probably aware of the very real problem of getting men to work well in this field. Much of the work, by its very nature, cannot be supervised closely, and many times it is difficult to determine if the job has been done properly in the first place. A worker may be asked to grease certain bearings, and if he fails to do so, maintenance costs and probably equipment breakdowns increase. But even if he did, the bearings might fail from time to time for other reasons. A bearing fails — did the man do his job or not? This sort of question may be very difficult to answer. Unless the man wants to or can be made to work properly, the firm is in trouble.

B 7.1: *Make or buy (materials, components, parts, services, etc., and the extent to which subcontracting is used).* Firms with complex machinery have complex parts inventory problems. If they order many parts from outside suppliers, they may find their inventory costs exploding. If they decide to make some key components in small lots, their manufacturing costs may explode. Decisions as to trade-offs here can be very complex.

These decisions are more complicated in situations where potential suppliers are far away, as is common in India. (Here we see a close relationship with B 7.2). Much of the machinery used is built in other countries, and long delays may result if the decision is to buy parts.

B 7.2: *Number, types, and locations of suppliers and B 10.2: Supplier relations.* The kinds of policies, attitudes, and relations a given firm has with regard to its suppliers are likely to be particularly critical in a sellers' market situation, or where suppliers of key items are not readily available. If the firm is willing to develop new and dependable local sources of supply by training and working closely with the personnel of supplier firms, giving financial help to suppliers or through various other policies and practices, the benefits in terms of the avoidance of equipment breakdowns may well be worth the costs entailed.

B 7.3: *Timing of procurement (major materials, critical components and parts, etc.).* It is often possible to avoid equipment breakdowns caused by critical spare parts and component shortages through careful and effective procurement planning. Such planning would provide for adequate lead times, inventory reserves, flexibility, and contingencies.

While the above B's appear to be most important, it is true that other B's also are relevant in this efficiency problem. The exact ranking of importance of each B might vary between observers, indeed, this is one situation in which the Delphi Technique might be used to determine which B's, and in which order, are most relevant. We will return to other, less important B's later.

The next step in this analysis is to consider which C's and/or I's are most important in affecting the managerial decisions and performance in connection with the strategic B elements. For the strategic B's, many C's were potentially important, but the ones used and analyzed further were those which seemed to be most relevant. They are the following (not presented in specific rank order).

C 1.3: *Higher education.* Equipment maintenance is a very complex technical problem, requiring the intensive use of many kinds of high talent manpower. This is particularly true in terms of the precise sophisticated technical talent required, and the technical and general management used in maintenance activities. Countries which have shortages of this type of manpower are typically in serious trouble with maintenance. C 1.3 seems to be more important in this case than C 1.2 or C 1.4, but these latter constraints were also relevant.

C 1.6: *Educational match with industrial requirements.* If a country has many arts graduates, lawyers, doctors, philosophers, and even economists, for example, but relatively few engineers, technicians, machinists, and electronic specialists, its social system may work relatively well, but its mechanical and electrical equipment is not likely to. Most maintenance problems require specially trained men to handle them properly, and general education reflected in various other C's do not typically do the job. Men must be educated and trained for the specific tasks at hand.

C 2.3: *Interorganization cooperation.* In all countries cooperation between the suppliers of critical spare parts and components and their customers is important in avoiding equipment breakdowns. This becomes even more critical where few if any alternative sources of supply are readily available, as is common in strong sellers' markets. Cooperation between firms which use similar kinds of parts can reduce the frequency and damage caused by equipment breakdowns, if they are willing to lend, sell, or exchange parts which they do not need at the time, but which are urgently needed by another plant. Where a government agency is responsible for allocating key parts and components to firms, if the agency is not interested in cooperating with the firms and trying to understand its problems and needs, the chances of equipment failures tend to be increased.

C 2.4: *View toward achievement and work.* As mentioned previously, the nature of many maintenance problems requires relatively unsupervised and conscientious workmanship. Attitudes of workers and supervisors do, therefore, significantly affect maintenance results.

C 2.7: *View toward scientific method.* This may be the most critical factor of all with regard to equipment breakdowns. If industrial personnel, including workers, typically have a relatively poor view or understanding of scientific, causal methodology, maintenance performance is likely to suffer substantially, even if men are otherwise trained quite well. Virtually all maintenance functions are quite scientifically oriented, and it takes good appreciation of planning and control, from the top to the bottom of the organization, to get good maintenance.

C 2.9: *View toward change.* Effective maintenance is a dynamic process, frequently requiring changes in specifications, procedures, and methods. Hence the view of change held by the people involved in maintenance activities is critical. If the majority, or even several of the key personnel are passive or resist change, it is not very likely that maintenance will be done well.

C 3.3: *Foreign policy and, I 2.5: Import-export restrictions for international firms.* If some machines, parts, and/or components must be imported, then the question of import restrictions, exchange controls, tariffs, and similar controls must be considered. A particularly important point here is that government planners may fail to appreciate the importance of obtaining spare parts and critical components for existing machines, with disastrous results for firms trying to maintain and utilize them. It is quite common for international firms operating in various countries to be subject to different import regulations or rules of the game than indigenous firms. Such regulations and rules may either benefit or hinder such firms.

C 3.5: *Political organization.* Where government agencies do allocate spare parts and components — either produced domestically or imported — to firms, the problem of serious and unpredictable bureaucratic delays in making allocation decisions can often be even more serious, in terms of equipment breakdowns, than negative decisions made within a stipulated and reasonable period of time. For it is often less difficult for the firm to plan and adjust its activities knowing that it will not be allocated certain items, than if it were to be in the dark as to when the decision will be made.

Arranging the above critical B's and C's in matrix form leads to Figure 2-3 below. The X's marked in this matrix have been inserted with the help of experts at the firms surveyed. The X's indicate the most significant relationships between the most important critical elements of the management process and the environmental constraints which relate to equipment breakdowns.

FIGURE 2-3 Equipment breakdown C-B matrix

	C 1.3	C 1.6	C 2.3	C 2.4	C 2.7	C 2.9	C 3.3 & I 2.5	C 3.5
B 1.4	x	x			x	x		
B 2.3	x	x			x	x		
B 3.3		x			x			
B 4.10	x	x			x	x		
B 5.7				x		x		
B 7.1	x	x	x	x	x	x	x	x
B 7.2 and B 10.2		x			x	x	x	
B 7.3			x					x

How can the above matrix help explain differences in equipment breakdown performance among the firms studied? Intuitively even nonexperts are likely to feel strongly that many and perhaps all of the C's noted in the matrix are not very good in India relative to the U.S. Our kind of empirical research helps separate myths from reality and give substantiation to such intuitive feelings. More importantly empirical research reveals the actual concrete kinds of efficiency problems caused by the C's through their impact on specific B's. At this state of knowledge, low C scores arrived at without intensive research at the firm level often tell us little if anything about their real impacts on productive efficiency.

The U.S.-based plant has strong advantages in every area noted on the above matrix. One could reasonably infer, particularly if a much larger sample of firms were studied, that firms in the U.S., in general, would be in a much better position to avoid unanticipated equipment breakdowns than firms in India. Good C's tend to lead to good performance of the B's most related to this type of efficiency problem.

The American firm in India can and does transfer some relatively favorable factors to India, and thus reduces the negative impact of various local environmental constraints. What can be transferred are better staffing policies and skilled personnel — including some American and other foreign managers and specialists — training programs, perhaps various incentive programs, together with various behavioral attitudes and values that are more conducive to productive efficiency. For example, the U.S. subsidiary did better than the Indian firm, but in most cases not as well as the U.S. based plant, on B 1.4, B 2.3, B 3.3, B 4.10, B 5.7, and B 7.3, in spite of such local constraints as C 1.3, C 1.6, C 2.4, C 2.7, C 2.9, C 3.3, and C 3.5. The U.S. subsidiary also made a number of spare parts not made by the Indian firm, largely because it did a better job in overcoming various educational constraints. With regard to B 7.2 and B 10.2, the U.S. subsidiary did a better job than its Indian counterpart in searching out and cultivating new and fairly dependable local spare part and component suppliers, and this served to reduce the negative impacts of C 2.3, C 3.3, and C 3.5. Furthermore, the U.S. subsidiary had somewhat more flexibility in importing certain kinds of critical spare parts than the Indian firm, because of I 2.5 regulations bearing on its operations.

On the other hand, the U.S. subsidiary was faced with more serious environmental constraints across the board than the plant located in the U.S.

In general, the U.S. firm in India is still bound substantially by the local environment in terms of the education, training, and attitudes of its employees; the attitudes of other organizations whose cooperation it may desire; and import controls and bureaucratic delays imposed by the Indian government. It may be able to adjust to such constraints more effectively than the Indian firm, but it can never escape them completely. The Indian firm is clearly in an even more difficult position. Rarely can a purely local firm effectively recruit abroad to obtain trained men with certain kinds of attitudes.

The matrix shown in Figure 2-3 suggests that much of the total equipment breakdown problem might be explained by the variables indicated therein. But this type problem is complicated, and it is not easy to find a small number of C's and B's which explain everything. It is useful in such complex situations to build a Level II matrix, to determine if anything important was overlooked. In this case, additional B elements are identified, and the C's and I's relating to these B's are also covered. Some of the same C's and I's used in Figure 2-3 may again be relevant, but they now refer to different B's. The analytical process proceeds in the same manner as for Table 2-3.

We should point out that the above approach does not adequately deal with or answer a very basic question. That is, are the managers of firm A in environment X (say India) as effective as the managers of firm B in environment Y (say the United States), given the environmental constraints which they must contend with? Or more specifically, were the managers of the above U.S. subsidiary actually more or less effective than their counterparts in the domestic company with regard to the equipment breakdown or other efficiency problems, given the considerably less favorable environmental conditions in India? Even though efficiency performance was significantly better at the U.S. based plant, this does not necessarily mean that its managers were more effective, since the level of efficiency is a function of both managerial effectiveness and external environmental factors which are largely if not totally beyond the control of firm management. This is reflected in the following equations:

1) $e = f(x)$ 2) $x = f(Bm.n)$ 3) $Bm.n = f(Cm.n)$

4) $\therefore x = f(Cm.n)$ and, 5) $e = f(Cm.n)$

In the above equations the variables are defined as follows:

e is a given efficiency indicator or measure
x is managerial effectiveness as summarized in an index score made up of individual scores for various B's
$Bm.n$ are elements of the management process critical to the efficiency problem
$Cm.n$ are relevant environmental constraints

The only way that the question regarding superior management performance in two different environments could be answered in any definitive sense would be to determine the incremental impacts that differences in relevant C's (and I's if applicable) have on the related B's which, in turn, bear on efficiency (the e's). In other words, one must determine the relationships between ΔC's and related ΔB's. If a given C is improved by say, 10 percent or is 10 percent better in country A than B, what impact will this tend to have on the related B's and e's? To answer this kind of question, the relevant C's and B's must be quantified in a meaningful way. Then the difference between the sum of the C scores in the two environments must be compared to the difference in the sum of the B scores for the firms under study with regard to the efficiency problem being considered.

If this can be accomplished, it may be possible to conclude that a 10 percent increase in a given C (say within the United Stated vis-a-vis India) tends to increase the efficiency or improve the performance of the related B's by 20 percent. If the B scores at the U.S. subsidiary are only 5 percent lower than those at the domestic company, we might conclude that the subsidiary's managers are more effective, even if their efficiency performance is lower. If two firms are operating in a similar environment the comparison is much simpler, since one can usually conclude that the firm with the best efficiency performance has more effective management in the area or areas involved.

We have not attempted such a rigorous or quantitative type of analysis in this book. However, more qualitative assessments of these kinds are made at various appropriate points. A more rigorous quantitative approach is essential if management, international business and economic development are to evolve into the realm of true science. We hope that the above conceptualization of approaches (which may prove fruitful for both theory building and practice) has a significant impact.

CHAPTER 2   FOOTNOTES

1. Our colleague, Richard Farmer, can speak for Saudi Arabia, where he has work experience. We can speak for India and other developing countries in which we have lived. With regard to the Soviet Union and China see the following books by Richman: *Soviet Management: With Significant American Comparisons,* Prentice Hall, Englewood Cliffs, N.J., 1965; *Management Development and Education in the Soviet Union,* Institute for International Business and Economic Development Studies, Michigan State University, East Lansing, 1967; *Industrial Society in Communist China,* Random House, New York, 1969 and Vintage Books, 1972.

2. The following works have helped us classify managerial functions: H. Koontz and C. O'Donnell, *Principles of Management,* 4th edition, McGraw-Hill Book Company, Inc., New York, 1967; W. Newman, *Administrative Action,* 2nd edition, Prentice-Hall, Englewood Cliffs, N.J., 1963; W. Newman and C. Summer, *The Process of Management,* Prentice-Hall, Englewood Cliffs, N.J., 1961.

3. See R. Farmer and B. Richman, *Comparative Management and Economic Progress,* Richard D. Irwin, Inc., Homewood, Ill., 1965; Farmer and Richman, *International Business: An Operational Theory,* Richard D. Irwin, Inc., Homewood, Ill., 1966; B. Richman, "A Rating Scale for Product Innovation," *Business Horizons,* vol. 5, vol. 4, Summer, 1962, pp. 37-44.

4. See the books cited in footnote 3. See also, R. Farmer and B. Richman, "A Model for Research in Comparative Management," *California Management Review,* Vol. VIII, No. 2, Winter, 1964, pp. 55-64; and, Richman, *Industrial Society in Communist China,* Chapter 8.

5. The country constraints or C's are dealt with in Farmer and Richman, 1965, *op. cit.* The international constraints or I's are discussed in Farmer and Richman, 1966, *op. cit.*

6. For a thorough review and discussion of the efficiency problem see Farmer and Richman, 1965, *op. cit.,* Chapter 5 and Appendix B, and the numerous sources cited therein.

7. For a discussion on the Delphi Technique see *Ibid.,* pp. 329-334; N. Dalkey and O. Helmer, "An Experimental Application of the Delphi Method with the Use of Experts," *Management Science,* Vol. IX, No. 3, April, 1963; O. Helmer and N. Rescher, "On the Epistemology of the Inexact Sciences," *Management Science,* Vol. VI, No. 1, October, 1959; T. Garden and O. Helmer, *Report on a Long-Range Forecasting Study,* The Rand Corporation, Santa Monica, Calif., 1964.

PART 2
ENVIRONMENT

CHAPTER 3
EDUCATIONAL
ENVIRONMENT

One of the building blocks most basic to the process of industrial and general economic development is the educational environment within a country. The term "environment" is used rather than "system" to reflect the fact that education is more than just the product of formal schooling. It represents an amalgamation of the school system, of cultural and ethical philosophies concerning the value of knowledge and the worthiness of achievement, and of government and industrial attitudes and activities in this sphere.

In general, the educational environment in any country influences virtually every aspect of managerial and industrial life. It affects not only the specific skills and abilities of managers, technicians, workers, suppliers, and consumers, but also their methods of thinking and the speed at which new thought or values will be assimilated. It has great bearing on the entire staffing function, basic organization structure, degrees of work specialization, types of techniques employed, procedures, controls and technology used, costs of production, the overall productivity of firms, and many other aspects of performance.

Similarly, the education and knowledge contained within non-industrial organizations — such as governmental, economic, legal, and regulatory agencies, banking institutions, transportation organizations, and port authorities — have a significant impact on the activities of industrial firms.

Executives and technicians sent to developing countries for the first time often are shocked to discover the extent and ways in which the educational environment of the host country affect the management process. They may have obtained some indications of this from secondary sources, but having lived, and worked in an advanced country, they often find it agonizing to adjust to the kinds of manpower and human problems which they find. On the other hand many international corporations have recognized the impact that a relatively poor educational environment has on managerial performance more readily than managers of indigenous firms who have lived and worked in such environments all of their lives. When this is the case, the foreign subsidiary often adapts to and copes with educational constraints more effectively than its indigenous counterparts.

In general, an understanding of the educational milieu is prerequisite to an understanding of the managerial processes necessary to direct industrial and general economic development. The most critical inputs to such processes are human elements, especially mental talents, and these are largely products of the educational environment. When the required abilities are unavailable, management faces strong challenges in dealing with the future. For example, if a large pool of well trained technicians is needed to implement a certain plan, it may be unrealistic to proceed if such technicians are unavailable in the local environment. The alternatives become clear, however. For the immediate future, one can try to import such technicians from elsewhere, switch to a method in which the quality of the technicians is not as critical, change plans entirely so that technicians will no longer be required, or look to the future and start training such technicians. Any one or a combination of these alternatives may be pursued from the start if one has examined the educational environment and recognized its significance to managerial action. It is not necessary to follow the time-worn path of so many companies and government agencies who act first and then analyze their errors later.

LITERACY LEVEL

Quantitative trends and language problems[1]

One of the most commonly used standards of general educational levels is the literacy rate. Adelman and Morris, two leading econometricians who use an interdisciplinary empiricist approach in their comprehensive quantitative models of environmental factors influencing economic development in 74 countries, point to literacy as one of the most critical factors.[2] This is supported by our own work in comparative management.

According to the 1961 Census, 23.7 percent of all Indian adults (over the age of 14) were literate, i.e., could read and write at least one language. This compares with a 16.6 percent rate in 1951. The U.S. rate is about 98 percent. Although more current official literacy statistics for India are not available, in 1966, Indian education officials indicated that the literacy rate was approaching 30 percent. However, several factors of special significance to the management process are concealed by Indian literacy statistics.

First, because literacy is defined in terms of the ability to read and write in at least one language, the figures say little about the ability of Indians to communicate with one another. The Indian constitution recognizes 14 distinct languages. About a dozen different written scripts, and several hundred more languages or dialects are used throughout the country. Hindi and its derivatives (Sanskrit based) are spoken by the largest number of Indians, but these languages are largely confined to Northern India. The languages spoken in the South are derived from a completely different root (Dravidian).

For firms that employ people who speak different languages and many dialects, and many firms in the larger Indian cities do, the communication problems tend to be substantial. A typical case was observed in a large Calcutta plant where managers and technicians frequently had to communicate through interpreters. Languages used were Bengali, Hindi, a Bihar dialect of Hindi, Urdu, Tamil, Assamese, and Oria. Similarly, workers in a machine tool factory in Southern India communicated in Tamil, Telugu, Hindi, Malayalam, Kannada, Urdu, or English.

[The only language which links all of India is English, a legacy of the British Raj, but it is the language of the elite, spoken primarily by relatively highly-educated individuals. Since most of the better educated Indian managers, technicians, and clerks, speak and read English, it is the major business language in India.] This gives Indian business and industry a potential advantage over many other developing countries because much of the pertinent management and technical literature of the world is published in English. However, the typical traditional Indian firm does not fully utilize English language publications or foreign experiences in general, probably due in part to the relatively low achievement drive of many of their managers.

A second factor which clouds the issue relates to the validity of the measure. What constitutes literacy or the ability to read or write? There is reasonable justification to suspect that the census figures err on the side of leniency, and that many of the individuals who are classified as literate are probably barely so, and only in certain types of situations (e.g., ability to write one's name, read numbers, and interpret newspaper headlines or advertisements).

On the positive side, however, are a number of factors of interest to students of management. First is the growth rate. An increase of seven percentage points (from 16.6 to 23.7 or from 23 to 30) may seem insignificant, but when this is translated into absolute figures it represents well over 20 million people. The impact of such a change can best be placed in perspective by recognizing that this number far exceeds the total populations of all but a handful of African and South American nations.

The breakdown between literacy rates for males and females is also of significance since most of Indian industry's manpower input is male. An analysis of the 1961 statistics indicates that 33.9 percent of the male population was literate, as opposed to only 12.8 percent of the female population (as contrasted to 24.9 percent and 7.9 percent respectively in 1951).

An interpretation of the literacy rate figures must also consider the fact that there is little doubt that urban males are more literate than their rural counterparts. Since rural males are likely to be engaged in agricultural pursuits, business enterprises are primarily concerned with the most literate portion of the male population.

Finally, another important modification must be made to account for variations from region to region. These variations are the result of a number of factors, including state support to education (in many cases due to the progressiveness of former ruling princes), local cultural patterns, and circumstances (e.g., location of seats of government by the British). The total literacy figures have been broken down by states. Table 3-1 gives the numbers from the 1961 census for the most highly industralized states, and for the states with the highest and lowest proportions of literate citizens.

Several important facts are evident in Table 3-1. First, since Delhi is the center of government and much of the economic activity of the region is linked to government or commercial activity, a relatively high degree of literacy can be expected. The population of Delhi, unlike that of most states, is a mixture of people drawn from all over India. Second, the state of Kerala, which has by far the largest Christian population, differs significantly from all other states, both in total literacy and in female literacy rates. This is largely attributable to a relatively heavy emphasis on education which is part of the local cultural. Finally, there is a significant difference in literacy rates for males and females. This derives from the role of the woman as a housekeeper and child-bearer, and that of the male as the wage earner. Many urban male workers leave their wives and families back in the village, and only the male acquires the minimal educational standards necessary to perform industrial tasks. Education, in many rural

TABLE 3-1 Selected Literacy Figures — 1961 Census

Highest literacy rates	Male	Female	Total
Delhi	58.9	41.1	51.0
Kerala	54.2	38.4	46.2
Other (industrial)			
Gujarat	40.8	19.1	30.3
Madras	43.0	17.3	30.2
Maharashtra	41.8	16.7	29.7
West Bengal	40.0	16.8	29.1
Lowest literacy rates			
Rajasthan	22.8	5.7	14.7
Himachal Pradesh	22.6	6.0	14.6
Jammu and Kashmir	16.3	4.2	10.7
Total	33.9	12.8	23.7

areas, is seen solely as a means to a specific end; an end not associated with rural agricultural life. Little emphasis is placed on education for the sake of education. This may be attributable to the prevalent Indian sense of fatalism and the fear of angering the gods if one arrogantly tries to improve himself beyond the station to which, by birth, the gods have assigned him. (This will be discussed in more detail at later points in the book.)

The major industrial states have higher literacy rates than the agricultural states. This is to be expected. The figures for Gujarat (with Ahmedabad), Madras (with Madras), Maharashtra (with Bombay) and West Bengal (with Calcutta) are substantially influenced by their industrial centers. This seems to indicate that industrial activity either stimulates education, attracts it, or both.

Although exact figures are not available, it can be safely estimated that literacy in English is substantially higher in the South than in the North. This is supported by the recent riots over language which have taken place in the South in opposition to the elimination of English as an official government language. The reasons for this Southern expertise are numerous but perhaps the most important was the British decision to use both Hindi and English as official languages. The Northern Hindi speakers could enter government (civil service jobs have been and still are considered to be among the most prestigious forms of employment in India) without knowledge of English. For Southerners, entree to government required the learning of a new language, and an emphasis was placed on English. Inevitably, the British felt more comfortable with English speakers, and South Indians achieved great prominence in the Indian Civil Service. This, in turn, strengthened the emphasis on English education in the South.

One other point should be mentioned regarding literacy. Language has become an important nationalistic issue in India in recent years. Most of the states have been organized on linguistic bases. Recently, the State of Punjab was divided, after bloody rioting, into the States of Punjab and Hariana due to agitation between Punjabi and Hindi speaking residents. Each region takes fierce pride in its local language, its poets and its literary art forms. Furthermore, India has been subject to growing nationalistic trends which aim at erasing the influence of the British and removing all vestiges of the colonial period. This has resulted in a strong emphasis on local languages, and a strong deemphasis on English (and in some cases, Hindi). Some states (e.g., Gujarat) have gone so far as to cut off state aid to any schools which start teaching English "too early." If such trends continue, these states will become more and more isolated from the others, and major inbreeding will result (e.g., teachers from other states will not know the local language and, therefore, the only individuals who will be able to teach in such states will be products of the local educational systems). Certainly such situations must be examined carefully by industrial firms which are planning new ventures or expansions in such areas.

THE MANAGERIAL ENVIRONMENT AND ENTERPRISE OPERATIONS

The impact of literacy on the conduct of management and enterprise operations is substantial. Yet relatively few of the firms which were studied had explicitly looked at the issue in depth. Few had collected or analyzed any literacy statistics. And only a few companies — in almost all cases U.S. or other enterprises involving foreign ownership — tried to cope effectively with illiteracy constraints through conscious living practices or training programs. Yet managements repeatedly pointed to serious problems which resulted in large part or entirely from low literacy levels.

At the larger firms surveyed, the work force literacy rates typically ranged between 40 and 75 percent, but few of these workers had more than three to four years of schooling. Consequently, the managers of many of these firms felt that written communications would effectively reach only a small proportion of employees. U.S. subsidiaries were generally in the upper end of the range, while older Indian firms, especially those in the more traditional industries (textiles, jute, batteries, certain kinds of heavy engineering) had much lower literacy rates (in some cases only 10 to 20 percent). Relatively new Indian firms in such sophisticated industries as pharmaceuticals and chemicals were on the high side. Most of the foreign collaborators in these latter two sectors had literacy rates of at least 75 percent. Several had begun to restrict their hiring to primary school graduates, and some U.S. subsidiaries would not consider non-high school graduates except for such menial jobs as sweepers and cleaners. A few indigenous Indian firms claimed that they were going to follow a similar policy regarding primary graduates in the future.

A few U.S. subsidiaries had recently replaced literate or barely literate supervisors, foremen, and quality control inspectors with university graduates, and all new jobs of these types were to be filled by college graduates in the future. In many instances, the graduates were put in such jobs temporarily as part of a training program. This extreme change worked well in many instances, and led to serious problems in others. On the positive side, spans of control were broadened considerably, the number of supervisors or inspectors required was reduced substantially, control, and communication up the managerial hierarchy were improved, and better material usage and less idle operating time resulted. On the negative side, serious difficulties arose because of class and status conflicts between workers and supervisors, lack of mutual understanding and trust, poor communication, and ineffective direction and motivation involving workers.

One noteworthy exception to the emphasis on education placed by the foreign firms vis-a-vis the indigenous companies was the greater tendency of the Indian companies to set up their own primary and secondary schools which were often attended not only by the children and relatives of their employees, but also by children from the local community. This was an attempt to educate for the future, rather than the present. Although many U.S. executives recognized the shortcomings of the Indian education system, their responses were typically in personal terms — i.e., its affect on their own children. Usually, U.S. executives sent their children to special private schools in India, or in the case of older children, sent them abroad. They saw a clear distinction between the responsibilities of local government and private industry towards formal education. As in the United States, most professed the belief that formal or general education was not a desirable field of industrial activity. Furthermore, they focused their attention not on primary education, but on education specifically related to enterprise needs. More (but not many) of the U.S. subsidiaries established special literacy programs for their own work forces. Incentives such as free tea, snacks, and books were offered by some U.S. subsidiaries to get personnel to enroll in these programs which took place after working hours. One firm even gave a modest bonus and pay increase to those who successfully completed the program. However, only a small percentage of the illiterate personnel usually enrolled and only a small proportion of these completed the programs. For example, one U.S. subsidiary had run such a program for about ten years. In 1966 this firm had more than a thousand illiterate employees, but only several dozen people were enrolled in its literacy program, and only a handful had successfully completed the program as of that date. Many workers who had completed the program had regressed to a stage of bare literacy or virtual illiteracy as time passed.

In general, the problems associated with illiteracy were lodged both in the external and internal environments of firms studied. Specific problems and managerial reactions to them will be described in detail in Part 3, but is useful here to briefly examine, for illustrative purposes, the nature of some of them. The cement which effectively holds enterprises together, particularly larger ones, is the large amount of horizontal, upward, and downward communication which takes place. Much of this, such as job and time cards, must necessarily be written right on the factory floor. But who can perform this communication if personnel cannot read or write? Where workers, foremen, and supervisors are illiterate or barely literate, they must be instructed orally, which is difficult and time consuming. And often, instructions are not remembered completely and accurately. Because of the demands placed on the smaller number of well-educated personnel, they are overburdened at a cost to their efficiency, and the formal chain of command is often circumvented because it is necessary for top management to delve into detailed affairs at even the lowest levels. This tends to reinforce a high degree of centralization.

One cannot simply hand an instruction book or a blueprint to a barely literate employee. One must lead him, orally and visually, through every possible step of his job and its contingencies. Driving a truck or operating a lathe seems simple enough until one tries to train illiterates to do the job.

Illiteracy also creates striking planning and control problems. Wide and effective use cannot be made of written plans, procedures, policies, or methods. The typical modern business control system has at its heart a series of interrelated reporting documents, but who fills out and analyzes such reports when many employees cannot read or write? A preventive maintenance program may bog down because some employees cannot read gauges or fill out cards properly while others use the wrong or improper amounts of lubricants on equipment because they cannot read labels properly; job order reports for control purposes may not be completed properly because foremen are functionally illiterate.

One typically senses a pervasive feeling of apathy in an enterprise where a substantial portion of employees are illiterate or barely literate. Such workers lack self-confidence and seem resigned to the fact that they cannot get ahead regardless of how hard they work; they are trapped in their jobs since literacy may be essential to get a better job. Introducing changes and innovations in such an organization is difficult because of the amount of training, direction, and control usually needed to effectively implement them.

One U.S. subsidiary began using a computer for its payroll computations, but illiterate employees could not understand the codes or calculations on the paycards which accompanied their wages, and this led to distrust, suspicion, and conflict. Management in another plant decided to facilitate payroll calculations by eliminating paise (100 paise equals 1 rupee) and rounding off monthly wages in favor of the employees. This, too, led to considerable conflict and suspicion because illiterate personnel could not comprehend this new system, even though they benefited financially from it.

The administration of incentive schemes requiring detailed calculations by the worker, the completion of financial or operating reports, the use of suggestion systems, the issuance of a company newspaper, communication on routine matters between management and the work force, the recruiting of personnel, and even communications with international headquarters are all affected by the local literacy problems in Indian industry.

Another obvious problem arises with respect to reaching the market. Advertising cannot be prepared on a one-shot basis for a national audience (even assuming that media existed to reach everyone). Linguistic differences, and the limitations of the printed word in reaching a largely illiterate public present major difficulties and require substantial modifications of policies and practices which may be used effectively in the United States.

MANAGERIAL IMPLICATIONS

For management to be effective in India, or in any country where there is much illiteracy, it must be prepared to identify and analyze literacy data and problems, and, recognizing the limitations implied, be willing to adjust operations accordingly. Some firms, mostly U.S. subsidiaries, introduced various kinds of color and other visual schemes in place of the printed word, and this did reduce the difficulty in several instances.

Training, if it is to be effective, should in many cases, start with a basic literacy program, since this skill is so essential to rapid progress and improvement later on. This may be easier to accomplish in countries other than India, because of other relatively strong environmental constraints which exist in India. But even in India an increase in the literacy level even by only a few percentage points, may improve operations considerably, especially if those who complete company literacy programs become more dedicated and loyal employees. If enough firms bring about even modest increases in the literacy level of their employees, substantial benefits will also be felt in society at large.

In some cases firms may be wise to pay premiums to recruit literate employees, in view of the indirect and hidden costs and the inefficiencies that result from the hiring of illiterates. It will be easier to attract competent literates to do the jobs that illiterates would otherwise do, if there are opportunities for them to improve themselves further and advance in the organization.

PRIMARY EDUCATION

The most widespread educational activity in India is at the primary school level. Comprising grades one through five (occasionally six), Indian primary schools enrolled approximately 56 million children in 1968-69.[3] This represented about 75 percent of the six to eleven year-old children, up from 43 percent in 1950. However, the drop-out rate was high, and the effectiveness of the schooling was severely limited by several factors.

The key to the effectiveness of any education system is the quality of its teachers. Unfortunately, India has not been able to train a sufficient number of well-qualified teachers. Although the role of a teacher was revered in classical Indian mythology, the situation has changed considerably today with respect to levels of remuneration. Except for exclusive private schools, teachers are usually paid bare subsistence wages. Consequently, many of the people who gravitate to teaching jobs are individuals who have been turned out of the same educational system (inbreeding) with bare minimum standards, who cannot find better paying forms of livelihood. This has in many areas resulted in a downward spiral. The poorer products of already poor systems become the mainstays of the same system.

In some areas, Indian primary school education (grades one through five or six) is more progressive than many of its foreign counterparts. A greater emphasis is placed on science and mathematics at much earlier stages. However, the system is primarily based on rote memorization, and is not designed to develop creative thinkers. (This is also the case in numerous other countries in Asia, Africa, and Latin America.)

The result can be seen in many ways in the industrial scene. The relatively un-educated worker learns by an apprenticeship which consists of pure mimicry. He learns by rote and usually will not deviate from the patterns he acquires. Usually he learns from another worker who has learned in the same manner, without the benefit of formal training. Consequently, he may know "what" to do, but not "why." This results in situations which, if they were not true, would otherwise seem absurd. In one company studied in India, a major piece of equipment was idle for three months because the locally available replacement parts were stamped with a trademark which differed from that used by the original equipment manufacturer. The maintenance personnel were afraid to use the local parts because they were "obviously" not the same. The company waited until an "identical" imported part could be obtained.

One of the big problems which derives from the early education system in many developing nations is that the educational process is often divorced from national realities. Education is an abstract process. The Indian child does not play with building blocks. He does not have the opportunity to experiment with visual, textural, and other sensory characteristics. He does not pull things apart and put them back together. His toys are simple and non-mechanical. As a result, he does not develop a sense of how things mesh and work together. This has a major impact in later life if he moves into an industrial occupation.

Another related factor in Indian life is found in the games children play. Most of these seem to be non-competitive in nature. Even when games (e.g., card games) permit competitive scoring, more often than not scores are not counted. Competition, a major element which exists in the U.S. child's life, is either lacking or much diminished in importance in the life of the Indian child. Consequently, he does not feel pressure to excell nor is he as responsive to the pressures exerted by the accomplishments of his peers.

GENERAL SECONDARY EDUCATION

Indian secondary schools generally cover grades six through eleven without a junior or senior high school distinction. High school graduates, also called matriculates, who pass college entrance examinations and receive their "certificates" enter higher educational programs of at least three years in duration. Those students who finish high school but who do not do well enough to get into higher education programs may enroll in a variety of semiprofessional schools — technical, vocational, and other specialized programs — which are discussed in the next section. In some cases, students who complete only eight or nine years of general schooling can get into some of these programs.

In 1968-69, total enrollment in Indian general secondary education was about 19 million, a sizeable increase from the approximately five million enrolled in 1951. In the late 1960s more than one-quarter of India's population of high school age were enrolled in secondary schools.[4]

As is the case with primary education in India, secondary education is largely a rote process and most of the comments made with respect to elementary schooling apply here. Similarly, teachers present an especially critical problem, as they are underpaid and competent individuals are hard to get and hold. The entire system which generates teachers has built-in inefficiencies, and the system appears incapable of upgrading itself significantly.

A prominent Indian expert has summed up some of the major dilemmas of Indian secondary education thus:

> It is rightly pointed out that secondary education in India suffers from aimlessness, its primary aim being to prepare children for entrance into universities or for clerical jobs. Colleges are being clogged with undeserving students, and unemployed matriculates are running amuck for getting a job at a couple of rupees a day. Unfortunately secondary education is a victim of its own traditions.[5]

At the firms we surveyed in India, most secondary school graduates were doing menial clerical jobs, although some were employed as unskilled labor. High school graduates with no additional education or training are readily available at low wages, since there is considerable unemployment among this group. At a majority of the enterprises surveyed, matriculates ranged from 15 to 35 percent of total employees although some firms went as low as five percent. At the factory level, figures ranged from 1.5 to over 25 percent, with the lowest percentages found at older plants regardless of what industry they were in. Pharmaceutical firms typically had the highest proportions of matriculates, as compared to the other kinds of enterprises studied. By contrast, in a sample of companies within the United States, the lowest proportion of high school graduates found was well over 60 percent (40 to 45 percent solely within the plant).

SEMIPROFESSIONAL AND VOCATIONAL EDUCATION

In 1961, India's technical and vocational schools had a total enrollment of less than 400,000 students, and in the late 1960s it was still under 600,000.[6] Although the student-teacher ratio is only about 15 or 20 to one, compared to about 30 or 35 to one in regular secondary schools and 35 to 40 to one in primary schools, the impact of these schools has not yet been very substantial. This is the case even though they have grown quite substantially in number in the past two decades.

Table 3-2 presents some statistics on Indian vocational and semiprofessional educational programs classified by field of study. These programs train people chiefly for business and industry.

The overall Indian semiprofessional and vocational educational sector is less standardized, more confusing, and has changed more frequently in terms of types of programs and institutions than in the United States in the last two decades. In fact,

TABLE 3-2 Selected statistics on vocation and semiprofessional education[7]

Field of study	Number of institutions		Enrollment		
	1949-50	1961-62	1949-50	1961-62	1968-69 (est.)
Engineering	19	293	4,000	99,000	135,000
Industrial and technical	486	1,255	34,000	85,000	120,000
Commerce	110	412	28,000	117,000	158,000

different Indian published sources, including official government publications, give different statistics and other information about semiprofessional and vocational programs and classify them in different ways. There was disparity and confusion on this subject among Indian educators and government officials interviewed by the authors.

It was especially surprising to find that the managers, including several personnel managers, at many of the indigenous and foreign firms surveyed in India, knew little about and had little interest in semiprofessional and vocational schools in India. There were a few notable exceptions, to be discussed later, of cooperative work-study programs.

The most advanced type of semiprofessional education, in terms of formal schooling, is the diploma program. This is usually two to three years in duration, although there are some one-year programs in social work and a few other fields. Graduates receive diplomas in a variety of technical and engineering fields, and such areas as commerce, social work, and nursing. The better technical and engineering diploma programs are offered by polytechnical schools. They are typically a rough blend of American junior and community colleges and technical secondary schools, although the quality of training in most Indian polytechs is, no doubt, much lower than would be found in, say, California's junior colleges. Not all graduates from the Indian polytechnical schools become junior engineers, technicians, designers, or draftsmen. A sizeable number also become electricians, mechanics, and other types of skilled craftsmen. The number of Indian technical schools giving diplomas increased from 89 in 1951 to 284 in 1969. Enrollment increased from 6,216 to 48,000 students during this period, while the number of graduates increased from 2,626 to 25,000. In 1969, there were still fewer than 200,000 technical diploma graduates in India, and about 1.8 million craftsmen.

Students who receive a diploma in commerce typically are employed, if they can get a job, as junior accountants or bookkeepers, clerks, and stenographers. Indian diploma programs in commerce correspond roughly to secretarial colleges and secondary level "business" schools in the United States. Again the Indian programs are, on the average, of significantly lower quality.

By law, labor officers and their deputies must have a diploma in social welfare. A firm must employ a labor officer if it employs 500 people or more, and at least two if it has 2000 employees.

In general, students accepted in diploma programs are high school graduates who cannot get into higher educational institutions or who have dropped out of college. Some semiprofessional programs give a license rather than a diploma to their graduates.

India also has a variety of trade, vocational, and technical schools more junior and less semiprofessional in nature than the diploma programs offered by the polytechnical schools. Graduates of these schools usually receive certificates and are employed as toolmakers, mechanics, electricians, welders, draftsmen, machine operators, salesmen, bookkeepers, clerks, and in some cases as unskilled workers. A graduate of a certificate program would tend to get less pay and do somewhat less complex work than a graduate of a diploma program, but this is not always the case.

Certificate programs typically run from one to two years. Some of the better ones, such as those offered by certain Indian Training Institutes, combine part-time industrial practice, typically for about six months, with formal education. The certificate programs also take in high school graduates who cannot get into higher educational institutions, college dropouts, and individuals who cannot get into diploma programs. They also have more students who have not completed high school than do the diploma programs.

In our survey of industrial enterprises in India we found that for technical or skilled jobs more firms, both indigenous and foreign, preferred experienced recruits or personnel trained by the company to diploma or certificate holders. They did not trust the quality of the output of these programs.[8]

There is no doubt that the Indian system of formal semiprofessional and vocational education leaves much to be desired, in terms of quality and quantity. However, it has clearly improved in recent times. It is likely that many larger and older firms in India, including those with foreign interests, have a somewhat outdated view of India's semiprofessional and vocational education and assume that it is as bad and as sparse as it was ten or twenty years ago.

The difficulties in hiring adequate technicians of various kinds, technical supervisors, skilled workers, and craftsmen are more serious in some parts of India than others. For example, one multi-plant U.S. subsidiary found it easiest to obtain and develop competent personnel in Bombay, somewhat less easy in Calcutta, more difficult in Madras, and most difficult in Lucknow which contains substantially less industry than the other areas. Generally, firms in the more modern, relatively capital intensive, high technology industries had the greatest difficulty obtaining suitable technical and skilled worker manpower. This was also true for firms in industries which were made up of only a few companies.

Many firms in India experienced sizeable turnover rates, in some cases as high as 50 percent or more in a given year, involving semiprofessional personnel and skilled labor who were in particularly short supply. They would often spend considerable time, money, and energy recruiting and training such people, only to have them hired away by other companies.

But this is also true for technical personnel and skilled workers in short supply in American industry. The turnover rate for technicians at some of the plants surveyed in the United States ran as high as 30 percent in some years. Some U.S. firms have had to start their own training programs for various kinds of technicians and skilled workers because adequate supplies could not be obtained externally. One type of technical vocational education in India that received relatively strong support by a number of larger and more capital intensive enterprises was cooperative training programs involving schools and industrial enterprises. A good example of such a program, leading to a diploma, is the one offered by the Calcutta Technical School. This part-work, part-study program (roughly half of each) lasts four or five years depending on the student's background qualifications. Students are usually high school graduates The program is relatively intensive, normally involving a six-day week, and it has a significantly more practical orientation than the usual semiprofessional and vocational programs.

There are other programs of this type in the Bombay and Delhi areas, several offering certificates rather than diplomas, and these focus more on training skilled tradesmen and other workers rather than technicians or technical supervisors. However, total enrollment in all Indian cooperative educational programs is still small, in fact, very small in relation to regular semiprofessional and vocational programs, and minute compared to general secondary education.

In our sample of firms, more indigenous Indian companies were involved with cooperative training programs than companies with foreign ownership. They usually selected employees of their own to send to these programs, often relatives and friends. Many felt that this type of education led to more loyalty and greater identification with the company on the part of those personnel selected. A number of firms also stated that cooperative program graduates, particularly from the Calcutta Technical School, generally had more status at the foreman and supervisory level, and achieved faster advancement in the managerial ranks, than did polytechnical diploma holders. (They were also more likely to move into jobs otherwise filled by university graduates in engineering and science.)

All in all, it seems that it may be beneficial, not only for India, but also for other countries, particularly developing ones, to seriously consider the establishment of new cooperative educational programs of the type which seems to be quite effective in India.

HIGHER EDUCATION

Modern industries are voracious consumers of highly trained manpower. Even cursory examination of the varying managerial and technical tasks to be done in performing basic productive and managerial functions in a relatively modern industrial enterprise suggests that these tasks require numerous people possessed of higher education.

Take, for example, the production function. Here some essential skills are engineering, a variety of scientific and mathematical skills involving considerable sophistication, product design and development ability, ability to purchase materials and equipment logically and to efficiently integrate new equipment into older processes, quality control expertise; also required are analytical ability, ability to conduct statistical analysis of existing outputs in relation to factor inputs and production standards, knowledge of plant and layout planning, and value engineering, including analyses of utilization of materials and operations in order to obtain greater efficiencies. The ability to manage and implement maintenance and repair of machinery and plant, costing and preparation of cost effectiveness studies, knowledge of inventory planning and control are also necessary. Complex skills and much knowledge are similarly needed for the other enterprise functions, as well as the basic managerial functions.[9]

In advanced countries, such as the United States, most such skills are taught or developed in a systematic fashion at institutions of higher education: colleges, graduate schools, universities, and institutes. Some individuals may be able to teach themselves such skills, and some companies impart them to employees through their own training programs.

Most developing countries experience severe shortages of highly trained manpower, particularly in the areas of engineering, applied sciences, business administration and management. It seems common for such countries to overemphasize in their higher educational systems the humanities, arts, and law at the expense of training in the above fields. This is the result of various social and cultural pressures including the heritage from colonial rule, as well as financial costs, particularly in connection with education for engineering and the physical sciences. India has clearly made more progress with regard to education suited to economic development than many of the world's poor countries, but a sizeable number of the poorer nations, particularly the Communist states like China, have done substantially better.

SOME GENERAL INDIAN-AMERICAN COMPARISONS

Several features differentiate the Indian college student from his U.S. counterpart. First, he is younger by one to two years. Because Indian public education ends with the 11th grade, the typical Indian freshman is 16 or 17 years old, and 15 is not rare. Second, he has had a sheltered childhood. He has not sold newspapers, clerked in a store, worked in a plant, or done odd jobs. His major contact with business and industry has been with retail stores, but he does not know how stores operate or how merchandise reaches their shelves. He has never had a bank account. Because of traditional cultural patterns, he does not go out on dates, (although this is slowly starting to change). In essence, instead of accelerating the maturation process, the Indian higher educational system often tends to postpone or retard it by affording continued shelter from the real world and its responsibilities.

College in India is often viewed as a means for postponing the day when the individual must assume independence and begin to look after himself, and it is not unusual to find students who pursue one degree after another in arts, commerce, and law. When they finally finish, many are unemployable. Graduates with master's degrees from schools of commerce are often fortunate to find jobs as clerks or typists — many cannot really do much else and graduates in arts are often lucky if they can find any type of employment. Until recently, the individual who wanted to use education (as opposed to family connections or social background) as a spring board to opportunity, typically had to study abroad.

In the United States, a college degree is usually considered more than a symbol of the completion of formal education. College provides the student with opportunities to experiment with independence and develop ways of dealing with the real world.

Indian colleges are generally patterned after the British system, in that educational progress is based on a series of examinations. The student focuses most of his energy on preparing for these examinations, the most critical of which are administered at the end of the second year (and determine the avenues he can pursue to complete his studies) and at the end of his fourth year (to determine his final standings, and therefore his job opportunities). Unfortunately, the examination grade often becomes the entire thrust of education and the learning process degenerates into memorization and cramming for tests. Consequently, although large numbers of individuals are awarded college degrees, few have acquired skills or knowledge which will be of value in the working world.

In recent years, a more practical orientation has begun to emerge in a few institutions of higher education. As we discussed earlier some higher technical schools have embarked on cooperative programs, and some schools of management try to place their students in summer positions. In addition, a number of institutions (such as the five Indian Institutes of Technology, the two Indian Institutes of Management, and the few major universities of Delhi, Benares, and Bombay) are striving towards excellence in their fields. But much of the Indian university and college system is retarded by antiquated ideas, by the transplanted British system which does not seem to fit India, by low salaries and the resulting unavailability of talented instructors, and by a large number of students who are not yet ready to assume their roles as productive citizens.

QUANTITATIVE AND QUALITATIVE DIMENSIONS OF INDIAN HIGHER EDUCATION

An examination of aggregate statistics pertaining to India's higher education presents a much brighter picture of the high talent manpower available for economic development than is actually the case.[10] In absolute numbers, India has certainly done well as a developing country, but not in per capita terms, and more important, not in terms of quality and suitability of human resources. Moreover, a vast amount of the advanced knowledge and skills which exists among the Indian industrial population is greatly under-utilized because people either work at jobs where they cannot use much of their know-how or because they do not care to do so.

Total enrollment in Indian higher education increased 350 percent, from 383,000 students in 1949-50 to 1.27 million in 1962-63. By contrast, total enrollment in the United States has been five or six times greater, and in per capita terms over ten times greater. In recent times the United States has been graduating about 800,000 students annually from higher educational institutions. This is several times the Indian figure.[11] For every one thousand people in the United States in recent times, about 30 to 35 have been enrolled in higher educational programs, compared with less than 3 in India. More than ten years ago, in 1957, there were about 5.8 million higher education graduates employed in the U.S. economy, and today there are over 13 million. Even today there are no more than a few million graduates, at the very most, working in India.

The above gaps although large, are even greater when they are viewed in terms of industrial requirements, since employment in industrial enterprises is only about twice as large in the United States as compared to India, about 20 million versus 10 million.

Table 3-3 presents some statistics on Indian higher education enrollments by selected fields of study for 1956-57 and 1962-63 (the latest year for which such statistics are available).[12]

As will be discussed in more detail with some quantitative data in the section on educational match, there are large numbers of unemployed arts and commerce graduates in India, including many with master's degrees, and fairly sizeable numbers of unemployed law and science graduates. It should be noted that Indian commerce graduates typically obtain greatly inferior training to bachelors of business administration in the United States, and the same is true, with relatively few exceptions, with regard to B.A.'s and B.S. graduates.

Indian commerce and arts graduates except those from a few leading colleges, can typically only find work as clerks or semi-skilled workers, if they find employment at

TABLE 3-3 Enrollment in higher educational institutions by fields of study (1956-57, 1963-64)

	1956-57		1963-64	
	Enrollment (in 000's)	% of Total	Enrollment (in 000's)	% of Total
Arts	396	51.5	544	42.7
Science	210	27.3	386	30.4
Commerce	67	8.7	130	10.2
Engineering and technology	21	2.7	69	5.4
Law	19	2.5	30	2.0
Medicine	23	3.0	50	3.9

all. Many science graduates also find that they must work in rather trivial or menial jobs. At the same time, numerous firms are faced with critical shortages of competent managers, business administration specialists of various kinds, accountants, economists, psychologists, statisticians, mathematicians, applied scientists, and in some cases even legal experts who can perform the desired and required tasks effectively.

Engineering and technological fields present a two-fold problem in relation to managerial effectiveness and industrial progress. One is basically quantitative in nature, with critical shortages of certain types of engineers, particularly qualified chemical, aeronautical and electrical engineers, and an oversupply in other fields, particularly civil engineering, which leads to considerable unemployment. In recent times, about 30 percent of India's engineering graduates have been in civil engineering, compared to 27, 18, 4, and well under 1 percent for mechanical, electrical, chemical, and aeronautical engineering respectively. Approximately one-third of all mechanical and electrical engineering posts in the Indian economy have been filled by non-degree and non-diploma holders.[13]

In 1961, there were only 131,000 engineers employed in India compared to 785,000 in the United States. Whereas almost all of the latter were college graduates, only 58,000 of the Indian engineers had completed college programs. As of the early 1960s, India had only 2.4 engineers and scientists per 10,000 population compared to 61.7 in the United States in 1959.[14] As of 1969, there were about 332,000 engineers in India, 134,000 of whom had degrees. There were about 47,000 unemployed engineers with diplomas and 10,000 with degrees. One recent study estimated that this unemployment figure may be doubled by the early 1970s.[15]

Probably the most serious problem with regard to Indian engineering education is qualitative rather than quantitative. Many graduates of higher engineering and technical programs in India receive such deficient formal training that they do their jobs poorly and require considerable company training to bring them even close to a desired level of competence and effectiveness. Or they remain unemployed or unemployable as engineers or technical specialists. With the exception of a small number of first-rate engineering schools, Indian engineering and technical education is too general, abstract, and theoretical, and suffers from the lack of emphasis on problem solving, creativity, and analytical training.

The best Indian engineering schools, the five Indian Institutes of Technology or (IIT's), in Delhi, Madras, Bombay, Kanpur, and Kharagpur, have been set up in recent years with the assistance of leading American schools. They offer both undergraduate and graduate programs, but their total enrollment in 1965-66 was only 7,984 students. The IIT's provide students with the opportunity of combining their studies with projects and work in industry. There are only a few other relatively good Indian engineering programs, most notably those offered by Benares University and the Berla Institute in Pilani.

Several of the U.S. subsidiaries surveyed in India pointed out that it typically takes from two to six months to even place an engineering graduate from an Indian school in a permanent job, and from two to five years before he can work reasonably effectively on his own. Those who have hired IIT graduates say that the amount of time involved tends to be quite significantly reduced, but it is still usually longer than for graduates from good engineering American programs in the United States. In American industry engineering and technical graduates can typically be placed in a permanent job within a month or two, and can work on their own effectively within one year.

The content and quality of training in Indian business, management, economics, and social science education in general leave much to be desired in terms of the requirements of business and industry. Most of the Indian universities offer programs in commerce, quantitative methods and statistics, economics, and the other social sciences; and a growing number of higher schools, including institutes, are offering programs and courses in business administration and management. Some are now offering graduate programs. Although the quality of the business administration and management programs is generally significantly better than that of the commerce programs, most are far inferior to American programs, even those offered by mediocre schools.

Managers of industrial firms in India, particularly U.S. subsidiaries, complain that graduates from Indian commerce, economics, and social science, and even business and management programs, are inadequately trained in terms of their requirements, and that there is not nearly enough stress on practical application, analytical ability, or problem solving in such programs. Notable exceptions are the graduates of the two Indian Institutes of Management set up in the mid-1960s, one in Ahmedabad which was established with the collaboration of the Harvard Business School, and the other in Calcutta, set up with the assistance of MIT.

These two institutes offer graduate programs in management and business administration comparable to MBA programs at U.S. business schools, as well as a variety of management development programs for practitioners. The quality of training, faculty, and students at these two institutes compare favorably with that of American programs. In fact, some of their graduates who have come to the United States for doctoral work have ranked near the top of their classes. The two IIM's have close relations with many companies and their managers often cooperate in various ways with the institutes. Many of the students obtain summer jobs in business, and problem-solving field projects form part of some courses.

To date, the two IIM's have graduated only a few hundred students, most of whom have obtained positions at good starting salaries in business, industry, government, and even education. However, there has been feedback that some of the graduates have not been utilized well, especially those employed by relatively traditional local firms who tend to hire them largely for prestige reasons, because the progressive firms, including foreign companies, are doing so. A number of the IIM graduates have changed jobs, some more than once.

There is no doubt that these two management institutes, if properly operated in the future, will continue to be key sources of high talent managerial manpower in

India. Hopefully, quality will not be sacrificed for quantity as is so often the case in Indian education in general; for quality in business and management education in India, as in technical education, seems to be an even greater constraint on economic development and managerial effectiveness than quantity. Hopefully, industry will also encourage, make effective use of, and take advantage of the high talent human resources made available by the IIM's, the Indian Institutes of Technology, and the other first-rate higher educational programs in India. For if they do not, such training would tend to be largely fruitless. This also holds true for the first-rate higher educational programs set up in other developing countries.

DATA OBTAINED FROM FIRMS SURVEYED

One strong indication that quality, content, and types of Indian higher education are greater constraints on managerial effectiveness and industrial progress than quantity is suggested in some of the data obtained from firms surveyed. In our sample of companies, the proportion of employees having higher degrees ranged from 1 to 33 percent with the majority falling between 10 and 20 percent. These proportions are not greatly different from those found in the U.S. based companies studied (most fell between 15 and 25 percent, with the range being from about 8 to nearly 40 percent). Considering that the companies in the United States had substantially larger proportions (and absolute numbers) of people in research and development, most of whom were university graduates, and also that the U.S. based firms are larger and considerably more complex than their Indian counterparts, the quantitative higher education-employment gap is surprisingly small.

The firm in India with the greatest proportion of college graduates was a U.S. drug subsidiary, and its parent in the United States had the highest proportion in our U.S. sample. In a few cases, the U.S. subsidiaries in India had higher proportions of college graduates in relation to total employment than did their parent U.S.-based operations.

Generally, U.S. subsidiaries in India had larger proportions of graduates than similar types of indigenous Indian firms although this was not true in every case. Firm size was a less significant factor with regard to the proportion of college graduates than the age of the firm. Older firms in a given industry typically had smaller proportions of graduates and a lower level of educated personnel than newer ones. The probably reflects the generally increasing educational level of the Indian working population.[16] Pharmaceutical and chemical firms, followed by relatively complex engineering companies, typically had the largest proportions of graduates, with textile, paper and relatively simple light engineering companies at the other end of the spectrum. Location does appear to be a factor in our sample of firms in many cases. The number of college graduates in relation to total employment was found to be generally higher at firms located in or near Bombay, Calcutta.

Delhi, Kerala, and Madras than in less industrialized areas such as Lucknow, Allahabed, Jaipur, Assam, and Kashmir.

In our sample of firms operating in India, we found the proportion of managerial personnel of all types with higher degrees ranged from roughly 10 to over 90 percent, with the majority falling between 40 and 70 percent. In our sample of U.S. based companies, the range was from about 50 to over 90 percent, with most firms falling between 60 and 80 percent. At the corporate offices of the U.S. firms, the proportion was at least 90 percent in all cases. However, there were a few U.S. subsidiaries in India with higher overall proportions than their U.S. parents, and in several cases U.S. subsidiaries had significantly larger proportions of college graduates at the lower supervisory and foreman levels. At the plant level, U.S. subsidiaries generally employed larger proportions of college graduates than did indigenous Indian Plants in the same industry.

A substantially higher proportion of the clerks, typists, storeroom personnel, and other white-color workers had college degrees at the firms surveyed in India compared with the companies studied in the United States. As noted earlier, Bachelor of Commerce and B.A. degrees are the most common among such personnel in India, but Master's degrees, and B.S. degrees are also found.

In most cases U.S. subsidiaries in India employed smaller proportions of engineering graduates than their parent companies, but larger proportions than indigenous firms in the same industry. It was common for B.S. degree holders, and to a lesser extent personnel with other types of degrees, to be employed in jobs in India that are performed by engineers in the United States. With regard to managerial personnel, in most cases significantly larger proportions of them were technical graduates at the U.S. subsidiaries than at comparable local firms, but the proportion was not quite as high as in the U.S. based companies.

One striking finding involving U.S. subsidiaries in India, concerned the large number of graduate degree holders (Master's, Ph.D. and M.B.A.'s) that several of them employed. For example, one multi-plant subsidiary producing chemicals, batteries, flashlights, and various other products, had about 560 employees with graduate degrees, including several dozen with Ph.D.'s, in 1966. This represented about 10 percent of the firm's total employment, and a far greater proportion of graduate degree holders and Ph.D.'s than its parent company in the United States. One U.S. drug subsidiary had about thirty graduate degree holders including six Ph.D.'s, although it employed less than six hundred people. This too represents a significantly greater proportion than at its U.S. parent company. The proportion of graduate degree holders at a number of indigenous Indian firms, particularly pharmaceutical and chemical enterprises, though not as high as at some of the U.S. subsidiaries, was nevertheless surprisingly large, and larger than is common in many U.S.-based companies. In several U.S. and indigenous firms in India, more than half the managerial personnel were graduate degree holders.

Another striking finding was the number of employees having foreign degrees, primarily from the United States, particularly in some of the U.S. subsidiaries, but also in a few indigenous drug and chemical companies. The multi-plant U.S. subsidiary referred to above had 60 employees with foreign degrees, including some 24 Ph.D.'s and 15 M.B.A's. An indigenous Indian drug and chemical company employing about 2,400 people had 30 foreign degree holders (mostly graduate degrees) including seven Ph.D.'s and one M.B.A. However, among all of the graduate degree holders at the firms surveyed in India, only relatively small numbers were in business administration, management, economics, or the social sciences in general. The largest number were in engineering, technical, and basically scientific fields.

NON-COMPANY MANAGEMENT DEVELOPMENT PROGRAMS

This type of training, if effectively organized and conducted, can do much to raise managerial effectiveness by providing participants with new information, knowledge, and experiences applicable to their present or future jobs. In many underdeveloped and developing countries, non-company management training programs are rare or nonexistent. In such countries it is extremely difficult for managerial personnel to acquire information or knowledge which can improve their performance significantly. The only means of doing this may be to send people abroad for training, or for companies to run their own internal programs if they can obtain the suitable experts or specialists to do so.

Few of the world's poorer countries have more management development programs than India. Since the mid-1950s, increasing attention has been given to management training programs in India, and many, of different types, have been conducted to date.[17] However, for reasons to be discussed shortly, most of these have been disappointing in spite of the large numbers of such programs and their heavy enrollment. Nevertheless, they have undoubtedly contributed to a net gain in terms of managerial effectiveness and industrial progress.

The All-India Management Association, set up in 1957 with headquarters in Delhi, is a key organization with regard to management development programs in India. It offers some programs itself on a national scale, chiefly top management programs, and through its many member associations, numerous programs at regional and local levels. Its activities include live-in programs lasting for a few weeks or more, half or one-day conferences, evening lecture series, periodic conferences and seminars, and informal gatherings. Their content varies widely from general management, to emphasis on various enterprise functions and techniques such as finance, marketing, production, operations research, safety, and preventive maintenance.

Various management development programs are also organized by the Indian National Productivity Council and its local counterparts in different cities. In addition, teams and delegations of Indian businessmen periodically attend programs conducted by international and foreign organizations such as the International Scientific Organization, the Advanced Management Program in the Far East, and the International Labor Organization (ILO). There are also a variety of management training programs offered by various institutes and universities.

In spite of the ferment regarding management training in India and the talk about a "managerial revolution" which is taking place, evidence of such a revolution has not yet shown up extensively in practice. Many of the programs suffer from poor planning, organization, and content; unqualified instructors; participants who don't have the proper backgrounds or attitudes; and a general lack of commitment or maturation on the part of those involved. This includes instructors.

Even when a program is well run and potentially effective, frequently the participants either do not wish to or cannot apply what they have learned. All of these shortcomings can be found with regard to various management development programs in the United States, but they seem to be much more serious and pervasive in India.

In general, it is common to find that where management development programs do exist in developing countries, many participants fail to apply what they learn for a variety of reasons. Such reasons are often related to their basic attitudes toward achievement, change, risk-taking or scientific method. Frequently participants are not given the opportunity to apply what they have learned when they return to their firms. This is not uncommon even in the United States, but it is more common in less developed countries. Management training programs also tend to be viewed as social gatherings, as bonus vacations, or as places to make contacts, rather than as opportunities to acquire more know-how.

A Harvard University doctoral dissertation indicates that Turkish middle-managers who attended a management development program at the University of Istanbul did not change in their attitudes or behavior in the directions predicted or expected.[18] This probably applies equally to India. It seems evident that, in developing countries in particular, more consideration should be given to the attitude, values, and maturity of the participants selected to attend such programs, and to the likelihood that they will want to or be in a position to apply what they learn. This could greatly reduce the wasted time, effort, costs and resources expended on such programs. It may also be wise to have fewer programs of better quality and content.

A number of the larger and more progressive foreign companies in India, chiefly American, but also some British firms, prefer to operate their own management development programs or send people abroad for management training. A few leading Indian firms, such as Tata, also operate their own management programs on a fairly extensive and continuous scale.

There are some programs in India of generally high quality and content. These include the national top executive programs organized by the All-India Management Association, and some of the programs offered by the two Indian Institutes of Management.

A study of participation in several of the major management development programs indicated that U.S. subsidiaries send proportionately more people to top and middle management programs than do their Indian counterparts. However, the reverse is true at the lower levels, where the U.S. subsidiaries rely more on in-company training and recruiting to foster desired skills.

ATTITUDE TOWARD EDUCATION

"Attitude toward education" is an important environmental factor for a number of reasons. It has a direct bearing on whether or not individuals want to improve their skills and abilities through education, training, and self-development. Attitudes toward education can be important determinants of how much effort and sacrifice people are willing to undertake in educational and training pursuits. It also has a great bearing on the extent, quality, and content of the overall educational system within a given country. This in turn determines, in large part, the types and quality of people available to industrial enterprises and other organizations bearing on industrial and economic development.

Developing countries in general

The prevailing or dominant attitude toward education in a given country is a product of various cultural, sociological, and often political and economic factors. It is further complicated by historic and institutional views of what constitutes an "educated" man.[19] Many societies, especially less developed ones, still see religion, the classics, liberal arts, law, and medicine as being the only suitable fields of study for a "gentleman." As the society attempts to shift to a mass and diverse educational system in pursuit of economic progress, such attitudes frequently persist, and the better students and teachers pursue the traditionally elite fields and ignore such disciplines as business administration, engineering, and applied science. The result, in spite of expanded educational opportunities, is a critical shortage of such important skills for economic development.

It is important to point out that the dominant or prevalent attitudes of individuals in a given society toward education, training, and self-improvement depend largely on the opportunities for social mobility, career advancement, greater status, and material gain, as well as on their own attitudes toward achievement and work. For example, rigid class or social structures which prevent much of the population from getting ahead because of race, religion, caste, sex, family background, and the like, will frequently remove incentive for those discriminated against to attempt to improve themselves. This type of situation presents a serious obstacle to managerial effectiveness and industrial progress.

Indian society at large

Although Indian society places high regard on education, historically, education has played a very special and limited role in that country. India has not had the tradition of great universities and formalized education systems which developed in Europe and North America. Instead, education was the province of the Brahmin caste, the priestly group. The educated man was revered, but his education dealt primarily with things spiritual and philosophical. Practical forms of education were aimed primarily at the warrior, and largely consisted of the arts of warfare. All education was by apprenticeship. The lower castes, the businessmen and the farmers, did not "need" formal education, and in fact any attempt to secure it would have been interpreted as an attempt to defy the will of the gods. Education was for the higher castes. If a person was meant to be educated, he would have been born to one of those castes, according to general belief.

Although the caste system has been legally abolished it is still one of the most vital forces in Indian life, both in its structuralized aspects and in the way it has molded Indian thought. The masses still see themselves destined to certain roles in life by virtue of birth. To the typical farmer, higher education is unattainable. Partially this is a function of economics. But it is also tied to his philosophy of life and the role he envisions for himself. Changes are taking place, as the government places increased emphasis on primary schooling for village children. However, low aspirational levels tend to limit villagers' concepts of the opportunities their children may obtain through education. They do not see education as a stepping stone to wealth, power, or leadership. This same attitude can be found in the average Indian college graduate who is content to view his degree primarily as an entree to a job on the lowest rungs of the industrial employment hierarchy.

A related series of attitudes exists within the teaching profession. Teaching is largely a "caste" oriented occupation. A person is born into an academic family and continues in the tradition. Again changes are occurring, especially at the public school level, but the system already suffers from a type of "hardening of the arteries." In many cases, inadequately educated individuals provide minimal educations for people with low aspirations. Student products of this system often have their heads filled with facts and figures, but they have not been stimulated to think, and they often cannot make practical application of information they have acquired.

One consequence of this at the college level is the large number of professional degree collectors, many of whom have discovered that their educations have really not given them anything other than the credentials required to continue studying for advanced degrees. However, since a majority of college students still come from the relatively wealthy families, they may have the option of joining a family firm. In such cases, positions come not as a result of education but as a consequence of family connections.

Although engineering, applied science, business administration, and management have clearly increased in status and prestige as formal fields of study in India, they still only account for relatively small numbers of students and graduates. Foreign trained people in these fields, particularly those trained in the United States or United Kingdom, are more highly regarded than those who have local educations. Traditionally a British higher education, especially from Oxford or Cambridge, was the most prestigious, but now American trained Indian M.B.A's, engineers, and scientists from the leading U.S. universities, are typically the most sought after by companies. In fact, students who complete their graduate studies at India's first-rate institutes of management and technology often go to the United States for additional graduate degrees which involve programs similar to those they completed in India because of the prestige value of a U.S. degree.

Attitudes in industrial enterprises

Indian college graduates, because of their higher education, their disdain for physical labor and their distaste for being associated with uneducated workers, frequently prefer to take significantly lower paying white-collar jobs in offices rather than working in factories. This pattern seems to be less common, but far from rare, among graduates who have been educated abroad, particularly in the United States or Canada. College graduates at many plants surveyed, both indigenous and American, took great pains to avoid being identified in any way with less educated workers or with manual labor. For example, in some factories they refused to wear safety shoes or goggles, even in quite dangerous situations, because these were associated with the work force.

Although indifference to educational problems seems to be the prevalent attitude among companies in India, a few of the more progressive indigenous firms such as Tata, have begun to place considerable emphasis on the role of the corporation as a change agent in society. These companies are doing even more than U.S. or British firms in India in this regard. Some of them have identified the educational process as a key to both overall economic progress and individual corporate success. Realistically, they have concluded that the existing educational system has constraints and deficiencies of such magnitude that, given the intensity of current efforts and existing government resources, they will require many years to correct.

As noted earlier, several such firms have established their own primary and even secondary schools. Children of employees attend these schools either on a free or highly subsidized basis. Sometimes these schools are coupled with adult education. Several of these companies also contribute quite generously to the higher educational system (primarily in the engineering and science disciplines) and provide scholarships for outstanding children of employees. A small number of firms have been doing this with much success for many years. The students they educate and support usually flow into the firm's work force, and to some extent, management. Consequently, there is a continual upgrading of talent, and this also enhances favorable attitudes to education, as employees see their children actually getting better jobs through education.

As mentioned earlier, most foreign companies and non-Indian managers in India — and in most other developing countries, although Aramco in Saudi Arabia is a notable exception — drew clear distinctions between the responsibilities of government and private industry regarding formal education. These distinctions were usually based on patterns found in their home countries. Education was seen as a government responsibility, primarily because in the United States and in most European nations well developed educational systems have been established and are operated by local or national government.

Although most foreign managers felt the impact of the poor educational system even more severely than did their Indian counterparts, they tended to view it as a given. They had neither the emotional involvement or the personal commitment to institute change. In some cases, they were prevented from taking action not by their own preconceptions, but their perceptions of home office attitudes: "I think it is a good idea, but do you realize what New York would say if I included $5,000 in my budget to establish a primary school?"

In India, foreign firms and managers, particularly American, place significantly greater emphasis on the value of a college education in terms of its type, quality, and content than do Indian companies and managers. Nepotism exists in the foreign firms to a much lesser degree, and the individual's progress within the organization reflects a substantially larger element of merit. Consequently, foreign companies often attract some of the best educated and motivated talent in India. The attitudes (and successes) of such companies are bringing about changes, albeit slowly, in a growing number of indigenous organizations. However social considerations, including the caste system, are still major constraints on effective staffing in numerous instances, even in foreign firms, including U.S. subsidiaries.

EDUCATIONAL MATCH WITH REQUIREMENTS AND MANPOWER UTILIZATION

Introduction

Many of the poorer nations have educational systems seriously deficient in matching the manpower requirements of business, industry, and economic development. A leading study of education throughout the world clearly points out this dilemma: "The balance in any program of human resource development may be fully as important as the amount of investment in education. This is a crucial point, and is often neglected by purely quantitative measures of educational investment."[20] Too many B.A.'s, B. Comm's and lawyers may be produced, and too few engineers, accountants, technicians, and craftsmen, resulting in dysfunctional discrepancies in job opportunities and pay. At worst, such discrepancies can produce a large number of unemployed intellectuals sitting idly around coffee or tea houses plotting revolutions.

Such problems can be resolved, but certainly not efficiently if the task is left to productive enterprises who must expend considerable time, effort, and expense to retrain persons who have, in effect, wasted much of their own time and their country's resources by studying the wrong subjects. A more efficient role for industry is to train basically qualified candidates to fill specific roles in the firm, not to reeducate individuals.

Unemployment and critical shortages in India

In 1955, about 379,000 of India's high school graduates (matriculates) and 93,000 of her college graduates who desired employment were unemployed. This represented about 15 percent of all of India's 3.2 million employed secondary school and college graduates. By 1961, the number of employed high school and college graduates had increased to 6.2 million, but the proportion of those unemployed had reached 16.2 percent. In the mid-1960s, the unemployed included over one million matriculates and 83,000 college graduates.[21] The numbers increased considerably in the second half of the 1960s because of poor economic conditions.

There are large numbers of graduate degree holders, Masters, Ph.D.'s and lawyers, in the Indian economy, and the unemployment rate even among graduates from the best Indian universities has been discouragingly high. For example, as of 1959, 3.3 percent of all 1950 graduates of Delhi University, one of India's most pretigious and best, and 7.2 percent of the 1959 output were unemployed. Honor graduates in arts, science, commerce, and law, many with Masters' degrees, were working as clerks even eight years after they graduated. About 25 percent of all of Delhi University's 1950 graduates and 40 percent of its 1954 graduates were employed as clerks in 1959.[22]

India has more science graduates than any of the world's advanced industrial nations except for the United States and Russia which each have about 40 to 50 percent more. India's more than 100,000 science graduates compares very favorably *numerically* with only some 85,000 in the United Kingdom, 90,000 in Italy, 40,000 in France, 25,000 in Yugoslavia, and 20,000 in Canada. However, the impact of India's large number of scientists on technological development and industrial progress is relatively small. About 12.5 percent of India's science graduates are unemployed. Of those who are employed, 35 percent work as teachers, another 35 percent work in non-scientific and non-technical jobs, and of the remaining 30 percent who do scientific or technical work, not more than one-third of them work in business or industrial enterprises.[23]

It was noted in an earlier section that 37 percent of all the mechanical and electrical engineers in India do not have a college degree or diploma. At the same time about 10,000 engineering graduates (nearly 10 percent of all employable engineering graduates) have been unemployed in recent years, and about 47,000 engineering diploma holders (over 20 percent of the total employable) are jobless.[24] In 1968, Prime Minister Indira Ghandi told the Indian parliament that there were 50,000 unemployed engineers — presumably this includes all types of engineers — in India, and this represented over 25 percent of the country's employable engineers.[25] Civil engineers account for the greatest share of engineering unemployment. Numerous students who major in civil engineering hope to find managerial and other white-collar jobs in offices, especially with the government, rather than having to work with "dirty hands" work crews in the factories and fields.

In 1961, 15.2 percent of all new engineering graduates in India experienced delays of more than three months after graduation in getting jobs, and 3 percent had to wait more than six months. Difficulties in getting jobs has increased steadily for new engineering graduates in recent years. By 1965, 30.5 percent experienced delays of more than three months and 15.5 percent more than six months.[26]

Many other Indian graduates experience even greater difficulties and delays in getting jobs after graduating. There are a variety of reasons for this, which contribute to educational match problems in general, in addition to the sheer lack of jobs in relation to suitable qualifications. The absence of adequate information, cooperation, and contact between educational institutions and business and other organizations which employ their graduates is a serious constraint. There are also serious deficiencies such as a lack of employment agencies, career advice, and counseling. In addition, many graduates do not choose to take the jobs that may be open to them for various psychological, sociological, cultural, and economic reasons.

Another critical shortage area in India is that of accountants, especially cost accountants. India only has about five hundred certified cost accountants and around 7,000 regular chartered accountants or C.A.'s. This compares with over 40,000 cost accountants and 70,000 chartered accountants in Great Britain. Because the nation has had only one specialized institute for training cost accountants, most of those in the country have been trained by companies, primarily foreign firms. Yet cost accounting has become more important than ever in many industries, especially the pharmaceutical sector, particularly with the new government regulations, audits, and controls involving prices and cost analysis.

Still another example relates to computer personnel. While electronic computers are still not used very widely in India, the number of companies and other organizations acquiring them has been growing in recent years. Since few educational or training institutions offer programs or courses dealing with computers, a very critical shortage exists for computer specialists even though the total demand is not very great.

PROBLEMS AT THE FIRM LEVEL

In countries where the educational system meshes poorly with the requirements of business and industry, problems of managerial effectiveness and economic development are serious. Firms which are unable to find proper candidates must either make do with less capable persons or leave the positions unfilled. The entire staffing function tends to become much more time consuming and frustrating than in the United States. Costly training programs may have to be devised to bring personnel up to requirements, and much time, effort, and money may have to be expended on recruiting functions. Many key jobs can only be filled with people trained abroad.

If management does not have adequate knowledge about the kinds of skills needed for efficient performance, and this is often the case, the problem is compounded. Internal forces or conditions must be brought to bear to make management more aware of its human requirements in terms of productive efficiency. Where management knows the kinds of skills and abilities it requires, it cannot afford to wait for the country to overcome its serious educational deficiencies. It must take immediate action involving company training and effective recruiting if the firm's performance is to improve substantially and contribute increasingly to economic development.

The organization of the firm often has to be altered to adjust to less qualified personnel. At top management levels, the adjustment will usually be in the direction of less managerial specialization and more centralization, as authority tends to be concentrated in the hands of a relatively few key people. At intermediate and lower levels, jobs tend to become fractionated, the position of a U.S. technical manager may have to be split between two people: the technical specialist and the managerial decision maker. This pattern is particularly common in the functions of production, purchasing, and sales.

Control and communications procedures must be modified, since greater supervision will be required for less qualified employees. This places sharp demands on managerial time, and reduces the amount of effort which can be expended on innovation or planning for the future.

Most of the firms surveyed in India were seriously constrained in a variety of ways by the educational mismatch problem. However, their perceptions of the severity of the problem varied by nationality of the firm, and even more significantly by the number of foreign (especially U.S.) trained people they employed. In most cases, American subsidiaries perceived educational match problems to be more serious than did the local firms, primarily because they had more knowledge about the qualifications and skills required for efficient performance, and also set higher standards in many instances. However, some of the Indian firms which employed sizeable numbers of foreign trained managerial and technical personnel also had a good deal of insight and knowledge about the human requirements conducive to managerial effectiveness and production efficiency.

In general, the number of Western educated and trained managers and technical experts, particularly American trained, seemed to be more important that the nationality of the firm per se in determining its perceptions of the educational match problem and its willingness to deal with this constraint through more effective training and recruiting.

The better run companies experienced difficulty in hiring marketing and sales executives, marketing research and economic forecasting experts, cost accountants, financial specialists, computer experts and programmers, statisticians, operations researchers, maintenance and repair specialists, and qualified research and development personnel. They also felt constrained by the educational match problem with regard to qualified engineers, as well as upper level and middle managers in general. As a result several of the U.S. subsidiaries in India spent proportionately more time and effort planning and conducting training programs than their parent companies in the United States.

MISUSE OF HIGH-TALENT MANPOWER

Much of the high-talent manpower available in Indian industry is misused. This is partly due to poor educational matches and resulting shortages of various kinds of specialists and experts. Hence, it is common to find sales personnel performing legal and procurement functions, financial executives doing industrial relations and sales work, and top-level managers undertaking detailed production planning, engineering and marketing activities. This is particularly true in relatively traditional indigenous enterprises. It is also common to find, even at U.S. subsidiaries, persons with Master's degrees and Ph.D.'s in engineering and the physical sciences, often trained at leading Western universities, working in sales, finance, accounting, public relations, and personnel jobs. Similarly, top graduates in business administration, management, law, commerce, economics, psychology, and other social science fields are employed in engineering and technical jobs.

The educational match problem or constraint does not account for all such misuse of high-talent manpower. Another key reason for it is the attitude toward different types of occupation. For example, high-caste Indians trained in engineering or the physical sciences often insist on white-collar office jobs, especially at the head office, rather than work in a factory, while lower-caste Indians regardless of their fields of formal training, are often much more willing to take positions that involve work in plants or in direct association with personnel working in factories. In general, social or class structure, nepotism, discrimination, very limited individual mobility, the lack of suitable opportunities, and poor internal management, are significant constraints on the effective utilization of high-talent manpower in Indian industry. This is more pronounced in indigenous firms, especially the more traditional ones, than in U.S. subsidiaries.

CHAPTER 3   FOOTNOTES

1. Indian literacy statistics in this chapter are from official Government of India sources, primarily *India: Pocket Book of Economic Information,* Ministry of Finance, Delhi; and *Fourth Five Year Plan, 1969-1974,* Government of India, Planning Commission, Delhi, 1969.

2. See A. Adelman and C. Taft, *Society, Politics, and Economic Development,* The John Hopkins Press, Baltimore, 1967.

3. Primary education statistics are from the same sources cited in footnote 1 above, as well as *India: 1963* and *India: 1968,* Ministry of Information and Broadcasting, Government of India, Delhi, 1964 and 1967; and *Far Eastern Economic Review 1969 Year Book,* p. 168.

4. Statistics on Indian secondary education are from the sources cited in footnotes 1 and 3 above.

5. S. Mukerji, *Education in India Today and Tomorrow,* Acharya Book Depot, Baroda, 1960, p. 140.

6. Data pertaining to semi-professional and vocational training has been taken from the official Indian government sources cited above; D. Kidder, *Education and Manpower Development in India: Middle Level Manpower* unpublished MIT doctoral dissertation, Cambridge, Mass., 1967; various reports published by the Institute of Applied Manpower Research in New Delhi during the 1963-68 period; and L. Chandrakant, *Fourth Five Year Plan of Technical Education: A Draft Report,* Ministry of Education, New Delhi, 1965.

7. Table 3-2 has been derived from the source cited in footnote 1 above.

8. Kidder, *op cit.,* Chapter IV, especially pp. 118 ff.

9. Cf. R. Farmer and B. Richman, *Comparative Management and Economic Progress,* Richard D. Irwin Inc., Homewood, III., 1965, pp. 87-91.

10. Unless otherwise noted, Indian higher education statistics are from the sources cited in foot-notes 1, 3, and 6 above, and, *Chemical Industry News,* Journal of the Indian Chemical Manu-facturers Association, Vol. x, No. 2, April, 1965.

11. U.S. higher education statistics are from official U.S. government sources.

12. Table 3-3 has been derived from data presented in the source cited in footnote 1 above, and, *Chemical Industry News, op cit.,* pp. 755-756.

13. *Fact Book on Manpower,* Institute of Applied Manpower Research, New Delhi, 1963 and 1967.

14. *Third International Survey on the Demand for and Supply of Scientific Personnel,* Organi-zation for Economic Cooperation and Development, Geneva, 1962; and, *Stock Taking of Engineering Personnel,* Institute of Applied Manpower Research, New Delhi, December, 1963.

15. *Employment Outlook for Engineers,* Institute of Applied Manpower Research, Delhi, 1970; *Times of India,* Bombay, May 18, 1970.

16. This was also the finding from a study of five firms in the city of Poona. See R. Lambert, *Workers, Factories, and Social Change in India,* Princeton University Press, Princeton, N.J., 1963, chapter 11.

17. See N.S. Davar, *Management Training in India,* The Progressive Corporation Ltd., Bombay, 1962.

18. N. Bradburn, *The Managerial Role in Turkey: A Psychological Study,* unpublished doctoral dissertation, Harvard University, Cambridge, Mass., 1960.

19. For some excellent studies that deal with attitudes toward education and related problems, especially in underdeveloped and newly developing countries, see two books by F. Harbison and C. Myers, *Education, Manpower and Economic Growth,* McGraw-Hill Book Co., New York, 1964; and *Manpower and Education,* McGraw-Hill Book Co., New York, 1965. See also D. McClelland, *The Achieving Society,* D. Van Nostrand Co., New York, 1961, especially pp. 412 ff.

20. Harbison and Myers, *op cit.,* p. 185.

21. Indian unemployment statistics for high school and higher graduates are from *Stock Taking of Engineering Personnel,* and *Nature and Dimension of Unemployment Among Educated Persons in India,* 1953 to 1964, Institute of Applied Manpower Research, New Delhi, September, 1965.

22. *A Case Study of Delhi Graduates,* Asia Publishing House, Bombay, 1965.

23. From a survey by the Indian Council of Scientific and Industrial Research published in *The Statesman,* Calcutta, January 8, 1966, p. 7.

24. Statistics on the unemployment of engineering graduates and diploma holders are from the sources cited in footnotes 14 and 21 above, and *Engineering Manpower,* Institute of Applied Manpower Research, No. 2, New Delhi, November, 1967.

25. *Christian Science Monitor,* Boston, Mass. December 31, 1968, p. 6.

26. *Engineering Manpower,* 1967.

CHAPTER 4
SOCIOLOGICAL-
CULTURAL
ENVIRONMENT

INTRODUCTION

Every productive enterprise is part of a complex society. No firm can demand and obtain complete allegiance of its managers and workers twenty-four hours a day. Many of the attitudes, philosophies, values, goals, interests, abilities, and motivations of employees are developed before they begin to work for the firm, and others during non-working hours. Furthermore, the firm must accept as a given various attitudes, philosophies, values, and motivations held by other organizations and individuals with which it must deal.

In general, the dominant or prevailing culture in a given society is in continuous interaction with that society's industrial enterprises. However, productive enterprises are not only influenced by the local cultural environment; in time they also tend to modify it. The United States, for example, is clearly influenced by its large corporations; the cultural pattern which has evolved in this country over many decades is much different than it might be if productive enterprises were organized and operated in a different manner.

This process of two-way modification, adaptation, and adjustment tends to be gradual, often taking generations for really substantial changes to emerge.[1] At any point in time the sociological-cultural environment produces various constraints, factors which must be taken as "givens" for a large majority of firms operating in a given country. However, some firms, especially foreign operated companies, may have considerable leeway in overcoming or ignoring various negative and prevalent sociological-cultural conditions, and they can and often do act as a significant catalyst in the process of social change.

In general, most of the U.S. subsidiaries surveyed in India showed substantially greater accommodation to the rational requirements of industrialism as opposed to tradition, than did the indigenous firms. However, caution and gradualism often tend to be the wise courses to follow if substantial breaks from tradition are involved. We have observed several cases where too rapid "Americanization" or "over-Americanization" by U.S. subsidiaries, and in a few cases indigenous firms, has led to serious and unanticipated consequences.

American managers working in countries such as India which have a sociological-cultural environment varying greatly from that in the United States frequently find factors that are more frustrating, give them more headaches and problems, and take more of their time and energy on a constant basis than such other types of environmental constraints as foreign exchange restrictions, onerous labor legislation or transportation shortcomings. These factors or constraints embody the dominant attitudes, values, and beliefs of the society and tend to influence the motivation, performance, and behavior of individuals.

A number of basic sociological-cultural conditions which act as significant constraints on managerial effectiveness, productive efficiency, and economic development seem to be common to many underdeveloped and developing nations.[2] In fact, in numerous cases sociological-cultural constraints seem to be the chief cause of underdevelopment and poverty, although the way they actually manifest themselves may differ from nation to nation. For example, there are several common and basic aspects of *traditional* Hinduism, Islam, Buddhism, and even traditional Catholicism which relate to managerial effectiveness and industrial progress. Countries in which these religions prevail in their relatively traditional forms tend to be relatively poor in terms of economic development. It is not the type of religion per se that is significant here, but rather the values associated with it that provide standards for thinking and behavior. By contrast, the countries in which the dominant values are associated with the "Protestant ethic," or Calvinism, tend to be relatively affluent and advanced industrially.

A major difficulty involved in research concerning sociological-cultural factors is that they are hard to measure and quantify. This is always a problem when one attempts to deal with human attitudes and values. Although the variables are all clearly very important, it is often difficult to determine precisely how they affect management, enterprise operations, and economic development.

Furthermore, it is inaccurate to think of any nation as a single sociological-cultural entity. Nations are composites of many cultures and sub-cultures. However, within most nations, a single set of values usually dominates. And in comparing nations, the internal variations often fade into insignificance alongside the contrasts between prevalent cultural patterns. Although the extent or degree of the impact of the sociological-cultural environment cannot be measured precisely in any given instance, it is clear that it has a very substantial impact on managerial effectiveness and industrial progress. The creative, enlightened, knowledgeable international manager and his company can often take effective steps to at least partially overcome the impact of negative constraints, while simultaneously serving as a catalyst for social change and economic development.

THE INTERNATIONAL EXECUTIVE IN A FOREIGN SOCIOLOGICAL-CULTURAL ENVIRONMENT

The most critical elements which distinguish the knowledge, temperament, skills, and abilities required in international management from those needed for purely domestic managerial activities can be grouped under the broad category of "sociological" or "cultural". [In India the sociological-cultural dimension seemed to be the most significant barrier to the transferability and applicability of managerial practices which work effectively in the United States] In general, the larger the difference between the sociological-cultural environments of the United States and a particular foreign country, the more difficult will be the management transfer process. If it were not for intercultural differences in personal needs, priorities, and values, the extension of management activity to international dimensions would require only straightforward transmission of techniques and patterns. International management would differ from its domestic version chiefly insofar as environmental resources differed. However, the same patterns of thinking could be applied to problems of resource allocation and maximization.

The impact of sociological and cultural factors can best be discussed by envisioning a new environment where these factors have been imagined away and asking: "What kinds of problems would confront the foreign industrial manager and what responses would be required of him?" Our decision maker might face an environment which outwardly was very different from his home — different in climate, in political and social institutions, in resource and service availability, in population density, and a host of other tangible, measurable, physical characteristics. However, one variable would remain constant and upon this he could base virtually his whole pattern of action — the decision maker's thought processes would be largely in tune with those of the local population. His intuitive and instinctive reactions would still be valid since local attitudes, aspirational levels, and patterns of logic would either be a part of his own character or would be understood by him.

The problems faced by the U.S. manager in a country like India would evoke straightforward responses if we could discount the cultural factors. As he faced each new environmental challenge, the U.S. executive could base his responses on the answer to the questions: "What would I do if I faced this problem in the United States?" "If import licenses were required in the United States, what type of argument would convince U.S. officials that my needs are critical?" "If an employee cannot carry his load, what action would I take in the United States?" "If I want to motivate my people to greater achievement, what type of incentive would I give them in the United States?"

The waiver of "things-cultural" obviously contains critical flaws. The most critical is the assumption that one can distinguish between cultural and non-cultural factors. Why does a country select a particular form of government? What do the laws of a nation represent? Why is literacy high or low? Many of the institutions and physical characteristics of the environment reflect the local thought patterns and actually derive from and embody the local culture. They cannot be dealt with purely as physical phenomena. One must be able to identify and understand any cultural underpinnings. Where there are no such underpinnings, the transference process can be mechanical. Where such cultural ties exist, it is necessary to either modify managerial thinking and action or take conscious steps to modify the environment, or both.

As soon as we reintroduce the cultural factors, the nature of the problem assumes a new dimension. Our U.S. executive may find that more than just sound arguments are needed to obtain his import license. He may be required to establish personal relationships with the officials involved. He may have to approach them indirectly. His specific application may have to be preceded and supported by a series of social (and economic) interactions with various influential persons. The emphasis of the arguments supporting his application may have to be modified to appeal to local logic. Our executive may discover that any action he takes against an ineffective employee is viewed by the community (and reflects upon his and his company's character) in the same manner as if he had taken similar action against one of his children. How would U.S. society view the parent who throws his child out of the house because he doesn't do his chores well? He may discover that monetary incentives given to people with low aspirational levels can act as deterrents to productive output by allowing workers to fulfill their static aspirations by producing less. Perhaps a completely different pattern of personal behavior on his part may be the answer. Does a father motivate his children through economic "bribery?"

Few of these alternative courses of action are likely to be inherent in the U.S. executive's managerial thoughts or patterns. Instinctively he will fall back on what is familiar and what has worked for him in the past, although in time, and sometimes through serious mistakes, he will become more sensitive to the local sociological-cultural environment. No matter how much weight is given the image of the purely rational, organized, analytical decision maker, the manager does tend to salt his decisions heavily with his own learned value system. He does not have the time to analyze every problem. Furthermore, over the years, through the process of trial and error, he has built up a "common law" of decision precedents. His past decisions, many of which were based on analysis, provided a learning experience which resulted in the formation of decision-making habits.

When one party to a joint relationship is not familiar with the culture of the other and holds values which are very different, as in the case of interface between the U.S. manager and the Indian environment, the situation is ripe for conflict due to lack of communication and misunderstanding. The danger is multiplied when the parties use a common language. Each, while believing he is communicating, may be listening through cultural filters which distort what is actually being heard. The U.S. manager assigns a task to a subordinate, a local citizen, who, upon attempting to complete the assignment, finds that some necessary ingredient (which is "not really his responsibility") is missing. Our executive has probably assumed that the assignment of the task has imposed a responsibility for completion, or, at the very least, a prompt report of any delays. This may directly conflict with the subordinate's belief that he is relieved of all further obligation since it is obvious that completion will have to wait until the missing ingredient is supplied by someone else. The details have been communicated, and perhaps even the method for accomplishing the task, but the concept of "responsibility" is different.

Time will probably be highly valued by the typical U.S. executive. His personal time is important — he has many things he has to achieve or would like to achieve. In addition, time has an economic value to his company activities, and he thinks of it in terms of lost opportunities and specific dollar costs. On the other hand, less developed nations characteristically assign a very low value to time. In some cultures, time is almost a meaningless quantity. The language may not even contain words to express time dimensions. This life is often viewed as just a stage in an eternity of lives, and time moves at a pace set by the gods, not by man.

India has many of these characteristics. Time is seen as an endless, cyclic, flowing stream, controlled by the gods. Reincarnation and fatalism completely de-emphasize the quantum and value of time. This fatalism is similar to "Inshallah" (God's will) in the Moslem world, and the "bahalana" or fatalistic attitude in such Asian countries as the Phillippines. In Hindi, the words for "tomorrow" and "yesterday" are identical, and are only distinguished by usage; both mean one day from now. The different value and priority assignments often result in conflict — the U.S. executive who wants to get the new machine into operation immediately and the Indian employee who wants to wait for an auspicious day.

Many Indian business men, government officials, and educators, many of whom have been educated in Western countries, including the United States, appear to have Western values on the surface, and initially give the impression that they think like Americans, and even speak about business and managerial matters much like Americans. But most are still imbued with a good deal of traditional Hindu culture and tradition, and they live and act by it; e.g., placing considerable faith in astrology and various other mystical forces in arriving at their decisions, and consulting frequently with astrologers to discover auspicious dates or courses of action.

One of the major pitfalls facing the international manager is his tendency to examine situations from the viewpoint of what he wants or expects to see, based on preconceptions which may or may not be entirely correct. Edward Hall brings out this point, in not very flattering terms, when he states that Americans frequently "manage to convey the impression that we Americans simply regard foreign nationals as 'underdeveloped Americans.'"[3] A possible explanation for this attitude, supplied by Professor Hall, is that

> almost everyone has difficulty believing that behavior they have always associated with human nature is not human nature at all but learned behaviour of a particularly complex variety. Possibly one of the many reasons why the culture concept has been resisted is that it throws doubt on many established beliefs.[4]

Even when actions are the same, motivation may be different. In looking at Spanish America, Margaret Mead indicates that Spanish Americans ". . . accepted schooling but not the 'Anglo' motivation for education — the higher standard of living, the better job."[5] Similar differences can be found in the Indian situation, as discussed previously.

The manager who enters a new environment must, therefore, make a special effort to acquaint himself with the existing sociological and cultural patterns. He must do so not only because they are interesting and his knowledge will impress local nationals with his sincerity and interest in their country, but because the use of such knowledge in making decisions is vital to his own and to his organization's effectiveness. One of the primary tasks of a manager is motivation. He must work through other people. He must stimulate them, whether it be to perform effectively within the organization, to purchase his products, or to grant his export licenses. Unless he understands the sociological system and the cultural values which are important to the people with whom he is dealing, he is operating under a severe handicap.

A major key to the international management and economic growth process is, therefore, a thorough understanding of the sociological and cultural factors at work in the local environment.

> Not only is respect for the culture of the changing society necessary, but also understanding of how those habits and practices which must be changed *can* be changed; this is an important skill for the foreign members of the teams which come into a country.[6]

It is the recognition of the areas which need change, and of the most effective way to bring these changes about that must be the main focus to insure the success of foreign companies in "strange" environments. The other side of the coin which is just as important is the identification of those "strange" local practices which would be better left unchanged, and should be absorbed into the operating pattern of the foreign company.

The need for sensitivity to the interface between foreign and cultural indigenous patterns is just as critical for the "economic developer," whether he is of indigenous or foreign nationality. As indicated in Chapter 1, the host environment is under-developed because it has been unable to give birth to and sustain the concepts and practices which result in development. The process of change will therefore require an infusion of "things-foreign" into the local scene, and a thorough understanding of the transference process and the process of adaptation is essential. Technology and technical processes which are transplanted intact from more developed economies may run into problems similar to those faced by managerial practices which are similarly transferred. The practices or the environment must frequently be modified to affect a successful transplant.

Before proceeding with a detailed analysis of particular sociological-cultural factors which affect management and economic development, it is useful to identify some broad characteristics of the Indian environment. Such an overview is especially important for India, since there are certain characteristics which affect and relate to all of the specific sociological-cultural factors — and many of the other kinds of environmental constraints — considered in this study. This overview helps explain various attitudes which pervade Indian society and provides a reference frame which is useful in evaluating the significance of such attitudes for managerial purposes. Although this discussion focuses on India, its primary value derives not from the description of Indian culture but from the way such factors relate to the tasks of management.

Patterns as different from U. S. culture as these exist in many nations. And although they, in turn, will differ in many cases from those found in India, an examination of the Indian experience will sensitize the reader to the impact such factors can have. As a result of this exercise, he should be better able to analyze other environments and understand the problems which arise while attempting to link different cultures. It should be realized that modern management as we know it today is primarily a "Western" concept derived directly from the ethical and value systems of Western culture.

AN OVERVIEW OF INDIA'S SOCIOLOGICAL-CULTURAL ENVIRONMENT

A complete description of the Indian sociological-cultural environment is an impossibly complex task; however an examination of Hinduism provides a base for understanding India. Hinduism, the dominant religion in India (followed by more than 80 percent of the population) in its traditional form is virtually a way of life. It has not one single source of "authority" such as the Bible is to the Christian world. It has many different "scriptures," different interpretations, and even different forms. However, there are certain characteristics which permeate all of Hindu society. Although these are manifested to a substantially higher degree among the rural population, they are still quite widespread, although gradually declining in strength, in urban and industrial areas.

Some aspects of this culture have more significance to the manager or firm than others. In particular, two seem paramount in understanding the functioning of the Indian business environment. These are the joint family system and the caste system (with its related Hindu concepts of "dharma" and "karma"), which provide both formal organization and the traditions or working guidelines of life. As William Kapp aptly points out:

> Group membership shapes the aspirations and desires of the great majority of the people of India and these group aspirations are in turn moulded by the traditional patterns of behaviour prescribed for the various status groups of Hindu society. Hence, the premium is on tradition-determined action rather than on voluntaristic individual action. Thus, traditions are permitted to play a much more important role in India than in Western societies . . . . Not only are levels of aspiration dictated by the group and hence are as static or as dynamic as group tradition permits them to be but the failure to reach traditional goals need not be experienced as a source of individual frustration.[7]

The joint or extended family consists of a number of family units (i.e., father and mother, sons and their wives and children, nephews and their families, etc.) living together as one, sharing the same house and facilities, and pooling resources. The family is usually administered by a senior male member (although matriarchal structures also exist, especially in the South). He acts on behalf of the group as agent; however, although he may make ultimate and authoritarian decisions for the entire family, he usually does so only after consultation with the family council. Security is closely linked with family ties. Strangers are suspect, and alliances are very much dependent upon blood relationships, since these impose direct mutual obligations on the parties.

Caste presents a secondary type of kinship group providing common protective links, although these ties typically are not as strong as those of the joint families. The origins of the caste system are lost in time. However, references in ancient literature leave little doubt that the concept of caste has had different meanings at different periods in history. Today, caste seems to be a form of loose kinship group focusing around occupational activity. For example, virtually all of the foundry workers in a particular town may come from the same caste, and foundry work will be the only task in which they engage. Over the years, a very strong body of traditions has been established, traditions which indicate "pecking orders" among the caste groups, acceptable and unacceptable caste intermarriage patterns, and the prescribed duties and responsibilities for members of each caste.

Basically, the caste system divides Hindu society and culture into five broad segments. At the top are the Brahmins. The smallest group numerically, they are traditionally the priests, the educators, and, surprisingly, the cooks, since Brahmins have rigid dietary habits and customs. The next level contains the warrior class, traditionally the fighters and rulers, who now make up much of the military. This is followed by the business class, including various kinds of merchant-farmers and

landowners. The lowest level within the system contains the rural farming population, although this group, including sub-castes, is the least clearly defined since it has
experienced major occupational changes through history. The fifth and largest group
is actually outside the system and consists of the "outcasts," most of whom have
traditionally been referred to as "untouchables." Ghandi called this segment of
society the Harijans (Children of God) and in contemporary times they have been
given the constitutional name of "scheduled" castes. Traditionally these people have
been given the most menial tasks in the society — tanning, removing nightsoil,
cleaning, and other menial occupations. The caste-related mores and taboos which
evolved have become very rigid, although this is slowly changing. For example, the
traditional Brahmin who accidentally is touched by the shadow of the Harijan may
have to undergo extensive purification rituals before he is once again clean.

Each of the major caste groups is divided into many sub-groups, most of which
are occupation oriented, even among the outcasts. In traditional fashion caste is
inherited, and occupations are passed down from father to son. The entire structure
has become intimately linked with the religious structure, and castes are viewed as a
way of organizing temporal life. A person is placed in a particular caste by the gods,
as a means of rewarding him or punishing him for performance in past life. Rewards
consist of upward movement in subsequent lives, until the soul passes the upper level
of mortality and enters various stages of godhood, eventually breaking the cycle and
achieving nirvana, or release. Punishments consist of downward movement on the
ladder and can eventually result in rebirth in the animal kingdom (thus explaining
some of the value placed on the preservation of animal life).

The system of reward and punishment has important consequences for the management process. The two concepts embodied within the caste system which lie at
the heart of this are "dharma" and "karma." Dharma can be defined very loosely
as the body of duties required of a man to enable fulfillment of his role in life.
Karma introduces the aspect of "just rewards," and supplies the fatalistic and
religious notions of life cycles where a man's successive positions in the cosmic cycle
are determined by his observance of his dharma.

The belief that the gods have placed an individual in a particular caste (by birth)
must inevitably lead to the conclusion, if one assumes that the gods act with a purpose, that the gods wish that person to perform the duties and conform to the mores
expected of that particular group. Any deviation from established patterns is tantamount to defiance of divine will, and subject to punishment. The individual who
allows his worldly aspirations or achievements to run too high is in conflict with the
cosmic cycle, and will suffer perhaps not in this life, but definitely in the next.
Rewards come from absolute adherence to group norms.

> It is this iron law of inescapable retribution (karma) which gives Hindu culture its distinct
> character. By connecting the actual finite human situation with the individual's previous
> incarnations, cause and effect are spread over totally different lives. As a result, causation
> tends to lose all continuity and assumes a fatalistic tinge.[8]

> By advocating the acceptance of one's dharma as prerequisite of salvation and release and by enjoining the individual not to be motivated by a concern for the fruits of action, it [Hindu philosophy] not only tends to lower the level of human aspirations but places a premium on passive acceptance rather than amelioration of the human situation whether by hard work or by social reform.[9]

Although legislation has been enacted to diminish the "anti-social" aspects of caste, and although the melting-pot effects of industrial urbanization are also weakening the system, caste and its related concepts still pervade and dominate Hindu (and therefore Indian) thought. The joint family system, again undergoing a process of erosion as modern youth begins to seek greater degrees of independence with respect to new household formation, is still by far the predominant form of family organization. The need to consider the impacts of these features of Indian culture on the managerial process should be readily apparent. For example,

> A person whose springs of action are predominantly determined and whose feelings of security are derived from his dependency on his group will experience difficulties in developing an impersonal work discipline and commitments to an impersonal organization such as a firm (whether private or public). Indeed, discipline, orderliness, precision and punctuality for the sake of such an impersonal organization, may be rejected as pedantic, tyrannical and intolerable.[10]

Richard Lambert also finds that security is a primary motivating force behind the Indian worker.[11] The prevalence of extreme resistance to change which seems to be characteristic of many traditional societies is often directly related to needs for security. As Kapp indicates, individuals in traditional societies often react unfavorably to new ideas because they fear that resulting change might upset the status quo, and because the fear of benefiting rivals far outweighs the satisfaction that an individual might gain himself.[12] They see only a "zero-sum" game where one party can win only at the expense of the other. It is axiomatic that all non-family members are regarded as rivals in the traditional sense.

The concept of fatalism is another source of resistance to change. Because, to a Hindu, present life is only a transitory phase, temporal conditions are to be endured. Hindu culture lacks the conviction that man can make his own future or that social and economic progress or effective management, can depend upon human choices and action rather than blind destiny. Why should one bother to store food during good harvest seasons? If man is destined to survive, food will be provided. If man is to die of starvation, it is because the gods have willed it so. Storing food would be both impertinent and senseless, since the future is predetermined and inviolate.

This attitude offers a striking contrast to Western values, and specifically to values existent in the United States. The concept embodied in the quotation, "God helps those who help themselves" is diametrically opposed to Hindu philosophy. Indian literature extolls the virtues of being a good son or a good friend, of fulfilling one's dharma, above all else. It does not glorify the Horatio Alger ideals of entrepreneurship and initiative, to fight life's obstacles in an effort to rise above one's station.

> Somewhere in our American thinking is the idea that the individual feels pride in his performance and strives for excellence so that he will feel worthy and proud of *himself.* Traditional Hindu philosophy poses exactly the opposite notions: 'He attains peace who, giving up desire, moves through the world without aspiration, possessing nothing which he can call his own and free from pride.' [13]

The most important aspects of Indian culture which affect the managerial practices examined in this book include the strong need for job security, the conservatism of action, the distrust of non-family members, the lack of individual initiative, and the need for the close, supportive relationships provided in family and community (especially caste) situations, both implied and explicit. The fact that there are strong implications for industrial growth and development is fairly evident, especially when a new and dynamic culture based on achievement both for the sake of achieving and for the sake of increasing material belongings confronts one based on highly static approaches. The former has given rise to the type of industrial progress and relatively effective management systems which are trying to take hold in India, while the latter represents the traditional patterns which exist in the country. However, recognition of the fact that there are implications is quite distinct from the recognition of what these specific implications are.

There are many parallels between the Indian situation and that of other less developed groups. For example a study of the Spanish-Americans, mostly traditional Catholics, of New Mexico, revealed:

> Spanish American culture puts major emphasis on the established present. Things are as they are because 'These are the customs'. The past is not venerated, it validates the present; and the future is expected to be like the present. [14]

This is similar to the oft-expressed explanation of the lack of ambition evidenced in India: "it always has been, it is, and it will always be this way." In a tradition-bound society, this thought completely molds approaches to the problems of daily life. When it is linked with an emphasis on the passive acceptance of one's lot, the result is a static society, a society which cannot, *by definition,* be in tune with Western ideas of change, growth, and industrial development.

The Mead study reports that the Spanish-Americans

> do not consider work itself a virtue. It is not common sense, in their view, to work just so as to keep the hands occupied, or even to earn money when there is money for the current needs of the family because some other adult male is employed. [15]

The need to keep busy, the desire to put aside for "a rainy day," the pride of achievement, none of these are present. Again, strong parallels with India can be seen: if bellies are full, there is no need for work. Work is required only if one is hungry. To attempt to anticipate and plan for tomorrow is to defy fate.

"The idea of higher pay does not immediately interest the Spanish-American."[16] "The assumption that all peoples have an incentive to improve the standard of living, and therefore of taking on employment, is not justified."[17] These correspond to prevalent thinking in India. As long as survival today can be patterned after the way survival was achieved yesterday, little more is desired and levels of aspiration are fixed accordingly.

In the course of a research project, Kusum Nair asked Indian villagers throughout the country how much land they would like to have if their greatest wishes could be fulfilled.[18] Instead of the "several thousands of acres" response that might be expected from the U.S. farmer, the vast majority of requests were for parcels of land so small that they were barely sufficient to provide food for the farmer's family. There were no thoughts of growing more to put aside for a rainy day, let alone to sell. In her conclusions, Miss Nair states:

> A great majority of the rural communities do not share in the concept of an ever-rising standard of living. The upper level they are prepared to strive for is limited . . . . it tends to be static, with a ceiling rather than a floor, and it is socially determined.
>
> If my observation is correct, it largely invalidates one of the principal assumptions on which present planning for economic development in the rural sector is based. For in a situation of limited and static aspirations, if a man should feel his requirements are just two bags of paddy per year, he works for two bags but not for more. If he looks to the stars, it is only to worship them, not to pluck them . . . . In fact, often, the peasant does not consider it moral to want more . . . .[19]

The Spanish-American study gives one significant explanation for the low levels of aspirations:

> There is an attitude of acceptance toward the hierarchy combined with a fear of ostracism for standing out from the group that operates to keep Spanish-Americans out of competitive work situations. His status in his own community may be lowered rather than raised by achievement — and he has no other community. It is much more important to be than to do; to be a good son, or a good Catholic, or a good member of the village.[20]

Belonging and performing the roles required "to belong" become the utmost considerations. Attitudes toward work are similarly influenced:

> When authority was part of the structure of the family or extended family, the employee did not know how to obey a foreman, and the employer did not know how to treat the employee. And people to whom honesty was a matter of personal family relations acted

with dishonesty in terms of the industrial organization, the validity of which as a unit they did not recognize.[21]

and again:

Careful analysis of the habits and practices of a people shows that the traditional behavior practised between parents and children, for example, is systematically related to practices which obtain between employer and employee, audience and speaker . . . etc.[22]

There is little doubt that the cultural traditions of India have retarded effective management, as well as economic growth and development. They do not seem to fit well with the efficiency and dynamism required for rapid economic progress. The society does not adequately generate the entrepreneurs and the risk takers, the effective administrators, the confidence and trust necessary to develop effective credit and savings institutions, and the managerial personnel who can attain enough detachment from the culture to lead it off into new directions.

. . . so far India's development efforts have met with only limited success mainly because ancient traditions still pervade virtually every phase of Hindu social organization. Whether this limited success will be maintained or increased or whether it will be submerged by the weight of ancient traditions remains an open question. The answer to this question depends upon whether it will be possible to transform Hinduism into a world outlook that strengthens rather than weakens those aspirations and behaviour patterns without which sustained economic growth is impossible.[23]

The writer goes on to further state that:

. . . it can hardly be doubted that Hindu culture and Hindu social organization are determining factors in India's slow rate of development. It is not only the lack of capital resources or skilled manpower which impedes the process of economic growth but non-secular and pre-technological institutions and values such as the hierarchically organized caste system, the limited or static levels of aspirations, moral aloofness, casteism, and factionalism . . .[24]

and that:

Indeed it appears that there are no religious or intellectual reformers on the Indian horizon who may do for India what Luther and Calvin, or Galileo and Newton, did for the modern interpretation of the world in the West. And yet, such a reinterpretation is required for the transformation of a tradition-bound culture into a new society.[25]

George Litwin comes to a similar conclusion when he states that:

The great obstacles to any human development or behaviour change programs in India are provided by the culture itself. Complex, irrational and beyond the understanding of any individual, interlaced with religion, social forms, law, convention, language, and the very meaning of life, the culture provides the warp and woof of existence, and in fact stands in opposition to self-determined action of any kind. To me, the most important kinds of work that have been done in India by social scientists or anyone else concerned with human development are the education and training programs that attempt to give the individual some freedom from the culture, and some insight into his thinking about the culture network and his place in it . . . The aim of these programs, as I see it, is to provide some room, some freedom for the individual to develop new goals, new roles, new forms of thinking and action, *should he want to.*[26]

The viewpoint expressed in the above quotations is just as applicable to the patterns of individual firms as it is to the problems of overall economic development. Modern industry, as we know it today, does not flow naturally from Hindu thought and cultural patterns. As Farmer states (probably to an unnecessary extreme):

One solution [to the problem of development] which is implicit in the Western or American style, is to attempt to create a culture as much like the U.S. or Western Europe as possible . . . . Since no one knows how to be richer than the U.S. without being culturally similar to the U.S., the solution of taking it all or staying poor seems to be the only meaningful option available.[27]

The developed nations have much to offer the less developed countries in the way of managerial skills and techniques, and changing the local environment is a necessary step towards progress. However, one must know the environment in order to ease the transference and adaptation process. A few bad mistakes can result in total rejection. Companies can be forced to leave or even be refused permission to enter. The manager who understands the sociological-cultural milieu will be in a better position to anticipate the way the environment will react to a given stimulus and can therefore ease the traumatic aspects of change, either by altering the foreign inputs or by preparing the host environment. It is only with such knowledge at his fingertips that the manager can judge the validity and effectiveness of his own thought patterns and decisions.

VIEW OF BUSINESS MANAGERS AND MANAGEMENT

Introduction

Every society has its high-prestige careers and its occupational heroes. Some occupations are always considered better than others and are held up as examples of what the young may be able to achieve if they try hard enough to succeed. Often such occupations are better rewarded economically than other, less esteemed jobs, but at the minimum they carry with them substantial nonmaterial rewards such as prestige, status, power, or self-gratification.

The place of business (including industrial) managers in the prestige hierarchy of a particular country is important in terms of managerial effectiveness and economic development. Also important is the kind of people who become managers. If the high achievers, the most motivated, best educated, and most talented people tend to shun business and managerial careers, productive efficiency and industrial progress will be greatly retarded.

In an environment where managers are respected and highly regarded, one usually finds greater trust and cooperation and less conflict between managers, employees, and external parties with whom they have dealings. This results in more productive time and greater operating efficiency. Stringent direction and control can be replaced by greater reliance on self-control and individual initiative, and, if desired, authority can be decentralized in order to achieve still greater organizational efficiency.

An authoritative United Nations report on the world social situation has this to say about the status of various occupations in numerous countries:

> A common psychological obstacle to economic achievement is the fact that much higher status tends to be associated with land ownership or government position or professional or intellectual activity than is enjoyed by the businessman, engineer, mechanic, agronomist, or some other person concerned directly with material production.[28]

While there are other occupations with more prestige than management in the United States and in other countries where business managers tend to be accorded high status—e.g., Japan, Germany, and the Soviet Union[29]—the attitude toward managers in the United States is highly favorable when compared to the rest of the world. Moreover, management attracts a substantial portion of America's high achievers and generally competent well-educated people.

Negative social attitudes regarding managers are likely to interact with other types of environmental constraints that firms encounter. A country which has small regard for management and business activity is not as likely to have a government, or labor organizations, or educational institutions, or potential investors who are sympathetic to business problems. Hence, constraints such as tax laws, price controls, interorganizational cooperation, business codes, labor legislation, foreign policy, monetary and fiscal policy, availability of capital, and similar factors will frequently reflect such attitudes.

There are still many countries in Latin America, Asia, and Africa where enterprise owners and managers are viewed as a contemptible, corrupt group, whose main activities consist of the systematic exploitation of people. Often the educational system as well as popular folklore in a particular country reflects this attitude. Marxist propaganda assists in creating this image, but so do the activities of many businessmen. A given society's view toward managers is not determined solely by conditions over which firms and their managements have little or no control, but also by the actions and attitudes of the managers themselves.

In many countries the managers themselves do not view management as a profession. In fact the dominant view of society at large, and of some managers, is that management requires no special training, qualifications, or skills — only authority and power — and that managerial jobs need not be filled on the basis of personal ability or objective criteria. Nepotism, favoritism, caste, and other subjective factors predominate in staffing many firms. Some managers tend to blame environment and uncontrollable conditions, rather than themselves, for the problems, difficulties, and inefficiencies which confront them.

Negative attitudes toward business managers, and skepticism about management as a worthy profession, linger on in many countries, even long after a more positive management philosophy begins to emerge. This is what has been happening in India, although attitudes toward business managers and management have never been as strongly negative there as in some other countries.

One authoritative source sums up the current situation in India thus:

> Widespread criticism and suspicion of the activities of businessmen have been a striking feature of public debate on economic affairs in India since 1947. It has almost been a matter of habit with literate Indians to blame the commercial classes and financial interests for the country's economic backwardness.[30]

While the view toward business managers and management is gradually becoming more favorable in India than in the past, for the most part only the managers of a relatively small number of the larger and most progressive private firms, particularly U.S. and British subsidiaries, and a number of large public sector enterprises, are actually highly regarded. The owners and managements of the large majority of family controlled companies still appear to be regarded quite negatively.

The prestige and status of lower level managerial jobs in Indian industry is especially low; in fact lower than in many other poor countries. In India, as in many other developing nations, only the higher-level executives are considered as managers. Lower-level supervisors, and particularly foremen, are not usually viewed or treated as part of management. Not only are they accorded little status; they are also given little if any authority and receive relatively low pay, although this is gradually changing.

Scientific research reveals that people with a high need for achievement (n-ach) tend to make the most dynamic managers and the best entrepreneurs.[31] An important study correlated the achievement levels among samples of schoolboys aged 14 to 18 in five countries (the United States, India, Japan, Brazil, and Germany) with their liking or preferences for twelve occupations.[32] Four were business occupations (factory manager, buyer of merchandise, stockbroker, and advertiser), four were traditional (civil servant, lawyer, clergyman, and poet). The remaining four were scientific research worker, explorer, auto-racer, and politician.

The study showed that the Indian high achievers were most attracted to the more traditional types of jobs, and in fact "factory manager" ranked second to last. The occupational preferences of the American high achievers were almost reversed. However, including both relatively high and low achievers, "factory manager" ranked third among the Indian boys and only sixth among the Americans. "Buyer" ranked eighth amongst both groups, while "advertiser" and "stockbroker" ranked significantly higher among the American boys. The Indian boys low in need achievement were more attracted to the job of factory manager than the Americans low in n-ach; however, the reverse was true with regard to the high achievers.

AN EVOLUTIONARY OVERVIEW OF MANAGEMENT

The Western concept of management has gone through four evolutionary stages during the progression from primitive societies to modern industrial (non-communist) nations. An understanding of the particular stage (or stages) which a nation has reached is of great importance to potential industrial entrants, since it affects such crucial factors as the calibre of managerial personnel available for employment, their concepts of managerial roles and responsibilities, and the nature of competitive responses.

In the first stage, characteristic of very primitive societies, everyone performs the physical labor necessary for survival. Tasks consist of hunting and farming, and the individual is often accorded status on the basis of physical prowess. The functions of management are limited, and may be concentrated in the hands of the most able warrior who provides leadership in matters of defense. All tasks are regarded as important, although some (e.g., those of the warrior) may be regarded with more respect than others (e.g., those of the farmer). However, major distinctions focus primarily on physical abilities.

In the second stage, individuals start differentiating themselves from the group by developing non-physical skills which contribute to the society. The shaman and the witch doctor are probably the first to emerge in the primitive society, but they are eventually followed by the priest, the scholar, the doctor, the engineer, the scientist, the lawyer, and the other professionals. Somewhere along the way, true societal leadership also emerges, and eventually the politicians. These non-physical positions now share or surpass the status accorded to the warrior-athlete (the cleverest of whom have probably become societal leaders). Consequently, physical labor starts to move to the bottom of the status hierarchy, with agriculture (often associated with women) taking the bottom rung. The business units which start to form (i.e., units which start producing for others) are small and are run by the worker-manager (the family head). Although the chief of a tribe is also a manager, his function does not involve the production of tangible goods or services and is usually not classified as managerial in nature. This term is largely reserved for business operations. As a result, the "business management" function becomes associated with physical labor and is generally accorded low esteem.

A number of changes take place during the transition from stage two to stage three. One is that society starts to stratify. Whereas previously an individual could earn a place on the basis of physical or mental abilities, groups such as families and guilds tend to reserve functions and limit entry in an effort to retain power. Consequently, mobility decreases and the elitist groups become even more elite. Although managers of business enterprises are not among the elite initially, economic power starts to become respectable. Those family operations which have been able to transform physical labor into relatively large businesses controlling substantial wealth now establish an elite of their own. The business enterprise becomes, however, primarily a means for maintaining and enhancing family power. Consequently, it is a tight and secretive organization and because of this becomes suspect to society in general. Managerial positions are reserved for trusted family members and intimate friends, and the occasional outsider who is admitted must confine his activities to performing minor functions within the organizations.

At this point we have a society where the traditional occupations, government jobs (perhaps civil service), and various older professions attract most of the bright talent. Entry into business for individuals who are not already members of large powerful families is through positions associated with physical labor, which are low in status. A few groups, usually families which have managed to achieve great wealth and large economic empires, have become members of the elite, although they continue to be regarded with suspicion since their primary motivation has been self-interest.

In the final stage, the nation as a whole approaches the task of economic development. Family concerns grow so large and the total effort becomes so demanding that business leadership can no longer be provided by members of the elite families. The business enterprise assumes its position as an important institution of society and becomes less a tool of concentrated private power. Ownership becomes diffuse and the task of management becomes more respectable. A managerial "profession" develops. The industrial manager now moves up in social standing, mobility of individuals increases, and there may even be a trend away from disdain for physical labor. Finally, management is seen as a process which is no longer associated purely with business enterprises.

Most of the highly industrialized Western societies presently contain a mixture of stages three and four. In the United States we like to think that we are in stage four, but some strong elements of three still linger. The strong elements which linger from stage three bear much of the responsibility for the aversion of many bright college graduates to business careers, and for the frequent demands for the development of ethical codes for business management (although many of these demands are directed at "professional" managers who have not completed the transition, rather than at family groups).

Many developing nations simultaneously contain three or all four stages. Brazil offers all four. In India one can identify all of the last three, largely because India's society is so segmented that different groups are on completely distinct levels of economic development, although they intermingle in the economic activities of the nation. Within the villages, and wherever the caste system and the joint family system is strongest, stages two and three can be found, with the former predominating. Within the larger industrial centers, two is much diminished (but still existent) three predominates, and some traces of four can be found, most notably among foreign firms.

THE PUBLIC SECTOR

State-owned or public sector industrial enterprises can be viewed as a special case. In many (non-communist) countries where a sizeable public sector has emerged, the government often assumes that the management of this sector is characterized by the favorable attitudes and practices which relate to our fourth evolutionary stage: i.e., professional managers, good management-labor relations, an effective agent for economic development. In reality, especially in newly developing "mixed" economies such as India, but also in some more advanced nations such as England, this often does not turn out to be the case since many of the traditional attitudes and practices prevalent in the broad culture of the nation strongly influence the thinking of management. For example, personal friendships, kinship or community ties, favoritism, and politics, as opposed to merit and objective criteria, predominate in staffing decisions. There may still be considerable conflict in management-labor relations. Management tends to avoid responsibility and strongly resists innovation and change.

A sizeable public sector has evolved in the Indian economy, accounting for roughly 20 percent of total industrial activity (proportionately not much different from that in Canada). The Indian public sector is composed primarily of heavy industry such as steel mills, equipment, and machinery. It also includes some chemical companies, mining, defense firms (including aircraft), antibiotics, insurance and banking, utilities, and various other enterprises. Several industries contain both public and private firms. The public sector seems to enjoy somewhat more status than private enterprise. Many managers, technicians, and other personnel prefer to work in public sector enterprises at lower pay because of this and also because they assume they will find greater job security.[33] Managerial jobs in this sector are often viewed as civil service positions, since many of the public sector managers in fact come from government and civil service bureaucracy. But in recent years, there has been increasing disillusionment with India's public sector because of poor performance, favoritism, conflict, traditional attitudes and practices, and, at some firms, large cutbacks and layoffs of personnel.

Some Indian examples

It is worth taking a look at specific examples of prevalent patterns in India. These characterize in general the dominant, though gradually changing, evolutionary stages not only in India, but in many other underdeveloped and emerging nations as well.

The following is a very brief description of the managerial role of a small Indian businessman in a traditional stage two (with elements of stage three) society. The situation was observed by one of the authors in an Indian village and is typical of "cottage industry," within which the largest number of Indians find an industrial type of employment.

> The "manager" is a carpet weaver. He is a respected citizen of his village, but not as respected as the village headman, the priests, the school teacher, or the small number of wealthy merchants who also reside there. He produces fine wool carpets for one of the merchants. The merchant supplies him with yarn, but he performs the work in his own home, following traditional family designs and procedures. He is paid by the piece at what can only be considered bare subsistence wages. He "supervises" a work force of six children (his), ranging in age from about six to fourteen. The work is very fine, the hut is ill-lit, and the children work from dawn to dusk, often on only one meal per day. By the time they reach their early teens, their eyesight has deteriorated to the point that they are no longer capable of the fine discernments necessary for weaving. The father, who lacks the agility and eyesight to weave, confines his activities to dealing with the merchant, training the children, and supervising the design and quality of output.

> His productive capacity is strictly a function of his reproductive capacity. He is neither content nor dissatisfied. His is the lot of the "typical" village "businessman." Few would aspire to his position in life, certainly not the sons of the upper-level families of village society, none of whom work with their hands. His daughters look forward to early marriage, his sons to continuing in their father's footsteps with their own families. Recently, however, events have presented his sons with the alternative of going to an urban center to find work as laborers in factories.

The merchant mentioned in the above sketch functions in stage three. He is the individual who has achieved a higher status through economic power. The example below illustrates the stage on a larger scale. It is drawn from a very large family-controlled managing agency in a large Indian city.

> This family is extremely wealthy and socially prominent throughout India, although discussions about the family with the general educated public invariably evoke questions concerning the motivation, morality, and ethics of family operations. Through a managing agency administered by a dominant elder brother (Mr. A), a vast and diversified industrial empire is controlled. Two younger brothers are also involved, but clearly in subordinate roles. The heirs apparent are the two eldest of Mr. A's three sons.

> Each of Mr. A's sons manages a major enterprise within the organization. Two (only one of whom is an heir apparent) were educated abroad, as were several of their cousins who staff second-level managerial positions within the various enterprises. All major decisions are made by Mr. A, with the advice of a family council consisting of his two brothers, two of his sons, one nephew, and a close family friend (a lawyer). None of the sons or brothers

have the authority to make major financial commitments, and the nephews have virtually no power at all.

Two conversations, one with the second eldest son (foreign educated), and the other with a foreign educated nephew were very revealing concerning methods of operation. In the first interview, the son was asked about exchanges of information with his brothers (one of whom was managing a group of companies in the same industry). His response indicated that the only coordination whatsoever was the communication of overall financial data to the father. He firmly believed that an exchange of operating information was both unnecessary and a hazard (i.e., the more people who knew, the greater the chance of disclosure). Although the sons' social relations with one another were close and cordial, their business worlds were absolutely distinct. The nephew, a young man functioning at a level equivalent to vice president under one of the sons, was ready to resign as a result of his frustration. Although he received a substantial income and was accorded a good deal of status and prestige in the community, at least on the surface, by virtue of his family connections and position, he had virtually no power to make decisions of any kind. Everything had to be referred upward to the son. Unlike many of his contemporaries, he was not content to allow the education he had received abroad to become a mere status symbol.

The important elements of this sketch relate to the secrecy and the concentration of control in the hands of the family members. Even though this family was respected — or feared — for its power and influence, it was regarded with suspicion and distrust by the general public. Furthermore, its method of operation contributed towards discouraging bright young non-family talent from entering the managerial profession, and even had an inhibiting effect on family members who were not admitted to the true inner sanctum.

In traditional societies, entry into business pursuits is often a closed process. One enters either at the top (via birth into a wealthy business family) or at the bottom (via birth into a trade class). It is the rare individual who has both the motivation and the ability, as well as the good fortune, to move up the ladder from the bottom to the top, and it is also rare to find the individual from the top who is willing to undertake the physical work associated with striking out on his own.

Consequently, the bright young students without family connections tend to be anti-business. Many seek civil service appointments and go into government positions which frequently relate to issues of economic growth, and regulation and control of business enterprises. They distrust business interests and are unfamiliar with the way industry functions. Their distrust is heightened by the secrecy with which most Indian firms surround themselves — secrecy often directed at tax evasion.

Consequently, in a nation such as India, many of the government decisions made with respect to industry seem to be anti-business. Some undoubtedly are intentionally so. Others result from ignorance of the impact that such decisions will have on industry or the role industry plays in the process of economic growth. Industrial operations are seen strictly in terms of personal operations, and business firms are viewed as the tools with which a few individuals control the masses.

THE ROLE OF INTERNATIONAL MANAGEMENT

For the foreign firm entering such an environment, the pitfalls are many. Even though its operating concepts may be very different from those of indigenous firms, it is still a business organization, and is *initially* subject to the same degree of distrust. Furthermore, it has other handicaps to overcome such as a possible lack of familiarity with local customs (although this has advantages too). It must therefore make special efforts not only to overcome the problems inherent in doing business on a multinational scale, but also to remove from itself the unfavorable local image of business firms.

In general, the stages of managerial evolution have been complicated by the introduction of foreign managerial forms. In India, for example, one finds first the British, and more recently, the U.S. influence. Unlike the "foreign" managerial practices which were brought to the United States during its early stages of development and became integral parts of the U.S. system, these foreign practices, as they have been introduced to developing nations, have come as overlays to existing patterns.

Perhaps the most important British managerial import which India received is the managing agency system which is now undergoing major change by law.[34] In the early days of the British Colonial empire, it became obvious that industrial enterprises could not be managed from England. A group of resident British managers were required. Yet the number of qualified Englishmen on the scene was limited. As a result, managing agencies were set up within India to look after operations. These were in essence top-level holding-consulting firms. One agency might manage a number of ventures for various London interests. Eventually, the agencies evolved into giant holding companies.

Initially, the managing agency was a purely British concept. However, as indigenous industry developed, it seized on the managing agency concept to solve a major dilemma. The joint family had limitations with respect to managing large operations, but the managing agency, which was a logical extension of this concept, provided the vehicle to maintain familiar and comfortable patterns and yet allow expanded activities. The family controlled industrial complex now had an effective means to organize — with a strong managing agency controlled by the head of the family at the center, and brothers, sons, nephews and cousins running individual operations and reporting directly to the agency. Many of the larger and more successful agencies (e.g., Tata's and Birla's) developed into India's present conglomerates. As business resources increased, the agencies, in an attempt to both put capital to work and free themselves from outside dependencies, expanded into industrial manufacturing operations of every sort, and into banking and other service businesses.

The more recent entry of U.S. firms into India has brought a completely different concept. Whereas both the British and the Indian managing agencies were closed systems, major managerial positions going to Englishmen and family members respectively, the U.S. corporations had to find their managerial resources, at least at lower and middle levels, in the local environment. They were not fettered by colonial traditions or family-type self-interest. As relatively impersonal entities, they provided the first opportunity for a sizeable influx of new Indian managerial talent. Furthermore, by placing much greater emphasis on professionalism and performance, the U.S. firms have opened new horizons for Indian youth. However, the impact of such ideas is just beginning to be felt, and these ideas are still far from dominant.

While there are a number of progressive British and indigenous firms in India which have pursued a similar management philosophy, and thus helped to bring about a more favorable attitude toward managers and management, the U.S. companies in India as a group have probably served as the most significant change agent. They have provided a model, albeit far from perfect, of the fourth evolutionary stage of management, which a still small but growing number of the more progressive indigenous enterprises are trying to emulate. This fourth stage must be the trend of the future, if India's growth and development plans are to succeed.

ATTITUDES TOWARD AUTHORITY, RESPONSIBILITY AND SUB-ORDINATES

The sociological-cultural environment tends to give rise to a dominant set of attitudes toward authority, responsibility, and subordinates in a given country or society. In turn, various patterns of behavior emerge from such attitudes. Exceptions can always be found to dominant attitudes and customary behavior patterns, but it still is meaningful to consider the representative majority.

Such dominant attitudes and related behavior patterns are much more "culture-bound" in relatively static, traditional, or homogeneous societies, than in others. In such cases the environment serves as a potent and pervasive constraint upon managements of all types, including the government bureaucracy, in their creation of authority, acceptance of responsibility, and in dealings with subordinates, and it would generally be difficult and risky to go against tradition on a significant scale or too rapidly. India seems to be a gradually changing, but still quite "culture-bound" country in this regard.

In Japan, managerial effectiveness and productive efficiency may suffer considerably if the enterprise deviates substantially and abruptly from the traditional Japanese conception and practice of paternalistic management. Similarly, it is likely to be much more costly, time consuming, and risky to introduce substantially greater participative management into industry in Peru, Saudi Arabia, India, or even Germany, as compared to the United States, Canada, Great Britain, Yugoslavia, Russia, or Red China at this point in time.

Research studies conducted in similar kinds of companies in Peru and the United States strongly suggest that authoritarian management and close supervision of subordinates are more acceptable and effective in Peru, as compared to the

United States.[35] The Peruvian employees, both blue and white collar, generally view participative management less favorably. If it were to be introduced extensively within a fairly short period of time in a Peruvian firm, it is likely that productivity would decline and employees would lose respect for their superiors.

A critical factor in the effectiveness of companies operating in foreign countries often rests in their understanding of authority, responsibility, and subordinate relationships as they are perceived in the local community or culture. The problem is quite different for foreign and indigenous firms. In the former, difficulties arise from cultural discrepancies in the interpretations of foreign and indigenous employees, each of whom may respond to authority and responsibility and view subordinates in a different manner. In the case of indigenous firms, the pyramidal organization form common to the West is often established without a real understanding of the types of authority and responsibility or roles of subordinates integrally embodied in such a structure.

FRAMEWORK OF ANALYSIS

In order to provide essential background information and definitions which have general significance, and before focusing our attention on India, we shall present a brief, essentially theoretical discussion which provides a framework for analyzing any country with regard to authority, responsibility, and subordinates.[36] In this discussion we shall deal with "ideal" types which represent the extreme points on a scale or spectrum. If enough research were to be conducted each country could perhaps be ranked with a fairly high degree of accuracy on scales in terms of dominant attitudes and resulting behavior patterns. We shall not deal with Communist countries in the following discussion since they represent a special case.[37]

First we shall consider the attitude toward managerial authority and responsibility by examining views that would prevail at each end of a hypothetical spectrum.

VIEW I
Authority is viewed as an absolute right of managers or other types of formal leaders (including enterprise owners). Top-level managers in particular feel they are born to manage and command others and that their authority is based on some type of natural law or charismatic endowment, rather than on a well-defined role in the organization, specific skills, knowledge, or other qualifications. This view of authority results in a high degree of centralization and little delegation of authority within the enterprise, accompanied by a strong reluctance to clearly assign or accept responsibility. This leads to much "buck-passing" and avoidance of blame when something goes wrong, and top-level managers are often consulted, and asked to approve even minor routine decisions. As used here, "responsibility" implies the obligation

to perform some task or make some decision, while "authority" connotes the power to require some task to be performed.

View I tends to dominate when the following conditions exist:

1. Where the economy is characterized by a preponderance of private firms operated under a system of patrimonial management and tight family control. While firms in such an environment tend to be quite small, many medium-sized and large firms may also be found under this type of system.

2. Where management is not viewed as a profession based at least in substantial part on concepts that can be learned and taught, and where it is believed that managerial competence cannot be evaluated on the basis of objective criteria.

3. Where subordinates only tend to respect a strong, domineering type of formal leader; and/or when there is a considerable feeling of dependency on top management by employees.

VIEW II

The amount of authority and responsibility a given manager should possess should and can be based on objective criteria, and careful evaluation of the requirements of the managerial job and of the qualifications of the incumbent or candidate. This view is accompanied by a belief that delegation of authority and acceptance of responsibility is conducive to growth, effective management development, and productive efficiency. The result is a tendency toward decentralization. View II dominates to the degree that the following conditions exist:

1. Where the economy is characterized by a substantial number of large and/or rapidly growing enterprises in which ownership and control are separated.

2. Where management is regarded as a profession having an operational, theoretical underpinning which can be taught and learned.

3. Where there is a sizeable professional managerial group or class consisting of well-educated and trained personnel throughout the managerial hierarchy, and where subordinate managers tend to be trusted.

4. Where the society places considerable emphasis on individual freedom, initiative, and achievement.

We shall now consider two sets of attitudes toward subordinates and employees in general (including workers) which comprise the extreme opposite ends of a similar hypothetical scale.

VIEW X

Subordinates are expected to be unquestionably obedient and totally subservient in executing orders and tasks issued by superiors. The result of this attitude towards employees is a high degree of authoritarian management and autocratic direction. Here, management issues orders and makes decisions without concern for the wishes or opinions of subordinates. At the ultimate extreme, we find dictatorial management under a system of forced labor or concentration camps, but it is unlikely that such a system would be very durable.

View X dominates:

1. Where management views its authority as a natural or divine right.

2. Where there is little or no concern for individual dignity, freedom, or initiative, especially where this is accompanied by an environment of much cheap, surplus labor.

3. Where employees are highly dependent on the enterprise because it is the major unilateral and independent supplier of welfare benefits which are urgently needed.

4. Where most of the working population is poorly educated and trained.

5. Where subordinates prefer and/or respect and obey a strong, domineering leader.

6. Where there is little or no countervailing power over personnel matters exerted by the government or organized labor.

VIEW Y

Subordinates and employees have a voice in all decisions that significantly affect them and their working lives. Here we have a high degree of participative management and consultative direction in superior-subordinate dealings. The advice, opinions, and suggestions of subordinates, whether they be managers or workers, are sought before final decisions are made. However, the superior manager does not necessarily relinquish his authority or decision-making powers. This view would be found under the following prevalent conditions:

1. Where the society places high value on individual dignity and initiative, and on the freedom of the individual to have a voice in determining his own present and future.

2. Where there is a widespread conviction that personnel respond best when they can participate in decisions that directly affect them and their work, and that they have something worthwhile to contribute. This is typically accompanied by a belief that people are not basically lazy, need not be pushed in their work, and do not respond only to material incentives or penalties.

3. Where personnel becomes increasingly less dependent on enterprise management because of greater opportunities through mobility, growing labor shortages, and/or rising living standards.

4. Where there is relatively little emphasis on class distinctions or status.

5. Where the labor force is relatively well educated and trained and possesses a relatively high level of job skill.

In general, authoritarian management tends to go hand-in-hand with centralization of authority, while participative management is more likely to be found where there is a tendency to decentralize authority. However, it is possible to have either a relatively high degree of centralization with participative management, or the converse, although the latter seems to be rare.

Two other important types of attitudes and related practices, which can also be represented on a scale, are worth discussing briefly. For each, we need only deal with one end of each spectrum, since the conditions conducive to the opposite end are implicit in our discussion.

VIEW A

It is natural, proper, and desirable for enterprise management independently to assume responsibility for the overall welfare of employees. The effect of this view is a high degree of enterprise paternalism. This view tends to prevail:

1. When the transition to industrialization in a particular society does not involve a major break from the feudalist tradition or traditional family type of relationships found in some parts of the world.

2. Where the enterprise is a major supplier of a wide range of welfare benefits, services, and facilities either by necessity or default — as where the government, organized labor, or society at large does not perform these functions adequately — or by choice, in cases where employees prefer this type of arrangement and favor being dependent on management because of cultural values or tradition.

Since a high degree of paternalistic management typically involves a father-son or master-servant type of relationship, and hence considerable dependence on the part of employees, it is generally conducive to a relatively high degree of centralization and authoritarian management.

VIEW B

Managerial authority regarding all important personnel welfare matters such as pay scales, dismissals, and working conditions are shared, and if deemed necessary, constrained by representatives of organized labor or the government. This type of arrangement is often referred to as "constitutional" management and is typically characterized by a concern for known and consistent policies and procedures in dealing with people at work.

View B dominates:

1. As economies develop and become more complex and as pluralistic societies evolve.

2. Where the expectations of employees are rising and strong; here labor unions or employee organizations are more likely to emerge.

3. Where the government plays an increasingly large and active welfare role.

Figure 4-1 presents a tentative and suggestive ranking of several countries on the authoritarian/participative and paternalistic/countervailing power scales. Each country is ranked in terms of dominant attitudes and related practices. It is true that there may be considerable variation among firms and their managements in a particular country. This variation is larger in some countries (e.g., the United States and Great Britain) than others (e.g., Turkey, Peru, and Japan). However, it is still useful from both a theoretical and practical point of view to talk in terms of dominant, or at least most common or typical patterns.

INDIA AND DEVELOPING COUNTRIES IN GENERAL

In India, as we have mentioned, dominant attitudes toward authority, responsibility, and subordinates are shaped in large part by values inherent in the joint family system, and perhaps to a lesser degree by the caste system and the related concepts of dharma (duty) and karma (just rewards).[38] In the joint family, decisions are taken by the head of the family and members are expected to abide by them. The interests of the family group, as perceived by its head, predominate over individual desires or interests. The family property as well as income is held in common, and expenditures are met out of a common pool.

An individual in a typical Indian joint family setup is judged not by the excellence of his personal achievements, but by the contribution he makes to the general welfare and aims of the family as a whole. A child brought up in this atmosphere tends to develop attitudes and patterns of behavior involving authority, responsibility, and superior-subordinate relations characteristic of the environmental situation within the family group. There is often a multiplicity of authority as far as the child is concerned. Praise and punishment, rewards and sanctions, are administered not only by grandparents or parents, but often by uncles, aunts, older siblings, and even older cousins. The orders, instructions, and advice given by different family members are likely to be conflicting.

The child's tendency is to so adapt himself that he may not be criticized or punished by any of the older members of the family. In most cases this may only be possible by avoiding action and responsibility altogether. This environment also encourages and enables the child to develop certain socio-political skills by which he gets around various members without necessarily accepting their views. Thus, if he is criticized for a particular form of behavior by one senior member, instead of justifying

FIGURE 4-1 Suggestive rankings for selected countries

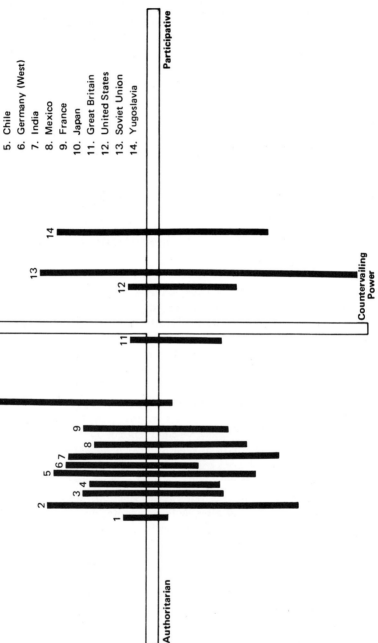

1. Saudi Arabia
2. Egypt
3. Peru
4. Turkey
5. Chile
6. Germany (West)
7. India
8. Mexico
9. France
10. Japan
11. Great Britain
12. United States
13. Soviet Union
14. Yugoslavia

it he approaches, for protection and consolation, another member who is likely to be sympathetic to such behavior. In such a situation, development of initiative and responsibility is retarded, while coalitions are encouraged. What is likely to develop is an innate ability to get around people, problems, and responsibility rather than face them.

> When such relationships are extended to the industrial sphere where organizational clarity, delegation and responsibility are of primary importance for efficient working as well as good relationships, inefficiency and frustration results. The members of an industrial organization are not bound together by the same ties of affection as members of a family . . . Because of this and because of the larger size of the industrial group, it is impossible to achieve the same degree of cohesion. Therefore, when organizational clarity is lacking in industry, high efficiency is impossible to achieve.[39]

One should also add that industrial enterprise calls for clearer authority and responsibility relationships than the joint family because closer coordination of many more interdependent activities is necessary for efficient performance. Moreover, efficient industrial enterprise calls for clear and consistent communication, rapid information feedback, and greater initiative at all levels.

Respect for seniority and age is a special feature of many hierarchical societies, particularly in India and other developing nations. This traditional respect is frequently transferred to industrial situations and business enterprise. A senior manager typically does not consult his subordinates on a policy matter or about the usefulness of a new process, even though they may be more qualified and knowledgeable on the subject, because he considers it beneath his dignity. Similarly, his subordinate does not offer his views because he feels it may be resented and he may be considered impertinent. The result is that the decision is not made on the basis of the best information available. The subordinate is conscious of this, and is frustrated as a result.

The formal organization structure of the Indian firm if diagrammed in Western fashion, often looks like a stubby inverted T with authority greatly concentrated in the hands of a very small number of top people, rather than a pyramidal type structure common in the United States.[40] Authority is jealously guarded. Spans of control involving only one or two deputies are common at the higher levels of Indian enterprises, but the chain of command is often violated with lower-level people dealing directly with the top manager and vice versa. An even better representation might be a circle, with the head man at the center surrounded by a considerable amount of role ambiguity. This type of organization is common not only in India. It is also embodied in the "patron" system of Latin America, the tribal system in Africa, and in the extended family, caste, and social-structure situations in other Asian and Middle-Eastern societies.[41]

Traditional authority and responsibility patterns and superior-subordinate relationships are accepted within Indian organizations. However, with rising expectations and aspiration levels a growing number of Indian industrial personnel of all types are now questioning these patterns and values, including management's attitudes, rights, and prerogatives. This is especially pronounced among Western-trained Indians who return home to work in industrial firms. As a result many people are caught between two worlds — the traditional and the modern — with regard to their own and others' attitudes toward authority, responsibility, and superior-subordinate relations.

As the concepts of managerial rights and authority (as well as the caste system) have come under fire, and firms have begun to place more emphasis on individual contribution, considerable frustration, role conflict, and insecurity have evolved among a growing number of industrial personnel. This results in substantially greater hostility, antagonism, disobedience, tardiness, absenteeism, and turnover, as well as more work stoppages and strikes. Such problems are more acute among workers at industrial enterprises in major cities than in rural areas where the break from tradition has been more gradual.[42]

The indigenous firm in a developing country

The indigenous firm basically experiences two kinds of problems with respect to responsibility, authority, and related superior-subordinate relationships. The first comes from maintaining traditional ways and the second from trying to change them.

Traditional patterns (the inverted T or circular organization) may prove effective when companies are small, but they become unwieldy when organizations grow. Consider the common and real case of an Indian executive in a 15-million-dollar-a-year company who took home every purchase requisition for his scrutiny and signature. Each night he would leave the plant at 7 P.M., with four or more brief cases full of purchase orders. The following morning he would return with each of the requisitions bearing either his signature or a question. Every box of paper clips purchased required his approval. A junior executive in the company complained to one of the authors that he was afraid to correct a twenty-cent mistake (eventually costing the company several hundred dollars) because it would involve the issuance of a purchase order (for 20¢) and thereby evoke the wrath of the managing director. The several-hundred-dollar cost would be hidden in routine operating expenses, however, and would not stand out.

The introduction of change in organization pattern presents many challenges to the indigenous firm, largely because the final result may be vague and unknown (i.e., outside its natural experience). However, the actual quantum jumps in the change process are likely to be smaller and less abrupt than in the foreign firm.

A classic example occurred in an Indian family company with which one of the authors is familiar. The elderly father had decided to retire, and his young son, just returned from study in Europe, took over the reins of the firm. The son immediately introduced controls in the manufacturing operations (quality was spelled out, and both authority and responsibility were clearly defined). The reaction of the work force came as a shock to him, and led eventually to his leaving the firm and striking out on his own. The workers believed their prime loyalty was toward his father, and that they had a responsibility to make sure the son did not ruin the company before he gained enough experience to know what it was all about. Consequently, every time he rejected a product, they would surreptitiously put it back into the manufacturing process. When he would give an order, they would obey it until his back was turned, and then carry out the task in the same manner that the father would have requested.

This same sense of loyalty was effectively put to use, however, by two indigenous firms — one in Central America and one in India. In the Latin-American case, the father had attended an executive training program conducted by a major U.S. university. He was impressed with what he learned about organizational structure. Even though his corporate empire was staffed with sons, nephews, etc., he resolved to establish a more decentralized, pyramidal, organization form to run his empire. He began by sending all of his sons and nephews to the United States for graduate work in business and engineering. When this process had been substantially completed, he used the "family council" as a forum. Each young man was given increased authority in response to his requests, but only if he could justify the need to the family council in terms of increased performance. Eventually, the father was able to divorce himself completely from day-to-day operations. His sons and nephews still play some of the roles of the patron; however, they have hired a substantial number of competent staff support people who provide middle management, although their roles as staff advisors vs. line managers are not always clear.

An Indian firm approached the same problem from a very different viewpoint, but again relying heavily upon U.S.-trained nationals. The head of the group began hiring non-family, well-trained (U.S. business and technical degree holder) Indians. He worked with them very closely and supportively — in a relationship somewhere between that of master craftsman and apprentice and father and son. They brought all of their problems to him and he supervised the evaluation and solution process. Over a period of approximately five to ten years, each of his key people began to think as he did. Eventually, he allowed them to start making decisions, checking with him after the fact to make sure that they were still in tune. The closer their thinking became to his, the more authority he gave them. He was eventually able to give up his daily involvement in company affairs and turn to other ventures, knowing that he was still "in control" of operations. Both he and his corporate managers agreed that the keystone to operations was personal loyalty. They spoke of each other as if they actually were father and sons (although many of the managers were his contemporaries), and their responsibilities toward him were those of sons to a father.

We came across very few Indian firms in which attitudes toward authority, responsibility, and subordinates, and the resulting behavior patterns were as modern or non-traditional as in U.S. subsidiaries surveyed in India. One notable exception was the vast Tata company complex; which literally has taken generations to reach its current stage. On the other hand, none of the firms surveyed in India, foreign or indigenous, approached the pattern achieved by the companies surveyed in the United States.

The foreign firm

The U.S. or other foreign company in a developing country is subject to organizational problems as a result of conflicts between attitudes toward responsibility, authority, and subordinates. Too often, managers view these concepts as absolutes, devoid of any cultural content. The U.S. manager who does not realize that his subordinates expect him to play the role of father can find himself in a very sticky situation. His subordinates look for the support and favors a father would bestow, and do not find them. Consequently, they fail to respond to his "authority" and his effectiveness is substantially reduced. Unless the manager behaves according to the "father" pattern, he does not evoke the responses that pattern will bring. He may think that his subordinates know what is expected of them because they have received his commands or instructions, but they are not prepared to respond in the manner he pects.

An example of this, drawn from India, concerned a Western (not U.S. in this case) manager who appeared to be indifferent to small problems of his work force. His organization chart indicated a pyramidal structure which he assumed was functioning in accordance with his concept of such structures. He therefore assumed that employee problems would be handled by middle managers. When workers came to him for requests, he would cut them short and send them to their immediate supervisors. These supervisors, Indians, felt powerless, since they interpreted their superior's lack of action to indicate denial of worker requests and they did not believe they had the authority to act (i.e., they could not conceive of the delegation process which was clear only in the managing director's mind). Consequently, tension characterized the organization. Interviews with workers revealed they had resolved the conflict (boss-not-acting-like-boss) within their own framework and had, consequently, downgraded the role of the top manager to the point where they felt they had little obligation to him. They had also noticed he referred many questions to his international headquarters for final decisions. Consequently, he was treated as another "underling." The big boss was a nebulous figure outside of India. The company was plagued by poor labor relations and poor middle-to-top management relations, largely because everyone missed the strong personality at the top and no substitute had been provided.

This presents another related area — the role of middle management. Two patterns emerge with respect to the authority and responsibility structure. In many countries middle-management positions are enigmas. Companies which install middle-management cadres without effectively preparing the way find confusion to be the result. The middle managers are confused with respect to their relationships in both directions, up and down. They do not have the respect of the workers or lower-level supervisors (who see power vested only at the top) nor are they clear about their authority. Strong effort must be made to develop effective middle managers and create an operating environment which will accept them. The top man, by virtue of his authority, must take the lead.

In the other pattern, the middle managers themselves begin to establish islands of authority. This problem seems to be more common among U.S. subsidiaries. In such cases, especially where top level control is relatively loose (as is more likely to be the case in non-authoritarian foreign companies), they may usurp powers of the top, and in essence, form small isolated kingdoms within the corporate empire. Again, the control systems necessary to prevent such occurrences can only originate at the top.

The U.S. or foreign company has an advantage, however. It is clearly an outsider. Just as the foreign visitor to many countries like India can deviate more from tradition than can nationals, so may a foreign company break more taboos. However, this must be done cautiously. One interesting case study (from India) involved an Americanized company which did develop an effective middle-management structure and was run by an aggressive American using a number of non-Indian practices. The company developed well, and then decided to fill its top jobs with nationals. One of the most Americanized of the Indian middle managers was promoted to managing director, and he continued to run the company in the same manner his predecessor had. The result was an internal revolt, and six of the firm's better managers eventually resigned. The "over-Americanized" Indian managing director also resigned. It was acceptable for a foreigner to act in non-Indian patterns, but it was not for an Indian to do so.

U.S. executives do not have to conform to local patterns in many instances. Many would find it difficult to take on a highly authoritarian or paternal role, and many would not want to do so even if they could feel comfortable. However, it is important for the manager to understand what is involved, and introduce change in a manner which increases the probability of acceptance. The U.S. executive in Central America who was unable to find any responsible local nationals (see page 4) overlooked the fact that his concept of responsibility might not be indigenous and that he might best find what he was looking for if he concentrated on developing it.

It is also necessary for an executive to be alert to the way his subordinates are responding to authority and responsibility. In one U.S. company in India, the U.S. managing director learned with a start that his Indian plant manager had staffed the plant almost completely with individuals with whom he had family-type relationships. Most of the supervisory positions went to cousins and nephews, and a large number of the workers had come from his home village, many miles distant. He had obligations to these people, and even though he had been "Americanized" (by visits and training in the United States), these obligations overrode all else. The managing director experienced great difficulty in changing this situation since the plant manager was of course strongly supported by his chosen employees. Several new plant executives were hired by the U.S. manager after the situation was discovered, but in every conflict situation between these new men and the plant manager, the latter received overwhelming support from plant personnel. Most of the good newly-hired people were ready to quit, yet the managing director felt he could not afford to fire the plant manager because plant operations were now dependent upon him and his "family."

Western managers tend to think of authority and responsibility in fairly clear-cut terms. A manual or contract, outlining both, is considered binding, and a very large body of precise terminology has evolved to clarify issues. However, many societies regard a manual, agreement, or contract only as an indication of intent — if it is convenient, it will be done. In many of these societies, the way to assure performance is not by a written document, but by creating obligations which are respected in the local culture. These are often of a personal nature, and the foreign manager who has not taken the time to develop these relationships finds himself at a loss. He gives instructions or delegates tasks and nothing happens. He may respond by repeating commands, often with greater and greater degrees of exasperation. Yet he receives blank responses, or responses of bewilderment. For one reason or another, the task cannot be done (or cannot "conveniently" be performed). "If it could have been, I would have done it. So what is the problem?" said one equally exasperated Indian manager, talking about a dressing down he had just received from his U.S. superior. The need for feedback must be learned — it doesn't develop naturally. The employee, unless specifically told, may not understand the effects of his non-performance and the possibilities for alternate action. The better-managed U.S. enterprises in India were substantially more decentralized than their local counterparts and had more effective delegation of authority and acceptance of responsibility. They provided more leeway for, and obtained more effective initiative and participation from subordinates at lower levels — but not always at the worker level. However, this had been achieved through a gradual evolutionary approach involving much time, patience, effort, and expense.

The relative success of these U.S. subsidiaries has not been achieved without critical problems and constraints which still persist; some of these have already been discussed. For example, one multi-plant, multi-division U.S. firm in India, probably the most Americanized company in India, has been working on a ten-year decentralization program which could probably be accomplished effectively in three or four years in the United States. In the process this company has overstaffed the managerial hierarchy, and structured very narrow spans of control, which have been rationalized as being necessary for long-run management development, training, and effective decentralization. Fortunately, this is a rapidly growing concern that can afford such overstaffing and also can provide advancement for many of its managers.

Two basic points stand out as being most crucial in the above discussion. The first is the important role of the top manager of a company operating in a developing economy. Traditional patterns generally correspond to family structure and thus employees look to the top man for guidance and direction. He sets the pace. Consequently, the choice of the proper individual is critical to the foreign firm.

The second point relates to the accommodation which must be made to assure a cultural fit. This has two aspects: the development of sensitivity to cultural factors in the environment, and the need for effective training and recruitment to introduce change. As we shall see in subsequent chapters, one of the most vital talents of the manager of a subsidiary in a developing nation is his ability to educate those who work for and with him.

INTERORGANIZATIONAL AND INDIVIDUAL COOPERATION

The extent to which various enterprises, organizations, groups, and individuals cooperate *voluntarily* with one another has a significant bearing on how efficiently the productive system of the country functions. A society marked by much suspicion between government and industrial firms, extensive labor-management conflicts, lack of cooperation among economically interrelated enterprises, mistrust of motives between businessmen and educators, and general distrust and suspicion among "strangers" or "outsiders" who deal with each other at work, will not be as productive a country as one in which such frictions are minimized.

Our concern in this section is with the extent of cooperation existing among industrial enterprises and other relevant related organizations and individuals, in connection with activities that are basically *voluntary* rather than legal or contractual. While the extent of voluntary cooperation that the management of a given firm has with other organizations, and the degree of cooperation which exists among the firm's personnel, are at least partially under the firm's control and an outgrowth of various of its policies, in most countries they appear to be dominant (or at least widespread) patterns with regard to the different kinds of parties involved. Such patterns are shaped largely by tradition in conjunction with a variety of historical, cultural, and sociological factors.

While friction and lack of cooperation in various areas are certainly common in the industrial sphere in advanced countries, it does appear that on the whole, this is a substantially greater problem in developing nations. It almost appears to be axiomatic that relatively high degrees of cooperation are difficult to achieve in developing lands, and what cooperation exists is closely guarded and limited to narrow and specific areas.

There seem to be a number of partial explanations for such lack of cooperation. One involves the reaction to "outsiders" or "strangers," which has already been discussed in reference to the Indian joint family system and community ties. It is more common in advanced countries, like the United States, to have fair impersonal dealings and general trust among virtual strangers in industrial endeavors, and this is conducive to more effective cooperation and greater managerial effectiveness.

Often closely related to the reaction toward outsiders, with regard to resistance to voluntary cooperation, is the fierce competition for limited resources which exists in developing economies. Unlike the U.S. environment, where most resources are relatively abundant, and obtainable at a reasonable price, the resources of developing countries are frequently scarce. Managers and other enterprise personnel are able to see virtually the whole pie and all of the units or individuals competing for pieces. This has a psychological effect which does not exist when the limits of the pie are not readily discernible. Foreign exchange, imports, raw materials, capital, cash, technology, competent managers, skilled workers — the quantities of all or many of these resources may be defined, limited, and far less than adequate. Cooperation, it is felt, will lead to a revelation of one's weaknesses, or to the sharing of one's strengths, and such things must be avoided.

To be effective in such an environment, the international firm must devote considerable time and attention to demonstrating, clearly and convincingly, the mutual benefits to be derived from cooperative activity of an essentially voluntary nature.

Cooperation with labor groups

In developing countries which have labor unions — or some other form of organized labor — there is a basic, deep-seated conflict between management and labor groups. Often the labor unions are directly involved with political parties, and conflicts which arise are frequently related to ideology, political identification, and class struggle. Labor groups want to change society, not merely to get more for the worker. And it tends to be much more difficult to reach a compromise on ideological, as compared to economic, issues. Labor unrest and bargaining are frequently based on non-economic grounds, and sympathy strikes on events far removed from company affairs are common. In many cases there is constant pressure to increase benefits without any concern for the economics of the situation, and pressure and political favoritism lead to the creation or maintenance of unneeded jobs. Unions are also inclined to take actions against their own members' best interest primarily because by doing so they may be able to embarrass opposing political parties.

Companies can find themselves caught in the middle of political disputes, and labor union cooperation tends to vary with political exigencies. Or, where there are rival unions in the same firm, the enterprise may be caught in the middle of inter-union rivalries, and even power struggles for leadership within a given union. On the other hand, managements as well as labor leaders, are often extremely stubborn, holding to their moral principles in spite of labor disruption, inefficiency, lower profits, and much worse.

In such an environment one is likely to find widespread and rather frequent strikes, work stoppages and lockouts, extensive informal restrictive labor practices and feather-bedding, and a great deal of unproductive time, effort, and expense absorbed in politicing and bargaining. Moreover, in such situations, it is likely to be difficult to retrench or dismiss workers, or to introduce more efficient technology and production processes.

India, in common with other developing nations, often reflects the above kind of environment. Many aspects of union-management relations there resemble problems common to the United States 50 or 60 years ago.

About 40 to 45 percent of India's nearly nine million permanent workers employed by registered industrial enterprises are union members. India's trade unions are grouped for the most part into four major federations.[43] The Indian National Trade Union Congress (INTUC) is aligned with the Congress Party which has ruled India since her independence in 1947, but whose political power, influence, and control have been greatly diluted in recent years. The All-India Trade Union Congress (AITUC) was the only major trade union federation in India prior to 1947. It was originally dominated by the Congress Party but was taken over by the Communists during World War II. There has been a sharp split in India's Communist Party since the Indo-Chinese War of 1962, and this has led to serious conflicts in many Communist-controlled unions at industrial enterprises. The party is split along pro-Moscow and pro-Peking lines. A number of Indian states including relatively industrialized West Bengal, are under Communist leadership, or at least are governed by coalitions dominated by Communists or Communists and Socialists.

The Hind Mazdoor Sabha — Indian Workers' Union — is affiliated with the Socialist Party, and was formed when the Socialists broke with the Communists, and hence the AITUC, in 1948. In 1949, another split occurred in the AITUC, when the United Trade Union Congress was formed with a view to separating the labor movement from parties and politics and confining its scope to the more traditional lines of trade union activity. This federation has never been as extensive, influential, or strong as the INTUC or AITUC.

Growing political instability in India in recent years has led to greater inter- and intra-union rivalries which in turn have seriously hindered union-management cooperation. At many enterprises, especially in areas like Calcutta, where coalition governments have been formed, various types of coalition union arrangements have emerged. For example, in the Calcutta region coalition unions have been formed at many enterprises under the coalition United Front Government — dominated by Communists and some Socialists — which has emerged.

While union-management problems arising from lack of cooperation are substantially more pervasive and constant in India than in the United States, it is difficult to say what kind of unions are the hardest to deal with in India.

This is largely a matter of the nature and attitudes of the local union membership, particularly the local leaders, at a given enterprise, as well as the attitudes of the

firm and its management. However, a number of Western executives of U.S. subsidiaries in India, initially greatly concerned when Communist-dominated unions
had taken over their plants, now prefer such unions to those dominated by the Congress Party with which they have had to deal. They feel that Communist-controlled
local unions, where there is no serious right-left split, tend to be more disciplined and
control their membership more effectively, especially once a labor agreement or
contract has been reached with management.

The lack of union-management cooperation is a much more serious problem and
constraint on productivity and industrial progress in India than it is in the United
States. Most managers admit that inept management is partially to blame, but they
usually claim that the unions are far more unreasonable and uncooperative than they
are themselves. From our own research, which includes discussions with union
leaders and workers and attendance at union-management meetings, the unions do
seem to be somewhat more unreasonable.

During the 1955-65 period, India, Italy, and the United States experienced more
official strikes than any other countries of the world.[44] However, the number of
official strikes is but one indicator — and often not of major importance — of union-
management conflict in a given country. If one takes into account unofficial strikes,
slowdowns, restrictive practices, lockouts, grievances, conflicts, bickering, and similar
activity, our research indicates that union-management conflict is a substantially
greater and more continuous problem in Indian industry than in the United States.

In India, union-management cooperation has deteriorated rapidly with growing
political instability. The number of strikes increased substantially from 1966 to
1968 especially during the ferment of the national elections, but seem to have
leveled out somewhat since about mid-1968. The number of reported company
lockouts increased from 138 in 1966 to 203 in 1967. In 1966, 76 of the reported
lockouts followed official strikes, while the 1967 figure was 107.[45] More quantitative data on labor problems in India will be presented in the chapter on union-
management relations.

Union rivalry leads to many problems for management at numerous Indian
firms. The local unions typically are relatively small, poorly organized, and financially weak. In many cases they cannot even collect nominal monthly dues, which are
usually only five or ten cents, from their members. Frequently plants contain more
than one union, each vying for worker allegiance by creating issues and agitating,
often without just cause. In many instances union demands are stated in such
vague terms that there is really no basis for negotiation or compromise. At the
other extreme, demands and grievances may be petty or unrealistic, involving such
things as the flavor of the tea served in the canteen or demanding the immediate
provision of free company housing or an unrealistic profit-sharing scheme for all of
the workers.

Serious problems also stem from the fact that it is common for even local union
leaders to be party workers appointed by politicians rather than persons elected by

the local union membership. This leads to vested interest problems far removed from factory affairs. A typical example of this involved a plant of one U.S. subsidiary located in the Indian state of Uddar Pradesh. The plant had a Congress Party union, and management relations with the union vice-president and treasurer (who were elected by the plant's union members) were excellent. Difficulties arose in dealings with the union president who was a politician and lawyer in the city, and the union secretary who was a full-time agitator paid by a number of different sources. Both of these officials were party appointees and dealt with a number of firms in the vicinity. Often the union vice-president and treasurer at the U.S. plant wanted to cooperate with management, but were prevented from doing so by great pressure from external union authorities.

We did not find many key differences in the union-management patterns of U.S. subsidiaries and indigenous firms. However, a number of comparative observations are worth mentioning. As is common in many countries, unions in India often try to use U.S. and other foreign subsidiaries as levers. For example, a union may feel that a foreign firm will be more responsive to a benefit package because the company provides such benefits in its home country. It may therefore use the foreign firm as a lever to gain the same benefits from local firms. On the other hand, it may attack the foreign company in the hope of building up anti-foreign sentiment to force unusual demands. This is done at times in India, but less frequently than in various other developing countries where anti-foreign feelings are much more widespread and deep-seated.

U.S. subsidiaries in India seem to be more frequent union targets than their indigenous or British counterparts. This is due in part to the way the managements of U.S. firms perceive and deal with unions. Quite often the Western managers of U.S. firms are more willing to give concessions and avoid strikes in the short run to make their records look better, thus enhancing their chances of promotion or relocation to a job in a preferred place. Union officials are usually aware of this and take advantage of the situation.

A number of U.S. subsidiaries are sensitive about the relatively large profits they make, and either they, their parent companies, or both do not want to risk strikes or adverse publicity, or to stir up anti-American feelings, including charges of exploitation. So they take a substantially softer stand against the union than they would in the United States. Capital-intensive companies are frequently under attack by unions, and are often the easiest targets for wage hikes because labor costs constitute a relatively small share of their total costs.

In general, Indian managers (and often British managers who have a flare for human relations) frequently handle union problems better than American managers, who may be effective in the United States, but who bring too many biases and preconceptions with them to India. The latter frequently appear to have difficulty understanding the motives of union leaders or workers.

Cooperation between government and industry

The extent of voluntary cooperation between government and industry in a particular country has a significant bearing on productive efficiency and economic progress. Antagonism or lack of understanding between government agencies and industrial firms gives rise to little cooperation, consultation, or communication regarding economic, technical, social, or other problems of common concern. In such situations, government agencies do not provide statistics and other information that would be useful for effective decision making in business and industry; and industrial firms are reluctant to supply the government with the information required for effective macro decision making. Government officials design and attempt to implement policies (and undertake various industry-related activities) without first seeking the advice, opinions, or knowledge of industrial representatives, while industrial managers refuse to cooperate in the achievement of national or local government plans and objectives. In this type of environment, governments render little economic or technical assistance to private firms. In less developed countries, the government is often seen as an arch-enemy of business, especially private business. It imposes import quotas, rigidly controls foreign exchange, often levies large taxes, develops complex labor laws, and imposes a host of other restrictions. This is especially true in nations which have only recently begun a major thrust toward economic development and a change from laissez-faire attitudes towards industrial operations.

A critical shortage of competent government administrators who understand industry and business tends to be a serious problem in poorer countries. In many of the newly-emergent nations, numerous government officials hold their positions by virtue of the patriotic spirit or military skills they demonstrated while overthrowing colonial powers, and not by virtue of their administrative talents or their abilities to deal with the process of economic growth. Many take government jobs either because they do not have the qualifications or connections to get substantially higher-paying jobs in business, or because they look down on careers in business.

Consequently, government activity and decisions affecting business often seem arbitrary, restrictive, or intentionally discriminatory. However, the process of economic development in countries which have severely limited resources requires many restrictions of the type to which businessmen generally object. (For example, it is much easier to identify taxable corporations and enforce corporate tax laws than it is to enforce tax laws regarding individuals.)

Many developing countries, including India, have introduced special agencies to help relatively small businesses become established and grow. They assist in various ways, from providing technical assistance to supplying capital for plant construction. However, such assistance programs are frequently poorly administered or misused. A study undertaken by one of the authors involved a visit to 15 small firms which had purchased imported equipment under the aegis of a government agency. The agency supplied 80 percent of the total funds and 100 percent of the foreign exchange required, and obtained the needed import license. Only five of these firms were legitimate. The rest were dummy corporations set up to obtain the equipment and then resell it (at substantial profit) to larger companies which could not obtain the necessary import licenses. This behavior, of course, reinforced the anti-business attitude held by many government officials regardless of whether small or large firms were involved.

A major constraint on effective cooperation in India is the size of the government bureaucracy that has evolved since 1947. It has become so complex and laden with internal rivalries that it is frequently extremely difficult for competent and well-intentioned government officials to cooperate, or make timely and effective decisions affecting industrial enterprises.

The tax situation presents another problem area. It is common for companies in many developing countries, including India, to keep many sets of books — for the tax collectors, for their stockholders, and for internal management. Tax evasion is rampant among indigenous firms. Foreign subsidiaries are less likely to engage in such illicit practices because they are more afraid of a major investigation and the resultant charges of exploitation, and also because their parent companies are generally opposed to such behavior.

The greater honesty of foreign firms with regard to paying taxes is, however, sometimes used unfairly against them. Indigenous companies which indicate substantially smaller profits by hiding much of their income, frequently claim foreign profit gouging. Since government figures support these claims, various governmental regulatory and investigatory groups also jump on the band wagon. Indian government officials, as well as indigenous firm managers, have expressed amazement at the conscientious manner in which U.S. companies pay their taxes.

Tax evasion and secrecy considerations contribute to the critical dearth of reliable statistical data about industry and corporations in many developing countries. Government questionnaires and forms are returned with blatantly false information (if they are returned at all). On the other hand, the lack of cooperation among different governmental offices also greatly compounds the collection, analysis, and dissemination of reliable data for both macro and micro decision making. For the above reasons, studies made by two or more government agencies, using different but supposedly comparable data, often show huge discrepancies — entailing several hundred percentage points in some cases. The whole process can and does degenerate into a game in which no side can possibly win. Decisions about investment, output, sales, foreign exchange, productive capacity, resource needs, and the like must frequently be made on the basis of highly unreliable and conflicting data.

The multinational corporation must seriously consider the temperaments and attitudes towards government of the executives it sends to a country like India. American executives too often bring with them preconceptions, biases, and fears with regard to government relations, especially in a so-called "socialistic" economy like India. However, American executives frequently obtain decisions from government officials quickly by being more persistent than indigenous managers.

While many indigenous firms in a country like India complain about government discrimination in favor of foreign firms, U.S. firms also complain about discrimination against them. However, they often have more confrontations with the government because they request more in the way of imports, foreign exchange, new product and expansion approvals, and profit remissions than do comparable local companies.

Apart from the above generalizations regarding U.S. subsidiaries and local firms, it is important to point out that some U.S. firms surveyed in India had better relations on the whole with government than indigenous firms in the same industry. For example, one U.S. subsidiary voluntarily cooperated with the government in the latter's defense requirements. It took on marginally profitable government orders at the expense of considerably more lucrative civilian production. In return, the government cooperated in various important ways with this company and granted it a number of major concessions. An Indian competitor refused a number of government orders which it considered relatively unprofitable, and this was one of the key reasons why the government was not responsive to the import, foreign exchange, or other supply requirements and requests of this company. The company actually had to shut down for several months in 1966 because it could not obtain critical materials.

In a more typical example, however, a U.S. subsidiary ran into great difficulties chiefly because it stubbornly refused to cooperate with government wishes for local participation in corporate ownership. At the time it was the only U.S. firm in its industry without any Indian equity participation. The company managed to buy some time (a few years) by agreeing to build its new plant in a part of the country the government wished to develop. (This move later proved to be unsound for the firm for a variety of reasons.) Furthermore, it was only a matter of time before the government renewed its demand that the firm divest itself of a sizeable amount of its U.S. ownership interest. When the company continued to stubbornly resist any move in this direction, the government brought even stronger pressure, threatening to revoke some of its licenses. Shortly thereafter, the company finally sold a considerable portion of its U.S. ownership interest, although it did not give up control.

Cooperation between firms

When the managements of industrial enterprises exchange information and ideas of common interest, all may gain in terms of greater productive efficiency. Furthermore, managerial effectiveness and productive efficiency may increase substantially where economic or increased revenues are derived through cooperative ventures, as in the case of: subcontracting; engaging in joint export promotion, procurement training, and research and development projects; establishing common repair facilities; exchanging critically needed supplies, and so on. Moreover, where firms present a united front in dealing with labor unions, industry's bargaining power is enhanced. The same is true with regard to various matters involving government, as well as other groups and organizations.

Cooperation of the above kind appears to be substantially less common or effective in poor than in affluent countries. However, firms in developing nations have much to gain from such efforts, since individually they are usually small and lack much of the know-how, capacity, and resources they require.

In general, foreign subsidiaries cooperate with one another to a greater degree than they do with local companies. Many exchange information regularly on such subjects as wages and salaries, personnel matters and employee benefits, and various aspects of operations, policies, or practices. The key managers of major American and British companies in India frequently play more active and effective roles in industry, management, and professional associations than do the managers of Indian firms.

It is also more common for foreign subsidiaries in India to help each other out when faced with serious supply failures by exchanging or loaning raw materials, components, and at times even equipment. They are also somewhat more inclined to embark on joint projects and cooperative advertising programs and to subcontract jobs. To the astonishment of a number of Indian managers, a large American subsidiary and major British company, highly competitive with regard to several of their products, have jointly used common electronic computer facilities for several years without any really serious conflicts.

One U.S. subsidiary in India takes pride in pointing out that its cooperation even goes as far as providing technical and managerial assistance to one of its major indigenous competitors. Although this company has provided urgently needed assistance and know-how which has helped keep its local competitor alive on a number of occasions, its motives have not been purely altruistic. If the competitor failed, or greatly reduced its output, the Indian government would be more likely to grant permission for another foreign — and more efficient — competitor to enter the Indian market. Nevertheless, the voluntary and earnest cooperation extended by this American firm has been very good for public relations.

Voluntary mergers and acquisitions are generally less common in developing nations, although the economic gains that could be realized are often much greater. A rare case of acquisition involved a large Indian pharmaceutical company which took over a much smaller firm in order to get its license for a strategic basic product. However, this was an exception to the pattern.

Many attempts to establish cooperative ventures fail because of distrust, suspicion, and conflict. For example, one case involved the producers of a certain line of electrical items sold primarily to national and local government agencies. The government overestimated demand for these products and a vast amount of excess capacity soon developed. Several producers went out of business, and the rest were operating at only a small fraction of productive capacity. The lowest cost producers decided to set up a syndicate whereby they would form a joint sales agency and put in one tender bid for orders. The orders would be divided among them, competition would be eliminated, and they could get higher prices and profits by cooperating this way. The need for bribery in securing orders would be eliminated. This venture was legal under India's rather weak anti-trust and collusion laws. However, the scheme failed because the firms could not come up with a mutually acceptable agreement.

Lack of cooperation between supplier and customer firms is frequently a great constraint on productive efficiency and industrial progress. A major reason for this is that relatively strong sellers' markets exist in many sectors of the Indian economy. However, even where competition exists, firms in their roles as suppliers typically have a "customer be damned" attitude. Enterprises, in their roles as customers, seldom engage in cooperative activities that would make suppliers — even in sellers' markets — more responsive to their needs. Instead, they continue to accept materials which do not meet their requirements as to variety, quality, and delivery time, and are faced with many production problems as a result.

Some U.S. subsidiaries surveyed in India provided know-how, technical and even financial assistance, as well as training, to their suppliers. This was rare in the case of indigenous companies. The U.S. firms were also more aggressive in searching out (at times among small workshops in garages and backyards) and developing new sources of supply. Several U.S. subsidiaries had special managers or staffs just to search out and develop new local suppliers, although this was relatively rare.

U.S. subsidiaries also paid their bills more promptly than did local firms. It is true, however, that many suppliers gave better treatment to U.S. subsidiaries than to indigenous firms because of the greater prestige attached to doing business with a major foreign firm, or because they were larger or growing more rapidly and hence bigger customers, or because they were more financially sound, and hence in a better position to pay their bills promptly.

Intra-firm and individual cooperation

Indian enterprise personnel seem to function as "islands unto themselves," to a greater degree than their counterparts in the United States. Communication among Indian personnel is frequently highly ineffective, and one senses great reluctance to exchange information freely. There generally seems to be substantially less interest or effort made to help co-employees solve problems of mutual concern, or to improve their skills and performance.

Even within a family-oriented Indian enterprise, cooperative efforts are often slight. Sons may compete for the top position, especially if the eldest son has neither the personality nor the competence to assume leadership. In such cases, brothers become rivals, and cooperation with respect to work relationships can break down completely. On the other hand, even when family pecking orders are clearly defined, cooperation may still be slight, since this implies a distribution of power, and often the power is concentrated in a single individual. One man requests, and the others comply — this is cooperation only in the sense that one cooperates by following orders.

U.S. firms in India have had varied experience in this regard. By increasing upward employee mobility, they create internal rivalries, and thus tend to inhibit cooperation (a common problem in the United States). On the other hand, by stressing cooperation (i.e., across horizontal planes) in the evaluation process, they emphasize its importance as a criterion for promotion. Typically, U.S. firms attract unusual types of nationals — ambitious, energetic, and anxious to advance their positions. Patterns set by top managers usually determine the extent of cooperation existing within the organization.

One of the operational patterns of U.S. firms abroad which tends to induce cooperation is widespread use of committees. In spite of their shortcomings, they provide contact, allow for inter-managerial scrutiny, and develop a sense of group belonging. Properly employed, and with effective top-level leadership, the committee can be a useful device for increasing cooperative efforts.

OTHER SPHERES OF COOPERATION

In the last chapter, mention was made of the lack of cooperation between educational institutions and industrial firms in India. The same also tends to be true with regard to cooperation between research institutes and business firms, although there are still not many independent research organizations doing work of importance to Indian industry. One notable exception is a prominent textile research institute established by a group of textile mills. It provides technical and other assistance that few firms could support on their own. It also provides a model for other such cooperative activities. Several countries in Asia, Latin America, and Africa have gone substantially further than India in setting up effective cooperative research and assistance programs for industry.

Another problem area previously mentioned is the lack of cooperation between employment agencies and business firms. Although India contains many government employment agencies, firms prefer to do their own hiring (often nepotistically), even for hourly and temporary workers. The red tape and incompetence characteristic of many of these agencies certainly contributes to their lack of use by industry.

Firms in India cooperate substantially less in community programs than is typical in the United States. Most show lack of concern with the many social and community problems which exist in an impoverished, problem-ridden country like India. This does not improve the image of business and businessmen.

A few indigenous and foreign companies play active roles in community affairs because of genuine concern, not just for tax write-offs, but they are the exceptions. Several leading Indian corporations have contributed much to the cities and towns in which they are located, and one major U.S. subsidiary encourages its key managers to take an active part in charity work and community leadership activities. These efforts enhance the firm's image, promote considerable goodwill, and progressively improve the profitability of the firm, especially since community service is very visible, and often has great impact in poor countries where few firms voluntarily engage in such activity.

ATTITUDES TOWARD ACHIEVEMENT AND WORK

Work for the sake of work, and the will to succeed and improve in the economic sphere rank very high in some countries — typically those making substantial economic progress. In these nations, achievement is often inseparable from time: in fact it is measured in part in terms of accomplishment per unit of time. Time becomes crucial, and goal setting, planning, prediction, scheduling, evaluation, control, and timely corrective action become essential. Underdeveloped countries do not usually share this ambitious attitude toward productive achievement and this is a key reason for their underdevelopment.

The pace at which economic growth and industrial progress take place, on both the macro and micro levels, is a function of the degree of achievement orientation in a particular society. It may be the most critical factor of all in terms of managerial effectiveness and economic development.

An outstanding pioneer study by David McClelland of Harvard, based on empirical evidence derived from numerous countries and sources, has this to say about achievement motivation and economic development:

> There is a strong suggestion that men with high achievement motives will find a way to economic achievement given fairly wide variations in opportunity and social stature. What people want, they somehow manage to get, in the main and on the average, though other factors can modify the speed with which they get it.[46]

Research reveals that people (or societies) with a high achievement drive or need for achievement — referred to as "n-ach" by McClelland — typically strive to improve themselves and their performance, and to reach towards standards of excellence. They have relatively high aspiration levels. Material gain is usually not the most important motivating force for them, and they derive satisfaction just from expending effort, hard work, and doing a job, especially a non-routine job, well. While they may be concerned with their failures, they are even more concerned with their achievements and successes. If they fail, they are inclined to move forward anyway and try again. They generally have a great desire to overcome obstacles. These individuals typically have considerable self-confidence, and view the world as neither particularly benevolent nor malign but neutral. They feel that they can at least partially control their environment, destiny, and events. Moreover, they tend to become bored by routine or the *status quo*, they are challenged by risk taking, but are inclined to take only rationally calculated risks.[47]

People with relatively high n-ach usually make the most effective managers, particularly of the entrepreneurial or dynamic type. Industrial managers with a high achievement drive are inclined to desire and strive to accomplish fairly challenging, but realistic, enterprise plans and objectives. Such plans and goals typically pertain to some notion of greater growth in sales, output, productivity, efficiency, or profitability. Such managers are also more likely to take calculated risks, to innovate, and be favorably disposed to change in the direction of greater economic progress.

Developing countries, cultural and religious values, and achievement motivation

In general, dominant attitudes toward achievement and work serve as severe constraints on managerial effectiveness and productive efficiency in most of the world's poor countries. It is vital to significantly raise the achievement motivation of the population at large if the pace of economic development and industrial progress is to be substantially quickened. That is not to say that virtually the entire population should become high achievers; this of course can never be done, and even if it could, it would probably not be a desirable state of affairs. However, a country which succeeds in raising the achievement drive of its population and bringing about a more positive attitude toward productive work, does much to spur economic progress and increase managerial effectiveness.

In a more productive achievement and work-oriented society it is usually easier for industry to recruit personnel willing to work reasonably hard and efficiently. It is also true that in any society the efforts of competent management may raise productive efficiency. However, where the culture is not achievement- or work-oriented, even highly competent industrial managers are likely to have difficulty in this area.

In planned, developing economies, it is important for adequate numbers of key government administrative personnel and political leaders to have a relatively high n-ach and a strong priority commitment to industrial progress, if such progress is to be achieved in substantial measure. Yet many emerging nations, including India, have large and conservative bodies of government officials who show relatively low n-ach. Tenure is provided to individuals not equipped or adequately motivated to administer the development process. Seniority becomes the major element in promotions and innovation tends to be downgraded. An official who accepts risk and fails may lose hope of advancement, while success will do little to hasten upward progress. The best strategy therefore appears to be simply to sit tight and maintain the *status quo.*

Prevailing religious beliefs and cultural values relating to parental behavior, child rearing practices, and the educational system are the key determinants in shaping dominant attitudes toward achievement and work in different societies. As early as 1904, the eminent German sociologist Max Weber discussed in convincing detail how the Protestant Reformation and Calvinism produced a new character type which infused a more vigorous spirit into the attitudes of both managers and workers, and which ultimately resulted in the development of modern industrial capitalism.[48]

Calvin saw in each man a basic imperfection which could be ameliorated in large part by prayer, thrift, piety, and work. The work notion was extremely significant. The argument here is that each man should attempt to achieve grace not only by being a God-fearing, pious person, but also a man who would work for work's sake. It was not enough merely to earn one's bread; work should continue constantly through life, even if the individual is already very wealthy. Luxurious idleness was seen as a certain prelude to sin.[49]

The beliefs of traditional Hinduism are not generally compatible with a high achievement drive, or hard productive work for work's sake. On the contrary, they explicitly teach that concern with earthly achievements is a snare and a delusion. In general, in the formal, ritualistic, ecclesiastical system of many of the world's great religions, the individual is "safe" if he does exactly what he is supposed to do, performs correct rituals, says his prayers often enough, calls in the right priest at the right time, and so on.[50]

From the above discussion it is fallacious to conclude that one who considers himself a Protestant necessarily has high n-ach, or that a Hindu, or a Moslem, Buddhist, or Catholic automatically has a low achievement drive. It is true that the Protestant ethic and Calvinism make this religion particularly achievement-, work-, and action-oriented rather than belief-oriented (involving dogma and ritual). However, it is the *values associated with* Calvinistic Protestantism, and particularly their implementations, that lead to a high achievement drive, and not Protestantism per se. In the same vein, the achievement drive of a member of one of the other great religions is related to the degree to which he adheres to the values and behaves in ways advocated by traditional religious doctrine, and how he interprets such doctrine. If he adopts values associated with Calvinism he can have just as high, or even higher, n-ach as any Calvinistic Protestant.

Research and experience show that there are clearly substitutes for Protestantism with regard to high n-ach and hard work. Communist ideology and the vast amount of publicity and indoctrination aimed at national or collective achievement, as well as dedicated hard work, have done much to spur economic progress and raise managerial effectiveness in various Communist countries.[51] Christian missionaries in various parts of the world have also succeeded in raising the achievement motivation of local populations.

It should be stressed that it is not essential that an individual be solely concerned with self-interest and his own personal achievement for him to have high n-ach or to work very hard, although in Calvinistically-oriented countries this tends to be emphasized. In other countries the individual's identification with a commitment to some notion of collective or even national achievement may have the same end result. This is the case, for example, in Japan, where the emphasis is more on group enterprise or collective achievement, and in Communist states, where the emphasis is on various combinations of individual, collective, and national achievement.

Class structure, individual mobility, and achievement motivation

Class or social structure and individual mobility are the subject of a later section, but a brief discussion is called for here since these variables are closely related to achievement motivation and attitude toward work. Class mobility and opportunities for individual advancement have a direct and vital bearing on the view toward achievement and work in a given society.

Studies dealing with management and entrepreneurship in a number of countries — including the United States, Turkey, Italy, Mexico, and Poland — indicate that the best place to recruit business managers is from the middle and lower-middle classes, because they are more likely to have a higher n-ach than if they come from an upper or lower-class background.[52] Moreover, available evidence derived from studies of several diverse countries suggests that people from the middle and lower-middle classes with high n-ach are frequently inclined to prefer, and if they are able, to pursue, business and managerial careers, since they feel they can succeed and achieve satisfaction in this type of occupation.[53]

Hence, as long as there is freedom and opportunity to enter business and industrial management in a particular society, there appears to be a built-in recruiting mechanism for attracting candidates with high achievement drives from the middle classes. A fairly sizeable and growing middle and lower-middle class may, therefore, be essential to achieve a relatively high level of managerial effectiveness and sustained economic progress. For underdeveloped and newly developing nations, however, a closed circle is frequently involved; development is typically necessary to create a substantial pool of middle-class managerial and entrepreneurial talent which in turn makes rapid development possible.

There is also convincing evidence that in many countries upper-class persons with high n-ach are not inclined to enter business. They generally prefer the traditional high prestige professions such as law, medicine, religion, politics, the military, and scientific research. Studies conducted in several countries, including the United States, India, Japan and Brazil indicate that upper-class boys interested in business careers tend to be highly conservative, not very high in n-ach, and probably more often than not ill-suited for a business or management career.[54] They pursue business careers because they feel that they cannot succeed in traditional, high prestige professions as a result of a poor school record or lack of confidence and ability. Sometimes family pressures may force them into the family business.

Such a picture as that painted above helps to explain further the dilemma that less developed countries are caught in. Because there is not a sizeable middle and lower-middle class, they do not have a steady flow of entrepreneurial and managerial talent upward. Hence, business and often political leaders in such countries must be recruited primarily from the upper classes where the capital and opportunities for establishing business can be found. But such persons very often are relatively low in n-ach. They tend to have an ultraconservative ideology, and believe strongly in family solidarity, so they establish family firms in which their sons are frequently expected to participate whether or not they have the talent or motivation to be effective. This situation is aggravated further by the "brain drain" in countries like India, where many of the most able high achievers leave the country, frustrated by the lack of opportunity.

Discrimination is also a significant constraint on achievement and work in many countries. In these situations, potentially productive members of society are often denied opportunity because of class, caste, racial or religious prejudice, sex, or other forms of discrimination.

On the other hand, members of minority groups or sub-cultures who have a positive self-image and high aspiration level in spite of significant obstacles, and who have some opportunities for getting ahead are likely to have relatively high n-ach and often make excellent managers of the entrepreneurial type.[55] In fact business may be one of the few relatively lucrative and satisfying activities open to them. The Chinese in Indonesia, Americans in the Middle East, Lebanese in Africa and elsewhere, and Jews in various poor (as well as advanced) countries are examples of groups with a relatively high achievement drive who perform crucial entrepreneurial and managerial roles in societies where most of the population is relatively low in n-ach.

Raising n-achievement

Usually, it takes underdeveloped countries decades, generations, or even longer to raise the achievement drive of the population, in the macro sense, and bring about a substantially more positive view toward productive work on a national scale. Various Communist countries have proved exceptions by drastically overhauling the educational system, culture, and social structure; by increasing adult literacy and providing functional education; by putting much of the child-rearing process in the hands of highly-motivated teachers and party functionaries; by providing greater opportunity for mobility for the "loyal" individual; and by placing a constant and intensive ideological stress on achievement and productive work.

Most non-communist nations, especially the more democratic ones such as India, do not wish to or cannot use the often coercive tactics, programs, and techniques of Communist countries. Here it typically takes considerably longer to raise the achievement motivation and improve the society's attitude toward productive work.

Can anything substantial be done to solve this on the micro level, rather than merely waiting for widespread change of the macro type? What about the individual manager and his enterprise?

Until very recently there was virtually universal agreement among Western psychologists and other social and behavioral scientists, that the crucial period for acquiring a relatively high achievement drive lies somewhere between the ages of five and ten. This has been supported by various psychological tests and studies.[56] McClelland and his colleagues also apparently held this view, at least until quite recently.

Then McClelland began to seriously question this assumption in spite of the evidence that had been accumulated to date. He has told one of the authors that his skepticism has been based in large part on the successes that Communist countries and Christian missionaries in various countries have had in raising achievement drive among adults. This has led him and some of his colleagues to establish programs for managers and businessmen — and more recently for other adult members of minority and underprivileged groups, including negroes and ex-convicts in the United States — aimed at raising their achievement drive.[57]

These programs, typically a few weeks in duration, are not concerned with the development of technical skills or the best way of doing things. They stress raising achievement motivation by correcting the self-image of participants. Their aim is to impart a growing conviction that people can change, can control and direct their lives, and that they can be change agents rather than pawns at the mercy of the environment. A variety of methods and techniques are used, among them: goal setting; problem solving and risk-taking exercises and related discussions focusing on what makes a high achiever and what the obstacles are; written assignments and films; brainstorming and group projects; and group acceptance and support of values associated with high n-ach.

Among the first of such achievement-training programs was one involving a large corporation in the United States. Managerial participants of the sample group in the program did significantly better on the average, in terms of promotions, greater responsibilities, better performance, after taking the course than the control group not undergoing such training. Since the American executives involved in this study, and in general, have on the average higher n-ach to begin with than typical managers in underdeveloped countries, this encouraged McClelland to set up such programs in poorer countries. He felt the results would be even more significant in terms of greater entrepreneurship and economic progress.

Similar programs have been established in cities in India, ranging in size from Kakinada with a population of about 100,000 to Bombay with several million. The results to date have been encouraging. For example, a follow-up study ranging from 6 to 24 months after the Kakinada program, showed that two-thirds of the participants had become unusually and concretely active in business. They had expanded their firms, added more employees and new products, gone into new businesses, or were making much larger profits. Only one-third of the group had been exceptionally active in similar ways in the two years prior to the course. Hence, the course seemed to have doubled entrepreneurship, since the favorable results achieved were not due to better business conditions.

The case of India

Fatalism, otherworldliness, apathy, pessimism, child-rearing practices and the joint family system, non-involvement, lack of initiative and dependency, the educational system and widespread illiteracy, lack of opportunities for individual mobility, the caste system, and various other elements of orthodox Hinduism and Gandhian type values are not compatible with a high level or achievement, not conducive to productive work in industry in India. The caste system in particular — though gradually breaking down — still has a tremendous effect on shaping aspiration levels, and hence achievement drive.

One knowledgeable and effective Indian industrial leader stated:

> The caste system in India has a great negative impact on aspiration levels and achievement motivation. The lower castes in particular have been rigidly restricted for many generations with regard to their ambitions and most of them have not yet been able to overcome the great obstacles which bind them. This has been further retarded by the difference in the social environment between urban and rural areas. Even when they make some effort to improve their economic status — by getting a job in a factory, for example — they typically do not aspire any higher and they stagnate. They may want to be a bit better than other members of their caste, but not so much better that they would be excluded from their peer group. If they leave that group, they usually have no other group with whom they can mix. Moreover, they are not accustomed to comparing themselves to anyone other than members of their own caste.

It appears that low aspiration levels, low n-ach, and a negative or at best passive attitude toward productive work in industry, and productivity in general, are more pronounced in India's rural areas, where the vast majority of the population resides. A U.S. subsidiary going into the Indian countryside is likely to be faced with substantially greater problems with regard to achievement motivation and attitude toward work than it would find in major urban centers.

Some of the indigenous firms surveyed in India made effective use of personal loyalty in motivating personnel toward high achievement and effort. Their employees personally felt greater obligations to and greater identification with the company and its objectives than they would under the types of relationships that exist in large impersonal corporations. However, personal loyalty pertaining to individual managers rather than the organization can lead to serious problems with changes in management, or if the firm grows rapidly. U.S. managers would frequently find it distasteful or very difficult to operate in this manner. On the other hand, if the U.S. subsidiary is not expected to grow rapidly, and if it is staffed by Indian managers who expect to remain with the firm or who can at least be counted on to effectively develop their successors, the use of personal loyalty to heighten achievement motivation and productive effort may prove effective.

Those Indian managers who have achievement drives comparable to U.S. executives are most likely to be found either among Western-trained Indians who have acquired a considerable amount of self-confidence and know-how, or among certain minority or sub-cultural groups, such as the Parsees, who originally came from Persia and typically have many Western values; the Marwaris, who are Hindus especially from the merchant caste; the Punjabis, particularly the Sikhs, who do not consider themselves Hindus; and the Indian Christians, who come primarily from Southern India, are often well educated in productive fields, and whose families are converts from the low castes. The largest business and industrial complex in India is controlled by a Parsee family (the Tatas), and the second biggest is run by Marwaris (the Birlas).

IMPLICATIONS FOR INTERNATIONAL MANAGEMENT

International firms can often do much to adapt to and partially overcome the relatively low level of achievement motivation which prevail on a widespread scale in developing countries such as India. This can be done by balancing modern approaches to management with effective adaptation to the local environment. However, it is rare for such firms to become as productive and work-oriented as comparable companies operating in the United States.

As a group, the U.S. subsidiaries surveyed in India did seem to be characterized by greater achievement-type activity and behavior within the managerial ranks than the group of indigenous firms. However, among non-managerial personnel, especially clerical and blue collar workers, there did not appear to be any significant differences between our samples of foreign and indigenous firms. In other words, U.S. subsidiaries did not seem to be more effective in "turning on" their workers. Those companies which seemed to be most effective were more successful in developing personal loyalty toward the organization, though not necessarily to individual managers or owners. They also seemed more inclined to treat workers fairly (though often firmly), to respect their dignity, to provide job security, to recruit and train employees more effectively, and to provide various types of worker benefits and incentives, frequently not of the cash payment kind.

Even the most achievement and work-oriented of the U.S. subsidiaries studied in India did not seem to be as achievement or work-oriented as the comparable plants and divisions of their parent companies surveyed in the United States. This is true at both the managerial and worker levels.

Even among the most dynamic and best managed American firms in India, it was difficult to get local managers and other personnel to take management plans, targets, and programs seriously during early implementation stages. Frequently, firms found it difficult to maintain gains in productivity and performance, and to motivate employees to strive for even better performance once a new high level was achieved.

A few of the U.S. companies in our study showed a tendency to send their less effective and less motivated managers to foreign assignments, while keeping the "cream of the crop" at home. Such thinking reflects a parochial rather than a global or progressive view of the multinational firm's role in the modern world. If the international manager is to be truly effective in such a relatively negative environment, he needs to have a high achievement drive and a high level of competence rather than the reverse. Several of the more effective U.S. companies have made a conscious effort to identify those sub-cultural groups from which relatively high achievers and work-oriented individuals are most likely to come, and actively recruit members of such groups. In particular, they have hired sizeable numbers of Western-, particularly American-trained Indians, engineers, and other specialists, many of whom have had work experience abroad. When recruiting experienced managers and other key personnel they pay particular attention to individuals working in industries which are subject to intensive competitive pressures, on the assumption that they are likely to be more achievement and work-oriented.

The most achievement and work-oriented firms — at least at the managerial levels — provide considerably more opportunities for advancement within the organization for well-motivated and qualified individuals. Of course this is much easier to do if the company is expanding at a substantial rate, and this is true of the more progressive and best managed U.S. subsidiaries surveyed in India. However, even these firms often fail to provide rapid enough advancement for competent high achievers, because of class structure, nationality, or seniority constraints (at times imposed by the parent company), inadequate planning and development, particularly with regard to managerial manpower, or overstaffing within the managerial hierarchy. In turn, this often leads to frustration, hostility, resentment, and the loss of key executives.

The most achievement and work-oriented U.S. subsidiaries in India also paid the greatest attention to fostering and maintaining on a day-to-day basis an organizational climate or environment encouraging to achievement and effort. This was accomplished in part by effective delegation of authority and decentralization, and by providing opportunities for initiative, innovation, and creativity.

SOCIAL STRUCTURE AND INDIVIDUAL MOBILITY

Introduction

Although a relatively small middle class is emerging in poor countries such as India, the social structure still tends towards a closed system with key jobs awarded predominantly to the relatively affluent, family members, close friends, or members of the same caste or community. Pay differentials in India at different levels of the enterprise hierarchy, especially in family firms, tend to be among the greatest in the world. The relative difference in income between the highest-paid manager and the average firm wage is much greater than in U.S. industry, with the exception of some giant U.S. corporations. India's caste system and its social structure may present an extreme example of class and individual immobility and differentiation, but similarly strong barriers exist in African tribal systems, and, perhaps to a lesser extent, in the social structures of various Latin-American and other Asian countries.

It is probably a natural tendency for family, friendship, caste, community, and other social ties to play the dominant role in staffing decisions in countries where there is much unemployment and a dearth of good job opportunities. In all fairness, it should also be pointed out that staffing decisions based on such factors often lead to loyalty, dedication, unity, effective communication, and relatively good performance in this type of environment. However, as firms grow larger, and technology, production processes, and product lines become more complex, and as expertise and motivation become more critical, such a staffing philosophy tends to have an increasingly negative impact on managerial effectiveness and productive efficiency. The problem becomes even more pronounced as greater competition, often involving foreign companies, emerges.

In general, where a substantial majority of citizens in a given country is prevented from entering the ranks of management or from obtaining other productive jobs, managerial effectiveness and economic growth are affected negatively.

In a society where social barriers to mobility are strong and extensive, it may be possible to bend local customs and attitudes to some degree, but gross violations may, especially in the short run, be both risky and costly. They may lead to considerable insecurity and friction among enterprise personnel who are accustomed to certain staffing patterns, and a certain status or class hierarchy linked to various occupations and jobs.

The case of India

In India all of the social factors limiting individual mobility discussed above still exist to a relatively high degree, although they are on the decline.[58] As one prominent Indian sociologist points out with regard to his country:

> Consideration of caste, community, and blood relationship persist at all levels and in all spheres of activity, whether it be industry, public service, or politics. Among the more sophisticated, it has become fashionable to decry any preference shown on the basis of caste, but it still makes its influence felt in various subtle and indirect ways . . . Every community blames the other community for this state of affairs, but they have all inherited the same burden from the past.[59]

In spite of social legislation embodied in India's Constitution aimed at eliminating discrimination in employment on the basis of caste, color, creed, etc., the enforcement of such legislation has not been effective to date, probably even less effective than similar legislation in the United States. Moreover, there are many more persons, both numerically and in per capita terms, who belong to underprivileged groups in India than in the United States. While India can point to some "untouchables" who have reached the top in society, including a few at the ministerial ranks of government, the fact remains that there still is much job discrimination. Research indicates that the correlation between job rank and status in the organizational hierarchy and caste-system ranking tends to still be very high at enterprises in rural areas. At the same time, industrialization even in urban areas has not yet served as a truly substantial social change agent regarding caste and the occupational hierarchy, and the caste makeup of firms in general still tend to reflect the larger society.[60]

Industrialization creates new professions and jobs not provided for in the caste system. This tends to break down traditional barriers, and members of different castes often work side by side in factories. However, caste considerations are still critical in many situations. For example, machinists do not want to keep their machines clean, and lower caste personnel, frequently "Harijans", must clean them. This results substantially in the need for more auxiliary personnel and, therefore, lower efficiency.

Nowhere does the American or other foreigner living in India encounter the caste system more dramatically than in staffing his own household. Individuals from different castes perform the tasks of sweepers (cleaners), bearers (waiters), cooks, gardeners, drivers, "ayas" (nursemaids), laundrymen, watchmen, and so forth. Americans are expected to have a wide variety of servants since they are relatively affluent. It is almost impossible to combine several jobs into one and interchange tasks among the personnel unless one hires non-Hindus.

In general, the division of labor along caste lines is most rigid at the highest and lowest levels of the social scale. Most Brahmins working at industrial firms — and many Brahmins still prefer not to work in this sector — have clerical, professional, managerial, or other kinds of white collar jobs. Few are employed as manual workers directly in production. At the other end of the social scale, members of the scheduled castes and tribes hold the most menial, unskilled jobs. Relatively few go much higher. It is rare to find such a caste member in a white collar or professional job, and especially rare in managerial ranks.

Brahmins are highly over-represented in educational programs, even those of a non-traditional technical nature. For example, in Kidder's study of technical personnel working for firms in the Calcutta area, 82 percent of the graduates of the Polytechnic schools and Industrial Training Institutes in the area during the 1960-1964 period whom he interviewed were Brahmins, most of them from well-off families.[61]

Not enough research has been done to date to conclude whether caste or education is a more critical factor with regard to upward mobility in industry. But the fact remains that the Brahmins on the average are by far the most highly-educated. In our research, however, we observed many cases where Brahmins held higher-level positions than personnel from other castes who had just as much, and often more formal education, and substantially better qualifications, including motivation.

Education does appear to be a slight leveler with regard to the class structure and employment, in that more opportunities are opening for the well-educated man (especially the foreign degree holder), regardless of class. However, the cost factor still largely limits higher education to the upper classes, and government scholarships and financial aid are still insufficient to have a major impact.

The caste system still contributes to various kinds of educational and training mismatch problems in the Indian economy. For example, in spite of widespread unemployment, there have been critical shortages of personnel in various fields such as carpentry, masonry, and the stone and leather crafts, while associated with employed persons from castes not associated with such occupations often prefer to work as unskilled labor at much lower wages. On the other hand, even if these persons wanted to learn a craft or trade other than that of their own caste, they are likely to find training unavailable. A carpenter or mason is not inclined to teach his trade to anyone outside his caste. Even within the caste he would first take his own kith and kin as apprentices. And in the rare case where an individual has learned the craft of another caste, it is doubtful that he could find work because employers would tend to feel that he was not really qualified and fellow workers might not accept him. In training programs set up in recent years by the government for craftsmen in various trades, carpentry classes are attended by carpenters' sons only, with very few exceptions.[62]

Community and language ties are also important in staffing at numerous firms in India. In some areas where provincial or regional chauvinism runs high, such ties are often at least as important as caste. It is common for firms in Calcutta to prefer native Bengali Hindu managers regardless of caste — with the exception of the lowest caste. For example, some firms owned or run by Brahmins would rather employ native Bengali managers of another caste than Brahmins from another part of the country. The same is true in governmental agencies and offices, where discrimination along caste lines may be more difficult to practice. Language differences contribute to such community chauvinism, and at times choosing a person for a job largely because he speaks the same language may not be an inefficient staffing decision.

Provincial chauvinism (as well as family ties) is also often a factor with regard to people leaving their community to seek a better job or get work in industry. In some states, this type of constraint on individual mobility is strong and extensive. In general, well-educated Indian citizens are more willing to migrate to other parts of the country in order to better themselves than citizens in many African, Asian, and Latin-American countries.

Although the late President of India, Zakir Husain, who died in 1969, was a Moslem, discrimination against Moslems in industry, especially in rural areas, is common in India. Moslems make up about 10 percent of India's population — numerically more than 50 million. Rarely does one come across a Moslem in a major managerial position in a Hindu company. Although Moslems make just as good workers as Hindus, it is frequently difficult for them to get suitable jobs or to better themselves.

In the second half of 1965 and 1966 discrimination against Moslems became particularly acute in India because of the Indo-Pakistani war. Moslems were laid off for "security" reasons, especially in the Calcutta region, which has the largest Moslem population. For example, about 25 percent of the employees of one Calcutta firm surveyed by one of the authors had been Moslem, and a majority of them were laid off during the 1965-1966 period. These included good mechanics and technicians, and the plant's efficiency suffered substantially. At that time the unions did not oppose such dismissals. One of the authors, who was then living in Calcutta, was even subject to pressure by various local authorities and Hindu citizens to dismiss his Moslem maid.

Discrimination against Anglo-Indians, particularly those seeking key managerial jobs, is also fairly common in Indian industry, although it is not as acute generally as in the case of Moslems.

The proportion of females employed in Indian industry is small (about 12 percent) compared to many other countries. The high rate of male unemployment and traditional attitudes toward the family and the role of women in general are major reasons for this. It is true that some Indian women, particularly those from influential or wealthy families, have achieved prominence in various professions, the most noteworthy example being India's current Prime Minister, Indira Gandhi. However, many indigenous companies do not employ any women. Males are employed even as typists, receptionists, and switchboard operators. It is rare to find a woman working as a manager, engineer, technician, or key staff specialist in any kind of industrial enterprise.

OUR SURVEY OF FIRMS AND IMPLICATIONS FOR INTERNATIONAL MANAGEMENT

With very few exceptions, the indigenous firms surveyed in India adhered in general to dominant social attitudes and traditional staffing patterns to a substantially higher degree than U.S. subsidiaries.[63] This was even true for the larger local companies. Typical was the case of a large indigenous (Gujerati-owned) firm. All of the 15 highest-level managers had the same mother tongue and were from the same merchant caste and community. Moreover, most of them were closely related, and 11 of them had one of two related surnames. Similarly, all of the key managers of a major Calcutta drug and chemical firm were Bengalis of the same warrior sub-caste. They were all either related or came from families that had long been intimate friends. Moreover, most of them had degrees in chemistry, primarily from Calcutta University. Virtually all of the managers, specialists, and clerks employed by this company were Bengalis, while most of the production workers were from Orissa.

The entire top management group of a large multi-plant equipment company owned by a Marwari family were Marwaris of the merchant caste. Most of them joined this firm around the same time and were previously employed in other organizations controlled by the same family. Moreover, a majority of them had B. Comm. degrees, and many of these were obtained from the same school.

It is also common for indigenous Indian firms to "import" key personnel from other parts of the country who belong to the same family caste or community as the owners. Typical of this was the case of an electrical metals firm in Rajasthan owned by Gujeratis living in Bombay. The key managerial jobs were also filled by Gujeratis of the same caste, most of them not college graduates, while almost all of the workers were Rajasthanis. Similarly, a Marwari-controlled chemical company in Assam in which a U.S. corporation had a minority 40 percent interest had its key managerial and key technical jobs filled by Marwaris — almost all relatives or close friends — mostly "imported" from distant parts of the country.

Because they are outside the system, foreign firms in India have had somewhat more opportunity to deviate from social-structure considerations in staffing, without adverse consequences, than indigenous firms. In actuality, U.S. subsidiaries in India have created a type of sub-culture with regard to staffing policies, inasmuch as they place significantly more emphasis on qualifications, merit, and ability than do most local firms. By providing more opportunities for advancement, without as many social barriers, they are in a substantially better position to attract, maintain, and utilize bright talent, as well as relatively young and highly-motivated individuals.

A still small but growing number of the more progressive indigenous firms, seeing the success U.S. subsidiaries have had with such staffing philosophy and personnel practices, have begun to move in a similar direction. Hence, here too, U.S. companies in India have come to play an important role as social change agents.

In general, U.S. firms had significantly more heterogeneous representation with regard to caste, community, region, religion, color, and sex, although few had managers drawn from the lowest caste or the female sex. Moreover, few members of the scheduled castes and tribes were employed in any capacity at all by most U.S. companies in India.

In some cases, it may be advantageous even for American subsidiaries to fill some types of important jobs with members of a particular caste or community. For example, it may be wise to have a purchasing agent or other administrator from the same caste or community as the key government officials or suppliers he must deal with. This can lead to more favorable treatment for the firm, as well as furnishing it with inside information not otherwise available. Similarly, it is often advantageous to have sales representatives from the same caste or community as their major customers, especially if a relatively competitive market is involved.

Although merit, ability, qualifications, motivation, and other objective criteria play a significantly greater role in staffing and organizational decisions at the American-controlled firms, the social structure still presents major constraints with regard to efficient staffing and personnel policies.

Let us cite one example involving the upper-management echelon. This is a particularly interesting case because it directly involves the head office of the parent corporation. The parent company in the United States felt it was time in 1966 to seriously consider appointing an Indian managing director for its Indian subsidiary, one of the largest American firms in India. The subsidiary was under a British managing director at the time, and all managing directors in the post had been Westerners. After much serious consideration, including a careful appraisal and review of potential candidates, it was concluded by head office management that only one manager employed by the subsidiary in India had the essential qualifications and motivation to fill the job.

However, this candidate was an Indian Christian whose family had converted some time ago from the untouchable caste. He was also relatively dark-skinned, and although color discrimination is not as acute as in the United States, it nevertheless is a delicate issue. Although he had moved up rapidly into the upper echelons of management because of his superior abilities, and in spite of his social background, corporate management decided that it would just be too risky to appoint him managing director. His social background was apparently the major reason. It was felt that not only would some other key executives be likely to leave, but that his advancement could also have adverse consequences with regard to other Indian personnel, as well as other organizations and individuals with which the subsidiary had to deal in India. In other words, from a public relations point of view, it was felt that this would be an unwise move.

VIEW OF WEALTH AND MATERIAL GAIN

General social attitudes toward wealth and material gain, and the views of wealth derived from different sources, influence the types, qualities, and numbers of individuals who pursue managerial and entrepreneurial careers in industry and business. They have a major impact on the way enterprises are managed and operated, and the way in which industrial personnel respond to material stimuli as motivational factors.

While most cultures are willing to utilize whatever wealth may be at hand at the moment, the general view toward wealth and material gain varies strikingly among people. On the one hand, it is possible to find completely economically-oriented men who calculate almost every step of their lives in terms of monetary gains or losses. Scrooge in Dickens' *A Christmas Carol* was perhaps the perfect characterization of this type of person. At the other end of the continuum, one can find men in religious orders who have taken complete poverty vows, and who demonstrate absolutely no interest in wealth whatsoever. Two societies peopled largely by types of individuals close to one or the other end of this continuum would be vastly different from each other in terms of managerial effectiveness and industrial development. One would expect that, in a world of economic men, every possible step would be taken to increase wealth as rapidly as possible; while in a world of men who had renounced worldly wealth, the society might be in constant danger of collapse for lack of production of even the most basic necessities of food, clothing, and shelter.

There are few present-day societies in which most of the population has an extreme negative view toward wealth and material gain. The number of basically closed, subsistence societies operating largely on a barter system with little notion of saving and investment has been diminishing rapidly in recent decades through exposure to the outside world. As this happens their members gradually adopt the economic motive and become more materialistic. Commonly-held American values and assumptions regarding wealth and material gain, when applied in Indian industry, often meet with considerable resistance, and result in serious conflict or even failure. This shows up in the way earnings are invested and distributed, in the incentive systems which are utilized, in various other personnel practices, in union relations, and even in connection with product design and marketing.

While suspicion and distrust of private managers still persist on a substantial scale in India, the industrial path to riches and material gain has clearly been gaining in respectability. So have managerial and entrepreneurial careers. However, numerous Indian business owners and managers — especially the more traditional ones — still stress quick profits, and derive much of their wealth through black marketing and other illegal or quasi-illicit activities, rather than through dynamic enterprise growth and reinvestment of earnings. In India much of the industrially-created income of firm owners and managers continues to be spent on non-industrial ventures such as religious festivities, weddings, material status symbols, conspicuous consumption items or pursuits of higher social status. Instead of using incomes and profits to substantially expand their firms, many managers and owners prefer to speculate and invest in land, goods, jewelry, gilt-edged securities, and foreign exchange (usually illegally).

U.S. partners in joint ventures often have bitter disputes with foreign collaborators over policies concerning the reinvestment of earnings, dividend payouts, sources and uses of funds, and various other issues involving money. Such conflicts reflect differences in basic attitudes regarding wealth and material gain. In choosing foreign collaborators U.S. companies should give serious consideration to such basic attitudes.

In economies where protected markets offer large and quick returns, even to inefficient managers, longer-range capital intensive ventures tend to suffer. This is one reason why the government in India has had to play a major role in the establishment of large capital-intensive industries (such as steel) deemed vital for economic growth. This situation is due not to a lack of resources in the private sector but to a lack of interest and motivation. In India, during the last two decades, the state has had to play a major role in capital accumulation and investment for industrial expansion. However, this has wasted vast amounts of wealth and income since many of the large-sector firms have been poorly managed.

Prevalent attitudes toward wealth and material gain have been substantially more of a constraint on India's development in the agricultural sector and within the rural population than in industry (especially the private sector) and the cities. The typical Indian villager is just starting to get a real thirst for increasing wealth by increasing his farm output and productivity, and seems on the verge of breaking out of his stagnant aspiration level. But to date, disappointing agricultural performance in India has seriously retarded industrial development. It has been a key factor in the foreign exchange crisis; it has greatly limited the funds available for industrial investment on a national scale; and it has greatly limited the amounts of various types of raw materials required by the industrial sector.

One of the real frustrations experienced by Indian economic planners has been the huge amounts of hoarded wealth which exist in the villages and which are not put to productive use. The typical villager husbands his wealth carefully — not for investment or emergency purposes, but because it is tangible and often a visible sign of status. Often the women wear the family fortune to the fields, in the form of jewelry. These items are passed from generation to generation, and are not to be spent or converted into income-generating ventures. The typical Indian farmer, rather than part with such symbols, will go into debt for years to provide a big feast and dowry for his daughter's wedding. Wealth is more important for the status it brings than for its purchasing power. Consequently, when an Indian villager moves to a factory setting, the promise of increased income is often not necessarily a major motivating factor in itself.

Numerous companies in India have had poor experiences with the introduction of monetary incentive systems, and merit systems have suffered even worse fates. The satisfaction gained by individuals who receive large merit raises is frequently more than offset by the dissatisfaction of those who receive little or nothing, often because of status implications. It has been common for monetary incentive systems to fail even when the personnel involved have earned more pay through them.

Material incentive systems which tend to work well in U.S. industry are likely to prove more effective with some types of Indian personnel or sub-cultural groups than others. Younger, Western-trained Indians in managerial and major technical jobs are more likely to respond in desired ways to American-style incentive schemes than relatively traditional Hindus, although this is by no means always the case. The impact of incentive schemes is often blunted by large statutory payments, which dwarf the salary portion of worker incomes. Government legislation requiring the payment of substantial "dearness allowances" (usually linked to a cost of living index) is one such factor. Bonuses and other fixed annual increments which must be paid by law, and are not related to job performance or merit, also contribute to this situation.

Industrial personnel in India frequently prefer lower-paying jobs if more fringe benefits or status symbols are provided, and if they feel that greater job security is entailed. Where piece rates and other types of incentives (including raises in many cases) are used by firms, absenteeism frequently goes up substantially once personnel achieve a certain level of pay. Bonus and incentive schemes designed to reduce absenteeism (including double pay in some cases) with very few exceptions have had no significant effect on attendance.

A U.S. subsidiary in Africa experienced serious absenteeism problems as a result of basically the same cultural factors that exist in Indian industry. This firm also tried various kinds of material incentives, but to no avail. Management then decided to try something entirely different. Most of its plant operations had been run on a multiple-shift basis. Workers were reclassified from hourly to monthly salaried employees so that they could be required to work overtime without violating the law. Then management introduced the policy of requiring workers to work a double shift if their co-workers or "buddies" on the next shift failed to report for work without providing a good reason in advance. This soon led to a substantial decrease in absenteeism which has apparently been maintained to date.

This is a good example of preconceived American assumptions about attitudes toward material gain being eventually discarded and replaced by another and much more effective strategy more in tune with the local culture. Motivational systems based on prevalent sociological-cultural conditions are often the most effective ways to accomplish desired objectives. For example, personal loyalty and personally felt obligations may often prove more effective as incentives than money in less-developed countries.

This is not to imply that U.S. firms abroad should abandon all forms of material incentive systems that work well at home. With proper planning, analysis, training, and preparation, such incentives can lead to favorable results as time goes on. U. S. companies can in fact be effective transfer and change agents with respect to economic development in this sphere. However, the use of material gain or wealth as a motivating force should not be based on preconceived assumptions or American values. Local conditions must be considered.

In general, U.S. subsidiaries in India have been more willing to experiment with various kinds of material incentive and merit rating systems than indigenous firms. However, they have not made as effective use of them as have their parent companies in the United States. In some cases material incentive schemes have been successfully utilized in India, although specific schemes that have proven effective at one company have often failed when applied at another firm or even in another plant of the same firm.

Those material incentive schemes which have typically proved to be the most effective in India have entailed at least some of the following characteristics:

1.   Sizeable numbers of personnel from the subcultural groups that are most likely to respond in desired ways to material incentives.

2.   Careful planning, preparation, analysis, and training on the part of management, as well as considerable patience.

3.   No strong union resistance.

4.   The use of group incentives, or at least some combination of group and individual incentives, frequently linked to a productivity or profit sharing program.

5.   Feelings of job security among employees.

6.   The linking of clear-cut standards of performance to rewards.

VIEW OF SCIENTIFIC METHOD

Scientific method here refers to the methodology developed for the analysis of various problems in the physical and social sciences. Critical to this notion is the idea that events can be described, explained, predicted, and controlled. The thinking runs, "if we do A then B will occur," with the idea that this hypothesis can be verified by trying A to see if B in fact occurs. If it does not, a new hypothesis might be proposed and tried. Another way of looking at this problem is to suggest that "event X depends on factors Y and Z," and then to relate, mathematically if possible, the relationship between the variables. Once hypothesized, the prediction is verified by observation, or experimentation.

This kind of thinking is not ancient. It dates back essentially to seventeenth-century England, most notably to the writings of Sir Francis Bacon, although limited effective use was made of scientific method in earlier periods (most notably by the Greeks, Romans, Chinese, Hebrews, and Arabs). All of the major technical and scientific gains in the past few centuries have been caused by application of such scientific methodology. In more contemporary times the scientific method has been largely a Western phenomenon, probably one of the most critical underpinnings of Western culture. It is part of the innovative and exploratory spirit which has led to the development of most Western technological and social advances. The lack of it is a major reason why underdeveloped countries are underdeveloped.

More recently, the same methodology has been applied to the social and behavioral sciences, with considerably less meaningful results. Even here, however, considerable progress has been made, particularly in the Western world. The major difficulty encountered in applying it is in trying to experiment, predict or control events in a situation where extraneous variables cannot be eliminated from the system, as in economics, management, sociology or psychology. But in any case, the notion of observing a system, proposing various hypotheses about behavior within the system, and checking results, is central to scientific methodology. This type of thinking is so common in advanced countries today that it is taken for granted in literally millions of relatively simple situations. Managers, technicians, machinists, electricians, salesmen, in addition to persons working in hundreds of other types of occupations, apply the technique without even considering what methodology they are using.

Hence a typical American skilled worker will plan his work, thinking intuitively: if A then B. In fact, even relatively routine types of skilled work involve such thinking on a fairly complex level, which becomes apparent if one looks more closely at how the worker functions. An American electrician does not use number 14 wire for 220-volt circuits as a matter of course — since he thinks about "causality" and can predict burnouts, short circuits, and fire hazards. Similarly an American machinist is inclined to make sure that his equipment is oiled at regular intervals, lest it function improperly and eventually break down. Only when one has lived in a culture where such apparently trivial rules are frequently violated does he realize and appreciate the nature of such an attitude and preconditioning in workmen and other personnel in advanced countries.

In management in advanced countries, the use of scientific methodology is even more pronounced. Managers spend much time predicting what will happen, given certain conditions, and in trying to prevent undesirable results by adapting to or changing the conditions. If we charge x dollars per unit how will this affect sales, profits and costs? If we introduce project A how much financing will be required and what will the net effect over time be? If we introduce a new piece of equipment how much will costs go down? If we introduce this incentive system will productivity increase x units? To fill a job opening effectively we need a man with qualifications x, y and z. The whole area of planning and decision making is basically this sort of activity, as are much of the processes of control, staffing, organization, and direction. In the functional business area — i.e., production, marketing, research and development, finance, etc. — a prime consideration is that the manager will be able to predict events and eventually control them as far as possible through his adaptation to and manipulation of his environment.

While considerable strides have been made in the use of the scientific method in Indian industry, it is still a very long way from being an accepted way of life or automatically used at an unconscious as well as conscious level, as it is in U.S. industry. As a result, things run out of control much of the time at Indian enterprises and it is difficult to plan effectively for the future. Fatalism, as well as various other cultural, religious, and educational factors, greatly retards the use of such methodology. The astrologer is often an important consultant on management decisions. Even in Indian scientific and engineering education, the emphasis is typically placed on facts, rather than on the testing, problem-solving, or analytical processes. Furthermore, until quite recently, few Indian managers had seen the connection between scientific method and managerial practice.

A kind of circular reasoning regarding scientific method has long operated in Indian management and industry. Since relatively few firms or managers have applied the scientific method in planning, plans tend to be ineffective. Consequently, pessimism about planning has been prevalent, and personnel have become even more reluctant to plan for the future. However, in recent years this has been gradually changing, largely as a result of the successes of foreign companies.

This is a critical area where education and training, encouragement, demonstration, dissemination of information, and other forms of assistance could be highly beneficial in terms of managerial effectiveness and industrial progress in India and other less-developed countries.

With only a few notable exceptions, U.S.-controlled companies surveyed in India make substantially more, and more effective use of scientific methodology in planning, control, and problem solving than indigenous firms. This is in large part due to the type of people they recruit and attract. Several firms stress this quality in interviews and appraisals, and a few even use formal or informal psychological and problem-solving tests to get at the candidates' true grasp of scientific methodology. Moreover, U.S. subsidiaries typically spend more time and effort in developing this aptitude among personnel, often by demonstration and example.

One of the main cautions for U.S. organizations in India regarding scientific method is a tendency to think that systems of logic are uniform and universal. The scientific method underlies (or is perhaps basically identical to) Western logic patterns. The lack of application of this methodology in developing nations often is a key cue to difference in thought patterns. Hence, such organizations are faced with the alternatives of modifying their own methods of thought, seeking out local nationals who have similar thought patterns and attitudes, or developing these patterns in those people with whom they must work.

ATTITUDES TOWARD RISK TAKING

People who have relatively high achievement drive tend to make the most effective managers of the entrepreneurial type. Therefore, many of the problems regarding achievement motivation in Indian industry also have a significant bearing on risk-taking attitudes and behavior. But there is more to risk taking than this.

In general, risk is an inherent part of economic activity. Since productive operations involve at least some degree of uncertainty, any economy or enterprise must assume some risks.

There are two dimensions of risk taking of interest here: 1) rationality and its boundaries and 2) degree of agressiveness or conservatism. Let us deal with the former first.

Rational risk taking in the truly optimal sense defies precise definition, since human beings and organizations are limited in knowledge and skill they have available for making decisions involving the future. However, it does make sense to talk in terms of the degree and boundaries of rationality in risk taking and decision making. The degree to which risk taking is rational in a given situation is dependent on the extent to which the following conditions are present:

1. The decision is based on the realities of the situation, including a well-reasoned — at times this may be basically an unconscious thought process — evaluation of the facts which are available.

2. The decision is based on logical assumptions and calculated courses of action incorporating weighted estimates of the potential risks and probabilities of success involved. Such weighting may be either unconscious or conscious, depending on the significance and uniqueness of the decision and the related risks involved.

Hence, rational risk taking and the effectiveness of risk taking depend largely on skill used in blending scientific method with the collection and use of pertinent information. The boundaries of rational risk taking may be enlarged through better education which imparts knowledge, through the generation and provision of more relevant information that the decision maker can draw upon, and by creating a more favorable attitude toward scientific method. All of these things must be done in India if substantially more favorable attitudes toward risk taking, and more effective risk activity, are to evolve in Indian industry.

Many basically rational persons in countries like India may, for example, expose themselves to typhoid fever by drinking impure water because they are not aware there is a potential connection between disease and water. Here the boundaries of rationality are clearly constrained by lack of knowledge. On the other hand an individual, because of mystical, religious, or other purely emotional forces, may behave irrationally and drink impure water even if he is aware that he may become ill. In a similar manner, many managers and politicians in India take risks that seem highly irrational and strange to Americans. They may take such risks either because they are in fact irrational in their decisions, relying on mysticism, faith, or ideology, or because they lack the knowledge, information, motivation, or skill necessary for adequate evaluation of the risks entailed. In the latter situation, it is also possible that relevant information available may not be utilized because knowledge of its existence is lacking.

A major problem in India is that industrial risk taking at both the macro and micro levels often appears to be irrational. Furthermore, the kind of information needed by industrial firms and their managers for effective planning and decision making is often scarce. Although vast amounts of information are disseminated by the Indian government, much is irrelevant and different agencies often provide dramatically different sets of data on the same topic. Numerous firms which have relied on government development plans, projections, estimates, and other information have run into great difficulties, including bankruptcy. On the other hand, industry is partly to blame for serious information gaps and deficiencies, since it frequently does not provide requested data accurately or in a timely fashion. The progressive and dynamic companies in India that take planning seriously, and which are the most effective risk takers, have to spend much time, effort, and expense on intelligence functions. They must collect and analyze much data which are readily available at a minimum or no cost to firms in U.S. industry. U.S. subsidiaries in India tend to do more of this, and are frequently more effective risk takers than their indigenous counterparts, although there are several notable exceptions. For example, probably no organization in India does a more comprehensive or better job in this regard than the Tata group. In fact, the data collected, analyzed, and made available by Tata is used by thousands of other firms in India, including U.S. companies.

Small firms in India are constrained by the lack of suitable information, as they are not usually in a position to perform their own intelligence function. As a consequence, they are either highly conservative risk takers or poor decision makers in a risk situation.

The second dimension of risk taking pertains to the individual degree of conservatism or aggressiveness. Here individual preferences toward risk taking under comparable conditions can be measured in order to determine general attitude and degree of conservatism or aggressiveness. Research suggests that in terms of managerial effectiveness and industrial progress managers (and other persons) possessing relatively high, but not highly-neurotic, achievement drives, tend to be the best risk takers. They are neither highly conservative nor overly agressive and speculative. They are inclined to undertake moderate, calculated risks which entail some challenge but, at the same time, offer a relatively good chance of payoff and success. Such persons also tend to prefer moderately ambitious operational objectives and plans and are receptive to innovation.

The highly conservative or ultraconservative risk taker is likely to have a low achievement drive, although in many cases such conservatism may be due to non-sociological-cultural factors, such as various economic, political or legal constraints which are operating on him or his firm. The conservative risk taker also usually opposes innovation and expansionary courses of action, and enterprises under this type of management usually remain static.

In India, U.S. subsidiaries appear to be significantly more aggressive — we should probably say less conservative — in their risk-taking attitude and behavior (in most managerial areas) than comparable indigenous firms, although there are a number of notable exceptions. The major reason for this is the types of managers and other personnel that the U.S. companies in India tend to attract. However, the U.S.-based parent companies that we have studied are, without exception, more aggressive in their risk-taking attitude and behavior than their subsidiaries in India.

ATTITUDES TOWARD CHANGE

The initiation and implementation of change — whether it be managerial, technical, economic, legal, political, or social in nature — is essentially a human process. Changes, however large, that are truly *desired* by the people involved can frequently be implemented quite successfully and assimilated with little social disruption. Changes that are not acceptable or desired, even small ones, can be put into effect only at considerable social, personal, and often economic cost.

In industry in any country, including the United States, one often finds considerable resistance to change and innovation at all levels. Regardless of basic environmental differences, people employed in industry resist managerial, technical, and other changes that affect them and their work for a variety of reasons. However, resistance to change in general is much more pervasive and stronger in firms in developing countries than it is in the United States, because of both external and internal environmental conditions, as well as individual personality factors.

As noted earlier, attitudes toward change are closely connected with attitudes involving risk taking and achievement, as well as scientific method and fatalism. And since relatively negative attitudes in these areas prevail in Indian industry, the initiation and implementation of change in the direction of greater efficiency and industrial progress is also greatly retarded. Moreover, Indian managers frequently do not want to undertake change, irrespective of the risks or potential gains entailed, because of personal values, beliefs, habits and customs.

Numerous Indian businessmen have become psychologically and culturally adjusted to stagnation, apathy, poverty, and the status quo in general. Authority is usually highly centralized and consequently there is frequently no flexibility or authority at lower organizational levels which would permit the effective introduction of even relatively minor changes in operations. Top managers constantly blame the "environment" or conditions beyond their control for their failure to initiate and implement changes, even though they may have considerable leeway to do so in numerous instances.

Highly inefficient firms in India have been able to survive and even reap lucrative profits with little or no progressive improvement in operations because of the protected markets in which they have been functioning. However, even when such conditions change, and competitive and other pressures calling for greater efficiency emerge, numerous firms do not effectively respond and merely keep on operating basically as they have been. The result is deteriorating performance and sometimes bankruptcy.

It is certainly true that when change is desired by management it is frequently resisted by union or other enterprise employees. However, enterprise managers in India frequently place too much of the blame on others, rather than on their own attitudes and abilities.

While U.S. firms in India fail to implement many of the changes they plan, they are more likely to carry out changes than are indigenous firms. This does not mean that all of the changes they introduce prove successful or effective. Often the reverse has been true. Sometimes lack of success has been due to "over-Americanization" of practices, policies, or operations. Often when beneficial changes are implemented, they take substantially longer and cost more than would be the case within the U.S. operations of their parent companies.

The U.S.-based operations surveyed usually had fewer difficulties in implementing change, and introduced new ideas more frequently and on a broader front than their subsidiary cousins in India. Where it took a few days to effectively implement a relatively minor change in procedures, methods, or organization in the United States it frequently took several weeks or months to implement similar changes in Indian operations. Similarly, where certain major changes were involved, it often took several years for effective introduction in India, as compared to only a matter of months in the United States. Not infrequently a desired change could not be implemented at a U.S. subsidiary at all, and in many cases a sizable number of U.S. personnel had to be sent over in order to carry out some concepts successfully.

The firms in India most successful in introducing change were more likely to communicate effectively to employees the reasons for the change and its expected benefits. They were also more prone to elicit the participation and opinions of those affected, during both the planning as well as the implementation stages, using committees and meetings for this purpose. Where feasible, they let those personnel directly involved in the successful introduction of change share in resultant productivity gains or economies — and put much patient effort into convincing personnel that their job security was not threatened. At times some even used a "demonstration effect" by relating the desired change to some previous change to prove that it did not offer a threat.

In general, change was viewed in substantial part as a marketing or sales job by managements of the more dynamic, effective, and change-oriented firms in India. The ways in which they handled the implementation of change were dramatically different from the practices of relatively traditional companies which did little if any planning for change.

Illustrative cases

The appendix to this chapter presents four brief case studies involving an interface between U.S. and Indian values. These are introduced here to provide the reader with specific examples of the characteristics we have discussed in this chapter, since it is always more effective to supplement a general discussion with specific illustrations.

CHAPTER 4 FOOTNOTES

1. For an excellent in-depth firsthand study of the mutual modification and accommodation process that took place in an Indian village and a nearby traditional industrial enterprise see J. Elder, *Industrialism in Hindu Society: A Case Study in Social Change*, unpublished doctoral dissertation, Dept. of Social Relations, Harvard University, Cambridge, Mass., 1959. For an excellent sociological study involving the modification process at five indigenous factories in the India city of Poona, see R. Lambert, *Workers, Factories, and Social Change in India*, Princeton University Press, Princeton, N.J., 1963.

2. Cf. R. Farmer, and B. Richman, *Comparative Management and Economic Progress*, Richard D. Irwin, Inc., Homewood, III., 1965, Chap. 7. See also the following unpublished doctoral dissertations; Lauter, *op. cit.,* B. Estafen, *An Empirical Study in Comparative Management: A Study of the Transferability of American Management Policies and Practices to Firms Operating in Chile,* UCLA, Los Angeles, 1967; F. Flores, *The Applicability of American Management Know-How to Developing Countries: Case Studies of Philippine Firms, American Subsidiaries and Affiliates Operating in the Philippines and Their Respective Parent Firms in the United States* UCLA, Los Angeles, 1968; M. Khalie, *Analysis and Evaluation of Some Environmental Constraints on Management in the United Arab Republic,* UCLA, Los Angeles, 1967; A. Papageorge, *Transferability of Management: A Case Study of the United States and Greece,* UCLA, Los Angeles, 1967; A. V. Phatak, *External Environmental Constraints and Their Impact Upon the Internal Operations of Firms in the Pharmaceutical and Engineering Industries in India,* UCLA, Los Angeles, 1966; S. Reksodihardjo, *Skills Investment in a Developing Country: Indonesia,* UCLA, Los Angeles, 1965.

3. E. Hall, *The Silent Language,* Fawcett World Library, New York, 1961, p. 9.

4. *Ibid.,* p. 50.

5. M. Mead, (ed.), *Cultural Patterns and Technical Change,* Mentor Books, New York, 1962, p. 151.

6. *Ibid.,* pp. 17-18.

7. H. W. Kapp, *Hindu Culture, Economic Development, and Economic Planning in India,* Asia Publishing House, Bombay, 1963, pp. 10-11.

8. *Ibid.,* p. 15.

9. *Ibid.,* p. 16.

10. *Ibid.,* p. 60.

11. R. Lambert, *Workers, Factories, and Social Change in India*, Princeton University Press, Princeton, N.J., 1963.

12. Kapp. *op. cit.,* pp. 50ff.

13. G. Litwin, "Some Notes on Motivation Development and Management Education," *The Asian Economic Review,* August 1963, pp. 564-565. The quotation is from *The Geeta,* translated by Pandit Swami, Faber, London, 1935.

14. Mead, *op. cit.*, p. 163.

15. *Ibid.*, p. 164.

16. *Ibid.*, p. 174.

17. *Ibid.*, p. 244.

18. K. Nair, *Blossoms in the Dust*, Cox and Wyman, London, 1961.

19. *Ibid.*, p. 193.

20. Mead, *op. cit.*, p. 175.

21. *Ibid.*, p. 246.

22. *Ibid.*, p. 14.

23. Kapp, *op. cit.*, p. 40.

24. *Ibid.*, p. 64.

25. *Ibid.*

26. Litwin, *op. cit.*, pp. 562-563. Italics are Mr. Litwin's.

27. R. Farmer, "Organizational Transfer and Class Structure," *Journal of the Academy of Management*, September 1966, p. 213.

28. *UNESCO, Report on the World Social Situation*, Paris, March 9, 1961, p. 79.

29. Cf. Farmer and Richman, *op. cit.*, pp. 112ff., and especially the sources cited in footnote 4, p. 113.

30. R. Bhambri, "Myth and Reality About Private Enterprise in India," *World Politics,* January, 1960, p. 186.

31. See D. McClelland, *The Achieving Society*, Von Nostrand, Princeton, 1961, especially Chapter VI; Farmer and Richman, *op. cit.*, pp. 154ff., and especially the references cited in footnote 3, p. 155.

32. McClelland, *op. cit.*, pp. 240ff.

33. Cf., D. Kidder, *Education and Manpower Development in India: Middle Level Manpower,* unpublished doctoral dissertation, MIT, Cambridge, Mass., 1967.

34. See P. Singh, *Essays Concerning Some Types of Entrepreneurship in India,* unpublished doctoral dissertation, University of Michigan, Ann Arbor, Mich., 1963, especially Chapter III.

35. W. Whyte, and L. Williams, "Supervisory Leadership — An International Comparison," *Proceedings of the International Management Congress* (C10S), 1963, pp. 481-488.

36. This framework of analysis was first presented in Farmer and Richman, *op. cit.*, pp. 123ff. It is based largely on the sources cited therein. See also Richman, "Employer and Managerial Attitudes Toward Employees as a Function of Nationality" in T. J. Gordon (ed.) *A Study of Potential Changes in Employee Benefits*, vol. II, Institute for the Future, Middletown, Conn., 1969.

37. For a discussion of Communist countries see the two sources cited in footnote 36 above.

38. See the excellent studies by K. Sreenivasan, *Productivity and Social Environment,* Asia Publishing House, New York, 1964, especially Chapters 4 and 5; and, M. Srinivas, *Caste in Modern India,* Asia Publishing House, Bombay and New York, 1962.

39. Sreenivasan, *op. cit.*, p. 70.

40. Farmer, "Organization Transfer," *op. cit.*, pp. 204-216.

41. See the doctoral dissertations cited in footnote 2 above.

42. See Elder, *op. cit.*

43. See Phatak, *op. cit.*, pp. 80ff.

43. See Phatak, *op. cit.*, pp. 80ff.

44. *The Statesman,* Calcutta, October 29, 1965 from *Ministry of Labour Gazette,* Great Britain, October 28, 1965.

45. *Indian Labour Journal,* January 1967, p. 22, and January 1968, p. 38.

46. McClelland, *op. cit.*, p. 105.

47. See *Ibid.,* especially Chapters 6 and 7; D. McClelland, and D. Winter, *Motivating Economic Achievement,* The Free Press, New York, 1969; J. Atkinson, "Motivational Determinants of Risk Taking Behavior, *Psychology Review,* LXIV (1957), p. 359ff; J. Atkinson, J. Bastian, R. Earl and G. Litwin, "The Achievement Motive, Goal Setting, and Probability Preference," *Journal of Abnormal Social Psychology,* LX, 1960, pp. 27-36; H. Green, and R. Knapp, "Time Judgment, Aesthetic Preference, and the Need for Achievement," *Journal of Abnormal Social Psychology,* LVIII, 1959, pp. 140ff.

48. See M. Weber, *The Protestant Ethic and the Spirit of Capitalism,* translated by Talcott Parsons, Charles Scribner and Sons, New York, 1948.

49. Cf. P. Tawney, *Religion and the Rise of Capitalism,* Peter Smith Co., Gloucester, Mass., 1962, pp. 110ff., and A. Hyma, "The Economic Views of the Protestant Reformers," in *Protestantism and Capitalism,* D. C. Heath and Co., Boston, Mass., 1959, pp. 94-106.

50. See McClelland, *op. cit.,* pp. 357ff., J. Gaheen, M. Srinwas, D. Karve and M. Singer, "India's Cultural Values and Economic Development," *Economic Development and Cultural Change,* VII, October, 1958, pp. 1-12; K. Sundaram, "Social and Human Problems in Introducing Technological Change," in *C105 Proceedings, op. cit.,* pp. 497ff.

51. Cf., B. Richman, *Management Development and Education in the Soviet Union,* Institute for International Business and Economic Development Studies, Michigan State University, East Lansing, Mich., 1967, and B. Richman, *Industrial Society in Communist China,* Random House, New York, 1969.

52. See the studies and findings presented in McClelland, *op. cit.,* pp. 252-266, 276-280.

53. *Ibid.,* see also, C. Mahone, "Fear of Failure and Unrealistic Vocational Aspirations," *Journal of Abnormal Psychology,* No. 60, 1960, pp. 253ff.

54. McClelland, *op. cit.,* pp. 255ff., S. Lipset and R. Bendix, *Social Mobility in Industrial Society,* University of California Press, Berkeley and Los Angeles, 1959, pp. 134ff.

55. Cf. E. Hagen, *On The Theory of Social Change,* Dorsey Press, Homewood, Ill., 1962; C. Savage, *Social Reorganization in a Factory in the Andes,* Cornell University, Ithaca, N.Y., The Society for Applied Anthropology, 1964.

56. See the studies and evidence cited in McClelland, 1961, *op. cit.,* pp. 340-356, 415. See also B. Rosen, and R. D'Androde, "The Psychosocial Origins of Achievement Motivation, *Sociometry,* 1959, 22, pp. 185-218.

57. See McClelland and Winter, *op. cit.,* D. McClelland, "Achievement Motivation Can Be Developed," *Harvard Business Review,* Nov.-Dec., 1965, pp. 6ff.

58. We have drawn on the following pertinent sources in our discussion and analysis of India's caste system and social structure in general. Sreenivasan, *op. cit.,* Srinwas, *op. cit.,* Lambert, *op. cit.,* Knapp, *op. cit.,* Elder, *op. cit.,* M. D. Morris, "Caste and the Evolution of the Industrial Workforce in India," *Proceedings of the American Philosophical Society,* 1960, Vol. 104, pp. 124-133; E. Dower, "Caste and Occupational Structure in Central India," *Journal of Social Forces,* October 1962, pp. 26ff; S. Jain, The Man in the Grey Flannel Achkan, *"Columbia Journal of World Business,"* Vol. 1, No. 4, Fall, 1966; A. Agarwala, "Management of Big Business in India," *The Indian Journal of Public Administration,* April-June, 1962, pp. 178ff., U. Pareek and T. Maulik, "Sociometric Study of a North Indian Village," *International Journal of*

Sociometrics, III, 1963, pp. 7ff; C. Vakil, "Business Leadership in Underdeveloped Countries," *Industrialization and Productivity,* No. 2, 1959, pp. 46-51; B. Nair, *The Dynamic Brahmin,* Popular Book Depot, Bombay, 1959.

59. Sreenivasan, *op. cit.,* pp. 76-78.

60. See especially Lambert, *op. cit.,* Elder, *op. cit.,* Morris, *op. cit.,* Dower, *op. cit.,* Sreenwasan, *op. cit.,* and Pareek and Maulik, *op. cit.*

61. Kidder, *op. cit.,* Chapter 2.

62. See Sreenivasan, *op. cit.,* pp. 64-65.

63. See also Phatak, *op. cit.,* pp. 155ff.

APPENDIX   CASE STUDIES INVOLVING
U.S.-INDIAN COLLABORATION

In this appendix four examples are presented in which "outsiders," in these cases American experts employed by Indian controlled companies, attempt to improve performance. They highlight the point that basic differences in attitudes, values, motives, and perceptions between foreign experts and indigenous managers make it difficult for the former to bring about substantial changes and improvements. Furthermore where local personnel do not actively cooperate it is unlikely that substantial improvements will be forthcoming.

Unfortunately, none of the experiences presented here have met with much success. However, this should by no means be viewed as a general argument against American collaboration with locally controlled firms in developing countries. Later in the book we will show that majority or even 100 percent U.S. ownership of a firm does not guarantee success, while collaborative ventures involving minority or even no U.S. equity ownership can be successful. However, the following cases do highlight the importance of sociological-cultural factors, especially in determining what collaborative efforts to engage in and how to choose local partners.

THE USE OF A RESIDENT CONSULTANT AT A LARGE ENGINEER-
ING COMPANY CONTROLLED BY AN INDIAN HOLDING COMPANY

This case actually began in 1965. At that time, Mr. B., an enlightened younger member of a large, family-controlled, Indian managing agency (holding company), decided he wanted to hire an American management specialist to modernize and improve the management of a large Calcutta-based multiplant engineering company for which he was responsible. The American expert would serve as a resident consultant for a minimum of two years. If this experiment proved successful it would be repeated at various other companies in the group.

A first-rate M.B.A. candidate was approached upon his graduation in June, 1966. This person had work experience in a similar company in the United States, and had also been an officer in the military. He was about 30 years of age. The company paid for a trip to India in the spring of 1966 where he met Mr. B. with some of the key managers of the engineering firm.

He decided to take the job and his terms were met. He signed a two-year contract which could be extended if he and the managing agency executive agreed. He was supposed to join the company in the summer of 1966, but he did not arrive until November. Indian-government red tape was largely responsible for this delay, but key executives of the firm also dragged their feet in various ways. The company president and vice-president were basically opposed to the idea from the outset. They felt the American was unfamiliar with Indian conditions, having never been to India before 1966, and that this would greatly limit his usefulness. They also felt he was too young and inexperienced to handle the job, and apparently also that he was being greatly overcompensated. They were worried about disruptions and their own status in the organization, and unclear about the role he was to play. In this regard, it was never clearly defined who he would report to until after he arrived. It was then decided that he would report to Mr. B. at the managing agency, would act as a consultant to the firm's top management, and would have to have their approval to implement changes.

Following his arrival in November, 1966, the American spent two or three months in familiarizing himself with the company. In February, 1967, the president of the company asked him to build an export-marketing organization and collect pertinent data in this area. This project was completed in 2½ months, and management admitted that some useful information and a few new ideas were derived from it.

In April, the American suggested that a team of four new graduates be hired from the Indian Institute of Management in Calcutta, and that it should contain individuals with backgrounds in inventory management, marketing, cost accounting, and personnel management. These were the areas in which the company needed most attention and improvement. The graduates would work as consultants, reporting to him, and if they proved effective they would stay on permanently with the company.

Management was not receptive to this proposal, but at the insistence of the American supported by Mr. B., it was finally accepted. Four graduates were hired, all with prior work experience in industry. The vice-president had final hiring approval. However, he felt strongly the new employees were to be paid too much — even though many of the IIM graduates had been getting similar pay. He and the president also felt that the new employees did not have adequate experience to be consultants. They were opposed to outside consultants in principle, anyway. They also felt that serious internal problems and friction would be created by bringing in young and inexperienced consultants who were to be paid more than many of the older managerial personnel. Their view was that young people should be assigned to specific jobs, that they should be trained only in connection with those jobs, and that good managers who move ahead tend to evolve without much, if any, formal planning or conscious development.

The graduates joined the company in June, 1967. Following their arrival, the American conducted bi-monthly seminars, lasting about seven months, for them and for eight department heads. The seminars covered such topics as general management, marketing, and cost accounting. None of the production managers ever attended these seminars nor did the vice-president. The president attended one. The American manager circulated articles and other printed materials to the seminar participants.

In August, 1967, two of the graduates were assigned to an inventory and costing project at one of the larger plants. They worked on inventory and control, cost analysis, information and reporting systems, and various other problems.

They finished the project in November. Few of their recommendations were implemented, and most of those that were did not remain in effect for very long. Management indicated that this was the least successful of all the projects involving the American or the graduates. The two men moved to another plant to undertake a similar project, but it never got off the ground. Top management admits that the plant managers did not cooperate with them.

One of the graduates was assigned to a sales and market analysis project focusing on a company product line that was faced with strong competition. The project involved an analysis of the sales organization, an appraisal of sales personnel, and the design of forms and information-feedback systems for sales depots, customers, and field salesmen. Management felt that this project was the most successful, although far from a complete success. Because of this project, some new sales personnel were hired, some organizational changes made, and improvements which were made in sales information and reporting systems facilitated somewhat faster and better decisions. However, many of the changes desired by the American were not implemented, and again, most of those that were either did not remain in effect for very long, or were not implemented very effectively.

Moreover, some of the personnel that the American thought should be hired, or assigned to various sales positions, were not hired or assigned. In fact a serious conflict arose because the American wanted to hire a marketing director whom he felt had outstanding qualifications, but the vice-president refused. Mr. B. backed the American, but the vice-president appealed to Mr. B.'s uncle, who was his senior and wielded greater power in the managing agency. The uncle was not directly involved with this company, but he was able to overrule his nephew and the American. The vice-president had previously worked for many years as this uncle's personal secretary. It is not clear what the president's role was in this case, but apparently he was involved in a power struggle with the vice-president. The American believed that the latter wielded more real power, and that the power struggle greatly hindered his own effectiveness.

The fourth IIM graduate worked on a project to modify existing personnel forms and design some new ones for job applications, recruiting, selection, and personnel appraisal. Management has made use of several of these forms and derived some benefits from them. However, some of them were discarded or ignored after a while. In general, the effective use of these forms has been hindered by various sociological-cultural factors bearing on the personnel function.

All of the above projects ended by mid-January, 1968, except the marketing project. By that time, the American had decided to leave before his two-year contract was up, and the graduates had decided that they, too, wanted to leave. During the following months all of them divided their time between working or the marketing project and trying to get other jobs. By June, 1969, all had left the company.

The president wanted to keep the marketing graduate and offered to make him a sales branch manager. But this graduate left suddenly in mid-May to take a position with another company in which Mr. B. was involved.

There appear to be a number of critical underlying reasons for the lack of success in this case, in addition to those indicated specifically. They revolve around basic differences in values, attitudes, motivation, and interests between the American expert and company management.

The American felt that much greater attention should be given to clear-cut formal organization, job descriptions, compensation based on the formal requirements of the job, ability, performance, and contribution to the company. Management gave much more emphasis to the informal organization and subjective factors. The president and vice-president felt that the effective delegation and execution of authority must be based on status, long experience, seniority, loyalty, trust, charisma, and various other subjective factors, with formal authority or position playing a secondary role. Their view of merit, ability, effective performance, and contribution differed significantly from that of the American. They also felt the American had a faulty notion regarding what motivates Indian personnel. In this connection they felt he placed far too much emphasis on material incentives, and far too little on job security, personal loyalty, inherent obligation, and status not necessarily connected with income.

When incompetent employees are shifted to lesser jobs, the company's policy has been to pay them the same salary as before; generally, however, they are allowed to remain in the same job. And management has also been reluctant to get rid of personnel who turn out to be ineffective in their jobs if they have been with the company for a considerable length of time. In these areas, too, there was much difference in opinion and attitudes between the American expert and company management.

U.S. MANAGERS SENT TO A JOINT VENTURE COMPANY WITH INDIAN MAJORITY CONTROL

This case concerns a medium-sized engineering company in Calcutta. The firm was founded in 1956 by Mr. R., who was the sole owner until 1960 when shares were issued to the Indian public. Several of his personal friends became major shareholders, although he remained in control with 50.3 percent of the outstanding stock and continued as managing director.

Until 1960, the company had engaged only in trade, including exports and imports. It had been quite profitable during this period since R. was an aggressive, energetic, and effective salesman with much personal influence and many important contacts. At the end of the 1950s he decided to go into manufacturing in the heavy engineering sector, and secured some small "educational" orders from the government to build railway wagons.

The firm began commercial production of wagons during the 1961-62 fiscal year, and by 1962 was also involved in structural fabrication work, as well as the manufacture of forgings, stampings, and pressing equipment. But government wagon orders continued to be the company's major business.

The company operated at large losses every year since it went into manufacturing. The chief reason for this was Mr. R.'s poor management and irrational decision making. Although he was a good sales entrepreneur, he knew very little about the management of complex manufacturing organizations, and he clearly did not have an aptitude for this kind of work.

In 1963 or early 1964, Mr. R. interested a leading American industrialist in the prospect of investing in his company in order to put it on a profitable basis. The American was a personal friend whom he had met through an international young presidents association. Serious negotiations for a joint venture began in early 1964.

A collaboration agreement was signed in July, 1964, not only with this American industrialist who had many diversified business interests, but also with a large West German company. The agreement took effect in the spring of 1965. Under this agreement the U.S. collaborator obtained 34 percent ownership and the German 7 percent; Mr. R. maintained 29 percent, and the Indian public 30 percent. Through the other Indian shareholders who were personal friends, Mr. R. was assured of maintaining control. The U.S. collaborator obtained the right to nominate three directors to a board of ten, and the German firm one director.

Both the U.S. and German collaborators entered this venture not only because of the profits they hoped to derive from existing operations, but also because they wished to eventually enter the steel-pipe manufacturing business. Mr. R. had secured the first government license for the establishment of this kind of industry. The U.S. collaborator was also interested in entering the housing construction business in India in the future, and he felt this venture with Mr. R. was the best way to pursue this goal.

As part of this agreement, the U.S. industrialist made it clear that an American financial controller and production manager would be provided by him, since these were the two weakest areas. These men would actually run the company, although they would officially report to R. who would remain as managing director. R. would devote his time largely to sales, new business, government and public relations, and would become involved in other areas only when major policy decisions were concerned.

With the endorsement of its U.S. collaborator the company was able to obtain a substantial AID (Cooley) loan in July 1965, part of which was supposed to be used in the future for the proposed steel-pipe project. Prior to securing this loan the company had been virtually insolvent.

The American financial controller, who had been involved in the initial negotiations, joined the Indian company in early 1965, before the agreement officially went into effect. An American production manager with considerable work experience in India joined the firm in May, 1965. And a U.S. engineer assigned to work on planning the housing venture was sent to the company in October, 1965.

Although R. never really relinquished his operating authority, and continued to make unilateral and often poor decisions according to the Americans, the American managers were able to function without excessive interference until about March, 1966. There were, however, constant conflicts stemming largely from basic differences in values and objectives, which the Americans believed hindered their effectiveness. In spite of this, they were able to make major changes and improvements in management and operations.

Without going into detail, some of the significant improvements and changes they made included the following:

1. Better overall planning and control, including the introduction of contingency planning.
2. Vastly improved and increased training within the firm.
3. Employment of new technical personnel, foremen, and supervisors.
4. Changes in personnel practices and staffing policies.
5. Implementation of cost accounting, cost control, information, and reporting systems.
6. Major improvements in production, procurement, inventory, and financial management.
7. Design of an integrated budgeting system. (This was never fully implemented.)

These improvements led to significant increases in operating efficiency and better overall performance during the 1965-66 fiscal year, ending in March. Utilization of plant capacity improved, and wagon production for the fiscal year increased by about 25 percent over the preceding year, reaching an all-time company high of 85 units in February 1966. Plant shutdowns, strikes, and labor problems in general, were greatly reduced and productivity rose substantially. Material wastage decreased and efficient use of scrap metals saved the company much money since it was able to reduce its purchases of high-cost supplies from the open or black markets. Sales increased by about 20 percent. The cost of goods sold, and net loss in relation to sales, improved, as did gross profit in relation to sales, and sales in relation to total assets. Although the company still showed a large loss, it was only about half of what it had been the previous year.

Then in March 1966, the situation changed drastically. For unexplainable reasons Mr. R., the managing director, assumed full operating control of the company. He began to make numerous decisions, some of which proved disastrous for the firm, without even informing the American managers. For example, in March he decided to reduce the labor force and factory administrative staff by 35 percent overnight. Wagon production fell by more than 50 percent that month as compared to February.

On April 1, 1966, the American production manager resigned, under great pressure from Mr. R. The American housing engineer resigned a few weeks later, and the financial controller several months later. Apparently Mr. R. convinced his American industrialist friend who sent these managers that many of the problems facing the company were due to their mismanagement.

Somehow, the company managed to stay in business during the 1966-67 fiscal year, although losses grew even larger. The company stopped all production in 1968, and declared bankruptcy in either late December of that year, or in early January 1969. A sharp cutback in government wagon orders and the general economic recession during 1967-68 greatly hurt the company. However, it is highly unlikely that the company would have been able to survive for long, even if these other events did not take place.

By the summer of 1969, Mr. R. was the custodian in the company's trusteeship and AID officials were evaluating the firm's assets in order to salvage part of its loan. Shareholders will get nothing.

THE USE OF AMERICAN EXPERTS AT AN INDIAN CONTROL-LED CHEMICAL COMPANY WITH MINORITY U.S. OWNERSHIP

This case involves a highly capital-intensive chemical company which produces a homogeneous product. It is a new firm with a modern plant. A large American chemical company owns 40 percent, a traditional Indian family owns 31 percent, and the other 29 percent is owned by the Indian public. Many of the biggest outside shareholders are close friends of the family, and this has insured that control remains in its hands.

The family member who has been running this company, Mr. L., is a highly traditional Indian manager. He does not believe in formal organization patterns. He rules largely through fear, and personal loyalty and obligation. He constantly undermines the authority — and status — of his subordinate managers by encouraging personnel at all levels to come to him with their problems, often even to his home. All of the managers, engineers, and staff specialists, as well as many of the workers, are either relatives, close family friends, or members of families which have close ties with Mr. L.'s family. The company has employed between 270 and 380 persons in recent years.

Mr. L. reserves even the most trivial decisions for himself. For example, he makes sure that the restrooms, canteen and ping-pong tables are orderly and arranged to his liking. He checks frequently on the guards, janitors, work-clothes menders and other menial service personnel, as well as the production workers. At the same time, major operating problems go unresolved since no one else has the authority, or wants to take the initiative or responsibility to deal with them. The company has no management development or effective training programs, and virtually no planning or control systems. Instead of instituting continuous preventive maintenance, Mr. L. shuts down the plant entirely every once in a while for several weeks, and everything is then checked out, and repaired if necessary.

This manager's main goal seems to be the maintenance of his status as undisputed king of his small empire, and to have people dependent on him for their needs. To this end, he dispenses largess as long as his employees show unquestioning obedience, and at least outward gratitude.

The company has been making a fairly good profit. Mr. L. draws a lucrative salary and derives many benefits from the company, including a good home, an imported car, servants, and paid vacations. However, it should be noted that it was not difficult to earn good profits in this industry since its product has enjoyed a highly protected sellers' market, most of the raw materials come from a nearly adjacent plant, and the product is used by only a few large firms in a single industry.

The American company has been concerned that profits have not been nearly as large as they could be. It has also been concerned about the possibility of newly-emerging competition that may place this firm in an unhealthy position if it does not improve its efficiency considerably. Labor productivity has been only 25 to 40 percent of that of the home plants of the U.S. collaborator, and the Indian company has been overstaffed well beyond the point of diminishing returns. Equipment efficiency has also been considerably lower. The unit cost-per-ton of output has been more than three times higher at the Indian plant. Higher material costs have accounted for a good part of this difference, but low productivity, relatively high overheads, and low operating efficiency in general have also been major contributors.

On a number of occasions, the American company has provided experts to try to improve the management, operations, and efficiency of the Indian firm. Few of their recommendations have been implemented effectively. Where the experts did succeed in raising efficiency, effects were short-lived. The U.S. company has apparently decided that it no longer pays to try to improve the Indian firm's management by sending over experts.

EXPERTS SENT BY AN AMERICAN COMPANY WITH A LICENSE AGREEMENT WITH AN INDIAN CHEMICAL AND DRUG FIRM

This final case involves a family-owned and fairly small Indian company which produces chemical products and a few pharmaceutical items. This company has had a license agreement with a medium-sized U.S. company that produces basically identical products. Prior to this agreement, the U.S. firm had been exporting its products to India.

The U.S. firm has permitted the use of its brand name, and has provided formulae and technical know-how. It also designed and helped install the Indian plant, assisted in procuring necessary equipment, trained a number of key people, and provided various standard procedures such as controls over product quality, methods of identifying and reporting rejects, and a standard cost system. In return it receives a royalty based on gross sales. The licensee is required to submit operating data to the U.S. firm, which is used for the purpose of trouble shooting.

While the U.S. firm has not been directly concerned about profitability per se, it has been concerned that operations run efficiently. It maintains a check on the quality of production by requiring the Indian plant to send samples of output to the United States for periodic inspection. The controls the licensor has had over the Indian plant have served a critical purpose with regard to protecting the company's product image, and in sales promotion. Since the inception of this license agreement, the U.S. company has been sending experts to the Indian company periodically. Originally they focused primarily on technical problems. But as time passed they became increasingly involved with managerial matters.

Serious and constant managerial problems have plagued the operation. These internal problems have been similar in many respects to those discussed in the preceding cases, and they have stemmed largely from sociological, cultural, and motivational factors.

Labor productivity at the Indian company has averaged only about 15 percent of what it has been at the U.S. company. The average total wage cost-per-unit of output is similar to the U.S. operation, even though wages are much higher at the U.S. company. Reject rates have been eight to nine times higher at the Indian plant. Output has consistently fallen below target, and cost goals have been exceeded consistently and substantially. The plant has been operating at only 20 to 30 percent of its designed (and licensed) capacity.

Sales have been far below forecasts and expectations. Although the company had made a profit during the initial years of the license agreement, in recent years it has operated either very close to the break-even point or at a loss. Environmental factors largely beyond the control of management have contributed to the Indian firm's poor performance; but internal managerial deficiencies have also been key factors. The U.S. company has been at a loss about what to do.

CHAPTER 5
POLITICAL-LEGAL
ENVIRONMENT

INTRODUCTION

Productive enterprises operate in environments in which legal and political factors directly affect their internal operations. A given law, or a political event, can cause firms to change the manner in which various critical elements of the management process are performed and, hence, directly affect productive efficiency.

The formal political and legal systems of a country are often the most easily identifiable of the important institutions which affect the management and operations of business enterprises. The nature of these institutions requires that their basic formal structures be described explicitly. A notable exception can be found in a number of traditional Arab countries, such as Saudi Arabia, where there is relatively little codification of the law. There are few clear-cut legal precedents, and rules are derived largely from Sharia (Moslem religious law).

For the foreign company, two common pitfalls related to the political-legal environment exist. The first is the assumption, based largely on conditions in most developed nations in the West, that the systems actually function as formally described. This may be far from the reality, and actual implementation or enforcement may differ greatly from what was intended by the written code. Law enforcement may be weak or corrupt. Political agencies may function in a highly inefficient manner and in ways very different from the intentions of "founding Fathers." These conditions are not peculiar to developing nations by any means, but the probability of encountering them on a substantial scale in less-developed countries is considerably higher than in advanced economies.

The second pitfall lies in the tendency common among businessmen to apply "universal" values of "right" and "wrong," or "logical" and "illogical." Such assumptions, usually derived from the cultures of home environments, may be at odds with local values incorporated in the political and legal institutions. The decision maker who relies on his instinct or intuition may thrust himself into dangerous situations. It is therefore vital that managers in both parent firms and subsidiaries make a special effort to familiarize themselves with both the structure and the actual workings of the local legal and political systems.

Typically, large numbers of managerial decisions must be made on the spot. In many situations, a manager cannot afford to delay his decision until he has studied its political or legal implications. He must instinctively incorporate these factors in the decision-making process. He must also know which decisions have major political or legal implications. In one environment certain situations may have none, while in another, the same situations may have many. Consequently, the manager must acquaint himself with the local political-legal environment to ensure that his decisions fit local conditions.

Political elements, extremely important in most developing countires, frequently exert greater influence on daily life than they do in more developed nations. Many developing nations are newly-formed, have not yet established firm political foundations, and are attempting to progress towards economic well-being through very delicate structures of power blocks. Existing governments may have precarious toeholds and are often involved in desperate fights for their very existence. Consequently, the survival motive often plays an important role in political decision making. Firms which operate in such environments must be fully cognizant of the impact which political considerations can have on operations and the paths which must be taken to secure operating needs of the firm. Short-range considerations may often suggest close alliances between companies and political groups or figures, while long-run considerations require companies to maintain political neutrality. Companies which become associated with a particular political group, or even an individual politician or government official, often find that their fortunes are completely subject to the vagaries of politics.

In developing nations, knowledge of the political and legal structure may be critical for survival. The effective manager needs this knowledge because his previous experiences may not supply him with the cues and guidance required to deal with a new environment. Furthermore, in developing nations, where relatively small — by U.S. standards — subsidiary firms cannot afford (or cannot find) adequate numbers of competent corporate legal advisors or political analysts, it is necessary that each individual manager be conversant with the legal and political systems, and that he be able to relate them to his own specific needs and requirements.

Finally, the governments of many developing nations make a wide range of corporate decisions which managers make for themselves in the United States. In India these include key decisions involving what to produce, where, how, how much, and for whom; what to change for output; when, where, and how much to invest; how much to import; and what is a reasonable return on investment.

This chapter explores those features of India's political-legal environment which exert a significant impact on industrial management and development.[1] It illustrates the importance of knowledge in this sphere for the effective conduct of enterprise operations. While we focus on India, our treatment has broad implications for management and economic development in most other developing countries, even though the political-legal environments of every nation will differ.

RELEVANT LEGAL RULES OF THE GAME

The legal structure within a nation is composed of a complex set of rules which delineate and control the relationships of various individuals and groups toward one another. These rules usually embody the moral and ethical values of the society, thereby formalizing patterns of behavior consistent with these values. They also attempt to clarify definitions and specify communications channels. In this section we will be concerned primarily with those areas which affect the operations of industrial enterprises.

Legal systems have both formal and informal dimensions. The formal aspects relate to procedures and court decisions which act as or influence legal interpretations. The informal elements relate to practices and tend to modify the system's actual functions from the formal or theoretical pattern. For example, certain laws, although on the records, may never be enforced. Another division within many legal systems involves domestic-international dimensions. Domestic legislation may deal with such subjects as wages and welfare benefits for workers, or contractual arrangements between buyers and sellers. On the international side, it may treat the establishment of licensing arrangements or the number and types of foreign materials a company can employ. In this section our interest is in domestic law. Its international dimension will be covered elsewhere.

We are primarily concerned with the impact of the legal system in three areas: company management; labor (including labor-management relations); and corporate relationships to external parties (e.g., suppliers and customers).

An Overview of the Indian Legal Environment and Some Significant Managerial Implications

The legal environment of India today is an amalgam of Western (largely British) legal jurisprudence and Indian values. The court system is largely based on the British pattern, and many statutes are drawn from British, United States, and other Western systems. However, a large number of Indian laws have been designed specifically to fit the Indian environment or to reflect typically Indian values and cultural patterns. The legal system, far from being in a rudimentary state, is highly developed, well institutionalized, and very active. However, great gaps between the formal and informal elements of the system cause major divergence between theory and practice. Law enforcement agencies (i.e., those concerned with supervising or enforcing the legislation applicable to the conduct of business) are frequently poorly staffed and organized, and often the people employed are poorly trained to handle their functions. Salaries for most jobs are low. In many instances, the required enforcement agencies have not been established.

In many situations the enforcement of laws enacted by the central government is left to individual state and local agencies. The constitution of India specifically relegates much of the control of industrial activity to individual states. However, law enforcement efforts at the state and local levels vary widely.

In a real sense, India's system is radical in avowed principle, but conservative in practice. This results in the enactment of many laws, frequently for purposes of appeasement of varying community forces, which are not effectively enforced. Gradualism and inaction in terms of implementation have frequently been used to safeguard vested interests and maintain the existing social order. Lack of vigorous enforcement is reflected in such general social spheres as the caste system and the prohibition of alcohol.

Within developing countries discrepancies between the formal and informal legal structures frequently lead to a major legal defect. Laws are passed to achieve some desired end, and if the laws do not accomplish their intended purpose, legislators typically respond in one of three ways. They may emphasize enforcement and take special measures to provide for or improve enforcement agencies. They may reexamine the law to make sure that it has actually been designed in such a manner as to meet its objectives, and modify or eliminate it as their study directs. Finally, they may add further legislation to plug loopholes and deal with the problems which still remain.

In developing nations legislative bodies frequently experience difficulties in dealing with the administrative mechanisms necessary to make laws work. They often overlook the first two legislative alternatives and concentrate solely on adding new legislation to bolster the failings of current laws. Instead of looking at the informal system, they focus on the formal and assume that problems exist because existing legislation is inadequate or has too many loopholes. This attitude reflects the backgrounds of many legislators in developing countries. They are people of substantial intellectual capacity but extremely limited administrative (and especially industry-oriented) experience.

When the legal system starts to break down, the passage of further legislation often spreads inefficient enforcement mechanisms even more thinly, which in turn leads to greater defeat of the stated intention of the law. In its turn, this results in legislative frustrations, and the process can degenerate into a type of vindictive punishment aimed at the sector concerned. Industrial firms then become frustrated by the legal red tape and restrictions, and defensive reaction mechanisms burst forth. Each party tends to develop a type of paranoia in which it is convinced that the other is uncooperative and primarily concerned with persecution, or illegal practices. This syndrome often leads to breakdown in enforcement agencies and the refusal of business organizations to comply with legislation without the threat of enforcement. By the time the cycle has run its full course the legislation often bears no relation to its originally stated purpose and has become onerous to all parties, as well as a hindrance to social and economic progress.

An example of this pattern in India can be found in the legislation concerned with the control of pharmaceutical products. Although the nation has a central (federal) drug control act, enforcement is the constitutional responsibility of the various states. The majority of Indian states, however, have not established appropriate agencies to enforce the legislation. In most of those which have, the drug control organizations are poorly staffed and cannot effectively handle their administrative burdens. The drug controller of one of the more progressive states in this respect has complained that the only firms he can supervise adequately are those which already essentially comply with the law. He does not have the trained manpower he needs to ferret out the many small companies which do not file required reports and which do not meet legal standards. The legislature, however, reacts to problems which still exist in the environment, and every additional piece of legislation passed makes filing more difficult for legitimate companies, and, by additionally burdening the enforcement agencies, makes it less likely that they will be able to deal with the true problem areas. Thus, the impact which such legislation is supposed to have is completely reversed.

Once legislators begin to experience frustration as a result of failure of laws to accomplish their intended purposes, almost anything can happen. A few years ago, in India, it was decided "once and for all" to put an end to the selling of spurious drug products in chemists' shops. To achieve this purpose, legislation was introduced to require the courts to impose a minimum mandatory term of one-year imprisonment for any chemist in whose shop a spurious product was found. The intention was to make the penalty so severe that chemists who were purposely selling bad drug products would give up the practice. On the other hand, the majority of chemists, reputable and honest men, would have been subject to mandatory imprisonment if, by mistake, such products found their way into their shops. Given the distribution system existent in India, the likelihood of such events is not remote. As part of the "paranoid pattern," the chemists fought the law (which was never enacted) on the grounds that they would now be susceptible to unethical pressures from drug inspectors.

Another example of this syndrome was the passage of a law a few years ago requiring that certain vitamin preparations be stored in areas which were cooler than 25 degrees centigrade (i.e., air-conditioned). This law was passed at the same time that many Indian cities, for lack of power, required all business establishments to turn off air-conditioning units which were not essential. Furthermore, few chemists shops were air-conditioned. In addition, many of the specified products were transported to the shops by government-owned rail. Yet at that time there were no refrigerated or air-conditioned cars available to move such items.

The intent of this legislation was to force manufacturers to reformulate their vitamin products so that they better survived (in terms of longer shelf life) the heat conditions of India. Again, the legislation derived largely from the frustration of legislators with respect to eliminating what they believed to be an evil (i.e., vitamin products of reduced potency). Regardless of the merits of the issue, the result placed the pressure on the retailer rather than on the manufacturer, where it was intended to be directed. Furthermore, arguments were made that most of the deterioration of the product occurred in transport — over a railway system owned and operated by the government. Yet legislators ignored the possibility that the problem might be somewhat alleviated by improving the transportation system, and the railways received none of their attention.

[Legislation relating to the industrial sector in India causes many conflicts which hinder effective enforcement. For example, one law requires housing to be provided near the plant for a certain proportion of the work force whenever companies above a certain size establish new plants. However, in numerous cases local zoning laws prohibit residential housing within reasonable distances of the plant sites. ⅃

Another informal impediment to law enforcement in many developing nations is corruption. Although there are many countries which have more severe problems, corruption is extensive in India. It is common for companies to extend bribes to factory inspectors, financial agencies, tax auditors, customs and police officials, other firms, union leaders, government personnel, and politicians. The low salaries paid to such "enforcers" contribute largely to such behavior. Over an extended time, informal price systems have evolved in many sections of the country regarding the payments to be made for various kinds of legal violations that go unreported, and such practices have eventually come to be viewed as socially acceptable.

While foreign firms in India do engage in such activities, the practice seems to be significantly more widespread among indigenous companies. The foreign companies are subject to closer government scrutiny, and this encourages them to adhere more closely to the laws than local companies. Furthermore, many of parent corporations discourage illegal activity by their subsidiaries. Often foreign subsidiaries encounter substantial competitive disadvantages as a result.

Some large American corporations have decided against establishing operations in India, largely because of its legal environment. Labor legislation in particular has been an area of concern. A number of American companies which decided to set up subsidiaries in India did so only after top management became convinced that many laws on the books were not enforced and were unlikely to be enforced in the future.

Basic Laws Relating to Company Management, Organization, and Control

One of the most important factors affecting the establishment and organization of companies in India is the national planning process. Since 1951 government plans have been drawn up to direct the emphasis of growth and development of various sections within the total economy. These plans have imposed a number of legal, as well as economic and political constraints on industrial activity within the nation.

India's history of planned government control goes back to the first industrial policy resolution in 1948. This resolution stated India's belief in a mixed economy (i.e., both private and government-controlled) and named a series of industries in which planning and regulation were believed to be in the national interest. This was followed in 1951 by the Industries (development and regulation) Act. The act, which has since been amended to cover all but relatively small firms, gave the government the power to regulate and control several dozen industries for which planned growth was deemed in the national interest. Companies covered by the act were required to obtain government licenses for new products, expansion of capacity, and new plant construction and equipment purchases. The government was also granted the investigative powers to look into the working of any industry or particular plant.

In 1956 a second industrial policy resolution was announced. It gave greater emphasis to the rapid development of the industrial economy (vis-a-vis agriculture), and the state decided to assume the exclusive responsibility for the development of a larger number of industries than those included in the first resolution. Industries were classified into three categories: those to be run exclusively by the government, those in which mixed sectors would be permitted, and those to be run by private interest. The resolution also reaffirmed the equality, in the eyes of the government, of public and private units in mixed sectors of the economy. Within those industrial policy resolutions, five-year plans were specifically designed to meet the goals established for the various stages of economic development through which India was mvoing.

In addition to requiring companies to obtain licenses for establishing new operations, expansion, obtaining foreign exchange and imports, and introducing new products, the government has also passed a number of specific laws regulating individual industrial sectors. Perhaps the laws relating to the pharmaceutical industry are among the most extensive. These provide industrial controls ranging from licensing of manufacturing and retail units to the establishment of quality controls and the specification of company reporting procedures.

The Companies Act, passed in 1956 and amended numerous times since, governs procedures for incorporation of firms and their subsequent regulation. It provides for two types of firms: public limited and private limited. A private limited firm has a limited number of shareholders and may restrict share transferability. A public limited firm may not have transferability restrictions and must have a larger number of shareholders. Under this act, companies must obtain approval for their names, their articles of association, their objectives, and so forth. They must register, establish a board of directors and submit periodic reports. The act also covers maximum compensation levels for managerial personnel and establishes titles for executives who manage the company. In essence, the incorporation of companies is performed by the central government rather than by individual states.

The Capital Issues (control) Act of 1947 provides that no company incorporated in India can issue capital without the central government's consent. The same applies to any companies incorporated outside of India but operating within the country with respect to capital issues in India. Again, the reason for this is to ensure that new projects fit in with the five-year planning documents.

The Indian constitution provides that no one shall be deprived of his private property except by authority of law. One amendment to the constitution, however, empowers Parliament to acquire any property and nationalize any business it deems necessary for the good of the country, but only on payment of fair compensation to private owners. Parliament may determine what is fair compensation. This is a situation where a legal issue really falls in the realm of policy. One must look at the record to get a proper perspective on the attitude of the Indian government toward nationalization and expropriation, and not at the laws themselves.

The government has stressed that it has no intention of nationalizing industries which are functioning in accordance with India's economic and social aims. There have been relatively few cases of nationalization, and all but a few took place before 1959. Major instances of nationization have involved life insurance companies, airlines, some mines, and banks. (The most recent of these took place in July, 1969 and involved 14 private banks.)

In the rare instances where industrial firms have been taken over by the government, they have been operating inefficiently, typically on the verge of bankruptcy. Only a handful of businesses having foreign equity participation have been involved, and in all cases decided on to date the amount of compensation paid by the Indian government has been termed "fair and adequate" in business circles.

In addition to the above federal laws, many states and local authorities impose their own restrictions on where and how businesses may be established. In some cases, positive incentives are given to attract companies to areas which have chronic unemployment or underdevelopment. Such incentives range from tax benefits to substantial assistance in cutting red tape and speeding up initial construction and licensing procedures.

In general, there are many matters relating to the above types of legislation which are open to "negotiation" between businessmen and central, state, and local government authorities in India. The rules of the game — as well as the government bureaucracy — have been and remain flexible, and unclear with regard to the regulations and control over industry.

Tax law

Tax laws influence management, operating efficiency, and industrial progress in major ways. The key impact, for our purposes, involves the ways in which taxes, or absence of taxes, pressure business firms to take actions which they would not otherwise undertake.

The major pieces of legislation relating to taxation in India are the Finance and Income Tax Acts. In general, taxation is a complex matter, even more complex than in the United States. Tax laws are less clear, change more frequently and substantially, and are less effectively enforced in India.

Indian enterprise and individual tax rates are among the highest in the world. There are a variety of taxes imposed in addition to base rates, which vary from time to time depending on immediate national needs. During the 1962-63 crisis with China, surtaxes were imposed which in many cases raised corporate profit taxation to as much as 85 percent. During the 1965-66 war with Pakistan, the related foreign exchange crisis, and the subsequent serious recession, frequent major charges were made in the tax structure — in many cases retroactively. This type of environment can wreak havoc on financial planning by industrial enterprises.

Supplemental taxes have been based not only on income, but also in inverse proportion to invested capital. This has hit hard those firms which tend to avoid capital-intensive operations. Dividends on inter-company transfers are subject to taxation. Individuals are taxed not only on income, but also on accumulated wealth, and in many instances tax liabilities have exceeded personal income during a given year.

A great deal of controversy has centered around the question of India's high levels of taxation. The issue focuses on whether the resource flow received by the state, and applied to development efforts offsets the negative effect it has on private enterpreneurial activity. It would appear that the overall effect is negative, since, due to the stringency of tax laws, much of the wealth of the country is hoarded or diverted into devious or marginal ventures designed to hide wealth and income. The tax structure frequently paralyzes efficiency, and encourages basically non-productive activities. It also encourages the transformation of honest money into "black money."

Within India tax evasion seems to be almost a national sport. One periodically picks up the newspapers to discover that a series of raids have been conducted in which axe-wielding government officials have uncovered thousands or even hundreds of thousands of dollars worth of "black money" that has been stashed in the walls and floors of the homes of Indian movie stars, industrialists, and other wealthy individuals, money which has not been reported, and therefore, has not been subject to income tax. The consequence of such raids is likely to be much status-providing publicity — indicating to the "raidee's" friends and the world at large that he has become very successful — and a financial penalty.

Because jail terms are almost never imposed for tax evasion in India, the wealthy individual can indulge in an interesting game of chance. The usual penalty for being caught is confiscation of the funds which are discovered, payment of the applicable tax, plus the imposition of fines which may approach 100 percent. However the probability of getting caught is very slim. The game, therefore becomes one of playing the probabilities, and most players conclude that the expected value of hoarding money and avoiding high taxes, given the slim chance of being caught is much greater than the value these same funds would have after tax payments had been made.

Because of the tax structure, many U.S. subsidiaries rely heavily on allowances and prerequisites to compensate their higher-paid employees. (There is no personal income tax in India on individual earnings of less than 4,000 rupees per annum.) High personal tax rates also hinder the use of bonuses as an incentive for higher-paid personnel.

The Indian government does provide a number of tax and fiscal incentives, especially for new companies, with the aim of encouraging industrial growth and development. These include tax holidays, development rebates over and above depreciation, special depreciation allowances, rebates based on export earnings, and various other exemptions, including relief from double taxation where more than one country is involved.

Complex rules relate to the production of goods which are subject to excise and sales taxes. They vary by regional municipality, and this further compounds matters. Such goods include alcoholic products, many drug and pharmaceutical preparations, chemicals, and glass bottles. These laws often require that such items be manufactured or stored in bonded storerooms and that they not be used until inspected, passed, and released by government inspectors. Often, excise taxes significantly increase price structures in industries in which the government is trying to reduce total costs to consumers.

Tax laws in India are clearly a significant source of frustration and inefficiency for firms as well as individuals. However, though businessmen are outspokenly critical about tax legislation, in private many admit that taxes are not of as great concern to them as are other environmental conditions, perhaps because they are relatively well-defined. In spite of the high rates of taxation, many firms make sizeable after-tax profits, and many individuals still make large personal incomes. In fact, U.S. multinational companies often earn higher net rates of return in India than at home.

Laws and regulations relating to the domestic flow of goods

India's individual states have the right to restrict the flow of goods across their borders. For example, some of the states with more highly developed drug control agencies occasionally restrict the sale of products from states which have weak enforcement agencies or specific problems of production involving poor quality.

Many states in India have prohibition and subject alcoholic beverages and alcoholic drug preparations to rigid government control and licensing procedures. Permits must be obtained to transport such products through the state, or to deliver or sell them in local state markets.

Regulations involving the flow of goods among different states frequently lead to bribery or other forms of illicit influence, employed to circumvent the law; for example, an engineering company which has been classifying unprocessed metal items as processed so that it can ship them from its Calcutta plant to its factory in another state without paying an excise sales tax. The firm's books show fictional processing charges. When necessary, government inspectors have been "paid off" to keep quiet. Some types of goods cannot legally be shipped to other states, even if taxes are paid. Here, too, bribes have opened the doors.

At the national level, the main instrument for controlling domestic distribution of scarce materials, such as coal and steel, is the Essential Commodities Act of 1955. Fertilizer distribution is also partially controlled through pooling arrangements. In addition, a number of commodities are reserved for state trading, including caustic soda and soda ash, sulphur, newsprint, tires, tractor petroleum products, and raw cotton.

Restrictive laws are also imposed on business activities by municipal governments. "Octroi" taxes are often levied on goods coming into a city from other areas. The levy of such taxes often severely retards the flow of goods, since trucks en route from one city to another are stopped in intervening cities, and goods and invoices are checked for tax liability. Local laws and regulations vary greatly among municipalities, and this poses a complex problem for firms.

Laws relating to suppliers and customers.

Relationships between suppliers and users of goods and services in India are patterned after conditions existing in Great Britain and other Western countries. Contracts, properly drawn, are considered valid and enforceable by law. However, due to major scarcities of materials, it is relatively rare to have cases brought into court. Industrial users often find it more expeditious to reprocess or make do with poor-quality products than to return them or bring suit. Often there are no alternate sources of supply. The time delays which would be introduced to replace the items, the animosity which could be created by a lawsuit, and other considerations would hamper the effectiveness of future operations, especially in the areas where sellers' markets exist.

The same situation applies with respect to customer attitudes, and regulations involving consumer protection. Quality of output tends to be low in many industrial sections. Yet the typical customer seems to be content with poor quality, and rarely will he resort to legal action even when he has a right to do so. When the expectation is for low standards, few people get upset when such expectations are realized.

However, this is an area where there are sharp differences between U.S. subsidiaries and indigenous firms in India, although there are exceptions. The U.S. firms are more concerned about product quality, usually because of parent company policy and control in this area. Even when Indian laws and regulations dealing with quality of specifications exist, the U.S. companies typically try to maintain product quality at U.S. levels, which are usually substantially above the levels prescribed in India. This is particularly the case in the pharmaceutical sector. Such behavior is desirable for both the consumer and India's economic development; however, in some cases, U.S. subsidiaries probably go too far in trying to maintain U.S. quality standards, because of the high manufacturing costs this entails.

Another area of Indian legislation that falls in this section involves exclusive distributorships. Such distributorship arrangements require government approval and must be reviewed every five years. One reason for this is that many indigenous firms appoint relatives and close firends as distributors, using transfer prices to lower tax liabilities.

Laws affecting commodity prices

Many commodities in India are subject to price controls. These range from regulations having the force of law to rather general policy statements which permit considerable leeway for interpretation and negotiation. A number of basic drug items fall within the first category, while various chemicals, batteries, and engineering goods fall in the latter category.

The Essential Commodities Act of 1955 has been a major instrument for price control in India. Specific orders or regulations have also been adopted at various times. At the peak, about 40 major commodities were subject to formal price controls. The recent tendency has been toward gradual liberalization of price controls, but informal price control is still in effect for many important products.

Price controls are also quite extensive at the retail level in India. Basic agricultural commodities are also subject to price regulations. Such price controls affect production costs of producers. Grain prices, as one example, affect the costs for manufacturers and users of industrial alcohol.

In general, India's system of price controls has led to a considerable amount of inefficiency, hard bargaining with government officials, lobbying, illegal practices, and black marketing activity. It has resulted in acute shortages in many items, and surpluses of others, because supply in relation to demand has been substantially out of line. A few years ago — at the peak of India's foreign exchange crisis — experts estimated that 40 percent of all business and monetary transactions involved black market activities. Since then conditions have improved somewhat.

Firms faced with enforced price controls for their output have found themselves in a serious profit squeeze since wages, raw materials, and other factor input costs have been increasing substantially in recent years. This is the case in the drug sector, where frozen price levels imposed under the Defense of India Act in 1963 (as a result of the crisis with China) are still largely in force. It seems likely that prices ceilings for various major drug products will be lowered further in the future; compulsory price reductions on many such products already went into effect in 1971. The profit squeeze is being aggravated further at those firms affected.

Many of India's price controls have been implemented in order to secure specific social or economic objectives deemed important by influential government officials and politicians. Even where the ultimate objectives have been commendable, price regulations have not been examined in terms of the actual overall impact they would have. As a result they have in many instances been self-defeating in terms of the objectives being pursued.

Patent laws and other intellectual property rights

India is a signatory to the International Patent Agreement. However, since the mid-1960s there have been many investigations and parliamentary debates concerning a change in posture. Foreign drug companies have been especially concerned about possible changes in patent regulations, since much of their output is protected by patents. Indigenous firms which do not do much research have tended to favor patent reform.

The more extreme advocates of patent law change feel that India should abrogate its patent laws to allow the production of needed items within the country without the need to export foreign exchange for royalty payments. The proposed changes that went to the Indian Parliament in 1965 included the following specific features:

1. A reduction in the terms of patents from 16 to 10 years.
2. A limit on royalty payments to 4 percent gross or 2 percent net, with licenses granted freely to interested users.
3. A change in the appeal process against decisions of the Controller of Patents by removing jurisdiction from the High Court and placing it in an administrative tribunal whose decisions would be final and unchallengeable in any court of law.

Although a final decision has apparently not yet been made at the time of this writing, the proposals have influenced discretionary policy decisions made by the government in such areas as royalty payments allowed to foreign companies. Industrial managers in India indicate uncertainty as to what the government's posture is regarding patent law. For example, top executives of several drug companies surveyed in the summer of 1969 made different interpretations of existing patent regulations. One firm thought that the life of patents for drugs was still 16 years, the second thought it had been cut to 14 years, and the director of the third company thought it had been reduced to 12 years with a 4-year extension possible. They all agreed, however, that there was a fair chance that patent life would eventually be reduced to 10 years.

Those lobbying against patent reform have pointed to the following effects that would be likely to result.

1. A reduction of the flow of private foreign capital in sectors significantly affected.

2. An adverse affect on the inflow of foreign technical know-how, scientific expertise, products, and processes critically needed for India's development.

3. A negative impact on research, development, and innovation.

**Controls and Policies Relating to Monopolies
and Restrictive Business Practices**

In India there are various policies and controls pertaining to monopoly power, collusion, and other forms of restrictive and discrimination business practices relating to pricing, distribution, market entry, and so forth. However, specific legislation does not exist, although there is a great deal of ferment and discussion regarding such legislation. Policies and controls have been ineffective in restraining undesirable behavior in this sphere. The government's industrial licensing system — involving the establishment of new firms, new products, and the expansion of capacity, as well as foreign exchange — has as one of its major aims the control of monopolistic behavior and excessive concentration of economic power. It has doon poorly in both respects.

Monopoly and restrictive practices legislation has been contemplated by the Indian government since 1969. A Monopolies Enquiry Commission, set up several years ago as a temporary investigating body, stimulated the preparation of a Monopolies and Restrictive Trade Practices Bill, which was placed before Parliament. although no final action had been taken on it at the time of this writing. This bill contains provision for compulsory registration and review of such practices. But its potential value depends entirely on the competence of the review and the proposed Monopoly Commission's view of the public interest. So far, the emphasis has been on concentration of power, and not on the economic considerations importnat to accelerated development. The government position seems to be that the large private houses are inherently socially undesirable. The Dutt Report — to be discussed in later sections — on industrial licensing reform has taken this posture as well.

In India — and to a greater degree in smaller developing economies — strong barriers exist to entry into various industries becuase of the large capital costs or the small size of markets. These constraints have been virutllly ignored by the Indian government.

Also missing from the current dialogue on monopoly control is explicit consideration of managerial and productive efficiency, innovation, productivity, market behavior, the economic relation between complementary products in the production process, as well as ways of specifically controlling monopolies when they are allowed to exist.

The critical question that India has to face is basic throughout the industrial world: since a growing proportion of future output will come from large firms, whether in the public or private sector, what is the best policy mix, and what are the best sanctions and incentives, to ensure that steady productivity improvements occur?

At this time, India badly needs legislation on monopolies and restrictive practices. To date, the only controls exercised have been through the overloaded and far from efficient industrial licensing procedures. And no clear guidelines have been provided.

A permanent, competently staffed, independent, and effective monopolies and restrictive practices commission, largely unaffected by power politics and strong vested interests, could do much to foster India's industrial development. Such a commission would have to be buttressed by sound legislation and effective enforcement based on clearly defined principles, as well as precedents as these evolve.

Laws relating to labor and personnel matters

One of the most pervasive and complex legal areas affecting business operation and management in developing countries is the body of legislation dealing with personnel, and particularly labor matters. In such countries, the strength and resources of employer groups are much greater than those of employees. A major reason for this is that job opportunities relative to the size of the labor force are scarce, and large surpluses of unskilled labor are available.

Because of the disproportionate position in terms of bargaining strength and countervailing power, and of the political and social issues involved — e.g., there are many more voting workers than firm owners and managers — and because labor movements make more noise than do managerial or employer associations, many governments have enacted labor legislation primarily designed to protect the worker against excesses or exploitation which may be committed by the employer. Such legislation places much of the responsibility for employee welfare on industrial enterprises.

Legislation dealing with labor and personnel matters in India contains all of the above characteristics. It is complex and it presents many problems and considerable frustration for enterprise managers. Firms spend a great deal of time filling out forms called for by various labor laws, and dealing with inspectors and union officials on a wide range of issues having legal implications. Day-to-day personnel decisions are substantially more centralized and time consuming, and involve proportionately more managers up and down the hierarchy in India than in the United States largely because of such legislation.

An example involves a relatively large, multiplant U.S. subsidiary in India. A shop manager at one of the firm's plants recently wanted to "charge sheet" a union official for falsifying workers' attendance records. Before a final decision could be made it had to travel five levels up the managerial hierarchy to the deputy managing director, primarily because of the legal issues involved. A number of company lawyers and other specialists were also brought into this decision.

Let us now briefly examine some of the major types of Indian legislation dealing with labor and personnel matters.

The Factories Act, which had its inception in 1948, requires the registration and regulation of all factories, except very small ones. It deals with such things as employee health, safety, working conditions, facilities, hours of work, child labor, and vacations. This act provides for elaborate inspection routines. However, various rules and regulations are unevenly enforced, if at all, and inspectors often ignore violations when they come across them. For example, according to this act a doctor appointed by the local government is supposed to examine all workers each year. However, at many plants visited no such examinations had been made for five years or more. All factories employing 100 or more employees are supposed to have a Works Committee, consisting of both labor and management representatives, to resolve day-to-day problems. Many firms do not have such a body, and many of those that do have it in name only.

Specific portions of the Factories Act come into conflict with the realities of the Indian employment situation, or with other laws and requirements. Shortages of trained personnel often force companies to work employees on an overtime basis which exceeds the relatively low maximum limitation imposed by the Factories Act. Government enforcement agencies tend to turn their backs on such violations.

With respect to other laws, little coordination exists between various legislative agencies. For example, the Factories Act requires that every facility in which manufacturing takes place must have at least two entrances. On the other hand, certain government excise procedures (governing the manufacturing of products on which excise duties are levied) require that these be manufactured in rooms with only one entrance. Enforcement is conducted by two entirely distinct organizations. Consequently, one can find manufacturers who, until they can get the matter settled, must alternately brick up and rip down doorway entrances depending upon which particular inspector is calling on them. Because of the deviations between the law and enforcement, companies are vulnerable to major pressure from individual inspectors under the acts. This encourages bribery and other forms of corruption.

Various laws have been passed in India relating to raising the status of women; e.g., encouraging birth control, and creating more and better job opportunities for females in industry. At the same time the Maternity Act tends to deter the employment of married women — and probably the effectiveness of birth control — since it provides for a six-week leave pay before and after birth. Even when pregnant or postpregnant women stay away considerably longer than this, the courts have stopped firms from taking disciplinary action, and have tended to sympathize with mothers and expectant mothers. The law also calls for companies which employ women with children to set up and operate nurseries at their own expense. However, this law is frequently not enforced.

The Employees Provident Funds Act of 1952 established the need for companies to provide retirement benefits for employees. The Employees State Insurance Act of 1948 provides for sickness, maternity, and employment injury benefits. In addition, there are a whole series of acts dealing with workmen's compensation, minimum wages, and various other personnel matters at both the central and state levels, as well as a host of regulations governing wage payments and working conditions.

The states having the most comprehensive and liberal insurance, sickness benefits, and leave provisions tend to have the highest absenteeism rates. Regulations and court rulings relating to the amount of leave personnel are entitled to without being subject to disciplinary action also encourage absenteeism. For example, industrial employees are typically entitled to 1 day's annual vacation for every 15 to 20 days worked, 7 days of casual leave without notice of explanation, and 10 days of sick leave with full pay. Where employees take much more leave than legally allowed without justification, the companies are frequently powerless to take strong punitive action. The courts typically have not allowed them to dismiss or even suspend the employees involved.

The number of legal holidays industrial employees are entitled to in India is also considerable. Although it varies from state to state, the minimum number found at any of the firms surveyed was 17. At some companies it ran as high as 30 or more. In addition to regular legal holidays, employees often take off for "special events" with impunity. These include general civic strikes and protests ("hartals"), typically to demonstrate against issues having nothing to do with their company (such as tram fare increases); food riots; other forms of civil and political unrest; monsoons and floods which make it difficult if not impossible to get to work; and so forth. It is also quite common for special holidays and company shutdowns to be declared when a prominent national and local government official, active or retired, dies. During a one-year period Calcutta firms were closed on nearly two dozen occasions because of such special events.

Most firms in India feel that a 10 to 15 percent annual absenteeism rate is normal and acceptable. Many calmly accept annual rates of 20 to 30 percent, especially smaller firms. Absenteeism during the marriage, harvesting, and festival seasons, and immediately following payday, typically runs to at least 20 percent and as high as 40 percent or more in Indian industry.

One major reason why firms in India have not shown great concern about high absenteeism — though U.S. firms are typically more concerned than indigenous companies — has been due to the large number of temporary and casual workers they employ. These workers usually receive low pay and few if any benefits. Management has the right to lay them off at any time and this is another important inducement for employing so many of them. They can be maintained in this status as long as they do not work continuously beyond a certain number of days, or more than a certain number of days in a year (the numbers vary from time to time and from area to area).

In reality, there are various ways in which firms have been able to employ the same casual and temporary workers for longs periods of time without giving them permanent status, bonuses, more pay, or benefits provided for by law. For example, they may lay them off briefly and rehire them, or they may record different names for the same person at different times in their records. Union officials and inspectors frequently shut their eyes to such practices.

However, in Bengal there has been a widespread crackdown regarding temporary and casual labor since the Communist-dominated, United Front Government first came to power in that state in 1967. The government froze the dismissal of casual and temporary employees and strongly pressured firms to give them permanent status. Many firms have been able to get around these new rules of the game but it has become difficult to maintain large numbers of non-permanent employees. This has reduced operating flexibility, and increased concern about high absenteeism. Other parts of the country may move in the same direction.

India has apprentice-training laws which have been enforced throughout the country, and enforcement has become more vigorous in recent years. This legislation requires that a certain proportion of jobs and related equipment be reserved for apprentice trainees at factories.

The Industrial Disputes Act of 1947 has a major impact on management and industrial operations in India. This act established a system of labor courts to settle industrial disputes between management and employees. It provides for arbitration in situations where disputes cannot be settled within the firms. It also specifies conditions under which strikes may or may not be called, and defines the rights of both workers and employers in cases of disputes.

The main effect of the Industrial Disputes Act has been to give the labor courts a major role in molding labor relation patterns through their interpretations and rulings. Both unions and management often hold out for unreasonable demands, in the hope that the matter will be referred to a labor tribunal, and settled in such a way that their constituencies cannot hold them responsible for any failure to obtain their demands or to uphold their positions. Government influence and the labor court decisions in India have been oriented toward providing more worker benefits, more secure jobs, and better working conditions.

In spite of problems and deficiencies, India's labor courts have generally functioned reasonably independently, fairly, and objectively. Delays in getting to court have been a major problem, however.

One of the areas in which India's labor tribunals have had considerable impact is that of worker compensation. Basically, the Indian pattern contains three elements. The first is a fixed-increment system, the second is a cost-of-living allowance, and the third is a bonus arrangement.

Under the fixed-increment system, a worker is hired at a specific salary which may be quoted as follows: 80-2-90-3-105-EB-5-115. This means that the employee will be hired at a salary of 80 rupees. Each year thereafter he will receive an increment of 2 rupees until he reaches a salary level of Rs. 90. At that point his yearly increments jump to 3 rupees, until he reaches the level of Rs. 105 per month. At this point he encounters an efficiency bar. Should the company decide that he is extremely able, he will then be granted two raises at the rate of Rs. 5 per year until he reaches the maximum. The labor courts have consistently ruled that the employee is entitled to this fixed increment and have overturned attempts of companies to pay merit increases in lieu of fixed increments. Consequently, a company which desires to recognize merit in its pay scales must do so by giving increments over and above the fixed amounts.

A permanent employee who does not earn more than 200 rupees per month in basic pay receives a "dearness allowance" which is pegged to a cost-of-living index. This allowance may be equivalent to or even greater than his basic salary. Once again, the courts play a major role in determining the formulas on which this allowance is to be based. Originally the dearness allowance started at the outset of World War II, when wages were frozen. In more recent times, where companies have argued for the abolishment of this allowance, often offering total pay packages providing for more compensation than does the existing system, they have been overruled by the courts. The dearness allowance arrangement requires a vast amount of paper work, and results in bickering and disputes. The size of the allowance is under constant review and subject to frequent change — e.g., even monthly — especially during highly inflationary periods.

Many Indian companies began to pay bonuses to employees during World War II. This was another attempt to get around frozen wage rates. As time goes on more and more firms have begun to pay bonuses semiannually or even quarterly, instead of annually. Also with the passage of time, the courts have established the bonus not as a gift from management but as an inalienable right of the worker. The courts have upheld the payment of bonuses, except where bankruptcy would result. Consequently, such bonuses have not been used for rewarding merit.

In 1965 India passed a standard national bonus law. All permanent workers now get a minimum bonus of 4 percent in relation to basic pay, regardless of the size of the company's profits or losses. Above this minimum, bonuses are linked to company profits. Workers are entitled to 60 percent of the company's net surplus, after all tax and dividend payments. There is a carryover provision of 20 percent to provide for bonuses during bad years. In many cases companies — especially U.S. subsidiaries — had been paying substantially larger bonuses than required by the 1965 law. Often these were tied to merit and performance. Such firms now typically award bonuses only according to the formula established by the law.

Fringe benefits are rather liberal in Indian industry, although in recent years the courts have been somewhat more sympathetic to cutting these back when they lower the efficiency of operations in return for higher wages or increased welfare packages. Recent legislation in India requires some new companies to provide housing for employees at subsidized rates. Although the number of industries covered is not very large, the coverage may be expanded considerably in the future. Firms provide not only subsidized housing, but subsidized meals, free tea and coffee, free medical service, and when companies are not located in large cities, they may even provide schools and recreation centers. A large number of firms in India which are located in outlying areas conceive of their operation as a large family-type structure with the employees living on company property and totally involved with company activities.

Much of India's labor legislation encourages firms to try to shift their combinations of factor inputs in the direction of less labor and more capital, especially in the case of new companies not yet locked into highly labor-intensive operations.

In general, companies in India find it difficult to discharge or lay off permanent employees, and can usually do so only with the permission of the courts. This contributes to low productivity, high absenteeism, and high costs, and seriously deters industrial progress and managerial effectiveness. High unemployment levels, in conjunction with inadequate unemployment compensation, are the key underlying reasons for the posture of the courts and the government in this regard.

The dismissal of permanent employees frequently involves such a time-consuming and complex process that personnel who are totally incompetent, or display negligence or dishonesty at work, are still retained. One of the difficulties arises from the huge backlog of cases facing many of the labor courts. It may take several years before a particular decision is settled. Should the settlement go against the company, the firm must pay back wages to the employee and reassign him under unpleasant circumstances involving a great loss of face. Consequently, it is not unusual to find that only minor disciplinary action is taken against employees who have been caught red-handed in theft. In order to function effectively, managements are forced to find tasks for these people which shunt them out of the mainstream of business activity, and yet keep them occupied and employed.

Surprisingly, India's public sector firms seem to have been somewhat more successful in getting permission to reduce sizeable numbers of employees than private companies. Usually public firms receiving such permission have been operating inefficiently and have been tremendously overstaffed. In general, where companies in India have been able to reduce a sizeable number of workers, they have been required to pay special and substantial compensation to them. However, there is no clear-cut law or policy in practice regarding the payment of such compensation.

Some concluding remarks on the law and the foreign company

Over and above the legal statutes on the books which apply to both indigenous and foreign companies in a given country, it is essential that the foreign firm assess the attitudes of local government, and of legislative and judicial officials toward foreign operations. In fact, international management must examine such attitudes specifically in relation to their own nationality. In this sphere, there may well be some major differences between the formal and informal legal systems.

Laws which apply uniformly to all firms within a given nation may in practice be administered differently depending on the nationality of the company. A foreign company may suddenly find it is being prosecuted or penalized for practices common in the country, and from which most indigenous firms seem to have legal immunity. Or it may find that the courts tend to levy heavier fines or grant worker and union demands more readily in the case of foreign firms in general, or those of a particular nationality. On the other hand, it is also possible that the converse may be true. In the same vein, special laws involving only foreign companies may not be enforced; they may be enforced differently according to nationality, or in other ways not consistent with the formal system.

DEFENSE AND MILITARY POLICY

All countries have some national defense posture, ranging from such massive military establishments as are found in the United States and the Soviet Union, to the small ceremonial guard forming the major defense force in such countries as Monaco. Advanced nations obviously can afford much more than poor countries. But many poor and developing nations also spend a large portion of their incomes and resources on this sector, resulting in a great drain on critically scarce manpower, materials, and capital.

India did not spend much for military and defense purposes until 1962. The Gandhian philosophy of non-violence and neutrality, and the policies shaped by key politicians, such as Krishna Menon, were major reasons for this. But the brief and sudden border war with China on the Himalayan frontier in October, 1962 led to big increases in India's military budget, and major changes in her defense policy. Defense spending doubled almost overnight, and it was later increased considerably more. This apparently paid off in the brief 1965 war with Pakistan, over Kashmir, in which India came out the victor, but much less decisively than in 1971 over Bangla Desh.

However, India's big increases in defense spending as well as her war losses, have contributed to serious resource drains, the severe foreign exchange crisis which reached its peak during the 1965-66 period, inflation, and the major economic recession during the 1966-68 period. With the outbreak of the first Indo-Pakistani war in September 1965, the West temporarily withheld all foreign aid, and cut off military assistance to both countries. The United States, as well as several other countries, has still not resumed military assistance of any significance to India. India has had to import various expensive defense items, while at the same time rapidly expanding her own defense production. This has led to a major diversion of resources. The manufacture of weaponry, aircraft, supporting equipment for troops, spare parts, and basic material and equipment has received a major thrust. However, sources of supply have come largely from imports and a small number of large domestic suppliers.

Most of the defense growth has occurred in the public sector and has not benefited living standards, economic growth, or the sustained development of civilian industry. India's defense policies and wars have not really had a substantial or durable impact on employment, the development of small enterprises, building a strong nationalistic spirit, raising the people's aspirations, or motivating the industrial work force to work harder and more efficiently. This has happened in China, and possibly even in Pakistan

(West not East) to a greater extent than in India. The benefits accruing to civilian production, such as research and development spin-offs, new technology, and the training of high talent manpower, have been minimal and are far outweighed by the negative effects.

India maintains a large standing army, both officially and in the form of armed police stations throughout the nation. This, too, has produced a substantial drain on resources which would otherwise be applied to furthering economic growth and development. India's military does not do nearly as much in the way of development work, such as the building of roads, dams, bridges, railroads, irrigation, water conservation projects, educational programs, as do the military in Red China, or in developing, non-Communist countries such as Columbia.

On the other hand, India's military establishment has stayed out of politics and still remains basically politically neutral. It is also called upon to maintain law and order in the face of riots, violent strikes and protests, and other forms,of civil disturbances.

In terms of industrial management, one of the most important aspects of India's defense policy has been the passage of the Defense of India Act following the outbreak of the Chinese crisis. As noted in the previous section, this act gave the government broad powers to regulate industry and commerce. Many of the laws and regulations which emerged from this act have been retained, and they are used to exert various pressures on the industrial sector.

Although the Defense of India Act has hindered managerial effectiveness and productive efficiency in many instances, it has also benefited various companies. For example, some firms producing chiefly civilian goods have been allowed to expand their licensed capacities substantially for defense emergencies. In many cases they have been using this additional capacity mainly, or even entirely, for civilian production, often against regulations, and the government has tended to shut its eyes in connection with such violations. The act has also enabled various companies to increase overtime work not only in factories, but also in offices, even where defense work has not been involved. The government has also liberalized imports for various types of firms, largely for defense reasons, even though many of them produce relatively little in the way of defense items.

Those firms surveyed in the drug, chemical, and engineering sectors of Indian industry which have been selling to the defense establishment have typically experienced a decline in defense business from the peak levels reached several years ago. At the peak their defense sales ranged from a few percent to roughly 20 percent of total sales. Their drop in defense business has been in the range of roughly 10 to 35 percent from peak levels in most cases. However, defense sales have increased somewhat at some first surveyed since 1968 or 1969, as the country pulled out of its major recession are tensions in relation to Pakistan mounted. A few firms surveyed have gone into some defense production only in the last few years. In India, U.S. firms have found themselves in a sensitive position at times because of the host government's defense policies, and especially during the war with Pakistan where their parent corporation also had operations in Pakistan. They have had to do some hard thinking — and in some cases in too much haste — about their public relations strategy.

In a number of cases, neither subsidiary nor parent company management have worked out public relations plans, strategies, or guidelines to deal with sensitive defense issues or crises. This critical area should receive serious planning and attention. If it is ignored, hasty and poorly thought-out decisions can lead to blunders which do harm to the multinational corporation as a whole, as well as to individual managers. The matter tends to be simplified if the subsidiary is entirely managed and operated by local nationals. But this is frequently not the case, especially in poorer and developing countries.

FOREIGN POLICY

Perhaps one of the biggest enigmas India offers to many U.S. corporations and businessmen is her position with respect to foreign policy. She claims to be neutral and unaligned, and for many years she claimed to be strongly against aggression or invasion of any kind. Consequently, Westerners were startled by India's sudden attack and takeover of Goa several years ago. They also point in wonderment to the naiveté shown by India's friendship with Red China right up until the border war broke out in October, 1962. Similarly, many have been amazed at India's war with Pakistan.

However, India has been highly successful in playing Communist and non-Communist powers against one another largely to her own benefit. In fact, she has set the model for many other "non-aligned" nations. She receives considerable aid from both blocs, although the larger amount of assistance has come from the West. No other nation has received so much aid from so many diverse countries.

Many of these have established businesses or plants in India; and India has sent people to study and undergo training in numerous countries throughout the world. She has also been an active participant in all kinds of international meetings, organizations, and training and information exchange programs.

Some U.S. subsidiaries have benefited considerably because of India's relatively neutral position in world affairs. For example, a U.S. drug subsidiary received substantial export orders from Egypt following the six-day war with Israel in June, 1967; and lucrative orders have continued to be filled for Egypt since then. Management believes that at least some of its products exported to Egypt end up in Communist countries. The reason the subsidiary has been getting these export orders is because Egypt stopped buying from its U.S. parent company. There are other cases where various countries have stopped buying from U.S. domestic operations but continue to buy from their subsidiaries in India and elsewhere.

One explanation for India's uncommitted position in foreign affairs relates to the precariousness of the balance of power within India: The country contains many diverse and active political groups. This is true even within the ruling Congress Party, which contains a sizeable number of extremists, mainly situated on the left, but also on the right. By maintaining a relatively neutral position the government has been able to avoid direct and unresolvable conflicts with these activist groups. Such situations are political realities in many developing nations.

Developing nations often find themselves walking a path between the avoidance of political uprisings at home and the maintenance of friendly economic relations abroad — relations which are crucial to the acquisition of resources which they cannot generate internally. An example of such conflict within India is the recent controversy over the development of the fertilizer industry. U.S. interests which were willing to put up capital, supply know-how, and construct and manage plants desired a relatively free market pricing mechanism for their products. This conflicted with the previously stated government policy of price controls for fertilizers. Serious internal conflicts developed when the government decided that the only practical way to obtain the fertilizer plants would be to yield to several of the major demands of foreign firms. Immediately various anti-government political factions raised the cry of exploitation and accused the central government of selling out to capitalistic dominance.

In many ways, India's foreign policy is pragmatic and geared toward self-interest in the economic sense. She has developed highly beneficial trade relations with various Arab and Communist countries which accept rupee payments (i.e., India can settle accounts in rupees, rather than with critically scarce "hard" foreign currency). There is little doubt that India's policies with respect to the Arab and European Communist nations reflect her dependence on these areas for critical foreign trade.

This situation prevails in many developing nations. They require every resource they can marshall in order to accelerate growth and development. Consequently, they must be as resourceful and crafty as possible to obtain these ends. Unfortunately, for industrial managers this often presents an unstable base of operations, since government policies and procedures fluctuate according to internal needs and pressures, and changing ideologies and external situations. Effective enterprise management must devote considerable efforts to obtaining and analyzing data relating to the country's foreign policies; and it must also anticipate likely changes that would have a significant bearing on its operations.

Foreign policy dilemmas which have a critical bearing on industrial management and international business in developing countries focus on the foreign exchange situation and on protection from foreign competition in order to build domestic capability. The developing country may strongly desire foreign investment, know-how, technology, and imports. Yet it may have serious reservations and suspicions about foreign influence and control. There is strong pressure at home to protect indigenous firms from foreign competition, and to protect jobs from the effects of automation and capital-intensive technology which advanced nations are in a position and willing to provide.

Moreover, because of critically scarce foreign exchange, developing nations put great emphasis on import substitution. They place stringent and often highly cumbersome restrictions on imports and foreign exchange, including profit remissions and capital repatriation with regard to foreign firms.

It is essential for international — as well as indigenous — firms operating in developing countries to understand the foreign policy dilemmas facing the host nation, if they are to be relatively effective in dealing with the government. This often involves making compromises to at least partially accommodate the aims of the government.

Another important factor relating to the foreign policy of developing nations involves the concepts of "pride" and "face". Many of these nations feel compelled to prove themselves the equal of more powerful and more economically advanced countries. India's government, for instance, has a strong feeling of pride which partially manifests itself in efforts to assume a major role in Asian and world politics and economics. Consequently, India often sacrifices internal growth and development for such purposes. She supplies troops to the U.N. peace-keeping missions, she supplies technical assistance to a number of other developing countries, and has even exported to developing countries products which were in scarce supply within her own borders. One can raise valid questions as to whether the world would be better off if India concentrated on applying these resources to her own problems; however, face and status are important motivators in these areas. In addition, there is little doubt that the world has benefited as a result of some of India's activities.

Face was one major reason why India refused to devalue her currency until strong pressure was brought to bear by major aid-giving countries, and she found herself in a severe foreign exchange crisis. Even her devaluation (from 4.75 to 7.50 rupees, per 1 United States dollar) in June, 1966, was probably too little, as well as too late. It has not had as favorable an effect on increasing India's exports or reducing imports as had been hoped for. But various other constraints are also to blame in this regard.

Few of the foreign firms surveyed took steps to hedge against India's devaluation in 1966. All those that did were either United States or British companies. Some companies which were either undergoing major expansion projects or putting up new plants at the time of devaluation could have saved hundreds, sometimes thousands, — and in a few cases millions — of dollars if they had predicted the devaluation and had taken steps to hedge against it. It is true that the timing of India's devaluation came as a general surprise. And it is also true that hedging against a devaluation that does not occur, or occurs much later than expected, can be very costly.

However, many companies overlooked strong indications that devaluation was likely to occur during 1966. For example, one U.S. subsidiary which was not caught by surprise constantly analyzed India's balance of payments and balance of trade positions, as well as her defense, foreign, fiscal, and monetary policies. It also gathered information and opinions from key foreign aid and government officials in

India and elsewhere, as well as from a number of influential foreign exchange experts and economic advisors. As a result, it engaged in foreign buying of hard currencies, prepaid or sped up payment of hard currency accounts wherever possible, got permission to make dividend payments, profit remissions, and service fee payments earlier than it normally would have, and so forth. The timing of this company with regard to the above transactions in relation to devaluation was nearly perfect, and it must be admitted that luck did play some part. But even if the devaluation had occurred later, the company still would have come out considerably ahead. This example emphasizes the need to keep abreast of current developments.

POLITICAL STABILITY

General overview

A high degree of political stability over a period of time by no means assures a high degree of managerial effectiveness or industrial progress. On the other hand, serious political instability can significantly hinder managerial performance and economic development. In assessing political stability in a given country, and in making predictions about it, business managers need to look beyond the words they read or the speeches they hear. They must examine actual behavior and events, and if possible learn what is really happening behind the political scene.

In a country, or region within a country, where political change is frequent and disruptive, managerial and firm performance suffer considerably. Where the new regime or political party that overthrows the previous one has a basically different philosophy or ideology, the impact is likely to be even more dramatic. Considerable uncertainty for firms can occur with major or sudden shifts in policy within a single ruling political party or faction. In fact, even the change of one or a few key political figures can have a major impact on industrial operations. A revolution of the Cuban, Syrian, Algerian, Congolese, or Nigerian type has such a traumatic effect on productive and managerial functions that firms invariably show large declines in productivity which may take months or years to rectify.

In general, political instability can manifest itself in a variety of ways and have a variety of effects on industrial firms and their managers. It may have substantially different implications for foreign firms than indigenous enterprises in a given country.

Political instability can sharply deter the establishment of new enterprises, as well as the expansion and diversification of existing ones. It can lead to strikes, riots, and other forms of labor unrest, work stoppages or slowdowns, often incited and organized by opposing political factions. Serious political instability and conflict between central, state, and local governments can disrupt the flow of resources — including people, commodities, and funds — from one area of the country to another.

Moreover, political instability can make it difficult if not impossible for enterprise managers to predict directions of change in government fiscal, monetary, foreign and defense policies; laws and their enforcement; product and factor input prices; availability of foreign exchange; and potential markets.

In many cases, political change may mean changes in relationships between the government and specific firms. Some companies may gain advantages, while others suffer as new people take over, new favorites are chosen, and new ideologies introduced. Drastic political change may even result in the nationalization or, occasionally, the denationalization of specific firms or whole industries, either foreign-or indigenously-controlled, or both. (Peru and Chile are recent cases in point.)

Political instability and conflict, especially within a ruling party whose rule is tenuous and based on feuding factions or coalitions, can lead to inaction. Because of a precarious balance of power, political infighting, and lack of concensus, governmental decision-making processes may come to a virtual standstill. As a result, firms may not be able to get approval to do the things they want to do, and critically needed changes in governmental policies, regulations, and legislation may be unduly held up or suppressed.

The case of India: Historical perspective

Until approximately 1965, the Congress Party generally provided national stability in India. When independence was won from Great Britain in 1947, the party emerged as dominant in Indian political life. It was fortunate to have two successive charismatic leaders. The first was Ghandi who gave the party its purpose and philosophy, and the second was Nehru who led the Congress Party through the first years of independence and actually guided the development of India as a nation. The strength of the Congress Party and the strong popular appeal of these two men provided stability to the central government. Opposition parties were weak at the national level and unable to elect more than an insignificant handful of legislators to parliament. However, the same factors which led to short-run stability eventually led to the growing and potentially severe instability which now exists in the central government.

Gandhi believed that the Congress Party had one key purpose in the Indian political scene, and that was the achievement of Indian independence. He indicated that the party should perhaps be disbanded once independence had been achieved. This was not carried out and the Congress Party continued in power. It is difficult to determine whether this was good or bad for India during her first years as a nation. The party did give the central government some stability, and certainly the introduction of the five-year plans was a step in the right direction. However, the leadership of the Congress Party was made up of the patriots who had fought for Indian independence, and unfortunately, patriotism is not necessarily synonomous with sound administrative skills.

The Congress Party started to harden at the arteries. Twenty years after independence, the leadership was still in the hands of these same, now elderly patriots — often referred to as the Syndicate — and there had been little infusion of young talent or new ideas. In essence, the leadership of the Congress Party had ceased renewing itself and had continued to carry on basically in the old tradition and the old ways, in spite of much rhetoric about change.

Politicians appointed to key government jobs, including those dealing with the regulation of industry and other matters of importance to economic development, have lacked the necessary qualifications and been ineffective in numerous cases. They have been shifted from job to job frequently. To a somewhat lesser extent this has also been the case with regard to government administrators in the Indian Civil Service, which involves little specialization and considerable job rotation. Few politicians and not many top-level government administrators have been professionally associated with a particular task prior to their appointments.

The dearth of administrative talent, the large numbers of discontented young people, widespread corruption, far from impressive progress, and the magnitude of the developmental tasks which had to be accomplished have given strength to opposition groups. Both right wing and left wing groups started whittling away at Congress' power at national, state, and municipal levels. Each time parliamentary votes of confidence have been held during the 1960s, the majority supporting the Congress Party has been slightly reduced. By 1967 the erosion had reached the point where more than one-half of the states and most of the major cities were no longer controlled by Congress affiliated groups. By now, however, the Congress as a party has become somewhat of a misnomer. It has become a loose confederation of a large number of groups with very diverse viewpoints. The only common link among these factions today seems to be the desire to avoid the struggle and chaos which would result from the total demise of the ruling party. As a result, these groups have banded together on critical issues which would lead to the dissolution of the government.

Even during the early period, the stability which existed at the national level eluded the political scene at the state and local levels. India was wracked by a series of conflicts, both ideological and physical. Many of these have revolved around linguistic issues. Others have focused on religious, chauvinistic and political differences.

The nation we now know as India would probably never have come into being save for administrative convenience. The British governed as one unit the large number of distinct kingdoms, diverse cultures, and varied language groups which they found on the Asian subcontinent. Many of these had little in common other than geographic proximity. As a result, when these subunits achieved independence in the form of a single nation, little existed to tie them together. Their only common link, the desire to achieve independence from the British, had already been eliminated. Local language and cultural differences were so diverse that the various groups soon started to divide.

As recently as 1967, bloody riots based upon the desire of different linguistic groups to achieve autonomy resulted in the division of Punjab into two states. The separatist DMK Party recently came to power in the state of Madras and fulfilled one of its major campaign promises of changing the states name to Tamilnadu. Tamil is the native language of this area. In general, there have been frequent conflicts in India deriving from religious differences — such as the Ahmadabad riots in 1969 — from partial differences between various political parties, and, from differences between cultural and linguistic groups. Consequently, many of the state governments have not been stable. At times the central government has had to step in and actually rule various states in an effort to provide some degree of order.

Within the last few years, a major change has taken place in the Indian scene. The opposition parties — both left and right — have become stronger and severely whittled away the power and secure position of the Congress Party at both state and central levels. At the same time serious friction and conflict within the Congress Party has increased sharply among leftists, rightists, moderates, and sheer opportunists. Perhaps the major turning point was the death of Nehru. His successor, Shastri, was able to buy some time for the Congress Party through a number of astute political moves, but his premature death heralded the rapid disintegration of the party. The selection of Indira Gandhi in an attempt to stem the trend by appealing to emotional reactions engendered by her father, Nehru's memory did not meet with much initial success and Congress became weaker and weaker. However, it would be unfair to say that Mrs. Gandhi has been the cause of this, since the Congress Party, in both concept and behavior, contained within itself the seeds of its dwindling strength. The elections in 1971 seem to indicate a reversal of this trend, but it is too early to determine whether this is a temporary or a more lasting state of affairs. However, there is little to dispute the fact that political stability in India today is made of gossamer — unless Mrs. Gandhi's impressive victory heralds a new era.

Perhaps the major factor which has saved the Congress Party what power it now possesses is the dissension and diversity of viewpoints which exist among the minority parties. India has dozens of such parties. Some have pursued political and economical aims. Others seek separation based on linguistic differences. Still others focus on racial or religious issues. Even among the various Communist and socialist parties there are basic conflicts in ideologies and aims. Because their objectives are so diverse, the opposition parties have been unable to unite in common efforts.

An examination of political stability must also consider the emotional content of the local temperament. Where large bodies of uneducated people are involved, emotional responses often override those based on rational analysis, and mobs may be swayed to action easily. In many ways, living in India is like living in a perpetual tinderbox, since only a small spark is needed to evoke a violent emotional outpouring which serves to relieve the extreme monotony of day-to-day life. Calcutta, a metropolitan area containing more than seven million people, is cluttered with homeless refugees from East Pakistan and untrained people who have been attracted to the city from the villages. They live in the streets, barely subsisting, and for all practical purposes can be considered outside of the existing social structure. Furthermore, the Bengali (including the East Pakistani) is noted for his depth of emotion — an emotion which leads both to poetry and to violent reaction. Responses to government laws and actions which are viewed as detrimental to the Bengalis often result in an emotional outpouring. Riots occur frequently on issues ranging from anti-Pakistani feelings (linked to the refugee problem) to dissatisfaction with the cost of living. Not too many years ago, the finance minister in the Indian Cabinet was asked how the government established the upper limit on certain types of taxation. His answer, given half in jest but containing a great deal of truth, was "we raise taxes until the Bengalis start overturning buses. Then we know we have gone far enough."

Nowhere in India during the last several years has political instability at the state level been worse than in Bengal: this has already led some companies to shift their head offices and other operations to other states, and it has contributed to widespread idle plant capacity and the serious outflow of capital that Bengal has been experiencing. It has also led to acute, widespread, and constant labor problems. Political activists have been inciting workers to agitate against firm management, frequently for unjustified reasons. In many cases the workers have been unhappy about this and with the general behavior of their union leaders.

Such problems have increased greatly since the coalition United Front Government first came to power in Bengal in 1967. This government has been dogmatic and Communist-dominated. However, the various types of Communist, socialist, and other factors which make up this most tenuous coalition government have been constantly engaged in severe conflicts and strong political infighting among themselves. This has had serious adverse consequences in terms of productive efficiency and industrial progress. Hopefully, national political leaders will learn from the Bengal experience and avoid the formation of an ineffective, warring, and highly dogmatic coalition government at the national level.

Even in states having substantially greater political stability than Bengal, emotional upheavals often occur. These may last for a few hours, for days, or even for years. The stimulus can range from personal slights to deep-seated issues such as linguistic, religious, and cultural differences. Responses can range from reactions within legislative bodies (which too often result in the passage of irrational laws) to large portions of the population taking to the streets with stones and clubs. Many such upheavals, however, must be distinguished from long-range political instability, as their effects are only temporary. Many states and municipalities do not have the police agencies capable of heading off such riots or putting them down quickly. However, after the initial emotional response, when the need for diversion has been satisfied, the issues are generally resolved or forgotten and things settle back to normal. But these upheavals must be factored into managerial thinking and, for the present, must be considered as elements of the environment.

The current political situation in India

Many readers no doubt know that political instability was a most critical and widely publicized problem in India during the second half of 1969 and early 1970. Reports of infighting at the top echelons of the ruling Congress Party appeared frequently in the mass media throughout much of the world. One day it looked as if Indira Gandhi might be on her way out as Prime Minister; the next day she mustered enough support to stay in. At this point it seems that she has the support she needs to push through her programs, but whether her strength will hold out through 1976 is another question. It is worth examining the 1969-70 situation to see what political power entails in India.

In order to maintain her power Mrs. Gandhi has had to appease the "leftists" and "radicals" not only within her own party, but also among opposition parties. This she did by making more and stronger pledges about moving India more vigorously toward socialism. However, rhetorical pledges were not enough and it was necessary in late July, 1969 for her to take the radical action of nationalizing India's 14 largest private banks. Whether she can avoid taking more radical steps and a too rapid shift toward socialism and still maintain her leadership position remains to be seen. If she does move in this direction this would no doubt do tremendous damage to India's fragile economy.

Since she became Prime Minister in 1966, Mrs. Gandhi has been under constant and increasing pressure from the "Young Turks," radicals and leftists on the one hand, and the more moderate and conservative elements of the Congress Party under the leadership of the "Syndicate" on the other. The Syndicate (which may now be defunct) is composed of old Congress Party hands, virtually all in their seventies or older. The leftists and radicals — including various kinds of socialists and Communists — have as one of their main targets the big industrial empires, most notably the Birlas. They want to curb further expansion of this kind, or if it is allowed they want it to be in collaboration with the public sector. Many politicians want to extend these curbs to foreign collaborations and subsidiaries as well. They also want representatives from government agencies and financial institutions to serve on the boards of directors of the large private companies, and to play an active role in their management.

Moreover, the leftists and radicals want substantially more of the overall industrial sector to be reserved for small-scale enterprises, and greater public financing provided for such enterprises. They want to expand the public sector in core and heavy industries and desire a greater role in the planning, regulation, and control of economic activity on the part of the government. This would be achieved through bank nationalizations, a major overhaul of the government licensing system, a powerful and permanent monopolies commission, the nationalization of import and export trade, the establishment of a central industrial pricing commission with broad powers, more comprehensive and detailed national economic planning, and various other reforms.

A number of committees, commissions, and ad hoc study groups set up in the last few years have advocated such measures. Most of them, such as the Industrial Licensing Policy Inquiry Commission (also known as the Dutt Committee) have been set up in response to strong pressures extended by the young Turks. And most have been dominated by leftists, including a number of influential members with strong Communist leanings.

The deep and possibly irreparable split within the Congress Party came into the open with the selection of a presidential candidate in mid-1969, The former president had recently died, and all members of Parliament were to vote for a new president. Normally the role of the president in India is basically a ceremonial one. However, the president has the power to designate a prime minister to put together a coalition government in the event no party gets a majority in Parliament. It was feared that this might well be the case in the next national elections. Mrs. Gandhi backed Mr. Geri, the leftist candidate, who was also being supported by most of the socialists and Communists. The Congress Party Syndicate under the leadership of Moraji Desai, who was Deputy Prime Minister and Minister of Finance, backed the more moderate candidate Mr. Reddy, who would probably not designate Mrs. Gandhi as prime minister in the event of a coalition government. In addition to strong disagreements on political issues, Reddy and Mrs. Gandhi are reputed to dislike each other personally. Geri won the election and Mrs. Gandhi's stature increased among the populace, as well as in political circles.

Shortly before the presidential election Mrs. Gandhi deposed Desai as Deputy Prime Minister and took over the portfolio of Minister of Finance herself. She also nationalized the 14 banks, which met with considerable support among the masses. Even though Desai and the Syndicate were opposed to bank nationalization, it was generally felt that some move in this direction was inevitable. However, the timing and extent of the bank nationalization came as a surprise to virtually everyone. Apparently, Mrs. Gandhi decided to nationalize the banks chiefly for political rather than economic reasons, and she did not consult with any of her key advisors.

Mrs. Gandhi's call for national elections in 1971, a year earlier than required, caught many people by surprise. Her stunning victory, giving her more than the absolute two-thirds majority which she needs to implement constitutional amendments, has changed the entire picture. The Syndicate was crushed, and she no longer has to rely on many of the groups upon which she was formerly dependent. Today, not only is she no longer as beholden to the industrial sectors, but she no longer needs the support of extremists on either end of the spectrum.

She has repeatedly pledged to accelerate India's move toward socialism. It is hard to tell what form this will take at this time, since she is no longer subject to extreme leftist pressures, but there is no indication that she has softened her approach toward private industry either.

Implications for company management

Whatever the outcome of India's political dilemmas, the wise firm doing or considering doing business in India does its best to keep abreast of the political situation on a continuing basis. But even the best managed firms are finding it extremely difficult to plan very far ahead; and most firms seem reluctant to embark on any substantial expansion or diversification programs, even if they are allowed to do so, in the prevailing political climate.

During the second half of 1969, government approvals and licensing for new projects, products, and foreign collaborations came to a virtual standstill because of the political situation. Such government inaction prevailed regardless of the priority of the project in terms of India's requirements for industrial development. Projects involving important drugs or chemicals have been held up, as have projects involving cosmetics and other non-essentials.

The situation improved somewhat in 1970. However, India's private investment climate is not likely to improve substantially until businessmen get a much clearer picture of what to expect in the political sphere. But this cannot happen until Mrs. Gandhi and other key politicians decide themselves what strategies, policies, and courses of action they should pursue.

POLITICAL ORGANIZATION AND GOVERNMENT CONTROL OF INDUSTRY

The structure of India's central government is patterned largely after England's Parliamentary system. The upper house, corresponding to the House of Lords, is the Rajya Sabah (the Council of States). It differs from the House of Lords in that members are both elected by the various state legislative assemblies and appointed by the president in recognition of outstanding accomplishments in the arts, sciences, or other fields. The membership of the lower house, the Lok Sabah (the house of the people) is elected by direct popular vote. This is the body in which the major legislative power resides. In both houses, representation is proportional to state population.

All legislation requires the consent of both houses of parliament. However, the Lok Sabah alone is responsible for taxation. It also appoints and has the power to retain or reject the ministers in whom true power resides.

The most important figure in Indian government is the prime minister, who is nominated by the constituency of the Lok Sabah as its acknowledged leader. However, he or she is formally appointed by the president, although the office is responsible to the Lok Sabah. The prime minister selects the various ministers who run the administrative functions of the government. The main power, therefore, derives from the Lok Sabah, through the prime minister and the cabinet.

As noted earlier in this chapter, India does not have a balanced two-party system such as the United Kingdom or the United States; yet it has selected the British form of government which is vulnerable to pressure exerted by opposition movements. The consequences of the British type of structure in a nation like India are quite evident to the businessmen who spends much time dealing with the government. Because the government can be dismissed should it fail to obtain a majority of votes in the lower house of Parliament, it is subject to many pressures and can only survive through compromise. The stronger the opposition parties, with their diverse views, ideologies, and interests become, the more difficult it will be for India to develop uniform and consistent governing policies. The overwhelming support won by Mrs. Gandhi in the 1971 elections may, however, change the picture.

The various legislative acts and decrees dealing with government planning, regulation, and control of industry which emerged in the late 1940s and 1950s led to the formation of a variety of central governmental ministries, agencies, commissions, councils, and the like. They were given broad powers to plan, regulate, and control industrial activity in the national interest. The subdivision of functions among different ministries and agencies often overlaps and presents serious problems of policy coordination. Of major concern here are those central agencies which control the licensing of new projects, new products, foreign investment and collaborations, and foreign exchange controls.

In India, industrial firms must deal with a variety of central ministries and other organizations whose basic organization is similar. A typical central ministry is headed by a union minister. Under him is a minister of state and one or more deputy ministers. Below the top ministerial level are the secretariats and departments staffed with civil service employees. Unlike the ministers, who hold political appointments and are subject to the vagaries of political life, the civil servants are permanent, and tend to be the mainstay of the administrative bureaucracy. Although the ministers have authority over policy, under normal conditions top-level civil servants in a particular ministry often wield more actual operational power than the top minister himself, due to their tenure in office. Businessmen who deal with Indian ministries soon realize that ministers come and go, while civil servants stay and provide longer-range continuity. On the other hand, political considerations often prevail at the expense of development in India's regulatory bureaucracy.

Under the ministers within a given Indian ministry the chief civil servant is called a secretary. Under him there are a number of joint secretaries followed by deputy secretaries, and undersecretaries. In some ministries there is also an additional special secretary directly under the top secretary. Ministries also have a variety of departmental, divisional, and section heads, and usually various kinds of advisory staffs and committees as well.

Probably the most important ministry with regard to government control of industry in India is the Ministry of Industrial Development. This ministry is concerned with overall industrial policy and is directly involved — or is at least supposed to be — in the evaluation and issuance of all industrial and foreign exchange licenses requiring central approval. It is also involved with price controls.

India also has a number of more specialized industry-oriented ministries such as Chemicals and Petroleum, Steel and Heavy Engineering, Irrigation and Power, Railways, and so forth. They focus on problems falling within their industrial sectors.

While these ministries do have discretionary powers, the Ministry of Industrial Development is supposed to have the final voice in all licensing decisions, since it is the central coordinating agency, and is therefore required to take an overall view of the national interest.

The Directorate General of Technical Development (DGTD), which is attached in a rather unclear way to the Ministry of Industrial Development, analyzes company applications from a technical viewpoint. Although it too has discretionary powers, it is primarily a service and advisory agency which makes technical feasibility studies for the various industrial ministries. Reporting to the director-general of this agency are industrial advisors concerned with particular sectors of industry. There are also departments, divisions, and sub-directorates. In mid-1969 this agency employed 15 industrial advisors, 150 engineers, 60 development officers, and approximately 600 other persons.

The Ministry of Foreign Trade has also been of great important to businessmen, although it has gone through some major reorganizations. This ministry has played a key role in formulating, coordinating, and implementing import and export policies. It has also been involved in the planning and allocation of various indigenous commodities in short supply. An agency known as the Chief Controller of Imports and Exports (CCIE) has been attached to this ministry and has offices throughout the country. It investigates and controls the issuance and use of foreign exchange licenses and import entitlements once they have been granted to firms. It is also involved in the control and scrutiny of export and incentive schemes.

The Ministry of Finance also has a major voice in formulating industrial policy, licensing decisions, foreign exchange allocations, and the economic and financial aspects of foreign collaborations and investment. The Reserve Bank of India plays a key role with regard to foreign exchange regulations.

The Ministry of Law is often involved in decisions affecting business enterprise, especially when constitutional issues are involved — as in bank nationalization — but also with regard to less dramatic decisions involving shifting production from one state to another, questionable sales promotion practices, patent infringement, and so forth. The Department of Company Affairs under the Ministry of Industrial Development is also involved with many legal matters. The Controller of Capital Issues must give approval for new securities.

The Ministry of Health and Family Planning plays an important role in the approval of new drug products, as does the Office of the Drug Controller. At times these agencies are also involved in a wide range of drug and chemical company operations, including such things as costs, prices, advertising, production processes, and personnel.

The Planning Commission is basically an advisory agency which has a voice in a wide range of economic and industrial matters. It drafts the country's development plans, but does not have final approval over them. Other commissions, councils, and agencies also have a say in shaping industrial policy and/or government decisions affecting business firms. Some of them are concerned with a particular sector of the economy, others with regional development, and still others with various specialized functions.

The government also contains a number of important inter-agency and inter-ministerial coordinating committees which are involved in industrial decision making. Among the most important of these have been the Licensing Committee, the Capital Goods Committee, the Foreign Exchange Committee, and the Foreign Agreements and Foreign Investment Committees. Special ad hoc investigative committees are frequently formed to deal with specific issues.

The supreme coordinating body is the council of ministers, reporting directly to the prime minister. It is composed of members of the Cabinet, ministers of state (individuals who may hold cabinet rank but do not sit with the Cabinet), and deputy ministers. Following the 1971 elections Mrs. Gandhi made major changes in appointments to cabinet and other key central government posts.

In general, companies of substantial size must still deal directly with many central government officials and many different agencies. It is not uncommon for larger companies to deal with hundreds of government officials and politicians and dozens of different ministries, agencies, and other governmental organs.

State and local-level government agencies and politicians are also frequent participants in government decisions involving industrial firms. State and local agencies have many of the same kinds of basic problems with regard to the regulation and control of industry as the central bureaucracy. However, they are primarily although not exclusively concerned with small-scale industry and are not of major interest in this study.

It will suffice to point out here that state legislatures have various exclusive powers as defined in the Constitution of India. These include such matters as the levying of state taxes, the granting of certain charters, and the control and regulation of industry located within their borders. The different structures within the states have led to a vast diversity of rules and procedures affecting business firms. There is no uniform national approach to local regulatory issues, and companies which do business in several or many states may find themselves subject to very different detailed regulations.

Basic underlying problems in India and consequences for industrial management

Any simple description of India's industrial strategy or government bureaucracy with regard to the control of industry is bound to be misleading. Government policies and regulation of industry are the sum of a large number of separate rules, procedures, and practices, each designed to meet some specific objective. A good many policies and objectives, each laudable in themselves, tend to conflict with one another as well as with the improvement of industrial efficiency. Moreover, the types and number of instruments used in the pursuit of national goals — industrial licensing, foreign exchange allocation and control, price regulations, to name but a few — have given rise to a situation in which the objective weighing of alternatives is very difficult and where a vast amount of discretionary control is called for.

In order to better understand why government control of industry in India has evolved and the way it constrains managerial effectiveness, one should know something about the national goals aimed at by India's overall industrial policy. The following is a partial list — not in any order of priority — of the large range of diverse objectives which the government seeks.

1. To achieve a high rate of industrial and overall economic growth.
2. To protect the nation's balance of payments, conserve scarce foreign exchange, and push for import substitution.
3. To promote new and expanded production in industries deemed to be of social importance and to discourage production of luxury goods.
4. To prevent the abuse of monopoly power, and of economic concentration.
5. To distribute income equitably.
6. To raise employment levels.
7. To balance new investment among the states and to develop backward regions.
8. To achieve price and general economic stability.
9. To prevent excessively destructive competition in order to conserve scarce economic resources.
10. To avoid excessive foreign domination and control without hindering desired forms of foreign investment, collaboration, and assistance.
11. To promote small-scale and cottage industries.
12. To promote economic self-sufficiency, balanced development, and the establishment of an overall industrial sector in the widest feasible lines of domestic production.

It is difficult to question the individual merit of these national objectives. However, by aiming at all of them simultaneously, national plans, industrial policy, and legislation provide little in the way of a systematic attempt to weigh one against another, or to establish reasonably clear-cut priorities. Without such a systematic attempt, serious contradictions, inconsistencies, and much discretionary power is inevitable. Because priorities are unclear, the personal values of officials play a key role in government decisions. Differences in interests, emphasis, and values among agencies frequently lead to long delays and red tape for company managers.

Not only do firm managers frequently not know whether to expect a positive or negative decision on their applications, but typically they also cannot predict even the approximate time when the decisions will be made — they may take one month, one year or even more than three years. Such uncertainty hinders efficient and effective enterprise planning and control. It is often better for a firm to receive a negative answer within a reasonably short period of time than to receive the go-ahead after it is too late, or at an unexpected time when it is not in a position to take advantage of it effectively. While discretionary power contributes to great delays in decision making, it can also lead to quick decisions which circumvent channels, if a particular government official or agency wishes to interpret the situation as one which calls for expediency in the national interest. Often the risks assumed by the decision maker can be made more attractive by special "rewards" provided by the petitioning company.

Another area in which the lack of clear-cut priorities has created problems is that of industrial licensing. In theory, the national plans determine the parameters of development for the future, and the licensing system becomes an instrument for its accomplishment. However, with little effective feedback, plans have often missed the mark by a wide margin, and little corrective action has been taken. In essence there has been little relationship between the plan and its execution. As a result, the licensing system has operated largely on the faulty assumption that the state plan will ensure that supply balances with demand for the period, when in fact extensive imbalances have persisted because the plan has not been implemented evenly or effectively.

At various times "priority," "key," "merit," "basic," "critical," "core," "essential," and "banned" industries have been defined in government lists for purposes of industrial licensing, import entitlements, allocation of scarce indigenous commodities, foreign collaborations, fiscal incentives, export incentives, and so forth. None of these lists is the same, and the government argues that the multiplicity of objectives is such taht a consistent list cannot be established. No clear basis has been established for determining priorities within each list (often dozens of industries or different products are contained in a particular list) or for changing priorities as time goes on.

Finally, priority in India's state control of industry has apparently not been conceived in terms of rate of return, or of potential for productivity gain, or some other economic or efficiency criterion. In fact, industrial efficiency per se has not been a well defined objective of major importance, nor has it been a basic value of the Indian way of life. The same is true for competition in the positive sense.

Major governmental administrative problems

In this sub-section we are primarily concerned with organizational and staffing problems within the Indian governmental bureaucracy which hinder industrial managerial effectiveness and productive efficiency. A basic organizational problem which already has been discussed in detail involves the lack of coordination and unclear roles and functions both within and among the many agencies involved in the regulation and control of industry.

Another serious problem involves special investigatory commissions set up by the government to examine various aspects of industrial control. Often such commissions are not given a clear definition of what they are supposed to do. This causes frustration, considerable uncertainty, and many other problems for the firms under investigation. A typical example of this involves the Tariff Commission — under the Ministry of Foreign Trade — which was given the task of investigating the drug industry a few years ago. Originally it was supposed to confine its investigation to price and patent issues involving 18 basic products. As it proceeded it investigated scores of different products with regard to detailed costs, advertising and sales promotion, investment, profitability, quality control, research and development, and so forth, in addition to prices and patents.

Another basic problem area is that of staffing policies and the types of personnel involved in government control of industry. One of the truly serious problems alluded to earlier and which is common to many developing nations, is the lack of business- or industrially-oriented political talent. Many of the Indian cabinet officials, other ministers, legislators, and major civil servants do not really understand the way firms operate, or the way their own activities and decisions relate to the overall economy. Yet they are called on to formulate plans and policies and make decisions dealing with such complex areas as capital investment, technology, product specifications, resource allocations, factor inputs, plant locations, and so forth. More often than not they do not have the ability — or if they do, the time — to properly analyze the masses of data which accompany company applications. And often much of this data is false or distorted in order to make a favorable decision certain.

The primary consideration in Indian ministerial appointments too often is political expediency — to ensure that a particular politician has a post. Sometimes shifts are made to remove ministers from posts in which their incompetence has been embarrassingly highlighted by a national crisis, and the ministers are given portfolios which are less sensitive. Often such appointees make their decisions on the basis of emotions and without a rational examination of the critical details of the problems.

The civil service aspect of Indian government is also very important to industrial decision making. Ministers are frequently shifted with considerable rapidity. However, the civil service is relatively immovable, although people are shifted to higher levels from time to time. The businessman normally deals not with the policy makers, but the implementors — the civil servants who are usually not subject to removal, and who, like most civil servants, tend to show relatively little imagination or initiative in their functions.

The emphasis on stability and the reluctance to change characterize the civil service ideology. Within civil service systems seniority, not ability or accomplishment, is frequently the most important criterion for promotion. Consequently, many civil service organizations instill among their membership an aversion to innovation. The man who innovates and errs may find himself on a blacklist which impedes further progress up the promotional ladder. The man who innovates and succeeds often receives little more than a pat on the back from his superiors — and possibly a bribe, gift, or special favor from a company representative. The safest route to promotion, typically not to "rock the boat," but to follow the rules to the letter and keep oneself as non-controversial as possible.

Such government officials are also reluctant to take responsibility for their decisions. Hence, numerous meetings are called in order to avoid individual responsibility and blame, and this creates endless delays in the decision-making process. The idea is to get as many other officials and agencies involved as possible. Consultations and communications are put in writing for the record, and this leads to further delays. The files on a particular company application are passed along from party to party for further comments and for "safety." It is also frequently difficult to get a mutually convenient date for all officials invited to a particular meeting. After the meeting the minutes must be approved and circulated in writing. And so on — while the firm waits for a decision to be made.

Although many of India's brightest college graduates go into the civil service, relatively few of them have had much contact with industrial life or economic activity. Consequently, the only systems and procedures they know are those employed in the government. But the application of government rules and procedures (the red tape) often introduces severe time delays for the businessman who is trying to accomplish an economic task with all of the deadlines and restrictions placed upon him by market conditions and other environmental factors.

Even the most able government administrators find themselves severely hamstrung by the political-administrative system in which they must function. It is common for the more able and better motivated officials to carry tremendous work loads while many if not most of those above and below them in the hierarchy are grossly underemployed. Gross overstaffing greatly increases unnecessary make-work activity and delays decisions. It also increases the discretionary powers of civil servants, including lower-level personnel who can influence the decisions made by officials higher up by making notations on company applications, determining what data to pass on to them, in what order and form, and so forth.

In general, Indian government administrators and politicians probably tend to be too accessible to people, including businessmen, who drop in to see them for all kinds of reasons, many without an appointment. This places large demands on the administrator's time. This situation goes back historically to the notion that Indian officials should be readily available to the public. But with vastly greater government regulation of industry this greatly delays governmental decision making. However, this is only a small part of the work load problems facing overburdened officials.

Let us look at a typical example of the work load of an able government administrator. This case involves a joint secretary in the Ministry of Industrial Development who is respected for his ability and integrity by both his peers and the industrial managers who deal with him.

This individual has a good education, and experience in production, engineering, and economics. In addition to his position in his own ministry, he also holds a number of other posts which consume much time. He is key man on a Parliamentary Committee on Public Undertakings, and he must reply to numerous parliamentary reports and questions pertaining to public sector enterprises. He is a member of both the Licensing and Capital Goods Committee. He is on the board of directors of a public sector company. He is secretary of the Materials Planning Board, and a member of the Invention Promotion Board, the Standing Committee for Industrial and Scientific Research, and the National Productivity Council. He is also joint secretary of a Productivity Project Coordinating Committee. He works closely with the Directorate General on Technical Development on clearing imports and investigating whether local substitutes are available. He is also involved continually in ad hoc meetings, has contacts with a wide variety of people in government, and usually sees anywhere from 6 to 15 businessmen a day.

Serious problems involving state politics

State level politicians and government agencies are often involved in central as well as local decisions involving industrial enterprises. Conflicts between various states and the central government, and among the states, have become substantially more serious with India's growing political instability and the ouster of the Congress Party from power in quite a few states. Because of such conflicts, many firms are prevented from locating plants in desired areas, from shifting production from one state to another, and even from expanding their capacities. Moreover, small-scale industry has also suffered in some states, such as Bengal, because the central government has been tightening up on the allocation of resources and various forms of assistance it provides to the states.

Problems of the above types are much in evidence. For example, in 1969, a U.S. subsidiary was being prevented from shifting some production from its Calcutta Plant to its newer Madras plant because of state politics. This shift, which would lead to more efficient operations, would not even require a significant reduction in the Calcutta labor force. An indigenous firm in the same industry wanted to build a new plant in Gujarat rather than in Maharashtra, where it has its head office and existing plant. Production would have been more efficient in Gujarat for a variety of reasons, but Maharashtra state politicians and government officials were able to wield enough power and pressure to block the project.

A large British firm had its letter of intent for a new chemical plant recalled by the central government in 1969, after it had taken about three years to get it in the first place. Two other foreign firms desiring to set up similar plants also had their letters of intent recalled at the same time. But a letter of intent had been granted to an Indian company to construct such a plant in Uddar Pradesh. The owners of this firm have high-level political connections within their own state of Uddar Pradesh, as well as in the central government. In fact, the area where they intend to build the new plant is in Prime Minister Gandhi's constituency. From all indications, the location of this plant would be highly inefficient, since the bulk of raw materials would come from Gujarat, while most of the output would have to be shipped to markets in the Bombay area, thus resulting in an uneconomical triangular pattern of commodity flows. The three companies originally granted letters of intent would have set up their new plants either in the Bombay area or in Gujarat.

Industrial licensing

Since late 1963, or 1964 there has been a modest trend toward liberalization of industrial licensing. For example, products such as paper, cement, tractors, scooters, coal, some kinds of chemicals, and various consumer goods either no longer require licenses or are licensed under simplified procedures. Generally, firms not in the small-scale sector which are no longer subject to significant licensing control have not required substantial amounts of foreign exchange. Moreover, most companies have been allowed to expand their capacity or output by 25 percent without a license if no foreign exchange is required, except perhaps for some minor items involved in equipment balancing and the like. Moreover, in the mid-1960s small firms exempt from licensing were reclassified as those having less than 2.5 million rupees in capital assets as compared to only 1 million previously. This liberalization of licensing has resulted in a steady decline in the number of centrally approved licenses.

This trend toward decontrol has undoubtedly been beneficial in terms of India's long-term industrial progress. However, reforms currently under study by the government could sharply reverse the trend.

License applications from companies are supposed to be first received and reviewed by the Ministry of Industrial Development and Directorate General for Technical Development, who then send them to other appropriate agencies and ministries for further review. The consolidated recommendations involved in a major decision are then supposed to go to the inter-agency Licensing Committee which may make a final decision in some cases, but more often makes a recommendation for action to the Minister of Industrial Development. This minister can then make a final decision, or, if he sees fit, consult further with other ministers and high-level officials. If a major decision is involved the Cabinet and even the Prime Minister would typically be consulted and involved in the final decision.

Civil servants at the secretarial level in the Ministry of Industrial Development are supposed to be able to make various relatively minor decisions without clearing them through the Licensing Committee or the ministerial level. Even joint secretaries are, at least theoretically, allowed to make various kinds of decisions not deemed of major importance. In some relatively unimportant cases, members of the secretariat of industrial ministers other than the Ministry of Industrial Development are supposed to have the authority to make the decisions themselves without further consultation, if they wish to do so.

The above picture of the licensing decision process reflects the official arrangements, but reality frequently differs considerably from the official situation in ways and for reasons discussed earlier. Further complications arise because what constitutes a "very important," a "major," a "not very major," and a "minor" licensing decision is often a matter of discretion and interpretation. We have come across cases where companies wanting to sell unneeded equipment have had to wait between three and five years to get the required permission. For reasons not made clear, this kind of decision was deemed an important one and had to be approved by a variety of different officials and several agencies. On the other hand, we have come across some amazingly fast — by Indian standards — decisions involving multi-million dollar plants and projects.

As noted earlier, before a company can apply for a license it must usually first apply for and obtain a letter of intent from the government. This can also take much time, and of course, even the issuance of such a letter is no guarantee that the firm will ultimately be granted a license.

Applications involving foreign collaborations and foreign investment typically receive special scrutiny from various government agencies. They must also be processed and approved by the inter-agency Foreign Agreements Committees, and also the Capital Goods Committee if capital imports or equity participation is involved. If the foreign venture involves more than 20 million rupees of foreign investment, more than 40 percent foreign equity participation, or more than a 5 percent royalty arrangement, it must also be approved by the recently formed inter-agency Foreign Investment Committee.

A Government of India Survey, published in the *Reserve Bank of India Bulletin,* presents some interesting findings with regard to time lags involving new ventures and projects. The period covered was from 1961 to 1967. It took a substantial majority of firms three to four years to commence production from the time of incorporation, and in quite a number of cases, five years or more. The time lag between obtaining the industrial license and registration of the new venture was more than 12 months in nearly all cases. Projects involving foreign investment collaboration took on the average one year longer in this regard. It took an average of four years between the date of the license to the commencement of production, and in a large number of cases more than four years.

The statistics quoted above involving delays are basically consistent with findings obtained from the companies we have surveyed. In general, we found that delays in obtaining letters of intent and licenses from the Indian government during the period of 1966-68 were not as long as in earlier periods. A key reason for this is that application dropped off because of the economic recession. However, by mid-1968, as the economy recovered, the number of applications began to rise considerably, firms began to try more vigorously to push them through, and delays became lengthier. With serious political instability emerging in the late spring of 1969, the issuances of letters of intent and industrial licenses came to a virtual standstill.

Imports and foreign exchange controls

The government officially obtained the power to control the country's foreign exchange, imports, and exports with the Imports and Exports Control Act of 1947. At the time India obtained her independence, the country had relatively healthy foreign exchange reserves. Since 1957-58 the country has been faced with acute foreign exchange shortages. Reasons for this will be discussed later in this book.

Since the late 1950s India's foreign exchange position has been uncertain. This has encouraged a continuous preoccupation with short-run foreign exchange savings. Import substitution has been pushed hard with very little regard for the longer-run effects on cost or efficiency of production, or the net impact on industrial development. Only in more recent years — since about 1967 — has the government come to emphasize export promotion as a means of reducing foreign exchange problems.

India's foreign exchange crisis reached its peak around the time of devaluation of the rupee in June, 1966, and did not begin to subside until 1967. Underlying this severe foreign exchange crisis was the Indo-Pakistani War in the second half of 1965, in conjunction with a very sharp drop in agricultural production in the 1965-66 fiscal year. Large defense expenditures were followed by abnormally huge imports of food grains. Industries dependent on agricultural commodities for their own production or for export were hit particularly hard, and this led to a chain reaction adversely affecting other interrelated industries not requiring major agricultural imports themselves. The temporary withholding of foreign aid by various of India's major benefactors, including the United States, primarily because of the war, also contributed heavily to the foreign exchange crisis.

In general, a large and complex body of foreign exchange policies and controls have evolved in India. They have probably hindered the country's foreign exchange position and industrial development more than if there had been fewer, but more carefully thought out regulations, providing greater flexibility. Few aspects of industrial control are unaffected by considerations of foreign exchange. As a result, foreign exchange control is very often the dominant factor in the issuance of industrial licenses and the clearance of capital imports. And, here too, short-run balance of payments considerations almost always tend to predominate rather than long-range considerations of industrial efficiency or productivity.

The widespread unavailability of imported items, in conjunction with the uncertainties facing firms trying to obtain foreign exchange and import licenses, has resulted in serious and widespread managerial and efficiency problems in Indian industry. This has had a negative impact even on firms which do not directly require foreign exchange but depend upon suppliers or customers who must have foreign exchange licenses to function adequately.

The government's import policies and regulations — which change, at times dramatically, from one period to the next — are contained in the "Red" and "Blue" books issued each year by the Ministry of Foreign Trade and Supply. Allocations to firms are made on a fiscal year basis covering the April-March period. Although tentative allocations are made to companies for the entire fiscal year, they are subject to revision — almost always downwards — for the second six-month period. The above ministry, as well as the Chief Controller of Imports and Exports (CCIE), the Ministry of Industrial Development, (DGTD) the appropriate branch of industry ministries, and often various other agencies may all examine company import and other foreign exchange applications before a final decision is made. This is especially likely to happen if a company asks for more foreign exchange or imports than is allowed according to official policies and regulations.

But such policies are often not clear, and discretion may be involved in their interpretation. Firms attempt to find "sponsors" in the different agencies, as they do with regard to industrial licenses. At times one agency may act independently and grant the foreign exchange license rather quickly, supposedly in the "national interest." A good example of this involved polyethylene imports a few years ago. Even though this product had been manufactured for some time in India, some users of this commodity convinced the Ministry of Foreign Trade and the CCIE that a severe supply gap would result if sizeable imports were not allowed right away. This agency apparently felt that large polyethylene imports would control what it viewed as monopoly practices in this sector. Large imports of polyethylene were approved without consulting the other ministries and agencies that should have taken part in this decision. The supply gap turned out to be greatly exaggerated and the producers of polyethylene in India found themselves with excess plant capacity for some time. Attempts to trace through the government bureaucracy to find out why this import decision was made, or by whom, have met with little success.

The government is supposed to make all of its import entitlement decisions for the forthcoming fiscal year by April, but rarely if ever does. In 1964 and 1965 firms were not notified about their import entitlements until the end of July. With the extreme foreign exchange crises during the period of late 1965-1967 the foreign exchange licensing system broke down completely, and tremendous cuts were made in import entitlements. During this period only firms producing one or more of 26 products labelled highly-essential got import licenses from the government.

Given the complexities, delays, and uncertainties faced by firms in India in obtaining imports, procurement and the planning of related activities are frequently difficult. Lead times of as long as 24 months may be required for getting critically needed imports. It is not uncommon for firms to be unable to execute their import licenses within the time allowed. Customs problems often add to the delays, and may involve rejection of a particular shipment for a variety of reasons, both valid and irrational. Companies are required to provide masses of data, often distorted or false, in order to justify their foreign exchange requirements, since the government uses historical consumption and production data as the basis for determining present and future allocations.

Government import licensing decisions are supposed to be based on two key criteria: product essentiality on the output side and domestic or local availability on the supply or import side. Both criteria involve considerable discretion. DGTD puts out a handbook of indigenous suppliers of different kinds of materials, equipment, components, spare parts, and so forth. Firms must refer to this book before requesting import entitlements. Even if local suppliers are not producing goods of the sizes, quality, ranges or specifications desired by the company wanting to import, the firm must get "reject" or "regret" letters from suppliers before it can be granted an import license. But domestic suppliers often do not send such letters, or else they quote impossibly long delivery periods or extremely high prices. Then the firm is faced by more red tape and delays if it wants to appeal the case and still try to import the needed goods.

It is not uncommon for DGTD — which is responsible for technical judgment — or other agencies to play an "innovative" role, suggesting that a particular manufacturer could and should produce a desired item, even if it has never made it before. Too often such innovators do not really understand the unique needs or problems of the company trying to get an import license. Considerations of timeliness and cost are typically ignored by government agencies and officials.

In 1967 a new foreign licensing system emerged with a new and expanded list of high priority and essential industries and products. It has made the "rules of the game" clearer and more consistent as well as more predictable.

Much of the process of granting import licenses to firms has been decentralized within the government bureaucracy as compared to several years ago. For example, in 1969 industrial advisors and development officers in DGTD, as well as less senior secretaries, particularly joint secretaries in the industrial ministries, have been routinely making many of the import and other foreign exchange decisions which would have been referred upward in the government hierarchy in former years.

However, the question of "local availability" continues to present problems and delays for firms desiring to import, although perhaps not to the same extent as in the past. During the summer of 1967 DGTD organized a conference involving potential users and suppliers of machine tools. Many producers agreed to modify their products while several users agreed to adjustments in the requirements with regard to design, quality, and detailed specification. DGTD claims that this has led to a sharp cut in import licenses. Although the estimated figure of 170 million rupees may be exaggerated, an appreciable reduction in imports in this sector has no doubt been achieved. This conference was initiated because of the recession and the great amount of excess capacity that existed at the time. DGTD resolved to hold similar conferences for other products in addition to machine tools at regular intervals in the future. This could prove highly beneficial, but to the best of our knowledge few if any such additional conferences have been held to date.

In 1969 industrial enterprises requiring imports seemed to be most hamstrung and frustrated by the Office of the Chief Controller of Imports and Exports (CCIE).

Many firms also were finding it difficult to obtain the incentives and entitlements forthcoming from their export performance. This agency (CCIE) functions in an amazingly centralized fashion even though it has 21 local offices throughout India. However, these local offices have virtually no formal powers, and they deal primarily in routine paperwork. They handle import licenses for small-scale local industry, export permits, and the replenishment of imports based on expert performance. All non-routine decisions and matter of any significance are supposed to be referred to Delhi headquarters. CCIE scrutinizes, investigates, verifies, controls, and audits the issuance and use of import entitlements and foreign exchange licenses once they have been granted to enterprises. It is also involved in the scrutiny of export incentive schemes. CCIE processes an average of about 2,000-2,500 formal import and export applications per day, and between 350,000 to 450,000 annually. It can hold things up for long periods if it wishes to, and it can request further information and details at its own discretion.

In this discussion, we have focused primarily on India's import controls. However, stringent foreign exchange controls are applied in many other areas, including foreign travel, royalty and service fees, salaries and expenses paid to foreigners, and profit remissions. More will be said about these additional areas in later chapters. Such controls can create much uncertainty and are generally of greater concern to foreign firms than to most indigenous companies, since the former have more international transactions, as well as foreign contacts and personnel.

An example of governmental decision making and discretionary control

A good way to end our discussion of the problems posed by governmental control of industry in India seems to be to present an actual case in some detail. This case, although unique in certain aspects, is nevertheless quite typical with regard to the inherent problems of Indian government regulations and control on a virtually continual basis.

The case was still not entirely resolved at the time this was written. It involves a large electricity project under the Ministry of Irrigation and Power which wanted to import nine locomotives from Japan. An Indian locomotive manufacturer discovered this and, desiring the order, began to apply pressure through friends in various government agencies. The manufacturer finally obtained support from the DGTD, which announced opposition to importing the Japanese locomotives.

The Ministry of Irrigation and Power appealed the DGTD decision and involved the Ministry of Industrial Development, which is loosely in charge of DGTD. The matter was then handed over to an able and energetic joint secretary. His conclusion was that the best solution would be to import five locomotives from Japan, and let the local company produce four, thus enabling the electricity project to proceed.

The Indian producer immediately appealed directly to the Minister of Industrial Development who directed the above joint secretary to investagate further before any final decision was made. After further investigation the following critical points were revealed.

1. The Ministry of Irrigation and Power had received an import license for nine locomotives nine months ago, and had received a tender bid from a Japanese company which was accepted.
2. The necessary foreign exchange had already been allocated to the Ministry of Irrigation and Power.
3. DGTD should have been involved before all of this happened, but it was not even informed. The same was true with regard to the Ministry of Industrial Development and various other agencies.
4. CCIE issued the import license at its own discretion, which it can do if it is felt to be crucial for expediting imports in the national interest. But CCIE apparently did not even inform DGTD or the Ministry of Industrial Development.

As the above facts came to light, the chief secretary of the Ministry of Industrial Development received a letter from the secretary of the Ministry of Economic Affairs stating that the local locomotive price was 143 percent higher than the imported price. At this time Economic Affairs began to exert pressure to have all nine locomotives imported. It was backed up by the World Bank. U.S. AID also began to exert some behind-the-scenes pressures to have the locomotives imported from the United States.

Meanwhile, the joint secretary of the Ministry of Industrial Development made a further investigation of the price quoted by the Indian producer. He concluded that the price differential would actually be substantially greater than 143 percent since the Indian quoted price probably would not even cover direct costs. Various kinds of expensive materials — especially certain types of steel components, wheels, and so forth — would have to be imported by the Indian producer. He then suggested that, in order to bring down the Indian price, the local producer should be given the required steel at international prices, that a 7½ percent excise duty drawback be given to the firm, and that custom duties be waived on all imported components.

The Ministry of Steel has to approve the allocation of steel at international prices, as does the Ministry of Finance. Approval on the duty drawback and waiver of custom duties has to be approved by the Department of Revenue, probably in consultation with other agencies.

The Japanese firm was now asked by the Ministry of Industrial Development to quote on an order of five rather than nine locomotives. This increased the unit price by 8 percent. This contact with the Japanese producer revealed that it had already produced three locomotives for the order which it started working on some seven months previously. The joint secretary finally obtained approval to honor an order for five locomotives, which satisfied the aid-giving authorities like the World Bank, as it would not result in undue project delays.

At an unspecified future date the other four locomotives will be forthcoming from the Indian producer who still has to go through the process of obtaining the required foreign exchange, imports, and other approvals and requirements to produce them. Hopefully, approval can be obtained soon to rush three or four locomotives to the electricity project from another project, but this will also require the approval of a number of different agencies and ministries. Meanwhile, the joint secretary is still trying to get various approvals regarding steel, duty drawbacks, custom duty waivers, and the like. He is also now exploring ways to get special concessions on import replacements.

SOME SUGGESTIONS FOR IMPROVEMENT IN INDIA'S GOVERN-MENT BUREAUCRACY AND REGULATION OF INDUSTRY

This section focuses on changes in India's governmental structure and control procedures which would enhance her prospects for attaining desired objectives in the area of economic and industrial development. Although these suggestions are more easily made than implemented, they may provide the basis for further and more detailed analysis. The one thing that is very clear is that unless the Indian government takes concrete steps to improve the current system of administration, regulation, and control over industry, firms and their managers will continue to be seriously constrained from improving their effectiveness and efficiency.

It seems apparent that government control of industry should move toward greater liberalization and decontrol. The simplified political machinery that this would require could then devote time to developing more consistent and clearer policies in a smaller number of key areas. Rules and procedures could be simplified and supervision and enforcement could be made more effective. A systems approach is required which will clearly define the inter-relationships between various decisions, the sequential steps involved in making decisions, the types of information required at each step, and the specific agencies or officials involved at each stage. As part of this process, elements must be collapsed so that, for example, the granting of a license automatically ensures the availability of necessary foreign exchange or other scarce resources.

The efficient handling of industrial resource allocation decisions could be aided by preplanned assignments of scarce resources to industrial sectors designated as top priority for purposes of industrial development. As projects arose in these sectors, they would receive immediate attention, and licenses would be granted whenever a firm could prove that its proposals would further national objectives. Lower priority projects or sectors would be dealt with at a later date, after top priority needs had been met.

Of course, not everything can be preprogrammed and clearly spelled out in advance. Some exceptions and inconsistencies will always arise, and there should be some leeway for discretion and interpretation. However, clear-cut and preprogrammed procedures should be used for dealing with exceptional cases, and also for handling appeals, instead of the current process where firms go from agency to agency and official to official to seek advocates for their causes.

Serious consideration should also be given in many cases to eliminating the letter of intent stage which precedes the actual granting of industrial licenses. Firms now have to go through the same process twice, with much more detail usually entailed the second time. With better and clearer planning, organization, regulations, and controls, such duplication may not be necessary.

In order to streamline the huge government bureaucracy, some major organizational changes seem to be required. The number of steps, officials, and agencies involved in a decision should be reduced in an effort to streamline the decision-making process. The use of integrated task teams having the skills and provided with the information to deal effectively with licensing decisions might also prove highly beneficial. So might a reduction in the number of administrative levels in the hierarchy.

The combination of various industrial ministries would also help. For example, several branches of industry ministries such as Chemicals and Petroleum, Steel, Mines, and so forth, could be reorganized as wings or major branches of the Ministry of Industrial Development. This would reduce many of the inter-ministerial conflicts that now exist and which must be resolved by the Cabinet or even the Prime Minister. This could provide faster, more coordinated, and better decisions.

In the same vein, DGTD should be more effectively integrated into the Ministry of Industrial Development. It may also prove beneficial for DGTD or various other agencies to organize coordinating conferences at regular intervals involving suppliers and customers in different sectors. As noted earlier, one such conference in August, 1967, apparently proved successful, and this approach could be expanded to cover expansion programs and other areas subject to industrial licensing and resource allocation, in addition to import problems.

It would also seem to be more feasible in terms of coordination for CCIE to be placed under this ministry rather than the Ministry of Foreign Trade. (In the past it was, and there seems to be no good reason for its having been shifted several years ago). There should also be considerably more decentralization of authority within CCIE.

Along with the above kinds of reorganization — and even without them — serious consideration should be given to reducing the number of personnel employed by various government agencies. Such reductions, particularly among lower-level administrators and clerks, would reduce the number of levels of hierarchy, and probably lead to faster and better decisions.

Retrenching government personnel is likely to be a distasteful and unpleasant task. However, out of necessity the Indian government in recent years has laid off many thousands of people employed by public sector companies. If it earnestly wants to improve administration the government may have no choice but to take similar steps in this sector. At the same time the overworked and able government administrators at the middle and upper rungs of the hierarchy should in many cases be provided with more qualified supporting staffs and assistants.

Recently greater emphasis has been placed on appointing government administrators who are involved in the control of industry on the basis of their knowledge of managerial and industrial problems. Many who have not had industrial experience have enrolled in training programs, and apparently have become less antagonistic toward businessmen and the private sector.

Furthermore, the appointments in the last few years of leading professional managers from private industry, such as K.T. Chandey and P. Tanden formerly of Hindustan Lever, as heads of such public sector companies as Hindustan Steel and the State Trading Corporation, suggest that Prime Minister Gandhi is now concerned and aware of the need for greater managerial competence and professional skill in government and government-operated enterprises. But, significantly more of this must be done.

THE USE AND MISUSE OF CONSULTANTS AND OUTSIDE EXPERTS IN BRINGING ABOUT IMPROVEMENT AND CHANGE IN THE GOVERNMENT BUREAUCRACY

A number of competent Indian government administrators earnestly want to take steps to improve the system in which they work. They seem eager to bring in consultants and other outside experts to help achieve this. In particular they feel that major improvements can be made in the areas of information systems, organization structure, mechanized data processing and information storage, including wider use of advanced planning and control techniques such as PERT (Performance Evaluation Review Technique), operations research, industrial dynamics, and systems analysis.

However, too often when outside experts and consultants have been called in to undertake studies in government agencies concerned with the industrial sector, their lack of knowledge of the real situation, their biases and preconceptions based on organizations and conditions in other countries, and their focuses and general frames of reference have led to virtually useless findings and recommendations. Often, they assume the stated formal organization to be the real organization, and they attempt to impose optimum theoretical or conceptual system changes on nonexistent bases.

Despite problems and limitations, it does seem that improvements in Indian government administration to facilitate more effective industrial management and development can be achieved with the aid of consultants and outside experts. But this requires high-level support and cooperation, and attention devoted not just to the *need* for a particular kind of study or change in the system, but also to the likelihood of a payoff in identifying and influencing the key officials who are in a position to actually implement change. This could result in a much more effective use of resources, time, and effort.

CONCLUDING REMARKS INVOLVING MANAGERIAL IMPLICATIONS

Although this chapter paints a rather bleak picture of India's political-legal environment, the reader should understand that its focus is largely on the negative constraints to industrial progress. In general, the government has tried to treat favorably and equitably both foreign and indigenous firms which have been willing to serve the nation's interest. And most major firms have continued to earn sizeable — although significantly declining in most cases — profits.

In general, India's political-legal environment presents the challenges, problems, and opportunities to businessmen present in most other developing countries. Perhaps the major difference is the diffuseness of the power groups in India. Unlike many Latin-American, African, or other Asian nations, it is difficult for an industrialist or manager to find one individual or group in India with whom an alliance would prove both politically and economically valuable in virtually all situations.

It is especially important for the foreign executive to recognize that India has and requires a more planned and regulated economy than do advanced capitalist countries. This means that activities of the firm must be consistent with national objectives if scarce resources are to be used effectively. The criticisms we have directed at the existing situation do not relate to the need for a planned or a regulated economy, but at the specific manner in which the planning and regulation process is being implemented.

Company representatives sent to negotiate with Indian politicians and government officials must make an effort to understand the values, motives, and priorities of these officials. In fact, it would generally be wise for firms to send executives who know the personalities and characteristics of the government personnel with whom the firm has dealings. It also often pays the firm to take into account region of birth, native tongue, and at times even caste of both the representatives they send to Delhi to negotiate and the key government officials involved in such negotiations.

The more impersonal, hardnosed, straight-forward, and objective approach which may work well in government-business dealings in the United States is much less likely to prove effective in India.

CHAPTER 5   FOOTNOTE

1. In addition to many Indian and United States government sources, United Nations and World Bank reports and newspaper and journal articles, we have drawn substantially on the following more widely distributed basic published works in our discussions of legal and political factors.

G. Myrdal, *Asian Drama,* 3 vols., Pantheon, New York, 1968; M. Kust, *Foreign Enterprises in India,* University of North Carolina Press, Chapel Hill, 1964; *A Handbook of the Companies Act,* Indian Chamber of Commerce, Calcutta, 1968; J. Baronson, *Manufacturing Problems in India,* Syracuse University Press, Syracuse, 1967; V. Sing, *Industrial Labour in India,* Asia Publishing House, New York, 1963; S. Kherd, *Government in Business,* Asia Publishing House, New York, 1963; A. Negandhi, *Private Foreign Investment Climate in India,* Institute for International Business Management Studies, Michigan State University, East Lansing, 1965; *India: Business International's Indian Roundtable* Business International, New York, 1961; N. Das, *Industrial Enterprises in India,* Orient Languanes, Bombay, 1962; L. Vidyarthi, *Leadership in India,* Asia Publishing House, New York, 1968; R. Bhaskaran, *Sociology of Politics,* Asia Publishing House, New York, 1967; G. Rosen, *Democracy and Economic Change in India,* University of California Press, Berkeley, 1966; H. Crauch, *Trade Unions and Politics in India;* Wand R. Chambers, Edingurgh, 1966; A. Aggarwal, *Indian and American Labor Legislation and Practices,* Asia Publishing House, London, 1967.

CHAPTER 6
ECONOMIC
ENVIRONMENT

The economic environment within any nation is closely linked to its political and legal systems, since the latter invariably are explicitly or implicitly built on ideologies and values which relate to both social and economic goals. This relationship is often more intimate in developing countries than in economically advanced nations such as the United States, primarily because resources are more limited and more direct government intervention is required in an effort to assure their desired utilization.

In reality economic constraints are not independent variables but are complex sets of interrelated phenomena. For analytical purposes, however, it is possible to examine each of them separately. Our major interest in this chapter relates to economic factors which affect managerial and firm performance.

OVERVIEW OF INDIA'S ECONOMIC PERFORMANCE[1]

While India's overall economic performance to date has been far from impressive, it has been better than that of many other countries. India has not stagnated, and many significant qualitative as well as quantitative improvements have been achieved.

The pattern has been erratic, especially during the decade of the 1960s. In particular, very poor agricultural performance for several years, the wars with China and Pakistan, the foreign exchange crisis, and more recently, growing political instability have seriously hindered industrial progress and general economic development. These conditions have contributed sharply to other serious economic problems such as inflation, economic and price instability, high costs, excess capacity, low productivity, capital shortages, and so forth.

During the 1950-69 period India's national and per capita incomes grew at annual average rates of about 3.4 percent and 1 percent respectively. Agricultural output barely kept pace with 2.5 percent population growth and some estimates indicate that it fell behind. Industrial production grew by about 6 percent; but if small-scale, handicrafts, and cottage industries output are included, the overall industrial growth rate was only approximately 4 percent.

Since the early 1950s industrial labor productivity in India has grown at an average annual rate of about 3 percent and industrial employment by about 2 percent while capital investment per industrial employee has grown by approximately 11 percent. India's capital-output ratios — which indicate the additional output derived from an additional unit of capital input — have been relatively poor in terms of international standards, especially in the public sector, and in fact this ratio has deteriorated by roughly 5 percent during the 1960s as compared to the 1950s. Labor productivity has also declined significantly during the decade of the sixties. In general, the performance of the public industrial sector has been substantially worse than that of the private sector with regard to productivity, profitability, and overall efficiency.

In absolute terms India ranks among the top 10 percent of all countries in the world in total GNP, overall industrial production, and agricultural output. However, it lags far behind the most advanced industrial nations, and, in per capita terms, is still a very poor country. India's total GNP is only about 5 or 6 percent of that of the United States — depending on what exchange conversion rates are used. Per capita income in around $100, less than 3 percent of that in the United States, while her current population of about 550 million is more than two and a half times greater. Total factory employment is less than half of the U.S. total, and total industrial output is less than 5 percent. Industrial output per worker (in all occupations, including agriculture), is less than 2 percent of the U.S. worker.

Two key policies have been basic to India's industrial strategy. The first is to accelerate growth and induce major changes and modernization in the industrial structure with the government playing the key role as regulator, investor, and innovator. The second is to greatly increase self-reliance, including import substitution, especially since the mid-1950s. In spite of the tremendous costs and inefficiencies entailed, these strategies, at least until quite recently, have generally succeeded.

Industrial growth has been significantly better than overall economic or agricultural growth. Before 1956 consumer goods accounted for about two-thirds of India's manufacturing output. Today it accounts for only about one-third. Since

1956 capital goods and intermediates have achieved annual average growth rates of more than 10 percent, while consumer goods output has grown by about 2 percent annually. The bulk of foreign investment has been in capital goods and intermediates. In 1950 textiles accounted for about 53 percent of India's industrial output, while today it accounts for only 24 percent. On the other hand, machinery output has doubled since 1950, and now accounts for about 19 percent of industrial output; chemicals and related products have doubled and now account for over 10 percent; and iron and steel production has increased by 50 percent and now constitutes about 13 percent of industrial output.

India's most serious economic crisis since the country achieved independence in 1947 began to emerge toward the end of the Third Five-year Plan, in the mid-1960s. Actually the economic system started to bog down and run into serious difficulties a few years earlier, but the government was slow in recognizing this and even drafted a Fourth Plan for the 1966-71 period which projected rapid growth rates. But during the Third Plan period rising inventories and excess capacity, a shortage of investment resources, as well as other serious resource scarcities and imbalances in the economy, all became increasingly serious problems. In addition, a widespread lack of confidence in the ability of the public sector to attain its objectives began to emerge, and this eventually led to the postponement or cancellation of quite a few public sector projects. The private sector also became increasingly pessimistic about the economic outlook.

The biggest blows to the economy during the mid 1960s were the war with Pakistan towards the end of 1965, and the poor agricultural performance in the 1965-66 fiscal year. Agricultural output fell by about 16 percent, and large military expenditures (including imports of defense items) were followed by abnormally huge imports of food grains. This resulted in India's most critical foreign exchange crisis, which reached its peak around the time of the devaluation of the rupee in June, 1966. Furthermore, the large imports required to complete projects initiated during the Third Plan period coupled with the temporary withholding of foreign aid by India's major benefactors (including the United States), primarily because of the war, contributed heavily to the foreign exchange crisis.

The situation gave rise to the decline of power and serious conflict within the Congress Party. Subsequently, the Fourth Plan was scrapped and the country operated without a five-year plan during the 1966-69 period.

In 1965-66, national income declined by more than 5 percent, and per capita income regressed to the 1960-61 level. Industrial output showed only a modest growth of 4 percent. In 1966-67 agricultural and industrial growth and national income stagnated. In 1967-68 agricultural production increased sharply — by more than 18 percent — national income increased by 8.5 to 9 percent, but industrial growth was stagnant again. However, by early 1968 an overall recovery in the industrial sphere was occurring, and an increase of 6 to 7 percent in industrial output was achieved in 1968-69 — about 2 percent below the target. National income increased from 2.5 to 3 percent during this period, while agricultural showed only a small gain in the range of 1 to 2 percent. However, for the 1969 calendar year, agriculture posted a gain of about 3 percent or slightly better.

Even though industrial output increased by 6 or 7 percent in the 1968-69 fiscal year, most of this growth was achieved by putting idle capacity and other resources back to work. Private sector investment dropped significantly in 1968-69 as compared to even 1967-68. During 1968-69 only 65 private sector companies — including foreign controlled firms — entered the stock market (raising a total amount of 434 million rupees) compared to 71 firms raising over 600 million in 1967-68. The combined project costs of all 65 companies in 1968-69 amounted to 1326 million rupees, as against 2037 million for the 71 companies in the previous fiscal year. Of the total project costs in 1968-69 only 180 million rupees was to be invested by new companies, while the balance of 1146 million was to be used by existing firms either to expand or diversify. The above figures reflect the increasingly pessimistic private investment climate that has evolved recently in Indian industry. The rate of foreign private investment has also fallen substantially in the last several years.

INDIA'S CURRENT FOURTH PLAN AND BEYOND

India's Fourth Five-Year Plan for the 1969-74 period projects an average annual increase in national income of 5 to 6 percent. Its annual average growth rate projections for industrial production, agricultural output, and net capital investment are 9 percent, 4.5 percent, and 13 to 14 percent respectively. Per capita income is projected to increase at a rate of about 3 to 3.5 percent while average annual population growth is expected to remain around the current 2.5 percent level. During this period it is anticipated that food imports from the United States under PL 480 will be eliminated, non-food imports will not grow by more than an average annual rate of 5 percent, and exports will increase at a rate of 7 percent. If these targets are achieved, net foreign aid would be cut in half by the end of the plan period in 1974.

This plan emphasizes various programs aimed at significantly improving agricultural performance, building up large buffer stocks of food, keeping inflation in check and maintaining price stability, significantly improving the country's balance of payments position, and greatly reducing dependency on foreign aid. It calls for relatively modest investment outlays — although they have been raised since the Draft Plan was completed. It also calls for a substantial expansion of the public sector with considerably more emphasis on profitability and efficiency. However, the public sector will not expand at as high a rate as during some earlier periods. In general, the plan calls for relatively balanced overall economic and industrial development, both by sector and by region. It also emphasizes restraint of excessive economic power, more dispersion of ownership, and greater income equality.

If the Fourth Plan is carried out successfully India's Planning Commission makes the following projections for the longer term. During the 1974-81 period national income is projected to grow at an annual average rate of 6 percent, population by only 1.7 percent, and per capita income by over 4 percent. By 1981 India would no longer be dependent on foreign aid according to these projections, and net capital investment will be 17 to 18 percent.

If India does achieve the above targets and goals, or even comes close to them, she will have accomplished impressive and sustained growth and development — a situation attractive to both foreign and indigenous private investment. However there is little hope that this will be accomplished unless greater political stability is maintained, along with a more effective and rational system of government regulation and control of industry.

The early results do not look very encouraging. Recent estimates indicate that in 1970 industrial production fell 3.5 percent from 1969. The wholesale price index rose by 6.8 percent, while a 2.2 percent increase in national income failed to keep pace with a 2.4 percent population growth rate. The estimated results for the fiscal period of 1970-71 were somewhat better, but still below the targets. In general, substantial improvements in many of the environmental constraints under study in this book will no doubt be required in order for India to perform as well as she hopes and plans to in the decade of the 1970s and beyond. Moreover, the severe refugee and political situation involving Bangla Desh which emerged in the early 1970s is also likely to place major constraints on the attainment of key goals in India's Fourth Economic Plan.

BASIC ECONOMIC SYSTEM

Every society must develop some type of system to answer the fundamental economic questions: What kinds of goods and services are to be produced? How much of each kind? By whom? How? For whom? At the heart of these questions is the basic problem of resource allocation. No country is wealthy enough to give all its citizens all of the goods or services they may want. Given this fundamental constraint, some form of rationing of scarce or limited resources must be developed. The resource allocation problem is most crucial in poorer and developing countries, and serious waste and inefficiency in the allocation and utilization of scarce resources tends to be a greater drain on the economics of poor, as compared to relatively affluent, countries. Yet inefficient resource allocation is frequently greater in the poorer countries, because of serious shortcomings in their basic economic systems.

Types of economic systems

At the extremes there are two basic types of economic systems available for handling the resource allocation problem: capitalist or free enterprise, and Communist or

Marxist. The former allocates resources through a competitive market price system where firms pursue profits as a key if not the paramount objective, consumer sovereignty reigns, and individuals pursue self-interest. The latter allocates resources through a comprehensive system of state planning, regulations and fixed prices, where enterprise profit is not necessarily a key objective, and where the interests of the state and its planners frequently take precedence over consumer sovereignty and individual self-interest. In both systems the aim is to allocate resources in the best way to achieve desired explicit or implicit objectives, and to equate supply with demand.

Virtually all economies have at least some elements of both Communist (state planning and resource allocation) and capitalistic (market forces) economic systems; and even in the more advanced countries — including Russia and the United States — there has been a noticeable trend towards convergence in recent times. However, in a majority of countries either the capitalist or Communist type of economic system still forms a distinctly dominant pattern. On the other hand, in contemporary times a growing number of "mixed" economies have emerged, particularly in developing countries, where the capitalist-Communist economic system distinction has become blurred, and where substantial elements of both market forces and state planning exist together. India is a country of this type, as are quite a few other countries in Asia, Africa, Latin America, and even Europe. Often such countries refer to themselves as "socialist" or "welfare" states, even though they may permit a considerable amount of private property ownership.

There seems to be a limit to the amount of comprehensive or detailed state planning that can be imposed on any type of economy, especially a relatively developed economy, strongly indicates that even relatively advanced Communist countries can no longer handle the crucial resource allocation problem either effectively or efficiently through pervasive or detailed state planning. A major problem has been one of information overload. It has become increasingly difficult to design information systems and feedback mechanisms that are responsive enough to show errors and discrepancies in plans and operations to enable timely corrective action, or to enable consistent and well-balanced comprehensive plans to be designed. The complexity of the task seems to balanced comprehensive plans to be designed. The complexity of the task seems to exceed man's ability to handle such problems, at least at the moment.

The more advanced Communist nations, including the Soviet Union, have run head-on into this problem.[2] Most are now altering their economic systems to rely more on capitalistic techniques, incorporating a greater use of scarcity pricing, more meaningful profit motives, industrial decentralization, and even enhanced emphasis on competition.

India's economic system: Organization of industry

Perhaps the most striking characteristic of India's economic system relates to her socialistic pattern of government and the mixed economy philosophy and partial state planning system that derive from this ideology. Business activities are a blend of government and private ownership, of highly regulated and virtually unregulated private firms, of some state-owned companies managed by private interests, and of indigenous and foreign independent and joint ventures involving both public and private ownership. In some cases the foreign involvement involves a foreign government.

Although India's public industrial sector has grown greatly since the mid-1950s, it still accounts for less than 15 percent of the nation's total factory output. If the small-scale private sector is excluded, it accounts for slightly over 20 percent. The public sector, however, represents roughly 35 percent of India's total industrial investment, and new investment in the Fourth Plan heavily favors the public sector. India has about 250 public sector industrial and mining enterprises, of which 60, accounting for 90 percent of total sector investment, are owned by the central government. The remainder are state owned. Most of the public sector output is in producer goods, and, to a lesser extent, intermediates, with little involving consumer goods.

The most dynamic and efficient force in India's economic development has been the larger private companies, including many foreign firms. However, individual companies show wide variation in terms of efficiency, dynamism, and managerial styles. Even the largest private firms in India are typically much smaller than their foreign counterparts in advanced countries. Many of the most dynamic and successful of these are influenced significantly by foreign practices and technology, through foreign ownership, collaboration or licensing agreements. These companies generally fall within the organized and regulated sector according to the Industries and Factory Act.

Most indigenous private firms in India are owned by single families or small groups of families or friends. Only a small number have broad public ownership — foreign firms now representing a disproportionately large share of them in this regard — but even in such cases management control is typically vested in the hands of small family groups. Again, foreign firms tend to be exceptions.

In general, one of the characteristics of private indigenous firms is the coincidence of ownership and management. There are relatively few instances where ownership is so widely dispersed that hired professional managers actually run the firm. In cases of such management it is primarily because the owning family is too small and has too diverse interests to look after daily operations. This pervasive coincidence of ownership and management control in India's private sector has hindered the effective growth of firms on a widespread scale.

India's largest private industrial empires are dominated primarily by family controlled managing agencies or conglomerates, although several have become increasingly involved with foreign collaborations in contemporary times. In the last few years they have come under strong attack by politicians and government officials because of their size. The six largest industrial houses which accounted for about 20 percent of India's industrial fixed assets in 1956 accounted for about 21 percent in 1967.

However, within this total the relative share of some industrial empires has changed sharply. Tata's, which in 1958 held over half the total assets of the top six, now holds less than one third, while Birla's, having doubled its assets since 1958, has slightly surpassed Tata's empire. Martin Burn also fell relatively while Mufatlal increased its relative share considerably. Those industrial empires with large holdings in basic metals — sectors in which government corporations have obtained large shares of the market — have grown more slowly than the more diversified houses like Birla's and Mufatlal's. Birla in particular has moved vigorously into new fields and has thrice the number of Tata's companies. Birla has been successful in getting new licenses, and this family has been a bigger backer, financial and otherwise, of the ruling Congress Party, than Tata or the other large houses.

By law, India's managing agency system terminated on April 3, 1970.[3] Managing agents typically received fees, ranging on a sliding scale from 4 to 10 percent of the net profits of the companies and affiliates that they controlled. Some 400 managing agents have now ceased to function under this law, but more than 100 have been trying to circumvent the law by managing affiliated companies through treasurers and secretaries. However, this loophole has now also been abolished, at least officially. Managing agents have also been appointed as selling agents by the affiliates they previously controlled, in order to preserve a fee or commission for them. While some former managing agents will relinquish or lose control of some of their subsidiaries and affiliates, most will probably continue to control them in much the same way that conglomerates and holding companies operate in the United States.

The largest numbers of companies and workers in Indian industry are in the small-scale private sector firms, which are relatively free of government regulation and control. In recent years, an increasing number of such firms have become interested in foreign collaboration, particularly licensing and technical know-how relationships. There are a number of definitions regarding the small-scale sector in India, and a brief explanation of each of them follows:

1. The conventional definition includes cottage and handicrafts industries which employ traditional labor-intensive methods to produce traditional products, largely in village households. They employ none or at most a few hired hands. The handloom textile industry is a prime example. This sector has been declining sharply and steadily, though it still employs millions of people.

2. The operational definition for policy purposes includes small factories registered under the Factories Act. Before 1967 it included all industrial units which had capital investment of not more than 500,000 rupees (then $100,000) irrespective of the number of persons employed. In 1967 the ceiling of capital investment was changed to include investment only in plants and machinery, and not land and buildings. This definition does not include unregistered manufacturing units which employ less than 10 persons with emergic power or less than 20 without power.

3. The third Indian definition of small-scale industries relates to national income accounting. This covers "all manufacturing and processing activities, including maintenance and repair services, undertaken by both household and nonhousehold

small-scale manufacturing units, which are not registered under the factories act." This is essentially a subfactory classification. There are few foreign firms in this overall sector. Contrary to popular belief, the small-scale industrial sector as a whole is still India's largest in terms of total output and value added, although its total share and growth have been declining steadily. It still accounts for roughly 50 percent of the nation's manufactured output in terms of net value added, and over 90 percent of India's industrial units, but it only accounts for a small share of the country's industrial capital investment. All in all, India's small-scale sector is unusually large even when compared to other poor and developing countries.

If we use definition 2. above — registered factories with Rs. 500,000 in plant capital investment — this sector accounts for about 27 percent of India's total industrial output, 20 percent of its net value added and 33 percent of its employment, but only 6.5 percent of its fixed investment.

About 75 percent of the output of the overall small-scale sector is comprised of consumer goods, with textiles accounting for by far the largest share. However, many of the small and more modern factories produce a variety of chemicals, plastic products, components, tools, machinery and semi-processed items which have industrial uses. At one time 73 industries were reserved for the small-scale private sector, and larger firms were banned from entry. However, there have been many violations by medium-sized and large firms. This number was reduced to 47 banned industries in more recent times.

The government now plans to increase this number considerably, especially in the consumer durables area; e.g., sewing machines, radios, bicycles and refrigerators.[4] Moreover, the capital investment limit for licensing and other purposes is being raised to 10 million rupees, although it is not yet clear exactly how this reform is to be implemented, especially with regard to control. A desire for increased employment and greater dispersion of income and wealth appear to be prime reasons for the government's interest in expanding the country's small-scale industries.

Unlike the common growth pattern in U.S. business and industry where many firms start small and eventually grow, few small enterprises in India become larger. Educational and sociological-cultural constraints in India seriously hinder both internal growth and mergers. Moreover, expanding small firms frequently subdivide — thus often losing potential economies of scale — in order to keep under established ceilings so that they can qualify for the special concessions provided for small business by the government. Larger firms in India are usually established on a medium-size scale and grow from that point.

India's machine tool industry is representative of a sector containing government-owned corporations, medium and large-scale private firms, and small-scale enterprises. The seven government owned corporations in this industry account for about 45 percent of its output. Of the 107 licensed private firms in the organized sector, five of them account for 50 percent of the total private output. The more than 1000 small-scale private units account for only a very small portion of its output.

India's economic system: Planning, resource allocation and control

The basic intention of India's five-year plans is to take stock of the nation's resources, project resource availability, and channel resources into activities which will maximize desired economic development and well-being. The plans also identify needs and deficiencies. In general, they are blueprints for overall development, and they indicate which sectors are to be stimulated, as well as policy and regulatory guidelines.

In reality, planners have been unable to identify in adequate detail the specific nature of interfaces between various sectors, or to pinpoint the effects that a given action will have on different sectors. This is largely due to a lack of understanding of the industrialization process, as well as to the uncoordinated nature of planning activities and the collection of statistics. The government has only recently begun to experiment with input-output analysis and has not yet applied it effectively to practical planning efforts. This approach could become useful as a tool for indicative planning. To date, economics has not really produced an effective optimizing instrument for India, nor does it seem likely to soon, given the country's nuclear priorities, diverse objectives, political system, economic problems, and basic economic system.

Controls are not effectively linked, nor are they closely tied to plans. Consequently there is often little relation between the state plan and its execution, especially with regard to the private sector, since no way has yet been found to enforce compliance to objectives set forth in the plan. As time passes, unrevised plans become less useful guides to action as projections become further divorced from reality. Often projections of physical quantities not only become inconsistent with one another, but also with the financial projections to which they relate. The licensing system — a basic form of control — has been far from effective in ensuring an allocation of resources which is consistent with the plan. Even where capacity targets have been achieved, output targets often are not met.

The design of India's economic plans suffers from serious deficiencies, largely informational. In many cases estimates and projections have been grossly overoptimistic. Capacity projections have frequently been based on unrealistic expansion plans for both public and private plans. Inadequate allowances have been made for long lead times, procedural delays, and inept management. Similarly, inadequate allowances have been made for resource and transportation bottlenecks as well as the development of adequate suppliers. Numerous illustrations of gross error abound. In the Third Plan period of 1961-66, the government projected a demand of 2.5 million electric meters, a product sold largely to state electricity boards and the railways. Actual demand and production turned out to be only about 1 million. In several industries, errors of similar size have caused more than half of the licensed producers to go out of business. On the other hand, in many instances demand has greatly exceeded supply.

Capacity calculations have presented another type of problem. Many firms successfully obtain licenses only to prevent competitors and potential competitors from getting them, and in spite of the fact that they are not used, the government often renews them. During the 1956-66 period one-third of all the new project and expansion licenses issued were not implemented.

A good, and quite typical, example of a case where demand has seriously exceeded supply in Indian industry because of planning and control problems involves alcohol. During the Third Plan period India's planners contributed to a serious alcohol shortage because key officials concerned with the licensing of alcohol capacity were uninformed about plans to construct a relatively large synthetic rubber plant which requires large inputs of this basic chemical. The latter's information and projections indicated sufficient capacity already was in existence and firms which requested expansion or new project licenses for alcohol production were turned down. When the new rubber plant came into being critical shortages of alcohol ensued, adversely affecting not only liquor producers and hearty drinkers, but more important, firms producing other important chemicals, drugs, etc.

Black marketing activity, as well as the activities of numerous unlicensed small firms, also distort planning projections and divert supplies from their intended uses. Firms substantially pad their requests for goods which are allocated by the government, since they know they will receive less than what they ask for and since the allocation process is often handled in an arbitrary manner.

The allocation of some centrally controlled items is handled by state governments. They negotiate with the central government and then reallocate what they get among small firms. Large firms deal directly with the central government. The same types of gamesmanship, personal influence, and corruption are involved at this level as in dealings between larger firms and the central government. One study of steel allocations conducted during the Third Plan period revealed that the percentage of requests actually received by firms varied from state to state from 14 to 60 percent.

Some major impacts on firms and their managements

In general, basic deficiencies in India's economic system contribute considerably to critical economic and managerial problems such as imbalances among interdependent sectors, huge bottlenecks, gross underuse and overuse of productive capacity and other resources, unfair competitive advantage and protected markets, enterprise profits which have little or no relationship with productive efficiency, and so forth. One finds excess capacity in various sectors (e.g., various engineering and capital goods industries), and at the same time critical scarcities of various commodities (such as various kinds of chemicals, metals, agricultural supplies and equipment, special tools, and components) which result in strong sellers' markets. To some extent this is true of all economic systems, including the U.S. economy; but the degree and extent of such problems are substantially greater in India than in many other countries. On the other hand, there are also other poor and developing countries which have even more severe problems in this area than India.

In this kind of environment it is difficult for even relatively well-managed companies to make future plans with precision. Control and day-to-day problems tend to
become more important than planning ahead or innovating. There are strong pressures
to centralize many of the operating decisions which are usually made at lower managerial levels at companies in the United States since they are more critical and much
less subject to preprogramming in Indian industry. Organizations are also structured
quite differently in India with more emphasis on procurement and government relations, since firm management there typically must devote more time and energy to
these functions than in U.S. industry (especially nondefense sectors).

The concept of managerial effectiveness is viewed chiefly in terms of how well a
company and its management "beat the system," work around government regulations
and controls, and thereby reap profits and other rewards. The profits and rewards too
often have little relationship with improving managerial performance within the firm,
raising productive efficiency, or otherwise contributing significantly to the broader
society. Many firms which play this game actually prefer the system since they can
make sizeable profits even though they produce substandard products at high costs,
have low productivity, great waste, spoilage and inefficiency, take few significant
risks, and do little in the way of real innovation.

Our conception of managerial effectiveness — which also tends to be much more
widely held in the United States as compared to India — does take into account
entrepreneurship and the way company management deals with the external environment. However, it also gives greater weight to how well management improves
its internal performance and firm efficiency. In India too little attention is paid
and too little weight is given to the concept of efficiency. A key reason for this is
the nature of India's basic economic system, which fails to provide enough pressure
on industrial enterprises to be efficient and effective in the way that Westerners
— and U.S. firms in general — typically view these concepts.

In spite of the problems relating to India's economic system, there is still considerable leeway to utilize modern managerial practices and techniques in order to
reduce the impact of negative constraints and improve performance. In this regard,
there are significant differences among various firms surveyed in India — and between
U.S. and indigenous companies. More will be said about this in later chapters.

ECONOMIC SYSTEM CHANGES UNDERWAY AND UNDER STUDY IN INDIA

We have referred in the previous chapter to the Dutt Report on Industrial Licensing
Policy which advocated major changes in India's economic and regulatory system.
The main thrust of this report involves restraining the size and expansion of large
private indigenous companies and foreign firms. It is not concerned with problems

of efficiency or abusive monopoly power per se. If it were to be implemented, it would lead to considerably greater government regulation and control of industry. The report was made public in July, 1969 and has since been considered by the Indian Parliament and the Cabinet.

On February 19, 1970 the government announced its New Industrial Policy, and this was followed by several statements of clarification.[5] While this policy has clearly been influenced by the Dutt Report, some of that report's key recommendations were rejected or modified. However, the new industrial policy and related changes in India's economic system still leave much to be desired.

The Dutt Report advocated the creation of a joint sector where the ownership and management of firms would be shared by government and private interests. Large indigenous firms and foreign concerns, particularly those obtaining substantial but unspecified, capital financing from public financial institutions, would be placed in this sector. Joint sector firms could be entirely reverted to the public sector at a later date. Under various conditions even private companies not requiring much state financing could be placed in the joint sector which would be subject to comprehensive state planning.

The government, at this point, clearly desires to expand the role of the public sector. Industries earmarked for public sector development in the Industrial Policy Resolution of 1956, and subsequent additions, will continue to be reserved for this sector. These include power, iron and steel, heavy electrical and mechanical machinery, petroleum, basic minerals, aircraft and shipbuilding. The government intends to expand the list of industries reserved for the public sector, and it also appears that more government firms will be entering consumer goods industries. Larger private companies will usually, if not always, be prohibited from setting up new ventures in industries reserved for the public sector.

Experience indicates that the granting of exclusive rights to government companies in all of these sectors without giving adequate weight to efficiency, productivity, and managerial considerations is an unwise course of action. In many cases, large private firms — both indigenous and foreign — have been, are, and will probably continue to be more efficient and effective than government corporations. In order for existing private firms to expand in the above industries a license will be required. Central government monopolies will continue to run air transportation, key defense firms, and atomic energy, with large private industrial houses and foreign firms generally confined to the core and heavy investment sectors.

"Core" industries include iron and steel, non-ferrous metals, oil and petroleum, fertilizers, petrochemicals, pesticides and various other major chemicals, synthetic rubber, cooking coal, newsprint, tractors and certain other agricultural equipment, various kinds of industrial machinery and machine tools, many electronic components, ship-building and dredges, and some other products. All investments over 50 million rupees are considered to be in the "heavy investment" sector. In this sector applicants will be required to give "full details" in order to justify the need for the high level of investment and the granting of a license. The government will prepare detailed plans for the core industries and essential inputs will be made available to them on a "priority" basis. The new industrial policy also states that "care" will be taken to ensure an "adequate" proportion of foreign exchange for non-core industries as well. Larger firms and foreign concerns will require expansion, as well as new project licenses in these sectors.

"Large industrial houses" are currently defined as those who have assets in land, buildings, plant, and equipment exceeding 350 million rupees. There are currently about two dozen such complexes in India. It is likely that before very long the government will reduce this figure to 200 million rupees, in line with the Monopolies and Restrictive Practices Bill currently under study. Assets are valued in terms of their original costs, and, where rented or leased, their capitalized value is to be used. A "foreign concern" is one in which more than 50 percent of paid-up equity capital is held by foreign interests.

Under the new policy, the de-licensed sector pertains to enterprises whose total investment does not exceed 10 million rupees. This exemption limit has just been raised from 2.5 million rupees which the Dutt Committee wanted to maintain. The new limit is the one recommended by the Hazari report, and it will cover many medium-sized as well as small companies. The larger industrial houses, foreign concerns, and "dominant undertakings" require a license in order to set up a unit or expand in the de-licensed sector.

A "dominant undertaking" is defined as one which either by itself or along with interconnected undertakings produces, distributes, supplies, or otherwise controls not less than one-third of the total goods or services of a particular type within India. The criteria for "dominant" also relate to the value, price, cost, output, or capacity of goods and services, or related employment. A firm and its affiliates will be considered dominant if any of the above criteria are met for any one of three calendar years immediately preceding the calendar year in which the question of dominance is determined. Many firms in India — including foreign subsidiaries and small firms — are dominant according to the above criteria, although careful scrutiny and considerable discretion would be needed to determine this precisely in many cases.

In the case of expansion of existing enterprises the exemption from licensing is to be provided only if the additional investment does not exceed 10 million rupees, and the overall investment including the existing one does not exceed 50 million, and also if the unit to be expanded does not belong to the larger industrial houses, foreign concerns, or dominant undertakings. Apparently, larger private companies can no longer expand their capacities up to 25 percent, even if no significant amounts of foreign exchange are involved, without government approval. This means even tighter control for them. License applications from parties other than large companies are to be given "special consideration" and shall be issued "liberally," except where foreign exchange implications necessitate careful scrutiny.

For industrial licensing exemptions the following foreign exchange conditions must be met in all cases: the enterprise's capital imports cannot exceed 10 percent of total capital required; imported materials cannot exceed 3 percent of ex-factory value of the products consuming their imports or 300,000 rupees, whichever is less; imports of components cannot be required beyond three years after production starts, but even then component imports will be regulated in accordance with the phased manufacturing program approved by the government. The new industrial policy clearly points out that the issuance of a license for a new undertaking, product, or expansion does not contain any commitment whatsoever regarding foreign exchange, imports, financing, or any other type of assistance. These things will still have to be determined separately and on their merits by appropriate government agencies.

The provision in the new policy for the re-licensing of industries which had been de-licensed since the mid-1960s indicates that of the more than 40 industries which were on the de-licensed list, about 6 now fall within the purview of licensing because their investment exceeds 10 million rupees per unit. Among the de-licensed industries for which licenses will now be required are paper, newsprint, cement, tractors, agricultural machinery, and continuous costing machines.

In the past "banned" lists were drawn up from time to time for the purpose of indicating the industries for which license applications would ordinarily be rejected automatically. These lists comprised products reserved for development in the small-scale sector and those for which adequate capacity had already been licensed.

The small-scale sector is to continue to include firms having a total fixed investment under 750,000 rupees. The new industrial policy still provides for the reservation of about 47 product lines for the small-scale sector, and the range of industries reserved for this sector is expected to be expanded substantially in the near future. The government has proposed that the following industries be added to the small-scale sector in the near future: steel furniture, cycle tires and tubes, electric horns, aluminum utensils, mechanical toys, pens, smaller hydraulic jacks, and tooth paste, among others. For agro-industrial licenses special preference is to be given to the cooperative sector.

The Dutt Report advocated a review of banned and reserved (small-sector) products every five years, while the more recently released Lokanathan Committee recommends an annual review. No government decision has been made in this regard at this writing. The Lokanathan Committee favors somewhat less licensing and regulatory control in general than the Dutt Report, though it has urged that effective measures be taken against the unauthorized expansion of larger firms in reserved areas because this limits the growth of small-scale and medium industries.

In general, there will still be intense scrutiny of projects and operations even in the de-licensed sector. Enterprises not requiring any industrial licenses under the new policy will still be faced with a registration procedure involving two detailed forms with supporting documents. One form will contain "full particulars of expected annual sales and production, phased manufacturing program and requirements for imports," and so forth, at the time when preliminary steps are taken to set up or substantially expand an industrial unit. The second form — which is even more detailed — must be furnished to the government immediately after commencement of production of the unit concerned.

With the end of the managing agency system in April, 1970, the licensing provisions of the new policy are likely to undergo substantial changes. A clear picture in this regard is not likely to emerge until the Monopolies Bill is put on the statutes, and this has still not occurred at this writing. Ultimately, the definitions of different industries and sectors as contained in the Monopolies Act are likely to become operative for industrial policy purposes. At least until then, considerable uncertainty and discretionary control can be expected to prevail.

The firms which presently have license applications pending with the government are required to review them to see whether they are covered by the new exemptions. If they are they may be withdrawn. On the other hand, those which are no longer exempt, even if they have taken steps to start production or have already started, must apply for licenses within three months. This also includes enterprises not falling within the limits of the new foreign exchange exemptions. The application form and related procedures in all of the above cases are very detailed and time-consuming.

It is by no means clear that India's new industrial policy will succeed in its objective of creating new entrepreneurship and stepping up industrial growth. Reservations for smaller firms and restrictions on the entry and expansion of relatively big ones cannot produce an economic miracle. Greater emphasis must be placed on encouraging and pressuring small, inefficient firms to grow and become more efficient, in addition to stifling the growth of larger companies.

Restrictions on larger and dominant firms will probably continue to be directed more by political than economic considerations. This is likely to retard industrial development and make India's high-cost economy even costlier. Stringent controls aimed at keeping down the prices of raw materials, producer goods, and components will seriously hinder the profitability of these firms, and hence their capacity to expand, especially in the core industries or heavy industry sector.

If, as expected, the definition of large private companies is reduced from 350 to 200 million rupees of assets, the range of government licensing and control would be widened considerably. Given a continuation of inflation and rising costs large numbers of companies in more and more industries will fall within this 200-million-rupee definition. New undertakings will therefore be at a significant disadvantage compared to those already established, since the cost and value of assets can be expected to continually increase, probably substantially.

The Monopolies and Restrictive Practices Bill, which is expected to become law sooner or later, focuses on absolute size and product concentration. According to this bill, if a firm's own assets, or those of the industrial house to which it belongs, exceeds 200 million rupees, or is one which occupies a "dominant" position as defined earlier, it must seek government approval in order to merge or expand by more than 25 percent. It must justify its position in terms of the public interest. However the Monopolies Bill, as it now stands, does not give emphasis to industrial efficiency or abusive monopoly power per se.

The government's new industrial policy gives the right to public financial institutions to convert loans made to private companies into equity capital, enabling them to have an "effective say" in the management and operations of the loanee firms. Such financial institutions will be required to exercise this right within a period of five years, and once this option has been exercised, it cannot be revoked. This right will presumably be exercised particularly in cases where the financial institutions think their loans are not being judiciously used or where expected profitability is greater than the interest rates chargeable on the loans.

In principle this may seem like a valid approach. But if "effective say" means that public financial institutions are to be provided with veto power (and this is not yet clear) in the affairs of the loanee company — for example, with regard to personnel recruiting and salaries, sales agents, procurement contract, sources and uses of funds in general, and so forth, even though they do not have a controlling interest in the firm, this will seriously infringe on the rights of shareholders or other sponsors and managers of the undertaking. In effect, this could amount to back-door nationalization, even without controlling interest in the company. More will be said about this in the sections dealing with banking and capital markets.

One other reform that deserves mention here is the establishment of a new Industrial Cost and Prices Bureau under the Ministry of Industrial Development.[6] The decision to set up such a bureau was made in December, 1969, following a proposal for a permanent pricing and cost committee or commission which was originally announced in the summer of 1969.[7] The new commission regulates commodity prices, investigates costs, and is generally given "wide" but rather unclear powers to do so. All industrial price disputes are now referred to this body rather than the Tariff Commission under the Ministry of Foreign Trade. The latter only determines the types and amounts of price protection with regard to foreign competition and trade.

This new bureau apparently has more limited powers than the proposed permanent commission. It is focusing on overall cost structures, possibilities for technological improvements, better use of resources, and import substitution in relation to prices and opportunity costs. It has the right to request detailed data from firms in major industries. The bureau is headed by a full-time committee of three members plus a chairman. It also makes use of outside consultants.

A truly nonpolitical, independent, and well staffed Industrial Costs and Prices Bureau having clear-cut powers involving pricing and cost analyses for a limited number of key commodities can lead to an improvement over the existing system of price regulation and control. But if politics continues to enter significantly into the picture, and the other above conditions are not met, it is likely that such a bureau will do more harm than good. In fact, it may well result in a greater number of arbitrary decisions, and more red tape, uncertainty, and inefficiency for firms. The experience of pricing bodies with relatively broad powers in Communist countries clearly points in this direction. At this point in India's development, fewer price controls rather than more would probably be the wiser course to follow.

It is difficult to predict specific changes the Indian government will implement in the future in an effort to improve the country's economic system. One must project political developments in order to forecast economic changes accurately, and at this time this is difficult to do with much confidence. Many crucial questions involving India's economic system and related regulations and controls remain unanswered. It does seem clear, however, that large size and large market shares in the private sector have become increasingly undesirable — chiefly for political reasons — to those who currently govern and run the country. All indications are that larger private and foreign companies will generally be discouraged and prevented from entering or expanding in all but specified "core" or heavy investment sectors, and even here government corporations are likely to play an increasing role.

SOME RECOMMENDATIONS: KEY ECONOMIC SYSTEM CHARACTERISTICS AND BASIC PRESSURES FOR EFFICIENCY

It seems that for managerial effectiveness and productive efficiency to increase substantially in a sustained manner and on a widespread scale, at least one of three basic types or sets of broad forces must be in operation. The first pertains to market forces and competition which pressure firms and their managements to be more efficient and effective. It appears that India now has a broad and diverse enough industrial base, and that the time is ripe to let this set of forces play a greater role in many sectors. Investment, foreign exchange, output, price, distribution, and other controls should be relaxed together in a systematic and consistent manner.

Strong fiscal and monetary policies are required for such a system to function well. In India's case, she should move towards a tariff-based import system, and possibly towards multiple exchange rates. Less emphasis should be placed on short-run balance of payments problems and highly rigid import substitution and greater emphasis on developing a sound and realistic overall development program which would tend to encourage more exports and attract the foreign investment and aid necessary to fill the gaps.

A second set of factors involves state economic planning, including effective planning of resource allocation and utilization. India could benefit considerably by implementing many of the best features of France's system of indicative national planning.[8] This would mean considerably more liberalization and decontrol in the Indian economy. The French plan is based on branches of activity rather than on specific companies or products. Its aim is not to dictate specific courses of action for private enterprise or to serve as a direct control device. Rather it states basic economic and social objectives for the nation and particular goals for each sector. Within this framework each firm is free to choose its own targets and strategies. The firm acts on the basis of better information, but still at its own risk.

The French government has been using both "carrots" and "sticks," but considerably more of the former, to get private firms to operate in accordance with "Le Plan." Nearly half of the country's total fixed-capital formation is in the public sector in any case. Credit controls and an array of fiscal incentives are granted to those companies supporting specific plan objectives. Incentives are supplemented by a limited number of regulations, and when necessary direct governmental intervention; but emphasis is on incentives and persuasion rather than direct control. Unlike India, where the government approves numerous things that firms can and cannot do, the French government is chiefly concerned with a relatively limited number of things companies cannot do. The French government intervenes directly only where there is danger of serious imbalances in the economy. The controls that do exist in France are, on the whole, more clearly specified than in India, and relate primarily to major investment decisions, some commodity prices, and credit regulations.

A major characteristic and strength of French planning is that it seeks to draw on all major decision centers in the nation, and this has tremendous informational benefits. About 31 planning commissions consisting of more than 2000 members are used for this purpose. Both the number of commissions and total membership have increased substantially since the inception of France's Five-Year Plans in 1947. These planning commissions are separate from the Permanent Planning Commissariat under the French government. The structure contains (vertical) branch-of-industry commissions and six (horizontal) coordinating commissions. About 20 percent of the members are business executives, and another 20 percent are from professional organizations including industrial and trade associations and various occupational groups. Labor union representatives comprise 14 percent of the total membership, government officials 29 percent, farmers and farm managers 3 percent, and various other experts 14 percent. The planning commissions are a key source of information in preparing the national plan. They also indicate measures that public authorities and private decision makers should follow in order to achieve the stated national and sector targets, make recommendations for improving conditions, review the implementation of the plan, analyze significant deviations, and come up with revisions or additional recommendations.

"Le Plan" has its greatest influence on large firms, and on major investment and other key financial decisions. It does not have nearly as great an impact on marketing strategy, production, procurement, personnel, or even R&D decisions. Foreign-controlled companies, especially large ones, tend to be less influenced or constrained by the plan. "Le Plan" provides considerable leeway for competition and market forces — even among large companies — but at the same time reduces waste and excess capacity and leads to better resource planning, allocation, and utilization.

Although French planning is not without problems and deficiencies, its positive effects clearly outweigh the negative. All in all, India could benefit considerably by moving in the direction of this kind of planning.

India's planners, policy makers, and controllers need to focus more on efficiency considerations, not merely on foreign exchange, import substitution, investment, or output. This would do much to help reveal real growth bottlenecks. To the extent that priorities are required, they should be spelled out much more clearly.

A particular problem with regard to allowing more competition and exerting less government control involves the marginal or inefficient producers, including many smaller firms, that might go out of business. Quite a few of them may unfortunately do so. This is in fact what happened on a substantial scale during India's last serious economic recession. But it is healthier for the economy in the longer run for inefficient firms to go out of business because of growing competition by increasingly efficient and expanding enterprises, than for other reasons.

On the other hand, some protection is required for relatively inefficient firms, particularly if there is a good chance that they will become more viable and efficient in the not-too distant future. Various kinds of assistance programs, as well as mergers, could be effective in this area.

The third set of forces that can spur enterprises and their managements to greater efficiency involves sociological-cultural factors which affect the attitudes, motivations, and related behavior patterns and performance of owners, managers, and other industrial personnel. These factors correspond to the variables or constraints which were covered in Chapter 4.

When enterprise personnel, especially key executives and owners, have basic attitudes which emphasize performance improvements, industrial development benefits. This seems to be the case regardless of the specific type of economic system of the country.

For example, leaving periods of intense ideological extremism aside, Communist China has been effective in terms of resource allocation and utilization, as well as growth and development. China seems to have developed a substantially better sociological-cultural environment with regard to economic development than India, and her industrial growth and development have been markedly better on the whole than India's to date.[9]

This is not to say that the type of economic system a country has is not of importance. However, in a developing country in particular, widespread or dominant attitudes and behavior patterns emanating from the sociological-cultural environment may well be even more significant with regard to managerial effectiveness, productive efficiency, and development.

The mere presence of market forces and competition does not *automatically* assure that firms and their managers will become substantially more efficient. The lack of basic attitudes and qualities that make for a competitive spirit tends to reduce many of the potential economic and other benefits that could be derived through reasonably healthy competition. On the other hand, a planned economy does not *automatically* lead to greater productive efficiency.

BANKING AND MONETARY POLICY

Overview

One of the problems basic to industrial management and economic development is that of providing credit to firms in the form of liquid capital. To achieve efficiency, the capital must be provided in the correct amounts to the right firms at the right time. This involves rationing out scarce monetary resources to the enterprises that will use this asset most efficiently and in the best interests of society at large.

A related problem is the control of the money supply in an economy so that there is neither too little nor too much on hand at any time. Too much will lead to price inflation, as excess money chases scarce goods and services; too little may well lead to deflation and recession, with correspondingly poor economic results.

The basic organizer of the money stream in most economies is the central banking system, or a similar institution which performs central banking functions. The central bank has various tools to accomplish its task, including the authority to set interest rates, create money or destroy it, set reserve requirements for commercial banks — regardless of whether they are state or privately owned — and rediscount commercial bank paper. The commercial banks, in turn, are also implementers of monetary policy in their dealings with firms and individuals, even though they are subject to regulations imposed by central banking authorities.

The manner in which the central bank and commercial banks perform their duties has a direct bearing on the management practices of industrial enterprises. Poor planning related to the available supply of money, or the establishment of unsound interest rates, can contribute to unnecessary crises and even depressions, causing firms to operate considerably below potential capacity or even to be literally destroyed. A sharp decrease in the amount of money in circulation will mean that less is available for loans, and this will have a direct effect on firm planning, organization, and staffing. It is also likely to lead to less demand for goods and services, with direct effects on company marketing, production, procurement, and financial policies. The same is likely to be true in the case of a sharp rise in interest rates. As aggregate demand shrinks due to recession, sales strategies, product lines, production needs, and inventory policies change in order to reflect these external conditions.

The availability of too much money at low interest rates can lead to artificial booms, excessive industrial expansion, imbalances among different sectors, and eventually, recession. In general, in a country where significant changes in monetary policy are uncertain or frequent, corporate planning is difficult; and the result is inefficient use of productive resources.

In many underdeveloped countries banking and monetary policy are ineffective or too passive to maintain economic stability. The caliber of the men who set monetary policies is frequently as great a problem as the regulations which constrain industrial progress. In recent years, major improvements have been achieved in banking and monetary policy in various developing countries — such as Brazil and Chile — by putting effective experts in charge. In other countries the reverse has been true.

Poor timing or shifts in the wrong direction cause an economy to fluctuate dramatically, bringing on depressions or severe inflation, and producing foreign exchange crises. This creates an atmosphere of uncertainty for industrial managers. Questions of timing can be critical, and the banking system may be guilty of actions which might be correct at one time, but are not at another. Political inteference can also seriously influence monetary policy.

It can be inferred that a banking system and monetary policy are effective if a particular country has experienced relatively little price-level fluctuation, if business recessions and booms are relatively mild, if the currency holds its value on international markets, if economic growth and industrial progress continue steadily, and if firms that deserve capital and can use it efficiently can get it at reasonable cost. Of course, by no means all of these conditions are entirely under the control of the banking system and monetary policy, but if economic stability and progress is to occur, it is usually necessary that banking and monetary policy be relatively effective.

The case of India

The banking system and monetary policy tend to be more effective in India than in many other developing countries. Nevertheless, there is still much room for improvement. As compared to the United States and other advanced non-Communist countries, relatively little effective or direct use has been made of monetary policy as a regulator of economic activity in India. Credit controls and interest rates have been outside the purview of India's Five-Year Plans, even though the plans focus on aggregate investment. Moreover, interest rates in India have been too low in relation to true capital scarcity; in fact they have been kept considerably lower than in most advanced countries. At the same time, India's money markets have been insulated from foreign markets.

With superficially low interest rates and capital costs the government has had to rely on other controls such as licensing, in an attempt to channel investment and other resources along desired lines. This has resulted in wasted and misused capital. It has also encouraged firms to become more capital-intensive at the expense of serious unemployment and a huge surplus labor pool.

Typically, interest rates and the cost and availability of funds are given relatively little weight by firms in their investment decisions. Most of the companies studied in India have not been concerned or constrained with regard to getting desired funds — as long as foreign exchange has not been involved. Government licensing approval and regulations and the availability of imports and required local supplies have been much more important factors.

India's banking system and monetary policies contributed to economic and price stability during the first fifteen years or so after India's independence. However, most of the 1960s have been characterized by serious economic instability, including a severe recession, acute foreign exchange crises, serious price inflation, and poor allocation and use of financial resources. But such factors as adverse weather conditions leading to poor crops, severe overpopulation, war, deficiencies in governmental planning and control of industrial activity have been more to blame for India's economic dilemmas than the banking system and monetary policy per se. Moreover, poor management and internal financial arrangements within many firms have presented greater constraints to productive efficiency and growth than external problems resulting from monetary policy and the banking system.

In U.S. industry, even a 1 percent difference in interest rates is a limiting factor in financial decisions. Certainly a 2 or 3 percent difference is of great importance, even during the inflationary and tight money situation that persisted in the late 1960s and 1970. This is not generally the case in India.

It is true, however, that in India inefficient companies, particularly small enterprises, often face a critical problem in obtaining adequate funds from banks and other financial institutions. It is common for such firms to have to resort to private moneylenders who charge monthly interest rates of 3 percent or more. However, stories of the unavailability of funds for smaller firms in India, and the discrimination against them by banks, seem to be somewhat exaggerated. In many cases the rejected enterprises are so inefficient and close to insolvency that banks would be taking undue and extreme risks in granting them credit.

On the other hand, favoritism, personal influence, and questionable practices (as opposed to merit or credit-worthiness) do seem to play a greater role in obtaining bank loans in India than in the United States. Moreover, Indian banks are more likely to "overlook" bad checks and overdrawn accounts for longer periods of time than banks in the United States. While indigenous companies in India are more likely to unduly influence banking officials than foreign firms, we have come across some instances where U.S. subsidiaries and managers have also resorted to bribes, "gifts," and other special favors.

Indian banks are less inclined to thoroughly scrutinize loan applications than U.S. banks. Often the bigger the pile of data submitted by the loan applicant, the better his chances of getting the loan. There also seem to be more violations and less effective enforcement of banking regulations laid down by central authorities in India than in the United States. For example, restrictions concerning loan limits, allowable time periods for various kinds of loans, and uses of funds are often not enforced.

In general, India's commercial banking system contains many inefficiencies, although foreign banks in India tend to be relatively more efficient. Indian banking operations are performed almost entirely by manual means and transactions between banks take long periods to clear. The system is laden with checks and counterchecks to make sure that everything is kept legitimate. For example, a study conducted by one of the authors indicated that, in a typical situation, as many as 13 signatures were required before a teller could cash a check 1) drawn on the branch of the bank at which the check was presented, and 2) presented by a person who had an account in that same branch. The process for making such payment usually required from 20 to 45 minutes' wait, and could take hours or even weeks if either of the two conditions were nonexistent.

Checking accounts are not widely used in India outside of intercompany transactions, and this limits bank resources for lending. Checks are rarely used in meeting industrial payrolls. Relatively few workers would know what to do with a check, and if they did, would have difficulty cashing it. A few firms surveyed which have used checks for meeting payrolls ran into so much pressure from workers that they had to revert to cash payments. Cash payments are also the rule in dealings with small traditional suppliers (leading to the generation of black money, as well as providing outlets for its use).

In many cases poor timing and political interference have rendered monetary policy ineffective in the Indian economy. A prime example of this was the devaluation of the rupee in June, 1966. Devaluation should have been undertaken at least several years earlier, and many experts feel that when it finally did come it should have been of a substantially greater magnitude. (The rupee was devalued from 4.75 to 7.5 rupees per U.S. dollar.) Internal political considerations were the causes for the delay and the limited extent of the devaluation. It was forced by rampant black marketing activity, strong pressures exerted by major aid-giving nations, and India's severe foreign exchange crises. Just before devaluation the Indian government estimated that roughly 40 percent of all business transactions in the country involved elements of black marketing activity.

Although devaluation has made imports more costly, direct government administrative control rather than market forces is still used in allocating all but a small share of India's imports. While devaluation has contributed to the substantial increase in India's exports, the impact of the increase in exports has not been that great, and prospects for further substantial and sustained increases in the future remain cloudy.

It is interesting to note that few firms or uncompleted new plants and projects hedged against devaluation. Most companies evidently became convinced that the government would not succumb to devaluation in the foreseeable future, or that there was just too much uncertainty regarding devaluation to warrant hedging. It is also surprising that a great many firms did not know how to hedge against devaluation, even if they had wanted to. One diversified U.S. company displayed considerable ingenuity in anticipating and coping with the devaluation. Management engaged in forward buying of foreign exchange to cover its inventories. It also made some early payments of dividends and other remittances. Whether this was mere luck, effective planning and intelligence, or some combination of both, is open to question. However, a careful and continuous analysis was made by parent company experts, as well as subsidiary managers, of foreign exchange reserves, balance of payment trends, the scope of black marketing activity, external pressures on the Indian government, and the prevailing opinions and apparent moods of key Indian politicians and government officials.

India's Reserve Bank (central bank) regulates the nation's money supply and shifts interest rates in an attempt to maintain economic growth and stability. Here too, poor timing and political interference have often rendered the monetary policy ineffective, particularly in recent years. The total money supply in India increased considerably and steadily during the 1952-65 period. Since 1965 it has been erratic, with substantial contractions and spurts within short periods of time. Credit squeezes have hurt many firms during periods of acute tight money. The aggregate deposits of the commercial banks have continued to increase in a more stable manner than the total money supply. On the other hand, the volume of commercial bank credit and check clearances have been erratic since 1966, and this has no doubt hindered planning and operations at many firms. However, other environmental conditions have been of greater concern to most of the firms surveyed. It is common for firms in India to be able to borrow short-term working capital funds from the banks of an amount up to 75 percent of their inventory value, and a ratio of 3 rupees for every rupee of their own is not unusual.

The timing and effectiveness of changes in interest rates in the Indian economy have also been far from ideal. During the 1951-63 period the reserve bank rate remained quite steady in the vicinity of 4 to 5 percent. The prime rate of commercial banks stayed within the 5 to 6 percent range, and the maximum legal rate was several percent higher. However, since late 1964 interest rates have been higher and have shifted more frequently than in the past. For example, banking interest rates were raised three times in the month of March, 1966. The Reserve Bank rate increased from 4½ to 6 percent within five months from September, 1964, to February, 1965. Since 1965 the reserve bank rate has ranged between 5 and 6½ percent, the prime commercial bank rate between 7 and 9 percent, and regular bank rates between 8 and 12 percent.

Interest rates paid by U.S. and other major foreign subsidiaries and large Indian companies on short-term bank loans and overdrafts have been basically similar. The affiliates of large managing agencies have been able to borrow money at interest rates in the vicinity of 0.5 to 1.5 percent less than if they were not part of these business empires. In 1969 U.S. subsidiaries and the more blue chip indigenous companies surveyed were paying 8½ to 9 percent on bank loans. In some cases these firms were paying slightly more, or 9½ percent, for rupee financing at U.S. and other foreign banks in India. Other indigenous firms surveyed, including a few small ones, were paying 9½ to 10 percent on short-term bank financing.

In the last several years a growing number of indigenous companies have been taking deposits from private parties which they use for their own financing. In quite a few cases such deposits are substantial, amounting to millions of rupees. Foreign firms in India have shied away from this kind of financing. They feel that it could create serious problems which would outweigh the potential benefits derived. Most companies pay from 9 to 12 percent interest on their private deposits, and a few prestigious firms pay slightly less. These deposits have provided a haven for much black market money, and largely for this reason the government recently passed more stringent disclosure regulations for such deposits.

At this time monetary policy could be a more effective regulator of the Indian economy if interest rates and the cost of capital in general were to reflect true scarcity values more accurately. Differential interest rates, selective but clearly defined credit controls, as well as a certain amount of financial rationing and earmarked funds, could be used to achieve clearly defined priorities, in place of heavy reliance on discretionary controls. Moreover, the undesirable expansion of large companies could be restrained by various monetary policies, as well as, possibly, a requirement for higher equity to debt ratios. Something along these lines seems to be essential if market forces, in conjunction with mere objective and automatic regulators and controls, are to play a greater role in the Indian economy.

The recent bank nationalizations can also provide the government with the means of employing more effective use of monetary policy.

Nationalization of India's banks

In July, 1969, Prime Minister Gandhi nationalized India's 14 largest private banks. This left only about 15 percent of the country's banking in private hands. The remaining private banks were either small or foreign-owned, the latter including a few U.S. banks such as Bank of America and First National.

When the 14 banks were nationalized the stated general aims for this action included a desire for greater monetary efficiency in business; elimination of black marketing activity, and corruption, and the placing of more emphasis on the needs of smaller firms and the agricultural sector. Although not officially stated, another purpose seems to have been increased use of the banking system to supply funds for public sector enterprises which have been obtaining the bulk of their funds from government sources.

Shortly after the banks were nationalized major shareholders brought the case to the courts. They charged that nationalization was illegal since it violated their constitutional rights. Their specific charges included unfair compensation and discrimination, inasmuch as not all of the private banks in the country had been nationalized.

In February, 1970, the Supreme Court ruled 10 to 1 that the nationalization law was unconstitutional. However, the court did not question the right of India's President to nationalize the banks or the right of Parliament to legislate on banking matters. To reassert the government's control over the banks, Mrs. Gandhi then turned to the same device she used in July, 1969, an ordinance signed by the President, V.V. Giri. This ordinance was turned into bill form and passed by Parliament.

The new bill was carefully written by leading experts in the Ministries of Law and Finance to meet the court's objections. The bill increased the amount of compensation to shareholders from $100 million (750 million rupees) to $113 million, and gave them the option of choosing their payment in cash or securities, or some combination of these. Originally, they were to be paid in bonds, but the court ruled this inadequate since the actual value of the bonds did not match their face value. In drawing up the new ordinance and subsequent law, Mrs. Gandhi turned aside the strong advice of many of her left-wing allies who favored nationalization of all 89 of the nation's domestic and foreign banks, in order to get around one of the discrimination charges. She apparently felt, no doubt correctly, that such a move would have a drastic effect on foreign capital, which India clearly still needs.

India's recent bank nationalization was motivated more by political than economic reasons. However, there is considerable justification for such a move on economic grounds, provided nationalization is effectively implemented. In France a major portion of the nation's banking activity is nationalized, and the banking system plays a key role in the context of French planning. India should seriously consider moving in this direction.

Nationalization of the Indian banks could lead to more effective use of monetary policy as an economic regulator. In turn, this could reduce the amount of discretionary control and cumbersome governmental regulations in the industrial area. It could also reduce and provide for more effective control of black marketing activity, corruption, illegal financial practices, and the misuse of funds in industry. Moreover, it could lead to a substantial increase in funds available to smaller firms and agricultural producers. In the past 15 years, India's financial institutions have given more than 50 percent of their combined credits to the 30 largest business empires.

However, such potential benefits as those noted above depend on whether politics can be kept out of banking, whether the banks themselves are effectively staffed and managed, and whether excessive and ambiguous regulations and controls hinder the banks from functioning efficiently. The banks could be forced to provide excessive funds for wasteful and efficient purposes, including the expansion of the public sector.

Apparently Mrs. Gandhi is taking a more moderate and realistic approach than many of her foes expected regarding bank nationalization. For the time being at least, she is letting the banks keep their separate identities, she has not yet made any major changes in their managements and staffs, and she is permitting more competition and flexibility to prevail in the banking sector than many persons anticipated. She has also acknowledged that banks should be managed by competent professionals, without any undue political interference. Hopefully, this will prove to be the case in the future.

Perhaps surprisingly, most of the industrial enterprise managers that we interviewed in India since the banks were nationalized were not seriously disturbed about this move. This has also been true of key executives of U.S. companies with regard to their subsidiaries and affiliates in India. Although some of them view bank nationalization with cautious skepticism, they have adopted a wait-and-see attitude. Their major concern is with the excessive delays, red tape, and controls might result from it. This has also been a concern voiced even by small firms that might otherwise benefit from the availability of more funds.

Most U.S. subsidiaries and other foreign companies surveyed in India had been dealing chiefly with the State Bank or other government financial institutions before nationalization took place. Several also had been dealing with foreign banks which have not been nationalized, but which have had restrictions placed on their deposits following the other bank takeovers by the government. (The foreign banks in India cannot expand their total deposits beyond what they were prior to nationalization.)

Many indigenous Indian companies surveyed, particularly those which have been part of large managing agencies, have dealt with a number of different banks, in some cases as many as ten or more. Most, if not all, of these banks are now nationalized, and owners and managers of such companies have been the most critical about the bank takeovers. A prime reason for this is that in many cases their firms could more easily engage in questionable financial activities and manipulations, illegal practices, black marketing, and hard bargaining under a system where they could use a sizeable number of different private banks than may be possible under a system of nationalized banks.

As noted earlier in this chapter, the government's "New Industrial Policy" gives government (public) financial institutions the right to convert their loans into equity so that they can have a direct say in the management and operations of loanee enterprises. With the nationalization of the country's leading commercial banks, the contribution of such institutions to the capital of business firms will increase considerably. This raises some obvious problems and fears.

FISCAL POLICY

Overview

The national budget is the basic instrument of governmental fiscal policy in all countries. The role of this budget is to allocate funds and transfer resources in accordance with government decisions from one area of the economy to another. In stagnant, underdeveloped nations, with poorly developed systems of public administration, government expenditures typically range between 5 and 10 percent of all expenditures. In developing mixed economies and advanced nations the government share ranges from about 10 to 35 percent. In both India and the United States it has been roughly in the vicinity of 13 to 20 percent in recent times. In Communist countries, where most of the productive effort is in the government sector, the percentage of government spending may run higher than 60 percent.

Governments or their closely controlled banks have the power to create money simply by printing bank notes, expanding bank deposits, and through various other monetary policies. They also raise money by fiscal measures, the most common being taxation, as well as bond issues and deficit financing. Taxes usually provide the major source of revenue in the national budget, particularly if the government does not follow a course of extreme deficit financing. Tax measures are also used to encourage and discourage various kinds of economic activity. The manner in which governments obtain the funds they spend, as well as how they spend it, has a direct impact on the economy at large, and on industrial enterprises.

Where the government channels too much spending too fast into certain sectors of the economy, serious imbalances and bottlenecks emerge. This leads to excess capacity in some industries, and excess demand, often accompanied by inflationary pressures, in others. Excessive deficit financing affects the stability of the country's currency, and can lead to inflation followed by depression, as well as a serious drain on foreign exchange. Overoptimistic and erroneous cost or revenue predictions further compound these kinds of problems.

Stability in government expenditures is also relevant for managerial effectiveness and enterprise efficiency. In countries where the national budget is relatively stable and consists largely of standard items which do not vary much from year to year industrial firms find it easier to supervise their activities efficiently than in countries where the budget and pattern of spending fluctuate widely. In the latter situation many firms may be required to shift their operations in order to adapt to new relationships and conditions that evolve in the economy.

Fiscal policies never reach perfection even in the most advanced nations, but they tend to be less effective in developing countries, particularly poor (and overpopulated) countries like India which have been striving for rapid development. It should be stressed, however, that there is often much that effective enterprise management can do to reduce the adverse effects of deficient governmental fiscal policies. In this regard, contingency planning in conjunction with effective information collection, analysis, and feedback are of particular importance.

The case of India: The national budget, government spending, and investment patterns

India's current economic dilemmas are largely attributable to the government's fiscal policies in connection with the country's first and second five-year plans. Her almost obsessive interest in heavy industry (90 percent of new public sector financing has come from the government budget) and over-investment in the poorly performing public industrial sector have contributed significantly to the nation's economic instability, inflation, and foreign exchange crises.

As is common in the public sector in many countries, enterprise managers and project administrators in India have not hesitated in appealing to the government for additional funds and other resources when cost and resource requirement estimates have been overrun. Such resources have typically been granted in India, since a denial would be damaging to prestige and might possibly curtail critical production.

Public sector profitability, productivity, and general operating efficiency have been much lower than in the private sector. Strategic production rather than profitability has been considered a prime objective, and has been achieved to a considerable extent, but at tremendous costs. All but a few of the major public sector firms — mainly oil and gas firms and heavy electricals — have been operating at large losses and have been able to obtain additional government financing. The successful public sector firms tend to be medium-sized and well-established. Combined gross profits in relation to gross sales at central government corporations dropped from an average of 6.5 percent in 1964-65, to about 4 percent in 1967-68. Gross profits in relation to capital investment dropped from 2.3 percent to 1.5 percent.[10]

It appears that the Indian government has become increasingly concerned about poor management and performance in the public sector, and now intends to place significantly more emphasis on efficiency. The usually liberal foreign exchange and import allowances and financing have been reduced for various government-owned companies and projects and sizeable cutbacks in excess manpower have been made. More emphasis is being given to managerial competence in key positions.

Highly overambitious plans in terms of revenue and cost projections, project completion dates, and foreign exchange and aid requirements have led to huge budget deficits and foreign debts. For example, fiscal experts predicted that actual foreign exchange requirements would be at least 25 percent greater than those provided for in India's Third Five-Year Plan. Government planners ignored this estimate, which proved to be too low. As another example, the actual gap between planned expenditures and available resources during the Third Plan period turned out to be significantly more than the $7 billion — roughly 20 percent of GNP at the time — anticipated by prominent fiscal experts and economists.

In many sectors demand has exceeded supply leading to strong sellers' markets, inflation and black market activity; while in other sectors supply has greatly exceeded demand, leading to idle capacity and inefficient use of other resources. In both cases, deficient fiscal policies have created considerable uncertainty for firms and contributed to sharply rising costs and profit squeezes in both the public and private sectors, leading to a decline in internal resource generation for investment and expansion. This has also had an adverse effect on tax revenues which have been much less than anticipated by the government. Profitability performance has generally been much worse in the public sector than in the private, although it has also deteriorated in the latter.[11]   In the late 1960s gross profits in relation to gross sales in the organized (licensed) private sector was around 8 percent, in relation to gross fixed assets about 11 to 12 percent, and to capital employed about 8 percent. Net profit in relation to net worth has been about 7 to 8 percent in the private sector.

As of the late 1960s government steel and engineering firms accounted for about 60 percent of all public sector investment; petroleum products and chemical firms, mainly in fertilizer, accounted for 20 percent; various mining and mineral undertakings about 8 percent; aviation and shipping around 4 percent; and all other sectors combined less than 10 percent.

It is interesting to note that while public sector investment has been substantial in Indian industry, both the magnitude and growth of private sector investment are considerably greater than is generally supposed. A recent study by World Bank experts indicates that two-thirds of India's manufacturing investment during the 1960s appears to have been in the private sector, and an even greater proportion since 1950. The impression conveyed by India's plans and other government data is that the public sector has dominated. However, such data are based on plans rather than actual accomplishments, and actual private sector investment has turned out to be considerably greater than planned.

The Fourth Plan (1969-1974) projects total net investment in relation to net national income as 13.8 percent by 1973-74. This compares with a rate of roughly 15 percent in the 1950s, and 11.5 to 12 percent at the end of the 1960s. This plan also projects a rate of 17 to 18 percent by 1980-81. Investment targets contained in the Fourth Plan are ambitious. In order to achieve them significant improvements in many of the environmental constraints described in this book will have to be forthcoming. Of major immediate importance is the political situation which is hindering both private indigenous and foreign investment in India. If this continues unchanged not only industrial investment, but also tax revenues, will suffer substantially.

In general, India's Fourth Plan suggests that government fiscal policy is moving in the direction of balanced economic growth and industrial development, given existing conditions in the economy. The projected pattern of investment shows a bigger share going to agricultural development than in the Third Plan (15.6 percent versus 14 percent). This is also true of transportation and communications (18.6 percent versus 16.7 percent). Industry and mining is slated to receive a slightly smaller share of total investment (23.4 percent versus 24.7 percent). Other categories, including inventories, are projected at about the same proportionate investment, with the exception of social services which is to receive slightly more.

A major share of the nearly 28 billion rupees in outlays earmarked for public sector industries in the Fourth Plan is to be used to complete projects already underway or committed. (About 95 percent of this is for central government projects, and the rest for those of state governments.) Most investment in new projects in the public sector is earmarked for high-priority industries like petrochemicals, mineral development, non-ferrous metals, fertilizers and pesticides. Some is earmarked for modernizing textile mills taken over by the government, as well as expanding paper production, especially newsprint. Only a modest amount will go for public sector growth in the engineering industries, and most of it is aimed at filling control gaps.

The total planned outlay for the private and cooperative sector is 24 billion rupees. If the more radical and socialistic-oriented Indian politicians get their way, public sector development is likely to be pushed considerably harder than indicated in the Fourth Plan, as it now stands. This could have a highly adverse impact on the private sector.

Taxation and fiscal incentives

Although India has among the highest company and personal income tax rates in the world, and tax revenues have increased greatly since 1950, the country's total tax revenues are still relatively small in relation to GNP, as compared to advanced nations. This is due to the fact that most of India's population pays little or no tax because the vast majority have very low incomes and those with higher incomes evade taxes. When the inefficient collection system is also considered, one can reasonably estimate that paid-in taxes represent only a minor part of the total tax revenues due to the government.

On the other hand, a tremendous amount of waste and inefficiency has resulted from the way the government has used tax revenues. The bulk of these come from various kinds of direct and indirect taxes on private firms, as well as from the more affluent individual taxpayers who are also the major private investors.

A key question is: could private firms and individuals have done a better job in spurring India's economic and social development, if tax rates had been lower and they, rather than the government, had spent the funds?

Businessmen in India, as in most countries, are outspokenly critical about the government's tax policies and laws. In private, however, managers of companies surveyed in India admit that taxation is not of as great concern to them as are many other environmental constraints. Concern is expressed about the frequent changes in corporate tax rates — including not only taxes on profits and dividends, but also on sales, and in excise, state, municipal, special, and various other taxes. During the 1965-68 period in particular, tax rates were changed frequently, often with no advance notice and sometimes retroactively.

In recent years, annual personal (earned) incomes under 3,000 to 4,000 rupees ($400 to $535) have been exempt from taxation. The tax on an annual personal income of 10,000 rupees has been about 7 percent. For annual incomes in the range of 48,000 to 84,000 rupees — key managers of major indigenous companies typically fall in this range — the tax has ranged roughly between 40 and 80 percent. The tax on incomes over 96,000 rupees has been about 83 to 88 percent. Dividends paid to individuals are tax-exempt under 1,000 rupees, and the average tax on company dividends has been about 30 percent. Maximum taxes on unearned income have been about 81 percent, when such income exceeds 300,000 rupees. Individuals are also subject to a wealth tax based on accumulated wealth. The taxes of some individuals in a given year exceed their income and hence reduce their net worth. These high taxes levied on those citizens who are in the best position to invest in business and industry undoubtedly have a dampening effect on the entrepreneurial spirit of the country.

The minimum profit tax rate for enterprises has been 25 percent. The basic tax rate for most corporations has recently been 50 percent, although a number of industries defined as priority — e.g., steel, mining, certain types of fertilizers and base chemicals, various kinds of machinery and equipment, and tractors — have had a base rate 5 to 8 percent lower. Super or excess-profit tax is imposed if earnings exceed a given firm's capital base. This tax goes as high as 50 percent where profits exceed 10 percent of the company's capital base. There are also dividend taxes, and special taxes, such as on the undistributed profits of certain kinds of closely-held companies. The maximum total tax rate on company profits has been about 70 percent recently. The total incidence of tax between a firm and individual shareholder on earned profits distributed as dividends can go as high as 96 percent. Most of the firms in the organized (licensed) private sector in India have paid total taxes on profits in the range of 40 to 60 percent. For major foreign companies such taxes have been somewhat higher on the average, ranging from about 55 to 65 percent.

The tax structure has encouraged capital-intensive operations. For example, one large, diversified U.S. subsidiary paid total taxes on earnings of about 65 percent several years ago. However, because it had undertaken more capital-intensive operations, and even though profits had not been declining, profit taxes had dropped to 57 percent by 1968 and were expected to drop further in succeeding years. The tax rate on patent royalties in India has been 50 percent since 1961, and still is about the highest in the world. Before 1961 it was 63 percent.

The Indian government has been offering a wide range of incentives to industrial enterprises in an effort to spur development. The incentives discussed here apply generally to both indigenous and foreign enterprises. Special concessions available only to foreign firms and foreign individuals will be covered in the next chapter.

In India new enterprises are exempt from paying taxes on profits up to 6 percent of their paid-up capital for their first five years of life. Recipients of dividends paid out of such profits enjoy a similar tax holiday. Both new and existing firms are granted a "development rebate" for new fixed investment, plus liberal depreciation allowances. Until around 1967 the normal development rebate was 20 percent. Since then it has been raised to 25 percent, with certain favored industries entitled to 35 percent, and a few, deemed to be of low priority, only 15 percent. Most foreign investment falls in the 25 to 35 percent bracket. Normal annual depreciation rates on plant and machinery vary from 7 to 25 percent, depending on the type of asset. More is allowed for multiple shift operations. The average depreciation rate for office equipment is 10 percent; for cars, 20 percent; for first-class buildings, 2.5 percent; and for office furniture and files, 6 percent.

Other fiscal incentives intended to stimulate new investment and enterprise growth are scattered throughout India's fiscal system. Some of these involve loss carry-forward privileges, special allowances for R&D expenditures, and various other tax holidays, exemptions, and rebates. Various export incentives are also available to firms.

Individual states, and in some cases even metropolitan areas, offer fiscal incentives under certain conditions. In addition to such special treatment on state and local taxes, it is sometimes possible for firms to negotiate attractive concessions on land, buildings, and various other items. India even has its "ecology" or "environment" incentives; for example, exemptions on capital-gains taxes can be obtained by industries which move out of congested metropolitan areas. However, in spite of serious air and water pollution, and other severe ecological problems in India's major cities, it is unlikely that India's government will use incentives, disincentives, and penalties to cope with such problems nearly as vigorously as the U.S. government is likely to in the foreseeable future.

The total package of fiscal incentives offered to firms enables many of them to deduct from income more than the amount of their actual investment. In some cases financial statements indicate sizeable profits, while for tax purposes the company shows a loss which can be carried forward to subsequent years.

Few people seem to question whether the various fiscal incentives available to firms in India are really needed to encourage industrial investment and expansion.[12] It is simply assumed that this is the case. Correspondingly, in order to prevent serious imbalances and excess capacity, licensing controls are exercised on a broad scale. The system often artificially inflates profits and makes effective planning difficult. There would probably not be a need for as much in the way of tax exemptions and other fiscal incentives in order to encourage industrial progress, if tax laws and fiscal policies were more effective.

GENERAL ECONOMIC AND PRICE STABILITY

Overview

Economic stability involves a condition of relatively full utilization of productive factors or the avoidance of abrupt and major disruptions in the employment of the country's available productive resources. Substantial underused capacity, excessive inventories, and high unemployment — including disguised unemployment — are indications of a generally unstable economic situation which is likely to be reflected in a serious recession.

An economy may be said to have a relatively high degree of price stability when various major indexes of price change remain quite stable over an extended time period. Price stability involves the prices of producer and consumer goods and agricultural products, and wage, interest, and foreign exchange conversion rates. Most countries now have price indexes for some if not all of these categories. Usually, but not always, substantial price fluctuations occur with general economic instability. Perfect price stability is rarely possible, and small movements of a few percentage points a year — typically upwards — are regarded as normal even in stable economies, given the complexity of the pricing problem.

The problem of price stability tends to be more acute in poorer or smaller countries than in advanced, larger, and relatively self-sufficient economies. Serious sectoral imbalances are also more likely to occur in the former. Moreover, in a country where many items must be imported, as domestic inflation proceeds the value of the country's currency in relation to other currencies declines, raising the cost of imports and foreign exchange even more rapidly. Speculators, seeing the decline, often force the local currency still lower, while flight of capital and extensive black marketing activity tend to increase. The problem may be somewhat alleviated — in the short run at least — by foreign aid, as has been the case in India. Countries which earn the bulk of their foreign exchange from one or a few key commodities, particularly agricultural products, also tend to be particularly vulnerable to sharp price changes on a widespread scale.

A disturbing impact is made on business firms by serious price inflation or deflation in the economy. When prices rise sharply firms are faced with the problem that future inputs will rise in cost. In acutely inflationary periods, inventories of finished goods also tend to increase rapidly in value. Such a situation can necessitate substantial change in a firm's inventory policy. Where possible, enterprises maintain large inventories and delay payment of their bills, since payment at a later date means less in real terms. At the same time, they try to collect on their own bills as quickly as possible, offering various incentives for prompt payment.

In general, in a highly inflationary period firms try to stay away from cash (the depreciating asset) in order to hold things (the appreciating asset). Where capital-goods prices are also rising rapidly, enterprises also tend to overinvest in fixed assets. This causes still more pressure on prices, encourages speculation and black marketing, and increases uncertainty and risks.

The end of an acute inflation can be painful. Even a significant slowing of the rate of inflation can cause illiquidity if a firm's anticipated capital and revenue gains are not realized. Countries trying to taper off their inflation rates in recent years have found that the cost frequently includes bankruptcies and the writing-off of dubious assets and inventories.

Substantial variations in rates of price inflation can further increase managerial uncertainty and risk. Constant increase of 10 or even 15 percent a year can be taken into account. But prices which increase 10 percent one year, 2 percent the next, and 27 percent the year after, make it almost impossible to plan with much confidence. In such a situation, contingency planning, variable budgets, and flexibility in operations can help firms to cope more effectively with erratic price changes.

In countries where prices fluctuate considerably, wise companies may set up special purchasing sections to engage in hedging and arbitrage activities. Sharp price inflation occurs. Enterprises scramble to get out of "things" and into cash. Excess firm liquidity, bare minimum inventories, and increased speculation about the further decline in prices occur, with serious negative impacts on productive efficiency and industrial progress.

In general, stable prices have a beneficial impact on managerial effectiveness and firm efficiency, while unstable prices tend to have the opposite effect.

Mere price controls to maintain stability will not by themselves create an optimum situation, since the result of such controls may be shortages of the items for which prices are artificially reduced, and such situations may be as disrupting to firms as actual price changes. At such times enterprises have to organize cadres or expeditors to obtain their share of the items in short supply. Black marketing activity and other illicit practices are also likely to become widespread.

The case of India

During the 1950s, India's economic progress was both substantial and reasonably steady, although a considerable amount of underutilized capacity existed in various sectors due to overexpansion of facilities and supply shortages.[13] Price increases in general averaged less than 3 percent per year.

During most of India's Third Plan period, until about late 1964, excess capacity in industry as a whole decreased steadily and substantially as the supply input position and infrastructure improved. Supply did, however, continue to be the key bottleneck, and agricultural raw materials became a greater constraint during this period.

Excess capacity in industry rose sharply and reached its peak during the economic crisis and sharp recessionary period of 1965-68.[14] Capital goods industries, particularly engineering goods, were hit the hardest. At this peak roughly 40 to 75 percent of capacity remained unused in most industrial capital goods, an estimated 40 percent in intermediates, and 30 percent in the consumer goods sector. Overall underutilized capacity for Indian industry as a whole probably reached a peak of around 40 percent, if not more.

In a 1967-68 survey, one-third of firms in a wide cross-section of over 800 companies from all major sectors gave inadequate demand as the reason for their excess capacity.[15] Another 8 percent gave inadequate demand as one among other reasons. Only 17 percent gave shortage of supplies as a major reason for underutilized capacity, and another 5 percent gave this as one among other reasons. Inadequate demand and supply shortages were indicated by 4 percent while 14 percent gave other reasons including labor troubles, technical problems, power shortages, inadequate finance, and start-up problems.

It is important to point out that even in those industries having the greatest excess capacity during the 1965-68 period, a number of products were being produced by firms operating either in excess of normal maximum capacity, or less than 20 percent below such capacity (which tends to be regarded as close to optimum capacity in most sectors). For example, in non-electrical equipment 28 out of 108 items were being produced at close to capacity.

By no means *all* excess capacity should be regarded as economically undesirable, especially in developing countries like India which contain a large number of highly inefficient enterprises. Underutilized capacity promotes the weeding-out of less efficient firms, as happened in India during the 1966-69 period.

However, when a real crisis occurs, as it recently did in the textile and transportation equipment industries, the government has been willing to take over failing firms, rather than suffer the unemployment consequences of a shutdown.

India now has an overall industrial base which can probably operate in most sectors at a reasonable level of capacity utilization as the 1970s proceed. Heavy engineering and equipment firms, particularly in the public sector, will probably experience the greatest problems regarding underutilized capacity. However, specific companies in other sectors will continue to experience considerable excess capacity in many if not most cases because of highly overoptimistic past estimates of demand. For example, the chairman of Indian Drugs and Pharmaceuticals Ltd. — a government corporation — recently stated that his company's capacity to produce tetracycline antibiotics will be well above demand for the next ten years.[16]

Inventory holdings in relation to annual sales in the public industrial sector increased from approximately 46 percent in 1965-66 to 64 percent in 1967-68.[17] These high inventory levels were largely due to inefficient management, and not only to external conditions. The private sector fared much better, with inventories in relation to sales only increasing from 29 to 31 percent during this period.[18] However, there is room for improvement in inventory management in the private sector.

Beginning in the early 1960s, and especially during the 1965-67 period, India's wholesale, food, consumer, and other price indexes have shown sharp and erratic jumps. Price levels rose about 50 percent during the 1964-67 period, and this does not include black market prices.[19] Prices often increased sharply within the same month, in frequent steps.

The general wholesale price index jumped 10 percent or more per year during the 1963-67 period. In fiscal 1966-67 it rose over 16 percent. This index reached its peak around August, 1967 when it was 80 percent higher than in 1962. It then dropped by nearly 10 percent by March, 1968, after which it began to increase again, but in a relatively steady and stable manner.

The wholesale prices of key industrial raw materials — especially oilseeds, and to a lesser degree fibers and minerals — rose more sharply and erratically than intermediates or finished goods. Raw materials had their sharpest average price rise, about 30 percent, in 1965-66, as did intermediates which rose nearly 12 percent, and finished products which rose around 10 percent. During the 1963-64 to 1966-67 period, textile product prices rose 20 percent, chemicals nearly 23 percent, machinery and transportation equipment 22 percent, and metal products 17 percent. All but the metal product prices had stabilized by 1967-68, while metal products posted an additional increase of nearly 10 percent during that fiscal year and stabilized thereafter.

The wholesale food price index (consisting of key agricultural commodities) increased 84 percent during the period of 1962-63 to 1967-68. The biggest average rise in one year came during fiscal 1966-67 when it jumped 24 percent. However, food prices actually reached their peak around August, 1967 when they were 120 percent higher than 1962 and 18 percent higher than the 1966-67 fiscal year average. By March, 1968 food prices had dropped 30 percent from their 1967 peak, and then began a modest but stable upward trend.

The price index for fuel, power, light, and lubricants rose about 53 percent during the 1962-68 period, averaging 8 percent annually from 1964. This index fell during the second half of 1967, but began to rise again in early 1968. Since the spring of 1968 it has been quite stable.

The consumer price index increased by over 60 percent during the 1962-68 period. In 1966-67 alone it increased by more than 15 percent, followed by an increase of roughly 10 percent in fiscal 1967-68. Since the latter part of 1967 it has been relatively stable.

By 1969, most commodity prices had stabilized in India and, in fact, early in the year some prices fell slightly. However, by mid-1969 inflation began again, though not as seriously as a few years earlier. For example, the general wholesale price index rose 0.5 percent during the last week of June, 1969, as compared to the previous week, and it was 3.8 percent higher than the last week of May, 1969, and 10 percent above the same week in 1968. Since the summer of 1969 price inflation has continued in the Indian economy, but through mid-1970 it was much less severe than during most of the 1965-67 period.

ORGANIZATION OF CAPITAL MARKETS

Overview

Liquid capital is the lifeblood of any business enterprise operating in the modern world. Lack of access to needed capital at a cost it can afford can force a firm out of existence, or at least cause it considerable harm. It can also mean that a new firm never gets started. A key problem for enterprises thus becomes one of obtaining adequate supplies of capital, primarily from the economies in which they function, although foreign capital may at times provide an additional source even for indigenous companies.

Hoarding is a severe problem in poor and less-developed countries, since it reduces the amount of savings available for productive investment purposes. This relates to various sociological-cultural factors, especially attitudes toward wealth and material gain discussed in an earlier chapter. Large amounts of capital which could be invested to yield both income and economic (and social) development are locked into nonproductive hoarded wealth. For example in rural societies most villagers, as poor as they may be, usually acquire some form of "savings" with the passage of time. Jewelry is often the form in which this wealth is maintained, and the entire family fortune may frequently be worn by the wife around her wrists and ankles, never to be otherwise employed.

The wealth of more affluent members of society is more likely to be invested in productive, income-yielding activities. However, the economy frequently loses a vast amount as a result of conspicuous consumption as well as the accumulation of "black money."

The demand side is affected by concentration of private business activity in the hands of the wealthy. The individuals and private enterprises in less-developed and poor countries most likely to employ the bulk of the nation's capital — apart from the public sector — are those who already have most of the private wealth, as well as greatest access to black money. They also do not want to allow "strangers" who are in a position to provide capital to have a significant voice in the affairs of their closely-knit companies. This lessens the need for the establishment of viable and efficient capital markets.

The case of India[20]

The kinds of problems discussed above have seriously hindered the growth and effectiveness of India's organized capital markets. However, India does have a better system of capital markets than many of the world's poor and developing countries. India's vast size, diversity, and total output, in spite of its very low per capita wealth, is one reason for this.

A few dozen of the largest industrial empires in India have obtained more than half of the credit extended by the nation's public and private financial institutions. Not only are major owners of the largest private indigenous companies represented on the boards of private lending institutions, they also constitute a large proportion of the government-appointed directorships of public financial institutions.

It cannot be denied that the bulk of capital and credit has been obtained by larger and growing companies in India, and that this has restrained, at least to some extent, the establishment and growth of smaller, struggling units. Whether this has been and is good or bad in terms of productive efficiency and industrial progress, however, is a question for debate. However, the shortage of capital faced by Indian industrial enterprises seems to be exaggerated by many. Few of the medium-sized or larger firms that we have surveyed indicated that lack of access to capital, or the cost of capital, has been a major problem. This includes some companies which have been operating at sizeable losses in the last few years.

The public financial institutions have become an increasingly important source of financing for private sector companies. These development finance corporations (or DFC's) are either directly or indirectly under the Ministry of Finance. There has been no organizational relationship between them and the other ministries and agencies directly concerned with industrial policy and development. Moreover, coordination among these financial institutions has not been effective. This situation has improved somewhat in recent years with the government's decision that the Industrial Development Bank of India (IDBI) — by far the largest of these institutions — should act as a coordinating agency.

IDBI was established in July, 1964, to provide large-scale financial assistance to new and priority industries, although the bulk of its funds have gone to established rather than newly-formed private companies. The Refinance Corporation — which has provided discounting facilities for plant and equipment investments, as well as replenishment funds to the banks for long-term loans to priority industries — has been amalgamated with IDBI. IDBI announced recently that it will enter the field of financing of public sector companies on a substantial scale.

The Industrial Finance Corporation (IFC) is the country's second biggest public financial institution. It has virtually become a subsidiary of IDBI. More than one-third of its funding has gone for the formation of new companies. IFC is empowered to subscribe to the shares of both private and public corporations to provide loans (mainly to larger firms), and also to underwrite securities and guarantee loans made by both domestic and foreign leaders. Another agency, the International Finance Corporation, also makes both loans and equity investments in private companies.

The Industrial Credit and Investment Corporation of India (ICICI) was established to provide medium, and in some cases longer-term loans to private companies, both in the form of local currency and foreign exchange. Roughly one-third of its loans have been to new companies. It also invests in equity securities, assists in the underwriting of new shares, and provides managerial assistance to firms. Capital provided by the World Bank, AID, the Export-Import Bank, and other foreign and international lending agencies for private sector projects is also channeled through ICICI.

The Life Insurance Corporation of India (LIC) was formed in 1956 with the nationalization of the country's life insurance industry. This institution, in conjunction with the promotion of insurance schemes, industrial provident plans, and the like, encourages the use of savings for productive ventures. LIC has grown greatly over the years, but it still attracts savings chiefly from the middle and upper classes. (There are income tax deductions for life insurance premiums.) However, the large but highly-segmented wealth of the villagers and the poor still remains largely untapped.

LIC provides loans to existing private companies, engages in underwriting activities, and takes equity positions as well. It also has a substantial shareholding in ICICI. LIC also invests in the securities of other public sector ventures such as electricity and housing organizations.

To date the role of India's development finance corporations, both as providers of medium and long-term loans and of underwriting and direct share capital, has increased steadily and substantially. Their total disbursements have risen from roughly 4 percent of gross fixed private investment during 1951-56 to an estimated 20 percent in the latter part of the 1960s. In most of the last several years loan disbursements from these institutions have exceeded the stock market in importance as a source of corporate finance. During the 1950s loan finance dominated their financial activities, but during the 1960s roughly 20 percent of the total stock issues floated by private companies have been taken up by them. In addition, they have sold about half the shares taken up under the underwriting arrangements.

About 40 percent of the development finance corporations' resources were borrowed directly from the central government or the Reserve Bank in the 1960s. After adding in the government's share of paid-up capital and other lending, the role of the public sector as a source of finance has approached 50 percent. The public financial institutions are therefore a major channel for government finance to the private sector. During the 1960s these institutions provided roughly 10 percent of the total financial needs of the private sector, and over most of this period the share increased. During the 1966-69 period, however, investment declined along with an even steeper decline in disbursements from the development finance corporations. But at the margin they still continue to play a major role in expanding companies and in the formation of new firms. For example, in 1966-67 companies which raised capital through prospectuses also planned to raise nearly 30 percent of their required finances from DFC's, and for new companies the proportion rose to 34 percent from direct loans alone. If share capital is included, the proportion would have been about 40 percent in that year.

In addition to the major public financial institutions discussed above, there are a number of other institutions of this type under both the central and state governments. For example, the National Industrial Development Corporation was set up primarily to provide funds to assist critical industries — especially major foreign exchange earners — which need to be revitalized. Funds are provided largely in the form of long-term modernization loans for the purchase of machinery and equipment. Many of these loans have gone to textile companies. The National Small Industries Corporation deals primarily with smaller firms and provides both financial and technical assistance. Through hire-purchase schemes it makes available both loans and foreign exchange to facilitate the purchase of machinery.

Various kinds of state-level financial institutions have also been created, and most of their financing also goes to smaller enterprises. However, the total resources of these state institutions are only a small fraction of those at the disposal of central financial organizations.

Direct foreign loans and foreign equity also constitute relatively small proportions of private sector financing in India, although they are of crucial importance in India's industrial development. In recent years foreign sources have provided roughly 5 percent of the total share capital among private corporations which have issued capital through prospectuses, while foreign loans have constituted roughly 4 percent of the medium and long-term loans of such companies.

In the last several years private companies have typically paid 8½ to 10 percent interest on medium and long-term rupee loans obtained from major Indian financial institutions. This has been about 2 to 4 percent more than they paid during easier money periods of the past. Major public sector corporations have often paid 2 or 3 percent less interest on government loans as compared to the cost of such loans to the private sector on the open market. Some U.S. firms — and at times other foreign companies — have been able to get medium and long-term rupee loans at lower rates, typically 1 to 2½ percent, than indigenous companies. Such loans typically come from AID or other foreign sources. Foreign subsidiaries generally have a better chance of getting more favorable interest rates on hard currency loans than indigenous firms. In the last several years, U.S. subsidiaries surveyed have usually paid 7 to 8 percent interest on foreign exchange loans, while indigenous firms have paid 8½ to 9½ percent. At times the parent corporation of a foreign subsidiary has provided attractive financing. For example, a large chemical company obtained from its parent a 6 percent tax-free foreign currency loan with a three-year moratorium on payments.

India's security exchanges are relatively unusual and advanced for a developing nation. Although the volume of transactions is small when compared to advanced countries, markets are well-established, brokerage firms and underwriters exist in fairly sizeable numbers, and there are adequate means for issuing and trading securities. The government has forced many foreign companies to allow local equity participation, and they have increasingly turned to the securities market. This has increased the volume of activity. Prestigious foreign and major indigenous corporations have frequently found that the new securities they have offered have been immediately oversubscribed and at highly advantageous prices. On the other hand, the daily markets for most issues is frequently very thin and a seller is not always assured of making a trade at or even near the previous trading price.

Many new capital issues are arranged by private subscription, particularly in the case of the more traditional indigenous firms, although some foreign companies also have done this for their Indian equity participation. Industrialists approach family members, close friends, and other people who can be trusted to permit operations to continue without interference. In most such situations, the right of transference of ownership is limited, and securities must be offered to existing shareholders before they can be sold on the open market. Generally, the more widely-held companies in India are larger than the tightly-held private firms.

India has securities exchanges located in seven major cities. Somewhere between 1500 and 2000 issues of common stock are traded, with the number of preferred stock, bond, and convertible debenture issues being much lower. The largest exchange, in Bombay, handles a majority of these issues, followed by Calcutta. India's securities exchanges are regulated by the Securities Contract Act of 1956. The Capital Issues Control Act of 1947 (as amended), and the Companies Act of 1956 are also basic pieces of legislation dealing with the activities of the securities exchanges and the issuance of securities to the public. The Ministry of Finance controls new security issues, and the central government approves only issues outside of India for all companies incorporated in India. On the whole, the government's objective is to channel investment into desirable sectors and regulate the capital structure of firms and their access to capital markets. Since regulations and guidelines are clear and well-established, such control is generally not a major hurdle.

Capital raised through the securities markets declined steadily in real terms after about 1961 and reached a low point in 1966. In 1967-68 attempts were made to raise 600 million rupees for 71 private sector companies. About 200 million of this was taken up by insiders, friends, various institutions, and so forth, leaving about two-thirds to be offered to the public. Virtually all of the remaining 400 million rupees had to be underwritten because of the relatively high risk of failure of the issues at the time. In the end, 58 percent of the amount offered to the public had to be taken up by the underwriters, and only 42 percent was subscribed by the public. Between 1964-65 and 1967-68 an average of 53 percent was left with the underwriters.

The securities underwriting business started in earnest in the mid-1950s. Initially the banks and brokers were the main agents, but more recently the major public financial institutions have come to dominate the scene. During the first half of the 1960s about 58 percent of the total issues were taken up by these institutions, and in the second half approximately 70 percent.

In 1968-69 out of 434 million rupees raised for 65 private corporations, about 93 percent was underwritten. Public financial institutions handled the bulk of this. LIC occupied the top position among all underwriters by underwriting 25 percent of the total issues during that fiscal year. Unit Trust handled about 22 percent and ICICI nearly 15 percent. Banks handled 7 percent and general insurance companies more than 5 percent; in both cases this was lower than in the previous year. However, with the nationalization of the banks and the government take-over of general insurance companies, public financial institutions can be expected to play an even greater role as underwriters in the future.

In general, since the early 1960s three major and interrelated structural trends have emerged in connection with financing and investment in the private industrial sector as a whole: 1) the role of the industrial securities market has diminished; 2) borrowing, particularly from the public financial institutions under the central government, has come to play an increasing role; 3) external financing has increased as profitability has decreased.

Borrowing as a source of funds in the private corporate sector accounted for about 29 percent of all funds during the Second Plan period in the second half of the 1950s. This source dropped briefly to 20 percent in 1961-62 during the peak of the bull stock market. It increased sharply to 28 percent in 1962-63, dropping off modestly to 26 percent in 1964-65, increasing again to 29 percent in 1965-66. During 1966-67 and 1967-68 it was 30 and 31 percent respectively.

Paid-off capital comprised 11 percent of all private sector corporate financing during the Second Plan. This source reached a peak of 15 percent in 1961-62. It dropped steadily and sharply to 6 percent in 1964-65, and increased to 9 percent in 1965-66. During the 1966-67 to 1967-68 period it was 8 percent. Other sources of external financing have remained quite steady, in the range of 23 to 26 percent in the 1960s, increasing from 15 percent during the Second Plan period.

Internal corporate financing dropped from 45 percent in the Second Plan period to 38 percent in 1962-63. It rose to 43 percent in 1964-65, but dropped off steadily thereafter. In 1967-68 it was down to 35 percent. Earned surplus and special reserves declined from 20 percent in the Second Plan period to 15 percent in 1962-63 as a source of corporate financing in the private sector. It rose to 18 percent in 1964-65, but declined steadily thereafter. In 1967-68 this source constituted about 11 percent of the total financing in this sector, and in 1968-69 it was estimated to be under 10 percent. Depreciation as a source of internal financing has remained quite steady, in the range of 23 to 25 percent, during the last fifteen years. Hence, the decline in internal financing has been brought about almost entirely through lower profits. The proportion of fixed investment financed by internal sources since 1964, and the declining overall trend, reflect the growth of inventories financed by borrowed capital. It is not uncommon for companies — including some U.S. firms — to violate regulations or commitments by using medium or long-term loans for financing inventories or other short-run purposes.

In sum, internal sources which financed about 45 percent of the financial needs of private corporations during the Second Plan have dropped in importance to about 35 percent, while sources external to individual companies have increased from 55 to 65 percent in the second half of the 1960s.[21] Among relatively well-established public sector corporations about 80 percent of all financing has been external in the past six or seven years. And because of the very low average rate of profitability in this sector — even lower if less well established companies were to be excluded — the great bulk of the internal financing has come from depreciation reserves.

FACTOR ENDOWMENT

Overview

In economics the term "factor" means an item or input of production necessary to create useful goods and services. The usual basic division of factors is in the form of land (which includes all natural resources), real capital, labor, and management (which includes entrepreneurship). The last is the most dynamic since it combines the other interrelated factors, and management is the central factor in our entire analysis. The relative supplies of the other factors of production are of course also relevant, since it is clearly much easier to manage in an environment where they are all present in abundance, than in an environment in which severe shortages exist.

In general, ample supply and good quality of one type of basic factor of production tend to reinforce the development of another. Poorer countries and their enterprises faced with serious deficiencies in all basic factors are confronted with significant constraints over managerial effectiveness and industrial progress, although some individual firms adapt much better than others. It is not impossible for specific firms or the country as a whole to considerably reduce the impact of such constraints with the passage of time. Thus, development of skilled and energetic labor and competent management tends to make possible the efficient use of larger amounts of more complicated capital equipment, while more extensive and efficient development of natural resources may well depend on greater development of various types of skilled and effective labor and management, as well as more real capital. Attempts to force the question by overrapid development of one factor — as is common in less-developed countries, most typically with regard to capital — may well prove less effective than an integrated approach which takes into account the simultaneous development of all basic factors.

Climate is also part of any country's factor endowment. In fact, it can have an impact on all of the basic factors of production. Weather conditions affect agricultural yields, soil, vegetation, types of crops, land use, and the like. Climate can also have a bearing on mining operations and the extractive industries. Similarly, it can affect human health, energy, and working capacity, as well as damage to and the condition of real capital, materials, components and products.

Natural resources

Although many poor and developing countries are rich in certain natural resources, few contain the proper balance of resources required for the construction of modern industrial nations. The resources of many countries are confined to a handful of key minerals or agricultural commodities. Even more important, the potentially abundant natural resources of many poor countries have not been adequately developed to provide easy accessibility or availability in large quantities due to difficult terrain or adverse climatic conditions, and lack of capital, know-how or motivation.

Critical resource gaps relating to labor or capital can be remedied with time and effort, although persistent critical food shortages can continue to have an adverse effect on the labor force. But deficiencies in indigenous natural resources are frequently facts of life to which the economy must adjust.

It is common to place the blame for a poor country's state of underdevelopment on its lack of natural resources. It is true that abundant natural resources make managerial and development tasks simpler. However, many countries which have achieved highly impressive industrial development have been far from favorably endowed with natural resources. Japan, Israel, and even the United Kingdom are cases in point. In such countries, favorable environmental conditions of other types — educational and sociological-cultural, for example — have more than compensated for critical natural resource deficiencies. On the other hand, many poor countries which are favorably endowed with natural resources — such as Brazil and Indonesia — have remained poor because of other serious environmental constraints.

The natural resources of a given country and the accessibility and effective exploitation of such resources have a substantial impact on the management and productive efficiency of industrial enterprises, and on industrial progress. Thus, if one country has large supplies of low-cost, easy to mine coal or petroleum, this will result in low fuel costs for industries using these minerals. Many production costs will be lower in a well-endowed country than in a poorly-endowed one. Production and procurement planning can be performed more effectively when natural resource inputs are in abundant supply.

A nation's natural resource base affects the patterns and quantities of imports and exports in the industrial sector, as well as the country's foreign exchange reserves and balance-of-payments position. Critical resource deficiencies can lead to serious economic problems and price instability. This is frequently most evident in connection with poor agricultural performance which leads to large food imports or sharp declines in exports.

In addition to the direct effect on industries which rely on agricultural raw materials, poor agricultural performance limits the country's ability to import goods essential to industrial and economic development. Even firms not directly requiring imports suffer if their suppliers or customers are dependent on foreign exchange and imports for their operations. Finally, low farm output in predominantly rural societies sharply reduces the purchasing power of the population. This leads to a sharp decline in the demand for consumer goods which, in turn, has an adverse effect on the demand for other goods and services produced in the country. It should be evident that industrial enterprises must be continually aware of the agricultural situation in subsistence-level, rural economies.

India's mineral resources

Unlike many other developing nations, India is a land relatively rich in mineral resources. Many of the country's basic industrial needs can now be met from her large reserves of iron ore, coal, gypsum, bauxite, chromite, mica, lime, clay, and various other minerals. India expects to achieve self-sufficiency in aluminum and most of its steel requirements during the Fourth Plan period (1969-74). Other minerals known to exist in substantial quantities include copper, gold, manganite, and lead.

Large oil fields and natural gas resources discovered recently are being developed. In fact, one U.S. subsidiary which produces polyethylene has found itself at a serious competitive disadvantage because it did not foresee this development and set up its plant several years ago to use alcohol in the production of polyethylene. A competitive polyethylene plant which uses naphtha — a natural gas distilled from petroleum — is much more efficient.

However, in spite of India's progress in exploiting its mineral resources, many minerals are still in short supply.

Several of the industries and mining operations which are required to extract and process the nation's minerals are highly capital-intensive and necessitate the importation of machinery and capital equipment which consume large quantities of foreign exchange. In addition, know-how is in short supply and many of the mining and processing enterprises which already exist have been poorly managed. Output rates have been lower than planned, considerable excess capacity has been the norm, and often the products extracted and processed are not in the forms or of the quality required by the economy.

India's Fourth Plan calls for increases in the production capacities and actual output of many of the country's major mineral resources. For example, an increase of 80 percent in crude petroleum output is projected along with a 60 percent increase in refining capacity. A twofold increase in iron ore and a 35 percent increase in coal production is projected. This will contribute to a projected threefold increase in pig iron, a 65 percent increase in steel ingots, nearly an 80 percent increase in finished steel, and a projected sixfold increase in the production of alloy and special steel products. The large increases planned for bauxite output and power generating sources is expected to lead to nearly a 100 percent increase in aluminum production. A nearly fourfold increase is planned for copper output. India did not produce any zinc until a few years ago, and nearly a threefold increase in zinc output is projected for 1973-74 as compared to 1968-69.

As India's mining and conversion industries develop, the country will be able to support an increasing number of sectors from internal raw material sources. Certainly the market afforded by her vast population — poor as it is in per capita terms — is sizeable enough to *potentially* sustain the bulk of the investments necessary to establish units capable of achieving adequate economies of scale. (However, foreign aid, assistance, and capital will no doubt still be required for quite a long time.) Unfortunately, this "market" will remain in "potential" status until a more solid agricultural base and a more diversified and efficient overall industrial sector is established.

Indian agriculture[22]

The improvement of agricultural performance is one of India's most crucial problems in terms of general economic development and with regard to managerial effectiveness and productive efficiency in the industrial sector. Many of India's vexing agricultural problems are common to other developing countries. However, India's vast population makes her situation more precarious and difficult than that of most other countries and although Red China has a like problem in terms of population, she has managed to solve her agricultural problems better.[23]

India's Fourth Plan projects substantial improvements in the agricultural sector and estimates that India will be self-sufficient in food grains by 1972. But in order to achieve the agricultural targets and goals of the Fourth Plan, major efforts must be made to solve certain basic and critical problems. Let us briefly examine some of these.

Between 70 and 80 percent of India's population of more than 550 million is located in agricultural areas. Major food crops include rice, wheat and various other food grains, tea, sugar cane, peanuts, and various fruits and vegetables. Of these, tea and peanuts are the major export items. Other major crops having commercial value, industrial uses, and export potential include oilseeds, cotton, and jute.

India has nearly three times the population of the United States, but less than one-third of the total land. Approximately 54 percent of her land is tillable as opposed to 47 percent of U.S. land, giving India only about three quarters of an agricultural acre per capita as contrasted with over 5 acres in the U.S., and India's current rate of population growth is about two and a half times greater than that of the United States. Moreover, there is little possibility of increasing India's approximately 372 million acres of cultivated farmlands, primarily because of topographical conditions and climate. Indian agricultural yields and productivity lag dramatically behind that of the United States. This issue is most critical since India's agricultural production has often been below the nation's minimum subsistence level, and the short-run goals associated with survival frequently have had to take precedence over longer-range goals of economic growth and industrial progress. In terms of per capita caloric intake, food consumption, and nutritional balance, India is clearly one of the poorest countries in the world.

If India is to achieve self-sufficiency in food production great improvements in farming efficiency and crop yields must be achieved. But the effort required to move from feeding people at a subsistence level to really eradicating hunger and serious malnutrition is enormous.

Unfortunately, agricultural production in India is only as dependable as the weather. India's climate is such that the great bulk of the farmland must be unused for large portions of the year when everything is dry. Consequently, the nation must take advantage of the monsoon rains to produce the crops she so desperately needs. When the rains are sparse, or when they are so heavy that they wash away seeds and inundate the land, the nation suffers bitterly and previous economic and industrial progress is destroyed.

On the other hand, the economy may move ahead rapidly — but typically in spurts and rather erratically — when the weather is good. Such dependency on the weather hinders effective medium and long-range planning in the industrial sector. Until India can build up her agricultural base and related infrastructure to the point that the weather only affects the amount of surplus she has left over, economic development will remain an undependable process.

India's problems are augmented by the lack of strong central government allocating procedures. Agricultural zones, maintained by the states, have been established throughout the nation to control output and prices. Frequently, one state will have a surplus of a key agricultural product while another experiences a severe shortage. Mechanisms and political pressures for distributing surpluses to deficit areas are generally ineffective, and it is common for agricultural produce to rot in some states while the central government spends foreign exchange to import food to cover deficiencies in other states.

The agricultural problem is also compounded by lack of adequate storage facilities; a high rate of destruction of foodstuffs by rats, other animals, and the elements; a lack of adequate transportation facilities to move food around the country; and by inefficient distribution and marketing methods. Estimates of lost agricultural output due just to poor storage facilities (so vital in a situation where major crops can be grown only during limited times of the year) and animals (not only rats and other vermin, but also cows and goats which roam the countryside) are often conservatively placed at 25 to 30 percent.

Much government attention has been given to land reform, since large land areas have been controlled by single families. However, land reform statutes limiting large family holdings — typically to about 30 acres — have not been widely enforced in most states. Small subsistence farmers still comprise about 40 million of India's 60 million farming families. And most of these small farmers, including tenant farmers and sharecroppers, have not benefited by what recent improvements have been made in Indian agriculture. In fact, many small farmers have been forced to leave the land because of higher rents in recent years. It is common for rents to run as high as 50 to 60 percent of total crop revenues.

The joint-family system and village traditions lead to further division of already small plots which are handed down from one generation to the next. Eventually, the plots become so small that it is difficult to make efficient use of them. To counteract this trend, the government has encouraged cooperative farming ventures in an effort to permit larger scale applications of advanced agricultural techniques. However, chiefly due to sociological-cultural factors, this has met with limited and scattered success to date. And until a considerably more substantial industrial base is developed, the fixed amount of land will be required to support increasing numbers of people. Population control is critical in this regard.

Difficulties in obtaining credit at reasonable interest rates have also plagued India's small farmers. Frequently they must resort to private, usurious moneylenders, since they will not use the wealth they have invested in jewelry.

The problems experienced during shortfalls in Indian agricultural production (i.e., vis-a-vis population needs) are augmented by a rigid adherence of various segments of the population to specific eating habits. For example, in the South rice is the staple while in much of the North wheat or corn are the basic elements of diet. A shortfall in rice cannot be offset by a large surplus in wheat because the rice-eating segments of the population will not modify their eating habits, and vice versa.

Another agricultural problem arises from the large number of cattle which roam the countryside causing great destruction to crops. Few of the cattle are productive with respect to dairy products and all graze on valuable grassland, creating erosion. They provide little or no meat since most of the population is vegetarian, and even the non-vegetarian population will not eat beef in deference to orthodox Hindu beliefs against killing cows. The 300 to 400 million cattle present a major problem — but one which is being overcome slowly through the application of birth control techniques.

The Indian government has been making efforts to sharply improve the nation's agricultural yield especially since the severe agricultural crisis that occurred during 1965-66. In that year, food grain output fell by about 16 percent from 88.5 to 74.5 million tons, and food grain imports reached a peak of 11 million tons, or 15 percent of domestic output. Agricultural production increased by 18 to 19 percent in 1967-68 over the preceding fiscal year, and then posted further, but modest, gains in fiscal 1968-69. In 1969, for the first time in several years, the government was able to put aside a buffer stock of 4 million tons of food. Moreover, farm prices stabilized in 1969 after several years of steady and sharp increases.

Improved agricultural performance has recently been achieved due to a number of factors in addition to favorable weather conditions. These include new varieties of cereal seeds; increased use of fertilizers, pesticides, and farm machinery; improvements in irrigation, water conservation, flood control, storage facilities, and transportation; and price increases raising official prices received by the farmer to levels close to those prevailing in the black market. All of this has also had a favorable psychological impact on millions of farmers — making them more willing to employ modern methods, raising their aspiration levels, and giving them a greater incentive for increasing production.

In spite of recent gains in output, India's agricultural sector is still beset by vexing problems. For the most part those who have benefited from the recent improvements and developments have been well-to-do farmers with relatively large land holdings. Agricultural growth has been accompanied by explosive social problems and agrarian unrest in the countryside, revolving largely around land reform. This has been most acute in Bengal and Kerala. As of 1970, less than 6 percent of the nation's cultivated farmlands had been planted with new high-yielding hybrid seeds; and despite irrigation expansion, only 15 percent of the country's 565,000 villages were assured irrigation, with the rest depending chiefly or entirely on the annual monsoons.

India's Fourth Five-Year Plan projects more ambitious agricultural growth than in any of the previous plans — an annual average rate of 4.5 percent. At the same time, it focuses more attention on agricultural development projects and efforts. The Fourth Plan projects the following increases in the output of major crops by 1973-74 as compared to 1968-69: food grains, 32 percent (from about 98 million to 129 million tons); sugar cane, 25 percent; oilseeds, 24 percent; cotton, 33 percent; and jute, 19 percent.

The Fourth Plan also calls for extensive improvements in irrigation, water conservation, flood control, rural electrification, plant production, storage facilities, transportation and marketing, as well as much greater use of high-yield seed varieties. Substantial gains are expected to be achieved through more efficient farming practices, such as multiple cropping and diversification, and greater use of modern technology, such as fertilizers, pesticides, tractors, and power tillers. For example, the availability of nitrogenous, phosphatic, and potassic fertilizers is expected to increase by more than 250 percent, 450 percent, and 600 percent respectively during this period. Farm tractor output is expected to expand from 14,000 to 50,000 units. Pesticide production — DDT and BHC — is planned to increase from 33,000 tons to 48,000 tons. If the Fourth Plan goes fairly smoothly there will be substantial opportunities for industrial enterprises which produce products for the agricultural sector.

Major efforts and projected gains in the field of animal husbandry are also set forth in the Fourth Plan. This includes cattle breeding, poultry farming, dairying, and the production of wool and hides. Programs involving better animal health and care, crossbreeding, and the use of more and better feeds are planned. This will benefit industries which rely on raw materials from this sector, i.e., food processing, leather goods, carpets, and textiles. It will also be beneficial in terms of exports, especially in view of widespread Indian attitudes involving food and cattle.

The Fourth Plan concentrates on helping small farmers to improve their productivity through community projects involving better water and power supplies, cooperative farming ventures, considerably more managerial and technical training and assistance, improved seeds, and greater use of modern agricultural methods. Bank nationalization has substantially alleviated the severe credit problems facing small farmers.

INDIA'S OTHER NATURAL RESOURCES

It has only been since the early 1960s that the government has made a serious effort to develop and expand the country's fishing industry. This action was spurred by the potential export market for fish and other seafood products. Although the oceans surrounding India — and to a lesser extent the inland waterways — abound with protein-rich fish, the development of this sector has been retarded because of the nation's huge vegetarian population. The only areas which consume fish are those located along the coast, and even here fish is eaten only by limited segments of the population.

Fish production increased nearly 60 percent during the 1960s — from less than one million to over 1.5 million tons annually. Moreover, exports have increased by close to 500 percent with shrimps and prawns largely replacing cured fish.

The Fourth Plan calls for a 33 percent increase in India's fish production by 1973-74, with continued emphasis on increasing exports and greater emphasis on deep-sea fishing and inland fish farming. To achieve this target major programs are planned to improve ports, cold storage facilities, and marketing channels, to expand and create new processing plants, and to increase the number of mechanized boats. In addition to planning outlays for such purposes the Industrial Development Bank, the Agricultural Refinance Corporation, and other financial institutions are expected to extend credit to the operators of fishing boats and fleets — including small fishermen. Fishermen's cooperative federations are also expected to be strengthened. Moreover, the Central and State Fisheries Corporations are expected to play a larger role in both domestic and export marketing efforts, as well as in the development and regulation of the fishing industry.

India's Fourth Plan also calls for development of the nation's forests. This sector has been one of low productivity. In spite of sizeable imports of forestry and timber-derived products, firms have frequently been faced with serious shortages of packaging materials, containers, labels, high-grade paper, newsprint, various kinds of wood, and other related items.

Plantations of quick-growing trees are planned to increase by 240 percent in 1973-74 as compared to 1968-69; plantations explicitly for industrial and commercial uses by over 160 percent, and farm forestry and wood-fuel plantations by nearly 160 percent. This will enable paper and paper board production to increase from 640 thousand tons to nearly 1 million tons, and newsprint from 30,000 to 150,000 tons. Consumption of industrial wood in 1968-69 was about 11 million cubic meters, while demand by 1973-74 is projected to be 16 to 17 million cubic meters. Domestic supply is expected to increase to 13.5 million cubic meters by 1973-74, still leaving a deficit of about 15 to 20 percent which will either have to be imported or go unfilled.

Labor and population

The most crucial resource of any nation is her people. However, the true measure of human resources with respect to industrialization and economic growth lies not merely in numbers, but in the ability and motivation of individual members to contribute productively to society. India, like many other developing nations, has no lack of numbers.

As of 1970, her population, numbering over 550 million persons, was expanding at an annual rate of about 2.5 percent — in spite of a relatively low life expectancy (50 years) and a high infant mortality rate (over 145 deaths per 1000 live births versus 23 in the United States). At this rate, India has nearly 14 million new mouths to feed each year not counting the millions of refugees from East Pakistan. This is an almost incredible figure when one realizes that of the 150 or so countries in the world less than one-third have populations of 14 million or more. If India's population continues to grow at 2.5 percent rate, it will exceed one billion before the year 2000.

To cope with her tremendous population explosion, India — with much foreign assistance — has been undertaking family planning and birth control programs in recent years. The Fourth Plan calls for more vigorous and extended programs to reduce annual population growth to 1.7 percent by 1980 and 1.2 percent thereafter.[24] Even if achieved, however, this would still mean a population of 870 million by the year 2000.

India has a vast amount of surplus labor which cannot be used efficiently with existing levels of arable land, other available natural resources, real capital, and managerial talent. Vast segments of the nation's population contribute only marginally to the economy, and population expansion greatly retards real gains in economic growth. Well over half of the population consists of the young, those in school, the old and retired, and the sick and disabled. If we include those who are unemployed all or most of the time, this proportion probably approaches 75 or 80 percent. If we also consider high levels of underemployment, and concealed or disguised unemployment, the proportion may well reach 90 percent or more. This latter category includes millions of peasants who work for a few months at harvest time and remain idle for most of the rest of the year.

Not only must India's farmers feed themselves and the urban work force, they must also feed hundreds of millions of dependent citizens who are not employed in any directly productive capacity. Where the typical American farm worker produces enough food to feed himself and 45 other people, millions of Indian farmers can barely feed themselves and their own families at a minimum subsistence level.

Because of the tremendous surplus labor problem, legislation has been passed making it difficult for firms to dismiss unneeded or undesired workers. It has also led to minimum-wage laws which are far higher than called for in terms of true supply and demand conditions, especially for unskilled workers.

Since India's leaders have been and are genuinely welfare conscious, much of the country's limited wealth is expended on public health, medicine, sanitation, schools, and similar items. Even though the amounts spent in these areas are small in per capita terms, they are sizeable in absolute terms and in relation to the nation's resources. Such expenditures, though certainly justified from an ethical or moral standpoint, nonetheless mean that substantially less of the nation's wealth is directly available for the expansion and development of industry. Furthermore, they tend to increase the population problem by lowering mortality rates and increasing longevity. On the other hand, such expenditures provide industry and other sectors with a better educated, healthier, more energetic, and more productive labor force. But in spite of such projects, given India's tremendous population and limited wealth, tens of millions of workers and other citizens suffer from serious health problems, malnutrition, and the like.

Per capita caloric intake and nutritional standards in India are among the lowest in the world. Each of her physicians must look after ten times the number of people that a doctor in the United States must cover. Whereas the United States has one hospital bed for every 100 persons, India has one for every 2200.

It has been estimated by experts that at least 95 percent of India's industrial workers live in housing which is unsatisfactory for healthful habitation.[25] This is especially chilling in view of a projected urban population of 160 million by 1981 compared with only 80 million in 1961. Although some cities, e.g., New Delhi, Madras, Ahmadabad, and Bombay, are better off than others, such as Calcutta, Howrah, Benares, Patna, and Lucknow, acute housing, health, sanitation, water, pollution, congestion, and similar problems exist throughout the nation. Great deficiencies in social overhead capital facilities, food shortages, illiteracy, and low income are all basic underlying causes.

As is common in many poor countries, most of India's industrial labor force is at least a little sick most of the time. Parasitic infections, respiratory ailments, venereal diseases, and other debilitating maladies affect a major portion of the work force. This contributes to absenteeism, tardiness, and low levels of productivity and performance. Personnel must be trained continually to take over the jobs of those who leave because of serious illness or death. Because the stamina and physical energy, frustration level, and motivation level of Indian workers are generally low, it often takes several people to do a job handled by one worker in more advanced countries; and it may take more time for the typical Indian worker to do the same job as his U.S. counterpart.

India's Fourth Plan places considerable emphasis on improving the health and well-being of the population.[26] However, the total problem is so enormous that progress must continue to be slow.

Industrial enterprises in India have been required by law to bear an increasing amount of the welfare costs of their employees. Although many circumvent such laws in various ways, others, especially the larger ones, go far beyond the law in providing welfare benefits and facilities. This increases both overhead and managerial burdens, and is motivated by both social consciousness and by the expected economic benefits to be derived for the firm.

While some American companies in India have been reluctant to provide employee welfare benefits beyond those legally required, a growing number have come to realize that by increasing these benefits they can improve productivity, profitability, and employee loyalty, as well as their public image. However, U.S. subsidiaries have typically been less inclined to provide worker housing — with the exception of plants located in rather remote areas — than many of the large Indian or other foreign nationality companies.

On the other hand, U.S. firms tend to provide better working conditions — including effective climatic control devices and safety measures — and in-company employee facilities (such as clean dining rooms and washrooms). One reason for this is that many U.S. companies and plants in India are relatively new and of modern design. Another is that these companies often adhere to the higher standards of their U.S. plants and offices.

U.S. companies in India also seem to place great emphasis on the recruitment and selection of relatively healthy Indian personnel. They are more likely to put potential recruits through comprehensive medical examinations and rectify curable health deficiencies which are found in employees.

Capital

India is interested in rapidly developing a broad, capital-intensive industrial base — particularly in heavy industry — to achieve a self-sufficient economy. The reasons for this are not only economic but also political, nationalistic, ideological, emotional, and military. This rapid buildup of plant, equipment, machinery, and the like, in many cases has seriously outstripped available supplies of other essential factor inputs, social overhead capital, and other supporting infrastructures, as well as available markets. It is necessary for India to build up a broad heavy industry base but it may have been wiser to try to achieve this over a longer period of time, and with a more balanced and integrated approach.

India should have done much earlier what it is now doing in terms of development. This includes placing greater emphasis on agricultural development and the buildup of supporting industries — such as fertilizers, insecticides, and agricultural machinery. It also includes more *effective* emphasis on the development of labor-intensive industries, particularly those having export potential such as handicrafts, assembly operations, and food processing.

On the other hand, while highly labor-intensive industrial operations are a natural development in India from a social as well as economic standpoint, there are many instances where this is carried too far. Government officials and industrial managers in India often assume that highly labor-intensive techniques are the most beneficial in many areas, primarily because wage rates are low. However, when one includes allowances, benefits, bonuses, and other overhead related to labor, along with absenteeism, training expenses, spoilage, low productivity, and strikes and slowdowns, true labor costs often exceed the obvious, direct labor costs. In fact, it is not uncommon for true total labor costs per unit of output to exceed that of firms in the United States producing similar products, even in situations where comparable technology is employed.

MARKET SIZE

It is a well known fact that in most lines of modern industry a firm's unit costs decline as production or volume of business increases. Such economies of scale are possible until diminishing returns set in.

For example, in automobile manufacture the minimum efficient size of a plant may require the production of tens or hundreds of thousands of vehicles per year. Steel, various basic chemicals, fertilizers, oral drugs, and oil also must be produced in big quantities in order to make reasonably efficient use of the production facilities. In other types of firms, such as those producing various kinds of machinery and equipment, intermediates, components, and consumer goods, the minimum-sized efficient plant may be much smaller, and a company with a limited output may prove as efficient as a larger one.

Also relevant to plant efficiency are marketing, procurement, warehousing, transportation, financial, R&D, managerial, and various other economies. The minimum size for an efficient plant and the size and characteristics of the market may be too small or too large to enable a relatively high level of efficiency in these other functions. Ideally the markets for all types of products manufactured by the overall industrial sector in a given country should be large enough for each branch of industry to be characterized by optimum-sized firms. Such enterprises would enable maximum economies of scale to be derived in all of the above productive functions, as well as in basic managerial functions.

In general, the wealthier and larger a country is in both absolute and per capita terms — reflected by effective purchasing power, income distribution, and population characteristics — the larger its markets are likely to be for a wide range of products. However, even the most advanced and affluent industrial economies fall considerably short of the ideal optimum-size situation regarding markets and location because of the existence of a variety of environmental constraints. Even an advanced country may be too small, from technical, marketing, or other standpoints, to support optimum-sized plants or a high degree of specialization in some sectors. And in certain sectors there may only be room for only one optimum-sized plant, and this may lead to serious problems of monopoly power. This problem is especially serious in poor countries, particularly those that are small.

Because India's population is vast, she has room for at least a few optimum-sized plants in virtually all consumer goods industries. Even if only 1 percent of the population could afford to buy a certain product, this would represent a market of some 5.5 million people. However, because there are many small-scale firms and because of India's licensing system, strange patterns of product diversification and the lack of industrial specialization, there are few optimum-sized firms in the consumer-goods sectors. Another consumer goods problem is caused by the widely dispersed rural population. Long distribution channels, with numerous small middlemen working on small margins, are required to reach the rural markets. Moreover, because of small-scale operations and widely dispersed markets, economies of scale in procurement, warehousing, transportation, R&D, finance, management, and so forth, suffer on a widespread scale.

In the case of producer goods and intermediates, India is better off because of her size and natural resources than many other developing countries. However, she is nevertheless confronted with serious problems relating to market size and economies of scale in these sectors as well. Many industries have substantial excess capacity, while others still cannot produce enough to fulfill demand.

The markets for most industrial raw materials and producer goods are large enough to support at least a few optimum-sized plants. However, poor macro and micro planning and control, and the existence of many small and inefficient firms have greatly hindered economies of scale. These conditions have also led to serious imbalances between the supply and demand for numerous products, and created critical regional imbalances regarding sources of supply, plant location, and output markets.

A serious problem confronting Indian industry relating to market size exists in the fields of intermediates, components, spare parts, and special kinds of materials.

Such items are critically needed by firms, but not in volumes which can support economies of operation. This means that the firms requiring such items must produce them themselves, make do with inferior substitutes, or import them. As a result there is a much higher degree of vertical integration in Indian industry than in the United States; for example, textile firms may operate their own small foundries to produce spare parts. Because the total potential market for some items is not large enough for producers to set up more than one plant in India, the firms' major suppliers and customers are often found in other parts of the country and costly and complex warehousing, transportation, and marketing arrangements are required. Where bulk commodities are shipped in tank carloads in the United States, they are typically shipped in relatively small drums in India.

In spite of these marketing constraints, firms in India could adapt more effectively. With better planning, they could minimize their excess productive capacity, and capitalize on unique market opportunities that arise. Contingency planning, greater flexibility in operations and in the use of facilities and other productive resources, and product diversification programs can be utilized for such purposes. Better supplier development programs, as well as vertical integration — involving comprehensive cost-benefit analysis — often bear much fruit. In marketing firms can often develop and expand markets through demonstration, education, and user-assistance programs, as well as more conventional sales promotion strategies.

SOCIAL OVERHEAD CAPITAL

Social overhead capital relates to the supply of public utility and welfare-type services available to firms and other consumers. Such services include transportation systems and related facilities; public warehousing and storage; electric power; gas transmission; water resources; communications networks, including telephone, telegraph, postal services and the mass media; housing; sewage; sanitation; hospitals and other medical services; and so forth. Equally as important as the quantity of such services available, are their quality, reliability and costs. Industrial enterprises in countries with poorly developed social-overhead capital facilities are faced with serious managerial problems which either do not exist or are much less serious in countries having relatively good facilities.

The management of the social-overhead capital facilities is a critical factor, and inefficient management of these facilities is particularly common in poor countries. This means poor service to users — which hinders the internal operations and performance of industrial enterprises.

In many areas, India is significantly better off than many other countries with regard to social-overhead capital in both absolute terms, and per capita terms. But in some areas — most notably housing and public sanitation facilities — India ranks close to the bottom with regard to world standards. By focusing on India, much can be learned about the impact of social-overhead capital on industrial management and firm performance in other countries, particularly poor countries struggling to develop.[27]

Power and water supply

Electric power and water supply are among the most important basic resources for the maintenance of an industrial society. The availability of these resources is often a key factor in plant location decisions. In poor countries well-established power grids are rare, and even where they exist, long distance transmission is often undependable. The industrial manager must think not only about the rated power capacity in any area, but also about the reliability of supply throughout the year.

It is common in less developed countries to find that electric companies cannot provide industrial power at times of peak demand, and firms may not be able to operate at all at certain times of the day (or year). An alternative open to such a firm would be to build and maintain its own power plant or emergency standby unit, but this is costly and increases the managerial burden substantially. The same is true in the case of inadequate or undependable water supply. Producers of aluminum, chemicals and drugs are particularly heavy users of water resources.

Inadequate, unreliable, or erratic power and water supplies have a direct impact on the efficient utilization of plant capacity, and other productive resources, hindering the establishment of new firms and the expansion of existing ones. Such deficiencies make planning and control much more difficult, and operations less stable.

Although India has made considerable progress in building power and water resources, the country's requirements still exceed the available supply. In areas where power is based on hydroelectric projects, a poor monsoon season usually results in the rationing of power supplies. Although India has large coal deposits, the heat content of her coal is relatively low and power generation from coal is expensive. Until recently, most oil had to be imported which also made it very expensive to use oil to produce electricity. India has been experimenting with all forms of power and has now several atomic power generating stations. However, per capita electric power generation and consumption in India are less than 2 percent of that of the United States. It has been estimated by experts that between one-third and three-quarters of India's total energy is still derived from cow dung. The country's Fourth Plan calls for a 50 percent increase in installed power generating capacity by 1973-74.

Transportation and storage facilities

Transportation and warehousing facilities have a direct impact on the supply and marketing of goods. Inadequate, unreliable, or erratic transportation leads to supply, production, and delivery failures for enterprises which can cause failure or bottlenecks involving interdependent firms and other parties. It also may cause the firm to carry considerably larger inventories or to vertically integrate more than it otherwise might, in order to overcome possible shortages and delays in the receipt of needed items.

Poor transportation and inadequate warehousing and handling facilities result in damage, spoilage, and pilferage of goods. Hand carts, rickshaws, bicycles, bullock carts, junks, sampans, and other human and animal-driven modes of transportation are widely used to transport a tremendous range of products in poor countries.

A country's transportation system also has a direct bearing on travel by enterprise personnel. Unreliable or slow transportation hinders timely face-to-face contacts between firm executives and customers, suppliers, government officials, bankers, and the like in other parts of the country. This affects firm organization and staffing as well as its communications networks and control systems. If local transportation is erratic or inadequate it is likely to lead to absenteeism and tardiness among enterprise personnel and it may inhibit the use of multiple shifts and the employment of women.

Transportation constraints often constitute a key factor in the location of enterprises in developing countries. Because of inadequate public transportation, it is common for firms to own and operate more of their own transportation services and storage facilities than in advanced countries. This considerably increases overhead costs and the managerial burden.

India's overall transportation system is superior to that of many other nations at similar economic levels. This is one clear-cut legacy of British colonial rule, although India has made much progress on her own. However, India's system is spotty, with some forms of transportation and certain regions substantially more advanced than others.

Rail, road, and air links connect the major cities in India. Many remote areas are also connected by air service. The road system, even in rural areas, is more developed than in many other poor countries. Unfortunately, few of India's rivers are navigable for larger ships. Most are shallow, and many only contain water during monsoon seasons. Because the rivers are flat, they often change course from year to year and may shift as much as a mile or two from their previous beds. This eliminates a cheap form of transportation available to many other nations.

State-owned and operated railways account for the biggest share of India's modern commercial traffic. In per capita terms, India still has less than 10 percent of the railroad track of the United States, and the total freight carried is only a small fraction of that handled in the United States. Rail freight traffic in India is far from dependable. In many sections switchovers are still needed because tracks change from narrow to broad gauge. Shipments often get sidetracked for weeks or months, and some are lost forever. In fact, many companies take the precaution of sending a paid guard along with their shipments. Should a train be sidetracked, the guard attempts to get word back to the shipper so that he knows at all times where his goods are located.

Many products which require special transportation and storage facilities (e.g., refrigeration) or which are hazardous to handle, (e.g., explosives, inflammables, resins) either cannot be sent by rail, or can only be transported at high risk and costs.

Agricultural products probably suffer the most from inadequate rail facilities and thus, many food items can be sold only in markets near the growing areas, and then in the season they are harvested.

Damaged goods are common in rail shipments in India; so is pilferage, which often exceeds 10 percent of the value of a given shipment. The proportion of damaged goods runs even higher. Insurance coverage is available, but at high rates; and claims are difficult to prove and settle. Most important, a firm is likely to find itself without critically needed goods. Because of these difficulties in rail transport, many Indian companies ship long-haul bulk commodities by truck, even though rates may be more than double.

Passenger rail traffic in India is generally handled more efficiently than freight. Three basic classes of passenger travel exist, ranging from boxcars with wooden benches to comfortable air-conditioned sleeper cars. Train fares are sharply graded so that even the poorest can afford to use the railroad. Most major intercity traffic is by rail. The best accommodations are usually the most difficult to obtain, and reservations must be made far in advance. "Gifts" are often necessary to ensure desired accommodations, and many firms whose personnel travel frequently by rail keep desired space available on a continual basis.

India's Fourth Plan focuses more on modernizing and increasing the efficiency of the country's railways than on adding capacity. The plan calls for more intensive use of rolling stock, accelerated conversion to broad gauge tracks, and better overall management.

India's major paved highways are narrow, often providing insufficient room for two trucks to pass. About two-thirds of the country's 15,000 miles of national highways are of single-lane width. The road system has many missing or uncompleted links, long unimproved sections, and many missing bridges. Only about 10 percent of the country's roads are suitable for all-weather travel. The roads and shoulders are poorly maintained and roadside facilities (gas, food, lodging, and so forth) are primitive in most parts of the country. Long trips by motor vehicle are far from pleasant.

Truck transportation is slow and costly. Fuel prices are high and maintenance costs on trucks are substantial. Moreover, trucking rates are not widely published and tend to vary greatly. Firms typically negotiate on each shipment. It is costly to send shipments of less than a full load and often truckers simply refuse to handle certain shipments. Trucking is largely a sellers' market, since there is a shortage of trucks in India in relation to demand.

Trucks are usually overladen, and frequent accidents occur when they have to leave the pavement to allow oncoming vehicles to pass. Indian roads are littered with trucks which have overturned or broken down along the way.

In general, the use of trucking to move goods is hindered by three major factors. As noted above, the first is cost of fuel, maintenance, and damage in transit. The second is a scarcity of trucks. For every hundred motor vehicles in the United States India has less than one. The third is the time factor. Trips which would take eight or nine hours in the United States may take three or four days — or longer in bad weather — in India. Some Indian bridges cannot take heavy loads and trucks must be unloaded at one end, driven to the other side, and then loaded by hand again before proceeding. The collection of tolls and taxes at various townships also slows down trucking time. Drivers must pull off the road and either pay the tax or convince authorities that their goods are consigned to other destinations. The authorities may check the driver's documents against the truck's contents and this may require an unloading operation.

Roads in major metropolitan areas are also spotty, poorly maintained, and usually highly congested. Because of poor sewage systems — Calcutta particularly suffers from this problem — roads flood and become unusable in heavy rains. Truck deliveries within the same city may take several days.

Bus lines link major cities, and also operate within cities and in rural areas. However, service is erratic, and buses are old, subject to frequent breakdowns, and extremely uncomfortable. Buses are also used widely as general-purpose transport, and a passenger may find himself sitting alongside a goat, a bunch of chickens, or even a piece of machinery.

India's Fourth Plan concentrates more on improving, modernizing, and maintaining existing road networks than building new ones. The plan calls for increasing the number of trucks from 300,000 in 1969 to 470,000 in 1974, and the number of buses from 80,000 to 115,000.

With regard to coastal shipping, the Fourth Plan emphasizes the development and expansion of harbors, dock facilities, and storage facilities for handling bulk commodities. A number of major new harbor projects are also underway. It is projected that by 1974 Indian shipping will serve about 40 percent of the country's overseas trade compared with only 15 percent in 1969. Total Indian shipping tonnage is expected to increase by about 70 percent.

Firms surveyed which have been using water transportation in India have been confronted with a variety of problems. For example, one company which has been importing chemical compounds in standard containers suitable for U.S. conditions has experienced considerable losses. The Indian stevedores use hooks which cut these containers open and have adamantly refused to do otherwise. (Labor problems and lack of cooperation on the part of dock workers have created serious problems in recent years.) This particular company recently bought its own boats and hired its own dock workers in order to deal with the problem.

India has three distinct airlines systems. The first is Air India, a government-owned but privately operated and relatively well-managed corporation which flies international routes. The second, Indian Airlines Corporation, is a government-owned and operated monopoly which handles all air traffic within India except in the extreme northeast. The final category contains some small private companies which operate between Calcutta and the northeast portion of India. The airlines connect all of the major cities in the country, and several smaller cities, and even some small towns which are not easily accessible by other modern modes of transportation.

All of India's airlines handle both cargo and passengers. Although the amount of cargo handled is relatively small, many firms do send things air freight when they are needed in a hurry, or when they are shipped to remote parts of the country. Air freight is very expensive, but it tends to be relatively dependable. Passenger air travel is fairly reliable, but is limited almost entirely to businessmen, government officials, leading educators, and the most wealthy classes because of its high cost.

The Fourth Plan provides for the modernization of India's major airports to handle the new types of jet aircraft, the construction of several new airports, and improvements in existing ones. It also provides for the acquisition of new planes which will add substantially to commercial airline capacity.

Communications

A country's overall communications system can be divided into three basic categories. The first contains the systems which are designed to facilitate direct, and chiefly long distance communications between individuals — telephone, telegraph, and postal services. The second contains the mass communications media — radio and television, magazines, and the like. The last group contains more localized, group communications media such as newspapers, magazines, movies, and so forth.

The first category — telephones, telegraph networks, and postal service — can have a major impact on industrial organization. Unless operations are confined to a central location, if telephones and postal and telegraph networks are poor and unreliable more travel by company personnel will be required. Poor communication systems necessitate frequent visits to other company locations, as well as customers, suppliers, government officials, and others. *De facto* decentralization is also more likely to occur, even where decentralization of authority is not desired or desirable. The decision-making process is also likely to be slowed down considerably.

This category of communications is also likely to have a major impact on managerial control and enterprise reporting systems. If facilities are inadequate, timely information feedback and effective corrective action are likely to suffer, as is planning for the future.

India's telephone system, although it connects all of the major cities, leaves much to be desired. First, units are few and far between. For every telephone in India the United States has 100. The Indian system is beset by widespread equipment, maintenance, technical, managerial, and facilities problems. Most of India's villages have not yet been linked to national telephone networks.

Within any one city, telephone service is usually adequate, although it varies considerably by city and during different periods. Although it may be necessary to dial a number several times before a connection is actually made, the voice transmission, when the call is finally linked, is usually adequate. Two major problems exist, however. The first is the long waiting time (up to several years) to obtain a telephone. Even industrial firms face great difficulties in getting an adequate number of telephones to relieve the bottlenecks on their switchboards. Small firms and those in outlying areas often cannot get any telephones for long periods of time. It is common to use all kinds of influence, and even outright bribes in order to obtain telephones. Problems in the telephone system are largely due to a lack of facilities ranging from telephone poles to relay switches. In fact, to speed the process, the telephone user often supplies his own telephone poles if he desires service in an area where service did not previously exist.

The second major problem is cultural. Many Indians dislike using the telephone for business purposes. It is viewed as being too impersonal, and lacking the desired face-to-face contact. Consequently, the telephone's use is frequently more limited than it might otherwise be.

Conditions with respect to intercity telephone communications are very different from the intracity situation. Trunk lines are usually overcrowded. All calls must be placed through an operator over these trunks. Calls are designated as one of three levels — "ordinary," "urgent," and "priority." "Priority" calls are the most expensive and may be placed only by government officials and people with special authorization. "Urgent" calls can be placed by anyone who wishes to pay a substantial premium over the cost of "ordinary" calls. Priority calls are placed first; then come any urgent calls which are pending. When both of these categories have been cleared, the ordinary calls are handled. Within any one group, calls are processed in the order in which they are received.

It often takes a day or more to complete an "urgent" call of 300 to 500 miles. Frequent breakdowns occur in the circuits and line overloads are common. Naturally, the waiting time will vary with the time of day. When a local or national crisis occurs and government officials are on the telephone, it is almost impossible to get a call through to another city. The situation with international calls is even worse. Such calls must go through a system of trunk lines. It usually takes several days to place such a call and when it is finally connected, the transmission losses at each of the connect points along the way is so great that voices often cannot be heard.

In addition to the telephone, some internal radio communications on a person-to-person basis are employed. However, the use of radio is highly restricted and is largely confined to government agencies such as the police.

India's telephone system is superior to that of many poor countries, and adequate telegram transmission facilities link all of the major and many of the small cities. Although most villages are not connected, telegraph offices in towns or cities nearby usually service them. The transmission system is good enough so that a growing number of firms have recently been linking their operations via direct teleprinter communication or telex systems to speed up data transmission. They are frequently within the same city. Most companies which have their own computer installations also have their own telex networks. Some firms even cooperate with each other by relaying telex messages to suppliers, customers, and other parties. This practice tends to be more common among foreign firms. Indigenous companies seem less inclined to cooperate in this way.

The major difficulty with India's telegraph system is not in the transmission system, but in what happens with the output at the end of the system. Delivery of telegrams can be extremely erratic and as a result, it may take several days to receive a telegram.

The Indian postal service is a large operation, probably as efficient as any in developing nations. There are problems within the system, however. For example, mailmen often have no way to protect the mail against the elements. This means that, during monsoon season, mail and packages are often delivered in thoroughly soggy form (resulting, in the case of letters, in illegibility). Another problem relates to the temptation placed before postal clerks by large amounts of postage. A large package or an overseas airmail letter may carry postage equivalent in value to a week's salary for a postal clerk. Despite these difficulties, the postal service appears to be one of the more efficiently operated government agencies.

A number of firms have begun to use selective mailings for advertising purposes. This is primarily aimed at commercial customers rather than private individuals. Mass mailings of literature addressed to "resident," so common in the United States, are relatively rare in India, as a result of the cost of printing and distributing such material and the need for selectivity in directing advertising pitches.

The other two categories of communications, involving mass media, tend to have their greatest impact on the marketing function of firms, particularly advertising and sales promotion. In a company's role as customer, these media may also influence procurement activities. Newspapers may also have a bearing on the recruitment of personnel through advertisements.

Communications facilities within India are poor by standards of most modern countries, presenting problems deriving not only from physical facilities but also from the general cultural milieu.

Because of the high illiteracy rate in India, written communications do not reach a major segment of the population. Verbal communication runs into a similar problem with respect to the diversity of languages and dialects. It is impossible, at present, to communicate in any one language with all or even a majority of Indians, although English is the most widely understood language within urban business circles. The alternative, visual mass-media communications such as movies and T.V. are expensive and usually require verbal support, presenting some of the same problems.

Hence, India cannot be considered as an entity for communication purposes. Instead it consists of large pockets, each of which must be addressed individually. In addition to the language problem, there are differences among various segments of the population based on religion, class, caste, geography, and so forth. This has important implications for companies promoting their products on a national or multiregional basis as well as for government planners.

India has only about one radio broadcasting transmitter for every sixty in the United States, and only a single radio for every five hundred in the United States. The radio networks in India are government-owned and controlled by All-India Radio. Since government policy does not permit commercial use, firms must turn elsewhere for advertising. Television is in its infancy in India, and a factory has recently been set up to produce a small number of sets, but it is likely that the government will prohibit commercial advertising when this industry becomes more established.

The primary means of advertising for most companies in India is through local mass-media, such as newspapers, movies, and billboard displays. There are a number of advertising agencies in the country, and a few U.S. and other foreign affiliates are among the most successful.

India's movie industry is one of the biggest in the world, and movies play an unusual role in Indian life. They represent a form of escapism enjoyed by people in all walks of life, in urban and rural areas. This medium is widely used for advertising, with considerable time devoted to commercials in movie theaters, both in slide and moving picture form. The government also uses this medium to promote major social and economic programs.

Newspapers and, to a lesser extent, magazines are also used for commercial advertising, but they reach limited segments of the population. Circulation figures are extremely small by U.S. standards. Newsprint consumption per capita in India is only about 1/1800 that of the United States. A large India newspaper typically has a total circulation of less than 100,000. Because of transportation costs and problems, newspapers are usually available only within the particular city where they are published, and only a few of them have national distribution.

An analysis of the communications systems of developing nations often reveals, as in the case of India, the nature of the problems which must be faced by economic developers and private industry in reaching specific individuals and organizations, as well as large segments of the population. Such factors must be carefully considered in planning and carrying out strategies and activities.

Other social overhead capital facilities

Sewer defects in a country like India create serious health problems. If an industrial firm has to dispose of large amounts of wastes, lack of an adequate sewer system can result in delays, as production is stopped or slowed down to clear the factory area of noxious wastes, typically by hand. It often pays the firm to build and maintain a costly waste-disposal system. The same is true in the case of facilities to cope more effectively with floods, leakage, and other weather and environmental conditions.

In general, there is relatively little public or corporate concern about pollution in most of India's major, congested cities — although this varies somewhat by city. In Calcutta, for instance, the situation is so bad and there are so many other acute problems, that serious pollution problems tend to be treated with apathy. U.S. subsidiaries and other foreign companies frequently do more on their own to reduce pollution (and the impact of adverse weather) than do indigenous firms. This is probably due to an instinctive desire to try to maintain standards prevailing in the affluent countries in which their head offices are located. Their top managers are also often more aware of the seriousness of pollution and other ecological problems because of their familiarity with ecological conditions and standards of advanced countries, although these are far from adequate in many instances.

Consulting services are not conventionally considered as part of social overhead capital, although they may provide beneficial external economies. The consulting business has grown considerably in India, and the country now contains a wide variety of practicing consultants covering such fields as general management, engineering, marketing research, advertising, accounting, and other specialized technical and business fields. However, many of these are inadequate. Larger and more progressive firms have set up their own consulting groups, in some cases making them available to other organizations on a fee basis. International firms benefit from the services of experts provided by the parent company. Demand for private foreign consultants in Indian business and government has been growing in recent years. However, there is frequently much red tape, including foreign exchange problems, in employing them in India.

CONCLUDING REMARKS

It should be obvious by now that it is not only necessary for managers and government officials to identify and describe environment. One must *understand* it well enough to project ahead for the future. Decisions must be made today to prepare for tomorrow.

While the economic environment is important, economic insights yield only partial results for decisions which must be made by industrial managers and government planners. The problems of production techniques, sales promotion, and worker incentives, for example, relate to economic considerations but they also involve problems of education, sociology, psychology, cultural anthropology, law, political science, and various other disciplines. The four environmental chapters presented thus far have attempted to bridge the gap between relevant disciplines, external conditions or constraints, and internal firm management, operations, and performance.

CHAPTER 6 FOOTNOTES

1. For quantitative data in particular we have drawn on a wide range of sources compiled by Indian government agencies, the World Bank, U.S. Agency for International Development, the United Nations, and various other governmental and international organizations. We have also drawn on special studies authorized by the Indian government in our analyses of India's economic constraints and problems. These include reports and documents prepared by the Dutt, Hazari, Karre, Lokanathan, Santhanam, and Swaminathan Committees, and the Administrative Reforms and Monopolies Commissions. The Statistical Outlines of India, published annually by Tata Industries Ltd., have also furnished us with pertinent data, as have the as yet unpublished industry studies conducted by the Higher Education Research Unit of the London School of Economics.

In addition to the above, we have drawn on the following major works in our study of India's economic environment: G. Myrdal, *Asian Drama,* 3 vols., Pantheon, New York, 1968; J. Lewis, *Quiet Crisis in India,* The Brookings Institute, Washington, D.C., 1962; W. Malenbaum, *Prospects for Indian Development,* Free Press, New York, 1962; A. Phatak, *External Environmental Constraints and Their Impact on the Internal Operations of Firms in the Pharmaceutical and Engineering Industries in India,* unpublished doctoral dissertation, UCLA, Los Angeles, 1966; A. Negandhi, *Private Foreign Investment in India,* Institute for International Business and Economic Development Studies, Michigan State University, East Lansing, 1965; M. Kust, *Foreign Enterprise in India,* University of North Carolina Press, Chapel Hall, 1964; J. Baranson, *Manufacturing Problems in India,* Syracuse University Press, Syracuse, 1967; W. Reddaway, *The Development of the Indian Economy,* Richard D. Irwin, Homewood, Ill., 1962; B. Shenoy, *Indian Planning and Economic Development,* Asia Publishing House, New York, 1963; T. Sharma, and S. Chauhan, *Indian Industries,* Agarwala and Co., Agra, 1966; S. Iyengor, *Fifteen Years of Democratic Planning,* Asia Publishing House, New York, 1965; B. Bhatra, *India's Economic Crisis and Fourth Five Year Plan,* Atma Ram, Delhi, 1967; G. Janger, *Our Economic Problems,* National Publications, Delhi, 1966; A. Mann, *Investment for Capacity Expansion,* MIT Press, Cambridge, Mass., 1967; D. Singh, *Economics of Development: With Special Reference to India,* Asia Publishing House, London, 1966; R. Kulkorim, *Deficit Financing and Economic Development: With Special Reference to Indian Economic Development,* Asia Publishing House, London, 1967; S. Ghopal, *Agricultural Financing in India,* Asia Publishing House, London, 1967; K. Sastri, *Federal-State Fiscal Relations in India,* Oxford University Press, London, 1966; G. Rosen, *Democracy and Economic Change in India,* University of California Press, Berkeley, 1966. See also a more recent article by A. Ghosh, "India! Drifting Toward Chaos," *The Wall Street Journal,* New York, April 5, 1971.

2. Cf. B. Richman, *Soviet Management: With Significant American Comparisons,* Prentice-Hall, Englewood Cliffs, N.J., 1965.

3. See "Managing Agencies Will Go from April 3," *The Times of India,* Bombay, March 27, 1970.

4. *Times of India,* Bombay, Jan. 6, 1970, p. 1.

5. This new industrial policy is presented, discussed, elaborated on, and analyzed in *Eastern Economist,* Feb. 27 and March 20, 1970.

6. See *Times of India,* Bombay, March 24, 1970.

7. See *Times of India,* Bombay, July 30, 1969, p. 1.

8. For an excellent study of French planning and its impact on business management see H. Schollhammer, *French Economic Planning and Its Impact on Business Decisions,* unpublished doctoral dissertation, University of Indiana, Bloomington, Ind., 1967; and H. Schollhammer, "National Economic Planning and Business Decision-Making," *California Management Review,* Vol. XII, No. 2, Winter 1969, pp. 74-88.

9. For a comprehensive study of Red China with Indian, Soviet, and U.S. comparisons see B. Richman, *Industrial Society in Communist China,* Random House, New York, 1969 and Vintage Books, 1972.

10. Public sector profitability figures can be found in Indian Reserve Bank surveys, data compiled by the Central Government's Bureau of Public Enterprises, and annual company reports.

11. Profitability figures for the private sector can be found in Reserve Bank of India surveys, as well as data presented by the *Financial Express,* Feb. 19, 1968 and July 13, 1969; and *Economic Times,* July 22, 1968; *Business International,* April 17, 1970.

12. One notable exception is Gunnar Myrdal. See his analysis in this regard in Myrdal, *op. cit.,* vol. 3, p. 2103.

13. Underutilized or excess capacity figures in this section are computed on a one-shift basis. They have been derived from a variety of sources. The most useful in this regard have been a recent confidential report prepared by World Bank experts, *Underutilization of Industrial Capacity* National Council of Applied Economic Research, New Delhi, 1966; R. K. Koti, *Utilization of Industrial Capacity in India, 1966-67 and 1967-68,* Gokhale Institute Monograph Series, Nos. 2 and 9, Poona; and Indian industry surveys conducted by members of the Higher Education Research Unit at the London School of Economics, *op. cit.*

14. See sources cited in footnote 13.

15. See Koti, *op. cit.,* No. 9.

16. As reported in *Financial Express,* Bombay, May 17, 1969.

17. These figures have been derived from reports compiled by the Bureau of Public Enterprise which is part of the Indian Government.

18. Private sector inventory data have been derived from Reserve Bank of India bulletins and surveys.

19. The price data in this section have been derived from Reserve Bank of India bulletins and surveys and from Indian Planning Commission reports and draft plans.

20. The statistics and other relevant data presented in this section have been derived from the following sources: Reserve Bank of India Bulletins and surveys; annual and special reports issued by the Department of Company Affairs, the Bureau of Public Enterprise, and public financial institutions under Indian central government ministries; the Dutt Committee Report on Industrial Licensing Policy; Reports issued by the Indian Investment Center in New York; World Bank studies; and Kurst, *op. cit.,* especially Chapter X.

21. Figures have been derived from the annual reports of the Department of Company Affairs under the Ministry for Industrial Development. See also *The Times of India,* Bombay, March 27, 1970, p. 13.

22. The following sources have been drawn on most heavily in our analysis of Indian agriculture: *Fourth Five Year Plan: 1969-1974,* Indian Planning Commission, Government of India, New Delhi, 1969; *Near East and South Asia: Economic Growth Trends,* Agency for International Development, Washington, D.C., Nov. 1968; various studies by World Bank experts; S. Schonberg, "India Bedeviled by Agrarian Unrest," *New York Times,* Jan. 19, 1970.

23. Cf. Richman, *Industrial Society in Communist China, op. cit.,* pp. 534-547.

24. *Fourth Five Year Plan 1969-1974, op. cit.,* Chapter 17.

25. Cf. Myrdal, *Asian Drama, op. cit.,* p. 554, and the sources cited therein.

26. For details see *Fourth Five Year Plan, op. cit.,* Chapter 17.

27. National statistics relating to social overhead capital in India and the U.S. have been derived from *Fourth Five Year Plan, Near East and South Asia: Economic Growth Trends,* Myrdal, *op. cit.,* pp. 540ff., and the sources cited therein; *Selected Economic Data for the Less Developed Countries,* Agency for International Development, Washington, D.C., April, 1968.

CHAPTER 7
INTERNATIONAL
ENVIRONMENT

The domestic environment of every country is partly molded by external conditions deriving from its relationships with foreign groups and nations, for example, foreign trade or defense expenditures. In addition, a whole international environment is born as a result of these relationships. Factors which make up this environment include foreign policy, international treaties, common markets, and the like. Although these could be considered as a subset of the domestic environment, they are of great significance to business enterprises, especially those which are not indigenous to the country in which they function, and therefore, merit separate treatment.

In reality the foreign subsidiary is concerned with at least four sets of environmental conditions: the domestic and international environments of both the parent company's country and of the host country in which it does business. A multinational corporation with operations in 60 or more countries would be dealing with 240 different sets of complicated and interrelated environmental conditions, since the international outlook of the parent will differ with respect to each of the 60 nations. While some of these might be similar or identical, many would not be, and these would force the company into different patterns of management and operations and varying patterns of productive efficiency. International business is clearly very complex.

Although we have dealt with the domestic environment first, the process of analysis for a multinational company wishing to expand in other countries would tend to first focus on the international environment, seeking key veto factors. These would include the investment climate, profit remission, exchange control, import and export restrictions, international trade patterns, balance of payment trends, national and political ideologies, attitudes toward foreign firms and foreigners, and special legal rules for foreign business.

We have divided the international environment into three basic categories corresponding to those used in analyzing the domestic environment: sociological, political-legal, and economic. Education can be viewed entirely as a domestic constraint, since people are not usually educated in an international environment per se, although they may be educated in several different countries. But the other kinds of environmental conditions frequently differ enough between domestic and international segments of a given country to be considered and analyzed separately.

OVERVIEW OF SOCIOLOGICAL FACTORS

The sociological and cultural aspects of the international environment are probably the most difficult to recognize and deal with. They are embedded in a complex structure of attitudes, beliefs, and ideologies, many of which are not readily identifiable to the foreigner, and rooted in cultural concepts which are among the most resistant to change.

The sociological environment is likely to have both a direct and an indirect effect on foreign firms. Its indirect effect is manifested in various laws, policies, and regulations which, in turn, have an impact on industrial management and enterprise performance. Its direct impact is shown in various kinds of attacks on foreign firms or foreign personnel, boycotts of their products, labor agitation, and other forms of harassment. While the sociological environment may contain many elements favorable to the foreign firm, the majority are frequently unfavorable in less-developed countries.

Within developing nations, three of the more important of these elements are national ideology, the nature and extent of nationalism, and the local view of foreigners. Although a nation is not a living being, the prevalent attitudes of its citizens give it a type of anthropomorphic life derived from an amalgam of individual viewpoints. This character must be identified and understood by multinational corporations.

National ideology

A national ideology is made up of a country's dominant ideals, attitudes, and viewpoints. Particularly important are its self-image and its image in the international sphere. Dominant ideologies, in terms of their impact on business firms, are not necessarily based on majority concensus. They may be based on the ideals and values of the most active or influential citizens of a given country. However, political leaders both reflect and shape many of the attitudes and ideals of their people.

Many countries present clear-cut ideologies to the rest of the world. At times, however, there may be significant differences between the image and the reality. Moreover, few nations are monolithic when it comes to ideology. Nevertheless, to describe a person as American, Irish, French, Indian, Egyptian, etc., is to define in part the kind of man being considered. Politics and law, as well as much of economies, tend to follow the stereotypes. Attitudes toward property rights, private profits, welfare, foreign relations, wages, different kinds of products and foods, prices, contracts, treaties, competition and innumerable other matters often differ according to the nationality of the group under consideration.

Public opinion and reaction along ideological lines are subtle and complex issues which should be carefully studied by firms and their managers. This is much more of an art than a science, although some scientific poll-taking can be done in any country. Pulse-taking of this type tends to be especially difficult in revolutionary or rapidly changing societies or those characterized by political instability. Algeria, Jordan, Libya, Syria, the newer African countries, Southeast Asian nations, countries such as Peru, Chile and Argentina, as well as India, fit into this category. A key problem in such countries is the identification of who really represents the prevailing state of public opinion — the radicals or revolutionaries, the more moderate segments of the population, or the conservatives or reactionaries. The question is made more difficult in countries where there exists a mass of illiterate peasants and workers whose ideological attitudes are even more difficult to discover.

Political speeches, the mass media, and special white papers may reveal much about a country's ideology. On the other hand, both oral and written rhetoric may be misleading in terms of implications for industrial firms. Overt manifestations of hostility toward a particular country are often overemphasized for political reasons. One political leader may damn the United States, while a key minister of the same country is trying — not necessarily quietly — to obtain American aid, private investment, or collaboration.

Perhaps a country's novelists, satirists, artists, and poets give truer insights into the society than official speeches, pronouncements, or newspaper articles. In any event, the wise corporation will attempt to get at true ideological currents by developing close contacts among those segments of the society that are of greatest importance with regard to the effectiveness, mobility, and profitability of the firm. Company management should try to identify actions that are likely to be either taboo or particularly favorable in terms of prevailing values, customs, and attitudes. Fortunate indeed is the manager who knows what the ideological situation really is, for he will be in good position to adjust to it in ways which benefit his company.

A major means of protection for the international company is to be aware of national ideology and be a responsive and responsible corporate citizen of the host nation. This does not imply complete conformity to prevailing attitudes. Good citizenship usually means taking an active, not a passive role, and the multinational corporation can be one of the most effective catalysts for economic development and social change. However, the approach should generally be evolutionary rather than revolutionary. The changes foreign firms introduce must be presented in such a manner as to minimize disruption, further the direction in which the society desires to move, and be perceived as beneficial.

Of course there are situations, such as those arising from abrupt change in government, where even those foreign companies that have behaved as good citizens come under heavy attack and are even expropriated. This happened in Cuba after Castro came to power and more recently in Peru, Bolivia, Chile, the Arab world and Zambia. However, many of the foreign firms which were taken over have not been model citizens of their host countries.

A number of major American corporations have decided not to invest in certain less developed countries, including India, largely because their key executives felt that there was a sharp conflict between their own ideologies and objectives and those of the countries under consideration. One U.S. corporate chief executive indicated that he did not want to invest in India because it was moving vigorously down the socialist path, because government involvement in industry was too great, and because too many employee welfare benefits were required. This despite the fact that he believed that substantial profits might be derived from such a venture.

National ideology has implications for many elements of the management process, and any of the enterprise and management functions may be affected. In Moslem countries, for example, production schedules must be adjusted to prayer times, and in many Arab nations the assignment of a Jewish manager, no matter how competent, may not prove to be a wise course of action. Similarly, research and development on birth control methods should probably not be assigned to a subsidiary in Spain or Ecuador. In one country, foreign investment in a particular industry may be favorably regarded while in another, it may be considered treachery.

Firms unaware of or insensitive to the histories, feelings, and traditions of the countries in which they operate may find continuing difficulties created by friction between their managers and host country citizens. A company can ignore this factor only at its own peril.

Some American companies abroad have avoided severe problems by sustained efforts to blend in effectively with the ideology, aspirations, and needs of the host country. The Trans-Arabian Pipeline Company (Tapline) is a good case in point. During the Suez crisis of 1956-57, Arab anti-American and anti-European feelings reached fever pitch. Mobs attacked embassies, foreign firms were struck, and anti-Western demonstrations took place. Damage to the property of foreign companies was great, and the pipelines of the Iraq Petroleum Company, running through Iraq, Syria, and Lebanon, were blown up to prevent oil from reaching Europe.

However, Tapline continued to operate normally in Saudi Arabia, Jordan, Syria, and Lebanon. Its oil traffic was not interrupted because for years prior to the Suez crisis, Tapline management had worked out a *modus vivendi* with its local hosts. The task did not consist of sending out propaganda. It involved years of demonstrated good deeds which benefited society as well as the firm, and systematic hard work in building up local relationships which endured through trying and violent times. In a few days, those responsible within the company managed to gain more for the firm than their combined lifetime salaries. And again during the Six-Day Arab-Israeli War in June, 1967, Tapline came out unscathed, while various other Western companies in the Mid-East were subjected to extensive damage and harassment.

This kind of adjustment to local ideologies, aspirations, and politics is seldom widely noticed when it works. Only when expropriations occur, or when firms are sabotaged does this area come into public focus. But then, it is usually too late to undo the damage of years of defective adaptation and inept public relations.

American national ideology often has a direct impact on U.S. operations abroad. For example, for many years the U.S. government has either banned outright or greatly restricted trade with most Communist countries. However, many countries do not have such bans or restrictions, and U.S. subsidiaries located in them are free to import from or export to various Communist nations (within certain limits). But surprisingly few do. The reason in many cases is neither legal nor economic, but ideological. Such dealings may be considered "unpatriotic" or "un-American," and relatively few American firms — even under foreign managers — seem inclined to consciously violate this American attitude, even when considerable profits might be made.

Another illustration of American sociological pressures on international business was seen several years ago when President Johnson asked for "voluntary" restrictions of capital exports by firms and banks in an effort to solve U.S. balance of payments difficulties. A majority of companies did comply, and in so doing reduced potential profits, shifted types of financing and sources of capital and paid more for funds. Although government pressures were applied to secure compliance, and even though the program did become compulsory in the late 1960's because of persistent and serious balance of payments difficulties, a great many corporate executives felt that voluntary restraint was the proper response to help in solving a serious problem for the government.

One final aspect of American ideology warrants comment here: that is, the widespread negative attitude among U.S. corporations with regard to engaging in joint ownership ventures with foreign governments which would place them partially or largely in the public sector. Although more U.S. multinational firms have become involved in such ventures in recent years, probably a majority still find this repugnant from an ideological standpoint. International companies in most other developed capitalist countries seem to be more open-minded in this regard. Many highly lucrative business opportunities are foregone by American businessmen in ruling out joint ventures of this type.

Many U.S. companies seem to overlook the fact that the government may be a major indirect partner, anyway, through the regulations and policies it imposes on the firm. Even 100 percent ownership does not necessarily mean that a foreign subsidiary will have freedom to do what it wishes. On the other hand, having a foreign government as an equity partner often provides major advantages.

Let us now turn our attention to India. India considers herself a democratic nation, and is particularly sensitive about her position of neutrality. Consequently, an earnest attempt is generally made to avoid arbitrary discrimination between indigeneous firms and foreign subsidiaries, or between foreign companies of different nationalities. However, foreign subsidiaries are invariably linked in the thoughts of the local population to the countries of their parent firms. Serious tensions or positive feelings with respect to the parent nations are often reflected in local attitudes toward the companies.

India has tended to be ambivalent about private foreign investment. Foreign investment has been welcomed and is needed for rapid economic development, but concern is voiced about foreign domination and influence in Indian affairs. Such ambivalence contributes to the lack of clearly defined and consistently enforced policies, and the uncertainty faced by foreign companies negotiating with the Indian government in connection with private foreign investment and collaboration.

Because of India's intense national pride and desire for economic independence there has been growing pressure on foreign companies to allow more local equity participation. Those firms which have been adamant about maintaining 100 percent ownership have come under increasing attack. This has included governmental pressures and harassment of various kinds, with adverse publicity being disseminated to large segments of the population. Foreign firms have been subject to increasing pressures to support import substitution programs, increase exports, place Indians in key positions, and conduct more research in India. Those firms which have been complying have better relations with the government and a better public image than those which have made relatively little effort to cooperate.

Private enterprise profits are viewed with more suspicion and antipathy in India than in the United States. In fact, many U.S. subsidiaries surveyed in India do not publicize profit maximization as a key objective. Some go even further and restrict profits to avoid the possibility of serious negative reactions, absorbing them in higher pay or benefits for employees, modern — even luxurious by Indian standards — facilities, overstaffing, lower prices for their products than the market can bear, and so forth.

U.S. subsidiaries tend to be more sensitive about large profits than indigenous firms. Often this has been the case because they have, in fact, been making substantially larger profits. However, with profits declining on a large scale in Indian industry in recent years, fewer and fewer firms — either foreign and indigenous — have had to worry about this problem.

Two basic factors warrant some attention with respect to India's self-image in the international sphere. The first relates to passivism as manifested in Gandhi's "Ahimsa" philosophy — the passive resistance and nonviolence which was so effectively employed to achieve independence from the British. The second is the desire to obtain a position of importance in the world by acting as a neutral fulcrum on which the diverse ideologies of the East and West can be balanced. These two factors are closely interrelated.

Hindu philosophy, as seen through Western eyes, is a paradoxical mixture of peaceful and cruel elements. Basically, it is a nonagressive, passive philosophy, stressing virtues of love, friendship, and duty. However, its passivity also results in the condoning of many acts which would be considered cruel and abhorrent within other religious and ethical philosophies (e.g., the killing of female infants in the past). Perhaps the explanation lies in the emphasis of Hindu philosophy on the spiritual rather than the temporal, as opposed to other, more pragmatic patterns of religious thought which devote more attention to the physical aspects of life.

India's posture is full of similar "inconsistencies" (to the Western mind) which affect her relations in the international sphere and which, unless understood, make it difficult for diplomats and businessmen to take effective action. One of these inconsistencies relates to the use of violence to achieve national aims.

Although the events which led to the achievement of independence were not without violence, the major thrust of the Indian patriotic movement, directed by Mahatma Gandhi, was nonviolent in nature. This is emphasized as the prime example of Hindu philosophy in action. However, it can be argued that passive resistance was not the direct application of Hindu culture per se, but instead was a technique adopted by an extremely astute leader to achieve a desired end. It is difficult to predict the subsequent development of this concept had Gandhi survived; however, it is evident from present conditions that passive resistance, if an element of Hindu philosophy at all, is not a very strong one.

India and the individual groups of people within the nation, both in recent and long-past years, have rarely hesitated to employ violence to achieve their needs. Prior to becoming a country, the subcontinent now known as India was comprised of a large number of kingdoms, many of which were constantly at war with one another. Many of these principalities bitterly fought the British to the very end, and the names of their warrior kings, like Tippu Sultan and Shivaji, are revered. India's history and literature is full of references to war and warriors. In more recent times, the country has been wracked by violent internal disputes concerning language differences, food shortages, labor problems, and conflicts of political ideologies.

Although India has attempted to play a major role as a peace-maker in the world, she has not hesitated to use violence herself to achieve desired objectives. At the time of independence, troops were moved into Hydarabad to make sure that the Moslem ruler of the largely Hindu population acted in the best interests of his predominantly Hindu subjects, while at the same time troops moved into Kashmir to ensure that a Hindu ruler would be able to do "what was right" for his largely Moslem population. Later, the nation did not hesitate to employ force to throw the Portuguese out of Goa. Each of these actions, however, was rationalized by philosophical arguments which essentially elevated them to special situations in which the use of force was justified. Yet India professes the need for the nations of the world to settle their problems through the use of nonviolent means. The issue has been brought home to India in a direct and personal manner as the result of the war with the Chinese in 1962 and again with the Pakistanis in 1965 (prompted largely by India's refusal to discuss the issues of Kashmir), and again in 1971.

With respect to her role in the world balance of power, India is probably unique among the developing nations in terms of her success and stature. Many nations try to walk the line separating commitments to any power bloc. By so doing, they hope to gain more of the vital resources required for development than they could by aligning themselves with any one group, and to be able to "bid up the price" for their friendship and good will.

However, some government leaders within these countries do not really understand the cultural values of the more affluent nations with which they must deal or realize that many of these nations react negatively toward this tactic of "being played-off against an adversary." On the other hand, few affluent countries, and the United States is no exception, give assistance for purely humanitarian or even economic purposes. Assistance is usually tied to political and commercial objectives. This, in turn, upsets local political leaders and populations. The international company may get caught in the middle of ideological conflicts and government interactions. It must understand such situations in order to adapt effectively to them and assert its influence to increase understanding and bring about constructive change.

Nature and extent of nationalism

The form that nationalism takes in a particular country is actually part of that country's national ideology. However, the concept of nationalism warrants separate consideration because of its importance. Those countries characterized by extreme nationalistic fervor present the fewest opportunities for international trade and investment. In general, firms considering new ventures or already operating in highly nationalistic environments must take these feelings into account in formulating their major objectives and strategies. The proper response to such situations may require alterations in critical elements of the management process. Even where a particular country is not presently supernationalistic, the firm should assess the nature and extent of nationalism, and attempt to forecast any significant shifts in the foreseeable future, since these may influence regulation and legislation in the country.

Overt symbols of supernationalism are likely to be disturbing to foreign firms, especially after a few acts of expropriation have taken place and frequent political expressions of animosity toward a particular country, like the United States, have become the vogue. In such circumstances, it is easy to conclude that foreign business activity is virtually hopeless.

However, such countries are usually badly in need of capital and know-how and often the image is worse than the reality. Furthermore, the public view toward foreigners and things foreign is frequently not nearly as hostile as loudly expressed political rhetoric would indicate. Multinational companies willing to explore such countries closely may discover lucrative business opportunities, as well as an unexpectedly warm reception in both official and unofficial circles.

The multinational corporation should evaluate nationalistic feelings within a particular country on several different levels. This can be illustrated by using a hypothetical U.S. multinational corporation.

First it must examine the prevalent nationalistic attitude toward the U.S. government. The country may truly dislike or even abhor the American government for various reasons. If such negative feelings are already present or are increasing and can be expected to remain for some time, it may be unwise to invest there, even if such investment is allowed. It may even be wise in some cases to pull out existing operations as soon as possible, in order to minimize future losses.

However, a country which on the surface seems to be highly nationalistic and unfriendly toward the United States may not in fact discriminate unduly against American firms doing business there, especially if they are viewed as good corporate citizens. If some U.S. companies — or other foreign firms — seem to be treated more favorably than others, an effort should be made to find out why.

Attitudes toward American personnel (and often other kinds of foreigners) should also be assessed. In some countries, foreign employees may be viewed unfavorably. Here it may be wise to recruit and train as many local nationals as possible. It is common for U.S. subsidiaries to be viewed more favorably in various countries if all or nearly all of their personnel are locals. In other countries, it may not matter very much. If there is no discernible pattern regarding attitudes toward American (or other foreign) personnel in a particular country, an attempt should be made to discover the traits of those who are viewed most favorably by the local society.

The firm should also assess the local acceptance of U.S. and foreign products in general, and the firm's own products in particular. Various forms of discrimination against U.S. firms or American personnel may not preclude an attitude so favorable to U.S. products that substantial profits can still be realized.

Exporting to a country may be the alternative where products manufactured abroad are considered superior, or where the country is so hostile toward the mere presence of U.S. firms or Americans that it becomes too risky to operate there.

Nationalism can do much to raise the aspiration level of the local population, motivate them to greater productive efforts, and generally improve the overall sociological-cultural environment of the country. Healthy nationalism of this type need not go hand-in-hand with hatred of or excessive discrimination against other countries, foreign business, or foreigners. Japan is a good example of this kind of country, as is Mexico.

One of the great modern Indian paradoxes relates to nationalism. Although India, as a nation, gives an outward show of great nationalistic feeling, internally she is wracked by dissension which frequently erupts into intense conflicts and even violence. Language differences, regional chauvinism, the caste system, and social stratification probably split India more seriously than the feudal system ever split medieval Europe. The lack of true cohesion contributes to political instability and has a negative impact on India's sociological-cultural environment.

The spirit of Indian nationalism was largely forged by the common desire to achieve independence from the British. India does not have a cultural heritage as a united nation since it was born chiefly as an English administrative convenience. When the British withdrew, there was no longer a common target for national unity. Divisive forces began to grow, and the central government became weaker. Since independence has become a reality much of India's nationalistic feelings seem to be reserved primarily for foreign consumption. Moreover, while there is still resentment toward the British, there is also respect for, and emulation of things British. Thus, a type of love-hate relationship seems to exist between India and Great Britain.

Although, in the name of nationalism, foreign business comes under attack from time to time, this is not a critical problem. To date, those foreign companies which have made an earnest effort to accommodate to the country's needs and aspirations have been treated favorably and justly.

True Indian nationalism asserts itself in several ways to which foreign firms should be sensitive. On the positive side, India's pride manifests itself in an emphasis on the cultural heritage of various portions of the nation. Indian art and literature is rich, although internal language and cultural differences give rise to regional chauvinism. Science and mathematics were highly developed very early in Indian civilization. That part of the national pride which derives from the "golden ages" — starting with the early Indus Valley civilizations and going through the kingdom of the Moguls — has led her to feel that she must recapture a leading world position and assume an active role in world affairs of importance befitting her size.

There is still a strong movement in India, represented by various vocal and active minority groups, to abolish everything reminiscent of colonial days. Often mob psychology is used to swing portions of the population into strong emotional reaction against foreign influences. The move to abolish English as a national language and the defacing of monuments dedicated to events of the colonial days are indicative of these sentiments. Some minority groups would like to see India only for Indians, or just for Hindus. Many react on an emotional basis with no understanding of the consequences to a nation which is so dependent on non-Indian, non-Hindu support and know-how. While it is unlikely that such supernationalistic groups will gain control of the central or even of state governments, they may get a bigger voice in governmental affairs.

Flashes of national emotionalism tend to erupt and can assume violent and irrational forms. Indian mobs can be whipped into a frenzy over relatively minor issues — although they tend to be less inclined to attack foreigners than other Indians. It is almost as if much of the population, having few diversions, looks for outlets for its energy. Such outlets may result in attacks on or agitation at industrial enterprises, especially in a volatile city like Calcutta. Situations flare up rapidly but, if flames are not fanned by opposition groups, disappear just as quickly. In other words, although the major thrust of national — or regional — pride may seem to be reasonable, individual expressions of such pride can present serious problems and must be monitored closely.

Another factor that should be considered seriously by foreigners is the desire of most Indians to achieve self-sufficiency as quickly as possible; dependency on foreign influence and support is always uncomfortable and sometimes demeaning to large segments of the population. India has needed and still needs large amounts of foreign aid.

From the time she gained her independence through 1970, India received foreign aid of all types totalling around $17 billion, more than $9.5 billion of which came from the United States. Because of India's position of neutrality she has received aid from nearly two dozen organizations and countries which vary greatly in terms of ideology.

India's dependence on foreign inputs and assistance to maintain her growth and development would seem to imply some degree of security and stability for foreign companies since it is in her interest to maintain reasonably favorable relations with the parent countries of such companies. However, this assumption is no substitute for good corporate citizenship, and India, like most countries, does not always act in her own best interests. Emotional responses creep into any governments' actions, and it is dangerous to put too much faith in the dependency relationship. Moreover, India hopes and plans that by the early 1980s foreign aid will no longer be required, and that food imports from the United States under PL480 will not be required after the early 1970s.[1]

Although India is grateful for foreign aid, her national pride is clearly hurt because she has to accept it in such huge quantities. Every string tied to assistance which restricts India's freedom of action is viewed by large and influential segments of the population as an attempt at foreign domination. On the other hand, granting nations tend to expect gratitude and friendship in tangible forms. This places India in a difficult position since she accepts assistance from both the East and West bloc, and is sensitive about her neutralist posture. The pressures exerted by foreign powers often result in anti-foreign statements by the Indian press and government leaders. This prompts anti-Indian sentiments in foreign countries, which, in turn, alters the perceptions and plans of business firms which are planning to invest in India or are already there.

The immediate outlook for reduced dependency by India on the more affluent nations does not seem to be hopeful. It is important to note, however, that foreign firms operating within less developed countries like India can be of great assistance in reducing foreign aid dependency. Numerous development tasks cannot be performed effectively by government-to-government activities due to political reasons or governmental inefficiencies. Foreign firms in the private sector are often in a position to assist with such projects and thereby help alleviate anti-foreign sentiments.

View toward foreigners and things foreign

The prevalent view toward foreigners and things foreign — organizations, products, ideas, and so forth — in a particular country is closely interconnected with national ideology and the nature and extent of nationalism.

The outsider may be viewed as a threat, representing a different way of thinking, a peculiar type of ethics, and a potential menace to the stability and well-being of the local culture or country. On the other hand, he may engender feelings of somewhat friendly curiosity, particularly if he comes with intriguing tales to tell, and brings interesting customs and artifacts with him.

The foreign firm is also an outsider. And it too is viewed with the same mixed emotions. It is a carrier of new methods, ideas and technologies which evoke varying degrees of resistance in different areas and among differing populations. In less developed countries, it is usually a wealthy outsider, representing tantalizing possibilities of wealth. Both the foreign firm and its foreign personnel must demonstrate by their actions that they are desirable citizens of the host country in order to ensure their success over time.

In addition to speaking to and observing people, one way to obtain a rough orientation regarding attitudes toward foreigners is to look at the foreign influences in evidence in daily life. This may provide insights about the acceptance and tolerance levels toward "things foreign" and to things which come from specific countries. However, such impressions should be carefully evaluated since other factors may help account for the presence or lack of foreign features. Some factors worth noting include the amount and nature of tourism, tourist facilities and foreign cuisine available; architecture and public statuary; foreign movies, art, music, and publications; coverage given to different foreign countries — including foreign language training — in the educational system and in the country's own mass media; and the degree of penetration of foreign customs, hair styles, clothing and other items.

Perhaps one of the most important aspects in the search for foreign elements within a nation, at least for international companies, is the comfort of foreign personnel who will compare local conditions to those which exist at home. In poor countries, the "comforts of home" typically can be approximated only in the small foreign enclaves which are established in the major cities where high concentrations of foreign residents exist. This has important positive and negative consequences for foreign firms and personnel.

The selection of individuals sent to a foreign country can be an important factor in the success of whatever venture is being attempted. Basically, there are two ways to keep such individuals and their families content. One is to construct enclaves which provide the expected food, plumbing, publications from home, air-conditioning, etc., in a form as close as possible to that of the home country. In doing this, the foreigner isolates himself from the local population but, at the same time, obtains comfort in relatively familiar surroundings. However, this often creates resentment on the part of the local populace, and deprives the foreigner of vital stimuli which would give him a feel for the day-to-day life of the countries in which he is living.

The second alternative is to select people who can adapt with only minor modifications to the local environment. Unfortunately, many organizations focus almost entirely on "non-adaptive" (e.g., job skill) attributes in selecting personnel for foreign assignments and this frequently results in both ineffectiveness and unhappiness.

A third alternative is to eliminate the need for foreign personnel by filling jobs with qualified local nationals. However, educational and sociological-cultural constraints may limit the available number of really or potentially qualified local nationals.

Most Indians have a positive attitude toward foreign manufactured goods. Imported items carry high status, both because of quality considerations and because they are symbols of sufficient wealth to permit the payment of high import duties (or bootlegging fees). Western products, especially those from the United States, are held in especially high esteem, much more so than products from communist countries.

Major foreign subsidiaries in India — particularly American and British companies — are highly esteemed, and their products are close behind imports in the prestige hierarchy. This frequently gives them a competitive advantage which is understandably frustrating to indigenous competitors.

The individual foreigner in India is usually treated with a genuine display of warmth, respect, and even deference. He typically meets with friendship and curiosity wherever he goes. The fact that he is a foreigner usually works in his favor in establishing good relationships, except in unusual situations, such as that which prevailed during the fighting between India and China. India's Chinese restaurants disappeared and Japanese who lived in India took to decorating their cars with large signs indicating they were Japanese, not Chinese.

The reception of the white foreigner in India is also influenced by the fact that India is extremely color-conscious. The original Aryan invaders were light-skinned, and there is strong evidence to indicate that at its inception the caste system was at least partly predicated on differences in skin color. The lighter a person's skin, the higher his prestige in many sections of India. This was reinforced by the skin color of India's masters — the British. As a consequence, the task of the light-skinned foreigner is often greatly lightened and his potential ability to get things done, assuming he does them in ways which are reasonably compatible with the society, is likely to be substantial.

With regard to business operations, it is also important to note that tolerance for the actions and practices of foreigners tends to be greater in some areas of India than tolerance for similar acts by Indians. The foreign manager is frequently permitted to do things which would be viewed with hostility in the case of an Indian (who is supposed to know what is in accord with custom and tradition and what is not). Westernized Indian managers have often encountered more difficulty than U.S. managers when they behaved in the relatively impersonal and efficient manner of U.S. executives.

POLITICAL-LEGAL FACTORS

The relationships and interactions which occur at a macro level between nations invariably affect international business activity. The astute businessman finds it advantageous to be informed about current governmental discussions and the international arrangements which are presently in force in countries of significant interest to his company, even though they may not have an immediate or direct impact on his firm's activities.

Political ideology

A key element in international business planning is the determination of major changes in political ideology which are likely in the foreseeable future. The problems which result from not being able to anticipate changes were probably most clearly highlighted for U.S. firms when Castro came to power in Cuba. By studying the backgrounds, actions, words, and relationships of the leaders or revolutionaries who are vying for power in a given country, the businessman will be in a better position to predict changes in political ideology. He would also be wise to explore the mood of the local population in order to foresee the possibility that the existing government will be ousted, and if so, the type of political ideology that is likely to emerge. When prevailing political ideology is at odds with the values and aspirations of influential segments of the local population, foreign firms must be especially wary.

The usual trend in the modern world is for poorer countries to move leftwards politically. A sharp and abrupt shift in this direction is likely to offer considerable danger to private foreign companies. Takeovers by nationalistic military groups often result in harsh restrictions being placed on foreign companies, and sometimes, in expropriation. Foreign companies, particularly large ones, offer tempting targets for local politicians.

The Indian government has been favorably disposed toward foreign investment and collaboration where it has been deemed to be in the national interest, and where it has not been perceived as unduly threatening the nation's independence or posture of neutrality. In theory and on paper, the government has indicated those sectors in which foreign investment is welcome and those where it is prohibited, and such lists have been altered from time to time. There are also rules and regulations regarding the proportion of foreign equity participation allowed, royalty fees, and other arrangements permissible. These, too, have changed from time to time. Furthermore, the official government policy precludes discrimination on the basis of nationality once a company has been licensed.

Actually, rules and regulations involving foreign business in India have often been more flexible in practice than they have appeared in official documents or statements, and foreign companies have been granted special exceptions and more favorable terms than those officially prescribed, (usually after hard bargaining). Once arrangements involving foreign companies have been approved the Indian government has had a good record to date in honoring them.

However, with growing political instability it is becoming more difficult to predict the direction that political ideology is likely to take with regard to private foreign business. The Fourth Five Year Plan says very little with regard to the role of foreign business. One day the government makes negative pronouncements about foreign business, and the next it announces that a multimillion-dollar joint venture with foreign equity participation has been approved. Government representatives are trying to encourage private foreign investment through the Indian embassies and missions abroad, while various government committees take a hostile view toward such investment.

At this time, it seems that foreign private investment will continue to be allowed in India as long as it can be justified by the government as serving the national interest. But the range of investments allowed is likely to decrease in the future, and the terms may not be as favorable to international corporations as in the past. Any significant increase in discrimination against foreign firms operating in India is likely to be based on their size and apply to large indigenous firms as well.

Legal rules for foreign business and foreign personnel

Many countries have laws which either discriminate against or favor foreign firms. Restrictions may take such forms as limitations on the percentage of foreign corporate ownership, the employment of foreigners, and the ability to transfer funds abroad, as well as special taxes. On the other hand, favorable treatment may include special tax concessions, liberal import allowances and foreign exchange for profit remission, and promises to cut red tape.

Over and above the statutes, it is essential for a foreign company to assess the attitude of local government officials and law enforcers toward their own operations specifically, and foreign operations in general. Laws which apply uniformly to all operations within the country may in practice, be administered differently depending on the nationality of the firm. A foreign firm may suddenly find it is being attacked for certain practices while its indigenous counterparts seem to have legal immunity. Or it may find that local firms receive various kinds of favored treatment involving the abuse of official regulations. The reverse may also occur.

In general, legal rules pertaining to foreign business are highly complex, often more complex than domestic laws. They may also change greatly in a short period of time. The wise international company will seek legal advice in this area early, which should include the services of competent local attornies in the countries in which they operate, or plan to. It is often useful also to discuss such matters with executives of other international corporations and subsidiaries in an effort to determine how laws are actually applied. U.S. government agencies and private organizations — including embassies, the Department of Commerce, banks, and accounting and consulting firms may be able to offer valuable information in this regard.

Poorer countries often require that some stated minimum percentage of company employees must be local nationals. This tends to have its greatest implications for firms in countries which have a relatively unfavorable educational and cultural climate. Thus in Costa Rica, 90 percent of all employees must be nationals, and they must receive 85 percent of the payroll. Mexico requires that 90 percent of each category of skilled and unskilled workers be nationals.

When foreign (or even indigenous) firms cannot recruit adequate numbers of key managers or technical specialists locally, and are also prohibited from bringing in foreigners to fill such jobs both the firm and the economy tend to suffer. If foreigners were permitted, even on a short-term basis they could often train local nationals to take over. Many companies are overstaffed or have much larger payrolls than necessary, so that they can satisfy the percentage rules and yet bring in critically-needed foreign personnel. In many countries, the proportion of native employees required is not precise but is controlled by the issuance of work permits to aliens. This can lead to confusion and resentment, for example, where a firm wants to bring in a controller, and the host government argues that such a job could be filled adequately by poorly trained local commerce graduates in accounting.

India has no precise legal percentages relating to the employment of foreign and local personnel. However, it is usually difficult to employ foreigners who are not categorized as "technicians" according to Indian rules. Those who do get technician status are entitled to tax exemptions under certain conditions. Engineering and related technical and scientific personnel can get income tax exemptions of one year without prior government approval and of up to three years if this governmental approval is granted prior to the end of their first year of employment. They can get extended exemptions of several years beyond this, as long as their employer pays their personal income taxes — which are deductible as business expenses.

Managerial personnel can get income tax exemptions for only six months, and then only with prior government approval. It is generally difficult to bring in foreigners under this category although an engineering degree holder can be employed in a managerial job.

Indigenous companies have somewhat more difficulty in bringing in foreign technicians — including consultants — than do international firms. But the government will usually approve a valid application eventually.

There are some advantages in employing citizens of British Commonwealth countries in India. They do not need special visas, nor do they have to register with the local police. However, once they are within Indian boundaries, all foreigners have great freedom of movement throughout most of the country.

The impact of taxes on international firms can be very great and can affect all elements of the management process, as well as net profitability. The extraordinary variety of taxes and tax policies pursued throughout the world make this topic very complex, especially since a vast array of bilateral and multilateral tax arrangements exists between different countries. The wise international company will seek advice from appropriate tax experts.

In some countries foreign firms may receive special treatment. For example, Saudi Arabia has an income tax which applies only to foreign firms and foreigners; local firms and citizens are taxed at different amounts. Chile has a special tax on corporations which are owned at least 75 percent by nonresidents. Many oil producing nations in the Middle East and Latin America have special concession agreements with foreign oil companies which provide for special taxes and payments in return for concessionary privileges.

The reverse of discriminating taxation is tax exemption, which is usually available to encourage desired forms of foreign investment. Pakistan, Ireland, West Berlin, and many other countries offer special tax holidays, reduced taxes, or other concessions to foreign companies. Puerto Rico, which has long had its own taxing powers, has used such tax incentives for many years with great success.

India does not generally discriminate against foreign firms in the field of taxation and tax incentives are available equally to new foreign as well as indigenous ventures. However, occasionally a new foreign venture may get special tax concessions over and above those normally available.

India does allow relief from double taxation on company profits, intercorporate dividends, royalties, fees, and other forms of income. India has reciprocal tax arrangements with many countries, including the United States. Such arrangements demarcate zones of taxation between India and other countries according to the nature and sources of income, and also ensure the application of allowable tax credits and incentives. However, in many cases Indian tax concessions to U.S. firms may be offset by the U.S. foreign tax credit — i.e., when the U.S. tax rate is higher.

Tax considerations generally favor incorporation rather than the establishment of foreign branches in India. The tax rate on branches is presently 65 percent, higher than in most other countries. The intercoporate dividend tax in India is currently 25 percent, also still higher than most other countries, as is the 50 percent rate on patent royalties and licensing fees. The foreign tax credits allowed by the U.S. government can cover all Indian corporate taxes, unless the Indian tax rates are higher than the U.S. rates, which is often the case. Interest payments on foreign loans are exempt from Indian taxation, upon approval of the Indian government, which is usually a formality. However, the terms of the foreign loans require government approval and this can be difficult if interest rates are judged to be too high.

Because laws involving foreign business are different in different countries, international firms cannot expect to operate in set ways, independently of the specific foreign environment. Managers of foreign operations must be able to adjust their operations to the special legal constraints they face.

International organization memberships and treaty obligations

Virtually every country has at least some international organization or treaty obligations with other countries which affect national and international business. Since each country's obligations to other nations are different, each must be examined separately.

While India is a member — and generally a reliable upholder — of international organizations and treaties of various kinds, she has generally avoided agreements which would affect her neutral position or which are not judged to be in her national interest. For example, India is a relatively active member of the United Nations and its various agencies, the Colombo Plan (initiated by the British to coordinate modest bilateral aid projects), and most of the other international organizations and banks, but with only a few significant exceptions, she is free to go pretty much her own way.

India has investment guaranty treaties with a number of countries, including the one signed with the United States in December, 1959. The agreement with the United States covers both expropriation and the lack of currency convertibility. In the case of disagreement on what is fair compensation, the issue is to be submitted to impartial arbitration, and the decision is to be accepted as final and binding. India has honored treaties of these types, and to date there has been no expropriation or confiscation of U.S. manufacturing firms there.

The International Convention for the Protection of Industrial Property is concerned with the protection of patents, trademarks, copyrights, and other intellectual property. This a multilateral agreement among the majority of the important — mostly relatively advanced — nations. The Communist states and many other countries, including India, do not belong to this convention. Although India feels that such a treaty is largely a one-way street, with most of the benefits accruing to the advanced nations, she has a good record of protecting the intellectual property rights of foreign companies through other legal means. However, India's patent laws, especially with respect to drugs, have recently been under attack and may be modified, as discussed in Chapter 5.

India is a member of the General Agreement of Tariffs and Trade (GATT). This organization is principally concerned with the reduction and elimination of tariffs and other trading restrictions between member nations. The ultimate goal of the organization is a multilaterally oriented, totally free trading system between all countries. In general, members are not supposed to use quotas, but, as usual, several loopholes exist. The major one concerns the case where a country has balance of payments difficulties, as has happened in recent years in both India and the United States. In such cases, the country may levy discriminatory quotas against other countries where it lacks foreign exchange to buy. Such discriminatory quota restrictions are to be eliminated through consultation with the International Monetary Fund (IMF), and many have been reduced or eliminated in this way. All of the GATT members are also IMF members. The significant constraints placed on India by GATT have involved only a limited number of commodities — mostly agricultural — such as sugar and coffee.

GATT operates through annual meetings, where members negotiate, usually bilaterally, to reduce tariffs on selected items. This is a sort of horse-trading operation, where one nation gives tariff reductions to another in exchange for comparable reductions on items which might be exported to it. When agreement is made between the bargainers, the "most favored nation" principle is applied. This means that any reduction made to one country applies immediately to all other nations. This has resulted in effective tariff and quota reductions for a variety of exports from many nations, although advanced countries have generally been more affected than poor countries.

India is also a member of the Economic Commission for Asia and the Far East (ECAFE), a U.N. organization which deals with regional trade agreements and other matters. However, the agreements are essentially more symbolic than binding, with emphasis given to the principle of cooperation.

In general, India makes more use of special unilateral agreements than formal or long-term treaties in the field of international trade. No more than 20 percent of India's trade has been based on bilateral agreements in recent times. Most of these have involved Communist nations, and in some cases other soft currency countries. At times India has entered into bilateral agreements involving technical cooperation and other matters with non-Communist countries, such as Japan.

International oil companies — and various other kinds of mineral exploration and extraction firms — operating in less developed countries, have devised a type of concession agreement between the company and the host government which allows for exploitation of mineral resources in given geographic areas in exchange for payments and other types of assistance. India has entered into such special agreements with foreign oil companies. While such relationships have been relatively trouble-free, much negotiation has been entailed. In fact, in mid-1970 the government announced that it had decided to revise existing arrangements with foreign refineries to better suit national needs.[2] The Ministry of Petroleum and Chemicals began negotiating with the companies, and it was indicated that a government corporation will take over all imports of crude oil. A new pricing arrangement — involving mostly lower prices for the foreign oil firms — would be worked out, and the government also requested foreign oil companies to review their remittances abroad, especially in respect to items not covered by their agreements, with a view to reducing them and, "over a period of time eliminating them altogether."

As previously mentioned, India is an active member of the United Nations. This organization can be of great benefit to businessment. However, few companies — either international or indigenous — take advantage of the tremendous stockpile of specialized knowledge available for the asking. Membership in international organizations need not entail only obligations; significant benefits may accrue. For example, a publishing firm considering the production of textbooks in or for a developing nation would be wise to find out if it is a member of the U.N.-administered Universal Copyright Convention. If it is not, proper protection of valuable copyrights might prove difficult. If it is, the company may then find it worthwhile to explore provisions of the Universal Postal Union if its books or other materials will be sent by mail. If the country is largely agricultural, the Food and Agricultural Organization may be able to contribute important information about the production problems, the kind of books which may prove most relevant, and other data of interest to the marketing department about local farming and agriculture. The U.N. Technical Assistance Board might be able to recommend experts in the publishing field who could be of service, and UNESCO might assist with valuable data on population, social reform, and educational requirements.

Power or economic bloc groupings

Most countries belong to political and/or economic blocs, which have significant implications for business and industrial activity. A bewildering variety of such blocs exist in the world today. There is a Communist bloc, subdivided presently into the Chinese, Russian, and neutralist segments; an Arab bloc; an African bloc; a "Third-world" neutralist group; and advanced Western groups such as NATO, and the Organization of American States (OAS). Another type of bloc is the economic customs union or common market such as the European Economic Community (EEC), the European Free Trade Association (EFTA), the Latin American Free Trade Association (LAFTA), the Central America Common Market, and the Comecon Association of the Soviet Union and other Eastern European Communist countries.

Formal membership in an organization for non-economic purposes (e.g., NATO or SEATO military cooperation) often spills over into and affects business matters. For example, production specialization and uniformity of weapons systems may be facilitated, and joint ventures between firms in member countries may be formed to take advantage of this situation. Thus an American aircraft manufacturer may team up with an Italian firm to develop or produce new types of aircraft to be used by defense forces in England, France, and West Germany.

Even less formal alliances or power blocs can have an impact on many companies in various ways. The Arab bloc's boycott of Israel and foreign companies doing business with or in Israel is a clear case in point.

Customs unions, aimed at economic integration of member countries, have the greatest and most direct impact on firm management. They can also benefit economic development by bringing about lower tariffs and costs, greater economies of scale, larger markets (including export markets), and a freer flow of resources and goods and services.

A major problem faced by less developed countries in forming a common market is that most of them — at least within the same region — tend to export similar kinds of products, and possibilities for extensive trade increases tend to be small, particularly in the short run. They also may import similar kinds of products. Hence, sales within the groups are likely to remain small until more diversified economies can be developed. The situation is further complicated by the absence of adequate transportation and communications facilities between the countries.

Another critical constraint is that the losers in economic integration among countries are usually the inefficient local firms which require a high level of protection in order to remain viable. Less developed countries usually have a higher proportion of such companies than relatively advanced nations. The formation of customs unions or common markets is liable to be damaging to such companies, and few governments are willing to risk such consequences on a broad scale.

India has avoided formal associations with either the Western (capitalistic) or Eastern (communistic) blocs. For example, although she has received much U.S. military assistance, especially after the 1962 war with China, she has refrained from committing herself to SEATO or any other formal defense plan. Moreover, India has not allowed foreign private investment in her defense sector.

India is a member of the British Commonwealth, which still includes scores of countries throughout much of the advanced and developing world. However, Commor wealth membership no longer imposes many constraints or obligations on member countries as compared to the past; it also provides little in the way of benefits. However, most Commonwealth citizens can travel to and even work in member countries with fewer formalities or red tape than those required of nonmembers. The Commonwealth also offers some trade advantages to member countries; however, with the United Kingdom entry into the EEC, these may be eliminated.

India is a prominent member of the so-called "third-world" neutralist bloc, although no formal alliance makes her so. Because of this informal commitment, the Indian government is unlikely to take actions which would be interpreted as a significant move from her neutralist position. She has, however, taken non-neutralist positions at various times, based primarily on economic, not political, needs. An example of this is the government's strong pro-Arab stand in the Middle-East situation — due to the fact that India has much critical trade with Egypt and other Arab countries.

IMPORT-EXPORT REGULATIONS

Every government interferes to some extent with trade passing beyond its country's frontiers. Here, we shall first briefly consider some of the basic features of import-export controls in general, and then focus on the situation in India.

Overview

Many countries tax imports primarily to gain revenue, and a few even tax exports for this purpose. A second major purpose of import restrictions, especially within poor countries seeking rapid development, is to protect local firms from the competition of foreign goods. Countries with acute foreign exchange problems restrict imports to conserve this limited resource. Export restrictions, which are much less common, may be imposed in order to achieve some national purpose as when the United States prevents trade with Cuba and Red China or completely bans the export of a highly strategic military item.

Endless arguments, both logical and irrational, have raged for centuries about the propriety of import and export controls, and clear resolution of the problem is not in sight. The basic reason for this controversy is that presumably, in the absence of protection, costs and prices would be different than they are with protection. This means that some parties suffer while others gain.

Three basic methods used to restrict imports are: tariffs (taxes on imports); quotas (restrictions on the quantities of certain goods which can be imported); and exchange controls (restrictions on the funds available to pay for imports).

The process of tariff collection tends to be a complex one in most countries, and the United States is certainly no exception. The method of levying duties, the definition of commodities, and the administrative requirements of a customs police are matters which have developed over centuries, and in most countries an army of specialists is necessary to guide a firm's goods through the procedures. An incredible array of documents, licenses, bills of lading, special permits, official seals, and other trivia is required for clearance. Firms are frequently faced with great frustration in clearing goods, and bribery or special favors are common facts of life in many countries.

Tariff policy is frequently designed to pressure both local and international companies to do things they might not otherwise do. For example, a country wishing to establish a new industry may first set high duties on finished products and much lower ones on components and raw materials. Production, marketing, and planning are clearly affected, not only in the given country, but also in the parent country of international firms involved, since the company must now send its exports out in kit form rather than as finished items. Differential duties may also be set on components and raw materials. Duties for items which are relatively simple to produce or locally available may be assessed at high rates while items difficult or expensive to produce locally may be imported duty-free. This affects supplier relationships, make-versus-buy decisions, and inventory planning. The process can proceed until the entire product is produced locally.

Tariffs may force substitutions. For example, a high duty on petroleum may lead to more extensive use of coal, or the use of alcohol rather than naphtha in the manufacture of basic chemicals such as polyethelyne. On the other hand, it may lead to more rapid development of the country's own petroleum resources. Quite often, duties may have unanticipated effects. A country wishing to protect its cotton spinners and textile industry may levy high duties on cotton goods only to find that rayon, nylon, and other synthetic imports start to rise.

A more direct method of restricting imports is the use of quotas. This kind of restriction tends to be used widely in poor countries and Communist states. It can be more effective than high tariffs since someone may be willing to import an item and pay the high price caused by the imposition of tariffs. On the other hand, quotas often encourage smuggling and black marketing activity. The legal holder of a quota for an item for which there is demand has a valuable license, and there are frequent abuses of the privileges extended. Countries which use quotas extensively always have "fast-buck artists" who have the necessary connections to get quota licenses even though they cannot justify the need for the items they import.

Quotas, including outright bans of various products, can also be used to force firms into desired molds, as is the case with tariffs. For example, the Indian government recently denied permission to a major U.S. computer manufacturer to import computers into the country. However, it did allow the importation of parts equivalent to ten complete computers which were then assembled in India.

Exchange controls are utilized to control various import requests. With exchange controls, a firm has to justify the importation of a particular item in order to obtain the foreign exchange it needs. Like quotas, exchange licenses may have a value of their own, and many nations have active markets in them. The usual problem is that the demand for foreign exchange exceeds the supply. Countries sometimes have several rates of foreign exchange for different classes of imports. A machinery importer may get a more favorable rate than an importer of nonessential consumer goods. One major potential problem with multiple exchange rates, however, is that they can be in a state of constant flux as the government shifts regulations to reflect rapidly changing economic conditions. Discretionary control and value judgments can also enter into the picture here as well.

India's Import Restrictions and Import Substitution

The Indian government derives substantial tax revenues from the high tariffs imposed on imports. The duties paid on most of the imports used by the drug, chemical, engineering and other firms we have surveyed in India have ranged from 50 percent to well over 100 percent. However, quotas, licenses, and foreign exchange controls are the chief instruments used by the government to restrict and allocate imports to enterprises on a priority basis. This is done to bring about rapid import substitution, to protect industry within India, and to conserve scarce foreign exchange.

The Indian government began its vigorous import substitution effort in earnest during the Second Plan (1956-61). However, it has frequently cost the country more than the benefits or savings realized, because of high costs, excess capacity, high investment in inventories, poor production planning, and a tremendous drain on executive time. Little or no attention has been given to comparative advantage considerations, and every venture requiring imports tends to be treated as a separate and special case.

In spite of huge costs and tremendous inefficiency, gains have clearly been made in import substitution per se in Indian industry. According to official calculations, in the mid-1950s over 40 percent of the basic materials used in India's drug industry were imported. As of 1969, the proportion was less than 10 percent, and some government officials have placed it as low as 6 percent. Import substitutions have mostly involved small firms, but big gains have also been made among the larger companies. Sizeable gains in import substitution have also been made in the chemical, engineering, and especially capital goods industries, as well as many other sectors, even though official statistics tend to be exaggerated.

In the aggregate, according to data compiled by the *Annual Surveys of Industry,* 16 percent of the market for manufactured goods in India in 1960-61 was met by imports. By 1967-68, the proportion had dropped to 11 percent. If various industrial inputs are included, such as raw cotton and crude oil, then the overall dependence on imports appears to have declined from 21 percent in 1960-61 to 14 percent in 1967-68. According to *Reserve Bank of India* data, the decline in India's total import dependence has been even more rapid, falling from 24 to 15 percent over the 1960-68 period.

The trend in import substitution has been less marked in intermediate goods, showing a drop from 21 percent in 1960-61 to 19 percent in 1965-66. In the consumer goods field, import substitution is virtually complete and by 1965-66 only ½ percent of this market was met by direct imports of manufactures,[3] although some of the imported basic intermediate materials also go into consumer goods. The pace of import substitution in Indian industry seems to be slowing down in most sectors, and it appears that a point has been reached where it is becoming increasingly difficult and costly to make substantial gains.

Indian firms have generally been more willing to engage *voluntarily* in import substitution efforts than their American counterparts. However, where Indian governmental pressure has been brought to bear on U.S. subsidiaries, they have frequently responded faster and more effectively. They often have a major advantage over local firms, as they can draw on the know-how and resources of the large multinational corporations of which they are part. On the other hand, their parent companies have frequently resisted import substitution because they have supplied many of the imported items at a good profit.

Import controls became most stringent during the 1965-66 period, when India experienced its worst foreign exchange crisis to date. Imports came to a virtual standstill when the crisis reached its peak around the time of devaluation of the rupee in June, 1966. Shortly thereafter, the government announced a liberalization of imports, made possible by renewed foreign aid on a substantial scale. As a first step, 59 priority industries were allowed to import raw materials, components, and spare parts needed to bring production close to full capacity for six months.[4] These industries included most of the major ones in the country such as drugs, chemicals, and various kinds of machinery and other producer goods. Export-oriented industries, as well as small-scale firms making products similar to the priority industries were also included. By the late 1960s import restrictions, although not as serious a constraint as they had been during 1965-66, were still a problem, and substantial premiums were being paid for import licenses and foreign exchange through legal channels as well as the black market.

In 1970, premiums paid for imports and foreign exchange, black marketing activity, and overbuying, were tapering off somewhat. The political situation had stabilized to a degree, India's foreign exchange position was relatively comfortable, and the Aid-India Consortium had indicated greater foreign aid commitments for 1970-71.[5] India had also been granted permission to divert sizeable sums of unused Soviet aid to new projects.[6]

On March 31, 1970, the Indian government announced its own import policy for the 1970-71 fiscal year and beyond.[7] Under this policy, the raw material and component requirements of the 59 priority industries in 1970-71 generally continued to be met on the basis of their actual needs for maintenance and sanctioned expansion of production. Greater emphasis was given to the import needs of small-scale industries, major exporters, and those firms in a position to increase their exports substantially. Nonpriority firms continued to be allocated the imports they desire or need subject to the availability of foreign exchange; preference with regard to capital goods imports was given to firms with substantial export potential. This included capital goods imports for modernization, expansion, diversification, and research and development.

The new import policy also gave the public sector a greater role in foreign trade, and this trend is likely to continue in the future. This involves the nationalization of some trade, and means that firms will no longer be allowed to buy the nationalized items directly from their foreign suppliers. Government trading corporations — the largest being the State Trading Corporation (STC) followed by the Minerals and Metals Trading Corporation (MMTC) — is taking over the importation of 38 more products, in addition to 22 items previously taken over. These items include a variety of drugs and chemicals, raw silk, stainless steel, steel sheets, powdered milk, tinplate and tin, and nylon molding powder. In the near future they will take over raw cotton, and other items.

Firms have experienced serious delays in receiving approved imports of nationalized trade items and they are not always able to get goods which meet their precise specifications. Firms in the drug industry experienced the greatest number of problems and were also the most concerned about the anticipated increase in the nationalization of foreign trade.

Economies deriving from bulk purchases, shipments, and transportation charges may result from one government agency placing large orders for the entire nation's needs for a given commodity. This may also lead to faster shipments to India from abroad, and cut down on black marketing activities and the importation of products from parent corporations at inflated prices. However, such benefits may be more than offset by losses in managerial effectiveness and productive efficiency.

In 1969-70 government trading corporations handled imports amounting to 1450 million ruppees. With the 60 items now nationalized, it was estimated that the government could handle at least 3000 million in 1970-71. Under the new import policy, more stringent import quotas for private trading companies have been placed on 29 additional items, including various drugs, chemicals, spare parts, tools, and instruments. Total imports by private companies dropped from 440 million rupees in 1968-69 to 420 million in 1969-70.[8] Moreover, in the near future they are likely to drop much further and eventually, such traders may be phased out entirely.

In an effort to provide more flexibility for industrial enterprises STC and MMTC and some other government trading corporations now import goods in demand and sell them to license holders. STC is now creating an Industrial Raw Materials Assistance Center (IRMAC) for this purpose, and its chairman feels that the "new scheme would give the public sector a sense of competition and dynamism." The kinds of materials to be offered for sale will be announced from time to time, but the types have not yet been determined in detail at this time. Smaller firms will apparently be given special consideration. In general, firms will now be able to buy various items "off-the-shelf" against their surrendered valid import licenses — possibly saving considerable time. STC will determine the prices to be charged in consultation with the Foreign Trade Ministry. The government expects prices to be reasonable, since there will be no obligation for firms to buy from this source.

As an alternative, such a system might work considerably better if off-the-shelf imports were auctioned off to the highest bidder at regular or predetermined periods, or when a sudden surge of demand for certain commodities emerges. In this way, firms willing to pay the price would be able to obtain critically needed imports quickly.

Under the new import policy registered manufacturer-exporters who had minimum exports of one million rupees in 1969-70 in nontraditional goods will be eligible for "on account" import licenses in the future. This means that they will be able to get imports before actually exporting up to a value of 50 percent of their approved import-replenishment licenses.

Imports for small-scale industries are being liberalized. The upper limit for initial raw material import licenses for firms in this sector is being raised from 50,000 to 75,000 rupees. Such licenses probably will not be too difficult to obtain. Small-scale firms will also generally be entitled to 50 percent of their imports from preferred sources, as compared to 33 percent in the past, even if they have not been exporters.

Under a more rigid provision of the new import policy, 56 more types of imports formerly allowed to priority users without restriction will now be permitted only on a restricted basis. These include various kinds of drugs, chemicals, dyes, ball bearings, components and motor vehicle parts. In addition, 159 additional kinds of goods formerly imported in varying quantities have been added to the banned list, since the government feels that indigenous sources of supply are adequate or that certain items are not essential. These items include various kinds of drugs, chemicals, machinery, tools, ball bearings, and instruments.

Once permissible imports arrive in India, customs clearance can prove time consuming and frustrating. For example, a firm may import camshafts which have been disassembled in order to prevent damage in shipping. It may be necessary to assemble them on the spot for customs inspectors — to make sure they are the specified imports — in order to avoid long delays in getting them cleared. Inspectors also tend to examine drugs and chemicals very closely — but typically lack the expertise to know exactly what they are doing. At times such shipments may be rejected because of claimed quality or specification deficiencies. When this happens the firm must obtain permission to import replacements.

Quite often firms themselves cause delays in clearing customs by not filling out the required forms in the *exact* manner prescribed. Indian customs officials demand precision to the smallest detail in filling out forms. For example, if you write the date as 7/1/71 instead of July 1, 1971 — or vice versa — the form may be held up and have to be redone. Often an under-the-table payment can provide the satisfaction required.

A new company, especially a foreign concern, may be able to get liberal import commitments including machinery, raw materials, components, spare parts, for several years as part of the overall agreement under which it was approved. This is most likely if the new venture is considered of strategic importance or of very high priority. The government has at times even been willing to extend the import privileges of such new ventures — foreign exchange reserves permitting — beyond the time initially agreed upon, especially when the firm has demonstrated that it is a good corporate citizen.

The Indian government may also allow a foreign firm to "borrow" certain items from its parent company or affiliates against import entitlements, if it is in a bind. In some cases, the government may also allow a foreign subsidiary to obtain a foreign exchange loan from its parent company or other sources, against orders to be exported in the future, which can be used to import needed items. However, the government is not likely to approve such loans if the interest rate is too high — typically no more than 6 percent is allowed.

India's Export Regulations and Incentives

India only began in earnest to pressure firms to increase their exports of nontraditional goods following the peak foreign exchange crisis and devaluation in 1966. Prior to that time major attention was focused on traditional exports such as tea, jute, and textiles.

Shortly after devaluation in June, 1966, the Indian government adopted a new export promotion scheme in conjunction with some import liberalization. This scheme has involved both "carrots" and "sticks."[9] Export incentives have been used which provide price or cash subsidies, import entitlements, and duty drawbacks and refunds. Such incentives have clearly had a favorable effect in the engineering and heavy industry sectors in particular; but there has been a recent slackening-off as firms have put much of their idle capacity back into operation and shifted their attention increasingly to the high-priced and more profitable domestic market. Export incentives have generally not been as important in most other sectors, including drugs, chemicals, and batteries.

The export incentive scheme for the engineering sector has, on the average, provided for a cash subsidy of about 25 percent of value added or F.O.B. export value, a 25 percent import entitlement in relation to export value, and duty drawbacks and refunds of around 5 percent. Some types of firms have been able to get substantially more, and there has been considerable flexibility in negotiating with the Indian government on large tenders in foreign markets.

In the pharmaceutical industry, the cash subsidy has typically been 15 percent of F.O.B. export value where the firm has been exporting at least 5 percent of its output, and 20 percent where exports have been 10 percent or more. The import entitlement has been 20 percent of export value, and duty drawbacks and refunds have averaged about 7½ percent. However, because of high domestic prices for drug products in India, and because pharmaceutical firms have not had as much excess capacity, export incentives have not had a very significant effect to date.

For many industries, the "stick" has generally been more important in spurring firms to export. In this regard, ten major industries — most of them also included in the list of 59 priority industries — have been categorized as obligatory export sectors. These include drugs, batteries, and various other kinds of producers. In these ten industries, official government policy has required firms to export at least 5 percent of their output or suffer sharp cuts in their import entitlements. For many companies the official minimum obligatory export target was later raised to 10 percent. However, the government has not enforced this policy vigorously as long as firms have made a genuine effort to increase exports.

Official government policy permits firms in many sectors, including the ten obligatory export industries, which export at least 10 percent of their output, to purchase imports from the cheapest foreign source, using free foreign exchange. (In other cases, firms must import from prescribed countries or sources.) However, this policy has also not been followed closely, primarily because of the limited amount of free foreign exchange at the government's disposal.

In general, firms have experienced serious delays and much red tape before receiving the export incentives due them. Their applications for the incentives must be scrutinized by the Chief Controller of Imports and Exports, the Finance Ministry, and various other government agencies. Some companies do not even bother to go through all the trouble involved in getting excise duty drawbacks of customs duty refunds. Problems and delays pertaining to the receipt of export incentives seem to be easing, however.

The new import policy announced in March, 1970 provides greater export incentives than before.[10] It also adds three new industries to the existing ten obligatory export sectors: pipes and tubes, transmission towers, and weighing machines. The government also claims that it intends to implement its obligatory export policy more vigorously than in the past and announced that 250 enterprises in the ten original obligatory industries which failed to export at least 10 percent have had their import quotas reduced — apparently only modestly or symbolically in most instances. At the same time, the government decided to consult with these firms on their difficulties and help in resolving them so they could significantly contribute to the export effort.[11]

In 1968-69, it is reported that 300 firms qualified for special treatment because they exported at least 10 percent of their output. In 1969-70 the number rose to 658, of which 465 were in the small-scale sector.[12] In view of their export contributions, these small-scale firms were rewarded with a 100 percent increase in the allocation of foreign exchange for their imports.

It has also been reported that the long tussle between the Ministries of Foreign Trade and Industrial Development over permitting "monopolistic or dominant" undertakings to set up export-oriented units has finally been resolved. Many foreign firms and foreign collaborations in India fall into this category. Guidelines have been prepared by the two ministries for granting industrial licenses to such export-oriented units, and these have gone to the Cabinet for approval.[13]

The essential feature of the scheme will be that monopolistic and dominant companies[14] wanting to set up a new unit or undertake an expansion project will have to execute a bond in which they undertake to export a specified minimum percentage of their production. The bond will provide that if there is a shortfall in the exports guaranteed, twice the amount of the shortfall will be given to the State Trading Corporation to be exported at the best price available in world markets. The STC will then remit the export proceeds to the defaulting firm after deducting its standard commission.

Where such a firm claims that its proposed venture or expansion will be export-oriented, the licensing authorities will examine its past export performance. If a license is granted, the government will decide what proportion of the firm's existing production should continue to be exported, as well as specifying the proportion of the new or increased output which must be exported. In both cases a bond will be required of the firm.

In the past the Ministry of Industrial Development has found that firms which gave export assurances typically have not lived up to their promises, in spite of warnings of penalties. Hence, this ministry has been reluctant to grant new licenses to dominant firms. The Ministry of Foreign Trade feels that such firms are generally in the best position to export in substantial quantities, and has pressed for a more flexible approach in industrial licensing. By making firms execute guarantee bonds in the future, it is felt the problem will be resolved. As a result, various dominant firms which have been pressing for expansion or new projects — including certain battery and cycle component producers — are now more likely to get licenses if and when the Cabinet approves the new scheme.

Foreign subsidiaries, have generally achieved better export performance in the last several years than their indigenous counterparts in the same industry. However, U.S. subsidiaries have tended to increase their exports significantly only in response to strong government pressure, such as the need to export to get essential import entitlements or desired industrial licenses. Quite often U.S. parent corporations have restrained their subsidiaries from exporting in order to maintain international markets for other units in the complex.

U.S. investment and capital export restrictions

The United States has a number of restrictive rules concerning direct foreign investment — and to some extent, even local investment — in a limited number of industrial sectors, particularly public utilities, transportation, and atomic facilities of all sorts. In recent years, it has also placed restrictions on U.S. private investment and other capital exports in an effort to alleviate the country's balance of payments problems. This was formalized in 1968 by an executive order of President Johnson,[15] and was still in effect under President Nixon in 1971.

The mandatory controls were largely aimed at appeasing the severe criticisms of U.S. balance of payments deficits by influential European central banking authorities. The controls were directed primarily toward private U.S. loans and investment in Western Europe, not in developing countries.

U.S. INVESTMENT GUARANTEES

The Agency for International Development (AID) of the U.S. government administers a broad investment guarantee program, established in 1961. The program has involved developing countries which receive American assistance or aid. AID has insured American multinational corporations against such risks as expropriation and confiscation of investments; inconvertability of local currency into dollars; and damage arising from wars, revolutions, or insurrections — in some cases up to 100 percent of the value of the investment. This program applies only to new investments which have not been implemented before such insurance has been taken out. The purpose is to encourage American firms to take risks in areas of the world that might not be attractive otherwise. Reasonable payment is required of the company for the insurance protection it gets. In many situations the risks may be so large as to preclude private insurance companies' interest in such programs, leaving the government to fill the gap. Actually, however, the U.S. government has made a profit on such insurance business to date.

Foreign Investment and Restrictions Within India

In India foreign business investments of all types have increased from 2.65 billion rupees in June, 1948 to 12.3 billion rupees by the end of the 1966-67 fiscal year.[16] This entailed nearly a 500 percent increase in less than 20 years.

As of March 31, 1967 direct foreign investments in India — involving branches, subsidiaries, and affiliates of foreign firms — accounted for 53 percent of that country's total outstanding foreign investment. It had increased by over 300 percent — from 2.1 billion rupees to 6.5 billion — during the 1948-67 period.[17]

Foreign "portfolio" investments[18] in India increased 13-fold — from 447 million rupees to 5.8 billion — during the same period. Portfolio investments include equity as well as creditor capital (securities, suppliers' credits to firms, and so forth). Foreign portfolio investments accounted for only about 17 percent of India's outstanding foreign business investment in 1948, and increased steadily and sharply to 47 percent as of March 31, 1967. At that time, equity accounted for about 11 percent of all foreign portfolio investments, and creditors the remaining 89 percent. In the "creditors" category 60 percent was loans, with 28 percent representing suppliers' credits. More than 75 percent of the increase in outstanding total foreign business investment in India during the 1965-66 period came from portfolio investments, and less than 25 percent from direct investments.

The United States was India's major supplier of total foreign capital during the 1965-67 period, accounting for over 40 percent — 950 million rupees out of 2.36 billion — of the total increase. The United States' proportionate share of all long-term foreign business investment in India was only 5.5 percent in 1948, increasing to 25.2 percent as of the end of the 1966-67 fiscal year.[19] The United Kingdom's share has dropped from 80 percent to 48 percent during this period, but Britain still ranks first. West Germany's share as of March 31, 1967 was 5 percent, Japan's 3.7 percent, France's 2.6 percent, Italy's 2.2 percent, Switzerland's 2 percent, and Sweden and Canada's about 1 percent.[20] Germany and Switzerland had only negligible amounts of foreign investment in India before 1949, while the other countries cited above — other than the United States and United Kingdom — had none.

Since 1960 the United States has provided over 50 percent of India's direct private foreign investment. The number of American subsidiaries and collaborations in India has more than doubled since 1950. There are now well over 400, most of them manufacturing enterprises. In 1950, U.S. direct private investment in India was only $38 million. It increased steadily and sharply to $159 million by 1960. It continued to increase substantially until 1965, when it reached $255 million. It declined to $237 million in 1966, but rose to $267 million in 1967, and then to $281 million as of the end of 1968.

American direct private investment in the manufacturing sector accounted for nearly half of all such investment at the end of 1968. Trade within India accounted for about 15 percent, and other sectors — including finance, banking, service industries, public utilities, — accounted for the rest. About 35 percent of all U.S. earnings derived from direct investments in India were reinvested in 1967, and 33 percent in 1968. In 1968, the reinvestment rate in the manufacturing sector was 17 percent.[21]

India's approach as a recipient of foreign investment has much in common with that of other developing countries. Although she has laid down some general guidelines in accordance with her Five Year Plans, most approvals have been decided on a case-by-case basis.

Table 7-1 indicates the pattern of India's foreign business investment by sector in 1948 as compared to 1967.[22] The distribution among sectors reflects the extent to which foreign investment has been encouraged and discouraged in each sector since 1948. The overall pattern of emphasis is representative of many developing countries.

Foreign investment in India has grown most sharply in manufacturing (including mining). During the 1948-67 period the proportionate share of foreign investment in this overall sector increased from 40 to 65.5 percent. Within the overall manufacturing sector, it is clear that the Indian government has given greatest preference to foreign investment in chemicals and drugs, petroleum, and metals and metal products. It has also given preference to machinery and equipment and electrical goods in general, although the public sector has increasingly played the major role in these industries. Restrictions on foreign investment have been greatest in those relatively traditional sectors, such as textiles, and foods and beverages, where the indigenous private sector has been dominant. Restrictions on foreign investment in the mining sector have also been stringent.

Official policy on foreign private investment (including collaboration) for the Fourth Plan period of 1969-74 does not involve a dramatic departure from the approach followed in the past.[23] Foreign ventures which can fill a critical and long-term gap in the economy, and which do not interfere with the maximum utilization of domestic know-how, resources and services, will generally continue to receive preference, as will those entailing the importation of know-how or technology in sophisticated industrial fields, especially if the public sector cannot handle the task by itself. Foreign ventures involving consumer goods will not ordinarily be permitted except where they generate substantial increases in exports. The major changes from the past are a narrowing of the range of acceptable foreign private investments, as India moves toward self-sufficiency, greater emphasis on the export potential of foreign ventures, and closer scrutiny of proposals. Any foreign project entailing more than 20 million rupees in foreign capital, 40 percent foreign equity participation, or a 5 percent royalty fee must now be approved by the Indian Cabinet, and the interagency Foreign Investment Board, as well as the various interagency licensing and other committees.

It will probably be more difficult for a foreign firm to obtain majority ownership in India than in the past. Although India's 1956 Industrial Policy Resolution generally ruled out majority foreign ownership, many exceptions were made; in some cases, majority ownership has been approved only for a limited time. But this has become rarer in recent years and will probably be eliminated.

TABLE 7-1 Pattern of long-term foreign business investment in India (percentage breakdown by sector)

	June, 1948		March 31, 1967	
Total: all sectors	100% (2.65 billion rupees)		100% (12.3 billion rupees)	
All manufacturing and mining		40%		65.5%
Chemicals, drugs and allied products	3		14.9	
Petroleum	9.2		13.4	
Metals and metal products	3.4		9.5	
Transportation equipment	negligible		5.4	
Electrical goods and machinery	1.5		4.2	
Textile products	11		4.2	
Food, beverages, etc.	4		3.4	
Machinery and machine tools	negligible		2.9	
Mining	4.3		0.8	
Miscellaneous	3.6		6.8	
Services		40%		25.4%
Trading	15.5		4.4	
Financial	6		5.4	
Construction, utilities, and transportation	12		13.9	
Miscellaneous	6.5		1.7	
Plantations		20%		9.1%

Majority ownership has usually been granted to foreign companies in India only if at least one, and usually several, of the following conditions were met:

1. The foreign venture was in a field judged to be vital, a big investment was entailed, or advanced technical know-how was involved.

2. A substantial number of Indians would be trained in major and skilled jobs.

3. India's foreign exchange position could be improved significantly, (through import substitution, exports, or both).

4. The domestic production of the products under consideration were small but judged to be highly important, and a rapid increase in purely indigenous production was not expected.

5. The capital investment entailed was fairly small, and the industry was not deemed to be strategic.

In the future, foreign majority ownership is not likely to be granted on the basis of points 2, 4 and/or 5, in particular. When and if it is granted, points 1 and 3 will no doubt have to be met, as a minimum. The joint venture between Birla's and U.S. Steel which was approved in 1970 involves a $75 million fertilizer complex which is deemed highly strategic to India's development. However, U.S. Steel has apparently been granted only 40 or 45 percent equity participation in this venture.

Where the Indian government has been willing to grant substantial (but not majority) foreign ownership, the following arrangement has typically been favored: 40 percent ownership to the foreign firm, 20 percent to an Indian partner, and 40 percent to the Indian public. Many foreign firms have been able to maintain effective control under these conditions.

There is no formal pattern for the foreign investment or collaboration agreement in India. The agreement may be only a few pages in length, or it may involve huge volumes of very detailed data. It may be split into two or more subagreements covering equity participation, licensing fees, technical collaboration, managerial and technical control, and so forth. In any event, the overall agreement is the basic document that forms the basis of governmental approval or rejection. Under certain circumstances, the government may permit a foreign company to take equity in lieu of royalties and/or fees, and this may be advantageous from a tax standpoint. The firm may also be permitted to give machinery, goods, etc., in lieu of cash for equity in some cases; but this is likely to entail hard bargaining over asset value. In general, the international firm is not likely to be able to maximize its equity position, royalties, and fees, and it will have to determine what trade-offs are most advantageous to it.

In the last several years, a small but rapidly growing number of Indian firms have been seeking investment and other collaborative ventures abroad, especially in hard-currency countries. The Indian government provides liberal foreign exchange to these firms to cover the travel and other out-of-pocket expenses incurred in negotiations and exploratory trips abroad.

Most foreign ventures involving Indian firms are not in developed countries, and this is to be expected. Indian firms typically have more to offer other developing or poor nations where they can fill critical gaps. As of the beginning of 1969, the Indian government has approved 64 joint ventures involving Indian companies — mostly fairly large and progressive ones — in 25 foreign countries. However, all have not yet been implemented. Of these ventures, 32 involve African countries, 15 are in Southeast Asian nations, and most of the others involve other Asian, Latin American, mid-Eastern, and West Indian countries. Only a few involve Western European countries, North America, or other advanced nations.[24] Some of the products covered by these ventures are textiles, drugs, light engineering goods, paper products, pipes, tractors, sugar, re-rolling mills, sewing machines, trucks, transformers, air conditioners, foodstuffs, asbestos, and cement products.

Profit remission restrictions

The kinds of profit remission restrictions which exist in a given country may determine whether or not a given foreign investment should be made. A record of frequent and severe restrictions, or signs that a country is likely to move in this direction in the foreseeable future, can increase investment risks substantially.

Even though an established U.S. subsidiary may be earning a good rate of return in the local currency, the operation may not meet overall corporate objectives if local earnings cannot be converted to dollars. In such cases, as blocked funds pile up, shifts in local financial planning, procurement, and spending patterns may be required. For example, an expensive second-hand machine available locally may become more attractive than a cheaper, new, and more productive machine which has to be paid for in hard currency. As a result, production processes may become very different because of the existence of stringent profit remission and exchange controls. Or possibly the firm might decide to provide more benefits to personnel and increase local spending in other ways which it otherwise would not consider.

A fairly common reaction in international business is that any currency but the relatively strong ones, e.g., dollars, Swedish Kronor, Swiss francs, Japanese yen, pounds sterling, German marks, becomes a type of "gamblers' money" which can be spent more carelessly than "real" money. This attitude can lead to carelessness in financial dealings which may do neither the firm nor the host economy any good in the long run. When profit remission and exchange controls are altered or relaxed, such ingrained thinking and behavior may become both risky and irrational.

Many developing and relatively unstable countries interested in attracting foreign capital and know-how offer to guarantee profit remissions for a fixed number of years or in stated amounts or percentages in order to reassure nervous investors. Special deals may be made for particular investments which are deemed of major importance for the host country. Often profit repatriation is an item of special bargaining between government officials and company representatives.

India has been fair and relatively liberal with regard to profit remission, especially in view of her foreign exchange problems.[25] Although government approval is required for all profit remissions or other currency outflows involving foreign exchange, foreign firms have been able to remit profits in accordance with agreed terms. The Indian government has pressured foreign firms to increase their reinvestment of earnings, but such pressure has not usually been strong. It does appear, however, that preference with regard to industrial and other licensing decisions has sometimes been given to those foreign firms which have reinvested relatively large shares of their earnings.

Conflict has arisen between some of the parent corporations and their subsidiaries surveyed — in India and elsewhere — with regard to the share of profits to be remitted. The subsidiary often desires to retain a larger share of its earnings than the parent firm wishes. In recent years, most of the U.S. firms surveyed in India have reinvested between 10 and 25 percent of their profits, although there seems to be a slight downward trend.

The Indian government may impose more stringent restrictions on profit remissions in the future. For example, certain remittances of foreign oil firms not specifically covered in agreements are now being cut. This primarily involves special payments for engineering, technical, and managerial services and other overhead expenses allotted to Indian operations; costs incurred by parent firms; and royalties and licensing fees. It may eventually involve profit remissions per se.

On the other hand, the minister for Industrial Development recently rejected a suggestion calling for a ceiling on the profits earned by foreign firms and for more stringent restrictions on the repatriation of profits of minority foreign ventures, royalty payments, and other remissions involving foreign collaborators.[26] He claimed that this would be bad for India's development, pointing out that only a few foreign companies now make net profits as high as 14 percent on their investments, while others average only about 8 percent. To the specific question of whether a foreign collaboration involving a soft-drink manufacturer which had a capital of 30 million rupees, but which had been sending 50 million rupees to the foreign parent company annually, was really necessary for the country, he replied that the collaboration was entered into long ago and, according to the agreement, "whatever has to be repatriated has to be repatriated." However, on other occasions, this same minister has taken a much more negative position towards outflows of capital to foreign parent operations.

Exchange control restrictions

In many countries faced with serious monetary or development problems, exchange controls are applied to every type of monetary transfer involving conversion of local currency to foreign currency. Frequently all foreign exchange earned or spent by firms or local citizens, must be approved by and processed through government channels. Such pervasive foreign exchange control affects foreign travel, sales promotion abroad, the maintenance of an office or service facility outside the country, or even the small matter of taking prospective customers out to lunch in Hong Kong.

One good indication of how much a country's currency is overvalued, and how strong is the demand for foreign exchange within the country, is the premium paid for different kinds of foreign currency on the open or black markets. In some countries, such as India, both types of markets exist, since certain kinds of foreign exchange credits received by enterprises may be sold legally and at premiums to designated firms under certain conditions. These firms may then use the foreign exchange entitlements primarily to procure various allowed imports.

Indian rupees are traded openly on the basis of supply and demand in Thailand and Hong Kong. The free exchange rates there tend to be higher than those charged on the "open" or black market within India, and the spread between the buying and selling prices is also larger than within India, primarily because rupees bought outside of the country must be smuggled out and then back in, and stiff penalties can be imposed.

The premiums paid for hard currencies within India reached their peak right before devaluation of the rupee on June 6, 1966. At that time, one could get 17 or more rupees per U.S. dollar, while the official exchange rate was only 4.75. After the rupee was devalued to 7.5 rupees per dollar, premiums reached a low of about 8.5 to 9.5 rupees per dollar during the 1967-68 recessionary period. By mid-1969, the selling rate had risen to 10 to 11 rupees per dollar, and the buying rate to 9 to 10 rupees. The selling rates outside of India have generally been within 10 percent of the black market rates prevailing within India in recent years.

Indigenous firms in India usually make more use of the black market to procure foreign exchange than do foreign companies. This may be due to better planning and management on the part of foreign firms, making them less likely to be caught short in a critical foreign exchange crisis. In some cases, corporate policy strongly prohibits foreign subsidiaries from obtaining foreign exchange through illicit channels. And in others, foreign firms have been able to get more liberal foreign exchange allotments from the Indian government than their indigenous counterparts, or else their parent companies have helped them obtain critically needed foreign exchange.

Foreign exchange restrictions on local citizens are often much more stringent than those applied to foreigners. For example, Indian citizens are not allowed to leave India without special permission from the government, and even then they are usually provided with only token amounts of foreign exchange to support their needs abroad. A foreigner in India, especially one who receives at least part of his income in hard currency, has much more freedom to travel and to obtain hard currency.

Stringent foreign exchange restrictions generally hurt the export promotion and foreign expansion efforts of indigenous firms significantly more than those of foreign companies. It has been particularly difficult for Indian manufacturers to send representatives on extended business trips abroad, to maintain or open sales offices in foreign countries, or to engage in much sales promotion activity abroad. A few Indian firms surveyed have even had to close down sales offices because of foreign exchange problems and rely solely on independent agents or representatives abroad.

INTERNATIONAL ECONOMIC FACTORS

The balance of this chapter focuses on three critical international economic factors or constraints. These are 1) general balance of international payments position; 2) international trade patterns; and 3) membership and obligations in international financial organizations and foreign aid.

Balance of payments

An important international factor is a nation's balance of payments position. Most of the developing nations run chronic balance of payments deficits, but even where balances are positive, the countries may be vulnerable to future changes. It is important for firms to understand the balance of payments concept, its implications, and the key causes and potential solutions to the problems it raises.

OVERVIEW
The balance of payments (B of P) of a given country is essentially a double-entry statement of all transactions of that country with the rest of the world, usually for a period

of a year.[27] Total expenditures in other countries (including loans) must balance with total receipts from all countries (including loans). In other words, outflows must equal inflows, although a key factor in achieving a balance may be a large "current accounts payable," which puts pressure on the country to earn more abroad or spend less. To buy abroad, one must earn or borrow the necessary funds, since no country can create the money of another country. The generally acceptable international medium of exchange, gold, can be used as a settlement medium of last resort, but this commodity is also limited in supply.

Debit transactions on the B of P are any transactions which involve payments by domestic organizations or individuals to foreigners. Credit transactions are all those involving receipts from foreigners. Debits, in effect, represent demand for foreign currencies needed to pay debts, while credits are supplies of these currencies received in payment.

Balance of payments statements are usually divided into current and capital account categories. Imports and exports are the best known current account items, and net performance here determines whether a particular country has a favorable or unfavorable balance of trade. However, a nation can have a favorable balance of trade, but run a significant balance of payments deficit because of its debtor position regarding "invisible" current-account items or in its capital account. In some cases, the reverse may be true.

Invisibles in the current account consist of such items as transportation, insurance, and other services which the country provides to foreigners (credits) or which they provide to it (debits); tourist expenditures abroad and the spending of foreign tourists at home; income (such as dividends, interest, and other earnings) remitted from abroad or paid abroad; private gifts sent abroad or received from abroad; and so forth. Hence an invisible item, such as the expenditure of an American for a drink in Paris has the same basic effect on the final B of P as does his import of French wine to be drunk in his home in Los Angeles.

Governments also deal heavily in foreign exchange. Payments by government controlled banking agencies are usually carried as central government transfers and flows. In a country's overall current account major governmental items may include military goods and services exported or imported, foreign-aid grants, and payments made or received.

A nation having a net deficit on its current account can offset it by settling in gold or by net borrowing which involves capital movements. In general, the more a country can earn, the more it will be able to purchase from other countries, and the stronger its credit will be. As a result, most countries are concerned with possibilities for increasing the supply of foreign exchange by exporting more, selling more services, and attracting more foreign tourists. Like most individuals, countries usually find that they have little difficulty in spending available funds on badly needed or desired items from abroad. The usual problem is how to earn enough to achieve or maintain desired standards of living or other national goals.

The capital account deals with capital movements. These include the long-term and short-term loans private citizens or firms make or receive from foreign private sources and investments in businesses or securities.

The concept of money throws a veil over the real aspects of capital movements.[28] Usually a foreign borrower borrows money from the United States, for example, rather than capital goods or other commodities. He gives an IOU in the form of a bond, note, or stock certificate, and he gets dollars. If he simply holds the dollars or puts them in an American bank or invests them in an American security, no net capital movement takes place. However, when he uses the loan to purchase goods of a value in excess of his sales to the lending country, a capital movement does take place. When the time comes to make interest payments on the loan, the foreigner must sell us more goods and services than he buys in order to obtain the extra dollars he needs. If he can't do this, he will have to borrow even more to meet the necessary payments.

Capital movements also include long- and short-term government loans and credits made or received through various direct or intermediate channels (e.g., the World Bank). When the U.S. government makes a loan to India, it is reflected as a credit in the Indian account, and as a debit in the U.S. account. As repayments are made, the entries are reversed.

If, after all debits and credits are listed for a given period, a country still is short of meeting its total international requirements, it may ship gold abroad to balance its accounts. Gold has been universally accepted as payment at a price of about $35 an ounce. This presupposes that the country has enough gold. In the modern world, a common way of holding reserves is not in gold, but in dollars or another relatively hard and stable currency, and the final adjustment may be made by writing a check on the central bank's dollar account in the United States to cover its requirements. Since dollars cannot be manufactured, except by the United States, this assumes that the country has acumulated reserves some time in the past.

Most currency exchange rates are defined in terms of accepted standards of "value," mainly gold, sterling, or dollars. Since all currencies are defined the same way, an international monetary comparison is then possible. The definition implies that the monetary authority of the country stands ready to buy and sell at this stated rate any of its own currency (usually a small difference in the buying and selling rates is quoted). The price may fluctuate within an allowable small margin depending on the supply of and demand for the currency at a particular point in time.

This short-term fixity of exchange rates presents a variety of problems to governments and firms. In effect, the entire economy is expected to rotate around this fixed price for foreign currency. If domestic prices increase, competitive imports become relatively cheaper, since their prices have not changed, assuming there is a stable exchange rate for foreign currencies. This could lead to increased imports, more demand for foreign exchange, and an increasing deficit in the current account of the country. If the situation persists for long, the supply and demand situation for local currency become unbalanced, and severe economic disturbance can result eventually leading to a redefinition of the value of local currency (i.e., devaluation) to reflect a lower exchange rate. This makes prices within the country more attractive to foreign buyers at one stroke and simultaneously raises the price of all foreign goods and services to local residents. Rationing of existing supplies of foreign exchange is another alternative which can be employed.

STAGES OF A COUNTRY'S BALANCE OF PAYMENTS

In general, the United States, United Kingdom, and various other advanced countries, have gone through four balance-of-payments stages typical of the growth of an agricultural nation into a well-developed industrialized one.[29] From about 1776 to 1870 the United States was essentially a "young and growing debtor" nation, as is India today. This means the country imports more on the current account than is exported, since borrowing from abroad is required to build up its capital structure.

The second stage is that of the "mature debtor" nation. This characterized the United States during the 1870-1914 period. India is struggling to enter this stage, and hopefully will be successful before 1980. In this stage a favorable balance of trade evolves and the surplus offsets dividends, interest, and other payments that must be remitted abroad on past borrowing and investments. Capital movements also tend to be not too far out of balance, with borrowing not substantially exceeding lending. The third stage is that of the "new creditor" nation. The United States found itself at this stage during the 1914-1930 period, with exports expanding rapidly and loans and other forms of assistance starting to flow outwards in large amounts.

The fourth stage is that of the "mature creditor" nation. England reached this stage some years ago, and the United States more recently. The United States now finds herself requiring the income from previous loans and investments to meet her huge current-account outflows.

INDIA'S BALANCE OF PAYMENTS

India's balance-of-payments deficit on her current account exceeded $1 billion during the 1965-68 period. It dropped sharply to only about $500 million in fiscal 1968-69, and preliminary estimates for 1969-70 indicated a further though modest improvement. The net inflow of capital — derived for the most part from foreign aid — slightly exceeded the current account deficit in 1965-66 and 1967-68, and was nearly $200 million larger than this deficit in 1968-69. During the 1965-68 period India drew about $225 million from the International Monetary Fund (IMF), but since 1968-69 has been paying back funds to IMF ($78 million in 1968-69, about $165 million in 1969-70, and about $200 million in 1970-71).[30]

India's total foreign exchange reserves have also been growing fairly rapidly in recent years. At the end of fiscal 1966-67, India's official foreign exchange reserves (including commercial bank holdings in foreign exchange and gold) stood at $700 million.[31] At the end of 1969 they approached $900 million, and as of mid-1970 they stood at around $1 billion.[32]

This improvement in India's current account has been brought about by a marked increase in exports coupled with a considerable slowdown of imports, especially food-stuffs. India's trade deficit in 1965-66 was a huge 9.5 billion rupees (nearly $1.3 billion). By 1968-69 it had dropped to 5 billion rupees, as exports increased by 13 percent over the previous fiscal year. However, exports in 1968-69 were still only about 4 percent higher than the country's previous peak year of 1964-65.[33] The 1969-70 export target called for a 7 percent increase over 1968-69. During the year the target was lowered several times, and actual export growth turned out to be only 3.8 percent.[34] In spite of this, India's unfavorable trade balance in 1969-70 was lower than it had been for 14 years. Imports totaled about 15.7 billion rupees in 1969-70 compared with over 19 billion in 1968-69. Exports totaled around 14.1 billion rupees compared to 13.6 billion in the preceding year.

Hence, India's trade deficit declined from about 5.5 billion rupees ($730 million) in 1968-69 to 1.6 billion ($213 million) in 1969-70.[35] Lower food grain imports was the most important single factor in the trade deficit drop. Fertilizer imports were also down quite sharply, as were purchases of some kinds of capital goods abroad.[36] India achieved a trade surplus for five months during 1969-70. She achieved an all-time monthly high of 1.45 billion rupees in exports in January, 1970, 300 million rupees more than in January 1969. In March, 1970, however, exports were only slightly ahead of imports.[37]

In spite of the recent improvement in India's balance of payments — achieved mainly by the substantial reduction of her trade deficit — world trade over the past 15 or 20 years has expanded significantly more than India's (more than 6 percent versus about 4 percent). India's relative share, instead of increasing, has been de-clining. Her absolute share is still less than 1 percent of total world exports.[38] Even if India achieves a 7 percent annual growth rate in exports during the 1970s, this would still represent no more than 2 percent of the present value of world export trade.

India must increase her exports at an annual rate of over 6 percent, and probably at least 7 percent, while keeping import growth down to 5 percent or less, if the coun-try is to resolve its balance-of-payments difficulties during the 1970s. To do so a series of constraints on exports which currently persist will have to be removed. These include the following factors: as domestic demand picks up and output surpluses decline, pressure to export tends to decrease; traditional exports are tapering off due to increasing foreign competition; high costs and lack of economies of scale in produc-tion, procurement, distribution, R & D, and other areas; and inadequate quality and varieties to meet foreign competition.

India's Fourth Plan (1969-74), if it reaches its goals, will do much to alleviate the country's balance of payments and related foreign exchange problems.[39] It calls for an annual (compounded) increase in exports of 7 percent during the five-year period and beyond. It also calls for growth in nonfood imports of not more than 5 percent a year, with food imports being eliminated entirely during the course of the plan. It projects major improvements in the service and tourism categories of the country's B of P current account. By the end of the Fourth Plan, India hopes to reduce foreign aid net of debt servicing (interest and loan repayment) to half of the level at the end of the 1960s, and to entirely eliminate dependence on net foreign aid by 1980-81. However, India's planners have pointed out that during at least the first two years of the Fourth Plan foreign aid requirements would continue to be high, and aid must be obtained well in advance to enable programs and projects to progress in accordance with the Plan.

Hence, India hopes that income, output, and investment targets will be achieved without requiring any significant increase in foreign debt beyond the Fifth Plan (1975-80). This implies that the internal savings of the economy after 1978-79 will be sufficient to finance required investments and that the economy will have a foreign trade surplus (inclusive of invisibles) equivalent to at least the interest payments to foreign creditors. It is projected that internal savings will be adequate to achieve this if a marginal savings rate of around 28 percent were sustained throughout the period.[40]

If India does achieve the above targets, it will emerge from a young growing debtor nation to a mature debtor nation, within the next decade or so. It will also lay much of the groundwork necessary for becoming a new creditor nation in the more distant future. In order to achieve this, however, there will have to be sustained improvement in many of the environmental constraints under study in this book. This would have to be accompanied by major improvements in managerial and productive efficiency in the industrial and agricultural sectors.

International trade patterns

OVERVIEW

Countries have widely differing patterns of exports and imports, depending on such key factors as level of economic development, factor endowment, and competence and know-how in differing economic sectors.

In general, more industrially advanced nations have more complex import and export patterns, reflecting their ability to produce many kinds of products competitively. Poor countries usually rely on a narrow range of export commodities — often only one or two — to earn the foreign exchange needed to import other goods.

Countries with the ability to sell a wide variety of products abroad are not usually nearly as troubled by inability to export as nations with a narrower export list. At the extreme, a one-crop nation with a widely variable price (e.g., coffee) will be in serious balance of payments trouble every time the price of its basic commodity falls — or even if the weather is bad in a particular year. Countries which depend upon tin, wheat, coffee, wool, cocoa, jute, tea, cotton and similar products for which world prices are determined largely or entirely by aggregate supply and demand may face export earnings fluctuations of as much as 25 percent per year as prices shift in international markets. Petroleum, iron ore, and copper producers are more fortunate, as prices for these products are partially controlled by large multinational corporations, with active governmental support in many cases. But virtually total reliance on export sales of one to three primary products, which characterizes most of the world's less developed nations, has the effect of making export earnings and import potentials relatively unstable.

Many international firms are the key commodity exporters in less-developed countries. Petroleum in the Middle East and Venezuela, copper in Chile, iron ore in Liberia, coffee in Colombia, and specific agricultural commodities in various Latin American nations and elsewhere form the largest single exports of these nations and are all controlled by large international companies. The companies are in the "hot seat" at all times because of their critical importance to export earnings, and they tend to be among the earliest targets of political pressure.

International trade statistics can be of great use to an individual firm, especially a multinational company. Specific import and export figures often point to opportunities not immediately obvious, as well as to potential problem areas. They may reveal areas in which domestic markets are oversupplied, where critical shortages exist, and the kinds of products for which the country generally has a favorable or unfavorable competitive advantage in world markets. They may also indicate whether a particular project is likely to be approved by local authorities, as well as the kinds of controls likely to be enforced or established.

Evaluation of import-export figures — in conjunction with national or regional plans may also reveal areas in which government pressures to establish import substitution or export promotion ventures can be anticipated. Each firm should evaluate the situation in terms of its own plans, products, and areas of expertise. For example, many foreign pharmaceutical companies entered India with the idea that they would import virtually all of their products in bulk form (usually from their parent companies), repackage them for distribution within India, and market them there. Over a period of years, successively increasing pressures have been applied by the Indian government to force backward integration, first to the manufacture of bulk intermediates and then to the manufacture of basic raw materials. Moreover, in the last several years, increasing pressure has also been applied to get drug firms to export more of their output. Companies which do not anticipate such pressures may find themselves in very awkward positions.

THE CASE OF INDIA

Pressures for import substitution and export promotion in Indian industry will no doubt continue for a long time, with little or no relaxation likely during the 1970s.

The role of traditional exports as India's chief foreign exchange earner can be expected to continue to decline. In 1955, tea, jute, cotton and related textile items accounted for 70 percent of the country's total exports. By the end of the 1960s they accounted for less than 50 percent. Even product diversification with regard to India's traditional exports — e.g., instant tea and jute laminates — is not expected to do very much for their export potential. India must continue to diversify her exports on a broad front in order to achieve and sustain economic development.

India exported practically no engineering goods until the second half of the 1960s. As of 1970-71 about 10 percent of the country's exports consisted of engineering goods, which doubled during 1967-69, and increased by another 30 percent in 1969-70. During the Fourth Plan, 65 percent of the country's projected increase in commodity exports is slated to come from minerals and manufactures, with engineering goods and chemicals playing the biggest growth role.[41] Particular attention is being given to exports of products for which world demand is expected to grow at a rapid rate. These include metals and metal manufactures, iron ore, various drugs, chemicals and allied products, and batteries. Good potential is also seen for fish items, various minerals other than iron ore, some handicrafts items, and some smaller agricultural commodities such as tobacco, and vegetable oils and oil-cakes.[42]

At this time, on the basis of international price comparisons and other key factors,[43] India seems to be generally most competitive in world markets for the following kinds of products in addition to her traditional key exports discussed above: pig iron, coking and noncoking coal, footwear, some kinds of structural steel, steel bars and rods, various kinds of metal manufactures and engineering goods (especially those in which India has had long experience), some types of textile machinery, smaller electric motors and transformers, certain basic machine tools, telephone equipment, some cables, cement milling machinery, and a limited range of consumer goods. It is also possible that, if India achieves self-sufficiency in food grains, an increasing amount of her superior qualities of rice could be diverted for export purposes. Products for which India has fair to fairly good export potential include: sugar, various kinds of steel items, zinc ingots, truck tires, spinning frames, a limited range of chemicals and allied products, and various kinds of consumer nondurables and light durables.

India's chief imports during the 1960s consisted of foodstuffs, chemicals (including fertilizers), petroleum products, paper and paper products, steel and nonferrous metals, nonmetallic minerals, and a wide range of machinery, equipment, electrical goods, components, spare parts, and intermediates. While the Fourth Plan calls for only modest annual increases in India's imports, they are likely to increase quite substantially during the earlier years of the Plan because of improved economic conditions, vital commodity shortages and bottlenecks which have recently emerged, and large new outlays of investments for public sector projects. By the end of the Fourth Plan (1974) and during the Fifth Plan it is anticipated that imports of most items will be sharply reduced or eliminated entirely. At the same time, significantly increased imports of some commodities are still planned for. This includes goods for which there are inadequate indigenous resources or substitutes or which cannot yet be produced economically within India.[44] Such products include: fertilizer materials (e.g., sulphur and rock phosphate); nonferrous metals other than aluminum; crude oil (which is currently a controversial item); certain kinds of machinery; transportation equipment and metal products; various kinds of components and spare parts; and a limited range of specialized materials and intermediates.[45]

In recent times, about 40 percent of India's imports have come from the United States, with less than 10 percent coming from the United Kingdom, and a similar proportion coming from all Communist countries combined.[46] Although India trades with a wide variety of diverse nations, her heavy U.S. imports result from the wide range of needed commodities which the United States can supply and ties between aid and purchases. With a decline in the United States' relative share of aid to India, the proportion of imports coming from the United States has also been declining. Many of the imports from the United States have involved foodstuffs, as well as goods used to build up India's public sector and other indigenous industries.

India's export trade is distributed more evenly than her import trade. However, the United Kingdom is still her biggest customer, accounting for about 20 percent in recent times.[47]

India makes use of bilateral trade agreements primarily with Communist countries and other soft currency areas. Where money cannot be freely exchanged (which almost always implies an overvalued rate), the bilateral agreement frequently results in overpriced items being swapped on each side of the deal. India trades in this manner with countries that accept rupees in payment in order to arrange for a flow of goods on a basis which will not require use of hard currency. Many of these arrangements are direct barter arrangements, while others permit payment in local currencies for deferred trade at a later date.

In general, firms in countries which advocate bilateral trade arrangements may be forced to purchase imports which are not really desired, do not meet their specifications, and are not worth the price paid. The usual machinery of trade restriction is responsible for this.

Membership in international financial organizations and foreign aid

In recent decades a number of important international financial institutions have evolved. Most of these are potential sources of foreign capital. Others provide for support of the local currency in time of crisis. Consequently they have significant implications for business firms, especially multinational corporations.

Also of considerable importance, especially to developing countries, are foreign aid programs. Some of these programs are administered by international financial organizations, most notably the World Bank, which coordinates the Aid-India Consortium, in recent times the largest foreign aid program of all. Various relatively advanced countries also have their own foreign aid and development programs, in some cases (like the United States) in conjunction with or in addition to the World

Bank consortiums, and in others (like the Soviet Union and other Communist countries) entirely separate from such programs. Foreign aid also has an important impact on the recipient's economic environment and on firms doing business with or within the country.

INTERNATIONAL FINANCIAL ORGANIZATIONS

The International Bank for Reconstruction and Development (IBRD), also called the World Bank, is perhaps the most important of the international financial institutions which have evolved since World War II. It is now a multi-billion dollar institution. Initially it provided capital for reconstruction of war damage, but recently most of its loans and activities have been concentrated in development activities of its poorer member nations. Its 80-odd member countries contribute capital to the World Bank roughly in proportion to their income and political importance. The bank also sells bonds to obtain additional funds for lending. The United States has been and still is by far the largest contributor, although its role has been declining somewhat because of its own balance-of-payments problems, and as other relatively advanced countries have become more affluent. In effect, countries buy shares in the bank, and have voting rights in a manner analogous to any joint stock corporation. Any nation is free to join, provided it abides by the rather simple and straightforward rules, although Yugoslavia is in fact the only member from the Communist world.

The World Bank lends at commercial rates of interest to public (e.g., governments) or private customers who qualify in a commercial sense for loans. Only member nations and their dependencies are eligible for loans. There is no particular subsidy involved in the bank operations, since loan applications are carefully analyzed both in terms of the potential economic returns of the project and the possible balance-of-payments problems that might arise as a result of servicing the debt (i.e., interest and repayments). A unique feature of the bank's regular commercial activities is that it routinely deals in large international loans to borrowers who may have no other adequate source of funds. To date, the bank has made multi-million dollar loans for such things as electric power projects, roads, irrigation and flood control, mineral development, steel production, and other kinds of industrial production.

While all World Bank loans must be guaranteed by the country's national government, many loans are made to private firms. The country or firm involved is expected to contribute substantial equity itself, and the bank may only lend the amount of money needed for foreign exchange. The generally cautious attitude of the bank is reflected in the fact that it has never yet had a default in a loan. India has obtained over $450 million to date, as has Japan, the two largest borrowers.

Firms often benefit directly from projects financed by the bank — new highways, power plants, water facilities, and the like. They also receive indirect benefits since important by-products of the bank's activities are research and advice on the types of economic activity most suitable for a specific country. The bank has prepared numerous "country" studies under its own auspices, indicating what economic development policies and programs might prove most desirable in the given country, and these contain invaluable information for individual firms.

Another major international agency is the International Finance Corporation (IFC), which is an affiliate of the World Bank. It was formed in 1956 in recognition of the fact that, in many cases, private firms could not expect to obtain the guarantees of their governments for World Bank loans. The IFC makes fixed-interest long-term loans, and also engages in equity participation in industries in member countries. As a lender to private firms, this organization is a source of capital for both international and indigenous firms. Loans are usually much smaller than those made by the World Bank, averaging only about $1.25 million each.

Like those from the World Bank, loans from the IFC are essentially commercial in nature, and are only made after close examination of a firm's potential. The applicant must provide detailed data on its activities, as well as a carefully devised plan. And here, too, no defaults have occurred to date.

IFC insists on substantial equity participation by borrowers, and as a result, for each dollar of loan elicits the equivalent of three to five additional dollars of invested capital. Firms borrowing from IFC pay interest rates comparable to those paid by similar firms in countries where the private money market would perform this function. Actually this is frequently a form of concealed subsidy, since a Brazilian firm borrowing at 6 percent from IFC may not be able to obtain local capital at less than 15 or 20 percent.

Since the IFC and the World Bank apply commercial lending criteria, many less developed nations have not been able to make much use of their funding. Consequently the International Development Association (IDA) was formed in 1960 as an affiliate of the World Bank, with initial subscriptions from member countries of one billion dollars. Countries were divided into developed and underdeveloped categories, with special, easy subscription terms to the less developed.

The general purpose of IDA is to make subsidized development loans to poorer countries. Capital is typically provided interest-free to such countries, payable over 50 years, with a 10-year period of grace at the outset of the loans. While IDA maintains that it carefully selects its loan projects, it is clear that it is willing to support much riskier projects than the World Bank. IDA will lend to either public or private organizations, and government guarantees are not required.

The Inter-American Development Bank (IDB) was organized in 1959 by 20 of the 21 North and South American countries (Cuba is not a member), through capital subscriptions. All countries are eligible for loans except the United States. IDA performs three types of lending activities. The first is similar to the hard commerical loans made by the World Bank; the second is analogous to loans made by the IDA; the third type of loan is generally made to improve social conditions (such as education, health, land settlement, and housing), rather than economic situations.

The more recently-formed Asian Development Bank also extends loans and various kinds of assistance to member countries in that part of the world. Most involve relatively modest projects in smaller Asian countries. Japan plays the major role in this institution, being Asia's most advanced nation.

The International Monetary Fund (IMF) was another major international financial institution to arise out of World War II. It has been dealing primarily with problems associated with sudden or sharp changes in balance of payments for member countries. Before IMF, if a country had a crop failure, leading to acute short-term pressures on the balance of payments, its only recourse might be the imposition of exchange controls, devaluation, or possibly a quick international loan from another country or a bank. IMF was created to eliminate such short-term disturbances which also affect countries other than the one directly involved.

IMF provides short-term loans of foreign currencies which are needed to ease balance-of-payments problems in the drawing country. Each of the nearly 100 members contributes a funds quota in gold (25 percent) and its own currency. The IMF reserve has been well over $15 billion. Member nations have an almost automatic right to draw on the first tranche (or the 25 percent of their quota in gold); however, additional loans are increasingly difficult to obtain. Thus a country in temporary balance-of-payments difficulties has an immediate source of funds available to cover the first shock of its deficit, and if it can convince the IMF of the validity of its position, it can draw considerably more to cover deficits. The United States has had over $5 billion in drawing rights, by far the largest of any other country. This drawing right serves as a major cushion against attacks on the dollar, and as such is an important weapon in the whole balance of payments question.

In general, the ability to obtain more credits from the IMF basically rests on the ability of the country in question to convince the fund that its plan to restore equilibrium in its balance of payments is sound. This tends to ensure that a country in trouble will be forced to consider meaningful economic alternatives at home to solve its problems. The member country also has access to skilled technical advice on corrective measures.

The IMF requires that member countries define their currencies in gold, and that these par values be maintained within plus or minus 1 percent. Thus each member is under pressure to maintain a stable currency at all times. Changes in the par value can be made, although the IMF must approve such changes. (At times, it may even strongly encourage either devaluation or reevaluation.) Fund members are generally not supposed to have exchange controls, multiple exchange rates, restrictions on capital flows, or similar discriminatory devices. However loopholes in this rule do exist, primarily with respect to countries in transition from wartime dislocations, or poor countries having very acute balance-of-payments and development problems, such as India. However, the fund is generally reluctant to expel a member for violating the rules. (Only Czechoslavakia has been expelled to date.)

The IMF deals only with national governments, typically through their central banking agencies; private businessmen do not have direct dealings with the organization. However, membership implies that the country will constantly be under pressure to maintain freer currency, and fewer exchange control restrictions and barriers to free movement of funds, and that it has available, to meet emergencies, expert advice and a reserve of scarce currencies to be used in the short term. The availability of such assistance is of great interest and benefit to the businessman.

FOREIGN AID AND U.S. ASSISTANCE PROGRAMS

Foreign aid has played a vital role in the development of many poor countries. It has also benefited — both directly and indirectly — numerous firms, both international and indigenous. It has led to environmental improvements of many kinds which have a significant bearing on business and industrial activity. Many international and indigenous enterprises have obtained loans through various foreign assistance programs, and many more have increased their business considerably because of the demand for goods and services created by such assistance. Companies in more advanced countries have also benefited through larger exports made possible by foreign aid.

In general, foreign assistance to developing countries takes several forms. There are gifts and nonrepayable grants which may involve commodities (including foodstuffs), cash, services, technical assistance programs, debt relief on outstanding obligations (interest payments and even principal payments may be waived), and so forth. Often this form of aid is earmarked for purposes such as industrial or agricultural development, social overhead capital, health, education and training, and community development.

Another basic category consists of project aid in the form of loans, credits or commodities tied to specific projects. In this case, loans and other forms of assistance are repayable to the donor under varying terms. Project aid loans may be repayable either in local or hard currency, depending on the conditions imposed by the donor. Developing countries, of course, greatly prefer loans and credits which are repayable in their own currency or payable with local goods and services.

The other basic category of assistance involves nonproject aid. This also takes the form of loans, credits, and the like, but it is not tied to specific programs or projects, giving the recipient more freedom of action. However, there may be some strings attached even to nonproject aid; for example, much of it may have to be spent in the donor nation. Nonproject aid may also be repayable either in local or hard currency, depending on the terms imposed by the donor.

As noted earlier, some countries (most notably Communist nations) handle all of their assistance directly on a government-to-government basis with the recipient developing country. Other countries may give some aid on this basis, but are also Consortium members under World Bank chairmanship. There are such consortiums for a number of developing countries, including India whose consortium consists of a dozen relatively advanced nations.[48] The consortium agrees in principle each year how much aid of various types India should ideally get, but actual allotments are usually decided through bilateral talks between India and the individual consortium members. The United States is a member of all of the World Bank consortiums, and plays the leading role as donor in most.

Developing countries often face considerable uncertainty regarding the aid that they can expect from year to year, and this makes it more difficult to carry out medium- and long-term development planning. This in turn creates greater uncertainty for firms operating in and doing business with the recipient country. Uncertainties in the legislative procedures regarding foreign aid authorizations of many donor countries, including the United States, have increased in recent years. Few make definite aid commitments for more than one year, and quite often such commitments are late in coming. Moreover, the amount of aid agreed upon in principle by a World Bank consortium or individual donor country with regard to a recipient country often turns out to be significantly more than the actual amount finally provided.

Consortiums and major individual country donors tend to have a voice in what should and should not be done with the foreign aid provided, apart from the specific strings tied to project aid. However, in recent years pressures of this type have been geared more directly to the economic needs of the recipient nations than in the past, and there now seems to be fewer political or ideological overtones on such transactions.

The United States has been providing foreign assistance through three major agencies or sources. The most important agency has been the U.S. Agency for International Development (AID) which has had missions in many developing countries. It appears, however, that AID will soon be abolished. Its tasks will be partly taken over by a new International Development Corporation, as well as some other recently established organizations.[49] Through its Technical Cooperation Programs AID has provided outright grants and the services of specialists for a wide variety of projects and purposes — e.g., industry, agriculture, family planning, education, and health. AID has also provided both project and nonproject loans of many kinds, some repayable in dollars and others in local currency. Most AID assistance involving hard currency expenditures by the recipient country must usually be spent for American goods and services. Loans typically run for 40 years, with a 10-year grace period, and bear interest of 2 or 3 percent.

Interested firms frequently have received valuable help and support from AID if they have tied-in with its programs and priorities. AID has also tended to have at least some vested interest in those organizations which obtain loans from it. A number of enterprises — including some U.S. firms — have violated the terms of AID loans, and used the funds for unsanctioned purposes. Several have defaulted on AID loans.

The second major source of U.S. foreign aid has been Public Law 480 or the Food for Peace Program. This involves agricultural commodities (mostly foodstuffs, but also some other items like cotton and oils). Under PL 480, Title I, the United States sells commodities to developing nations on concessional terms. The bulk of the commodities is paid for in the local currency. However, the U.S. government typically returns much of the payments to the recipient government in the form of grants and loans (mostly loans) to be used for development purposes. Some is reserved for local currency loans to private firms as Cooley Funds.[50] American firms operating in the host country, indigenous firms having an affiliation with a U.S. company, and purely indigenous enterprises which facilitate the disposal of American agricultural products — e.g., flour mills, warehouses, and so forth — are eligible for such loans. The terms of the loans made to private firms are usually not nearly as liberal as those extended to the governments of developing countries. However, typically they are at least as favorable as those for any other types of borrowing that may be available.

Some of the funds returned under PL 480 are also reserved for U.S. government uses abroad.

Title II of PL 480 also provides assistance. It covers donations of agricultural commodities to help meet famine or other urgent and extraordinary relief requirements, and for distribution through voluntary agencies such as CARE, UNICEF, and church groups.

A third form of "assistance" involves loans from the U.S. Export-Import Bank. This bank authorizes loans, guarantees, and insurance to facilitate U.S. exports. It lends at commercial rates of interest related to its own cost of borrowing money. All loans are made and repayable in dollars. They may be short-term or medium-term in nature, but they are very rarely for more than 10 or 15 years. Both public and private sector organizations are eligible for Export-Import Bank loans if they qualify, as are purely indigenous firms, those having a foreign affiliation, and U.S. companies.

INDIA'S FOREIGN ASSISTANCE

India has received more total foreign assistance than any other developing country.[51] During the 1950-70 period, India's foreign assistance from all sources was around $17 billion and, of this total, over $9.5 billion (57 percent) has come from the United States. The World Bank and its affiliates have provided 13 percent; West Germany 7 percent, the United Kingdom 6 percent, and the Soviet Union 5.5 percent.

India's total foreign assistance, though still large, has been lower recently than in the past. Table 7-2 indicates India's gross aid (excluding assistance from the Communist bloc) during the 1966-71 period. "Gross aid utilized" consists of actual disbursements. The table also gives debt servicing figures, as well as net utilization figures for each fiscal year. To arrive at the net utilization figure, debt servicing and PL 480 food and nonfood agricultural imports have been subtracted. Net aid utilization is essentially the amount actually spent by India for development purposes. (It does not include drawings or repayments made on India's IMF account.)

Table 7-2 indicates that although gross aid utilization continues to be over $1 billion per year, it has dropped substantially from the $1.5 billion level of several years ago. The amount of project aid utilized has also been declining, while nonproject aid utilization shows no clear-cut pattern. PL 480 food aid has also been dropping off

TABLE 7-2 India's utilized foreign aid, 1966-71 period[52]
(in millions of dollars converted at the official exchange rate of $1 = 7.5 rupees)

	Total (gross aid utilized of all types)	Project aid	Nonproject aid (includes debt relief when extended)	PL 480- food	PL 480- nonfood	Debt servicing	Net aid utilization (for devel- opment)
1966-67	$1494	$497	$424	$538	$35	$365	$556
1967-68	1575	380	672	447	76	444	528
1968-69	1211	368	548	260	35	500	416
1969-70	1217	300	620	230	67	549	371
1970-71 (Projected)*	1140	280	590	230	40	550	320

*Although no definite figures on 1970-71 aid could be located at the time of this writing, indications are that total aid was at least $200 million below the projected figure of $1.14 billion.

quite substantially, while PL 480 nonfood aid utilized — e.g., cotton, oils, etc., which form only a small part of total PL 480 aid — shows no clear pattern. Debt servicing has continued to rise — in spite of some debt relief in some years — as outstanding debts have continued to grow. (India obtained about $76 million in debt relief in 1968-69, $94 million in 1969-70, and hopes to obtain $100 million in 1970-71). Perhaps the most important trend revealed in the table is the steady decline in the amount of net aid utilized for development purposes. Net aid utilization reached a 15-year low in 1969-70, and is expected to decline further in 1970-71.

Total aid "in the pipeline" (authorized but not utilized) declined from about $2.7 billion at the end of 1967-68 to $2.1 billion as of April 1, 1970. Of this $2.1 billion, about $1.6 billion was project aid and the rest nonproject. The amount in the pipeline has dropped as the Indian economy has recovered and picked up steam. Two billion dollars in pipeline aid is about enough to cover six month's import improvements.

Total aid authorized for India by consortium participants, excluding PL 480 aid, was $777 million for 1968-69, of which $135 million was project assistance and $642 million nonproject. In 1969-70, total authorizations were about $822 million, of which $292 million was project aid and $530 million nonproject. (This includes $160 million from the United States, all in nonproject aid, which was authorized after the Indian fiscal year ended, but just before the end of the U.S. fiscal year on June 30.)

In May, 1970 the Aid-India Consortium members, affiliates, and observers met and agreed in principle that a total aid authorization (excluding PL 480) for India of $1.1 billion was warranted for 1970-71. Of this, $400 million would be in project aid and $700 million in nonproject assistance (including $100 million in debt relief). The consortium also concluded that around $1.1 billion of annual aid during the entire Fourth Plan would be desirable for India. However, total authorizations in recent years have been roughly $400 million less than the one billion or more dollars agreed on in principle by the donors. This has apparently also been the case for 1970-71, although final figures for this period could not be located at this time. It appears, however, that India actually obtained between $850 and $900 million in 1970-71, which is more than was actually authorized in the several years preceding. The World Bank feels there is a serious underestimation of the foreign exchange needed to implement India's Fourth Plan. It is also concerned that India's overemphasis on self-reliance may lead to slower economic growth than India's planners have assumed.[53]

India is hoping that aid-giving nations and organizations will provide more in the way of nonproject aid and debt relief in the future, as well as longer-term aid commitments. The Fourth Plan originally called for gross foreign assistance of about $5.4 billion, but this has since been revised downward to $5.1 billion.[54] This compares to $4.7 billion received during the Third Plan period. The Fourth Plan estimates total debt service payments (amortization plus interest on foreign loans) — excluding IMF loans — at about $3 billion. This leaves only about $2 billion of external assistance for implementing the plan. If PL 480 aid is deducted from this, it leaves only about $1.5 billion, or an average of $300 million per year, which is significantly less than annual net aid utilization during the Third Plan period. (See Table 7-2.)

The chances of India getting as much as $5 billion in foreign assistance during the 1969-74 period do not appear to be favorable. Four to four and a half billion dollars seems to be a more realistic projection. This could lead to serious difficulties in achieving some key Fourth Plan objectives. This does not include the special aid going to the hordes of refugees from East Pakistan in the early 1970s.

Firms interested in or already doing business in India or other developing nations would be wise to keep track of the country's foreign aid situation. By so doing they can better anticipate the kinds of policies, controls, and restrictions the government is likely to retain or impose on business activity. U.S. companies may also be able to benefit from U.S. foreign aid commitments.

CHAPTER 7   FOOTNOTES

1. Cf., *Fourth Five Year Plan, 1969-74,* Planning Commission, Government of India, New Delhi, 1969, chap. 2.

2. Cf., *The Times of India,* Bombay, May 11 and June 2, 1970.

3. These figures are based on data compiled by The Reserve Bank of India and The Annual Survey of Industry. For a good qualitative presentation and overview of India's progress toward self-sufficiency in industry, see the *Financial Express,* Bombay, July 7, 1964, Export Supplement, sponsored by the Federation of Indian Export Organizations.

4. See *The Statesman,* Calcutta, June 22, 1966. The list of 59 priority industries — which is still in effect — can also be found in *Import Trade Control Policy* (The Red Book), Vol. 1, Ministry of Foreign Trade, New Delhi, for the year April 1969-March 1970, appendix 1.

5. See press releases from The World Bank dated May 28, 1970, issued from its Paris office, *Times of India,* Bombay, May 8, 17, and 30, 1970.

6. *Times of India,* Bombay, June 2, 1970.

7.   See *Bank of India Weekly Economic Survey,* April 9, 1970; *The Statesman Weekly,* New Delhi, April 4, 1970; *Times of India,* Bombay, April 1, 1970; *India News,* Indian Embassy, Washington D.C., April 10, 1970.

8.   Statistics on imports handled by government corporations and private traders are from sources cited in footnote 7.

9.   Details can be found in the annual Red and Blue Books put out annually by the Indian Ministry of Foreign Trade. Figures and other data presented in this section are also based on our own first-hand research in India.

10.   For details see the sources cited in footnote 7 above.

11.   See *The Times of India,* Bombay, April 1, 1970.

12.   *Ibid.*

13.   For details see *The Times of India,* Bombay, May 30, 1970.

14.   A dominant firm or undertaking is defined as a company which either by itself or through its affiliates produces, supplies, distributes, or otherwise controls not less than one-third of the total goods or services of a specific type, and of any description, within India.

15.   Executive Order 11387 (1968). See also G. Haberler and J. Willett, *Presidential Measures on Balance of Payments Controls*, American Enterprise Institute for Public Policy Research, Washington, D.C., 1968.

16.   These figures are from *Monthly Newsletter,* Indian Investment Centre, New York, November 15, 1969. See also the foreign investment survey in *Reserve Bank of India Bulletin,* August, 1969.
      In order to facilitate a comparative assessment of India's foreign investment position in 1966-67 with previous periods, the date for 1966-67 have been corrected to exclude the appreciation following the devaluation of the rupee on June 6, 1966. If no correction is made in this regard, the corresponding total outstanding foreign business investment figure as of March 31, 1967 would be 14.8 billion rupees rather than the 12.3 billion reported in the text. The 14.8 billion figure would be comprised of 7 billion in direct investments and 7.8 billion in portfolio investments.

17.   See sources cited in footnote 16.

18.   For a more precise definition of foreign portfolio investments in India see sources cited in footnote 16. Equity with regard to such investments includes scattered minority holdings of equity shares of firms, including indigenous firms, held by foreign nonresidents.

19.   See sources cited in footnote 16.

20.   See sources cited in footnote 16.

21.   Earnings is the sum of the U.S. share in net earnings (or losses) of foreign corporations and branch profits after foreign taxes but before U.S. taxes. Reinvested earnings are computed as the difference between the U.S. share of net earnings of foreign corporations and the U.S. share of gross dividends (before withholding taxes).

22.   Table 7-1 is based on data presented in the sources cited in footnote 16 above.

23.   Cf., *Fourth Five Year Plan 1969-74,* pp. 241-42.

24.   For more details, see *The Times of India,* Bombay, December 31, 1968. Kenya is the leading country in terms of actual and contemplated Indian joint ventures with 9, followed by Etheopia with 7.

25.   Cf., the results of a questionnaire survey in Negandhi, *op. cit.,* pp. 71-75. A. Negandhi, *Private Foreign Investment Climate in India,* (East Lansing, Mich.: Institute for International Business Management Studies, Michigan State University, 1965), pp. 71-75.

26.   *Times of India,* Bombay, May 13, 1970.

27. For sample balance of payments statements and related analyses for the United States and other selected countries see P. Samuelson. *Economics,* 7th Edition, The McGraw-Hill Book Co., New York, 1967, pp. 631-639; and R. Farmer and B. Richman, *International Business,* Richard D. Lewin Inc., 1966, pp. 167-174 and 246-257.

28. See Samuelson, *op. cit.,* pp. 638-639 and pp. 691-701.

29. These four stages are discussed in Samuelson, *op. cit.,* pp. 636-37.

30. Balance of payment and IMF drawings data for India have been obtained for monthly issues of the *Reserve Bank of India Bulletin* (see especially January, 1970 volume, pp. 9-15); and the *Statistical Abstract of India* (annual volumes). Estimates for the latest years have been derived from a number of personal sources, including Professor Martin Grossman of Harvard, a leading authority on the Indian economy.

31. *Near East and South Asia: Economic Growth Trends,* U.S. Agency for Industrial Development, Statistics and Report Division, Washington, D.C., November, 1968, p. 33.

32. *Times of India,* Bombay, May 30, 1970.

33. *Times of India,* May 13 and 19, 1970; *India News* (published by the Indian Embassy in Washington), April 10, 1970; *Fourth Five Year Plan, 1969-74, The Statesman,* Calcutta, July 29, 1969.

34. *Ibid.*

35. *Times of India,* May 19 and 30, 1970.

36. For figures on food grain imports and other key items for 1969 see *Asian Student,* May 23, 1970.

37. See sources cited in footnote 33 above.

38. See *Times of India,* Bombay, May 19, 1970; and *Fourth Five Year Plan,* p. 39.

39. See *Fourth Five Year Plan,* pp. 7-8, 13, 31-32, 38-41, 91-95, 275-76.

40. *Ibid.,* pp. 13-14, 31-32, 39.

41. *Ibid.,* p. 40.

42. *Ibid.,* pp. 39-41.

43. Categorization of products produced in India in terms of their degree of competitiveness in world markets is based in part on data provided in the *Fourth Five Year Plan, op. cit.,* a recently compiled World Bank report; industry studies recently completed under the auspices of London School of Economic's Unit for Economic and Statistical Studies on Higher Education; and price data compiled by India's Ministry of Industrial Development.

44. Data on India's imports can be found in the sources cited in footnote 43 above, as well as *Monthly Statistics of Foreign Trade of India* (published by the Dept. of Commercial Intelligence and Statistics, Government of India). See also *Times of India,* Bombay, May 8 and 30, 1970.

45. See *Fourth Five Year Plan,* pp. 38-39.

46. Cf., *Near East and South Asia: Economic Growth Trends,* Office of Program and Policy Coordination, AID, Washington, D.C., November, 1968, p. 33.

47. *Ibid.,* pp. 26-27.

48. The 12 members of the India Consortium are the United States, Canada, United Kingdom, West Germany, Japan, Italy, Austria, Denmark, Sweden, Holland, France, and Belgium. Norway, though not an official member, sends a representative to consortium meetings. So do IMF, OECD, and at times other international organizations.

49. More details can be found in various reports issued by the U.S. State Department, the U.S. Agency for International Development, as well as U.S. newspaper and magazine articles around April of 1971.

50. Named after Harold Cooley, former Chairman of the Agriculture Committee of the U.S. House of Representatives. He initiated the Cooley Ammendment to U.S. Public Law 480 which provides that a portion of the local currency proceeds from the sale of U.S. agriculture commodities shall be made available for lending in the private sector.

51. Data on India's foreign aid has been obtained primarily through World Bank and U.S. AID sources, Reserve Bank of India reports, and Indian government planning documents. We are indebted to Professor Martin Grossman of Harvard, a leading expert on the Indian economy, for helping us to resolve inconsistencies in some of the data given by different sources.

Among the recent unofficial sources also consulted were the following: *The Times of India,* Bombay, April 24, May 8, 9, 17, 30, June 2, 21, and 24, 1970; *Statesman Weekly,* Calcutta, June 27, 1970; *Asian Student,* May 4 and 9, 1970.

52. Table 7-2 is based on data provided by the sources cited in footnote 51. The figures for 1969-70 are tentative. The ones for 1970-71 are projections made by Professor Martin Grossman which are based on a careful examination of current sources, as well as firsthand information obtained recently from World Bank, AID, and Indian government sources.

53. This is the opinion of a number of experts consulted by us. See also D. Mukerjee, "India and the Donors," *Times of India,* May 30, 1970.

54. See *Fourth Five Year Plan, op. cit.,* pp. 91-92; and *Asian Student,* May 9, 1970.

PART 3
THE
MULTINATIONAL
CORPORATION

CHAPTER 8
THE MULTINATIONAL CORPORATION: BRIDGE OR BARRIER TO DEVELOPMENT?

Although the terms "multinational" and "international" corporation have been, and will continue to be, used interchangeably here, there is a conceptual difference between the two. The distinction, a matter of degree rather than an absolute notion, involves a spectrum or continuum of possibilities with the traditional international company at one extreme and a genuine multinational corporation at another. Few firms are actually at either extreme; however, a substantial majority will probably be closest to the international end of the spectrum.

MULTINATIONAL VERSUS INTERNATIONAL CORPORATIONS

The true multinational corporation has a unimodal global outlook. It recognizes environmental differences in different countries, but also realizes that many managerial methods and technical processes can be transmitted effectively to different countries. In fact, it approaches the whole transferability question in an empirical way, utilizing centralized controls and uniform policies in strategic areas, but only after a close examination of their true effects. It recognizes the fact that it can often learn much from host countries and is, therefore, a student as well as a teacher.

The genuine multinational corporation has also been called "geocentric" or "cosmopolitan."[1] If profitability is one of its key goals, it attempts to maximize returns in the course of time for the whole system, rather than overemphasizing profitability of its parent country operations. For example, if the parent country is the United States, and greater overall profitability on a global scale can be realized by cutting back U.S. operations or profits, the true multinational corporation would do so. In other words, the objectives of the overall system would take precedence over those of any one component.

The multinational firm usually provides for stock ownership in the parent company — if it clearly still has one — in the various countries in which it has operations, and other countries as well. Managers and other subsidiary employees are encouraged to obtain stock in the parent company. Each year, the annual stockholders meeting may be moved to a different country, just as many American corporations now move them from place to place in the United States.

Executive positions and other key jobs in the parent corporation, as well as abroad, are filled on the basis of merit and ability rather than nationality. Talent is recruited from around the globe.

The multinational corporation has a genuine global outlook, which emphasizes the need for comprehensive and integrated planning in conjunction with an effective system of strategic controls. It can be a powerful agency for regional and global economic unity, as well as a key instrument for providing progress, raising living standards, and peaceful coexistence. However, the structure of most nations and the parochialism of most private citizens limit such roles.

Few international corporations qualify for true multinational status. Unilever, Royal Dutch Petroleum (Shell) and Nestle, headquartered in the United Kingdom, Holland, and Switzerland, clearly are leaders in this regard. IBM and Union Carbide are among the front runners in the United States. However, the French president of IBM World Trade Corporation which handles IBM's international business, does not sit on the parent company's board of directors and IBM World Trade is still basically a subsidiary of the parent IBM.

International corporations see themselves largely as domestic companies (i.e., domestic in reference to their parent country), even those which have large and well-structured foreign operations. They operate abroad but retain ownership and management, and usually view the world from the vantage point of their country of origin. They are bimodal in that parent company operations are not seen as elements of the multinational or global system. Instead, international activities are viewed as appendages to domestic operations. They may be considered important, but they are subservient to the objectives and interests of the parent firm. They frequently insist, within subsidiary operations, on the primacy of methods used at home and often even of the laws and values of the home country.

Such corporations tend to display rigid attitudes of superiority and to assume that any methods that work at home can and will work abroad. Final decisions relating to international operations often rest with people primarily concerned with domestic matters, who cannot adequately take into account significant local environmental differences. In the interest of uniformity, they frequently impose procedures and controls on foreign affiliates which lead to serious problems and have unintended effects. This kind of international corporation is referred to by some authors as being "ethnocentric" or "monocentric."[2]

Many firms combine some of the characteristics of multinationalism and internationalism. They regard domestic operations as separate and distinct from foreign activities, with coordination confined largely to areas in which domestic operations have strong interests. But they tend to be more sensitive to local conditions and traditions abroad, and respect local jurisdiction and national policies more than ethnocentric firms. They also make a greater effort to accommodate to the requirements and aspirations of host countries, and give their foreign affiliates more autonomy than do ethnocentric corporations. Local subsidiaries are also more likely to be run by local nationals. However, many do not provide solid central control in key managerial areas. As a result the overall operation is likely to run less efficiently than it would otherwise.

The kind of international corporation just described has been referred to as "polycentric."[3] A common problem with the polycentric corporation, especially in its more extreme form, is that it tends to be sensitive to foreign environmental differences and significantly underestimates the extent to which methods which work at home can be transferred and utilized successfully abroad. It is not as effective a change agent as is the multinational firm since it operates under the assumption that local managers usually know what is best for the subsidiary, and that unique solutions are needed to deal with most local problems. In many cases, this kind of international corporation is actually a confederation of rather loosely connected affiliates.

In general, traditional ethnocentric international companies tend to be the most vulnerable to negative criticism, hostility, and attacks abroad. Polycentric corporations are less vulnerable but where too much emphasis is placed on accommodating to local environmental conditions, serious suboptimization problems are likely to result. Geocentric corporations are less vulnerable to attack than ethnocentric enterprises, and more efficient and effective on a global scale than either ethnocentric or polycentric firms. However, they may be more vulnerable to criticism in some countries – at least in the short run – then polycentric companies; they are change agents and they place greater stress on overall corporate objectives and efficiency. In the long run, the geocentric approach to international business will no doubt prove to be by far the most effective. In the short range there will continue to be notable exceptions.

ENVIRONMENTAL CONSTRAINTS AND THE EMERGENCE OF GENUINE MULTINATIONAL CORPORATIONS

The emergence of true multinational corporations is constrained not only by parent company policies and objectives, but also by external environmental conditions beyond the corporation's control. Domestic and international legal rules; monetary and fiscal policies; political, military and national security considerations; economic conditions; ideologies; and sociological-cultural factors seriously interfere with the notion of the multinational enterprise. Such constraints strongly inhibit flows of capital, goods, services, people, and ideas, across national boundaries.

What is needed are reasonable and effective supranational coordinating and regulating mechanisms to "de-politicize" international business and reduce major disparities in national policies which bear on multinational corporations. [4] Ideally, one may visualize a World Corporation Authority, possibly established under the aegis of the United Nations, to charter and regulate multinational enterprises. This would require some basic departures in the way the U.N. and other international agencies currently operate; but it is by no means beyond the realm of possibility. A true world government may well become a possibility, as men come to recognize and accept the fact that the present order cannot effectively deal with such problems as the arms race, the population explosion, human misery, pollution, and the awesome technological and social revolutions taking place. Critical environmental conditions which currently influence the emergence of multinational corporations include:

1. Balance of payments difficulties: in the United States, these have placed pressure on international companies to restrain their foreign investments and capital outflows, increase their repatriated income from abroad, decrease their imports, and increase their exports. For example, pressures to increase exports often impel U.S. parent operations to impose U.S. products on their foreign subsidiaries at the expense of less costly sources of supply, and inhibit the freedom of the subsidiaries to develop and exploit their own export capabilities.

2. Parochial profit interests and foreign trade protection: as overseas activities have expanded, a new force has come into prominence. For example, many U.S. firms have foreign affiliates which are now major suppliers to U.S. markets, as well as foreign markets. Consequently, imports which "hurt" domestic operations may benefit foreign subsidiaries. Although the total operation may benefit from such subsidiary operations, U.S. companies still pursue what is best only in terms of the interests of their domestic operations.

3. Taxation: many tax regulations extend beyond national boundaries and tax the operations of subsidiaries even though they have little contact with the parent country.

4. Domestic legal and value systems: the application of U.S. anti-trust regulations to foreign operations is an example of the way a parent nation can attempt to assert its values abroad. The same is true of sanctions in connection with trading with various communist nations.

COMMON CHARGES AGAINST INTERNATIONAL COMPANIES

The international or multinational corporation is, among other things, a type of private "government," often richer in assets and more populous in employees and stockholders than some of the national states in which it conducts its business. Most also carry strong identification with their parent nations — an obvious political problem in some areas.

U.S. international companies are among the most vulnerable to criticism and attack for reasons apart from how they may actually behave. They are seen as representatives of the world's richest and most powerful nation. They are often accused of being instruments of imperialism and exploitation, especially by leftists and radicals. Traditional and conservative elements view them as threatening invaders who upset the status quo by disrupting "orderly" markets, engaging in "reckless" financial practices, paying "extravagant" wages and salaries, and by being "insensitive" to local customs and traditions. The realization of this vulnerability must play a significant role in the decision-making processes of the astute U.S. international executive.

Instruments or promoters of imperialism

American international corporations are viewed by many as collaborators in the U.S. government's efforts to enhance its national power in the world. Conversely, they are also perceived as influencing U.S. foreign policy to act in their own interests. While there may be truth to these charges in some cases, most critics do not recognize that the era of U.S. "gunboat diplomacy" and "dollar blackmail" in international business has been on the wane for some time.

American firms now carry much of the risk of doing business abroad, and they cannot always count on the U.S. government to bail them out or even apply pressure on their behalf. This is evidenced by the number of recent expropriations of U.S. corporate properties abroad without U.S. government intervention and by the many stringent restrictions and strong pressures imposed on U.S. operations abroad by many host countries.

Exploitation

Exploitation is another common charge still made against U.S. operations abroad. Unfortunately there is good historical evidence to back such charges in many cases. International firms, particularly in the extractive and mining industries and agriculture, did frequently obtain highly favorable concessions from local authorities through power plays or corrupt practices. They also often made huge profits, thus contributing little and taking much from the host nation.

In recent times this pattern has become the exception rather than the norm, but frequent charges of exploitation still persist. In some cases they are valid, but in most they are greatly exaggerated, if not wholly unjustified. Often the charge of exploitation is based on the naive idea that the foreign company expends irreplaceable natural resources without providing a *quid pro quo*. However, critics commonly overlook or underestimate the risks assumed by the foreign firm in searching for and developing local resources, and the contributions made to the host country's material welfare by the foreign company that succeeds. It is easy to point to "extravagant" profits being realized by successful foreign operations and forget the unsuccessful ventures, uncertainties, hard work, skill, and long delays experienced in creating a profitable enterprise.

Exploitation arising out of the monopoly power of foreign companies has also been reduced on a broad front in recent times. In fact, indigenous firms are likely to have greater monopoly power than international firms in most countries as more and more nations place greater restrictions on the monopoly power of international firms, and U.S. anti-monopoly laws reach abroad.

Charges of exploitation involving U.S. companies are not nearly as common in India today as they are in other poor countries. They come mainly from the more extreme leftist and radical quarters in India. Most of the foreign-owned and operated plantations, and firms engaged in the extractive industries in India, have been British rather than American. Hence, exploitation charges have been more common against the British. Furthermore, in the area of wages and salaries, U.S. firms in India are usually criticized not for exploitation, but for being too "extravagant."

Local equity participation

The wholly-owned subsidiary is still the predominant form of American direct corporate investment abroad, and this is a source of conflict and resentment. Due to national pride and economic considerations (especially if the foreign enterprise is profitable) the host country wants its citizens, or at times its government, to have a major piece of the action through equity participation.

On the other hand, the international company frequently requires a majority position to ensure management control so that decisions will be based upon "objective" economic criteria. However, it is worth repeating again that an inflexible approach of this type frequently leads to serious difficulties.

A common source of conflict relating to joint equity participation involves what the international company "pays" for its equity position. If it provides equipment, or other commodities, services, or know-how, at substantially inflated prices in lieu of cash, conflict can develop as times goes on. If the foreign firm acquires a majority equity position by this means, difficulties are likely to be even greater.

It is common for a specific international company to be in a particularly strong bargaining position — especially in poor countries or high-risk situations — because of its unique products, patents, special know-how, and the like. In such situations, it may be unwise for the company to use its strength to "buck the inevitable tide." This is likely to lead to deep-seated resentment on the part of the host government or local partners which can manifest itself in adverse ways in the future.

Repatriation of earnings and service fees

Hostility over majority foreign ownership of firms, is likely to be accompanied by strong resentment over the repatriation of earnings by international companies which own such firms, especially if the parent company regularly repatriates all or nearly all of the earnings it may be entitled to by law, leaving little or nothing for reinvestment with the foreign affiliate. Such a policy regarding the repatriation of earnings is viewed by many as a form of exploitation.

Many international companies — especially of the ethnocentric type — do "milk" various foreign subsidiaries in order to increase their profitability at home. It may be the wise thing to do if the viability of the foreign affiliate is in serious doubt, or even if stringent restrictions or a local currency devaluation is expected in the near future which would greatly reduce the amount of earnings that the parent will be allowed to repatriate. But, often the best strategy from a global viewpoint, taking into account longer term considerations, would be to reinvest more of the foreign earnings in the host country. If international companies do not do this voluntarily, they may eventually be compelled to do so under unpleasant and unfavorable circumstances.

Another common criticism of international firms relates to the fees charged by the parent for services provided to its foreign affiliates. Such service fees are usually paid in hard currency and, therefore, constitute a drain on foreign exchange. Critics overlook the substantial benefits derived by the host country, which may include: training activities; the importation of know-how; the implementation of new plants, projects, and products; more effective production processes; import substitution; and greater operating efficiency.

On the other hand, many international firms continue to provide services to their foreign affiliates which could be performed adequately — and often much more cheaply — by the affiliates. Also parent companies sometimes charge questionably high fees for some of the services they provide.

Research and development

A common criticism of American international companies is that they centralize research and development activities — including engineering as well as scientific research — in the United States, while relegating foreign operations primarily to routine tasks (e.g. "hewing wood and drawing water"). This can also be a major issue in the conflict over service fees and royalty payments. However, most less-developed countries present educational and sociological-cultural constraints which severely limit the nature and amount of R & D that the international firm can effectively perform there. Often, the risks are higher and economy of scale considerations make local R & D impractical.

On the other side of the issue, many firms assume that R & D should be centralized in the parent country, while R & D activities which are assigned abroad go usually only to other advanced countries. The available and potential supply of local scientific, technical, and engineering talent in many of the less advanced countries is overlooked, as is the opportunity to develop products, materials and production processes which are more suitable to local conditions.

Import and export restrictions

A charge frequently made and often valid, is the allegation that foreign affiliates of U.S. corporations are obliged to pursue import and export policies that serve United States interests rather than those of the host countries. Affiliates are often required to purchase goods and services from their parent companies, restrict their exports to the United States or third countries, and forego the use of imports from, or exports to, various communist nations. Some U.S. parent companies have voluntarily eased such policies where they are able, in recent times. However, actions taken by host governments seem to be the major change agents in this area.

Intracorporate transfer prices

Criticisms about the intracorporate transfer price of international companies is common in government circles. Multinational corporations often establish the prices of goods and services which flow from one part of the overall company to another so as to increase revenues and profits at certain points while reducing them at others. The minimization of overall tax liabilities is usually the chief reason for this sort of action. In many cases, the amounts are grossly unfair to one of the trading partners. But, this is stimulated not only by corporate policy and objectives, but also by national disparities in tax regulations and other matters.

Use of foreign nationals in key managerial jobs

Gone are the days when international firms can send large numbers of personnel from the home country on a relatively permanent basis, to manage and operate their foreign ventures. More and more countries have adopted laws which restrict the number and types of foreigners that firms can employ. At the same time, rising educational levels and improvements in sociological-cultural environments abroad have made it easier and more feasible for international companies to obtain competent local nationals for their foreign operations. Moreover, even if local nationals are generally not as effective as, say Americans, they may still perform adequately and their pay is usually considerably less — much less in poor countries. Hence, there are sizeable net economic benefits derived by employing them.

Criticisms of multinational corporations over inadequate use of local nationals now tends to be most common and harsh in connection with key managerial jobs (as well as engineering, scientific, and technical work which has already been discussed). Often critics do not understand the kinds of training, abilities, experience, motivational factors and personality traits that are required for effective and efficient management. They overlook potent educational and sociological-cultural constraints in their country which severely limit the supply of managerial talent which comes anywhere close to U.S. standards. Nor do they comprehend the risks entailed for the international firm if seriously deficient and unqualified local nationals assume key managerial jobs.

Many international companies do not do as much as they could (and should) in developing and utilizing available managerial talent in host countries. Some companies will staff top-level managerial jobs with local citizens only in countries where language, values, and the educational system closely resemble those of the home country. For example, an American international firm would probably staff its Canadian, and possibly its British and Australian operations, with local managers.

However, if the international firm took the time and effort to seek and train local citizens for key managerial jobs, benefits would often outweigh the costs and risks. These managers better comprehend the value system and overall environment of the host country, usually receive salaries much lower than those required to attract a U.S. employee, and can frequently provide better governmental, union, employee, and general public relations in the host country.

The most effective local nationals for top-level subsidiary jobs have usually had substantial training in the firm's parent country, or in some other advanced industrial nation. This training may have been derived through formal education, management development programs, company training or work experience. Managerial experience and special training programs abroad seem to be significant factors in contributing to success, and a well-trained local national placed in a top-level subsidiary job who has also been exposed firsthand to parent company operations is frequently in the best position to blend local environmental considerations with the interests of the parent firm in the decision-making process. Often he is also the best person to determine which of the U.S. policies, practices, and techniques are most applicable in his own country.

Insenistivity to local customs, values, needs, and practices

U.S. international firms, as represented by their foreign affiliates, are frequently said to be insensitive to local values, practices, and customs. Such criticism is more likely to be the case if an American or other foreigner is in charge. But it is quite often so even when a local citizen is put in charge, because of the type of person selected for the job or because of the constraints and policies imposed on the subsidiary by the parent company. Such charges are frequently justified.

The international company often goes too far in imposing its own notions about government's role and how it should be dealt with. The same is often true with regard to welfare matters, union relations, and personnel policies and practices. Where the foreign environment is substantially different than the U.S. environment such an ethnocentric approach not only upsets local citizens, but also hinders the firm's performance.

Overcentralized management

Another common complaint levelled against the international corporation is that it overcentralizes decision making in its head office, leaving only routine management decisions to its foreign subsidiaries and affiliates. Excessive overcentralization often gives the subsidiary a "foreign" image in the host country, and this results in great resentment. In fact, overcentralization is a prime cause of many of the other criticisms against international corporations which have already been discussed.

Some key decisions and policies should be centralized in any multinational corporation. But most decisions would best be made at the local level, within a broad set of global policies and guidelines.

International firms too often rationalize the lack of delegation of authority to foreign subsidiaries on the grounds that they do not have enough qualified and trustworthy managers for these operations — people they could discover, train, and assign such responsibility to if they made the effort.

A strong argument can be made for decentralization of authority to countries which have environmental conditions very different from the parent nation. Uniform policies and standardized methods are less likely to prove applicable or effective in such countries, and faulty assumptions by headquarters management about unique local conditions are likely to be more common. Hence, multinational corporations should expend considerable effort to develop capable managers for their operations in less developed countries.

MAJOR BENEFITS DERIVED BY HOST COUNTRIES FROM INTER-NATIONAL BUSINESS OPERATIONS

In spite of the many criticisms of multinational corporations, host countries derive substantial net gains and benefits from foreign operations in their nation. While some foreign operations are clearly more beneficial to the host country than others, virtually all contribute at least something.

Direct private foreign investment by multinational corporations usually provides desirable risk capital to host countries. In contrast to most foreign government investment, apart from gifts and grants, the recipient country does not incur the same kinds of direct interest and debt repayment obligations which exist regardless of the effectiveness of the aid. If the foreign venture proves successful the international firm will, of course, want to repatriate profits and possibly capital as well. However, success for the foreign company usually means various kinds of benefits for the host country. Moreover, private foreign business investments and also frequently licensing agreements tend to be inherently superior to governmental aid as an instrument of development because they combine direct transfers of technical and managerial assistance with that of capital.

In developing countries multinational corporations provide capital and undertake risks in sectors where private firms in the host country and its government do not have the resources, motivation, or interest, to go. Foreign capital investment frequently leads to new and better products, more productive technology, more efficient processes superior management, and better development and use of the country's resources.

The foreign operation contributes directly to national income and public revenues through the additional wages and salaries and net increases in employment it provides, the rent it may pay on land and facilities, the interest it pays on local borrowing, the taxes it pays to the host government, and the profits it reinvests for further expansion or pays out as income to local investors. It contributes indirectly by creating derived demand effects and stimulating various indigenous firms in the economy. For example, it stimulates the sales of local suppliers and helps its customers expand and improve their operations by the goods and services it provides. This, in turn, increases its suppliers' and customers' net value added, resulting in contributions to national income. U.S. affiliates abroad also often render various forms of direct assistance to improve the operations of the local organization with which they interact.

On the average, U.S. subsidiaries tend to be more efficient than indigenous firms, especially in developing countries. This means that the U.S. firms are likely to economize on the use of national resources through internal operating efficiencies. Through their activities and positive income-generating and public revenue effects, foreign firms also stimulate greater external economies in the host country — particularly with regard to infrastructure and social overhead capital items such as transportation industrial parts, roads, housing, hospitals, welfare, schools and public utilities. This also benefits other users since they can obtain and use such facilities and services in greater quantities, at lower costs, and often of higher quality and dependability. More-over, benefits are achieved to the extent that foreign firms bear the costs of building, operating and providing such facilities and services themselves, either voluntarily or by law.

Subsidiaries and affiliates of U.S. multinational corporations usually do a better job of training personnel and upgrading local talent than do indigenous firms. They can also act as an effective catalyst for social change by recruiting, developing, and utilizing personnel who have attitudes and motivations more conducive to productive efficiency, economic achievement, and national development. U.S. subsidiaries also tend to be more dynamic in stimulating new markets.

Perhaps most importantly, U.S. subsidiaries frequently bring with them a host of new ideas, concepts, approaches, values, and attitudes, many of which are applied successfully and benefit the host country's development. As time passes indigenous enterprises come to utilize those which have proven most effective. U.S. firms also tend to spur a greater quest for efficiency and competitive spirit in many of their indigenous counterparts, and frequently develop local entrepreneurship by taking in local partners, by their collaborative activities, and because personnel they have trained leave to work for local enterprises or to set up their own businesses.

In general, too few international firms even attempt to make a careful assessment of how their foreign operations could and actually do benefit the host countries in which they operate or how they come into conflict with the interests of these countries. They need to do a better job of identifying the interests of their subsidiaries with those of host nations in every possible way that is likely to have favorable mutual effects. They must also do a more effective job of publicizing the genuine benefits host countries derive from their operations, as well as the risks and costs that they assume.

COMPARATIVE ADVANTAGES OF MULTINATIONAL CORPORATIONS

Most international firms fail to capitalize on many of the potential competitive advantages available to them. All tend to have some significant potential competitive advantages over most of their purely domestic and indigenous counterparts, especially in less developed countries.

Multinational corporations and their foreign affiliates have greater access to more sources of capital, and often can obtain funds at significantly lower costs, than their indigenous counterparts. They can derive competitive advantages from their ability to shift funds and other resources among operations in different countries, and by manipulating their profitability and tax positions in ways which benefit or suit them. Because of their size and diversity, they can also afford to take greater risks which can result in higher profits — and can better deal with crises, e.g., a serious recession, a major strike, or government threats. As a result, they are often in stronger bargaining positions than are local firms.

International corporations usually have superior technical, scientific, and managerial know-how. Effective transmission of such information to their foreign affiliates leads to substantial competitive advantages over local firms. In fact, competitive advantages may often be possible in all enterprise and managerial functions. However, these corporations usually do a more effective job with the transfer and application of technical know-how than they do with managerial know-how.

The foreign affiliates of international firms have access to considerably more new and better products and personnel, including local nationals working or studying abroad. Moreover, in many countries the most talented and best motivated citizens of the host country (especially those not members of the elite class) prefer to work for a foreign subsidiary since they will have greater opportunities to use their talents and better themselves.

Major multinational corporations endow their affiliates with much of their own prestige via brand names and general image. This provides the subsidiaries with a distinct competitive advantage in local marketing. Furthermore, the contacts of the parent firm can provide the foreign affiliate with competitive advantages in procuring imports and marketing exports.

The many potential and actual competitive advantages that the affiliates of multi-national corporations have over their counterparts in host countries is an understand-able source of resentment on the part of their indigenous competitors. In fact, it is often the root of local condemnation of international firms. However, when properly used, these advantages can benefit the host country significantly. These companies must want to, and be free to, act as "good citizens" in their host nations. In any event, excessive protection from foreign competition over a prolonged period of time is likely to do more harm than good in terms of the host country's development.

FOOTNOTES FOR CHAPTER 8

1. See H. Perlmutter, "Social Architectural Problems of the Multinational Firm," *AISEC Quarterly Journal,* August, 1967; H. Perlmutter, "L'Entreprise International: Trois Conceptions," *Revue Economique et Sociale,* Lausanne, May, 1965; and H. Thorelli, "The Multinational Corpora-tion as a Change Agent," *Southern Journal of Business,* July, 1966.

2. *Ibid.*

3. *Ibid.*

4. Neil Jacoby also expresses this position in his recent comprehensive article, "The Multinational Corporation," *The Center Magazine,* Vol. III, No. 3, 1970, May, 1970.

5. Jacoby considers some of the same criticisms in his article cited above. However, he focuses chiefly on relatively advanced countries.

SELECTED BIBLIOGRAPHY

Barber, R., "The Political Dimensions of Corporate Supranationalism, *"Worldwide P & I Planning,* Sept. — Oct. 1969.

Behrman, J., *Some Patterns in the Rise of the Multinational Enterprise,* University of North Carolina Press, Chapel Hill, 1969.

Behrman, J., *National Interests and the Multinational Enterprise,* Prentice Hall Inc., 1970.

Blough, R., *International Business: Environment and Adaptation,* McGraw-Hill Book Co., New York, 1966.

Boddewyn, J., "Le Defi Americain: Challenge and Response," *Business Horizons,* June, 1969.

Broehl, W., *The International Basic Economy Corporation,* published by the National Planning Association in its series titled "United States Business Performance Abroad," New York, 1968.

"The Man Who Makes it One World for IBM," *Business Week,* July 18, 1970, pp. 90-92.

Special Report, Multinational Companies, *Business Week,* December 19, 1970, pp. 57-146.

Donner, F., *The Worldwide Industrial Enterprise,* McGraw-Hill Book Co., New York, 1967.

Dunning, J., *American Investment in British Manufacturing,* Allen and Unwin, London, 1958.

Dunning, J., "The Foreign Investment Controversy," *The Bankers Magazine,* (U.K.), May, 1969 and June, 1969.

Farmer, R., and Richman, B., *International Business: An Operational Theory,* Richard D. Irwin, Inc., Homewood, Ill., 1966.

Fayerweather, J., *Facts and Fallacies of International Business,* Holt, Rinehart and Winston, New York, 1962.

Hitchen, D., *Canadianization of United States Controlled Corporations in Canada*, UCLA doctoral dissertation, Graduate School of Business Administration, Los Angeles, 1965.

Ingram, J., *International Economic Problems*, Wiley, New York, 1966.

Jacoby, N., "The Multinational Corporation," *The Center Magazine*, May, 1970.

Johnson, H., *The World Economy of the Crossroads*, Oxford Univ. Press, New York, 1965.

Kindleberger, C., *American Business Abroad*, Yale University Press, New Haven, 1969.

Kindleberger, C., *International Economics*, 4th ed., Richard D. Irwin, Homewood, Ill., 1968.

Krause, W., and Mathis, F., *International Economics and Business*, Houghton Mifflin, Boston, 1968.

Mason, E., "The Corporation in the Post Industrial State: at Home and Abroad," *California Management Review*, Summer, 1970.

McCreary, E., *The Americanization of Europe*, Doubleday, New York, 1964.

McMillan, C., Gonzales, R., and Erikson, L., *International Enterprise in a Developing Economy*, Michigan State University Press, East Lansing, 1964.

United States Business Performance Abroad, a series of 13 studies dealing with the operations of multinational corporations in different countries, chiefly developing nations, published by the National Planning Association, New York.

Perlmutter, H., "Social Architectural Problems of the Multinational Firm," *AISEC Quarterly Journal*, August, 1967.

Perlmutter, H., "L'Enterprise International: Trois Conceptions," *Revue Economique et Sociale*, Lausanne, May, 1965.

Polk, J., "The New World Economy," *Columbia Journal of World Business*, Jan. − Feb., 1968.

Richman, B., *A Firsthand Study of Industrial Management and Economic Development in India*, Agency for International Development, Office of Program and Policy Coordination, Research Report, Washington, D.C., December, 1969.

Robinson, R., *International Business Policy*, Holt, Rinehart, Winston, New York, 1964.

Rolf, S., *The International Corporation*, International Chamber of Commerce, Paris, May, 1969.

Root, F., "The Expropriation Experience of American Companies," *Business Horizons*, April, 1968.

Rose, S., "The Rewarding Strategies of Multinationalism," *Fortune*, Sept. 15, 1968.

Saforian, A., *Foreign Ownership of Canadian Industry*, McGraw-Hill Book Co., Toronto, 1966.

Servan-Schreiber, J.J., *The American Challenge*, Atheneum, New York, 1968.

Tannenbaum, F., "The Survival of the Fittest," *Columbia Journal of World Business*, March − April, 1968.

Tanzer, M., and Cordell, A., "Multinational Corporations: Price to Host Countries," *The Nation*, July 6, 1970, pp. 17-20.

Thorelli, H., "The Multinational Corporation as a Change Agent," *Southern Journal of Business*, July, 1966.

Vernon, R., "The Multinational Corporation," *The Atlantic Community Quarterly*, Winter, 1967-68.

Vernon, R., "Multinational Corporations and Foreign Sovereignty," *Harvard Business Review*, March − April, 1967.

Yoshino, M., "International Business: What is the Best Strategy," *The Business Quarterly*, Fall, 1966.

Zenoff, D., *Private Enterprise in Developing Countries*, Prentice-Hall, Englewood Cliffs, N.J., 1969.

CHAPTER 9 MANAGEMENT OF MULTINATIONAL CORPORATIONS

The multinational or international corporation can be viewed as a three-element system in which each element functions within a different set of environmental conditions. The first contains the headquarters operation of the international firm. The second element consists of its subsidiary operations. The third element contains the linking devices which connect the center or headquarters to its foreign subsidiaries and affiliates; linkage which provides channels for the information flows and controls necessary between the center and its subsidiaries. This element is the main focus of this chapter.

SPECIAL ASPECTS OF THE MULTINATIONAL ENVIRONMENT

We have already examined the sets of environmental conditions which relate to the first two elements of the multinational corporate system; i.e., headquarters and subsidiary operations. We have not yet considered the environment surrounding, and in part evolving from, the linkages between the headquarters and its foreign affiliates. This is the most difficult environment to identify or measure, although it is highly important and central to the management process. Unlike the other kinds of environmental conditions, it does not have substance in itself, and it tends to be considerably more abstract and difficult to quantify. It does not have an average annual mean temperature that can be recorded, a literacy rate or average educational level which may be quantified, geographical characteristics that can be clearly mapped, or measurable economic indices. Yet it is as real as these other environmental conditions.

Both the subsidiary and head office environments concern specific countries and peoples contained therein. The special environment surrounding the multinational corporation, however, relates to the interaction between the various foreign country environments and the environment of the headquarters or parent country; and also directly between the headquarters and its affiliates. We refer to this as the "multinational environment."

The existence of a separate "multinational environment" is often denied by academicians, and by others as well. The subject is dismissed with the statement "all of the elements contained in multinational business are found, to one extent or another, in domestic business, and, consequently, any environmental differences are solely questions of degree, and are not unique in themselves." To some extent, this may be true. However, very different environmental conditions can result when similar components of systems are mixed in varying degrees. For example, few people would deny the existence of a significant difference between a beautiful sand beach along the shores of a clear blue lake, and a bed of quicksand. Yet both may contain identical components of sand and water. Certainly one would not deal with the two situations in the same manner nor would one expect the two environments to react to stimuli in similar fashion. In essence, we have two distinct although related environments. New inventions are also recombinations of already existing ideas, e.g., sophisticated electronic computers evolving from relatively simple desk calculators.

The same kind of chemistry takes place when a firm begins to operate across national boundaries. However, because this multinational environment is less tangible than the others, it is often overlooked, and consequently becomes the source of many problems. It is not related specifically to the locus of operations, but pertains more to the *mix* of environments in which the company must function. The multinational environment has four basic components: 1) relationship between operations of the parent firm and the international headquarters; 2) distances; 3) degree; 4) diversity.

Elements deriving from the proximity of domestic operations

In the United States and elsewhere, most international activities of corporations are outgrowths of domestic activities. Usually, occasional foreign orders evolved into the establishment of export departments which in turn led to the establishment of operations within foreign countries and the formation of additional organizational units to direct them. As a result of this historical pattern corporate management often views international operations as an appendage to domestic operations. This does not readily lend itself to an organizational concept that places global management at the focal point and relegates domestic operations to the position of one element within a total system. The result is an ethnocentric entity as discussed in the previous chapter.

In such corporations, the international "appendage" is subservient to domestic goals, policies, and other domestic considerations. Many of the executives responsible for international operations will have at least two titles, one relating to their position in the parent organization (often synonomous with domestic operations) and another relating to their position in the international organization. The chief decision-making executive with respect to international activities is frequently located one or more levels below the chief executive officer of the overall corporation, who is usually the chief executive officer or board chairman of the domestic operation. Figure 9-1 contrasts this type of structure with that of multinational firm.

The view of international operations as a "sideline" has major implications for foreign activities. As space is curved as a result of the gravitational forces of large bodies, the environment of international management is altered by the proximity and interests of the domestic parent. Where executives who must make or sanction decisions for the total enterprise are oriented primarily toward domestic conditions, requests by managers of foreign operations tend to be viewed within a priority system based on domestic considerations.

For example, for many years the federal and local governments within the United States have assumed primary responsibility for providing or controlling services in such fields as education, welfare, transportation, power generation, and so forth. Because

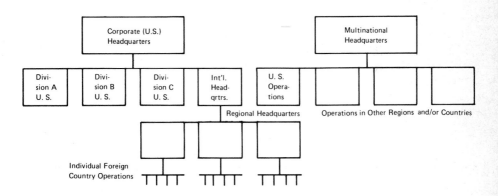

FIGURE 9-1   Structural differences between the international and multinational company

they do not have to spend a great deal of time and effort thinking about these matters, U.S. Corporate executives frequently take them for granted. They tend to overlook the importance which such services have for industrial activities. Many foreign countries do not or cannot adequately provide similar facilities. Consequently, the overseas executive concerned with managerial problems in such nations who suggests that his firm assume a significant part of this role can usually anticipate substantial resistance from headquarters personnel who believe that such activities are the responsibility of government agencies and not of private industrial enterprises.

Similarly, the installation of automated equipment in subsidiary operations instead of employing labor intensive processes is often based on experience derived directly from domestic operations. The needs and conditions of the local situation abroad are ignored.

It is common for headquarters individuals to see serious and foreboding precedents in the kinds of actions which should or must be taken abroad (e.g., the establishment of "socialistic or welfare states"). Even when the subsidiary manager is able to win his case, he may have to expend an inordinate amount of time and effort to do so. Consequently, the decision process is seriously retarded.

Distance

Problems relating to distance are not unique to international operations. The domestic corporation with plants or branches situated in New York, Atlanta, Chicago, Houston, and Los Angeles must deal with the question of distance every day. Basically, the geographic dispersement of subunits within the organization tends to complicate the overall logistical and linkage functions, including the processes of communication and control. The same areas are affected when operations are extended to foreign countries. However, two major factors tend to make international distance problems more complex than domestic. These relate to facilities and attitudes respectively.

The facilities available for operating across national boundaries are more limited — often dramatically so — than those existent within the United States. Hence, logistical support becomes more difficult.

Frequent and dependable air service, prompt rail freight, and efficient postal and trucking services between New York and Chicago make it easy for a domestic firm to shift inventories or other resources from the New York to the Chicago operations, should the need arise. Similarly, the domestic firm's purchasing agents are able to deal in a country-wide market with the assurance that in most cases, only small price differentials (arising from transportation cost) will modify their search for the best and cheapest items. In most cases, procurement time differentials are slight from one geographic area to another because of the efficiency of the means to move goods and the lack of trade barriers. With respect to supply and market area within the United States, the company needs only to consider the economics of transportation costs when it develops its logistical network, and it may decide to ship to a given area from a nearby plant or from a plant at a great distance. Transportation costs are also well defined.

The situation changes substantially when operations are extended abroad. Lead times increase dramatically. Extra handling (often resulting in increased damage) is involved in transporting goods overseas. Consequently, additional constraints are placed on international logistical networks which do not exist on the domestic scene. The locus of the supplier of goods, or the geographic relationship of the market to manufacturing facilities becomes much more important and options become more restricted. In many cases, transportation rate structures become more complex. If overland shipping is required, it may necessitate several transfers between carriers, and it may take considerable guesswork to determine costs and delivery times. Packaging must be changed to withstand the greater rigors to which goods moving in the international area will be subject. Provision must be made for the goods to be inspected at borders or other points of entry. Documentation can increase to burdensome levels.

In similar fashion, communications also become more complex. Days may be required to place an overseas telephone call — the same call which could be made in a matter of seconds within the domestic environment. When the call goes through, voices may be unintelligible due to noise and static. The excellent communications facilities which exist in the United States lend themselves readily to integrated communications networks, where data may be fed from the various operating subunits of the firm into a central location to generate timely pictures of overall corporate activities (often employing direct inputs to centrally situated computers). This becomes expensive, and currently, sometimes impossible, for most networks which extend overseas. Consequently, the magnitude of the communications problems increase, as do the number of limitations imposed on what management can do.

Basically, however, the distance problems that arise from poor facilities and time lags can be treated in the same manner as if they occured in the domestic environment. The limitations are usually not that difficult to identify, and adequate means exist to work around them. In essence, their primary implications for the international corporation are that: 1) it needs to employ people who are specifically familiar with these limitations; 2) it must incorporate the increased expenditures necessary to overcome or circumvent these limitations in its cost structure; 3) it must, in many cases, modify its operations and methods to accommodate these limitations.

There is another class of problems relating to distance which is attitudinal in nature. Problems of this sort are frequently more difficult to deal with. The establishment of an overseas operation (perhaps with the exception of Canada, but clearly including Mexico) is typically accompanied by a change in attitude. It is a function of psychological as well as physical distance, and frequently the former has an even greater impact than the latter. In many cases it relates to language changes, and it may also be a vestige of the past when the United States considered itself a self-contained, semi-isolated entity. In general, this attitudinal change manifests itself in different approaches to dealing with the operating unit which is located 3,000 miles away on the other coast of the United States as opposed to the one which is located at the same or even a substantially lesser distance, but in Latin America.

An executives' attitudes about distance in relation to international activities tend to have as significant an impact on overall logistical considerations (vis-a-vis domestic operations) as the lack of adequate facilities. For example, most domestic firms view the United States as an entity, and many have established integrated procurement-manufacturing-marketing systems to deal with it. Granted, there are clearly difficulties in operating such systems across international boundaries. However, few international companies even attempt to view their international activities in the same manner. When they do, they often treat overseas activities as a separate unit, seldom integrated with the domestic or overall system, except insofar as import, export and technical informational linkages exist between the two sets of operations.

Communications are in similar fashion affected by "distance" attitudes. Within the United States, a call from the New York office to the San Francisco office is made without a second thought. Conference calls often replace face-to-face meetings, and most people are reasonably comfortable with the information conveyed over the telephone. The mail service is reliable, and is commonly used to transmit important documents. However, when the communication must go overseas, it assumes a much more formidable nature. This is not only a function of the cost and the time required to place the call (which is small to many European countries). It is also the result of a feeling of grappling with the "unknown" and the "unusual." Consequently, the U.S. executive often approaches foreign communications cautiously and may rely more heavily on infrequent personal visits, to "find out what is really going on" and sometimes even to deliver important documents in person.

As a result of both poorer facilities and communications channels and the attitudes which surround them, companies frequently establish different control procedures for foreign operations than they do for domestic units. This is not to imply that all controls are a function of logistical and communications considerations relating to geographical and psychological distance. Many other environmental and managerial factors also exert great influence on controls. But where headquarters personnel feel uncomfortable about foreign operations, and because they desire accurate and timely information concerning them, they tend to centralize more of the decision-making authority in the headquarters than would normally be done with a domestic operation.

When decisions are made in the headquarters, headquarter's management often deludes itself into thinking that it knows what is happening in subsidiary branches, even though it may not have knowledge of the current state of affairs. Such centralization severely restricts the ability of subsidiary managements to react promptly to new situations. Some subsidiary managers may risk independent and unauthorized action. But many do not, and when the issue is complicated by factors of degree and diversity (to be discussed shortly), the subsidiary manager may have to wait months or longer for a decision which is no longer applicable because local conditions have not remained static.

An actual example which illustrates long-distance control problems involves a subsidiary located in a congested city in a developing country, in which good office and warehouse space was at a premium. As a result of historical developments, subsidiary office and warehouse operations were located in five different buildings scattered throughout the city. Traffic problems and the poor telephone service available presented severe communication and coordination problems for the company. Consequently, subsidiary management began a search for a new building which would permit consolidation of all operations. Such facilities became available infrequently, and even when a building did open up, demand was so great that it was usually committed to a new tenant within a matter of a few days. When the opportunity to acquire new space arose, it was necessary to act immediately. However, this subsidiary required approval from its headquarters before any such action could be taken (to give headquarters control over both the locus of activities and any lease commitments). During a two-year period, three opportunities to move were discovered. In all cases proposals were finally approved by the U.S. headquarters, but the two-month average delay between the request and the approval was so great that the opportunities were all lost.

This illustration is by no means an isolated example. The managing directors of a majority of U.S. subsidiaries surveyed in India reported that, often, the only time they could get prompt answers concerning certain matters was when the responsible executive from the international headquarters happened to be visiting them. Distance, delay in communications, other decisions which are competing for the parent organization's executives' time, and internal organizational problems within the headquarters all contribute to this kind of situation.

It is wise for international firms to decentralize many of the decisions which relate to and result from distance problems. This in turn, requires that subsidiaries be staffed with competent and trusted managers who have the guidance and a broad enough view to operate in the best interests of the overall corporation.

Degree

Extending operations across international borders gives rise to a whole class of problems which are essentially similar to problems experienced in widely dispersed domestic operations but are intensified in degree. This intensification derives primarily from the increased number of environmental constraints placed on the method of conducting international (vis-a-vis domestic) operations. Problems relating to degree can frequently be handled in a fashion similar to that employed in domestic operations, but they may require greater attention and because of their magnitude, somewhat modified approaches as well.

One of the managerial functions most affected in terms of degree is that of planning. Time delays can be substantial in the conduct of international business. Raw materials and funds which must be transported across international boundaries, finished products which follow similar routes, and the sheer complexity of global coordination, demand special attention from planners. New investment criteria must often be devised to evaluate opportunities at stages much earlier than would be justified by stateside standards. For example, a company may have to undertake a venture long before local market conditions justify profitable operations so that it can establish a foothold before competitors enter the field and the government closes the possibility of entrance. Often, such markets hold great promise for intermediate to long-range development.

Another important area in which problems are intensified is inventory control. Any attempt to control inventories on a global basis must deal with long and unpredictable shipping times, higher transportation costs, the dependability and quality of local sources of supply (both existing and future), government policies affecting the continued use of imports or shipment for export, and the kinds of storage facilities available. Therefore production levels which must be coordinated with these inventory levels take on an increased degree of complexity.

The augmented problems of packaging are also basically a matter of degree. Extra handling, and handling by less gentle means, must be factored into the selection of packaging materials. In like fashion, products must be modified to better withstand the rigors of international transport and different or changing climatic and storage conditions.

Another important area affected in degree is that of information relating to basic managerial functions, planning in particular. The relevant macro information needed for managerial decision making is scarcer in most countries than it is in the United States. Dun and Bradstreet type of credit reports may not exist. Adequate, reliable, and relatively current industry statistics, as well as data on a wide range of other conditions of interest to the firm, are frequently lacking. Consequently, decisions must be made on considerably less data than are available and utilized in domestic matters.

Less information frequently results in increased risk, and this, in turn, leads to the imposition of more and tighter controls. The controls, in turn, may slow down the decision-making process considerably. Contingency planning and greater flexibility in operations may offer a better solution, one which would often be used in domestic operations when serious informational limitations confront the firm.

Staffing problems may also be a matter of degree. Even in the United States, firms experience difficulties in recruiting, maintaining, or training various kinds of personnel. Because of greater educational and sociological-cultural constraints in many other countries, staffing problems are intensified for U.S. subsidiaries.

Diversity

The most critical aspects of the environment surrounding multinational linkages derive from the diversity of the varying environments in which the international corporation operates. They are generally the most difficult to deal with because they introduce complex sets of environmental conditions which limit the ability of the corporation to apply uniform policies, practices, methods and controls, or even to establish uniform goals for the conduct of its operations in different countries. Consequently, new and special approaches and operating patterns must be developed to deal with the diverse nature of the multinational environment. Unlike problems of distance and degree, the problems which arise from diversity frequently are difficult to identify because of their greater complexity. They are also considerably more difficult to solve. Diversity, more than any other set of elements, is the "quicksand" of the multinational environment.

Educational constraints in different countries relate to the staffing, direction, and motivating functions of management in particular. Where differences in the educational environments of countries in which international firms operate are great, problems of diversity tend to overshadow those of degree. Different policies, practices and approaches will be required by the firm if it is to build an effective work force and managerial cadre.

The diversity of cultures also plays a role in shaping the environment surrounding multinational linkages. Because the international executive may have to deal with many different cultures, most or all of which may have a different value system, he may find it difficult to establish the rapport he needs for building satisfactory personal relationships with subsidiary and affiliate personnel. Consequently, international firms frequently employ detailed control systems which are introduced to compensate for this lack of comfort and assurance. Language barriers enhance this gap. Rather than overemphasizing controls for these reasons, many companies would be wise to devote more time to selecting and developing executives who can establish a comfortable relationship with the foreign personnel with whom they must deal.

Managerial styles often come into conflict in international corporations — much more frequently than is usual in domestic operations. For example, the United States tends to emphasize participative, decentralized management patterns. In many countries, management styles are more authoritarian in nature, centered around family-type groups. Frequently, the subsidiary manager will have to conform to such patterns more than was anticipated, even if he is a U.S. citizen. He may have to act paternalistic, or make it obvious that he makes the decisions. This, in turn, may bring him into conflict with the ideologies of the head office, which tends to increase communications barriers, again resulting in the imposition of greater controls.

A major question relating to cultural diversity is that of mobility of individuals. The truly multinational organization should be able to move people freely, not only within a particular country but from country to country. A great deal can be gained from the development of international atmosphere within the headquarters and the subsidiaries. Yet there are cultural barriers to such mobility. The peoples of many countries have developed strong animosities towards other nationalities. The German salesman may still have some difficulty in France. The black Kenyan and the white

South African will probably not relate to one another very well. Companies must think carefully before transferring a Greek executive to Turkey or vice versa, and firms doing business with Israel will find relationships difficult with Syria.

Another cultural issue relates to product standardization. The U.S. manufacturer of trucks may have difficulty in selling the domestic version of his truck in areas where people are physically small and unable to reach the floor pedals. On the other hand, a great deal of expense may be involved in designing and retooling to produce "nonstandard" vehicles. There is a definite economic advantage in amortizing U.S. development costs over as large a production of standard items as possible. Yet somewhere a compromise must be achieved between local needs and the economics of the parent corporation. Again there is also the danger of setting precedents — if a company tailors its products to the needs of one economy, should it not do the same for others.

Numerous other problems derive from cultural matters and related environmental constraints. For example, differences in either concepts or requirements for product quality can arise from sociological-cultural, economic, educational, or political-legal factors. The U.S. corporation that wants to maintain a uniform and high quality image on a world-wide basis may find conflict with various foreign markets which neither desire nor understand such quality or may not be willing or able to pay for it. Consequently, the international company may have to face the questions of risk which would arise if multiple quality standards were applied to the same product (and brand) in different parts of the world.

The diversity of political systems in which the international company must operate also presents major problems. A key issue relates to the subsidiary as a citizen (e.g., its responsibility to initiate positive local social and economic change as opposed to the need to repatriate high profits to the parent and to avoid controversy). What role should a U.S. corporation take in improving the local environment in another country, especially a developing nation? As policies are formulated in this regard, can they be applied uniformly, or must they be tailored to specific situations? In some countries, the activities of foreign subsidiaries in introducing change are considered to be "outside meddling," and are regarded with suspicion or antagonism. On the other hand, these "foreign" firms are expected to contribute to the development of their host nations. Where is the line between the passive and active responsibilities of such corporate "citizenship?"

Another issue relating to political diversity concerns equal treatment of foreign governments with respect to their requests. Because so many U.S. firms overcentralize their control in the headquarters, foreign governments must often deal directly (whether they go through the subsidiary management or not) with the parent firm. Consequently, there is a tendency on the part of such governments to look at the global operations of the parent. A particular concession granted in one market or to one government frequently generates demands from other governments for identical treatment. Yet in many cases, internal situations are very different. Parent companies can impose harmful decisions upon particular subsidiaries for fear of setting precedents which may be detrimental to other overseas operations. For example, one large U.S. pharmaceutical firm refused to grant permission for a developing nation's public sector firm to manufacture an obsolete product. The U.S. company was afraid that other governments might use this as a lever to ask for rights to manufacture more important products. Subsequent government reaction caused disruption and financial loss to the company's local subsidiary.

A frustrating and time-consuming problem relating to the diversity of legal environments often arises from the large amount of documentation required for international transactions and contracts. Although attempts have been made to standardize the papers used in international business and trade, much still remains to be done in this area. Different countries require different kinds of justifications before permission will be granted for the establishment of foreign subsidiaries, licensing agreements, and so forth. Errors in documentation can delay projects for long periods of time. Consequently, the international company must obtain the services of individuals who are familiar with specific problems, or know how to ferret out information. Labor legislation and regulation is another legal area which differs considerably among countries.

Laws relating to taxation present another legal problem area. On the positive side, the multinational company can use the diversity of tax laws within its international environment to assist in the achievement of its financial goals and objectives. But difficulties can arise if specialized advice is unavailable.

An issue relating to taxation which moves into a less defined area is that of transfer pricing. When subsidiaries in different nations do business with one another, the establishment of prices for the transactions will often determine the locus of profits. Subsidiary A (in country A), by charging subsidiary B at cost, can show no profit while the total difference between cost and final sales value appears on the books of B (in country B). Most host countries have strong feelings about the effects that such practices can have on their internal tax revenues. Consequently, overall tax considerations (used to maximize returns to the parent company or overall international organization) must be tempered by some knowledge of "the degrees of tolerance" which local governments have in this regard. For example, if country A has a very high tax structure while country B has a low one, it will be to the advantage of the multinational firm to transfer as much of the profit as possible to company B. On the other hand, should the multinational corporation incur the ire of country A, the net result may be detrimental to overall global operations. An equitable position must be achieved, but the balance point is not always easy to identify.

One of the most serious difficulties relating to the diversity of the legal "structure" is that there are often no final bodies of appeal for the settlement of disputes which cross national boundaries. The framework of international law leaves much to be desired. Various countries have different interpretations of "what is just and what is not," and each wants to maintain its own sovereignty in legal matters. Consequently, international subsidiaries may find themselves operating in markedly different legal frameworks than those which exist in the home country and, with respect to international transactions, may find themselves in a state of legal limbo. Even where the legal structure is explicit, companies find it different in application from what they would normally anticipate. In international matters, the only way to obtain satisfaction may be through negotiation, either from a position of power or of weakness, and the legal structure may be totally impotent to deal with the situation.

One of the most noticeable areas in which existing legal systems have shown their inability to deal with multinational problems relates to nationalization or expropriation. An international company may have established subsidiary operations under agreement with the then existing local government. A new government takes over and refuses to honor the previous agreement, charging that exploitation and corruption were at the base of the original negotiations. The legal system in the local country may no longer be of any help in settling such a matter to the satisfaction of both parties. It may even have been changed retroactively. In addition, there are few mechanisms to deal with such situations at the international level. Consequently, the individual company is left to attempt to negotiate a settlement.

Often, international legal issues are clear, but legal interpretations differ. For example, the United States has been engaged in serious confrontations with Ecuador and Peru over fishing rights. While both agree that a country's dominance of fishing rights extends to its offshore limits, the extent of these limits is in question. Consequently U.S. fishing boats operating according to the U.S. legal interpretation, have been impounded by Ecuador and fines have been levied for failure to comply with the Ecuadorian interpretation.

Another kind of difficulty relating to interpretation is the question of "meaning" or "intent." The legal structure in the United States, for example, is fairly specific about contracts. A contract, if properly drawn, is binding on all parties concerned. In many countries, the contract is considered to be an expression of intent, not commitment. In essence, it may only indicate that one party intends to perform the terms of the contract as long as it is "convenient." In other situations, the signing of a contract may be solely a means to avoid unpleasantness. One party may never have intended to fulfill the terms of the contract, and signed only because it did not wish to upset the other participants. Even in countries where the legal structure is designed to offer redress for broken contracts, the social structure can make it difficult to obtain such relief. Consequently, the multinational corporation must continually consider the diversities of both the explicit legal structures and local interpretations of the concepts embodied therein. It must also be continuously alert to the fact that it often cannot protect itself by falling back on legal remedies.

Political and legal considerations can combine to present a formidable challenge to international managers. Two specific examples which face U.S. based corporations deal with antitrust issues and situations involving trade with communist nations.

The United States has well-established statutes designed to eliminate or reduce practices which restrict trade. These antitrust laws have been applied to eliminate price fixing, various kinds of collusion, and lately, even size. On the other hand, many foreign countries (notably Japan and until very recently, most of Europe) have allowed and even encouraged restrictive cartels and other arrangements. The U.S. government's attempts to extend U.S. antitrust laws to the operations of U.S. companies in foreign nations has frequently led to intergovernmental conflicts which present serious dilemmas for the companies caught in the middle. The company which, for competitive reasons, needs to belong to a "cartel" which the U.S. government prohibits can find itself in an extremely awkward position.

Similarly, U.S. laws relating to trade with communist nations, though relatively clear-cut in respect to purely domestic companies, become complex when international boundaries are involved. Consider the plight of the U.S. subsidiary located in a depressed section of a major European nation which received an order to produce automotive machinery for Cuba. Since the subsidiary was an arm of a U.S. corporation, the U.S. government maintained its "rights" to prohibit such a sale. As an entity incorporated and operating in the host country, the local government insisted, since it had no regulations restricting trade with Cuba and since it needed the jobs which would be created, that the company accept the order. Here we have a combination of legal and political considerations. In any one nation, the answer would have been clear, but because multinational elements were involved, the issue became complex and difficult to handle.

Economic diversity clearly plays a critical role in the management of international firms. The sizes of markets for given products vary dramatically within different countries. However, potential export markets that may be obtained by setting up operations in a particular foreign country may be even more important for the firm than its internal market. The development of common markets and free trade zones has led to a totally new method of conducting international operations. Economies of scale can be achieved by centralizing manufacturing and assembly facilities in certain nations which can then supply a number of countries without much concern for the incurrence of tariffs or onerous red tape. International operations must be carefully planned to take advantage of the kinds of benefits (and sometimes to work around the problems) which result from such confederations.

Fiscal and monetary policies differ greatly among countries, as do levels of economic and price stability. This has a major impact on enterprise planning, as well as finance, marketing, and production functions. Some countries have strong and organized capital markets where reputable firms can usually obtain funds at reasonable costs, while others have weak or nonexistent capital markets. Exchange restrictions prohibit certain kinds of fund transfers between subsidiaries and their headquarters and among subsidiaries, and often require innovative approaches for the achievement of parent company objectives. For example, in countries where exchange controls are rigorous, it may be necessary to enter completely new business lines so that profits from a main thrust of activities can be returned to the parent in the form of goods and services. The whole issue of repatriation of capital and earnings arises only when operations transcend international boundaries.

Sharp diversities in wage structure in different countries — which result from a variety of economic, educational and other environmental conditions — also directly affect the conduct of international operations. Some are questions of degree: e.g., the political issues surrounding the establishment of U.S. assembly plants across the Mexican border to take advantage of low wage rates may be more intense, but are similar to those engendered by the New England textile manufacturer's shift to North Carolina. But new dimensions are introduced in some situations as a result of diversity. Consider the expected reaction by the local national to the U.S. executive who is sent abroad to work with him, where both men perform similar tasks and yet one is paid five or ten times more than the other. Similar predicaments arise with respect to employee benefits. In some countries, the law requires the provision of extensive and expensive benefits. In other countries, no such requirements exist, yet the question arises "should a company treat its employees differently in one area than another just because an international boundary intercedes?".

Each of the factors relating to distance, degree, and diversity alter the managerial process when international boundaries are crossed. Each adds to the complexity of the multinational environment, and many give rise to new managerial environments. The major challenges they offer to the multinational firm are the need to develop managers who are flexible and familiar enough with such situations to act in the best long-range interests of the total entity, and the need to develop organizational structures and policies which are responsive to the challenges and yet stable enough to provide direction and goal orientation for the entire global enterprise. The alternatives of rigid centralized control and complete anarchy are equally discouraging. A middle position must be achieved and this can only be done when a thorough knowledge of the operating environments, and the ability to cope with them are available.

THE MANAGEMENT PROCESS AND EFFECTS OF THE PARENT COMPANY ON FOREIGN OPERATIONS

One of the most important tasks facing a headquarters organization is the establishment of guidelines to assure that subsidiary goals and objectives are consistent with the achievement of overall corporate aims. A well-developed set of overall objectives can increase subsidiary management's efficiency by eliminating much of the anxiety and uncertainty that derives from not being sure how actions will be perceived back in the headquarters. Naturally, it is necessary to tailor the reward systems to the achievement of these overall goals.

Policy guidelines should be as broad as possible — to allow local management the greatest possible flexibility in dealing with local environmental conditions. Since timeliness is important, local managers must have the authority to make most of the important day-to-day operating decisions.

On the other hand, the parent firm clearly cannot cut the subsidiary loose. It has an investment and a reputation to protect, and it also has the responsibility of ownership. Depending upon the particular environment involved, international corporations can and should do a better job of tailoring their control systems to achieve a better balance between essential headquarters control and the ability of local management to react to immediate and varying situations. The key to this lies in the selection and development of competent subsidiary managers. The parent company must have confidence in the managers who are making decisions for the subsidiaries. Only then can it feel that broad decentralization is likely to result in decisions which are in the best interests of the total enterprise.

PLANNING, GOAL SETTING AND POLICY FORMULATION

Perhaps the most important factor distinguishing the genuine multinational corporation from the traditional international firm is the way it plans and sets goals and policies. The multinational company treats its global operations — including those of the home country — as an integrated entity, while the international firm deals with foreign activities as a secondary or separate adjunct to domestic operations. Consequently, in the latter case, the plans, policies and goals of the domestic parent too often take precedent. Moreover, its actions are frequently based on short-run considerations.

One of the keys to success in the multinational sphere seems to be flexibility. Plans which are not versatile enough to deal with the complexity of diverse environmental conditions give rise to operating policies and controls which compel subsidiary managers to take devious actions if they are to operate effectively.

The parent company must formulate a master plan for global operations and make strategic policy decisions with regard to basic product lines, types of business activities to pursue, division of international markets, areas of production specialization, major capital expenditures, the staffing of key positions, and perhaps a limited number of other areas deemed truly critical. The broad objectives and policies of the corporation as a whole should deal with such things as protection of the company's reputation, the global image it wishes to have, and the minimum levels of profitability and growth and related maximum risks that the firm is willing to accept in any of its operations over a period of time, typically at least five to ten years.

Integrated global planning cannot be done on a short term basis. Many worthwhile international projects take years to develop and mature. Plans should include projections of expected performance in key areas, as well as the basic role of each foreign subsidiary during the ensuing five to ten years, taking into account existing and anticipated critical environmental conditions. This permits strategic daily decisions to be made within a framework of anticipated comparative strengths and weaknesses for each of the company's major operations in the longer run. As a result, the multinational firm is in a better position to balance production and markets among its operations in different countries based on opportunity, costs, comparative advantages, risks, and profitability considerations.

There is always uncertainty in global planning of this type. However, contingency plans can be formulated in order to alleviate this difficulty. Such plans can outline alternative courses of action and reduce lead times and costs as unanticipated conditions arise.

Once headquarters has made known the risks it is willing to assume on a given project (in terms of total resource committments), and has determined the minimum level of profitability acceptable over a given period of time (usually no less than five to ten years), subsidiary management should be given considerable freedom to pursue its own courses of action. The parent need only make sure that it has an effective feedback and analysis system to monitor progress.

Table 9-1 presents some of the uniform but restrictive policies commonly established by international firms in an attempt to achieve their objectives, and some of the related problems which result in their foreign operations. No attempt was made to make this table complete. It only provides an illustrative sample of such policies and related problems. Since most of these have been discussed in detail elsewhere in this book, only a few comments are presented here.

Many parent companies use domestic operations as a basis of comparison for foreign activities. Before permitting a particular subsidiary to expand operations, for instance, they may require detailed analyses of rates of return, and then base the final decision on comparisons of projected income with the returns expected from domestic operations. This procedure, although often applicable to inter-company comparisons within the United States or even between countries of fairly equal levels of development, leaves much to be desired when evaluating opportunities in developing nations. In the United States, most projects should pay for themselves before five years have passed. However, it may be necessary to spend five more years to develop a potential market in a foreign country before showing substantial profit.

A common problem which arises in the marketing area in the multinational environment is the use of uniform methods of distribution. In some countries, for example, distribution channels are weak and company-owned and operated channels may prove the best. In other countries, the connections an established distributor may have, even though he might not be the company's image of the ideal working partner, may be a major key to success. Some countries contain strong and independent distributors, while others may have voids in this area.

Many international firms use their subsidiaries as training grounds for home country personnel under the assumption — frequently false — that "smaller operations" (vis-a-vis domestic operations) equates with fewer problems or risks. This is the "minor league club" treatment of foreign activities which may be greatly resented in the host country. Smaller operations usually do equate with smaller staff support functions, giving top-level subsidiary executives fewer experts to rely upon. At the same time, the complexities of, and too often unfamiliarity with, the local environment

TABLE 9-1 Problems and policies in international firms

Areas	Common policies	Examples of problems
FINANCIAL	1. 100% ownership, or at least a majority equity position	— Conflict with national interests and trends — Inability to get approval for foreign ventures — Balance of payments difficulties — Greater risks
	2. Application of uniform return on investment criteria	— Failure to enter markets which could prove lucrative over time — Selection of less favorable projects in terms of long run
	3. Repatriation of earnings, service fees, and/or capital	— Conflict with local governments — Draining of subsidiary resources
	4. Tax minimization	— Conflict with local governments — Conflict with local revenue needs and subsidiary operations
	5. Detailed and overstandardized financial control systems and forms	— Failure of subsidiary personnel to understand headquarters needs or requests — Poorly filled out forms — Unnecessary work
MARKETING	1. Central control over product lines and specifications	— Imbalance in local product mixes — Unsuitability to local conditions
	2. Uniform price policies	— Restrictions on subsidiaries to effectively meet local market conditions
	3. Selection of uniform distribution channels	— Poor fits with local buying patterns
	4. Centralized control of promotional activities	— Failure to effectively stimulate local markets
	5. Rigid restrictions on exports	— Conflicts with local governments — Local balance of payments problems — Longer term potential of subsidiary hindered

TABLE 9-1 Problems and policies in international firms (continued)

Areas	Common policies	Examples of problems
RESEARCH & DEVELOPMENT	1. Centralized R&D	— Products and processes not tailored adequately to local conditions — Failure to take advantage of local opportunities — Conflict with local governments and subsidiary personnel's desires to upgrade and utilize local talent
PRODUCTION & PROCUREMENT	1. Duplication of U.S. manufacturing processes	— May not conform to local conditions or economies
	2. Restrictions on changes in facilities	— Hampers local management to adapt to local conditions
	3. Centrally prescribed equipment, material or other input specifications	— Conflicts with local manufacturers or with government import restrictions
	4. Uniform quality standards	— Does not mesh with local supply conditions or market requirements
	5. Central approval of quality control samples	— Delays
	6. Imposing imports on subsidiaries	— Conflicts with local governments — Local balance of payments problems — Deters import substitution and vertical integration
STAFFING & PERSONNEL	1. Uniform policies relating to welfare benefits, incentive systems, merit increases, recruitment, promotions, dismissals, layoffs, discipline, union relations, etc.	— Conflicts with local personnel, labor unions and/ or local governments
	2. Restrictions on employment levels	— Hamstrings local management
	3. Criteria for selecting key personnel	— Selection of people who relate to headquarters rather than local operating environment — Resentment created in host country

TABLE 9-1   Problems and policies in international firms   (continued)

Areas	Common policies	Examples of problems
STAFFING & PERSONNEL (Continued)	4. Use of subsidiary as training ground for U.S. personnel	— Inability to relate effectively to new environment and breadth of functions — Resentment created in host country
	5. Selection of subsidiary managers and experts on basis of limited functional performance in larger U.S. operations	— Failure to recognize need for training abilities — Failure to provide them with adequate staff support at subsidiary level

may add a whole layer of problems beyond those which exist in the domestic situation. Consequently, casual selection of key subsidiary personnel can severely handicap operations. (Unfortunately, the effect may long go unnoticed because many foreign subsidiaries still operate in sellers' markets, at least for the present, which can absorb a great deal of inefficiency and ineffective management activity and still make the profit and loss statement look "O.K." or even good vis-a-vis U.S. figures).

In essence there is a tendency to transfer intact to foreign operations, many policies which have proven to be reasonably successful in U.S. domestic activities. When it becomes obvious that such policies do not apply abroad, there is a tendency to move in the direction of increasing the number of restrictive measures and controls rather than toward more permissive approaches. Too often, companies attempt to force the local environment to adapt to them, rather than meet it half, or at least part-way.

CONTROLS

Financial controls placed on foreign subsidiaries by parent companies are typically (and understandably) the most extensive. They often hinder the subsidiary's operating flexibility. Some of the problems can best be seen by examining an actual case where rigid financial control by a parent created difficulties for the subsidiary.

The head office of a particular company limited the capital expenditure authority of the managing director of its Indian subsidiary to $200. (This figure has been raised substantially recently, but is still lower than that for managers in charge of smaller and less diverse operations within the United States.) No one interviewed in the headquarters was able to justify the low capital spending limit figure of its Indian subsidiary — or that imposed on various of its other foreign operations as well. It seemed obvious that the selection of the figure had been made with little consideration for the effect it would have on subsidiary operations. The low figure also raises a serious issue concerning the staffing policies and practices of such a corporation. If the best this firm could do was to find a managing director for its Indian subsidiary who could be trusted with no more than $200, was it really worth the headaches to operate the subsidiary? Although the question is somewhat facetious, it does have significance in that many international firms still use their foreign operations as a way of "exiling" managers they want to get out of their domestic hair.

In the above example, one of the reasons why the $200 figure had not changed much sooner was because the Indian subsidiary managers developed methods to work around the controls and had not raised the issue in parent company discussions because they knew that financial control was a sensitive area. In addition, the outlooks of most of the U.S. and other non-Indian managers in India were largely derived from the fact that they knew their assignments there were only of a relatively short-term duration (two or three years at most).

In general, many of the policies of international corporations are formulated not really as policies to *guide* foreign operations, but rather as controls — controls which then implicitly give rise to corporate policies, rules and even objectives when they become ends in themselves rather than means. The controls impose not only rules, but also goals as well, when they are so specific that they severely limit alternative courses of action available to subsidiary managers. Because of major differences in operating environments, strict controls frequently lead to very different results in various nations. Consequently, the stringent imposition of uniform controls may be inconsistent with global goal attainment for the corporation.

There is no question that some degree of parent control over financial and other matters is essential. Effective controls can also have considerable positive value in that they compel people to give more serious thought to their plans, proposals, and actions. Yet, although rigid in some areas, many parent companies are lax in key sectors which are necessary for effective control and decision making. For example, of the Indian subsidiaries studied relatively few were required to submit budgets or forecasts which projected beyond three years into the future. Interestingly, several submitted one-year budgets to parents who employed five and ten year projections for their U.S. operations.

Once subsidiary budgets are approved, controls should focus on the causes for *major* deviations, in either operating results or the environment. This is the essence of "management by exception." Although most of the U.S. international firms surveyed basically used this approach in their domestic operations, a majority of them did not with respect to their foreign subsidiaries. One could argue that an effective control system for international operations might be akin to the approach taken by many sensible people who enter a gambling casino. They study the odds, decide how much they are willing to bet and lose, and then let it ride. The situation with respect to foreign operations is not quite analogous because the odds are much more often potentially in favor of the bettor (there is no house cut *per se*), and as the environment changes the situation can always be re-evaluated.

However, all too often international headquarters react to "changes" which are really the result of poor homework or planning. Their reactions are based on the acquisition of knowledge of certain factors previously overlooked. Greater emphasis should be placed on the initial study and evaluation process to decide whether or not to engage in a particular foreign venture, on the periodic review processes which take place (or should take place), and on the functions of planning, communication and direction. Only then can it be determined whether or not a system is truly out of control. Merely responding with even more excessive restrictions is likely to cause much more harm than good.

ORGANIZATION

Even domestic companies which have multiple product lines and operations in many parts of the country have difficulty in devising optimum organization structures. The best managed firms continually seek improvement by experimenting with and modifying their organizations in response to changing conditions. At the heart of the problem is how to best balance the functional, (e.g., marketing, finance, production), product line, and geographical aspects within the total organizational setup, and still provide for reasonably effective authority, responsibility and reporting relationships.

The organizational problem for a multinational corporation is more complex. It must effectively balance and integrate geographical operations with functional expertise and product line considerations on a global basis. Line and functional authority and related control must still be exerted by the parent company, and possibly even domestic staff and service units, but only in areas which are deemed essential and appropriate after careful examination and periodic review. In general, it is best to decentralize as much functional authority and staff support as possible to local operations. Adequate staff and service support must also be provided at the subsidiary level itself. The whole problem is complicated by distance, diversity, and degree considerations.

Several multinational firms have established separate regional corporations with their own boards of directors. In these situations, much of the functional authority and staff support which was formerly exerted by the parent organization and domestic operations has been delegated to the regional organizations. An essential condition for this to be effective, is that the regional organizations have an adequate volume of activity to make full use of their personnel. Even then some centralized control, both line and functional, and staff support at the parent level itself, is still required in some critical areas (e.g., finance, R&D, dividing up international markets and product lines, and so forth).

In well-managed multinational corporations, adequate provision is made for planning, coordinating and controlling product lines on a global basis. Specific product lines are often assigned to product managers or liaison personnel who serve as key information centers with regard to all significant aspects of the products for which they are responsible. In some cases, they may also be given functional authority over certain aspects of their product lines. They are most commonly found in the parent organization, and in some cases in major domestic product divisions. However, where various product lines are concentrated in particular regions, it may be feasible to place more of these product specialists at the regional level.

Because of the complexity of the organization structures of international corporations, attention should be given to clarifying and updating all of the kinds of authority and responsibility relationships: e.g., functional, advisory, and so forth; that exist within the overall organization, as well as the roles assigned to specific key personnel. Many firms fail to do an adequate job in this area. But even the well-managed multinational corporation must rely heavily on the informal organization for smooth functioning because of the complexity of its structures and operations. This involves a great deal of information flow and communication, vertically and horizontally. Competent personnel must be placed in major jobs, and there must also be considerable mutual trust and understanding among the people who deal with each other regularly.

In the better-managed multinational firms communication channels tend to be direct. Subsidiary managers are better able to identify and communicate with people in the headquarters or domestic operations who can best help them.

Many international companies require all correspondence to go through complex and cumbersome "official" channels prescribed by the formal organization. The routing of a request for assistance or clarification from a subsidiary production manager, for instance, may have to go through the managing director and possibly some of his deputies as well. Then it goes to the regional office, then to one or more people at international headquarters who are concerned with production problems, then to the specialist who deals with the particular problem area involved, and then, perhaps, to someone in domestic operations who can supply the answer. The reply may travel a more direct route back, although copies of it are likely to be sent to everyone involved with the initial request. The complexity of this process is based on a "need for control" and the desire to keep everyone informed of what is going on. The result, especially if authority and responsibility relationships are not well defined, can clearly be negative.

Although some multinational corporations do an impressive job of designing relatively effective and efficient organization structures, new organizational concepts are clearly needed in international business. This will demand both creativity and experimentation. For example, it is possible that the best way to organize in many cases is not by geography, which tends to lump together such diverse countries as Japan and Hong Kong with India and Indonesia, or Spain and Portugal with Sweden and West Germany, but to organize on the basis of similar levels of economic development, environmental conditions, and possibly the size of potential markets. Grouping countries along these lines may well strengthen the capability of the total organization to evaluate and deal with diverse conditions. It is possible that considerably more authority may be effectively decentralized under such country groupings; moreover, much in the way of specialized staff and service support may also be pushed down to levels below the parent organization, or shifted from domestic to international operations. The increased managerial and organizational efficiencies obtained by grouping Brazil with Indonesia, Japan with West Germany and Spain with Peru, for example, may more than compensate for the increased travel and other costs related to the greater distances involved.

STAFFING AND MANAGERIAL MOTIVATION

Although it has become less common for multinational firms to assign their "second stringers" or "duds" to overseas operations, a number of serious problems still exist in the assignment of foreign nationals to key foreign subsidiary jobs. Too often, managers with limited functional backgrounds and experience are sent abroad in order to "broaden" their experience. They frequently lack the skills and abilities to train subordinates, nor are they given the staff support they are accustomed to at home. The best managers sent abroad have broad experience and proven training ability. Most have also spent considerable time familiarizing themselves (and their families) with the local environment before they take over operations there. A number of devices can be used by the firm to achieve such familiarization in addition to informal chats at the home office or special courses and training programs in the home country. These may include temporarily assigning the person to a staff job at headquarters which relates to the operations of the country to which he is to be assigned; sending him on familiarization trips abroad before he takes over; and having him work for some time (typically a few months) with the manager or specialist whose job he is going to take over.

Another major and common problem arises from the lack of continuity in top management at the subsidiary level. Most of the U.S. subsidiaries we have studied change their managing directors every two or three years. Often it takes at least a year for a foreign manager to get an adequate grasp of local environmental conditions. Such turnover of key foreign personnel tends to create adverse motivational effects. The manager, knowing that his assignment is only temporary, will often make decisions which are not in the best long-term interest of the subsidiary or the corporation as a whole. In order to look good in terms of the short-run targets stressed by headquarters (most typically profitability, and possibly sales growth or market share) he may fail to deal effectively with labor unions (giving in to avoid a strike, even though capitulation may hurt in the long run); fail to make desirable organizational changes (to avoid disruptive conflict); or implement new projects (which will, initially yield low returns), for example. He has to look good for his next step up the career ladder.

Frequent changes in top-level subsidiary jobs also tend to be unnerving for local personnel. A succession of key executives may make it difficult for local nationals to adjust to varying personalities, leadership styles, values, and special interests. This is even more likely to be the case when managers or specialists of different nation-alities — e.g., American, British, Australian, Indian — succeed one another.

Longer-term assignments of foreign nationals (e.g., at least five years, and even longer), and the selection of local nationals for key jobs reduces or eliminates the above kinds of problems. Once the subsidiary is fully and effectively staffed with local nationals, continuity and succession problems are usually greatly alleviated, since qualified locals can be promoted as vacancies open. The appointment of well-trained local nationals to top executive jobs also often results in better personnel relations, as well as better union and host government relations.

It is common for U.S. international firms to select local nationals for key sub-sidiary executive posts because they seem to be like Americans. Often they are only superficially so. If they really do operate just like Americans, severe personnel prob-lems can ensue, since they may be out of harmony with the expectations of other local nationals.

International firms frequently give inadequate attention to the various role con-flicts which confront the top managers of their foreign subsidiaries. They must somehow blend parent company interests with those of the subsidiary, as well as the national interests of the parent company nation with those of the host country. If one of their roles is expected to be innovative, they must gain local acceptance to implement their ideas and programs. They must adequately identify with the local community at large, as well as the local business community. If they are members of and identify with professional groups at home — e.g., engineers or accountants — they are likely to be concerned with their status at home and will want to keep up to date in their professional field.

A competent local national placed in a top-level subsidiary job may often be able to handle such role conflicts better than a U.S. manager. He is likely to understand the factors relating to the local environment better, and he may need not worry about his professional status in the parent country. Of course, he would still have to be familiar with and responsive to the legitimate interests and goals of both the parent country and parent company. In many cases, a third-country national may do a better job of resolving his role conflicts as manager of a U.S. subsidiary than an Amer-ican manager, or even a local national. He may operate with fewer preconceived ideas or faulty assumptions, and on a more neutral and less emotional level. As a result, he may be able to balance his conflicting roles more objectively.

Few international companies have devised reward systems for key foreign sub-sidiary executives which are effectively tied to the achievement of both key sub-sidiary and overall long-range corporate objectives — a difficult task in the domestic area as well. However, the potential benefits that can be derived from developing more creative and effective reward systems in the international sphere may greatly outweigh the costs entailed. Many of the conventional managerial reward systems which work well — e.g., profit sharing plans, stock options, various kinds of special bonuses tied to performance, and so forth — are overlooked by U.S. multinational firms for motivating top-level managers of their foreign subsidiaries.

LEADERSHIP, DIRECTION, COMMUNICATIONS, AND INFORMATION CHANNELS

No international corporation is likely to move very far down the road of becoming a genuine multinational firm unless leadership in this direction is exerted at the top echelons of the parent organization. Top management must set the course through all its basic functions and provide an effective example and inspiration for those lower down in the organization to follow. Generally, top managers who have had considerable experience in international operations themselves are most likely to exert this kind of leadership and inspiration. It is, therefore, no coincidence that in recent years an increasing number of executives appointed to top-level jobs in relatively progressive U.S. multinational firms have had substantial international experience.

Considerable effort must be expended in sensitizing both foreign and home country members of the firm to the value systems, customs, and philosophies of each other — not so that they will be adopted or accepted as immutable, but so they will be understood, factored into decision-making, and, where feasible, modified through effective leadership, communication, and, training. Eventually, the truly multinational firm must eliminate a "we-they" attitude. It must contain only employees, not domestic employees and foreign employees.

In general, international firms need to find better ways to increase the effectiveness of their communications and information flows. The problems relating to increased data flows are not usually as difficult to deal with as those relating to increased understanding and trust. Ways must be found to increase desirable interaction. More frequent meetings, rotation of personnel, newsletters, and greater emphasis on participative management in planning and decision-making are some of the practices that can be employed for this purpose.

Although the transfer of technical information and know-how has become a well developed art in many U.S. international corporations, a common shortcoming is the lack of effective channels for disseminating information of a managerial nature. Requests for data on new products, technical processes, and manufacturing problems are often answered promptly; however, few subsidiary managers request information dealing with managerial problems, and those who do are typically disappointed with the results. This is an area where international firms can improve substantially.

CONCLUDING REMARKS

Most U.S. international corporations have not yet learned to live in a multinational world. Global approaches tend to be rejected in favor of extensions of U.S. domestic policies and interests, and objectives and plans are formulated largely with U.S. corporate management and U.S. stockholder interests in mind. As a result, U.S. international corporations are probably much less effective than they could be. However, effectiveness is a relative concept, and American subsidiaries abroad, especially in developing countries, are usually more effective than their indigenous counterparts.

But this is no justification for complacency. By "multinationalizing," most U.S. firms could substantially improve their performance. This will not only benefit them, their stockholders, their subsidiaries, and the United States; it will also benefit the host countries in which they operate, as well as general world order and development. To accomplish this, new managerial approaches, new philosophies, and a whole series of new and more creative concepts are needed, not just by corporations, but also by national governments and international agencies and public organizations.

SELECTED BIBLIOGRAPHY

Ashton, D., "The International Transfer of Management Skills," *AISEC Quarterly Journal,* August, 1967.

Behrman, J., *Some Patterns in the Rise of the Multinational Enterprise,* University of North Carolina Press, Chapel Hill, 1969.

Bivens, K., and Greene, J., *Compensation of Overseas Managers,* National Industrial Conference Board, New York, 1969.

Blough, R., *International Business: Environment and Adaptation,* McGraw-Hill Book Co., New York, 1966.

Boddewyn, J., *Comparative Management and Marketing,* Scott, Foresman, Glenview, Ill., 1969.

Charafas, D., *Developing the International Executive,* American Management Association, New York, 1967.

Copen, M., "Manufacturing Management in Developing Nations: A Comparative Study of Problems and Practices of U.S. and Indigenous Companies in India," doctoral dissertation, Harvard Business School, Cambridge, Mass., 1967.

Davis, S., *Comparative Management,* Prentice-Hall, Englewood Cliffs, N.J., 1971.

Donner, F., *The Worldwide Industrial Enterprise,* (New York: McGraw-Hill, 1967).

Duerr, M., and Greene, J., *Foreign Nations in Multinational Management,* National Industrial Conference Board, New York, 1969.

Estafen, B., *An Empirical Study in Comparative Management: A Study of the Transferability of American Management Policies and Practices to Firms Operating in Chile,* doctoral dissertation, UCLA, Los Angeles, 1967.

Farmer, R., editor, *International Management,* Dickenson, Belmont, Calif., 1968.

Farmer, R., and Richman, B., *International Business: An Operational Theory,* Richard D. Irwin, Homewood, Ill., 1966; revised edition; Cedarwood Publishing Co., 1971, Bloomington, Indiana.

Fayerweather, J., *International Business Management: A Conceptual Framework,* McGraw-Hill Book Co., New York, 1969.

Flores, F., *The Applicability of American Management Know-How to Developing Countries: Case Studies of Philippine Firms, American Subsidiaries and Affiliates Operating in the Philippines and Their Respective Parent Firms in the United States,* doctoral dissertation, UCLA, Los Angeles, 1968.

Fouraker, L., and Stopford, J., "Organizational Structure and Multinational Strategy," *Administrative Science Quarterly,* June, 1968.

Gonzales, R., and Negandhi, A., *The Overseas Executive: His Orientation and Career Patterns,* Michigan State University Press, Lansing, Mich., 1967.

Ivancevich, J., "Predeparture Training for Overseas," *Training and Development Journal,* February, 1969.

Ivancevich, J., "Selection of Managers for Overseas Assignments," *Personnel Journal,* March, 1969.

Kindleberger, C., *American Business Abroad,* Yale University Press, New Haven, 1969.

Kolde, E., *International Business Enterprise,* Prentice-Hall, Englewood Cliffs, N.J., 1968.

Lauter, G., *An Investigation of the Applicability of Modern Management Practices by Industrial Managers in Turkey,* doctoral dissertation, UCLA, Los Angeles, 1968.

Lee, J., "Developing Managers in Developing Countries," *Harvard Business Review,* Nov.-Dec., 1968.

Lavell, E., *The Changing Role of the International Executive,* National Industrial Conference Board, Business Policy Study No. 119, New York, 1960.

Maisonrouge, J., "Education of International Managers," *The Quarterly Journal of AISEC International,* February, 1967.

National Planning Association, New York: Under a series titled *United States Business Performance Abroad,* NPA has published 13 studies dealing with the operations of multinational corporations in different countries.

Negandhi, A., "Profile of the American Overseas Executive," *California Management Review,* Winter, 1966.

Organizing for Worldwide Operations, Business International Corp., New York, 1965.

Perlmutter, H., "Social Architectural Problems of the Multinational Firm," *AISEC Quarterly Journal,* August, 1967.

Papageorge, A., *Transferability of Management: A Case Study of the United States and Greece,* doctoral dissertation, UCLA, Los Angeles, 1967.

Phatak, A., *External Environmental Constraints and Their Impact Upon the Internal Operations of Firms in the Pharmaceutical and Engineering Industries in India,* doctoral dissertation, UCLA, Los Angeles, 1966.

Prasad, S., editor, *Management in International Perspective,* Appleton-Century Crofts, New York, 1967.

Pryor, M., "Planning in a Worldwide Business," *Harvard Business Review,* January-February, 1965.

Raymond, L., *The Influence of Managerial Factors on Enterprise Performance: A Study of U.S. Subsidiaries and Local Firms in Britain,* doctoral dissertation, UCLA, Los Angeles, 1970.

Richman, B., *A Firsthand Study of Industrial Management and Economic Development in India,* Research Report, U.S. Agency for International Development, Office of Program and Policy Coordination, Washington, D.C., December, 1969.

Robinson, R., *International Business Policy,* Holt, Rinehart and Winston, New York, 1964.

Robinson, R., *International Management,* Holt, Rinehart and Winston, New York, 1967.

Rolf, S., *The International Corporation,* International Chamber of Commerce, Paris, May, 1969.

Schollhammer, H., "The Compensation of International Executives," *MSU Business Topics,* Winter, 1969.

Simonds, K., "Multinational? Well, Not Quite," *Columbia Journal of World Business,* Fall, 1966.

Steiner, G., and Cannon, W., *Multinational Corporate Planning,* Macmillan, New York, 1966.

Thorelli, H., "The Multinational Corporation as a Change Agent," *Southern Journal of Business,* July, 1966.

PART 4
ENTERPRISE MANAGEMENT, OPERATIONS, AND PERFORMANCE ABROAD

CHAPTER 10 OVERVIEW OF MANAGEMENT AND PERFORMANCE

This part of the book focuses on the management, operations and performance of enterprises surveyed in India. While the emphasis is on India, this section has relevance to and implications for other developing countries and for companies and public authorities in relatively advanced nations other then the United States. The particular emphasis will be on a comparative analysis of U.S. subsidiaries abroad and indigenous firms although some attention will also be given to the performance of other foreign affiliates as well as to U.S. parent companies. The transferability and applicability of U.S. management know-how and practice is of central concern, as well as the processes of adaptation and accommodation.

TRANSFERABILITY OF MANAGEMENT SKILL AND PRACTICE

The establishment of a new foreign subsidiary usually occurs when a company has experienced success — at least by its own standards — in its domestic operations. This success is generally attributed to a particular set of managerial practices and philosophies. It is only natural, therefore, for the firm to think of structuring managerial patterns for the new subsidiary in a similar manner. Yet, as we have seen, the new environment may differ greatly from that of the parent organization. Consequently, the successful graft of managerial know-how and practice from one environment to another may require a substantial amount of adjustment in basic patterns and the development of new approaches.

Managerial practices are integral products of the environments which spawn them. To a large extent they embody the specific values and mores of the cultures from which they derive. Furthermore, they are frequently designed to deal with problems which arise in a specific environmental setting.

In general, the transferability and applicability to developing nations of management concepts and practices proven successful in an advanced country like the United States are becoming increasingly important issues. Until recently, the primary focus has been on the transference of modern technology and technical processes. But increasing attention is being directed toward the managerial processes, especially in nations such as India.

There are a number of reasons for growing concern about managerial problems in Indian industry. First, as firms have grown over the years, their operations have become more varied and complex. Greater managerial competence is required if further and sustained gains in efficiency and growth are to be forthcoming. Increasing competition and the breakdown of strong sellers' markets for many specific products also call for greater managerial effectiveness, as do inflationary pressures, and rising factor input costs (often coupled with controlled selling prices). Many firms, especially (but not exclusively) in engineering and heavy industry sectors, are faced with considerable excess capacity, and this too is leading to greater concern about effective management. Finally, more and more local enterprises are becoming aware of and wish to emulate those foreign companies and progressive indigenous firms which have achieved success largely because of their use of modern management methods.

THE RELATIVE SUCCESS OF FOREIGN VS. INDIGENOUS FIRMS IN GENERAL

Available evidence indicates that U.S. companies are generally more efficient and successful (in terms of profitability, growth, productivity and other conventional measures) than indigenous firms. Nevertheless, the more progressive indigenous firms frequently succeed in time in closing the gap substantially between themselves and their U.S. competitors. These generalizations are based not only on available studies of India, but also on studies of such diverse countries as the Philippines, Greece, Chile, the United Kingdom, Western European countries and others.[1]

Superior technology and technical know-how, greater access to capital at better terms, economies of scale and firm size, superior products, and international prestige and reputation contribute to the superior performance of U.S. subsidiaries. However, superior management is also a critical factor. Available studies of the largest and most successful companies in India indicate that on the average foreign firms fare considerably better than local companies. Of the 50 largest private industrial firms in India (in terms of total assets) in the early and mid-1960s over half were affiliated with international corporations. By 1970 the proportion had reached 75 percent, and the proportion of U.S. affiliated firms had increased from about 10 to 20 percent.[2] In general, an increasing number of U.S. firms have come to rank among the largest and most successful companies in India in recent times.

Although profitability and growth have deteriorated considerably in both India's private and public industrial sectors since the mid-1960s, the performance of U.S. and other foreign firms in India has not been hurt as badly as has that of indigenous companies. For example, the average return on capital for the 50 largest private industrial corporations in India fell from 10.9 percent in 1967-68 to 10.3 percent in 1968-69, while average net return on sales fell from 5.4 percent to 5.1 percent. However, the 37 firms affiliated with international corporations did better as a group with an average return on capital of 11.7 percent in 1968-69 and a profits-to-sales ratio of 5.5 percent. The nine companies with U.S. equity fared even better as a group than the 37 foreign affiliated firms as a whole.[3]

It is interesting to note that in the past, U.S. subsidiaries surveyed in India typically did better in terms of profitability and growth than the comparable domestic operations of their parent companies. However, since about 1964, the pattern has become more mixed, with a substantial number of American subsidiaries in India faring considerably worse than their counterparts in the United States.

MANAGERIAL CHANGE

A good argument can be made that many subsidiaries in India and elsewhere would be considerably better off today if they had focused much earlier on improving the managerial process rather than waiting for strong environmental pressures to force them to do so. Largely in response to such pressures, most of the U.S. companies surveyed in India have introduced substantial changes to improve their management processes since the mid-1960s. In contrast, few of the Indian companies surveyed had made many significant changes in their management processes during the 1960s, although a number of them continuously claimed that they were about to do so. Typical in this regard is a fairly sizeable but traditional drug and chemical company: for more than five years top management has been talking about greater decentralization of authority, and the grooming of a young and energetic man to step into the managing director's shoes. But to date this still has not happened. Similarly, in spite of much talk, there have been no significant changes in its management practices.

Many Indian companies feel they have accomplished a great deal if they succeed in introducing even relatively minor changes in the management process. For example, one company which is very pleased with its record has made the following changes, and only these, during the last five years: 1) the purchasing and public relations executives have swapped jobs; 2) the maintenance function has been switched from engineering to manufacturing where it is still highly ineffective; 3) a special group of quality control inspectors have been assigned the task of checking on incoming materials with some positive results; 4) somewhat more use is now being made of committees and meetings for coordination purposes, in the absence of comprehensive or integrated company plans; 5) the individual incentive scheme for salesmen has been changed to a group scheme, based on keeping down sales expenses, with little effect to date; and 6) an electronic computer was introduced in January, 1969. As of mid-1969 it was still too early to tell whether the computer decision was a wise one, since the machine was only being used on a limited experimental basis.

The most progressive Indian firm studied made an impressive number of changes and improvements in management. It has entered into technical collaboration agreements with major foreign companies and, in many ways, is better managed than many of the U.S. subsidiaries which were surveyed. This company employs a sizeable number and proportion of American and other foreign-trained managers, technicians, and specialists.

MANAGERIAL ADAPTATION

The successful transference of managerial skill and practice from a more developed to a less developed country requires considerable adjustment in basic operating patterns. An accommodation must be made to the local environment, not only to deal with new physical factors, but also because the accomplishment of objectives requires motivating and selling ideas to people (local nationals) whose value systems differ from those of the parent country. As a result, it is axiomatic that a U.S. domestic enterprise, if transported intact (key personnel, equipment, practices) to India, would still have to undergo some major changes in order to accommodate to the local operating environment.

Conversely, the nature of business operations within a developing nation like India changes with the entry of "Western" companies. Such companies introduce Western values — values which are intimately related to industrial societies. As a result of the competition these firms offer and the examples they set, the local business environment is altered, and indigenous firms are pressured to change, although they often do so slowly. Industrial development, as we know it today, is based chiefly upon Western values. Consequently, economic growth, as well as the operation of successful enterprices in a developing economy requires, on the one hand, a break from traditional patterns, and on the other an adaptation of Western practices to local environmental conditions.

If one were to depict this graphically on a horizontal scale, placing the traditional indigenous values at one end, and Western values at the other, one could hypothesize a point (or a region) lying between the extremes, at which a company is best equipped to deal with the local environment at a given point in time. By adding a vertical scale to measure the relative success (most commonly economic) a given firm achieves, we can prepare a diagram which we have labelled the "Adaptation Spectrum." Before exploring such a spectrum in more detail and applying it to firms studied in India, it is useful to identify more fully its two extremes. The points used to anchor the adaptation spectrum on its horizontal scale are, in this study, the managerial processes and values of the traditional Indian company and those of the highly Americanized or stereotyped U.S. operation.

STEREOTYPE OF THE HIGHLY TRADITIONAL INDIAN FIRM

At one extreme of the spectrum or continuum we have the traditional Indian enterprise which manifests in its management, organization, operations and business dealings the traditional values and cultural patterns of Indian life. Many of the characteristics of this kind of firm are common to traditional indigenous enterprises in other developing countries.

In reality, there are few companies of any significant size or complexity in India which operate in a purely traditional sense unless one confines the examination to cottage industry or remote rural areas. However many more indigenous firms are closer to the traditional end of the spectrum than to the Americanized end. Most indigenous firms modernize slowly; moreover, most of the progressive Indian firms where one is likely to find truly substantial departures from traditional patterns are relatively large or relatively new. They are usually in competitive industries where there are significant numbers of foreign firms and they employ complex modern technology.

What follows is not an exhaustive picture of the characteristics of the traditional Indian firm. Rather it is a thumbnail sketch which focuses on some of the stereotype's most salient features.

In general, the traditional company is characterized by all of the prevalent attitudes, values, and behavior patterns discussed in the chapter dealing with the sociological-cultural environment (Chapter 4). It is a family type of affair, dominated by one man — usually the father or an elder brother.

Due to a distrust of outsiders, key positions in the firm are filled by brothers, uncles and cousins; in addition, many posts are assigned to more distant relatives and close family friends. The operation of the firm is visualized more as an extension of family life (providing many of the functions of the joint family, including mutual aid and security), than as a purely economic operation, although outsiders seldom see anything but the economic facade.

The top man makes all decisions concerning expenditures, regardless of the amounts involved, and very few decisions of any kind are made without his approval. All disputes within the managerial group are referred to him for settlements. He hires, disciplines, promotes and rewards.

If the top man is the father, the sons are continually "jockeying for position," to the extent that they may withhold information and assistance from one another. Other managers resign themselves to lesser positions in the company, because the top is reserved. Correspondingly, non-family members have little expectation of progressing far above the levels for which they were hired initially.

Promotions in the lower supervisory levels are based on who you are and who you know. Seniority is the basis for worker advancement (which is limited). Hiring practices are lax, and often follow caste or community lines. A great deal of consideration is given to the employment of capital and very little to the employment of labor. Matters regarding worker performance and motivation tend to receive little attention. ("Labor is cheap.") However, the company deals with its workers in a paternalistic manner, with the top man frequently meeting individual workers, discussing problems, listening to their complaints, lending money for weddings or illnesses, and so forth. Employees tend to regard him as a father. In making direct contacts throughout the organization, the top man ignores any existing "chains of command."

The organization structure is both vague and nebulous. A rough "pecking order" exists, based on position in the "family," but it is difficult to pinpoint specific responsibilities and very unusual to find much authority below the top level. The whole structure of lower-level supervisors is very weak, and most can be regarded as workers rather than managers. Management development is practically unknown, and few, if any, of the company's managers have had contact with management education. Worker training typically consists solely of on-the-job observation of other workers.

Managers and workers are generally secure in their positions; as long as the company can survive, the employee knows he has a job for life. His aspirations are limited, and he soon discovers exactly where he stands in the hierarchy and how far he is likely to go. Each year a fixed increment may be added to his pay. His duties and responsibilities are prescribed not by decree, but by the working relationships which develop with his superiors. He is extremely conservative (he has found that the penalties for taking initiative and erring are much greater than the rewards for succeeding), prefers to refer decisions upwards (often because he doesn't have the authority to make them), and tends to go by established traditions.

Conservatism pervades the entire firm. A great deal of inertial resistance to change exists, especially in regard to managerial techniques, which do not receive much attention. The primary focus is on getting goods out the door and counting the receipts. Quality has never been an important consideration. Development of truly new products is minimal, and a major "innovation" is the introduction of a "new" product which a competitor has already proved in the market.

Supplier relations are dependent on individual relationships between managers in the supplying and the purchasing companies, not on quality or (to a lesser degree) cost. Gifts are freely offered and accepted.

A systems approach to problems is practically unknown, as are planning and control in the modern sense. Procedures for determining inventory levels, work loads, production schedules, etc., are based on "intuition" and "past experience," with very little quantitative analysis. Frequently such problems are ignored and left to seek their own solutions. Cost data is very scarce and is only compiled at top levels to give an overall statement of profit and asset positions. These figures are guarded jealously, lest they give competitors useful information.

The firm usually maintains a complacent internal attitude, and except for the brothers near the top who are fighting for position, the incidence of managerial ulcers is probably very small. Informality is the watchword, and there is little pretense of "democracy in action," although family councils may be called at higher management levels to discuss problems. However, such meetings serve primarily to obtain "unanimous" approval and support for the top man's decision. In summary, the main strength of the traditional Indian firm probably lies in the strong internal bonds which tie the organization together, while its main weaknesses, highly static and inefficient management, conservatism, complacency, and the maintenance of large numbers of inefficient employees, result from the same factors which give rise to this strength.

STEREOTYPE OF THE HIGHLY AMERICANIZED FIRM IN THE CONTEXT OF A DEVELOPING COUNTRY

It is assumed here that the reader is generally familiar with the operating patterns of Western companies, and especially those of U.S. firms. For the other extreme of the adaptation spectrum it is meaningful to consider not only the stereotype of the economically motivated, systematized (if not computerized), orderly, efficiency-oriented company which represents the American ideal, but also the stereotype of the impersonal and unyielding firm as seen through the eyes of local nationals. This kind of enterprise makes an absolutely minimum adaptation or accommodation to the local environment. In reality, probably no U.S. subsidiaries in India are at the very extreme Americanized end of the spectrum. (If there are any it would be a good bet that they won't survive very long!)

The stereotyped, highly Americanized company is commonly viewed by Indians as very cold, impartial, and unfeeling in its business dealings. It is characterized by a great emphasis on economic considerations and a lack of humanistic characteristics. It pays well, and it offers considerable prestige to employees just by virtue of its name and product reputation. But it is not a pleasant place to work. (The common view regarding British companies is that they are not as far to the right on the spectrum as U.S. firms.)

This image is certainly true in a relative sense, because in comparison with their traditional Indian counterparts, U.S. companies are much more likely to emphasize the economic aspects of operating a business and to give substantially less attention to the types of personal relationships which exist in Indian firms (or society). However, compared to their U.S. domestic counterparts, U.S. subsidiaries in India are usually more paternalistic and their activities tend to be influenced by human and emotional factors to a great extent.

THE ADAPTATION SPECTRUM

The adaptation spectrum, as shown in Figure 10-1, is a graphic representation of the managerial transference and environmental accommodation process. This approach can be useful for evaluating responses to specific problems; for example, analysis of relationships between various intrafirm efficiency indicators (e's) — such as machine downtime — specific elements of the management process (B's), and environmental constraints (C's). The graphic representation would tend to change, in some cases dramatically, depending on the specific kinds of problems studied, the nature of the external environments involved, and often the time period covered as well. It can also be used in analyzing overall company managerial patterns and aggregate performance, although this would prove more effective if such aggregate analysis were built on more detailed micro analysis of specific e's and B's, as well as relevant C's. In the case of aggregate firm analysis, the graphic representation would differ depending on the countries under study, and often also on the specific industries or types of firms studied.

The vertical scale of the adaptation spectrum measures relative success. It should be noted that the use of "economic success" introduces a pro-Western bias, since it involves concepts and performance measures which are most closely associated with Western business. The peak point in reality, probably a region — on the adaptation spectrum is the one at which a company tends to be best equipped managerially to deal with the local environment. This is the point where the adaptation process has most successfully blended the managerial know-how and practices of the

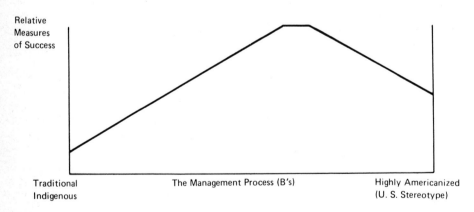

FIGURE 10-1 Adaptation spectrum

more developed nations with the local conditions and dominant values of the less developed country. Between the two extremes, a large number of blends (i.e., degrees of adaptation towards the ideal point) exist.

A number of the characteristics of the adaptation spectrum warrant elaboration. First, the peak point or region lies closer to the right end than the left end in the above figure, which probably holds true for most modern industrial sectors — e.g., drugs and chemicals — in India and elsewhere. The exact location of the peak region depends on the industries and the specific countries considered.

On the basis of logic or *a priori* reasoning alone — apart from available empirical evidence — it seems justifiable to place the peak region closer to the right than the left of the horizontal scale of the spectrum in most situations. The process of industrialization is largely a Western phenomenon, and Western companies have developed skills and practices which allow them to compete successfully in industrial situations. Over the years an evolutionary process has taken place which, through a type of natural selection, has tended to stress those values and practices which are most conducive to industrial activity. On the other hand, traditional patterns in India (and elsewhere) did not emerge from an industrial milieu, and even though the physical environment is still India, the challenges and opportunities offered by industrialization require many responses which are largely Western in nature.

The peak region, however, would tend to move further to the left the more under-developed, traditional, and environmentally different a particular country is in comparison to the United States. For example, the peak region for Afghanastan, Ethiopia, Niger, Uganda, and Somalia would probably be further left than for India. In primitive societies, it would probably be quite far to the left. Similarly, it might even lie closer to the left than to the right extreme for traditional handicraft industries in more developed societies.

Although a country's level of industrialization and affluence tends to be a critical factor in determining how far right or left on the spectrum its peak region is, its environment must also be considered. Some relatively developed countries have industrial environments very different from that of the United States; e.g., Japan. In such cases, their peak adaptation region may actually lie closer to the left end than that of a less developed country.

One may question the *exact* points on the adaptation spectrum for any particular case. It is impossible to claim perfect accuracy since the graphic representation is based on estimates requiring considerable judgment and experience. However, they do provide useful, if not exact, depictions of reality.

Another related characteristic of the adaptation spectrum as shown in Figure 10-1 pertains to the height of the spectrum line at the extremes. The value at the Americanized end is higher since most U.S. international companies have already developed a sizeable body of managerial skills and practices which they can effectively use to deal with industrial problems. (Of course, some firms do much better than others in this regard.) The traditional indigenous firm in India and other poor countries must not only develop such skills, but it must also break with established patterns of thought, motivation, and behavior. It should be noted, however, that a highly over-Americanized firm may eventually approach the zero point of relative economic success, since it may be so imcompatable with the local environment that it does not continue in existence. On the other hand, highly traditional indigenous firms which stay that way may also eventually be forced out of existence due to their failure to compete effectively.

It should also be pointed out that the spectrum provides no indication of the costs, degrees of effect, or frustration which accompany the adaptation process. Although frustration levels may be similar at either end of the spectrum, survival considerations may give the traditional firm to viable alternative but to adapt and change at least to some extent. This process is typically a gradual one, in which the firm puts out cautious feelers to introduce changes with as little internal disruption as possible. Once the need for change has been both recognized and accepted, the company slowly starts to initiate change, largely through trial and error, and a gradual erosion of old habits takes place, often at an accelerating pace. A newly created indigenous firm can often move away from the traditional end of the spectrum quite quickly since it is not yet locked into traditional patterns. This is what has happened in various Indian public sector companies where administrative fiat has prescribed much of the management process at the outset.

The U.S. subsidiary tends to change in distinct phases, some of which take longer and are more difficult than others. Ethnocentric U.S. firms and managers, in particular, frequently have preconceived ideas of what situations "should be," and which of their practices are "up for change" and which are "inviolate." Often, these ideas originate in the parent office, without the benefit of a detailed examination of the requirements of the local situation. Some are related to the maintenance of uniform worldwide policies. Others reflect the fact that the foreign subsidiary is often regarded as little more than a small extension of a large corporate entity — one which can be terminated under "unfavorable" conditions and written off as a calculated risk that "did not pan out." This is an option which is not available to the Indian firm.

The image of what things "should be" is usually based on principles, values, and practices which have proved successful in the home environment and are deeply rooted in the domestic (U.S.) culture. In resisting change in these areas subsidiaries fight a battle of principles — to prove that their way is best or more moral; they are frequently forced to fight this battle with their workers, local unions, the local government, and their own managers. In many cases, they are forced to yield, but only after threats (sometimes backed by action) from government agencies, labor organizations, and other interested organizations.

In reality then, the adaptation process tends to occur in steps, as each successive battle is won or lost, rather than in the linear fashion depicted earlier. In some cases, the starting point is an emphatic refusal to compromise on anything, in particular, the maintenance of 100 percent ownership. The final stage is usually a departure from the initial position and is often characterized by substantial local ownership of the subsidiary, a higher degree of participation by local nationals in subsidiary (or in a few cases even international) management, and considerable reductions in tension between the subsidiary and government, labor, and other local groups.

Figure 10-2 presents a modified and more realistic diagram of the adaptation spectrum.

It often requires five or ten years or more for the subsidiaries of strongly ethnocentric U.S. international corporations to shift from the far right to a position approaching the optimum adaptation point — if they reach this point at all. For example, most of the U.S. subsidiaries studied in India indicate a trend towards Indianization of upper management positions within a five-to-ten year period, although very few have fully completed the process yet. The adaptation spectrum clearly represents an open system with managerial behavior in productive enterprises causing both environmental and value changes on a macro scale. The peak region, in term's of a firm's economic success, tends to shift further toward the Americanized end of the spectrum in a developing country and as a given country develops. However, as the United States moves further in the direction of a post — industrial society — the world's first genuine society of this kind — the peak region for this country might begin to shift leftward as new values and environmental conditions emerge; or it might take on some entirely new characteristics which will require a sharp break or discontinuity in the spectrum.

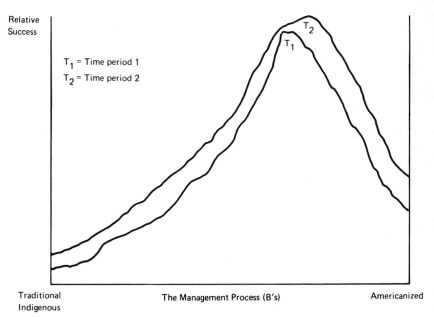

Relative Success

T_1 = Time period 1
T_2 = Time period 2

Traditional Indigenous

The Management Process (B's)

Americanized

FIGURE 10-2   Modified adaptation spectrum

One of the most significant findings emerging from our studies is that the companies which have the largest number and proportions of relatively Westernized, and particularly Americanized, Indians in key positions are generally the most successful in their respective sectors, regardless of the nationality of company ownership or control. These are Indians who have been educated and trained in the West (particularly in the United States), but who are also relatively Westernized in their attitudes, motivational patterns, and behavior.

The correlation between the number and proportion of Westernized Indians of the above type and relative firm success is evident in the pharmaceutical industry. The most successful Indian company in this sector has had a substantially greater number and proportion of relatively Westernized and U.S. trained local nationals than any of the other indigenous drug firms. It also compared favorably to several U.S. subsidiaries in this regard, and it has been about as successful as they have been.

In general, the nationality of top management, more than the nationality of ownership, is the most critical factor in determining whether a particular firm falls to the right or the left of the peak point or region of the spectrum. However, this statement deserves some qualification. Almost all of the U.S. subsidiaries in India that have been examined have had either foreign (not only Americans) or Indian top managers from their inception. Managers who had set the basic pattern in the formative stages of the operation have generally had successors who have worked along similar lines if they have been of the same nationality (although there are a few notable exceptions). Few of the U.S. subsidiaries surveyed which started out with foreign top managers have yet switched to local nationals.

APPLICATION OF THE ADAPTATION SPECTRUM AND INDICATORS OF RELATIVE SUCCESS IN THE PHARMACEUTICAL INDUSTRY

In this section we shall apply the adaptation spectrum to ten relatively large companies (by Indian standards) in the drug industry. Firms A, B, C, D and E are indigenous Indian companies, and firms F, G, H, I, and J are U.S. subsidiaries with 100 percent or majority American ownerships. A majority of these ten companies are ranked among the top ten pharmaceutical firms in India in terms of market share, and all are among the top twenty drug companies in the country.

Figure 10-3 plots diagramatically the position on the adaptation spectrum and the relative economic success of the five private indigenous firms and the five U.S. subsidiaries studied. The plotting of firms along the horizontal axis of the spectrum reflects how the overall management process has been handled by each company, i.e., where each firm falls on the "traditional − Americanized" scale. Although we have taken into account managerial performance during the 1960s as a whole, more weight has been given to how each firm was being managed in the

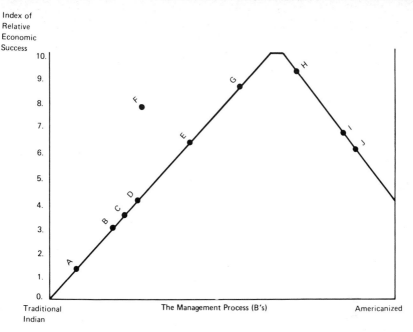

Index of Relative Economic Success

FIGURE 10-3 Application of the adaptation spectrum for ten firms in India's pharmaceutical sector

latter part of the decade. The plotting of firms along the horizontal scale is admittedly subjective and speculative. However, it is based on intensive study of the way in which many specific and critical elements of the management process (B's) — and related e's — have been dealt with in the firms surveyed.

The vertical scale indicates relative aggregate economic success for each firm. It is based on the 13 aggregate indicators presented in Table 10-1. These include such factors as overall firm profitability, growth, and productivity. The vertical scale is based on a composite index score for each firm which ranges from 0 to 10. In turn, the index score for each firm is based on its rank order with regard to the 13 performance indicators — which have been weighted equally — presented in Table 10-1. Table 10-2 presents the composite index scores for the ten drug companies and elaborates further on how these scores have been derived. More sophisticated mathematical techniques and statistical analyses could have been employed, but, frankly it would not have been worth the effort. A rank order and computer analysis[4] has also been done for the kinds of micro intrafirm efficiency indicators (e's) to be covered in the following chapters, including: product yields, productivity in various areas, unanticipated equipment breakdowns, idle capacity, material wasteage, scrap, rejects, unit product costs, returned goods, late deliveries, inventory levels, absenteeism, indicators of product and technical innovations and improvements, planned versus actual

TABLE 10-1   Rank orders of ten pharmaceutical companies in India in terms of economic success during the 1960s[1] (Companies A, B, C, D, E are Indian and F, G, H, I, J are U.S. controlled)

Average annual (compounded) sales growth %	Sales — Gross profit[2]	Sales — Profit (before tax)	Sales — Net profit	Total Assets — Sales	Total Assets — Sales per employee	Total Assets — Operating income[3]	Total Assets — Net profit	Total Worth — Net profit	Net return on common stock equity[4]	Average annual growth in earnings per share of common stock[5]	Profit (before tax) per employee	Net profit per employee
F	J	H	F	H	G	H	H	H	H	H	G	G
I	F	J	H	E	H	G	G	G	G	D	H	H
G	H	F	J	D	F	E	F	E	J	G	I	F
H	I	G	G	G	–	F	I	F	D	J	F	E
E	G	–	–	–	J	–	E	I	B	C	E	I
D	B	E	E	F	E	J	J	J	C	B	J	J
C	E	B	C	J	D	C	C	D	A	A	C	C
J	C	D	B	C	B	D	D	B			B	B
B	A	C	D	B	C	A	A	C			D	D
A	D	A	A	A	A	B	B	A			A	A

[1] Rankings are based on average performance for each measure during the 1960s. For a majority of firms rankings are based on nine operating years, but for some data has only been obtained for eight years.

[2] Gross profit = sales minus cost of goods sold.

[3] Operating income is computed as net profit before taxes and before subtracting for interest payments or dividends. This ratio is similar to the Dupont method of computing rate of return on total investment.

[4] Data not available for firms E, F and I.

[5] Data not available for firms E, F and I.

TABLE 10-2   Aggregate rank order and scores for ten pharmaceutical companies in India
(Derived from Table 10-1)

Final rank	Final scores: Index of relative economic success*
H	9.3
G	8.4
F	7.9
I	6.7
E	6.2
J	6.1
D	4.0
C	3.5
B	3.0
A	1.3

*Final scores have been obtained from rank orders for each of the 13 economic indicators presented in Table 10-1. Equal weight has been arbitrarily assigned to each indicator. The firm ranking first on each indicator received ten points, for second place nine points, and so on down to one for last place. There are 13 economic indicators in Table 10-1. The total scores for each firm have been divided by 13 to arrive at the final scores, except for firms E, F, and I where data was only available for 11 of the 13 economic indicators, and 11 was used in the denominator. For the two economic indicators where data was only available for seven firms, those firms ranking first received ten points and the last placed firms received four points rather than one point. Firms E, F and I received scores of zero but, as noted above, their total scores have been divided by 11 rather than 13.

performance in various areas, and so forth. This shows a close and generally significant correlation between how individual firms rank with regard to their aggregate performance and how they rank with regard to the micro intrafirm efficiency indicators. The correlation generally holds true for firms in various other industries in India, in addition to the drug sector.

As shown in Figure 10-3, with only one notable exception, the firms closest to the optimum adaptation region are those which have achieved the greatest relative economic success. The exception is F, an Indian-managed U.S. subsidiary.

A brief comment on each of the ten drug firms is warranted before turning our attention to their relative economic success. Company A is by far the most traditional firm. It is run in strict — but paternalistic — authoritarian and highly centralized fashion. Its facilities are antiquated, though here and there one finds some modern technology. Effective maintenance, repair, and modernization could do much to improve existing facilities, even if more modern technology were not added. The firm is diversified and produces many highly unprofitable items — for both sentimental reasons and because management is not sure of unit costs. Company A has operated at a substantial loss in the last several years and its viability seems to be in serious question. This firm has traditionally shunned even foreign technical collaboration, but for reasons of survival it has been considering the possibility of such collaboration recently.

The management of Company A has had as a top priority objective making the firm "a good place to work by providing job security." It has also had a basic policy of providing employment to chemists and other scientifically and technically trained individuals who have received their education at institutions in the city or state where the firm is located. Very few of its personnel have had any education or training abroad. In spite of its basic objectives and policies the firm has ironically been plagued with critical labor problems and much union agitation in the last several years. Moreover, demand for many of its products has fallen sharply, and it has been badly hurt by supply problems, including import restrictions. Such critical problems could have been in substantial part prevented or at least alleviated through better management. However, profitability and growth per se have historically not been priority objectives, and they have been valued largely to the extent that they have been essential to survival.

Company B has also been fairly traditional, though clearly less so than Company A. It is highly diversified, though many of its products make little or no money. The firm has few foreign-trained personnel, and it has been going along in about the same managerial manner and at the same pace for some time.

Company C, like A and B, is old and well-established, but less diversified. It was taken over by a larger and relatively progressive Indian company in the first half of the 1960s, primarily because it held some desirable product licenses. It has had some foreign-educated managers and specialists — including a few trained in the United States — in recent years, who have introduced some changes and modest improvements in operations and performance. However, the magnitude and extent of changes and improvements have been considerably less than hoped for.

Company D is also an old and established family-controlled Indian firm. It is fairly diversified and has as one of its key objectives a high degree of vertical integration. It has been generally successful in achieving this goal, but the methods used have been uneconomical in many respects. Company D does more research and development than probably any other indigenous drug firm in India. Traditionally it has shunned foreign collaboration of any type, but in the last few years it has modified this position, and has been actively trying to negotiate technical collaboration agreements with foreign firms for a few major products.

Company D differs from A, B, and C in that most of its key managers, as well as many technical and scientific specialists have been educated abroad, several of them in the United States. In spite of this, most of its key executives are closer to the traditional end of the spectrum than the Americanized (or Westernized) end in terms of their attitudes, motivational patterns, or behavior. Company D still has many vestiges of the traditional Indian firm, e.g., more than 75 percent of the managers in the top three levels were related, and the head of the family made all major decisions, as well as many minor ones, especially in the financial area. On the other hand, modern managerial techniques were substantially more in evidence than in Company A, and somewhat more than in Companies B or C.

Company E is by far the most progressive and least traditional of the Indian firms. Once an indigenous firm reaches a breakthrough point in unshackling itself from tradition change becomes relatively easy. This has been the case with Company E for some time. It has been run largely by "professional" Indian managers and specialists, most of whom have been educated in the United States. Several have also worked in the United States. This firm has entered into various kinds of technical collaboration agreements with foreign companies.

Although Company E is controlled by a family, it has developed an effective middle-management group. It has experimented with different types of organizational forms, and has made use of computer-based quantitative techniques, and innovations in communications technology. It has been the most profit-oriented of the Indian firms, although it has tended to give careful consideration to both the humanistic and economic aspects of most decisions.

Company F, a wholly owned U.S. subsidiary, deviates from the adaptation spectrum. The explanation for the deviation can be found largely in its limited but profitable product line which embodies advanced technology. The firm's major products are highly specialized, some are patented, and they include relatively high-profit-margin items for which India has a growing and unsatisfied demand. This firm, though competing on a national basis with some of its products, has really been filling a special niche in the industry. Although it ranks third among the ten drug firms in aggregate economic success, it ranks only about fifth or sixth overall with regard to performance on the types of intrafirm efficiency indicators (e's) to be considered in later chapters.

The management of Company F has been Indian and of a semitraditional nature. The top manager has always been an Indian who has had some training and work experience in the U.S. parent company's operations, and he has made all of the major local decisions. Many of the parent's policies, procedures, and rules have been outlined in manuals, but the subsidiary has often deviated from them. This company has probably been able to maintain its 100 percent U.S. ownership because it is significantly smaller than any of the other U.S. firms studied. Having appointed an Indian top manager from the outset may also have been a contributing factor.

Company G, one of the most successful and best managed U.S. subsidiaries, appointed its first Indian managing director in 1968. In general, it has done a relatively good job in balancing American management methods with local considerations. From the outset this firm provided 40 percent equity participation to an Indian collaborator who has also served as its distributor. The collaborator is part of one of the largest, most progressive, and most successful Indian industrial empires. Company G has maintained relatively good relations with the government, its own employees, and the recently formed labor union in its plant, as well as customers and suppliers. It has generally been willing to make some compromises and to grant feasible concessions before extreme pressure was brought to bear.

Until a few years ago Company G, being quite new, had been preoccupied with technical problems. More recently, it has turned its attention increasingly to managerial improvements, and has done so with notable success. Like other drug firms in India — especially foreign companies — it has become greatly concerned about more stringent price controls and shorter life patent protection.

Company H has shifted from a position far to the right of the spectrum to a more moderate position during the past decade. Under great governmental pressure it finally allowed Indian equity participation, to the extent of 25 percent, in the mid-1960s. (More recently it has come under pressure to further increase local equity participation.) The firm fully Indianized its management several years ago, and appointed its first Indian managing director. Following this it was able to normalize its relationships with the labor union, after a stormy past, and it achieved efficiency levels approaching those of its U.S. parent in several areas. However, the Indian managing director soon resigned, along with several other major executives. He was followed by two "interim" foreign top managers — neither of them American — and in the second half of 1969 it appeared that another new managing director, probably foreign, was soon to be appointed. Serious labor problems erupted again in 1968, but they were largely resolved by mid-1969.

Company H owes much of its economic success to two factors — a specific product line and a relatively effective and efficient management. Most of its major managers and many of its key specialists have been educated or trained abroad, chiefly in the United States. The company has also done a good job of training personnel within India.

Company H has placed great emphasis on the economic aspects of decisions, and defined its key objectives in terms of sales growth and profitability. It has done a relatively good job of applying American management practices and techniques, but it has clearly gone too far in a few areas. Although Company H has been economically successful to date — the most successful of the ten firms — it could run into serious difficulties in the future if it moves significantly further to the right in these areas.

Company I has, proportionately, substantially fewer managers who have been educated or trained in the United States than G or H. However, in this company, managerial decisions have been more highly concentrated at the upper levels of the parent corporation, and this accounts for its higher degree of over-Americanization. The parent of Company I has exerted strong, pervasive, and detailed controls over its operations. There has been more of a "we" and "they" split between the Indians and non-Indians, and considerably less trust on the part of either group in the competence and attitudes of the other. Company I has given 35 percent equity participation to an Indian company which has also been serving as distributor for various of its products. Company I appointed its first Indian managing director in the late 1960s; the company was not studied after that point of time.

Company J matches the U.S. stereotype most closely. The parent company and local management have defined clearly what they will and will not do to adapt to the local environment, and they have been adamant in this regard. Less adaptation has taken place than at any of the U.S. firms. Company J has had a non-U.S., foreign managing director who in many ways more closely resembles the stereotype U.S. manager than do most U.S. executives in India. The foreign and local managers have been distinctly divided into two groups — even more so than at Company I — both operationally (in terms of authority and responsibilities) and physically (i.e., socially). Bitter labor disputes and poor government relations have characterized this firm over the years, and it seems to have moved from one crisis to another. This company would not have been as successful as it has if it were not for the nature of some of its key products, which have enjoyed relatively high growth and profit margins — though both have been deteriorating in recent years. Company J has allowed only about 15 percent local equity participation, in spite of strong government pressure to provide for more. All of this 15 percent is held by one Indian distributor whose organization was taken over by Company J several years ago.

Now let us turn our attention to the actual performance and relative economic success — as reflected on Tables 10-1 and 10-2 — of the above ten drug companies. The poorest of the U.S. firms averaged a 12 percent annual sales growth during the 1960s. One averaged between 15 and 20 percent with three averaging better than 20 percent. Only three of the indigenous firms averaged over 12 percent sales growth, two over 15 percent, and none 20 percent or more.

All of the U.S. firms averaged at least 40 percent in terms of gross profits in relation to sales (computed in terms of sales minus cost of goods sold). Only one of the Indian firms did this well. All of the U.S. firms averaged 20 percent or more in terms of profit before tax in relation to sales, while none of the Indian firms did so. Four of the U.S. firms averaged 10 percent or better with regard to net profit (after tax) on sales, and all averaged over 9 percent. None of the Indian firms averaged 9 percent or better. Four of the U.S. firms achieved a sales to total asset ratio of 1.0 or better, and all did better than .9. Only two Indian firms did better than .9. All of the U.S. firms achieved sales per employee of more than 50,000 rupees, while no Indian firm achieved 50,000 — the best was over 40,000, however.

All of the U.S. companies averaged rates of return — computed in terms of operating income divided by total assets employed — greater than 18 percent, and all but one did better than 20 percent. Only two of the Indian firms did better than 18 percent, and only one did better than 20 percent. Four of the U.S. firms averaged better than 10 percent with regard to net profit divided by total assets, and all did better than 8 percent. Only two Indian firms did better than 8 percent, and only one did better than 10 percent. With regard to net profit to net worth all U.S. firms averaged 10 percent or more while only one Indian company did so.

Of the three U.S. firms for which data has been obtained for return on common stock equity, all averaged better than 15 percent. None of the four Indian firms for which such data was obtained did this well. All of the three U.S. subsidiaries for which growth in earnings per share of common stock data has been obtained averaged 13 percent or more. Of the four Indian firms for which such data has been obtained, only one did this well, and two of these companies has negative earnings per share growth rates for the period.

With regard to before-tax profits per employee, all of the U.S. firms averaged better than 10,000 rupees. Only one indigenous firm did this well. As for net profit per employee, all of the U.S. firms averaged better than 5,000 rupees, while, here too, only one Indian firm did this well.

Two indexes which were computed for each firm are not shown on Table 10-1 or reflected in Table 10-2. These are total capital (i.e., total assets) per employee and fixed assets per employee. This was done to see how relative firm differences in economic success compare with relative differences in capital intensity. They have shown that differences in the economic success among the ten firms have been significantly greater than differences in capital intensity, giving added weight to our contention that managerial factors tend to play a key role in economic success.

It is worth commenting briefly on three other major drug companies in India which have not been included in the above discussion, in Figure 10-3, or in Tables 10-1 and 10-2. They comprise a large public sector corporation and two major British subsidiaries.

The public sector firm would rank seventh or eighth (out of eleven firms) in terms of overall economic success in relation to the above ten firms. All of the U.S. firms plus one of the Indian companies have done better. Indian Company D has done just about as well. The public sector firm did best during the 1960s with regard to both before and after tax profits in relation to sales, ranking fifth and fourth respectively. A major reason for this has been its dominant sellers' market position with regard to its basic product line, as well as the fact that it has imported large amounts of basic commodities which it has sold domestically at several times the world price. It ranks near the bottom in terms of sales divided by total assets, sales per employee, and growth in per-share earnings. It ranks around seventh on most of the other performance indicators. This government corporation was set up originally in the 1950s with relatively advanced technology.

Many modern managerial practices were prescribed for this government firm at the outset by administrative fiat. However, it regressed in many areas, and the kinds of inefficiencies common to public sector firms grew along with the organization. In terms of total capital and fixed assets per employee it compares favorably with the U.S. subsidiaries as a whole. In fact it has had more assets and capital per employee than all of the indigenous private companies and a few of the U.S. firms, even though it has been considerably overstaffed.

Partial data obtained for a leading British drug subsidiary in India — 75 percent U.K.-owned — indicates that this firm ranks higher than one of the five U.S. firms, roughly about as high as one or two of the other U.S. firms, but significantly behind the other two (G and H). It ranks near the top on sales in relation to assets, and quite high with regard to return on net worth, common equity, and total assets. It ranks lower on sales growth, and lower still on profits in relation to sales.

A second British drug firm (60 percent U.K.-owned) which is also among India's ten largest pharmaceutical companies in terms of market share was analyzed. This firm ranks above all of the Indian companies, except E, and behind all of the U.S. firms.

No clear-cut patterns exist — using the indicators presented in Table 10-1 — between the aggregate economic success of U.S. drug subsidiaries in India and their parent company operations in the United States. On various measures the subsidiaries have done substantially better during the 1960s, and on others they have done significantly worse.

For example, subsidiary G has done worse than its parent U.S. based operations on all except sales growth and growth in earnings per share. On the other hand, subsidiary H has done better than its parent company's operations in the United States on almost all the indicators, including sales per employee and profits per employee. The parent company of G has done better on all but one indicator — sales growth — in the United States than parent H, but H has done better overall than G in India. In terms of total assets per employee, parent G has had about three times more than its subsidiary in India, and about 40 percent more than parent H, while parent H has had about two and a half times more than its subsidiary. Subsidiaries G and H have been about the same in this regard. In terms of fixed assets per employee, parents G and H have been quite close, and both have had roughly twice as much as their subsidiaries. Subsidiary G has actually had about 20 percent more than subsidiary H.

The one general pattern that does emerge from aggregate parent company-Indian subsidiary comparisons (and not only in the drug sector) is a chronological one: the aggregate economic performance of the subsidiaries has generally deteriorated significantly more than that of the U.S. based operations in recent years.

As noted above, it is usually more meaningful to deal with the more internally controllable intra-firm efficiency indicators (e's) when comparing operations in countries which have substantially different environments. Such comparisons are often even more meaningful when they are expressed in real or physical terms, in the form of ratios, time units, or in terms of changes over time, rather than in purely monetary terms. Even then, it is often difficult to determine whether uncontrollable environmental conditions, technology, economies of scale, or managerial factors are the most critical with regard to relative levels of performance. The U.S. based operations studied in the drug section have generally been doing much better with regard to the vast majority of intrafirm efficiency measures investigated than their subsidiaries in India. And where such performance *has* been better at subsidiaries, it has typically been due to intentional avoidance of excessive suboptimizations in the U.S. based operations. Although environmental conditions, economies of scale, capital intensity and various other essentially non-managerial factors are largely responsible for superior firm efficiency in the United States, managerial factors also play an important role.

Overview of firm performance in some other industries

One of the firms studied most intensively in India is a relatively large and diversified multiplant U.S. subsidiary that manufactures batteries, flashlights, chemicals, plastics, some carbon and metal products, and various other items. In spite of substantial deficiencies and problems, this company has been among the best managed in India.

No comparable indigenous firms produce the same broad range of products. Therefore, in order to evaluate and compare operating efficiency with local companies, economic success indicators for the separate product groups manufactured by this U.S. subsidiary were compared to aggregate indicators of indigenous firms producing similar products. In some cases this posed problems since values had to be computed and estimates made for such things as the allocation of overhead items and capital costs among different product lines for the U.S. subsidiary. However, this task was simplified by the company's excellent cost accounting system.

With regard to batteries — its chief product line — the U.S. subsidiary had only one significant Indian competitor during the 1960s, although some new competition has been emerging in the last few years, and more is anticipated in the near future. The U.S. firm did much better than the indigenous firm with regard to profits (gross, as well as before and after tax) in relation to sales, sales and output per employee, and before and after tax profits per employee. It also achieved somewhat higher average annual sales growth and a higher rank on net return on assets. The Indian firm did better with regard to sales in relation to total assets. If we look at the overall performance of the U.S. firm — including all product lines — it fared slightly better than the indigenous firm on net profit on total assets, net profit on net worth, return on common stock equity, and much better on earnings growth per share of common stock, while the Indian firm did better on operating income in relation to total assets. However, the aggregate performance of the U.S. firm in these areas is considerably understated in terms of batteries, since batteries have been by far the most profitable business of the company, while chemicals and plastics have dragged down overall profitability considerably.

The U.S. firm has had substantially more total capital and fixed assets per employee in terms of both overall operations and for batteries alone than the Indian company. However, superior management has clearly been a more important factor than greater capital intensity in the performance of the U.S. subsidiary. It has also done much better on nearly all of the intra-firm efficiency indicators to be covered in later chapters. In fact, the U.S. firm has given managerial and technical assistance to its Indian competitor on various occasions in the past. If it were not for the unsatisfied demand for batteries in India and restraints placed on the U.S. firm — not only by the governmental licensing and other authorities, but also by the company itself — it is unlikely that the Indian firm could have survived the competition at all.

In flashlights, a comparison of the economic success of the U.S. firm and its leading indigenous competitor during the 1960s yields less obvious conclusions. The U.S. firm made some major mistakes and experienced several serious setbacks in its flashlight operations, especially in the areas of marketing and product design and development. However, it has done considerably better in terms of sales and output per employee, and profits per employee. There is little difference in before and after tax profits in relation to sales. The Indian firm has achieved considerably higher annual average sales growth and somewhat higher sales on total assets. This firm has had a German in its key technical job for many years, and has been sending some of its key people — mostly family members — to Europe for training.

If we look at the overall performance of these two firms — including all of the products of the U.S. subsidiary — the indigenous firm comes out better on return on assets, net worth, and common stock equity, while the U.S. firm has an edge with regard to growth in per share earnings. The U.S. firm has considerably more total assets and fixed capital per employee. Again, the U.S. firm has done substantially better on most of the intrafirm efficiency indicators studied.

The operations of the chemicals and plastics division of the above U.S. subsidiary have been beset by critical problems and the results, especially with regard to polyethylene, have been disappointing. This has been due chiefly to factors beyond the company's control, which will be discussed further in later chapters. However, management — especially in the parent company — has also made some costly mistakes. A key problem has been the uneconomical size of its plant and the production processes employed. Another major problem was caused by the large amount of polyethylene imported by the Indian government several years ago, which flooded the market.

The U.S. company has had no comparable indigenous competitors in this product area. It has had a major British competitor in India, however. A limited amount of comparable performance data which was obtained from both of these firms seems to indicate that the U.S. company has had an edge in terms of economic success and internal efficiency. The British subsidiary has been faced with the same kinds of serious and largely uncontrollable problems as the U.S. firm in its chemicals and plastics operations.

In the late 1960s a major new competitor went into production. This British-Dutch-Indian venture has a more economically-sized plant and more efficient production processes. It is emerging as a significantly more successful competitor than the U.S. and British chemical and plastics operations.

Another firm studied was a highly intensive chemical concern that produces a homogeneous type of carbon. This is a joint venture between Indian interests and a U.S. company which holds a 40 percent interest. The management of the subsidiary is firmly in the hands of the relatively traditional Indian partners. Unfortunately, there are no comparable indigenous firms of this type in India. However, it is interesting to compare the subsidiary with the U.S.-based operations of the parent company.

Although U.S. plant capacity was about ten times greater than that of the Indian firm, the latter was large enough to derive basically the same economies of scale. The U.S.-based operations did better on nearly all of the aggregate indicators contained in Table 10-2. Labor productivity averaged about 250 percent more in the U.S. operations, and the unit cost per ton of output was about three times higher in India. The U.S. firm also did considerably better on most of the intrafirm efficiency indicators studied. One notable exception was waste (the reverse of product yields), where the Indian firm averaged 9 percent compared to 15 percent in the U.S. operations. The basic reasons for this were the superior grade of crude cake used in production by the Indian plant and the newness of the Indian plant.

One of the best managed and most prestigious firms studied in India was a relatively large and diversified British firm with 85 percent U.K. ownership. It has employed exclusively Indian managers for a considerable period of time. This company produced toilet articles, cosmetics, various cooking products, and agro-industry items. It was more successful than a smaller but competitive U.S. subsidiary on all aggregate indicators except for net profits on sales. (U.S. firms in India often do better than British firms with regard to profits in relation to sales, while U.K. companies do better in terms of return on capital. A major reason for this in many cases is that the British firms are older, and therefore have a lower capital base in terms of current value.) It also did better on more of the intrafirm efficiency indicators investigated and appeared to be managed significantly better.

Also studied was the aggregate performance of three firms in the Indian rubber industry. One was 61 percent U.S. owned, another 25 percent, and the third was 51 percent owned by U.K. interests. The firm with majority U.S. ownership has had significantly better overall performance with regard to the success indicators contained in Table 10-1, ranking first on a majority of these. The relative performance of the other two firms was mixed during the 1960s. The minority U.S. firm had substantially better sales and earnings growth — it was a much newer company — and better net profits in relation to sales. The British firm did better on return on assets, net worth and equity, and on sales in relation to total assets.

Only a few meaningful aggregate performance comparisons can be made for firms studied in the industrial engineering or heavy industry industries. Unfortunately, there are very few comparable U.S. and indigenous firms in these sectors, since the range and types of products produced differ considerably from firm to firm.

In the case of a U.S. joint venture (with 50 percent U.S. ownership) and an indigenous firm producing similar kinds of diesel engines, the former has done somewhat better, on the average, during the second half of the 1960s with regard to the economic success and intrafirm efficiency indicators for which data was obtained. However, the joint venture experienced sharp start-up losses in the mid-sixties. It was beset by very serious managerial — as well as technical and external — problems. Neither firm fared very well in the engine business — external conditions have been a major factor, although both have had highly deficient management by U.S. standards. However, somewhat better management seems to have evolved in the joint venture in the last several years.

The performance and management of the U.S. joint venture discussed above have been greatly inferior to those of its parent company's U.S. based diesel operations. The U.S. operation has had dramatically superior capital output and sales to capital ratios, its labor productivity has been several times higher, and its unit costs several times lower. Technology, economies of scale, and other such factors account for much of this; however, managerial factors have also played a significant part in the greatly superior U.S. performance.

An intensive study was made of a multiplant, indigenous electrical engineering company that produces transformers, switchgear, elevators, electric meters, and various kinds of motors, pumps and engines. This company has had some technical collaboration agreements with foreign international firms. There were no comparable U.S. subsidiaries in India, but a wholly owned British subsidiary did produce many of the same products. In general, the British firm has achieved better economic results — particularly if one compares intrafirm efficiency indicators — although the Indian company has done nearly as well or somewhat better in some areas.

If one compares the efficiency of companies in the United States which produce similar electrical engineering products to that of the Indian company, the U.S. firms come out dramatically ahead. For example, labor productivity in the manufacture of similar kinds of transformers typically runs about fifteen times higher in the United States (30 units per man-year versus two units in India).

One of the best examples of the transferability and applicability of American management skill and practice involves the heavy engineering firm described in the case at the end of Chapter 4. This Indian firm took on an American partner to the extent of 34 percent of its equity in the early spring of 1965. Prior to this time it had suffered huge losses. A financial manager and a production manager, both American, joined the firm and took over most of the internal management, functioning for a year without much interference from the managing director. During that time — from about April, 1965 until March, 1966 — the Americans were able to move a considerable distance along the adaptation spectrum towards the Americanized end. Sales and output increased by more than 20 percent, and the company's operating loss dropped by 50 percent. All of the firm's aggregate economic indicators improved significantly, and the improvement in many of the intra-firm efficiency indicators was even much more dramatic. However, the managing director resumed his old ways and patterns in the spring of 1966, and in a very short time the management process regressed to, or perhaps beyond, the point where it used to be on the adaptation spectrum, and the company went out of business in the late 1960s.

CHAPTER 10   FOOTNOTES

1. See for example the following studies dealing with India: *India — A Review of Trends in Manufacturing Industry*, 2 vols. plus a statistical annex, prepared by E.B. Waide, A. Nowicki, and B.S. Lee for the World Bank, December, 1969; *Business International*, April 17, 1970, pp. 124 ff., *Economic Times*, Bombay, December 20 and 27, 1965; A. Negandhi, *Private Foreign Investment Climate in India*, Institute for International Business Management Studies, Michigan State University, East Lansing, 1965; S. Kannappon and E. Burgess, *Aluminium Limited in India*, National Planning Association, New York, 1961; A. Negandhi and B. Prasod, *Comparative Management*, Appleton Century Crofts, New York, 1971 (This study contains data on a number of other

countries in addition to India); A. Phatak, *External Environmental Constraints and Their Impact Upon the Internal Operations of Firms in the Pharmaceutical and Engineering Industries in India*, UCLA doctoral dissertation, Los Angeles, 1966.

For studies dealing with various other countries see: F. Flores, *The Applicability of American Management Know-how to Developing Countries: Case Studies of Philippine Firms, American Subsidiaries and Affiliates Operating in the Phillippines and Their Respective Parent Firms in the United States*, UCLA doctoral dissertation, Los Angeles, 1968; B. Estafen, *An Empirical Study in Comparative Management: A Study of the Transferability of American Management Policies and Practices to Firms Operating in Chile*, UCLA doctoral dissertation, 1967; L. Raymond, *The Influence of Managerial Factors on Enterprise Performance: A Study of U.S. Subsidiaries and Local Firms in Britain*, UCLA doctoral dissertation, Los Angeles, 1970; A. Papageorge, *Transferability of Management: A Case Study of the United States and Greece*, UCLA doctoral dissertation, Los Angeles, 1967; N. Jocaby, "The Multinational Corporation," *The Center Magazine*, May, 1970; J. Dunning, *The Role of American Investment in the British Economy*, Political and Economic Broadsheet 507, London, February, 1969; J.J. Servan-Schreiber, *The American Challenge*, Atheneum, New York, 1968; B. Estafen, J. Anzizu and T. Korsvald, "Hunting Down the Famed European Management Gap," *European Business*, No. 26, Summer 1970.

See also the country and industry studies published by the National Planning Association of New York under its series *United States Business Performance Abroad*.

2. *Business International*, April 17, 1970, pp. 124 ff., *The Economic Times*, Bombay, December 20 and 27, 1965.

3. See *Business International*, April 17, 1970.

4. The computer program was based in part on one developed by Professor David Eiteman of UCLA.

CHAPTER 11
PLANNING AND
INNOVATION

INTRODUCTION AND OVERVIEW

One of management's primary functions is planning. Plans are required to channel the energies and resources of the organization toward desired goals. But they are also vital to anticipating and preparing for the problems and opportunities which the future may bring. Planning for the first purpose (i.e., to give the enterprise direction) is equally important in both developing and developed nations, although data limitations and other factors may make the process more difficult in the less developed countries. However, the second type of planning (i.e., the anticipatory kind) is often more critical in developing countries where greater uncertainty exists and where major environmental changes tend to be more difficult to predict.

Effective overall managerial planning consists of more than just preparing for an inevitable future. It is a dynamic, interactive process which helps shape the future for which it is preparing. The effectiveness of planning is, therefore, also linked to the innovative capability of the firm.

In India — as in other less developed countries — U.S. firms generally do a significantly better job of planning than their indigenous counterparts. However, in most cases these U.S. subsidiaries could be even more effective. Careful investigation reveals

431

that much of their planning is superficial and not taken very seriously. Managers often go through the formal motions of comprehensive and detailed planning only in order to seem responsive to the pressures, policies, and procedures imposed by the parent corporation.

Lack of information, lack of understanding of the planning process, inadequate training, poor communication, and ineffective motivation are the major human constraints which hamper managerial planning at indigenous firms, in particular, though they operate at U.S. subsidiaries as well. But when environmental pressures become strong enough to make planning critical in terms of viability, profitability and growth, U.S. subsidiaries tend to improve their planning faster and more effectively than their indigenous counterparts. The parent company often assists this process by placing judicious pressure on the subsidiary.

In addition to environmental constraints, some fundamental human and cultural problems confront planning and innovation efforts in many developing countries, India included. Because these efforts are directed toward influencing the future, they often conflict with the fatalistic values so common to less developed lands. A characteristic of social value systems in such countries is the belief that a man's life is predestined, and that he can do little to influence the inevitable outcome. In many societies even an attempt to influence the future is considered imprudent and immoral.

The concept of planning, and the harnessing of creativity to economic endeavors are both peculiarly Western ideas. Because they are often diametrically opposed to local beliefs and practices their introduction is often slow, and a great deal of conscious and concentrated education is required to develop local nationals' skills in these areas. This educational process must go deeper than just acquainting nationals with techniques of planning and innovating. It must reach the basic foundations of their cultural value systems and convince them that man can influence his own future, that planning is "good" and that it is neither a waste of time nor an arrogant challenge hurled at the gods. In essence, the introduction of these concepts is comparable to a missionary effort.

BASIC ORGANIZATIONAL OBJECTIVES

Few of the firms surveyed in India, regardless of national ownership, had explicit statements of basic organizational objectives. However, in most cases they did have fairly clear-cut implicit objectives which had evolved over time, and which were reflected in the actual behavior, policies, and decisions pursued by management. Explicit statements of firm goals were generally more to be found in Indian companies (both traditional and relatively progressive) than in U.S. subsidiaries. One possible reason was that the U.S. firms assumed profitability and growth were desirable key objectives, and therefore no formal statements were required.

Neither Indian nor foreign firms did a good job of communicating the overall goals of the company down through the managerial ranks, although the U.S. firms generally did somewhat better than the others. A desire to treat various objectives as confidential — including some established by parent companies — and top management's view that communication was not needed were two major reasons for this. Nevertheless, more effective communication of organizational objectives down through the managerial hierarchy, as well as greater participation by the managers in formulating operating objectives and plans, could help motivate managers and provide them with better guidelines for action.

One firm in India which has been most successful in recent years in setting long-term objectives, translating them into concrete operating targets and plans, and communicating them to appropriate managerial levels is the U.S. battery, flashlight and chemical producer. The ultimate objectives of this company have been, for some time, "to produce and market high quality products in India and for export at a minimum price which will return a reasonable profit. The company will also expand and diversify its activities, as necessary to meet customer needs, to render better service, to obtain better quality or to effect economies in operation." This firm has also spelled out supporting objectives dealing with such things as financial health and aims, the provision of as steady and secure employment as conditions permit, compliance with local laws, and effective discharge of moral and social obligations to the Indian government and local communities in which the firm operates. In addition, the company has explicitly defined many broad long-term policies to serve as guidelines in achieving corporate objectives. These policies pertain to virtually all managerial and enterprise functions, and to specific strategic areas such as exports, import substitution, and public relations.

Although the firm has experienced some serious problems and has made some costly mistakes, it has been relatively successful in blending economic, humanistic, and environmental considerations in both the formulation and pursuit of its objectives and related principles and policies. Few indigenous or foreign firms have done as well.

Virtually all of the medium-sized and larger companies surveyed established at least some quantitative objectives or targets on an annual or shorter-term basis. These generally included profitability, sales, and production objectives. Most also (explicitly or implicitly) had some kind of growth objectives and some general guidelines to help determine those areas in which the firm would concentrate or expand its efforts. However, relatively few defined longer-term objectives clearly. Attempts at quantification were typically based on simple projections and extrapolations of past and current trends.

When a firm can sell virtually everything it produces and can get adequate factor inputs, planning becomes less important and objectives may be achieved even if the enterprise is highly inefficient. But conditions have been changing considerably in India, and firms that have continued to do little or no real planning have often not only failed to meet their objectives, but have found themselves in a precarious situation also.

PLANNING HORIZONS AND TYPES OF PLANS UTILIZED

There is a very widespread tendency in India for managers to use environmental uncertainty as an excuse for not doing more planning. In reality, this very uncertainty requires more rather than less concern. But environmental uncertainty was equated with low predictability and therefore, with low value from forecasting. Few managers, including many U.S. executives, saw merit in taking the opposite approach, i.e., trying to reduce uncertainties through planning and forecasting. Contingency planning, flexible plans, and variable budgets are some of the methodologies and techniques that can be effective in coping with uncertainty.

While more of the U.S. firms surveyed engaged in long-term planning than indigenous firms, a majority of these did little that was meaningful; however, in recent years an increasing number of U.S. subsidiaries and local firms have begun to take long-range and medium-term planning more seriously. It is surprising in many cases that they have waited this long, since failure to plan has led to many costly mistakes and lost opportunities. For example, many serious cases of excess capacity, uneconomical technology, unprofitable product lines, critical material and equipment shortages, and very strained employee relations could have been avoided or at least alleviated substantially by better long-range planning.

It is equally surprising that so many U.S. subsidiaries have done little or no planning in areas that most major U.S. domestic firms — including their parent companies — would consider to be critical. These include the introduction of new products, expansion, vertical integration, reorganization, alteration of ownership patterns, sources and uses of capital, import substitution, export promotion, and basic staffing issues (including the localization of management).

The long-term planning undertaken at firms surveyed was typically not systematized or integrated, and responsibility for such planning was not clearly defined. For example, planning with regard to product diversification was often not tied in adequately with market considerations, distribution channels, pricing and sales promotion strategies, capital, capacity, inventory, material, facilities and manpower requirements, and so forth.

The firms surveyed in India which have been doing the most effective planning beyond one year included one Indian and two U.S. drug companies, and the diversified U.S. firm referred to earlier. One U.S. subsidiary had recently switched from a five- to a three-year plan because it had found the five-year forecast to be too inaccurate in view of environmental uncertainty, and of little value for decision-making. Its parent company in the U.S. still uses five-year plans.

The diversified U.S. subsidiary had a very broad 15-year plan, as well as more operational plans extending beyond one year. The 15-year plan for the 1966-1980 period focused primarily on investment, diversification, and expansion projections and was not really operational. It did, however, force management to extend its planning horizons. One of the U.S. drug subsidiaries had a similar 10-year plan.

Only a handful of all of the firms studied had even attempted to establish an overall model or plan for growth and development. Even fewer had master plans extending beyond one year which considered alternative courses of action, and those which had defined long-term growth had seldom formulated any comprehensive strategic plans for achieving their objectives.

One U.S. drug company did attempt to establish an overall model for long-term growth and development, but the model was never implemented. Shortly after this firm decided to expand its operations in India, local management prepared three different scenarios based on likely courses for the future development of the company. Based upon these patterns, they then projected three sets of probable operation results for the coming five-year period. The projections included sales figures, profits, and capital requirements. The scenarios included such intangible factors as relationships with the government, local suppliers and unions, as well as projections of overall economic conditions.

The first scenario assumed that the existing corporate structure would remain unchanged, that U.S. ownership would continue at 100 percent, and that product lines would stay basically the same. The second considered splitting operations into two companies, one of which would have a different capital structure, including local ownership, and would move into new product lines. The third considered a single company with a new organization and capital structure and an expanded scope of activities. These plans, although reviewed by top-level international headquarters management, were never used except in an indirect manner, i.e., they may have stimulated some thinking on the part of the people who read the documents.

Because most U.S. subsidiaries did not have explicit plans for long-term growth and development, they were vulnerable to charges of exploitation. Both government and union officials often felt that these firms were in the country to draw out what they could without making substantial long-term investments in the economy. Unfortunately several statements by U.S. managers, in response to proposals for legislation which would seriously hinder the flows of raw materials and funds across Indian borders, gave support to the suspicion that their firms would pack up and leave if conditions worsened. Instead of reasoning with the government, and trying to work within the system, U.S. managers often resorted to threats of this nature, emphasizing the fact that Indian operations were a small, and perhaps insignificant portion of the company's worldwide activities.

The attitudes expressed or implied by such U.S. managers conveyed feelings of impermanence not only to outsiders, but also to their own subordinates. The following statement was made by a top level Indian executive in a U.S. company:

The British firms are here to stay. There's no doubt about it. However, I don't know if [the name of his company] is here to stay or just to get what they can while the climate is favorable. The company doesn't seem to care about making any compromises.

The compromise referred to above was the company's refusal to permit local ownership, in spite of strong government pressure. Yet at the time this statement was made, U.S. management had already decided to permit a substantial amount of local stock investment. None of the Indian executives were aware of this fact, and when the decision was announced it came with little advance notice and appeared to many to have been made on the spur of the moment.

Only one of the Indian firms surveyed — a drug producer — did a truly thoughtful job of developing a long-term growth and development model. It identified explicitly a desirable position to strive for several years in the future and designed specific strategies to reach it. The firm has not done as well as it hoped, but it has undoubtedly been more successful than it would have been without such thoughtful long-term planning. This firm established specific three- and five-year goals for market share and profitability. To attain the desired long-term goals, the company decided to forego current profits and plow income into major advertising efforts. Through promotional campaigns, it planned to build its market share, even though profits would be negligible during the build-up period. Management felt that once it had obtained the share it desired, it could retain the market, and by concentrating on cost reduction (including a cutback in promotional activity), earn profits which would more than compensate for the income lost during the initial period.

Few firms studied in India have engaged in in-depth product planning extending beyond one year. Although some U.S. companies, and a few local firms, have recently established competent marketing research groups — or at least assigned the task to a qualified specialist — such companies are still few and far between.

The lack of effective product planning and marketing research has led to serious problems and foregone opportunities for U.S. as well as local firms, in spite of the competitive advantages many American companies have with regard to their product lines. In most cases, the introduction of new products was chiefly a function of top management's "best" personal estimates of what might or might not sell, rather than a carefully researched or planned decision. U.S. subsidiaries typically introduced "new" products taken from the parent country, fully engineered, and fully tested — in terms of the U.S. environment. New products were also introduced in response to government restrictions on imports, or to meet (rather than lead) competition.

An example of poor product planning involved a large U.S. company which introduced a new agro-chemical product to take advantage of opportunities in India's largest economic sector, agriculture. By U.S. farming standards, there was little doubt that there would be considerable economic benefit to the farmer from use of the product. However, the firm grossly overestimated market demand. It failed to assess adequately the impact of cultural values, attitudes toward risk, the small amounts of cash available to the average farmer, and so on. In its enthusiasm, the company also overlooked several raw materials supply difficulties. Consequently, many unnecessary problems were generated, and it took much longer to make the new product line profitable than was originally anticipated.

An important area for establishing organizational plans is that of future expansions. Such plans should consider markets, distribution channels, capital requirements, facilities, manpower, and other factors. Although extensive surveys are generally performed when a firm plans entry into India, or when a new plant is being considered, few foreign or indigenous firms devote adequate planning effort to expansionary programs. In most cases, expansionary plans which do not involve totally new facilities look ahead no longer than one year.

In general, planning processes and plans at firms studied in India focused on the short run, and in particular on short-term projections of monthly, weekly, and daily operating data. Planning documents consisted mostly of sales forecasts and some kind of operating budgets. However, these were prepared more for control purposes than for future planning. The only planning activity found in most of the major firms was the translation of sales forecasts into requirements of imported raw materials and the ordering and stockpiling of these items, and even here the effectiveness and quality of such planning varied widely, with U.S. firms generally doing a better job than their indigenous counterparts. In only a few cases were accurate forecasts of capital requirements or productive capacities made.

Financial, organizational, and manpower planning ranged from mediocre to poor. An extreme situation was found in several major traditional firms. For example, a fairly large, traditional Indian company operated with extremely small cash balances. Yet the firm did not engage in any type of financial planning activities. When questioned about this situation, the managing director indicated that there was no need for planning. When the company found itself in a tight financial situation, pressure was placed on customers in order to reduce the company's always large and overdue accounts receivable. Expansionary projects were generally undertaken in small segments, and only in good years when current income was sufficient to cover all capital expenditures. Employment expanded or contracted in the same manner.

Most of the major firms prepared some kind of sales forecasts for major product lines for the coming year. Generally, annual forecasts were divided into months, although some used quarterly break-downs. The more traditional Indian firms merely divided their annual forecasts by 12 to obtain monthly targets, rather than computing seasonal or other variations. The relatively few companies — mostly American — which projected forecasts beyond one year typically used either three- or six-month periods for the second year and beyond. A few firms — again mostly U.S. — also tried to predict not only sales for broad product lines, but also sales volumes of individual products and, where applicable, even package sizes. However, few of them achieved a high degree of accuracy with such forecasts.

In a number of cases, U.S. parent firms supplied sales targets by product lines for their subsidiaries. These goals were established in consultation with the subsidiary's top management. They then became basic sales objectives for the coming year, as well as constituting a sales plan.

Although sales projections were common, few firms genuinely planned for capacity requirements. Sales goals were not converted into concrete or specific requirements for future production, manpower, working capital, etc., except when the introduction of a new product which would clearly require new allocations of resources was being considered, or when it suddenly became evident that the market or resources for a certain product had already become exhausted.

DETAILED AND PREPROGRAMMED NATURE OF PLANS

U.S. firms in India engaged in more planning — especially short-term — than indigenous companies, and also more than most British companies, making greater use of labor, cost, material, working capital, overhead, quality control, and equipment utilization standards. These standards were updated frequently; in contrast, the few Indian firms which used standards seldom updated them. Also, while the U.S. subsidiaries often used normative standards, those used by the indigenous firms were invariably historical in nature.

It is quite common for U.S. parent companies to impose on their subsidiaries detailed planning procedures and standards which are not applicable to local conditions. As a result they are often ignored or circumvented by the subsidiary managers. Where they are implemented, significant problems and inefficiences tend to arise. One U.S. drug firm prepared a detailed five-volume annual budget each year which was reviewed by international headquarters. One of the top subsidiary managers admitted that much meaningless data was placed in these budgets just to satisfy the parent organization. Nevertheless, the pressures exerted by parent companies do compel most of the U.S. subsidiaries to do a more thorough planning job than they would probably otherwise undertake.

With few exceptions, indigenous firms did a poor job of defining and integrating interrelated elements in their plans. For example, operating budgets were usually very crude and were not broken down in useful detail: only one budget figure for "direct labor" might be listed, and it would include direct labor expenditures for the entire plant for the month or quarter. Seldom was there an attempt to identify how much of the total applied to each department or product, or to compare actual with anticipated amounts.

FLEXIBILITY OF PLANS

Careful, detailed planning, especially in the short-run can increase operating efficiency. However, detail coupled with rigidity may do more harm than good. If an organization draws up a rigidly detailed plan and events do not turn out as anticipated, the firm may have to scrap the entire plan and start planning again from scratch, thus losing much productive time. Moreover, the need for revision and corrective action in one part of such a plan is likely to call for revision in many if not most other parts. With inflexible plans, information feedback and corrective action in all interrelated areas may be very difficult to achieve in a timely or efficient manner.

Flexibility with regard to plans implies the ability to detour or change course without undue cost or friction, or to keep moving toward organizational objectives despite changes in the environment or failure of initial plans. Firms can provide flexibility in a number of ways; some are costlier and require more time, effort, and skill than others, but in many cases the benefits outweigh the costs. In general, building flexibility into plans is desirable under conditions of high uncertainty; where the stakes or risks are sizeable; where relatively long lead times are needed to adjust to changing and unforeseeable conditions; and where the cost of error is likely to be significantly greater than the costs of designing more flexible plans.

One way to provide for flexibility is to allow for reserves or slack in key areas, for example, by providing the resources and capability to achieve a sales or output volume ranging up to 120 percent of the most likely forecast. The use of supplemental monthly or quarterly plans which update longer-range plans is another method. Firms can also build flexibility into their plans by clearly assigning priorities in advance, in the event that resources available turn out to be smaller than planned, or when all specific product mix targets cannot be met.

Variable plans, designed to vary according to levels of activity, can also be used. Step budgets are one variety of these plans. Conversion factors are commonly used, and the variable plan is based upon an analysis of resources required to achieve certain volumes of outputs. To be truly effective, such plans require an open-sequence control system so that corrective action and revision of plans in one area automatically leads to changes in closely related and interdependent areas. Variable plans and budgets may be expressed in physical as well as monetary units; for example, they may be used to determine the best product mix choices depending on how much materials, components, spares, manpower, and/or productive capacity turns out to be available.

Flexible plans of the above types are used effectively in American industry when sales volume is very difficult to predict, particularly in the case of new products; when future government spending is highly unpredictable and the government is a major customer; and in other situations where economic trends and future conditions involve much uncertainty. All of the U.S. parent companies surveyed were making at least limited use of flexible plans in their domestic operations, although only about half were making substantial, continuous use of them.

Indian industry requires more flexible planning than does U.S. industry, since greater uncertainty exists in many areas, and lead times required to adjust to changing conditions are often much longer. Yet few U.S. subsidiaries were doing much flexible planning and those which were, were not doing a thorough job. Only one indigenous drug firm studied was doing anything substantial in this regard.

The firms which had the best flexible plans generally experienced less serious disruptions or loss of productive time than those that did little or no planning of this type. They were also able to shift their plans and activities to achieve their aggregate targets more effectively as conditions changed. Their projections were frequently wide of the mark with regard to their more detailed targets — e.g., specific product sales — but they were able to come closer to their overall growth and profitability objectives. The additional costs and efforts entailed in designing more flexible plans were clearly worthwhile in most instances.

The diversified U.S. subsidiary studied has been making the most effective use of flexible plans. It has apparently learned the value of doing so from costly mistakes and foregone opportunities of the past. Flexible plans are used for some of its expansion and diversification projects, in the areas of procurement and imports, export orders, managerial career patterns, and elsewhere. For example, when supply bottlenecks occur the firm knows which products should and which should not be cut back on the basis of profitability and other key criteria. If production must suddenly be cut back the firm has alternative plans for changeover, overhauling equipment, training, etc. It also has plans for overproducing certain products in the short run under certain conditions, as well as alternative product mix schedules tied in with variable budgets. It has been geared to implement major expansion and diversification programs rapidly if and when government approval is forthcoming.

PLANNING METHODOLOGIES, TOOLS, AND TECHNIQUES

The starting point for the planning process at nearly all firms surveyed in India was the sales forecast, and a number of companies indicated that they used trend projections. However, in most cases, the projections were rough and based on little genuine analysis. The typical forecaster would sit down with a column of figures representing past monthly sales performance — usually for no longer than the preceding 12 months — would "eyeball" the data, and estimate figures for the coming year. Relatively few firms — mostly U.S. — undertook in-depth analysis, drew graphs, estimated seasonal factors or used mathematical methods to approximate trends. Sales planning and analysis are one area in which even the best U.S. subsidiaries lagged far behind their parent companies in terms of modern techniques and methodologies.

In many indigenous firms and a few U.S. subsidiaries the sales managers were not even asked to provide estimates of unusual situations likely to affect sales (e.g., special advertising campaigns, promotional activities, special competitive situations, etc.). Often the sales forecasters would forget or neglect to do this and in many cases, the individuals preparing the forecasts were not part of the sales organization.

Under conditions, prevalent in India, much time could be saved by focusing first on procurement planning to identify possible procurement and import constraints. Possibilities could then be assigned with regard to the availability of major types of supplies, and more meaningful sales plans could then be developed. However, very few firms approached planning in this way; as a result much time was wasted, since procurement problems eventually arose, causing sales and other plans to be discarded or revised. It was particularly common for indigenous firms to prepare detailed sales forecasts which assumed there would be no supply or other shortages.

At all but a few indigenous firms, and even at some U.S. subsidiaries, conversion of sales forecasts into budgetary data tended to be very imprecise. Historical standards and norms were frequently extended to the future with no allowance for changing conditions. In many cases, old labor rates were utilized even though labor contracts were about to expire and new wage demand levels were at issue. Budgetary calculations relating to the introduction of new products were based largely on estimates made by top management or accountants, and only occasionally were sales, production or purchasing managers involved. In general, the reasons why planning methodologies tended to be crude lay in the lack of technical knowledge, training, or motivation on the part of the people responsible.

The use of modern quantitative tools and methodologies in planning and control, e.g., operations research, linear programming, PERT and critical path methods, statistical analysis, model break-even analysis, or even less sophisticated marginal analysis, was very rare in India. The very limited number of electronic computers in India is one reason for this. However, these mathematical approaches could be used beneficially in numerous cases even without computers, since many of the conventional mechanical computing aids and devices are available in Indian industry — e.g., desk calculators, punch card and tabulating equipment.

Those firms which have computers — especially indigenous companies — make little use of such quantitative tools, techniques or methodologies. They confine their activities to a limited range of scientific or technical problems, and to some of the more routine business applications such as payroll preparation. Computers are little used for decision making, forward planning, or control.

In 1965 there were only about a dozen electronic computers in use in all of India. By 1970 there were several dozen at least. One of the first private companies to get a computer and put it into effective operation was the diversified U.S. battery and chemical firm. The project was initiated by the U.S. managing director in charge in 1961. The firm received an import license in 1964, and an IBM 1401 arrived in March 1965. For the first few years this computer was shared with a British competitor in the chemical industry which had its head offices in the same building, but in recent years the U.S. firm has taken over the computer entirely and has been using it on a three-shift basis.

There were a number of reasons why this company acquired a computer when it did. It wanted to be sure to get one while it could, in view of the need for governmental permission. It wanted to keep the number of its clerical and staff personnel down in order to avoid a white collar union, and it sought the prestige of being a pioneer computer user in India. Finally, it believed that the computer was economically justifiable, based on the cost-benefit analyses that were undertaken. In spite of considerable problems, the computer did pay for itself by around 1967.

Initially the firm used its computer for relatively routine financial purposes such as payroll, and for some technical and scientific calculations. In more recent years, the company has been making more effective use of the computer in planning, decision making, and control than possibly any other firm in India, in spite of various problems; for example, slow mail hinders timely inputs, although the firm has its own telex system, and there are still problems of human resistance, lack of know-how, and superficial and inaccurate data.

The company has had so much success with its head office computer that one of its divisions in Bombay has recently rented additional computer facilities there. Another division has been ahead of its parent company's corresponding division in computer applications and in quantitative methods in general. In most areas, however, it has lagged substantially behind its parent company.

None of the U.S. drug subsidiaries had computers, nor did they make nearly as much use of modern quantitative methods as the above company. In one or two cases, their size and the nature and complexity of their operations were such to clearly justify the use of a computer on economic grounds, and in most cases greater use of modern quantitative methods would have been beneficial. Here was another area where U.S. managerial know-how had not been adequately transferred. All of the parent companies of U.S. drug subsidiaries surveyed used computers in their domestic operations, and relied heavily on modern quantitative methods.

The most progressive indigenous drug company surveyed had been using a computer for some time. Not only did it employ quantitative methods itself, but it supplied consulting services to other firms. However, the use of such methods within this company has been cut back significantly in recent years, since much of the former applications were apparently superficial and ineffective.

One of the semitraditional indigenous drug companies started using a rented computer (comparable to the IBM-1401) in January 1969. Hiring and training competent programmers and other computer specialists has turned out to be a serious problem. The financial manager in charge of the computer attended a four-day computer course given by the manufacturer in England, and the vendor sent one of its own experts to the company for one year. During 1969 the company often used the computer more than eight hours a day, mainly for setting up and training purposes. It was the only user of the computer, although it expects to accept some outside jobs in the future. It has been using the computer chiefly for routine accounting and financial purposes, but has done some experimental work involving inventory and sales analyses, and production control.

EMPLOYEE PARTICIPATION IN PLANNING

The extent and effectiveness of employee participation in planning varied considerably among several of the parent companies surveyed in the United States. However, with only one exception, the U.S. based companies made much greater and effective use of employee participation than did their subsidiaries in India. In all cases this was true with regard to lower managerial and supervisory personnel and nonsupervisory employees. On the other hand, the U.S. subsidiaries generally involved their managers and specialists more effectively in planning than did indigenous or British companies.

Middle- and lower-management echelons seldom participated in financial and budgetary planning. The desire to keep cost, profitability, and other financial data confidential was a major reason for this. In some cases, top management also felt that lower-level managers were not familiar enough with such data or did not know enough about budgeting to contribute anything substantial. In several Indian companies, only a few trusted managers were involved in planning because of the various illegal and quasi-illicit activities and transactions engaged in by the firm.

At a majority of U.S. firms, and at nearly all local firms, personnel planning in such areas as managerial compensation and perquisites, and career projections and appraisals were also kept confidential with little or no middle- or lower-level participation. At U.S. subsidiaries, the same was also true in many cases with regard to various parent company plans involving the subsidiary, diversification and expansion plans, and plans for major changes in personnel or reorganizations. Often such plans were not known to anyone but the managing director until they were actually about to be implemented. In a few cases, they were not even known by the managing director.

A majority of the U.S. subsidiaries, and only a few of the Indian firms, had committees which were concerned with specific elements of the planning process (e.g., new-product planning groups). In general, the U.S. firms made greater use of such committees, and also used them more effectively for planning participation and joint decision-making than either Indian or British firms. However, in many instances these committees were used poorly. Even where participation was one of the stated aims of various committees, they were frequently used only to communicate already established plans and decisions, to give instructions, or as a means of avoiding individual responsibility. Discussions primarily focused around implementation rather than the actual plan formulation. This was especially true in the Indian firms that used committees.

Numerous situations existed in which more effective employee participation in planning in Indian industry could have led not only to better plans, but also to more effective control and motivation. This was probably truer in the U.S. subsidiaries than the Indian firms, since the employees of the former generally had more managerial and technical skill, as well as a more favorable attitude toward planning.

MANAGERIAL BEHAVIOR IN THE PLANNING PROCESS

Planning was invariably taken much more seriously by U.S. managers than by Indian executives. This is because management in the United States tends to engage much more in careful identification and analysis of alternatives, information collection, and genuine planning effort than management in India. U.S. management also tends to formalize the planning process more, rather than to rely on ad hoc or arbitrary decisions, to establish planning deadlines and take them seriously, and to accept individual responsibility and take individual initiative in planning. However, in a number of cases, well-trained and relatively Westernized Indian managers did a better job of planning than did U.S. managers. Because of their greater familiarity with the Indian environment, they were better equipped to predict certain events than their American counterparts. In such cases, the Americans tended to attribute more randomness and arbitrariness to the future than actually existed, and many of them felt that much of their planning experience at home was inapplicable to India. Frequent gripes were voiced about the unnecessary paper work required to satisfy their headquarters.

INFORMATION PROBLEMS IN PLANNING

Information problems which result in planning errors are generally more serious and widespread in Indian than in U.S. industry. Government statistics in India are meager and much less accurate. (Industry is partly to blame for this, since firms supply incomplete and distorted data to government agencies.) In spite of critical informational problems of the macro or external types, few firms were doing an effective job of gathering and developing their own information, even in cases where the benefits from doing so would have clearly outweighed the costs.

The lack of effective participation in planning at the lower echelons of the organization also greatly reduced the amount of useful information that entered the planning process. Horizontal communications were also limited, especially within indigenous firms which did not maintain downward hierarchical authority relationships for coordination, and in which key executives and departments tended to be viewed as islands unto themselves. Joint decisions were rare, and the sharing or exchange of information, and cooperation in planning were not encouraged in all but a few of the Indian companies. As a result different planning premises and inconsistent plans were frequently utilized by different but interrelated parts of the organization. This occurred less frequently in the U.S. subsidiaries, although they experienced similar deficiencies in varying degrees.

Even in the U.S. subsidiaries, it was quite common for many subordinates to give their boss — either when requested or voluntarily — the kinds of information or opinions they thought he wanted to hear. In many cases, information provided by personnel was based on a mere guess or on minimal analysis, but was implied or taken to be carefully thought out and analyzed. All of this was much more common at U.S. subsidiaries than in the U.S.-based operations of their parent firm.

A common problem among all types of firms in India in which middle- or lower-level managers and specialists were engaged in the collection of information for planning was the lack of knowledge among these personnel of the nature of the planning process. They were often told what information to compile without knowing the specific purpose for which it would be used. Consequently, when they had to exercise judgment in interpreting data, they had no way to relate their judgment to the intended purpose. Also, information which could have been obtained easily often was not collected or utilized simply because the people who had access to it did not know that it would be useful. Moreover, in many cases where data was requested, it was incorrectly compiled because upper and lower management had different concepts as to what was required. For example, overhead figures which higher management might request were often calculated in a manner far different from that intended (in many cases, because the lower-level personnel did not use standard U.S. accounting practices). Yet, men in top management would accept the figures and make decisions based upon them, on the assumption that uniformity of definitions existed throughout the organization.

INNOVATION, RISK-TAKING, AND CHANGE

Paradoxical mixtures of innovative thinking and unimaginative approaches to problem solving are very frequently found in U.S. subsidiaries in India and other developing countries. Innovation may be present in the introduction of new managerial methods, new products, and new technology; at the same time, the introduction of practices, processes and products may demonstrate a lack of imagination.

Far too often, U.S. subsidiaries and their parent organizations tend to introduce not what is most appropriate to the local environment but what is most familiar to *them*. In essence, they stick to the tried and true methods, products, and technologies which have proved to be successful in their U.S. operations. Although their impact on the local environment may seem innovative, in terms of doing the best job possible, it may be far from ideal.

By contrast, traditional indigenous firms usually show little creative thought with regard to managerial tasks and innovation, and generally resist change, though they tend to follow the lead of foreign companies or more progressive indigenous firms. However, the relatively few indigenous firms that *are* progressive in attempting to introduce new managerial thinking, new products or new processes, and in developing their managerial cadres are often truly innovative. Whereas the U.S. firm may casually introduce U.S. techniques, the progressive Indian company is more likely to thoroughly plan and study new methods or approaches before introducing them. As a result, modifications occur, and the progressive Indian firm may create and introduce patterns, approaches, and products, which are both unique and well-adapted to the local environment. They often blend the old and the new in a highly innovative fashion.

U.S. subsidiaries surveyed in India were more effective risk takers on balance than most of their indigenous counterparts. This was primarily due to better planning and more careful analyses, especially with regard to capital investment. They were thus less likely to find themselves confronted with unanticipated economic crises — such as great excess capacity or highly unprofitable products — than the indigenous firms.

U.S. subsidiaries were also more willing to incur the risks entailed in innovation and change than the more traditional Indian companies. However, in some respects they were more conservative and less effective risk takers than the more progressive and dynamic of the Indian companies.

Since it is a part of a large international corporation, the risks assumed when a U.S. subsidiary undertakes new ventures or uses new approaches are not as great as those experienced by an indigenous firm locked into the local environment. If a project falls through for the subsidiary, the international corporation is likely to be hurt only marginally, while the indigenous company may be damaged seriously in a similar situation. Moreover, most of the key decision makers and top executives of Indian firms are also the owners, and projects that fail may seriously damage their personal wealth and aspirations. This is not likely to be the case to nearly the same degree for the hired subsidiary manager who has little or no direct ownership stake in the business.

On the other hand, U.S. subsidiaries and their parent companies frequently incur risks that are not initially perceived when they transfer patterns which were successful in the United States without adequate evaluation of how they are likely to fit into the local environment. Moreover, potentially lucrative opportunities are often foregone by U.S. subsidiaries either because of more conservatism or because they represent opportunities which are not available to the parent company's domestic operations.

New products were not usually introduced by U.S. subsidiaries unless adequate markets already existed for them. Typically, these products were introduced in the exact form that they had been manufactured elsewhere, with virtually no local R and D. The reluctance of U.S. managements to introduce totally new products is understandable. They assume that less risk is involved in tested products, since the "bugs" have already been ironed out, and the product has a proven track record somewhere. Quite often, however, because of unfamiliarity with the local environment and deficient planning, U.S. firms misjudged local conditions, overlooking the fact that "bugs" are often related to the operating environment.

Indigenous firms, especially in relatively developed product areas, are often greater risk takers with regard to new product diversification, expansion, and vertical integration than U.S. subsidiaries. Although they also tend to be reluctant to invest in ventures perceived to involve significant risks, they usually have no alternative environment in which to invest their funds or pursue other opportunities. In the drug and chemical sectors, for example, as imports of critical supplies were increasingly curtailed by the government indigenous firms moved much more quickly to fill the void than did most of their U.S. counterparts. Invariably, the move to diversify was made in response to a crisis, but it was made, in many cases, without much hesitation. U.S. companies were more likely to pass these opportunities by and, frequently, when they finally decided to diversify or expand, licenses were no longer available.

While U.S. industry experiences considerable resistance to innovation and change, developing countries encounter more. It takes much longer to introduce even relatively minor changes in India in all areas, including procedures and work methods, machine speeds, plant layout or production processes, organizational activities, and the introduction of new managerial techniques. Changes which took months to implement in India took only a few days in U.S. operations.

It often took U.S. subsidiaries five to eight years or even longer to implement new projects and programs which would take a year or two at most in the United States. This was often due to serious delays in getting the required governmental clearances in India, and to procurement problems. However, several years time could have been saved in most cases through better planning and control. In general, the British firms surveyed did a better and faster job of implementing new projects than their U.S. counterparts.

A good example of slow project implementation involved a U.S. subsidiary's expansion and diversification program in the chemical sector. Implementation of a similar but much larger program in the U.S. took the parent company less than three years from inception of the idea until production started. In India it took more than nine years. The idea for the Indian venture was conceived in 1958 through discussions between headquarters and top subsidiary managers. A proposal was presented to the Indian government in early 1960, and production was planned for early 1965. A letter of intent was received from the government at the beginning of 1961, and the necessary license was obtained in mid-1963. Construction activity started in March 1964, with production expected to start by January 1966. In June 1965, management revised its start-up date to June 1966; then in February 1966 the target date was again revised to October 1966. Production did not actually commence until the second half of 1967. A British competitor implemented a similar new project in several years less time.

U.S. subsidiaries experienced their greatest problems involving change when a foreign managing director imposed changes without adequate analysis of the local environment. Too often the foreign executive would approach problems with almost missionary zeal, armed with solutions that had worked in another environment, and expecting the local environment to adjust to him and not vice versa.

With proper approaches, well trained and motivated local nationals often do a better job of planning for and implementing change than foreign managers. A good example of this in India involved a progressive indigenous company's approach to organization and staffing matters. It was one of the very few Indian firms surveyed that instituted substantial change in these areas during the study period.

The principal owner and managing director of this relatively large, successful, and not very old Indian firm anticipated a series of organizational changes from the time the company first started operations. He had diverse personal interests and intended to withdraw from daily operations as soon as things were on as sound a footing as possible. Consequently, he established a long-range plan whereby he could increasingly delegate authority and responsibility to his subordinates as he pulled back. A series of discussions were held and memoranda were written describing the nature of the anticipated changes, identifying the individuals who would be groomed for new responsibility, and indicating a rough timetable for the changes. Periodically, as each phase was implemented, further discussions were held and additional memoranda went out, reminding everyone of what had previously transpired, of the objectives of the changes, and of the plans for the future. In this manner, the entire Indian managerial cadre was able to accept the changes as part of the normal routine, and very little real anxiety was created. Because everyone knew what was going to happen, personal relationships could develop in anticipation of the eventual power structure. The changes involved a complete re-structuring of the functions of management, the introduction of cross-functional project groups, and the delegation of substantial responsibility to middle management; they took place over a period of approximately ten years.

This illustration exemplifies a firm which departed from the traditional pattern in two major ways, and yet was able to use existing social values and employee expectations to ease the transition. The major departures were 1) just the fact that major organizational change took place; and 2) the fact that non-family members were moved in to high positions of responsibility. (Nearly all were U.S. educated.) In the traditional Indian pattern, the granting of substantial authority and responsibility to non-family members would have come as a major shock — one which might have undermined morale, created intense rivalries, and fostered dissatisfaction. However, by preparing everyone in advance, organizational stability was maintained and everyone felt reasonably comfortable with the new, although unusual organization which emerged.

PLANNED VERSUS ACTUAL PERFORMANCE

The companies studied in the United States generally came significantly closer to achieving their long-term (3-year, 5-year, or longer) quantified objectives than similar firms in India. It was not uncommon for companies in India to miss by 300 to 500 percent or more their long-term sales growth, output, and profitability targets. Many new projects were never implemented or, when they were, became operational several years late.

With respect to short-term goals traditional Indian firms, as well as a few U.S. affiliates, often missed their annual sales, profitability, and output targets by 30 to 50 percent. In most cases, in recent years, their results have been below rather than above their projections. If they come within 20 percent of their annual targets they are usually reasonably content. On individual product targets, they have frequently been off by several hundred percent. They have also been very far off targets like production costs, labor productivity, equipment utilization, quality control, waste, delivery schedules, etc.

Most of the U.S. drug subsidiaries and the more progressive indigenous pharmaceutical firms come within 20 percent of their annual aggregate sales, profit, output,
and cost reduction targets and in many cases exceed them. The two best managed U.S.
drug firms have usually come within 10 percent, and have generally done a better job
of control and planning than even their relatively progressive indigenous counterparts.
They are also more successful in juggling their product mixes and their quarterly and
monthly operations in an effort to hit their aggregate annual targets. It has often been
easier for them to do this since they knew what their true unit costs and profit margins
were, had far fewer very low-profit and unprofitable items, and had more flexibility in
their operations.

For specific products, even the U.S. drug subsidiaries were often off target by 50 to
100 percent or more. However, they have generally come within 5 to 10 percent of
target on their high-volume individual items. Variations at the more progressive indigenous drug companies have been significantly greater on the average. The best managed
U.S. companies have also done better in meeting their cost, quality, scrap-equipment
utilization and other kinds of less aggregate targets and standards than the indigenous
firms.

The parent-company domestic drug operations studied in the United States generally came closer to meeting their annual targets and standards — but not always their
quarterly or monthly targets — than their subsidiaries in India. This was especially
true with regard to established products. There was no clear-cut pattern for new
products.

A diversified U.S. subsidiary that produces chemicals and plastics had poorer
results in achieving its long-term targets than its parent company in the United States.
Serious delays in implementing new projects and expansion programs, and the large
surplus supply of certain plastics in India during several years in the 1960s (brought
about chiefly by excessive government imports) were major reasons for this.

The U.S. battery producer in India did considerably better on the whole during
the 1960s in meeting both its long-term and short-term aggregate targets than its major
indigenous competitor. The U.S. subsidiary was furthest off target during 1967 and
1968, in large part because of serious labor problems, including major strikes.

In terms of aggregate profit, sales, and output targets there has been no clear
pattern between the U.S. subsidiary and its parent firm's domestic battery operations.
For some targets, and in some years, the subsidiary has come closer to plan, and for
others the U.S. based operations have come closer. Annual deviations in either case
have rarely been more than 5 percent below plan. Often they have been significantly
above plan — at times by 20 percent or more — and this has been more common at the
domestic company, especially with regard to profits.

The range of deviations from targets for individual products have generally been
greater at the subsidiary than in the domestic operations. Such deviations have generally been no greater than 20 or 25 percent in the United States, with the exception of
new products. At the subsidiary in India, such deviations have exceeded 100 percent

on many occasions, and in some cases they have been as high as 400 or 500 percent. However, small volume items or unpredictable export orders usually account for the biggest deviation. The domestic company has also done significantly better on the average in meeting its less aggregate short-term targets and standards in such areas as quality control, costs and expenses, equipment utilization, and labor productivity.

CHAPTER 12
CONTROL

The key to an effectively functioning organization is a well designed managerial control system. It provides assurance that the firm's plans are being carried out, and furnishes the feedback required to measure progress and evaluate the validity of these plans and objectives.

Planning and control are intimately related and form a continuous process. For the sake of analysis, however, these two basic managerial functions can be considered separately. The better the planning job an organization does — including the establishment of measurable objectives and standards — the better its control system is likely to be.

The establishment of an effective control system is a difficult task under any circumstances. However, environmental uncertainties, unfamiliarity with local values and practices, and the tendency of people to mistrust what they do not understand augment the problem for foreign industrial subsidiaries in developing nations. The environmental constraints that make control difficult in developing countries have the same effect on planning.

Control systems are "people oriented." They work well when they are in tune with the personal values of employees and when they incorporate meaningful rewards. They must motivate individuals to perform in a desired manner. Consequently, it may be difficult to move a control system from one culture to another without some modification — be it of the system, or of the knowledge, skill, and values of local personnel.

CONTROL STANDARDS

Two kinds of problems exist in Indian industry with regard to control standards. First, many firms, and especially traditional firms, fail to establish quantified standards in critical areas. Such firms rely more on "a feel for what things should be" than on specific and measurable performance objectives. Second, other companies — chiefly U.S. subsidiaries — establish too many detailed standards of a nature not easily applicable to local conditions — standards often formulated by the parent organization and imposed on the subsidiary.

Although both approaches have shortcomings, the control systems of U.S. subsidiaries are generally more effective than those of indigenous firms. In fact, the superiority of U.S. subsidiaries in this area appears to be even greater than in that of planning.

Marketing

Many standards are used by both U.S. and Indian firms in the marketing and sales area. The most common is a sales target for the coming year. Only a few of the most traditional indigenous companies do not establish specific sales targets for the coming twelve-month period. In many cases, these are broken down into monthly figures, by product line or product. In some cases — mostly involving U.S. subsidiaries — these targets are useful as performance standards, since they are highly refined and accurate. Few Indian companies are effective in this area. In numerous cases, individual breakdowns of sales targets and products is largely perfunctory, as when a year's forecast is arbitrarily divided by twelve to achieve monthly figures, in spite of substantial and determinable seasonal variations for both end-product demand and raw materials. Some U.S. subsidiaries also follow this practice, usually because it is the easiest way to satisfy the format requirements of the parent organization.

The use and accuracy of such standards relates closely to the perceptions of top management. When standards are seen as important and useful, more attention is given to their formulation and application. For example, relatively traditional firms that do establish monthly targets for sales often do not compile actual operating data until several months' time has elapsed. Consequently, most of their managers regard the formulation of standards as a worthless task.

Almost all of the major companies surveyed in the Pharmaceutical industry — but fewer in other sectors — had some standards relating to the performance of the sales force. In many cases, however, the standards were designed more to control the time of the salesmen than to measure the results of his efforts. For example, although most drug firms established standards relating to the number of visits a salesman should make, few had established targets concerning the amount of sales he should generate. This was typical of several of the U.S. subsidiaries where the parent firm placed emphasis on increasing the number of calls to doctors and pharmacists in an attempt to bring local medical representatives up to U.S. levels. They often overlooked transportation constraints, geographical differences, the hours kept by customers, the problems of getting to see them, and other environmental difficulties.

Differences in the geographical and economic makeup of each salesman's territory in India often make it difficult to arrive at one standard for all salesmen. Yet few firms had attempted to establish norms for each territory or group of territories. Only a handful of companies — mostly U.S. — set standards relating to the size of a given salesman's territory. In most cases, these were used in a general manner and decisions about new territories or dividing or combining old ones were made as a result of suggestions and complaints from regional managers and individual sales representatives, rather than after thoughtful analyses.

The lack of marketing research at most companies precluded the establishment of explicit standards related to market share, penetration, and so forth. Although managers in many firms talked about growth, objectives tended to be general in nature: "We want to be the biggest," "we want to be in the top five," or "we want to increase our market share."

Few firms measured the effectiveness of advertising and promotional activities, making no attempt to analyze media responses. Consequently, they often applied "rules of thumb." In the case of U.S. subsidiaries, these were sometimes derived from the parent company. Typically, ad hoc decisions were made whenever someone with authority felt that additional promotional activity was necessary.

Most U.S. subsidiaries and some indigenous firms established standards concerning the number of new products which would be introduced each year. In most cases, these were established on the basis of top management's "feel" for a reasonable amount of growth rather than on a planned analyses of market demand, capacity, and resource requirements.

Most of the parent organizations of U.S. subsidiaries — especially in the drug industry — watched the ratio of selling and administrative costs to total sales, as well as the ratio between total sales and number of sales personnel, closely. Although several subsidiaries had not set their own standards in this area, informal ones had evolved based upon reactions from the international headquarters to various mixes between sales efforts and sales results. In any event, guidelines were usually established in advance of each year's operations during the budgetary formulation process. Few Indian companies maintained similar standards. Instead, they allowed the size of their sales forces and marketing expenditures to increase or decrease in response to market conditions.

Production

In the production area, U.S. subsidiaries had comprehensive sets of standards. Standards at Indian firms — with the exception of a few progressive ones and those working with

U.S. or other foreign collaborators — tended to be meagre by comparison. Sometimes production standards were supplied to the U.S. subsidiary or affiliate in unaltered fashion by the parent company. This direct transfer was often coupled with a tendency to try to duplicate U.S. production facilities and processes. The U.S. subsidiaries and foreign collaborators imported a larger proportion of their machines, used layouts and manufacturing specifications supplied from abroad, and relied more heavily on imported raw materials. However, tighter import restrictions have been imposed on such firms in recent years, making many of these standards inappropriate and inapplicable. Yet, in many cases, standards have not been revised to reflect such changing conditions, thus weakening existing control systems.

The most common production standards, especially in the pharmaceutical industry, were those relating to quality control. Nearly all of the major companies studied had established standards to regulate product quality. The U.S. subsidiaries and foreign collaboration ventures generally set higher standards than their indigenous counterparts on comparable products. This was the result of several factors.

First, the foreign company usually had a world-wide reputation to maintain. Consequently, it tended to impose on all operating units the highest standards required in any part of the world in which it functioned. The Indian firms geared themselves to a much less demanding domestic market. For example, the indigenous company would be more likely to ship a product with an imperfect surface finish if it was not especially noticeable and did not detract from the product's performance, while the U.S. firm would rework or reject the same item.

Second, the U.S. firms devoted more attention to the establishment of standards for inputs to the manufacturing process than did Indian firms. Industrial raw materials often had to meet U.S. standards — standards not often attained by local producers. This led to intensive reworking of raw materials by U.S. subsidiaries.

While high-quality standards may be beneficial to a developing country, U.S. companies seemed to place too much emphasis on this area. Standards could be reduced or modified in ways that would not affect the international reputation of the company or hinder customer relations, would make greater use of indigenous supplies and thus reduce imports, and would reduce both the costs and problems confronting the subsidiary. A few U.S. firms studied handled this problem by marketing certain lower-quality items — such as batteries — under another brand name.

All U.S. firms and most of the Indian companies studied had some standards relating to the utilization of materials in production. In India (and other developing countries) where materials account for by far the largest portion of manufacturing costs (60 percent or more in most modern sectors) the control of raw materials usage received greater attention than other factor inputs. U.S. subsidiaries typically had tighter standards covering a wider range of material inputs (including such things as fuel, electricity, water, components, and supplies) than their indigenous counterparts.

The U.S. subsidiaries and other foreign collaboration ventures were supplied many of their material standards by parent firms and overseas affiliates. Precise figures supplied in this manner often presented problems since the figures were based on different climatic, transportation, and storage conditions; different kinds of raw material specifications; different levels of employee training; and different equipment (including that involved in materials handling). Pressures from the parent firm often resulted in subsidiary managers focusing on the achievement of parity with U.S. standards rather than on determining standards reasonable for the local environment. However, on the whole, the standards and figures provided from abroad did provide useful guidelines.

Standards relating to labor inputs were less common than those involving material inputs. Traditional indigenous firms in particular tended to treat labor as a fixed cost, and no attempt was made to determine productivity standards. Most other firms surveyed established labor standards only in highly aggregate and general terms.

A few U.S. subsidiaries were doing an effective job with regard to labor standards. Although most had received labor input standards from their parents, these were of little value in view of local operating and environmental conditions. Consequently, firms either evolved their own standards, or used gross measures of productivity (e.g., rupee value of output per man-day). In the former case, industrial engineering departments were assigned the task of establishing rough time standards. Time studies were made occasionally, but historical records were more frequently used as a basis for establishing standards. Only a few firms — almost all U.S. subsidiaries — used predetermined time standards and the industrial engineering departments at most firms that had them concerned themselves chiefly with methods of improvement rather than work measurement. The diversified U.S. battery and chemical company and a few U.S. drug firms did the best job in both areas.

Relatively few of the firms surveyed — and, again mostly U.S. and other foreign ventures — had established effective plant or equipment capacity standards. These were most prevalent in machine-oriented operations. For example, where a machine cycle controlled output (as in the case of a punch press which could stamp out "X" pieces per unit of time) and where products were relatively standard, most of the U.S. firms had developed capacity measures. Only a few Indian companies had done this. However, where facilities were used for a variety of products, each of which required different amounts of machine and labor time, only the most crude estimates were commonly found. In these cases, it was impossible for the parent or the equipment manufacturer to supply capacity figures and the people directly concerned with operations usually had neither the interest nor the competence to set standards. Consequently, in situations where the only limitation on sales was production capacity, many firms were unable to plan for the most effective use of one of their most critical resources. This factor, coupled with weak sales forecasting efforts, often resulted in profit levels which were lower than they might have been.

A key element relating to capacity is maintenance. Breakdowns of machinery hinder smooth production operations. Yet the maintenance area was neglected by all but a handful of U.S. companies. Few firms had established their own maintenance standards, and many discovered that the standards supplied by foreign equipment manufacturers were not applicable since they had been based on different qualities of material inputs, voltage reliability, and worker training. Even where good standards existed, little was done to translate them into effective programs. Many companies — including most of the traditional indigenous ones — did not even compile records which could be used at future dates to establish empirical standards. Consequently, maintenance consisted largely of emergency repair, and even at those firms which had maintenance standards — particularly the Indian concerns — these were either meaningless or were not used effectively for control purposes.

One class of standards that was uniformly absent in all but one or two of the indigenous firms surveyed was that related to meeting delivery dates. U.S. subsidiaries examined and controlled delivery performance more closely, but not as closely as their parent firms did in the United States. Several factors explained the lack of such standards. Many firms were selling everything that they could manufacture — although this has generally been less so in recent years. Consequently, production personnel devoted their major effort to fulfilling the marketing organizations' need for ever-increasing output. Under such circumstances, the "hand to mouth" nature of operations made the control of delivery dates less important than increased production.

In industries where products were made to order (usually for industrial users) there was a difference in the rationale underlying the lack of such standards in foreign as opposed to Indian firms. In the U.S. companies, substantial delays were encountered in obtaining raw materials, in repairing equipment, and so forth. Consequently, standards were often not set, and it was assumed that everyone would do his best to get production out as quickly as possible. Although the identical approach was found in indigenous firms, the affect was compounded by more traditional managers who tended to de-emphasize the value of time. Since local customers also seemed to place a low premium on time, there was little reason to emphasize time standards and maintain control on delivery performance.

Purchasing

The purchasing or procurement function was a highly critical area for most of the surveyed firms, but especially for foreign companies and collaborative ventures since they relied more heavily on imports, at least until recently. Purchases could be placed in three categories: imported items or products made largely from imported items; local goods or materials that were government controlled; and local items which were not controlled.

Few firms had standards to serve as meaningful targets or guidelines in either procurement or warehousing of any of the three categories. However, more companies, especially U.S. subsidiaries, have started to do so recently, as import restrictions have made procurement more critical for them. With regard to the first two categories, the rule generally was to purchase as much as possible, whenever possible. Imported and controlled items were in scarce supply, and the risks of overstocking were virtually negligible, since there were always buyers ready to take up surplus stock (usually through black market deals). Attempts to set standards were complicated and frustrated by continuous changes in the government restrictions, by alterations in the allocation process, and by often unpredictable time delays in government licensing and delivery procedures.

In the case of readily available and non-controlled domestic items, little lead time was required and inventories were maintained at relatively low levels. Consequently, few standards relating to either ordering or stockpiling had been established. However, even for many non-controlled items there was considerable uncertainty or long lead times involved. The U.S. subsidiaries generally did a better job in standardizing purchases than their indigenous counterparts, although there were a few notable exceptions.

Inventory control

Inventory control was another area where standards were spotty. More of the U.S. firms had established guidelines for gross-value figures (e.g., value of inventory to value of total yearly sales or production) than the Indian companies. In most cases, these were financial guidelines dictated by their parents. The great disadvantage of relying on such aggregate standards is that they do not take account of the internal inventory mix in both physical and value terms. A firm may have too much inventory in total, but it may not be carrying sufficient inventories of the right items at the right times. This may lead to production bottlenecks or stock-out losses in sales.

Of all the companies studied, a major indigenous drug firm was one of the first to apply a systematic approach to establishing inventory levels for individual products. In the first half of the 1960s it reorganized its inventory system and began collecting data needed to set standards in a meaningful way. To date, few firms surveyed in India have done as good a job. However, as of the late 1960s more U.S. subsidiaries were effective in this regard than indigenous companies.

Since many of the firms surveyed were able to sell whatever they produced as fast as they produced it, they did not feel the need to build comprehensive systems to control inventories of finished products or even goods-in-process. The de-emphasis of inventory control with regard to finished goods tends to spill over to other inventories, such as raw materials and spare parts. However, with the decline of sellers' markets for many items inadequate standards and controls even with regard to in-process and finished goods inventories has lead to serious problems at many firms. More of the U.S. subsidiaries have been successful in adopting their inventory control systems to such conditions than their indigenous counterparts.

Financial and cost standards

Within the U.S. subsidiaries, financial control usually received the greatest amount of attention, and almost all had comprehensive procedures directed toward the control of operating expenses and capital expenditures. However, in most cases standards were provided by the budgets, and these tended to be crude estimates. Only a few firms surveyed — almost all U.S. — had detailed, carefully thought-out, and effective standards relating to cost relationships or investment criteria.

Few companies had meaningful investment criteria, relating to the amount of money to be designated for investment purposes or to the expected return such funds were expected to yield. Some subsidiaries made use of payback period criteria with regard to investment decisions. In several cases, discussions with international headquarters personnel revealed that such standards were also lacking at the corporate headquarters in the United States, especially regarding foreign investment decisions.

In most cases, U.S. parent companies required detailed investment, cost, and income projections for new projects or major expenditures under contemplation at the subsidiary level. Once the capital expenditure budget had been approved it became the ad hoc standard against which the coming year's activities would be measured. Often, stringent limitations were placed on the spending or contractual authority of the managing director to assure that these could not be altered. However, in many cases subsidiary managers found ways to get around such financial control, often to the benefit of the company as a whole.

Many indigenous firms had no clear-cut investment criteria at all, and based their decisions on a "felt need" or intuition. Others used a rough payback period rule of thumb as their investment criteria, generally a two to three year period, although the period varied from industry to industry. Only two Indian firms studied were making any attempt to formulate detailed investment standards based on relatively long-term, discounted rates of return; however, this has not gone beyond the experimental stage in these companies.

Although virtually all U.S. companies and many of the Indian firms had cost accounting systems, few had accurate cost standards. The operating budget figures usually served as overall standards for use by top management. Cost standards by product were less common, and when available, were seldom used.

There are several reasons for the dearth of effective cost standards in Indian industry. Few accountants have been trained as cost accountants, and many Indian accountants working for U.S. firms were not familiar with the requirements of U.S. control systems. Invariably, they experienced confusion concerning the treatment of overheads and of any expenses which had to be allocated over several products or departments. Due to secrecy considerations, much cost data was not made available to lower-level personnel. As a result, the accounting department experienced little pressure (or feedback) from operating people to develop standards which could be used for measuring or controlling cost performance. This applied even to those companies which had established departmental or divisional cost or profit and loss centers, and in most of these cases, only gross cost information was communicated to top management, with little, if any, feedback going to the departmental or other lower-level managers.

Cost standards supplied to the U.S. subsidiaries by parent organizations were often not applicable in India due to differences in wage rates, material inputs and costs, worker and equipment productivity, and other factors. Many Indian accountants employed by U.S. companies did not know how to set up cost control systems and were concerned primarily with the collection of aggregate cost data. Their approaches were frequently consistent with the attitudes and practices found in the more traditional Indian firms.

In the traditional company cost control tended to be highly centralized. In many cases, the only approximation of a standard was an objective for overall profitability. The primary financial concern of the top men was usually how much money was available. Consequently, the accounting system often dealt only with the aggregates of cash inflows and outflows. This approach was reflected in the procedures of nearly all the accountants in the relatively traditional firms examined.

In most firms cost data was utilized only in setting prices and even there, market considerations tended to play the dominant role. In only a few cases was cost data used to achieve managerial control. Typically, control systems were designed to limit the outflow of company capital rather than to provide information which could be used to improve operating efficiency. The use of control systems as managerial development devices was almost totally overlooked at most firms.

CONTROL TECHNIQUES

The tools and techniques used in planning are also useful for control purposes. These include budgets, cost accounting, operations research and other mathematical and statistical methods, and the setting of detailed standards for labor, material, costs and expenses, profit margins, overheads, inventories, equipment, quality, and maintenance. In some cases firms that used such techniques in planning failed to make good use of them with regard to control. Most of the firms with modern control techniques were U.S. companies, but only a few of these approached the effectiveness of their parent's domestic operations.

Only one diversified U.S. firm among all those surveyed in India was effectively using a computer for control purposes. This firm was able to obtain relatively automatic and simultaneous revisions and changes in interrelated plans and operations. As information feedback and control led to changes in one area of the organization, changes were also made in interdependent areas via the computer. This reduced delays and imbalances in the overall system.

Many of the U.S. and British subsidiaries and affiliates used direct standard costing, but very few Indian firms were doing so. The latter either used historical costs, or had virtually no meaningful costing systems. Many U.S. subsidiaries were required to use standard systems by their parents. Some did not feel this was warranted under Indian conditions, and they did so half-heartedly only to please the parent company.

A common control technique, used more often in Indian than foreign companies, was that of surprise inspection. Many firms maintained a special auditor staff, the prime function of which was to swoop down on a particular manager or department and conduct a complete shakedown inspection to make sure that instructions were being followed and that nothing illegal was going on. This control by fear was generally an ineffective technique.

In one non-U.S. foreign company, managers lived in constant dread of a group they referred to as the "Gestapo." This team would show up in a department unannounced, stop all operations for periods ranging from several hours to several days, study all records, check all inventories and interrogate all employees. Similar types of "flying squads" were used by other companies although few of them went to the extremes described above.

INFORMATION SYSTEMS

At the heart of a control system is the data collection and dissemination process. Control data can be classified into three basic categories: information dealing with financial factors, primarily centered around the budget; information relating to physical factors such as input and output figures; and information concerning human factors including motivation, skill, and attitudes. In all cases the data is processed in the same fashion: standards must be established, data collected, and deviations or variances compared and analyzed. The end product is the corrective action which may result.

Both the U.S. and indigenous companies in India set up systems that were deficient, in varying degrees, in one or more of these aspects. The greatest information deficiencies involved the human factors. Next came deficiencies involving physical factors, followed closely by deficiencies involving financial aspects.

Both the design and use of information feedback systems for control purposes in Indian industry tends to be hindered by the dearth of effective control standards, reports, and techniques, along with excessive overcentralization. The more traditional companies had few formally prepared reports for control purposes, although some had begun to develop them. Most of the information flow was handled through informal contact between the managing director and other members of the managerial team, was not expressed in quantitative terms, nor retained for later historical analyses. Consequently, such companies had no real base upon which to construct an effective information and control system. Aggregate reports of financial and operating information proved of little use for control purposes. Moreover, most of the feedback that existed involved long reporting delays. Little systematic use was made of strategic controls.

Some of the more progressive companies (both U.S. and other), did compile detailed reports, in many cases daily, weekly and monthly, as well as quarterly and annually. Often they prepared considerably more reports per capita than similar kinds of companies within the United States. For example, one of the larger, diversified Indian industrial concerns — formerly a managing agency empire — compiled over 200,000 reports per year. Several of the better-managed U.S. subsidiaries compiled significantly more reports and memos per capita than their parent's domestic operations. However, few of the reports, especially at indigenous firms, were actually used. They came too late for timely corrective action, and available information was not adequately fed down the managerial hierarchy to enable lower-level operating personnel to adjust activities.

Most major firms systematically provided monthly aggregate figures for departmental and divisional operations (e.g., total monetary value of production and sales). In addition, they prepared reports on critical raw material shortages; the ratio of monthly sales to inventory; the physical quantity of output; the progress of new products and expansionary projects, and various other matters. However, no attempt was made to accumulate cost data which would give anything more than an overall estimate of profit and loss for any unit.

As already indicated, almost all of the U.S. firms had standard cost systems. These included the calculation and reporting of variances, among them computed material price and use variances and labor rate and use variances, for all of their production departments. However, individual production managers seldom saw the results of the analyses, and top management often decided that so many last-minute changes took place in product mixes on the production floor than it really wasn't worth the effort to try to obtain justifications for many of the variances which arose.

With only one or two exceptions, by far the best and most extensive reporting systems were found at a few progressive U.S. companies. Such systems included daily and weekly reports (most of which were current) and monthly production and sales reports covering the value and number of units by product lines; actual versus targeted figures, along with explanations for significant deviations; the status of critical supplies and inventories; the progress of new products, special projects, and sales promotions; labor and equipment productivity; and detailed analyses of cost variances. Figures were presented for both the current month (or shorter period) and for cumulative annual performance to date, and they were compared with similar figures for the previous month and the previous year to date. Unfortunately, in many instances the data was not relayed to operating managers down the line.

In summary, the information collection, analyses and feedback processes at firms studied varied from rudimentary to thorough. However, three factors played a major role in the effectiveness of these processes, and they warrant further comment. First, the accuracy of the information collected; second, who received the data; and finally, what was done with it.

The accuracy of data left much to be desired. Many examples of grossly inaccurate and imcomplete data were found, although this was typically a greater problem at indigenous companies, especially the more traditional ones. At the U.S. subsidiaries inaccurate data was frequently due to misunderstandings or lack of training on the part of Indian personnel. Detailed forms and formats were generally supplied by the parent firm; however, Indian personnel were not able to interpret the significance of this data (e.g., why it was required and how it was to be used). Rather than admit their ignorance, many attempted to use their own judgment and often supplied data that was misleading. In situations where data could be interpreted in several ways, the Indian accountants and other specialists often lacked guidance to select the most meaningful choice.

For example, in one U.S. company, the accountant computed a standard labor rate by dividing the average monthly wage of all workers in the plant by the number of days in the month. Consequently, the standard daily wage rate differed for a 30-day and a 31-day month. When it came to deriving standard labor costs for given products, he multiplied the "actual" number of man-days required (estimates given to him by production managers) by the standard daily wage rate. This resulted in the under-absorption of total labor costs since it did not account for weekends and holidays. In a flash of inspiration, the accountant concluded that the difference (the under-absorbed costs) must be what is known as "social overheads." He therefore incorporated these amounts in the plant overhead rate. The managing director based decisions on these computations for more than a year before the situation was discovered.

In an Indian plant, management decided that output should be measured in constant terms, and that the monetary value of production (based on sales price) was the only measure that would be suitable. During the first six months of operating under this system, figures showed that output declined in spite of the fact that the market seemed better than ever. The sales manager complained about shortages and pressure was put on the production manager to increase output. However, the production manager had never seen the output figures. Only when he and other members of his staff were called in and given an ultimatum to increase output was it discovered that special sales promotions and customer discounts had reduced the dollar volume (as measured at market price) of production in certain key departments, while physical output had actually increased. It was six months before this matter was cleared up.

The treatment of overheads presented continuous problems for most firms. The Indian accountants seemed unsure about how best to allocate them. In most cases, fixed overheads were assigned to every unit of activity. The accountants were unfamiliar with concepts such as contribution and marginal costing. Little had been done to develop their expertise in these areas by providing the necessary training. This situation was especially critical in the U.S. firms, since detailed forms had to be submitted to parent companies for decision analysis. The Indian accountants often supplied misleading data which top management used as if it were truly representative of operations.

At the more traditional firms data collection functions were often fractionated and individual tasks were allocated among clerical personnel in such a manner as to ensure that no one but top management was able to obtain a comprehensive picture of operations. One of the consequences of this was that there were few checks or counterchecks on the accuracy of data. The people close enough to actual operations to determine whether data was accurate never saw the information, while top management either did not have sufficient familiarity with lower-level operations or did not have the time to examine the details to verify the accuracy of information received.

In general, excessive centralization tends to create information overload problems at the top levels of an organization, and to result in ineffective control at lower levels. Virtually all the firms in India experienced this, to a much greater degree than any of the domestic companies studied in the United States. At some U.S. subsidiaries, the amount of information they had to compile for their parent organizations contributed considerably to information overload problems. But such problems were most acute at the traditional Indian companies and in some cases bordered on the unbelievable.

At these firms, the managing director was usually swamped with paperwork. He checked virtually all the outgoing and most of the incoming mail. Purchase requisitions and the very smallest expenditure authorizations waited for his signature. Typically, he concerned himself with a fantastic amount of detail and did not distinguish adequately between important and trivial things. As a result, his attention would be drawn away from critical areas of the business.

The best company surveyed in India, in terms of its information and control system, was the diversified U.S. battery and chemical subsidiary, which had developed an integrated information flow and feedback system cutting across interrelated functional and departmental lines. This was beneficial for decision making which involved relationships between sales needs, production capability, and materials stocks.

The company also generated reliable and useful information in a timely fashion for control purposes, and much more of it was used by middle and lower-level managers than at most of the other firms studied. Moreover, it involved lower-level personnel in the planning, budgeting, and standard-setting process, and this had positive motivational effects. In companies where managers received little direct feedback they tended to establish a "normal" working pace based on what they felt to be reasonable and to perform indefinitely at about the same rate. The above company had cost and profit centers which enabled it to pinpoint both critical trouble spots and high-performance areas, and to improve performance as time went on.

This firm also emphasized positive feedback (whereas most of the other companies transmitted primarily negative feedback down the managerial hierarchy). It's feedback and control system was more oriented toward people and results than those of other companies. It was also more attuned to two-way vertical communication and information flows, as well as horizontal flows. Even where middle- and lower-level managers did not receive detailed cost or other data concerning operations, they usually received regular evaluations of their overall performance. When problems persisted, upper-level managers tended to dig into the details of the performance failure and to work with the individual concerned to correct the situation.

TIMELINESS OF CORRECTIVE ACTION

The entire control process is defeated if it does not lead to rapid corrective action when performance is not going according to plan. In turn, the timeliness and effectiveness of corrective action depends on a number of other factors. These include: how good the plans and control standards were to begin with; how fast and accurate information feedback is; how quickly significant deviations and other undesirable events or trends are detected; and how promptly they are brought to the attention of those personnel who can take corrective measures.

In many of the less progressive firms, operating data was not compiled until three- or four-month time elapses had occurred. This had a negative impact on planning as well as control, since most managers came to regard the formulation of targets and other control standards as a worthless task. Consequently, the targets and standards themselves were useless for control purposes.

The following approach was typical of the traditional Indian firms. The top manager indicated that both the labor force and product mix tended to be constant. Therefore, he believed that it was not necessary to establish detailed standards for labor, materials, equipment, and costs, since all he had to do was monitor output. He felt that whenever output remained steady, everything was under control. Whenever it changed, especially in a downward direction, he looked for problems. Time delays in reporting data were so great that several months would pass before he became aware that problems existed, and because there were no detailed standards, it was difficult to pinpoint the areas which were causing the difficulties. Since there were no clear priorities in planning or control, there was a tendency to label all production job tickets and many other matters as "urgent," and no one really knew what was or was not truly urgent.

At the companies which had the best control systems, budget comparisons were usually available within ten days after the monthly operating period. In some critical areas, such as materials, inventories, and new product sales, control reports were prepared weekly or daily and were available shortly after the close of each day or week. Such information feedback facilitated corrective action. However, even at the best-managed firms in India, external (as well as some internal) constraints hampered timely corrective action. External constraints included slow mail, inadequate telephone and telegraph service, and transportation problems. However, those companies which set up their own telex systems were able to reduce information and communications problems.

The diversified U.S. battery and chemical firm used its computer to monitor its financial system and in process control activities, and to compile lead indicators and trends that could predict the need for corrective action before the results were in. It also relied much more on informal communications with regard to control than most of the other firms surveyed. Where other firms often experienced 10 to 20 percent lost time in productive operations because of bottlenecks resulting from errors or changes in sales, procurement, production, and other plans, the figure for this company rarely exceeded 5 percent.

TIGHTNESS VERSUS LOOSENESS OF CONTROL SYSTEMS

The nature of the control systems used in an organization tends to be closely tied to the philosophy of its management. Particularly important are top management's attitudes regarding centralization versus decentralization of authority and responsibility.

A well-balanced control system is not easy to achieve in any environment. Such a system involves the control of individuals, as well as control of enterprise operations, performance, and results. Tight control (as exemplified in highly centralized, one-man autocratic rule) is likely to stifle the creativity and motivation of managers and other personnel down the line, thereby depriving the organization of some of its most valuable talents and resources. Conversely, a control system can be so loose that it is ineffective as a guide to action. It does not pull the organization together so that its elements work toward common goals, and it does not provide for corrective action in a consistent or effective manner.

A balanced position is one where the control system serves as a guideline and information channel (in upward, downward, and horizontal directions) and, while delineating the boundaries of individual authority and responsibility, allows for adequate discretionary powers. In addition, it does not overemphasize the control of people at the expense of performance and results, or vice-versa.

The nature of this balance and the ways in which it is best achieved tend to be different under different environmental conditions. A balanced position in India is likely to call for more centralization and tighter control over people and performance than in the United States. However, even taking into account major sociological-cultural, educational, and other environmental differences, firms in India are usually further off balance in terms of control than companies in the United States.

In India, the tendency is to lean heavily toward tight, centralized control patterns. Indigenous firms usually placed greater emphasis on control of people, often at the expense of performance and results. Many of them established elaborate controls to prevent pilferage and spent a great deal of time going over time cards, and observing personnel. This was done because of a basic distrust of personnel not only with regard to honesty, but also with respect to competence, reliability, and skill. More effective training, staffing, and personnel development and motivation could have helped alleviate management's fears about the latter traits.

The most extreme cases of rigid and ineffective control systems were found in those relatively traditional companies which were owner-managed and in some of the public sector firms run by government bureaucrats. In these cases, attempts were made to collapse the control system to a single focus — usually the managing director. Since it is difficult, if not impossible, for an individual to effectively control all facets of a sizeable operation, the pattern was for top management to select a key area — usually finance — and reserve all decision-making power within this field for himself. In this manner, the head man tried to ensure that he knew all of the important things going on, and that money was being spent in a manner acceptable to him. However, he often overlooked other areas of the business that were running out of control.

This was typified in the case of one large Indian firm. The production manager lived in fear of the managing director because of occasional 20-cent expenditures. One of the production processes was dependent upon the use of a bottled chemical. The bottles were picked up the night before they were to be used, and were returned the following evening for refill. If a bottle was not returned on time there was an additional charge of approximately 20 cents per day. All expenditures had to be approved by the managing director, and since this was an unusual charge it was always noticed. Invariably, an inquiry was received as to why such unnecessary charges should be incurred. In some cases, the extra charge resulted because the planned production run for that day had to be postponed, due to equipment breakdowns or emergency requests from marketing for a run of another product. Or else it might be due to breakdown of the truck used to return the tanks. With the discovery of the additional charge, someone would be placed on the firing line by the managing director. In an effort to protect himself and his colleagues, the production manager adopted the practice of returning the tanks whether they had been used or not. A tank returned full cost the company significantly more than the overnight rental charge, but it would appear as a routine operating expense and probably go undetected since no control standards existed for the use of this particular chemical. The result was, of course, an increase in production cost.

Most of the U.S. subsidiaries had better-balanced control systems than their indigenous counterparts. However, in many cases control in certain areas — especially finance and accounting — was overcentralized and too tight. This was due to both parent company requirements and to the attitudes and practices of subsidiary executives. In nearly every case, management of the domestic operations of the parent was much more decentralized and greater use was made of management by objectives or results.

Many U.S. firms also tended to exercise rigid control in the personnel area — but not because of distrust per se. Once personnel levels had been approved by the parent, managing directors were not free to exceed the figures without obtaining approval from international headquarters. Interviews with executives from the parent firms indicated a common rationale on this issue. Because of the difficulty of firing and laying off personnel during recessionary periods, they wanted to make sure that staff was kept to a minimum. However, these controls caused difficulties both by limiting the flexibility to respond to given situations and by lowering the status and prestige of the subsidiary's top management in the eyes of lower-level managers and employees.

In addition to stringent financial and accounting controls, and limitations on non-budgeted expenditures and personnel levels, product prices, manufacturing methods, plant layouts, and promotional campaigns, various other matters required approval from the parent firm. Often no changes at all could be made by subsidiary management without obtaining explicit agreement from headquarters. Such controls sometimes stimulated greater efficiency and better performance; nevertheless, they also created problems. As one competent Indian manager of a U.S. drug subsidiary stated: "Our company is known to be one of the best managed and most decentralized in India. But much of this decentralization is really an illusion, given the array of stringent and often inappropriate controls that are imposed down the line both by the parent company and our own top management. This often results in serious efficiency and motivational problems, as well as other unintended effects."

This was an accurate statement. Nevertheless, this company was still one of the best managed and most progressive that we studied in India. Its control systems were not as balanced as they could have been, but they were superior to those of other firms.

UNINTENDED EFFECTS RESULTING FROM CONTROLS

The desire to build slack into plans and to pad budgets is a common tendency on the part of managers. This tendency is likely to be emphasized where there is uncertainty about whether production plans can be achieved; where plans are rigidly adhered to or difficult to revise; and where rewards or penalties are at stake. As managers build "safety factors" into their activities, they distort information, or at least bias it heavily in their favor. Top management may find it difficult to make adjustments, since they cannot determine how much "fat" is contained in any program.

Such behavior was more common and extensive at U.S. subsidiaries — and in parent company operations — than in indigenous firms. A major reason was that the U.S. firms allowed for more participation of middle and lower-level managers in the planning and budget formulation process. Greater use was made of formal plans, budgets, and related control standards, and clearer lines of individual responsibility were drawn. Managers were evaluated and rewarded on the basis of how well they performed in relation to plans, targets, and control standards. These factors were missing in most Indian firms. However, in the U.S. firms, the positive results usually outweighed the negative, unintended effects.

This kind of unintended behavior was common in connection with parent company-subsidiary relations. As the managing director of one U.S. firm put it: "We always build a great deal of padding into our budget requests, since New York holds us rigidly to the final figures. We can often make changes, but it just takes too long. To protect ourselves, we therefore build in enough slack so that we have some room to maneuver."

The danger of cutting away critical "meat" in certain areas when trying to eliminate excess budget "fat" is likely to be greater when the higher echelons are not familiar with local conditions, and when great geographical distances limit contact. On the other hand, it may be easier for a subsidiary to get away with padded requests. In any event, many cases exist where negative effects could have been avoided or greatly reduced with more appropriate and flexible controls.

Parent firms often exercised influence on subsidiary operations which created inefficiency, and morale problems. They frequently caused anxiety and frustration, and drained the energy of subsidiary managers by applying unrelenting pressure from international headquarters. Local creativity and initiative was seriously hindered in many instances. Frequently, subsidiary management responded by acting out a charade to satisfy the parent, and much wasted time and effort resulted.

In many cases subsidiary managers (especially if they were not Indians) refused to abide by controls, hatched devious schemes to get around them — e.g., to bypass rigid capital expenditure limits they bought equipment in pieces, each portion of which was under the limit, but the total of which would have required higher approval. In some cases, managers ignored controls, hoping that their actions would be demonstrated as beneficial before discovery occurred. And it must be said that probably more often than not such circumvention of parent-imposed controls did prove beneficial for the company as a whole.

Rigid one-man control systems drove many dynamic, non-family members away from Indian firms. They tended to seek employment with companies which would give them more discretion in the decision-making process, usually foreign subsidiaries.

It was common in several of the companies surveyed to divide the responsibility of inventory control, chiefly to prevent dishonesty. The storekeepers received only the incoming physical shipments, and did none of the paper work relating to the items. They took physical counts, and kept the store's records on the basis of physical inflows and outflows. All of the invoice information went to the accounting department. The accounting data was then used as a cross-check against physical inventories. The reason for this procedure was that the storekeepers would not know how much was supposed to be in stock and would therefore be forced to be scrupulously honest. This procedure, however, gave rise to many problems (sometimes consciously created by suppliers) since the storekeepers seldom had any way to verify whether or not the company was actually receiving what it had ordered. Physical inventories were usually taken by the accounting (or a special auditing) department. In one company a complete physical inventory of every major store area was taken twice each week. Due to poor inventory control practices, different batches of incoming materials were often not properly labeled, and frequently it was impossible to trace discrepancies to any particular shipment or to determine whether a shortage occurred in shipment or was due to in-plant theft or materials wastage.

In spite of the many and often serious unintended effects resulting from control systems, the U.S. firms, with very few exceptions, were more effective in exerting control than their indigenous counterparts, although their performance could have been improved. As one astute manager of a U.S. drug subsidiary told us: "We could improve our operating efficiency by 10 to 15 percent if we had a more effective over-all control system."

CHAPTER 13
ORGANIZATION

It seems reasonable to hypothesize that the organizational structures of a company will be closely linked to the cultural values and styles of its management, particularly top management. The organization structure is a manifestation of what people do and how they do it. Consequently, there is a predilection to adopt an organizational pattern which is both familiar and comfortable.

In India, drawing upon the earlier description and analysis of various key environmental factors, one can conclude the following:

1. Since the extended family, autocratically run and cohesive in nature, is the basic unit of society, the typical indigenous firm would tend to be organized along similar lines — highly centralized, authoritarian, and relatively paternalistic in nature.

2. Because the family unit has evolved to provide safety and security for its members, organizations might not only look like family groupings, but would also incorporate similar trust mechanisms, including a high degree of dependence (especially at decision-making levels) on personal, blood, and other intimate kinship relationships.

3. Authority and responsibility would follow the patterns of such family and kinship relationships, and personal relationships would provide the key organizational linkages.

4. An educational environment much inferior to that of the United States would tend to reinforce centralization, authoritarian management, and tight control at the top. It would also lead to considerable differences in the division of labor, types of positions, and other organizational arrangements.

By contrast, one would expect U.S. firms to be structured in patterns corresponding to those commonly found in the United States — a primary organizational principle being the division of labor according to task requirements and functional specialities, with people chosen to fit those specialities and requirements rather than the reverse. Authority and responsibility relationships would tend to be clearer in the U.S. firms; formal organization at all levels would be more important; more decentralization and participative management would be evident; fewer people would be related by blood or close family ties; and upward mobility from the lower ranks would be much higher.

The relationship between organizational patterns and the social environment has a significant implication for economic development. If one accepts the argument that development requires major changes in local social institutions, it follows that traditional indigenous organization structures must also alter, as they tend to be tied to the traditional values that have been ineffective in encouraging economic growth in the past. Since change is a slow process, these organization patterns will lag behind current needs.

SIZE

One of the easiest organizational parameters to measure is size — in terms of total assets, employees, sales, and so forth. The size of firms in developing nations tends to be smaller than in developed countries. In sectors where economies of scale are important, lower levels of efficiency and higher costs are the rule in developing nations.

Perhaps the most important factor affecting size is the magnitude of the market, including export markets. Transportation and other social overhead capital problems also limit a firm's size, by confining the scope of its markets and operations. The government's industrial licensing and planning policies in India are other limitations on size, as are stringent import restrictions, local supply deficiences, and an unwillingness to use outside capital for expansionary purposes. In addition, sociological-cultural factors — e.g., attitudes toward risk taking and change, lack of achievement motivation, concepts of authority, responsibility, decentralization, and participative management — are also limiting factors.

Foreign firms are faced with similar problems in a developing country, but they generally have more leeway (and desire) to expand. Foreign subsidiaries are usually among the largest within their industry, and grow at a faster rate unless the local government restricts their growth. In India, foreign firms are well represented near the top of the pharmaceutical, chemical, battery, flashlight, electrical, and petroleum sectors (the last being an area which has been subject to rapid changes in the last few years). Although they may be small by comparison to the domestic operations of their parent organizations, by virtue of know-how, capital, product quality, and reputation they tend to dominate local markets.

In addition to possible losses in economies of scale, another important consequence of the smaller sizes of firms in developing nations is that their organizations can support relatively few managerial functions, support staffs, or service units. With respect to the diversity and intensity of the problems faced, this can be of critical importance. While a large U.S. industrial firm may have an adequate staff to deal with the managerial and other problems it encounters, its subsidiary, producing the same broad product lines in a less-developed environment, may have to get along with a fraction of the specialized talent. This is true both for indigenous and foreign firms, and is especially important with regard to the selection of top managerial personnel – a subject which will be discussed in Chapter 14.

It is difficult to make direct comparisons between the sizes of indigenous and foreign firms in India because of the varied nature of operations and product mixes. Even within industry categories, differences can be great. For example, the indigenous firms surveyed in the drug industry tended toward more vertical integration in areas such as basic chemical production, equipment manufacture, and even plant engineering, consulting, and construction. The U.S. drug firms specialized more in pharmaceutical production.

CENTRALIZATION VERSUS DECENTRALIZATION

With few exceptions – all involving relatively progressive and large Indian firms – U.S. subsidiaries surveyed in India had significantly greater internal decentralization of authority than their indigenous counterparts. The domestic operations of their parent companies were in turn more decentralized – even taking size into account – than the subsidiaries.

In order to gain deeper insight into the question of centralization versus decentralization one should consider parent-subsidiary relations with regard to international companies. U.S. parent companies, directly or through their international headquarters, exert tight control on subsidiaries abroad, particularly in the areas of finance, personnel, R and D, and product mixes.

The British subsidiaries and British-Dutch-Indian ventures surveyed had greater decentralization vis-a-vis their parent companies than any of the U.S. subsidiaries surveyed. In most cases these ventures had Indians in top managerial positions. In fact, a few of their Indian managers had moved from U.S. subsidiaries largely to find greater decentralization with regard to the parent company. On the other hand, most of these foreign ventures did not practice internal decentralization to the extent that some of the most progressive U.S. subsidiaries did. It is interesting to look at the historical pattern of one of the best managed U.S. subsidiaries surveyed, a large and diversified company. In the 1950s an American headed the subsidiary. At that time the parent company was ethnocentric and even the U.S. managing director did not have much autonomy. He, in turn, did not delegate much authority. Small capital expenditures and such trivial matters as raises for watchmen required his approval, and he had to refer small issues to the parent, for final approval.

The American manager was promoted to a position in the home office's international division in the late 1950s and given responsibility for India. The new managing director was a man he trusted, and who was familiar with Indian conditions. At about the same time the managers were changed, the parent company became less ethnocentric. Consequently, the new man was given significantly more autonomy than his predecessor, and he developed a seven- to ten-year decentralization plan for the subsidiary which called for greater internal management development. (This kind of decentralization program could normally be accomplished in two to four years in the United States.) A large number of Indian managers — mostly U.S.- or Western-trained — were developed and promoted to key jobs as the firm grew. The number of foreign managers and specialists decreased.

In the early 1960s a British managing director was appointed (he was previously in charge of production). He continued to stress management development, and for a time to implement the internal decentralization program. However, greater parent centralization was evolving at this time, which was apparently due to a number of factors, among them a lack of confidence in the new managing director. The subsidiary was growing rapidly and had expanded into areas which required additional capital investment and know-how. This managing director also tended to check with international headquarters before making decisions to a significantly greater extent than his predecessor had. Moreover, overstaffing in management became an acute problem and the parent company began to exert greater control over staffing and personnel decisions. Centralized staff and service units began to proliferate, and these retarded decentralization and management development efforts.

An American deputy managing director was appointed towards the end of 1966, with the understanding that he would take over within a few years. At about the same time the parent corporation took a major step in the direction of geocentricity. It abolished its international division — which had become unwieldy — and set up a number of regional corporations with their own boards of directors. The aim was to decentralize authority to the regional level where a system of more applicable controls over individual subsidiaries would be established. When it was felt that the management of a given subsidiary was competent and could be trusted, it, too, would receive more operating autonomy than in the past.

The American deputy managing director became managing director of the Indian subsidiary at the beginning of 1968. He was also appointed regional managing director for India, which became a one-region country under the parent company's Eastern corporation. Under this setup the subsidiary was given more autonomy than in the past, and decentralization within the subsidiary accelerated. Although Americans and other foreigners still held several key managerial and technical jobs, the great majority of these positions had been filled by Indians, including members of the local board of directors.

One of the best managed and most successful U.S. drug subsidiaries had a succession of American and British managing directors until it appointed an Indian in 1968. Most of the people at international headquarters who were responsible for Indian operations had been involved directly with the Indian subsidiary. The parent firm recently organized regional management centers. While there have been some problems of overcentralization, the parent company provides greater and more balanced autonomy and flexibility than any of the other U.S. drug firms surveyed. The Indian managing director was groomed for his job for more than five years, and since he took over there has not been any significant trend toward recentralization either at the international headquarters level or within the subsidiary.

Another U.S. firm, although also one of the most successful and progressive in India, has not done as well in achieving a balance between centralization and decentralization. It has had a succession of foreign managing directors, interrupted briefly by the appointment of an Indian who did not work out well. Overcentralization problems have been most acute in the areas of finance and personnel. For example, a few years ago international headquarters approved the acquisition of 15 to 20 buses so the subsidiary could transport employees to and from its new plant, which is located at some distance from the center of the city. However, it would not approve the hiring of additional permanent personnel to drive these buses on the grounds that this would lead to overstaffing and possibly greater personnel problems. Only after serious labor problems arose did international headquarters give in.

The degree of centralization or decentralization permitted by U.S. and other foreign managers of U.S. subsidiaries appeared, in many cases, to depend on their confidence in the managers reporting directly to them, and their own knowledge of the areas involved. The broader their own backgrounds in the different operational functions, the more likely they were to take an interest in diverse areas, to get to know the abilities of their subordinates, and to set up procedures for operating in a decentralized manner. The top executive whose background was limited to a specific functional area frequently tended, somewhat paradoxically, to be more centralized in his decision making. Because he had limited contact with the operating managers in other functional areas, he relied on their judgments to a lesser degree and used his own more frequently. Often his decisions were based largely on intuition. This situation resulted in "self-fulfilling prophesies." Because he did not effectively communicate objectives and other critical information, his subordinates were not able to meet his expectations, which led to a further reduction in communications when his initial impressions were confirmed.

The type of manager described above, whether foreign or not, usually placed all or most of the blame for the lack of effective authority delegation on his subordinates. In general, the spiral with respect to the delegation of authority is a pervasive problem in developing countries. Superiors do not delegate because they feel that their subordinates are not competent and will not accept the implied responsibility or take any initiative on their own.

Most of the traditional Indian managers interviewed were conscious of the fact that they were not delegating authority. Many were opposed to the concept per se. Others echoed the managing director of a large public sector corporation who said, "Until we're on a firm footing and I know how good my lieutenants are, delegation is dangerous." It is important to know, however, that this statement was made approximately two years after the managing director assumed his position, and that during this time there had been virtually no change in top-level managerial personnel. Yet he was sincere, and his statement was indicative of the extremely high trust level he required before he would consider delegating any of his authority.

The most decentralized U.S. subsidiaries had not pushed authority as far down the hierarchy or achieved as extensive internal decentralization as had the domestic operations of their parent organizations. Real autonomy in decision making was rarely placed below the upper levels of plant or sales branch management. A plant manager in India often had decision-making powers equivalent only to a general foreman or section head in U.S.-based plants. The same patterns were also found in other functional areas.

In general, finance and personnel — including union relations in many cases — were the most centralized functions at U.S. subsidiaries. Much more of management's time throughout the hierarchy was occupied with filling out forms and reports in these areas, and in referring decisions upward, than in U.S.-based companies. Disciplinary action, personnel additions and cutbacks, overtime work, nonbudgeted money for meals for company drivers, and all kinds of minor expenditures required the approval of managers several levels higher up in the subsidiary organization than in U.S. domestic firms. The personnel function was highly centralized at many U.S. subsidiaries not only to prevent overstaffing, but also because few clear-cut policies existed for dealing with worker and union problems. Situations were handled on an ad hoc basis.

Purchasing decisions at U.S. subsidiaries, especially where imports were involved, were also more centralized than in the United States. The pattern with regard to government relations at U.S. subsidiaries was not as clear-cut. Some subsidiaries allowed more decentralization in this area than others. Those which allowed the most had competent, well-connected, and trusted Indians handling government negotiations and contacts. Marketing, production, and engineering were usually the most decentralized functions.

Overcentralization was more extreme at indigenous companies. Managers down the line in the U.S. firms had more latitude in determining schedules, assigning work, training, discretionary spending (albeit of a limited nature in most cases), initiating requests for capital expenditures, and participating in personnel decisions (including hiring and dismissals). At most indigenous firms, functional and other managers down the line were viewed chiefly as reporters and implementers, not as decision makers. They transmitted information to top management, received orders, and were expected to carry them out. Their chief managerial function involved personal contacts with subordinates and superiors, and centered around direction, communication, and to some extent motivation.

In the more traditional companies, the top man made virtually all of the financial decisions, and most other decisions of any significance. At some firms he was assisted by a trusted deputy, often called administrative director, who served in a line and staff capacity in a relatively ambiguous role. The range of decisions made by top management in traditional Indian firms — even large ones — was enormous. For example, top managers were often directly involved in assigning tasks to and checking on sweepers, drivers, and watchmen; the cleanliness of rest rooms and canteens; types of meals served to employees; the location of desks and ping-pong tables; and the authorization of 3-cent items.

The Indian companies under traditional managing agencies — recently abolished — were subject to even more stringent centralized control with regard to finance than the U.S. subsidiaries with the more centralized parent companies. However, in other areas such Indian firms often had considerably more autonomy vis-a-vis their parent companies than the U.S. subsidiaries, although they were more centralized internally.

In general, the centralization versus decentralization issue partly explains the tendency toward smaller-sized firms in developing countries. Under a highly centralized organization, the capacities of a single man or a small group of individuals who run the show can greatly limit growth and efficiency. Attention given to a vast amount of detail leaves little time for more critical functions, such as long-range planning. The highly centralized indigenous firm also restricts its growth by retarding the development of future managerial talent, and expansion is often linked to the size of the controlling family.

However, today one can see more of a compromise between family structure and qualified managerial cadres. Many families now send their sons abroad or to the best local schools to receive educations related to business operations. As a result, while the old principles of family control, support, and trust still apply, family members are being educated to the extent that they can provide a competent cadre of upper- and middle-level managerial talent.

It is in such companies that decision making begins to be decentralized down to the second and third echelons, and in some cases even further. Some of these firms eventually evolve into large, progressive organizations which employ sizeable numbers of non-family professionals in major jobs. However, few indigenous firms in developing countries have reached the stage where the family relinquishes direct control over the organization.

SPANS OF CONTROL AND ORGANIZATIONAL LEVELS

A comparison of the spans of control at the highest levels of management in U.S. and indigenous firms presents a clear and consistent pattern. The executives of the indigenous companies invariably had broader spans than their counterparts at U.S. subsidiaries.

This must be qualified in many cases, however, by taking into account the role of the "deputy." It was common for the organization charts of Indian companies to show a deputy as the only person officially reporting to the top man, with all managers at the next level below reporting to the deputy. In some cases the deputy was an "heir apparent." In others, he was an old compatriot of his boss and the two men would function as a team, although final decision-making power always rested with the senior man. In the case of some firms under managing agencies, the deputy was a trusted representative of the managing agents who really performed more of an audit function than a decision-making one.

In calculating span of control figures for managing directors, such deputies were ignored unless they were actually functioning as autonomous decision makers. This was more often the case in U.S. subsidiaries than in indigenous firms. In a few cases the managing directors of Indian companies were just figureheads with many outside interests, and the deputy managing director was really running the business. In such cases, the deputy was considered the true chief executive. Table 13-1 presents data on the number of managers reporting to managing directors (or other top executives) of U.S. and indigenous drug firms surveyed in India — it excludes clerks, secretaries, peons, drivers, and so forth.

The emphasis on centralization and the strong paternalistic patterns in the Indian firm gives rise to organization structures that are relatively broad at the top. This reflects the desire of the Indian top managers to be closer to the daily activities of their deputies as well as their strong reluctance to delegate. One might associate breadth with decentralization, since the superior's time is spread thin over the functions reporting to him. However, in the Indian companies, managers used the breadth as a substitute for an information gathering network. Functions and activities delegated further down the line in the U.S. subsidiaries — e.g., engineering, purchasing, inventory control, quality control — reported directly to the top man in the Indian firms. The more successful of the Indian firms had smaller spans at the top in most cases.

The pattern of spans in other sectors was not as distinct as in the pharmaceutical industry, but indigenous firms did have larger spans at the top in a majority of cases. It is also interesting to note that the spans of top executives of comparable domestic operations of U.S. parent companies surveyed (both drug and other) were in most cases broader than those of their subsidiaries in India. The subsidiaries had narrower spans in many cases because more on-the-job time was spent in training managers at the upper and middle levels.

TABLE 13-1 Spans of control
(Number of managers reporting to top manager)

U.S. Companies			Indian Companies		
Minimum	Maximum	Average	Minimum	Maximum	Average
3	9	6	6	14	10

A detailed study of spans of control at intermediate levels was more difficult to carry out because of the diversity of jobs involved. In general, the U.S. subsidiaries were better able to balance job requirements, and the abilities of both superiors and subordinates, in determining spans at the middle and lower rungs of the organization. The Indian companies determined spans in a more arbitrary manner. In areas where U.S. firms had substantial decentralization they tended to have significantly larger spans. In those areas where extensive training and personnel development was being undertaken, they had considerably narrower spans. The spans at the intermediate and lower rungs were usually narrower in subsidiaries than in comparable U.S.-based operations of their parent firms.

In most cases the number of levels between the top manager and factory workers and salesmen were greater in indigenous firms than in U.S. subsidiaries, especially if the line "deputies" at the various levels were taken into account. Although such deputies often had few decision-making powers they served as information transmitters and filters, and hence added more levels to the organization. The Indian pharmaceutical companies studied had from six to ten levels between top management and plant workers, and averaged eight. The number of such levels at U.S. drug subsidiaries ranged from three to seven and averaged five. The number of levels between the top manager and salesmen was not generally as large. The Indian companies ranged from four to eight with an average of six, and the major U.S. drug firms ranged from three to seven and averaged five. The same pattern held true for the nonpharmaceutical firms surveyed. On the other hand, U.S. subsidiaries in most cases had more levels in per capita terms — and in some cases, even in absolute terms — when compared to the domestic operations of their parents.

The degree of decentralization, the confidence superiors have in their subordinates, the abilities of subordinates, and the nature of control systems are key factors in explaining the differences in numbers of organizational levels between indigenous firms and U.S. subsidiaries, as well as between subsidiaries and their parent organizations. The desire of Indian employees for close personal relationships — which is greater in traditional organizations — and the limited ability of an Indian manager to deal on a one-to-one basis with many people also is a factor affecting the number of organizational levels. The structured relationships between the Indian manager and his subordinates were based more on personal friendships than in U.S. companies.

The more successful indigenous firms not only had smaller spans of control at the top, but fewer organizational levels, at least in per capita terms. They had achieved a better blend of Indian and U.S. patterns than their more traditional counterparts. The most successful U.S. subsidiaries had also achieved a type of compromise. Although their formal structures were distinctly American organizational forms, the informal interactions were derivatives of the working habits and patterns of the Indian managers and other personnel who filled the jobs.

BASIC DEPARTMENTATION AND GROUPING OF ACTIVITIES

With few exceptions, the firms studied in India were structured basically along functional lines of production, marketing, finance, and so forth. However, there were major differences in how these functions were actually organized and managed within U.S. subsidiaries and indigenous firms.

First, decision making within the various functions was more decentralized in U.S. firms. For example, purchasing agents had more authority at U.S. subsidiaries, and often operated several levels down in the organization. Engineering, inventory control, plant maintenance, quality control (except for pharmaceutical firms), as well as the more conventional line functions were also more decentralized at U.S. companies.

Second, the organization of various functions was considerably more fragmented at many Indian firms, and their performance often suffered as a result. For example, it was common to find engineering, R and D, and maintenance activities split among many different managers and departments whereas greater efficiency could have been achieved by integrating and consolidating them. Similarly, directly related planning and control activities were often divided among different managers. Such fragmentation was usually based on the personal interests or status needs of various managers, or on the desire for greater centralization and controls, rather than on any meaningful analysis of productive efficiency.

It was more common for U.S. firms to designate someone to be responsible for planning or budgetary control — such as a market planner responsible for market forecasts, or a budgetary officer responsible for coordination of the overall company budget. Few companies organized interrelated activities in accordance with an integrated systems concept — for example, having someone to coordinate inventory control, purchasing, and production schedules. A progressive Indian firm in the drug sector was the first of all the companies surveyed to move significantly in this direction. However, in recent years a number of U.S. firms — and a few other foreign companies — have begun to do so. A few companies — mostly U.S. — have also recently started to use project management and task teams.

Few of the companies studied had integrated product divisions. Those that did were relatively large firms (in a few cases, British subsidiaries) with diverse product lines. In a number of cases the manufacturing processes, engineering requirements, and distribution channels for a given group of products were clearly distinct from other lines carried by the company. But size and volume were often important limiting factors with regard to the establishment of self-contained product departments.

It was evident that it had never occurred to most of the companies to organize on a product basis, even to those U.S. firms which had been employing such organizational forms with success in the United States. In some cases at least, product organization would have probably proved effective in India. The desire to maintain a high degree of centralized control over operations was probably a key reason for not organizing in this manner.

Few firms had established integrated territorial or regional division management functions, even where they had geographically dispersed multiplant, multisales branch organizations. Many of the functionally organized firms surveyed could have benefited by organizing on such a basis.

Some companies in the drug and consumer goods sectors — mostly American and British — had several product managers responsible for the marketing of different product groups. In most cases they were staff people whose responsibilities were largely confined to developing sales promotion campaigns and coordinating marketing information on their particular product lines.

We also found situations where the parent company unwisely imposed various kinds of product manager jobs on the subsidiary — including some in the manufacturing area — just because this worked well in the United States. This was also true of various other kinds of organizational forms imposed on subsidiaries which sometimes proved ineffective in India.

WORK SPECIALIZATION AND DIVISION OF LABOR

At the lowest level of the organization — e.g., in production and clerical jobs — differences in degrees of work specialization were substantially greater between the U.S.-based operations of parent companies and their subsidiaries in India than between U.S. subsidiaries and their indigenous counterparts. Educational (including training) and sociological-cultural factors were chiefly responsible for this. The qualifications of workers in India and their motivation levels are lower than in the United States, and their values and attitudes are different. As a result, specialization of labor is more intense in India (and in developing countries in general) than in the United States and other advanced nations.

Social taboos such as the caste system, the great disdain expressed for various kinds of physical work, and status considerations are of major importance. A skilled Indian worker is frequently assigned a helper to carry things for him, clean his working space, and do other menial tasks that are beneath his status. Similarly, the typist who needs to move his typewriter will wait until an office "peon" can move his machine rather than pick it up and move it himself. A peon is assigned to serve him tea. The absence of modern material-handling equipment and other auxiliary technology also results in greater fragmentation of work and the need for larger numbers of ancillary personnel than in the United States. The government's desire to provide more employment and the rigid attitudes of trade unions support this pattern.

The U.S. subsidiaries in India had less fragmentation of worker and service functions than their indigenous counterparts. Superior training and the kinds of people the U.S. firms employed in terms of their basic education, values, attitudes, and motivations were usually the chief reasons for this.

A comparison of the organization charts of indigenous and foreign subsidiaries in India does not show many differences in the titles accorded to positions at various management levels. However, one must investigate how the organization really works to get at the question of division of labor in managerial and specialist positions.

Titles tended to be more descriptive and accurate in U.S. and other foreign subsidiaries. It was more common to find "managers" doing little real managerial work at indigenous companies. Such people were frequently little more than fact finders and communicators, with all information being passed on to higher managerial levels where the decisions were made.

On the other hand, managers and specialists at Indian companies often performed functions unrelated to their titles. For instance, at one Indian company the manager in charge of industrial engineering worked on sales incentive programs; the purchasing executive of another firm got involved in sales promotion; the financial manager in one company was involved in the maintenance function; and a sales manager in still another company was directly involved in some R and D work. Such lack of specialization was frequently due to prevailing personal interests at the time, status reasons, or because a particular manager felt he had nothing better to do.

Both indigenous and foreign companies frequently evinced confusion concerning the roles of managers throughout the hierarchy, but often for different reasons. In many cases, inadequate attention had been given to managerial or specialized training — especially in the more traditional firms — and individuals were left to fend for themselves. This was also evident in U.S. subsidiaries where practices commonly employed in the parent organization were not utilized because Indian managers either were not aware of them or did not have broad enough views of their own functions to see that these areas might be their responsibility. Sales forecasting provides an illustration. In many firms, forecasts were prepared in a centralized staff unit (often consisting of just one man) and were not seen as part of the function of regional or product sales managers.

The larger number of levels in the chain of command in Indian firms would seem to indicate a greater division of managerial labor. This was not the case, however; the many levels were probably the result of the managers' desire for status, the greater use of deputies, and the lack of decision-making authority down the hierarchy. In essence each manager had his own "messengers" or "tool carriers." The lower-level supervisor in indigenous firms has little direct decision-making authority. Yet he may have charge hands between himself and the work force. His boss, perhaps a department manager, may arrange daily work assignments, but have little to do with managerial decisions of consequence. At lower managerial levels, especially in the more traditional firms, individual managers worked basically as technical specialists.

USE OF STAFF SERVICES

The U.S. domestic operations surveyed (with one notable exception) had larger, and usually more effective staff departments and specialists serving the line organization than the U.S. subsidiaries. Many line decisions based on substantial staff inputs in the United States were based on few staff inputs in India. The scarcity of staff services in the subsidiaries resulted from their relatively small sizes but, in many cases, it also came from a feeling on the part of the parent that the smallness of the enterprise was synonymous with small problems.

Competent local specialists were not readily available for building staff functions, due both to the quality of local educational systems, and to the fact that the average Indian does not seem to be psychologically prepared to perform staff functions. The competent individual in a developing nation desires a position of command and leadership, and is uncomfortable in a staff role. The less competent person is likely to make an undesirable staff member. Some of the firms studied (mostly American subsidiaries) had "overstaffed" staff units, containing several levels of management, primarily to attract and keep well-educated Indians by allowing them to build their own "empires."

Research and engineering staff groups tended to be small in the U.S. subsidiaries. But with growing pressures to increase exports, engage in import substitution, and improve operating efficiency, they have recently been expanded at a number of these firms. Nevertheless, most of the support functions in these areas are still being supplied by the parent company. However, technical information supplied from afar often relates to environmental conditions that are not necessarily comparable. This is also true with regard to manufacturing instructions and product designs, and unless specific requests were made by a subsidiary, little attempt was made to tailor such information to local conditions.

Parent-company staff support in connection with managerial and other problems not of a purely technical or scientific nature was much weaker. However, this too has been improving in recent years, although not much is yet being provided on a direct basis. Indirectly, the parent's requirements that certain data be provided in specified formats, or that particular policies and procedures be followed, gave some managerial assistance to their subsidiaries. However, little direct help was forthcoming in such areas as managerial training, market research, data processing, and so forth.

Subsidiary managers were often reluctant to ask parent firms for managerial assistance. In many cases they were afraid that a request for help would be interpreted as managerial weakness. Consequently, the staff support normally provided within the United States was frequently missing in the subsidiaries, and the amount of staff analysis undertaken and of information available was dependent in many cases on the knowledge and scope of top subsidiary management.

In most cases, U.S. subsidiaries had more overall staff support than comparable indigenous firms. The exceptions to this usually involved engineering and R and D. Indian companies often had larger and more versatile staff groups in these areas, usually comprised of U.S. and other foreign-trained personnel. Some had even expanded their engineering and other staff groups to service other firms, often within their own industry. For example, foreign exchange scarcities forced several Indian chemical and drug firms to design their own plants and equipment, and some now provide engineering, design, and construction services to other organizations.

The U.S. subsidiaries had better developed personnel and training staffs than indigenous firms. It was common within indigenous firms for the personnel function to be considered little more than a paper work and filing unit. All decisions concerning hiring, firing, appraisal, promotions, raises, and training were made by top-level line management, frequently without inputs from the personnel manager. At most Indian companies and some U.S. firms the personnel department was concerned solely with nonsupervisory personnel records.

Greater use has been made by U.S. subsidiaries than indigenous firms of such staff services as marketing research, sales analysis, planning, customer services, distribution and merchandising, product and brand managers, sales promotion, maintenance and repair, industrial engineering for setting standards, quality control, data processing, cost accounting, systems and procedures, financial analysis, and various other functions. However, most U.S. subsidiaries were seriously deficient if not totally lacking in many of these areas, and in some cases indigenous firms were doing a better job. Moreover, it was common for companies — both Indian and foreign — which had such staff groups, not to make effective use of them. Very few U.S. firms had as effective staff support in most of these areas as their parent companies' domestic operations.

Only a few of the largest and most progressive firms had substantial staff groups concerned with advanced quantitative tools and techniques, systems analysis, sophisticated organizational analysis, management information systems, or electronic computers. And, here too, their effectiveness often left much to be desired.

USE OF FUNCTIONAL AUTHORITY

Functional authority is defined here as the power a department or individual may have over matters relating to activities undertaken by personnel in other units other than its own. If the principle of unity of command were followed without exception, functional authority would not exist. A typical example is that of a staff man giving direct orders to line and operating personnel in his own name instead of making recommendations to his boss or to other line executives. His instructions then have the same force as though they came down the regular chain of command. Functional authority may be beneficial where the managers lack specialized knowledge; when a minor part of the total operating job is involved; or where uniformity, standardized policy control or consistency in various line units is deemed essential. Nearly all of the U.S. parent companies surveyed exercised a great deal of functional authority over their subsidiaries. The more ethnocentric corporations exercised the greatest amount. Much of the functional authority imposed was beneficial to both the corporation as a whole and the subsidiary, but much was counter-productive. (See Table 9-1 in Chapter 9.)

U.S. subsidiaries exerted more internal functional authority on operating units than their indigenous counterparts. Probably more often than not this was beneficial, and it enabled top management to decentralize authority without giving up control in areas deemed strategic or critical. The indigenous firms were more inclined to have all authority and decisions emanate from top management. This added to top management's burden, and it failed to capitalize on the knowledge or skill of specialists.

BOARDS OF DIRECTORS, COMMITTEES AND GROUP DECISION MAKING

In relation to company size, the indigenous firms surveyed had larger boards of directors than U.S. subsidiaries. Very few large corporations of any kind had fewer than six directors or more than twelve. However, relatively small and medium-sized Indian firms often had thirty or more members on their boards. Substantially larger U.S. subsidiaries had no more than ten, and typically only six to eight.

The boards of most indigenous companies were dominated by senior (and often retired or semiretired) family members and close personal friends, many of whom did not play a direct role in company management. Outsiders were usually there for prestige or because they had valuable contacts. However, the outsiders ordinarily did not concern themselves with the major problems or potential opportunities confronting the company. These were handled by the senior family members in charge of management.

Indian firms operating under managing agencies or other kinds of holding companies often did not have their managing director on the board if he was not a member of the controlling family.

It was more common for Indian companies to have representatives from the various public sector financial institutions on their boards than for U.S. or other foreign subsidiaries. This was probably due to the fact that many indigenous firms obtain capital from such institutions. However, in at least some cases, representatives of the financial institutions had board membership because there was serious concern about the safety of funds which had been provided to the firm.

Only the best managed indigenous companies were likely to have outside directors who really contributed to the internal management and operations of the firm. A few firms had non-Indian board members, often representing foreign firms with which they had licensing arrangements.

Most U.S. subsidiaries surveyed had more active and valuable outside directors than their indigenous counterparts. However, the more ethnocentric U.S. international corporations typically had none of their Indian managers on their boards of directors. Their boards were filled with one or two of the top-level foreign managers of the subsidiary, several foreign executives from international headquarters, and a variety of Indians from the outside who had prestige or contacts.

The most geocentric U.S. companies maintained a close balance between foreigners and Indians on their boards, and in some cases these were mostly Indians. This was even more common among progressive British and Dutch subsidiaries and collaborations. Even where such firms did not have Indian managing directors, there were some high-level Indian subsidiary managers on the board. In a few cases, the board chairman was an Indian (usually an outsider). This was so in one U.S. subsidiary that had an American managing director. In general, the geocentric international companies seemed to have the most effective boards of directors.

The number of formal committees — both standing and ad hoc — and the amount of time spent in them varied considerably among the U.S. parent companies surveyed, and this seemed to be largely a function of managerial styles. Some U.S. subsidiaries had more committees and devoted more time to them than their parent companies did, while for others the reverse was true. There did seem to be some significant discernible patterns, however.

The committees in the U.S.-based companies were usually more productive than those at the subsidiaries. The latter also relied more on informal meetings and task groups for problem solving. There tended to be more genuine participation and two-way vertical, as well as horizontal, communication. Decisions were made more often in a group fashion. Moreover, more decisions were made among peers — e.g., between production, sales, and purchasing executives of equal rank — without involving higher-level executives.

The managers of those U.S. subsidiaries which made the greatest use of formal committees — and they were rarely Indians — often used them not only for communication and information purposes, but also as management-development techniques. However, meetings were frequently poorly-run, inappropriate people attended, committee heads often acted in ways which defeated the purposes of the committee, and subordinate managers failed to respond as desired.

The greatest number of committees was found in a large U.S. subsidiary run by a British top manager who had become interested in human relations and management development. (This was unusual since British subsidiaries in India made less use of committees than U.S. firms.) Titles of corporate-level committees which had been established included: long-range planning, policy, foreign exchange, product planning, financial planning, salary, provident fund, cost reduction, managerial responsibility and job descriptions. While some were clearly effective — especially foreign exchange and financial planning — much wasted time, effort and frustration resulted. Many committee meetings were used "to keep people busy" since there was overstaffing in the managerial ranks. Committees were also used as a means for avoiding individual responsibility and decisions.

Perhaps the biggest mistake the British manager of this U.S. subsidiary made regarding committees was the "Junior Board of Directors" he set up which met at least twice a month. It was chaired by him and was comprised of 15 other executives who were all subordinates of his own subordinates, who were not on the board. This caused resentment and insecurity on the part of his direct deputies. Not all of the executives at the third echelon were on the board, and this too caused insecurity. The managing director felt that this junior board would foster greater initiative, creativity, and decentralization within the organization. He also wanted to get a better firsthand feel for the people, problems, interests, and desires further down the management hierarchy. The board did not have any formal decision-making powers, however, so as not to violate the chain of command or usurp the authority of his own subordinates.

Although such a junior board might prove effective in U.S. industry, the odds are against its success in the Indian environment, and it proved to be a failure in the above case. When a new American managing director took over, the junior board was abolished, as were a number of other ineffective committees. Under this man, the effectiveness of the remaining committees, meetings, group decision making, and horizontal communication improved substantially.

In general, progressive companies, both subsidiaries and indigenous firms, made greater use of committees than traditional firms. Most committees at the Indian firms served in an advisory capacity to top management, and they usually dealt with specific matters such as insurance or inventory levels. U.S. subsidiary standing committees dealt with broad issues such as new product policy or expansion projects. They also reached group decisions more often, but this did not occur as commonly as in their parent companies. The Indian company committees were usually larger — often containing ten or more people. These groups often provided communication channels and a feeling of participation and sociability which was lacking in many of the more businesslike U.S. committee structures.

Committees at U.S. subsidiaries met more regularly than at Indian firms. U.S. subsidiaries also established task groups and ad hoc committees to deal with specific problems, and disbanded them once the problem had been dealt with. These ad hoc groups were usually comprised of representatives from the functional areas concerned. Within the Indian firms, such issues were handled either by a hierarchical decision or by an informal discussion at a standing committee meeting (much in the family council manner) followed by an executive decision. Even at most of the progressive indigenous companies, membership of these committees typically consisted solely of the upper levels of management, with little activity involving middle or lower managers. The U.S. firms exhibited more committee involvement and meetings at lower managerial levels. However, in most cases the time executives actually devoted to committees tended to be substantially less than their counterparts in their parent companies.

Managers in U.S. subsidiaries spent more time in committee meetings than those in Indian firms. For example, the managing directors of U.S. drug subsidiaries surveyed typically spent 15 to 20 percent of their time in committees, while the Indian drug company top managers spent around 10 percent, and in some cases much less. Most of the personal interaction in the case of Indian managers occurred on a one-to-one basis or in small informal gatherings.

The U.S. subsidiaries and less traditional indigenous firms usually scheduled periodic meetings among marketing, production, and sales, personnel to coordinate schedules, and within the manufacturing organization meetings between the various department heads and the production manager were common. Although meetings generally focused on problems, with the intention of coordinating along horizontal lines and making sure all viewpoints were represented in any final decisions, the committees did not function effectively as decision-making devices, but served the communications function much better.

It was much more common at the U.S. subsidiaries than at their parent companies for meetings to lack an agenda, and for issues to be raised on the spur of the moment. Emotional rather than logical or factual arguments usually dominated, and once the discussion was finished committee members automatically turned to the chairman for a decision. If the committee chairman was present and had the authority, the chances were that he would make the decision. If he was absent, the end result was more likely to be inaction, often with a complete repetition of the entire process (again unprepared) at the next session. Most Indian managers seemed to be comfortable with this process. And even in U.S. subsidiaries where top managers — including non-Indians — found such behavior disturbing, it was surprising how many of them did nothing to make these meetings more effective.

In a not untypical meeting within a U.S. subsidiary, an Indian department manager asked that he be allowed to deviate from the company's policy restricting the use of overtime. His request was presented in about three sentences, and was devoid of any factual data concerning need, cost, effects on production, and so forth. The issue, discussed for more than half an hour, focused primarily on his grievances against marketing personnel, who, he claimed, were continually changing their minds and causing him many problems. The production director asked that he provide more information at the next meeting. The type of information required was not specified, and the discussion was terminated with the understanding that it would be brought up again several weeks later. The department manager agreed, although his initial statement had indicated that this was a life-and-death issue. Later, in a private discussion with one of the authors, the plant manager stated that the problem was not solved due to the fact that the managing director was not present. If he had been, a decision would have been made. At a subsequent meeting of the same committee, the issue was again raised, almost the same discussion ensued, and almost the same results followed. Once again, the managing director was not present.

This kind of pattern was even more common at indigenous firms, but it was by no means unusual in U.S. subsidiaries. Committees, when used for decision-making purposes, functioned as court sessions, with the senior executive acting as judge and jury, and the various participants arguing their cases, attempting an emotional appeal to the executive.

The more traditional companies studied typically made less frequent and less effective use of committees. Where they had standing committees they were almost always top level, they met infrequently, and many of them existed more on paper than in reality. They tended to be employed primarily as communicating devices — basically downward — although sometimes they provided at least an element of participation, much in the manner of the family council. Decisions were always made by the top individual, although the committees may have permitted some exchanges of ideas.

ORGANIZATIONAL CONFUSION AND FRICTION

To the U.S. observer, the lines of internal authority and responsibility appeared to be clearer in U.S. subsidiaries than in indigenous companies. (In fact, many large Indian firms did not have organization charts.) However, the perceptions of Indian managers within various organizations were mixed, in this respect.

Responsibility and authority within the Indian firms tend to be largely a function of both blood and personal relationship to the top manager. Organizational structure is informal and seldom conforms to the lines which appear on organization charts. The production manager might turn out to be the chief advisor and most influential man with respect to financial matters, while the managing director actually makes the key production decisions. To the U.S. observer, the organizational picture is confusing.

The Indian organization experiences confusion and friction because roles are not clearly defined, the formal chain of command is by-passed in decision making, and personnel at different levels are inadequately informed of decisions relating to them. However, most traditional Indian managers appeared to be comfortable with the structure. Everyone knew where everyone else stood, the pecking order was clearly delineated, and few individuals were in direct competition for authority or promotions. "Heirs apparent" to the various managerial positions were clearly designated, and each man's position and future was established from the day of his employment.

In a few Indian companies, especially those facing strong competition, relatively young men had been elevated to high leadership positions with the expectation that they would eventually take over the reins of the company. In these firms, more tension and unrest was evident. In one Indian company, for example, a young man had been promoted to the position of marketing director. The managing director planned to retire within five years. He recognized the need for more aggressive policies to meet competition, but felt he had neither the ability nor the personal desire to move in that direction. He hoped that the new marketing director could breathe some life into the somewhat stagnant marketing organization, and eventually, after he was gone, assume the managing directorship and do the same for the entire company. This marketing director experienced a great deal of frustration. First, his promotion to such a high position at a young age had created problems with other members of the managerial staff. The big leap was contrary to the "rules of the game." Second, in trying to organize operations and identify the locus of responsibilities, he was appalled that he could never really pin anyone down to any specific area. The process by which lower-level decisions were made was vague; lines of authority were not clear; and he found too much overlapping of interests. His initial attempts at rejuvenating the marketing function led him to believe that a major restructuring and retraining program requiring several years would be necessary. He was not sure this could be accomplished without a number of personnel changes, and yet he knew that this was one area that the managing director felt to be inviolable.

In essence, then, because the traditional Indian organization was closely attuned to Indian social systems, most of the Indian employees felt comfortable and any deviation from the established pattern gave rise to feelings of insecurity. The attempt to keep tension and competition at low levels resulted in relatively complacent organizations which moved slowly. This could be seen in the marketplace as well, where Indian firms seemed subdued in comparison to the aggressiveness of foreign companies.

The U.S. organizations, on the other hand, functioned more along the lines of authority and responsibility which the organization charts indicated. Functions were clearly delineated and written job descriptions often existed. Most of the workers and managers knew basically what was expected of them, how far their authority extended, and how they could earn raises and promotions. Although tensions often ran high, job functions were executed relatively smoothly. The more traditional Indian personnel, however, experienced discomfort and insecurity in this kind of environment.

Most of the U.S. subsidiaries contained a number of young men who were highly competitive, and who served as driving forces. They also contained traditional types of Indian managers. The mix between the two varied, the most successful subsidiaries having the largest proportion of the former. Strong feelings of insecurity were voiced by the traditional managers, who were especially unhappy to see merit replace seniority and personal relationships as the basis for promotion. However, to some extent, even the younger, more aggressive managers shared the feelings of insecurity.

A related problem in U.S. subsidiaries was the unrest caused by frequent personnel changes at top levels. No sooner did people get to know the managing director, than he was transferred out of India and a new man arrived on the scene. The lack of personal contact between the managing director and upper- and middle-level managers was disquieting in many cases. The Indian firms showed greater organizational stability and far fewer managerial changes.

In sum, the degree of organizational confusion and friction was largely a function of the perceptions of the individuals involved. To the American or U.S.-oriented Indian managers, the U.S. organizational style with its clear lines of authority and responsibility, was more challenging, rewarding, and stimulating. These same characteristics frustrated the more traditional Indian managers who were comfortable in the more informal, personal and stable organizational arrangements of the Indian companies.

INFORMAL ORGANIZATION

As has already been discussed, informal relationships were the mainstay of the Indian organizations and, by comparison, tended to be de-emphasized by the U.S. personnel in the U.S. subsidiaries. The Indian managers of the U.S. subsidiaries still looked to the informal structure, but to a lesser degree than their counterparts in indigenous firms.

A striking deviation from the usual patterns was found in one of the newer and most successful Indian firms. This company had achieved a blend of the formal and informal in a manner that integrated both U.S. and Indian patterns. On paper, its organization structure looked much like that of the U.S. subsidiaries. Authority and responsibility were delineated along functional lines, and although no formal position guides had been written, assignments and scopes of operation were clear enough so that such documents could have been easily prepared.

The point which differentiated this organization from its U.S. counterparts was not the structure, but the basis upon which the structure had been established. In U.S. subsidiaries, organization structures were frequently formalized by fiat, with any accommodation to personalities and talents evolving over time. Individuals were hired to fit specific jobs, and were, in many cases, either sent to the United States for training or were U.S.-educated so that they would be able to adapt to the structure. However, in this Indian organization, the structure developed in a traditional manner.

When the company was founded, the managing director employed a highly authoritative style. However, he was careful to hire managers who had studied in the United States. As he hired them, he identified their "responsibilities," and although he made all significant decisions, they worked as his deputies in matters relating to their areas. He gave them close attention and developed strong personal ties with them. As they adapted their thinking to his patterns, he increased their autonomy. In essence, however, he was not giving them freedom to do as they pleased as much as he was turning on an "automatic pilot." Each of his executives was trained to act in a particular functional area as the managing director would have acted. Throughout this process he was supportive, and was able to build intense feelings of personal loyalty among his subordinates. This loyalty, coupled with the "training" he had provided, allowed him to relinquish some of his authority without fear of losing control. His managers were now his "sons." Eventually, he began to retire from the active operation of this particular venture and devote his time to other pursuits with the full realization that the business would be carried on almost as if he were there.

In this example, the managers did not have explicit policies or guidelines to follow. Instead, they had come to know the managing director's style and personality so well that they instinctively acted as he would have in similar situations. The degree of loyalty was such that, in several cases, top managers who had already reached the level where they had full decision-making authority, made decisions which were totally opposed to their own convictions. In one such case, a top executive initiated disciplinary action against an employee which might have resulted in a jail sentence, even though he knew the employee to be innocent. His explanation was that even though he had not contacted the managing director, he knew what the managing director's wishes would be, since the alternative — identifying the guilty party — would have initiated an internal feud which would have hurt the company's reputation. Although the decision was contrary to his own personal convictions, his loyalty was the overriding factor and he decided as he believed the managing director would have done. Later, a discussion with the managing director validated his analysis. In all cases, the guiding rule was, "we do what's for the good of the company" which, in essence, implied "for the good of the managing director." This company achieved a blend combining the clearly-structured, responsive U.S. pattern with the strong informal ties of the Indian organization.

In general, the informal links of the Indian organization seem to be one of its greatest strengths. They tie the unit together, make it cohesive, and drain tension. On the other hand, they are also one of its greatest weaknesses, as they impede effective decision making and inhibit managerial development and innovation. The U.S. organizational pattern tends to have the reverse effect. It would appear that there is much to be gained from the process of adaptation — a process which relatively few U.S. subsidiaries have begun to explore in a serious way.

One reason for the lack of such organizational experimentation by U.S. firms was the unwillingness of foreign subsidiary managers to change their patterns of behavior. Most brought preconceived notions of what the organization should be like and few knew India well enough to understand indigenous patterns. (It is necessary to add that, for many, this was their first position of overall responsibility.) To most managers, a passing acquaintance with organizational structures of Indian companies tended to confirm their faith in the "American way." Viewpoints seemed to crystallize in terms of absolutes rather than compromises, and thoughts of adaptation in this area were too often overlooked or quickly abandoned.

On the other hand, although many Indians saw U.S. organizational patterns as cold and inhuman, they were being forced to adopt them. They had to develop more flexible responses to survive, and the people who could provide such flexibility usually required greater authority and responsibility than was traditional. In addition, the U.S.

pattern was also associated with better pay and more opportunities for advancement, factors which appeal to many of the younger generation. Those who are older frequently express the philosophy that there is more to life than money or material things, or even power and prestige in the business world.

FLEXIBILITY OF ORGANIZATIONS TO MEET CHANGE

Changes in organization structure and related personnel changes were less common at indigenous firms than at U.S. subsidiaries. In theory, it should be possible to effect organizational change more quickly in the typical Indian firm, since the structures are more informal and a word or two from the top manager is all that is needed. However, because of the high regard for the personal relationships involved, the strong emphasis on stability, and also often because of the lack of knowledge of different organizational forms, the Indian organizations tended to be much more stagnant.

Changes came primarily as the result of the retirement of key individuals, and they were usually predictable several years in advance on the basis of the previous positions that people held and the authority they had received in anticipation of their forthcoming promotions. As each man's replacement stepped into the vacant position, some reorganization of responsibilities usually took place as a result of the individual's abilities and his relationship with the top man. But these changes, especially in the more traditional firms, were slow and evolutionary, and it is probably safe to say that change lagged far behind organizational needs in most cases. This also held true with regard to changes and additions arising from company growth.

The U.S. subsidiaries, as a group, experienced more frequent and extensive organizational changes than their indigenous counterparts. They probably had an advantage over the Indian firms with respect to flexibility, because they were organized more around functions, tasks, and job requirements than personalities. Change, though not without friction, seemed to be accepted as a way of life in these enterprises.

On the other hand, organizational changes were often made in a poorly planned manner, without adequate preparation. In many cases, this was largely the parent companies' fault. Some U.S. companies averaged several major reorganizations a year, which involved personnel at almost every level in the organization down through first-line supervisors. It was not uncommon for changes to come without any prior warning. This resulted in much uncertainty, insecurity, unrest, and confusion. Promotions and appointments, although reasonable, often surprised many of the people directly affected, and considerable anxiety was experienced both by people who were promoted and those who were not directly affected.

It was difficult to evaluate the net effects of such organizational changes, although in the longer run they were probably beneficial. If they had been achieved in a better prepared and better communicated fashion they would have been more effective, especially in the immediate time frame.

Most of the reorganizations moved more competent people into key managerial and decision-making functions, and they often led to structural changes which improved the company's capability to deal with problems and capitalize on opportunities. However, changes were sometimes made on a trial-and-error basis as problems were noticed, rather than as part of an overall organizational blueprint.

In general, few firms studied of any nationality had attempted to make a thorough analysis of the existing situation or of future expectations in order to determine the organizational pattern most responsive to environmental conditions — both internal and external. Indian firms typically attempted to duplicate the joint family type of relationship, while U.S. subsidiaries tended to employ the models used in their domestic parents' organizations.

CHAPTER 14
STAFFING AND
PERSONNEL

One of the most crucial managerial functions affecting the success of productive enterprise is staffing. It is people who establish the goals, policies, and direction of the firm. They determine the plans and strategies to achieve the goals, and they perform the tasks necessary to implement the plans. The quality of personnel determines how efficiently physical and financial resources are utilized, and how much and what kinds of these nonhuman resources are at the disposal of the enterprise.

Although staffing problems are important in all areas of the world, they acquire critical dimensions in developing nations. While labor may be readily available in these countries, the particular human resources required for efficient performance and industrial development are frequently in short supply. This applies to all levels of activity within the firm, but the problem tends to become more critical the higher up the organizational ladder one goes, and the greater the skill required.

At the lowest organizational level, involving unskilled labor, workers are easy to find. "Underdevelopment" implies underutilized or idle labor resources. However, even the most menial tasks can require abilities that are not found among the applicants. The man who is hired to move crates may not be able to read "fragile" or "this side up" labels, and he may have no concept of how much physical punishment a crate can take. The worker who is hired to keep the floors clean may have a different concept of "cleanliness" from that of management. In emergency situations, the unskilled worker may not be able to think or act effectively for himself.

Moving up the ladder to the skilled worker, critical labor shortages are usually the rule. Skilled work requires some education, and in most developing nations education and physical work are seen as antithetical to one another. The local national who has attained an educational level equivalent to that of the typical U.S. skilled worker (in terms of reading abilities and the specific technical abilities of the job) will not usually consider manual tasks. He wants a higher-status white-collar job.

Typically, the available supply of skilled workers consists chiefly of men who have learned through apprenticeship, and this presents both supply and quality problems. Again, the process of development implies that new enterprises are just emerging from a non-industrial milieu. These new firms generate increased demands for skilled workers (who are being developed by existing firms only to satisfy their own growth and replacement needs). The demand far exceeds the supply. Severe wage competition and pirating practices may result. Furthermore, learning through apprenticeship does not usually result in the acquisition of such basic skills as the ability to read and write. Consequently, a "skilled" machinist who is able to carry out verbal instructions may not be able to read a blueprint. Also, his skills are likely to be confined to a narrow range of activities or even to a few specific products.

Supervisory, middle management, and technical and staff specialist positions present another series of problems. The educational system does not provide a base sufficient for the development of competent managerial talent for lower- and middle-level positions. Even when bright, energetic individuals can be found, they may have an aversion to "rolling up their sleeves and pitching in." Distinct class differences between management and workers can result in management's misunderstanding of workers' problems, attitudes, and motivations. In many developing nations, the people who go into managerial jobs have little experience with the real nature of day-to-day business operations, and little understanding of how the various areas of a business firm relate to one another. Often they have not been trained in decision making, and tend to avoid the type of risk taking associated with innovation.

Top management levels offer special staffing challenges. Because the conduct of operations in most developing nations requires intimacy with the local political structure, top managers are often selected for their contacts. However, the local man who has the contacts may not have the managerial abilities. Where he works in a foreign subsidiary, he may not be able to relate well to the parent company. Or he may be engaged simultaneously in several external activities and not be able to devote the necessary time required to run the enterprise efficiently.

OVERVIEW

One of the most important findings of this study is the correlation between the proportion of Western-trained (and this includes formal education) local nationals employed by firms, both foreign and indigenous, and the firms' relative economic success. Those with the highest proportions of U.S.-trained managers and specialists have generally been the most successful in their sectors.

The U.S. subsidiaries studied in India have done a better job with regard to the staffing functions than their indigenous counterparts — although there were some exceptions. They have based their staffing decisions on a formal analysis of job requirements, necessary qualifications, merit, and other objective criteria. The more traditional Indian firms have placed greater weight on nepotism, personal relationships, and social criteria.

The U.S. subsidiaries usually did a better job in the area of personnel training and development. Their personnel departments did more manpower planning, and relied heavily on job descriptions and personnel appraisals for recruiting and selection, training, and determining pay increases and promotions. On the other hand, several U.S. subsidiaries ran into serious conflicts with local value systems. They projected more of an image of unconcern for such important questions as secure or stable employment, and respect for seniority and the dignity of older employees than did indigenous firms, or even British companies. In a sense, this has probably been true, but the image has been exaggerated in recent times in terms of the reality of the situation. In any event, the more traditional Indians have tended to feel uneasy about employment in U.S. firms.

Most of the U.S. subsidiaries were doing a poor job in the personnel area compared to the domestic operations of their parent companies. Since most of the parent companies studied have had years of experience and good if not outstanding records of success in staffing at home and in other advanced countries, it would appear that the transition to developing countries is not an easy one to make.

EMPLOYMENT DATA

During the late 1960s, within India's pharmaceutical sector, U.S. subsidiaries experienced greater growth, in general and in employment, than their indigenous counterparts. However, at the end of the decade, the largest firms in terms of employment were still indigenous companies. Of the ten drug companies examined in Chapter 10, three indigenous firms (A, D, and E) had more than 2,500 employees each. No U.S. firms had this many, and only one, firm H, had over 2,000.

There were noticeable differences in the patterns of employment of U.S. and indigenous drug firms. The former had higher proportions of managerial personnel, staff specialists, and salesmen. The latter were heavier on clerical personnel, "peon" types, and to a lesser degree blue-collar workers. The indigenous firms also had more temporary and casual workers. By way of comparison, the domestic operations of the U.S. parent companies generally had significantly higher proportions of staff specialists, salesmen, and managerial personnel than did their subsidiaries in India.

The major firms studied in depth ranged in size from under 500 to over 89,000 employees. (A public sector steel company was the biggest.) The largest U.S. firm examined employed 8,000 as of 1970.

RECRUITMENT AND PERSONNEL SELECTION

Basically, there are three sources of supply for personnel within a foreign affiliate or subsidiary: foreign nationals sent from the country of the parent company; foreign nationals coming from third countries, usually within the international sphere of the enterprise; and nationals from the country in which the subsidiary is located. Each of these sources raises a different set of problems.

Use of nationals from the parent country

Most U.S. international corporations send some U.S. citizens abroad to work in their foreign subsidiaries. Most often they are sent overseas to establish operations and to fill in until local talent can be found. They are rarely regarded as anything more than temporary, although on occasion top managers and key technical advisers may stay as long as five years or more. Usually the number of U.S. citizens assigned to foreign subsidiaries decreases with the passage of time.

The reasons for the temporary nature of assignments are several. First, considerable expense is involved in maintaining the U.S. expatriate. His salary is likely to be several times greater than that of a local national in the same job. It is also likely to be augmented by as much as a 25 percent overseas allowance. Moreover, many perquisites are usually provided which are not part of domestic benefit packages. Rental rates for "suitable" accommodations may be so high that it is necessary to provide company housing. A car, servants, and payments of utilities may also be included. Home leave, educational allowances, and job-related travel expenses add to the costs.

Second, local governments are often concerned with the upgrading and development of skills in their own citizenry. They place great pressure on foreign subsidiaries to replace overseas employees with nationals as soon as possible. A third factor is that, often, the U.S. manager does not perform effectively abroad. He may not be able to adjust to local conditions or operating practices; or his family may not be able to make the adjustment. Finally, companies often make the change to local personnel as a way of providing greater upward mobility and increasing morale among the local managerial staff.

Except in the case of the U.S. government, U.S. operations rarely move American personnel overseas to positions at lower levels in the organization, because of the expense involved. Furthermore, many developing countries have laws specifically prohibiting such employment practices.

The selection criteria used for expatriate top managers are often vague. The parent company may feel that it needs a "marketing man" or a "financial man" to look after the subsidiary. Beyond such generalizations, little effort is expended on defining skill requirements. Typically, the selection process falls into one of three categories, all of which draw upon existing personnel.

A formerly important practice in American business involved sending abroad a firm's "unwanted men." Domestic operations find themselves saddled with a relatively senior man who has become a problem. Not promatable for any of a number of reasons, he has lost much of his effectiveness, and yet the firm wishes neither to fire nor demote him. Assignment to a small foreign subsidiary seems to provide an ideal solution. This practice, largely a legacy of past eras when many companies considered their foreign operations unimportant, is decreasing. Pressure on profit margins in the developed areas coupled with the substantial untapped potentials and large profit margins afforded by developing countries, have changed this kind of thinking, and most U.S. firms now attempt to fill their overseas assignments with good talent.

A second and more prevalent selection pattern involves the appointment of young executives who are moving up the corporate ladder and who would benefit from the broadening experience of managing an overseas subsidiary. The subsidiary is seen as a means of providing a full scope of managerial responsibilities in an operation small enough to be easily manageable and in a manner which reduces corporate risk. Typically, the executive will be selected from a functional area (marketing, followed by accounting and finance, appears to be the most common although a production man may be chosen, particularly if plant construction is involved). Essentially, the foreign subsidiary becomes a training ground for expanding a competent executive's horizon. In some cases, the top man for a subsidiary in a developing country will be chosen from the corporate international staff or from a domestic operating division. In other cases, he may be one of the second-level managers in a large foreign subsidiary, located in a developed country.

Often, little is done in the way of preparing these men for their new positions. Assignments are frequently made on short notice. The manager moves into the new position not knowing what to expect. Consequently, many flounder badly at first, and some never recover. Often they come from organizations which maintain large supporting staffs. Personally, they have had exposure in only one or possibly two functional areas. When they are thrust into the developing nation, they find that they lack both the background required to deal with the managerial problems they face and the staff capable of handling them. They are reluctant to call upon the parent firm for assistance. They must rely upon the people currently occupying various positions and these individuals may not be well qualified. Too often, U.S. companies associate the small size of the subsidiary in a developing nation with small, simple problems — "just the right situation to give Bill a chance to cut his eye teeth and show his stuff." They overlook the complexity of the environment and the fact that competent operating personnel and staff support may not be available.

Probably the most necessary and the least-used approach to selecting personnel is that of examining the job, determining what is needed, and selecting individuals on the basis of these factors. One of the reasons why this seemingly "intuitively obvious" approach is not adopted is that managers in the U.S. operations who make selection decisions overlook many critical problems.

A careful analysis of the tasks faced by the U.S. manager in a developing nation reveals several important criteria.

Foremost, given the trend towards using local nationals and the inability of the local environment to provide these people in "ready-made" form, the U.S. manager must be a developer of people. He must be able to visualize operational needs, and find ways to enhance managerial skills, and develop modern attitudes in his employees. He must be able to identify organizational problems and structure tasks and relationships so as to best utilize available human resources. He requires broad knowledge in most if not all the functional areas and will probably find that he will have to develop not only the job related skills of his immediate subordinates, but their abilities to train and develop others.

He must be capable of evaluating abilities of middle managers throughout his organization. Initially, he cannot accept reports from the accountant or projections from his marketing department on face value. He must attempt to understand how these individuals think, how extensive their knowledge is, and what elements of professional development they lack — and he must be supportive about bringing about change. He must be sensitive to the attitudes of people around him, both within the organization and external to it. And finally, he must have a degree of tolerance for frustration, and a driving force coupled with patience. These qualities are not easy to find, but they are characteristics invariably required to run a successful operation.

Selection criteria of the type mentioned above often are not considered because "the proof of the pudding is in the eating" and many companies, using more vague selection criteria, have been successful in the developing nations. High profits lull companies into feelings of false security. But, relatively high profits do not necessarily mean that the highest profits possible are being earned. In addition, there are future considerations which also must be factored in. Continued corporate growth and profitability are usually viewed as desirable long-range objectives. Managerial practices which do not create a favorable base for the future, even though they generate profits today, may not be in the best interests of the enterprise.

At middle-management and specialist levels, many firms make use of U.S. nationals, especially during start-up phases. An engineer may be sent abroad to supervise the construction of a plant, or a marketing manager may be sent overseas to establish the marketing organization. In such cases, selection is made on the basis of the specific technical expertise required. The position is usually temporary (one to two years) and the man's primary function is to get things going smoothly. Occasionally, he is also given the responsibility of training his successor. However, this is not always the case, and even when it is, the man may not have the time or the skills to do an effective job.

The selection criteria used to pick specialists are often simple. First, a specific degree of technical competence is required. This immediately narrows the search to a few individuals within a company (for example, an engineer who is familiar with the equipment and manufacturing processes for producing a certain chemical). Usually another criterion is that the individual must have been with the company long enough to be familiar with its policies and operating procedures. Other criteria often used are: his availability (i.e., whether he can leave the job he is currently performing); his marital status (since it costs less to send a single man overseas); whether or not he has had previous overseas experience; and a record which projects a high degree of competence. These selection criteria seem reasonable, and the search is usually confined to experienced, younger employees within the company. At times older personnel approaching retirement are chosen.

Unfortunately, one of the major failings in the process is not so much in the selection, but in the preparation once the selection has been made. Often, the selection is made at the last minute, and individuals are shipped overseas with the most cursory briefing. They have not been prepared for the new environment and know little of the language, customs, and special environmental conditions to be encountered. Consequently, many have great difficulty adjusting, and even those who do so often operate ineffectively until they develop a feel for the environment in which they find themselves.

In general, the benefits from sending short-term U.S. experts tend to outweigh the problems and limitations. In fact, in many cases it would probably prove advantageous to send over more temporary personnel to train local nationals rather than to perform specific technical tasks. A few of the companies surveyed have done this recently, and experienced measurable improvements in operating effeciency.

Use of third-country nationals

As international corporations develop, a new pattern in staffing has become more prevalent — the use of third-country nationals in top-level subsidiary jobs. These are people whose nationality differs from that of both the parent company and the country in which they work. The increase in the use of such personnel in staffing subsidiaries has come about with the move by many corporations to multinationalize the international headquarters and overseas organization of the total global enterprise.

U.S. corporations tend to use third-country nationals only from other advanced countries. For example, within the U.S. subsidiaries surveyed in India during the 1960s, all were from England, Scotland, Australia and Canada.

The selection criteria for third-country nationals are almost identical to those applied in the case of nationals of the parent country. However, the final objective is often different. In the latter case, the ultimate objective for development is often a move into top-level positions in the parent company. In the case of third-country nationals, top-level staff positions in the international headquarters are usually envisioned as the ultimate in career development. However, as more firms become multinational in character, job mobility of non-U.S. citizens will probably extend to the very top organizational levels.

Although recruiting for third-country nationals is almost entirely a process of selecting people from the existing global organization, there are cases, largely legacies of the past, where third-country nationals have been hired from outside the firm. For example, in India, British citizens were occasionally hired to look after U.S. subsidiaries because they already were living in India, were familiar with the local environment, and cost less to hire than expatriate Americans. Furthermore, a common language and cultural heritage provided for a comfortable relationship with U.S. headquarters personnel.

In some cases, third-country nationals have been brought in as a consequence of old organizational structures. For example, the British subsidiaries of a number of U.S. firms directed the affairs of other subsidiaries located in Commonwealth nations. Consequently, Englishmen were used to staff the top-level positions. As the U.S. companies developed global orientations and Indian operations became more important, control was assumed directly by the U.S. international headquarters.

Most of the advantages and disadvantages outlined above with respect to a parent-country national apply to the third-country national, but there are a few significant differences. First, the salary and benefit requirements of the third-country national may be significantly less than those needed for the U.S. national. (The practice of differentiating, by country of origin, between individuals in the international organization is rapidly diminishing with time.) A second factor is that the third-country national may be better informed about the host environment. For example, he may speak the language, or his home country may have had a special relationship (e.g., a colonial situation) with the nation in which the subsidiary is located. Unlike the U.S. situation, where most people are monolingual and have had little experience with other foreign countries except perhaps as casual tourists, the European or the Asian may be comfortable with several languages and be intimately familiar with the people and environments of several nations.

Two distinct drawbacks may arise from the use of third-country nationals. First, in certain parts of the world animosities of national character exist between neighboring countries. Transfers of third-country nationals must take these factors into consideration and an oversight in this area could be costly. The second disadvantage results from the desire of the governments of developing countries to upgrade their own people. It is often more palatable to accept a U.S. national (on the rationale that the parent company is looking after its own interest) than to accept a third party even though he is an employee of the parent company. The feeling can be stated as: "if you don't send an American, you ought to employ one of our people."

Local nationals

Invariably, the bulk of the employees of a foreign subsidiary will be local nationals. Since staffing problems vary at different levels in the organization, problems relating to upper, middle and lower-level personnel will be considered separately.

The selection of local top-management personnel comes in one of two ways. First, when setting up a new venture, companies often use contacts with local distributors, bankers, etc. to identify the kind of individuals they are looking for. In almost every case studied, however, the individuals who were chosen participated in the financing of the capital requirements to get the company going. In essence, the companies try to seek good partners who have both capital to contribute and proven managerial ability or critical contacts. The other common method is to promote from within. When a firm decides to nationalize its top management, it selects local employees who have been working with the firm for many years, and who show promise. Often, even when the top job is not involved, the selection is preceded or immediately followed by an extended working and training visit to the United States in preparation for assuming higher responsibility.

In more recent years, two other methods have been introduced. Both are still rare, but are gaining in use. The first involves hiring top-level managers from other companies — either foreign or progressive indigenous firms. In most developing countries, inter-company job mobility, especially at the higher echelons, has been slight. However, as the need for top-level talent has become more acute, social values have begun to change. Industry associations have formed which have opened inter-company communication channels and there has been a growing tendency to raid the top-level talent of other, often competing, firms. In such situations, the acquiring company is able to obtain a good indication of the man's probable performance based on his record in the other firm. The company may also have to pay a premium to obtain and hold the individual if he is really good.

The other route, also growing in popularity, is to identify outstanding nationals while they are working or studying abroad. These persons may be assigned to work in the parent firm (or one of its subsidiaries elsewhere), and then returned to their home country to assume a high-level position or to understudy, for a short period, an American or other foreign executive who happens to be there. This method has the advantage of providing leadership which can relate to both the local and the parent company environment, but it may have the disadvantage of stifling the aspirations of other non-U.S.-educated or trained nationals within the subsidiary.

A few U.S. companies have used a hybrid form of subsidiary management. Here, two individuals, one local and one foreign, are given joint responsibility for top-level decision making. In this manner, the parent tries to combine both familiarity with the local environment and imported managerial practices. Only two such cases involving U.S. firms were observed in India. One was a situation in transition, while the other was a stable relationship which had lasted for years. In both cases, delineation of responsibilities and roles was clear-cut, and where differences arose, the American had final authority. These arrangements seemed to work in a manner most closely akin to the "deputy" system used so commonly in indigenous firms in India.

More of the European subsidiaries and affiliates surveyed had a hybrid form of management than did U.S. subsidiaries. This usually involved an administrative top manager and a technical top manager. In the case of India, the former was typically an Indian and the latter a foreigner.

There were some major differences in the channels used in recruiting high-level talent in U.S.-based operations as compared to U.S. subsidiaries. The former used executive placement services, consulting firms, and advertising. The subsidiaries relied primarily on informal contacts, suggestions of other key personnel in the firm, and applications sent in by interested parties. Advertising in newspapers and trade journals was used infrequently. Most developing countries have few, if any, of the kinds of executive placement firms that are found in the United States.

Recruiting for middle- and lower-management jobs, as well as for staff and technical specialists in India, took place primarily in the local country. (Less often, although the practice is growing in international companies, it took place in the parent country.) Local recruiting was nearly always done in a haphazard fashion. Most of the firms surveyed relied on personal contacts for the names of individuals, and letters of reference invariably were glowingly affirmative and superficial. Selection criteria tended to be ill-defined. College grades, personal references, and the general impressions of managers directing the interviews were frequently the only criteria used for selection. However, it became apparent in many cases that because of the applicants' relationship with a key manager, the decision had already been made prior to any formal selection process.

Even in U.S. subsidiaries where upper management did not concern itself intimately with the recruiting process, nepotistic hiring practices and emphasis on regional caste and social factors tended to be common — in spite of stated policies to the contrary. For example, in one U.S. subsidiary it was discovered that a sizeable proportion of the managers and other personnel hired by the Indian production manager were either his relatives or friends. This fact was uncovered only when someone happened to scan the personnel records and noticed that there seemed to be a disproportionately high number of manufacturing personnel who came from a distant Indian city — the same city which was the home of the production manager. A major reason why the personnel function was highly centralized in many of the U.S. firms was the desire to prevent this kind of situation.

Newspaper and other advertising typically meets with little success in personnel recruitment. In many cases, the ads appear to be a sham, to give the selection process the kinds of trappings that local employees feel the U.S. parent firm will require. However, in many nations there are good reasons for the ineffectiveness of advertising for recruits. First, tradition often stands in the way. Where good jobs have historically not been available through newspaper ads, qualified applicatns do not even read them. (More U.S. subsidiaries used trade journal and other specialized media than indigenous firms, with some success.) Second, many U.S. subsidiaries in India discovered that newspaper ads swamped their personnel offices with respondents, most drawn from the "unemployable" college graduate group. Because a great deal of effort is necessary to screen these people, many firms are reluctant to make use of direct advertising.

Recruiting on college campuses is more common than advertising in India, but it is generally used much less than in the United States. It is a relatively new practice in India which is starting to gain some momentum. One of the difficulties of campus recruiting is that few firms have taken the time to define for their personnel managers the qualities they desire in recruits, and it is impractical to have top-level managers conduct all of the campus interviews. Consequently, too little effort seems to have been made to develop good university contacts and engage in on-campus recruiting.

The more progressive foreign and indigenous firms tend to do the best job of camplus recruiting. They focus on the best schools — such as the Indian institutes of management and technology — and hire the most qualified candidates. When word gets around that major foreign companies are looking for new and recent graduates, recruiters are often swamped with applications. For example, one prestigious U.S. subsidiary had over 6,000 applications in one year for its six-men-per-year financial-management-trainee program. The firm tested the 600 best applicants and of these, 60 were selected for interview. The traditional Indian firms that do any campus recruiting tend to restrict themselves to the more traditional schools. The first-rate graduates they hire typically do not remain with them very long.

Several of the better managed U.S. subsidiaries preferred to hire recent graduates who showed great potential, and develop them along the lines required by the firm, rather than hiring older, experienced people. They also generally avoided direct raids on other firms.

One of the greatest potential resources of managerial and technical skills, and one which many U.S. companies overlook, is the large number of foreign students studying in the United States. One of the U.S. companies which recognized this fertile territory had established its recruiting efforts in the following manner: First, individual subsidiary managers notified the parent headquarters of the personnel required. Often they had to project ahead one or two years (to provide for any U.S. training activities). This information was conveyed to corporate recruiters who advertised in advance and visited U.S. campuses. They tried to identify nationals of the particular countries who met the specifications outlined in the subsidiary manager's requests. In addition, they looked for other likely prospects. Promising candidates were invited to company headquarters for interviews with the individuals who had corporate responsibilities for the region in which the subsidiaries were located. Where possible, interviews were scheduled to coincide with visits of subsidiary managers to the United States. When the prospect was hired he was usually employed in domestic operations for six months to two years before he was sent overseas. This gave him a change to learn the technical aspects of the job and absorb the management philosophy of the company.

Relatively few firms of any nationality surveyed in India made use of psychological or aptitude tests, problem-solving exercises, depth interviews, team or committee appraisals, or other techniques applied in the United States for selecting managerial or technical personnel, or workers of other kinds. The few firms that did used them superficially and ineffectively. For example, the personnel director of one semi-traditional Indian firm used a variety of tests, but they were rarely influential in the outcome of selection decisions. It was apparent that top management let him administer these tests — which were all developed in the United Kingdom and United States — just to keep him busy.

For the recruitment of skilled workers (both blue- and white-collar) in India, personal contacts, walk-ins, and unsolicited applications are the most common channels. Government employment agencies are rarely used. Many firms post notices of new vacancies on the company bulletin board (both in English and one or more local languages) and rely upon word-of-mouth to reach those people who cannot read.

In general, selection criteria were vague, especially in the more traditional firms. For example, a "skilled" machinist was probably not given any formal tests, and may have been hired on the basis of work he claimed to have done and the presentation of supporting letters. A new clerk or secretary might not have been asked to take a typing test. Instead the decision to hire was based on formal education, references, or general interview impressions, or personal contacts within the company.

At the unskilled worker level little effort was expended on recruiting, although U.S. firms paid somewhat more attention to the physical fitness and apparent aptitudes and attitudes of worker recruits than did indigenous firms. Usually, major foreign companies were besieged with workers seeking employment. One large U.S. subsidiary in India reported an average of over 300 people appearing daily outside the plant gates during a one-month period when a study was made. A considerably smaller U.S. firm averaged 40 a day over a period of several years.

Unskilled workers, especially for temporary jobs, (and less often skilled workers) are often hired solely because they are the relatives and friends of other company personnel. Random selection of people at the plant gate also occurs. Government employment agencies are also used to hire unskilled workers, usually by indigenous companies.

PERSONNEL RECORDS

A majority of the firms studied in India were characterized by a nearly total lack of useful personnel records. This lack caused little concern because of the rudimentary hiring, promotion, and appraisal practices which were followed. U.S. subsidiaries had considerably poorer records than their domestic counterparts, and at a number of subsidiaries top management made little attempt to become involved in this area and introduce new procedures.

Worker records frequently contained little more than name, address, birth date, perhaps schooling, and record of prior employment. Quite often, only the name was likely to be correct. In many cases, the files did not even contain an application form, since the employee was illiterate and unable to complete it. Sometimes, there were a few scribbled notes indicating the impressions of interviewers or line managers. Where firms did have formal rating forms, the forms were included in the file, but often contained only a simple, uninformative statement such as "OK" or "satisfactory."

In many cases, salary or wage information was not maintained in the personnel file. Instead, this data was held separately by top management or the accounting department, which was usually responsible for payroll. The personnel area was perceived as a department which looks after employee complaints about working conditions and administers group benefits such as company-supplied coffee or tea breaks, scheduling of infirmary appointments, and the like. The personnel manager, especially in more traditional firms, was a man with little power, and one of the lowest paid of the managerial staff. However, he often played a major role in union negotiations, especially if the firm was involved in disputes over benefits and working conditions, as as had been the case with a number of the U.S. subsidiaries surveyed.

One of the consequences of the low importance accorded to the personnel function was that little personnel effort was directed towards management. In many indigenous companies, no such records were maintained at all. The top man would carry all the information he required in his head and would either rely on the payroll department or his own scribbled notes to keep salary matters straight.

U.S. firms usually maintained at least minimal information. Some filed rating sheets in each manager's personnel folder, along with initial employment applications, and miscellaneous documents acquired along the way. In most cases, however, these records were maintained by the managing director himself. Because so much personnel information was centralized and maintained in secrecy, decisions relating to interdepartmental promotions were based either on personal contacts established by the individual or on information in the possession of the managing director. Even within departments, promotions were often based on less than complete knowledge of individuals due to the inacessibility of personnel files. The area relating to personnel records was generally one of the most neglected at the companies studied in India.

PERSONNEL APPRAISAL, PROMOTIONS AND PAY INCREASES

U.S. parent companies, with very few exceptions, did a better job of appraising personnel and preparing useful job descriptions in their domestic operations than did their Indian subsidiaries. In India forms were often prepared only as a formality, to conform to the directives of subsidiary management or the parent company. Many of the forms were similar to those used in the United States, and they would be completed annually (in some cases every six months) by a man's superior. However, several subsidiaries used rating forms that were neither job- nor performance-oriented. They dealt with such general characteristics as personality or cooperative spirit, which were sometimes ranked on numerical scales. Only a limited number of firms focused on an analysis of a man's performance, capabilities, and his record in reaching objectives.

In many firms evaluations were not discussed with the individual employee. For example, in one U.S. subsidiary, each manager completed rating forms on every one of his subordinates every six months, yet relatively few of the managers knew for sure whether they themselves were being rated, or had ever had an opportunity to discuss their ratings with their superiors. Most were convinced that the appraisals were unimportant because it was the relationship that they had with their own superior or higher management that determined promotion and raises.

Several U.S. subsidiaries concluded that they could not find or afford to have local specialists draw up job descriptions and that job descriptions and appraisal forms provided by the parent organization were not applicable because of differences in environmental conditions, scale, operational tasks, and so forth. Consequently, they did without them. None asked incumbent job holders to draw up their own job descriptions or to take part in their own appraisal.

In spite of such shortcomings the U.S. subsidiaries as a group did a better job of appraising personnel and preparing job descriptions than the indigenous firms studied. Top management of the U.S. firms had clearer ideas about the nature and scope of certain positions, and tended more often to fit qualified individuals to the task than managements in local firms.

At indigenous companies, particularly the less progressive ones, a man's job and advancements were usually a function of the relationships he had with his superiors, his social and educational background, and his personality. The jobs were usually tailored to the man who held the position. Consequently, there was little need for job descriptions or formal appraisal.

In the typical indigenous firm in developing countries promotion tends to be based on a man's family connections, his school, and so forth. These factors determine the highest position to which he can aspire. His time "in grade" will determine the pace of promotions. The only way this can be accelerated, under normal circumstances, is by the untimely death or departure of someone ahead of him.

U.S. subsidiaries place less weight on seniority and social factors than indigenous firms (but considerably more than do their parents' domestic operations). This provides incentives for highly motivated employees. Consequently, these companies attract qualified young people who are energetic and ambitious, who are not cast in traditional molds, and who may lack family connections. Nevertheless, the bulk of employees, even in U.S. subsidiaries, have traditional outlooks or at least vestiges of traditional thought patterns. They tend to become frustrated when their juniors are promoted above them. Indigenous companies adhere to a promotion-from-within policy even more rigidly than U.S. subsidiaries. However, some Indian companies have recently begun to select managers and specialists from outside. Where this has introduced only a small number of dynamic individuals into relatively traditional organizations, it has not proved very successful.

It was less common for people lacking college degrees to be promoted into managerial positions at U.S. subsidiaries than at their parent company's domestic operations. However, such promotions did occur. By contrast, they were virtually unknown within indigenous firms. The same patterns existed regarding entry of lower-level workers into supervisory ranks.

The U.S. domestic companies placed more emphasis on merit with regard to pay increases and upgrading than did their subsidiaries. These, in turn, emphasized these factors more than their indigenous counterparts. However, firms in India which have tried to base work pay increases on merit — almost all U.S. subsidiaries — have had to abandon this practice because of the acute problems that resulted. Strong opposition came from both the unions and the workers themselves, who prefer a fixed increment system that emphasizes seniority. Quite a few firms — mostly U.S. subsidiaries — introduce merit rating at the worker level for promotion and training purposes, although they do so only as an addition to the more traditional pattern.

TRAINING

Training and development of personnel is a more difficult and crucial task in developing countries than in advanced ones. It takes longer in a country like India to bring a local national close to U.S. standards. For example, U.S. subsidiaries in India have found that it usually takes at least twice as long to train indigenous engineers and technicians to desired standards, from 50 percent to several hundred percent more time for staff specialists, at least 50 percent more time for skilled workers and craftsmen, and even longer to develop line managers at all levels. Of course, where local nationals have been trained in the United States and are Westernized in their attitudes and motivation, the training period is reduced.

In India the U.S. subsidiaries surveyed have done a better job of training and personnel development, sometimes with much support from the parent company, than their indigenous counterparts. However, few have done a really effective job in this regard. Time and time again, local middle and lower managers, conscientiously attempting to act in the best interests of the firm, pursued courses of action detrimental to company objectives because they lacked knowledge which could have been imparted easily through training. This is an area in which the transference of U.S. know-how is scanty, because top-level managers do not recognize this as their responsibility, or are not qualified to develop their lower-level managers or specialists.

It is common for U.S. subsidiaries to send key individuals to the parent's domestic operations to get practical experience for a period of a few months to a year. It is presumed that this provides invaluable experience which hastens the managerial and technical development the company desires. There is little question that such practices contribute to an organization's success but the "training" often leaves much to be desired. Most commonly, the employee is assigned to a technical slot in the domestic organization in a position similar to the one he occupies in the subsidiary or similar to the one to which he is destined to move, but little attention is given to the development of his managerial skills per se.

Only a few U.S. subsidiaries, and even fewer indigenous companies had made strong efforts to develop internal management. Nor was someone on the top levels assigned specifically to management development or training. The most progressive company in this regard has been a large, diversified U.S. subsidiary. It has its own training staff, sometimes augmented by outside experts, and a training center which is now also used by other companies. Only a handful of other companies in India ⊣ including a few indigenous ones — have done this. This subsidiary offers a variety of formal management-training programs, including fairly long-term administrative, financial and computer training courses for recent college graduates. It conducts many shorter-term programs for all levels of management, many of which are initiated by the requests of various managers. Some programs stress human relations and personnel management; others stress various functional areas; and still others provide a mixture of both managerial and technical training. This firm also makes use of job rotation, training pools, task teams, team training and special projects for personnel development purposes. There has also been considerable stress — at least by Indian standards — on coaching and counseling by superiors, and on other methods of informal and self-development.

In recent years, the establishment of management-training programs by management associations and newly-formed institutions of business administrations in India has led firms to send personnel out and to bring consultants in to provide managerial development activity. However, the effectiveness and use of such programs have been limited because their quality has been spotty. Firms sometimes send the wrong people, or people are sent for the wrong reasons, or the personnel involved either cannot or do not wish to apply what they have learned. In many cases, limitations have been budgetary in nature. In many U.S. subsidiaries expenditures for such training activities are outside the spending power of the managing director and require approval from the parent company unless they have been anticipated a year in advance and included in the firm's budget.

In many U.S. subsidiaries, Indian personnel strongly felt the lack of management training. Many conscientious executives recognized that their prior backgrounds and training had not provided the managerial know-how required for their current positions. The blanks on the control and decision-making forms they were expected to complete (often decision-making requirements of the parent), particular demands for certain types of information from the managing director's office, and so forth, raised questions in their minds concerning their ability to provide what was required. This contributed to their feelings of insecurity. Many of these managers spoke of a need for management development, and in the course of interviewing the authors were frequently asked to suggest books and articles which would help. In a number of companies, these needs as expressed particularly by middle managers, when related to the managing director, resulted in formal and informal programs aimed at strengthening managerial skills — programs which were quite successful.

Within most of the indigenous firms surveyed, the only training activities were usually apprenticeships in which people at all levels of the organization served. As deputies or assistants, managers understudied their superiors and thus learned to assume higher responsibility. This process was often ineffective.

At companies where little emphasis had been placed on the development of lower management, meaningful rating schemes and training for new employees were usually lacking. Basically, the new employee was left to do his job and if he did not cause his supervisor severe problems (such as breaking machines or causing serious conflicts) he was confirmed in permanent status. Top managers perceived the process differently. High-level executives complained that workers on probationary status "work like hell," but once granted permanent status, go into semiretirement. However, detailed examination often revealed that the real difficulty arose because upper management was not aware of the process by which workers moved from temporary to permanent status. Many — especially foreign managers — could not believe that their subordinates were so naive. Even in those firms which had specific rating procedures tied in with some intended form of training for new employees, the process operated in a similar fashion. For example, one company required a new man's immediate supervisor to rate him at three-month intervals during the first year (after which he would become permanent) and required his supervisor's boss to review the ratings at six-month intervals. In actuality, the immediate supervisor used no rating criteria other than personal observations about the man's willingness to work and learn; at the next higher level, the rating was rubber-stamped and filed in a desk drawer. Documents were forwarded to the personnel file only if they were to be used for dismissal purposes.

At traditional companies in particular, it is not unusual for a machinist (or other type of skilled worker) to be hired off the street and turned loose on a machine with no formalities other than the completion of a single application form (sometimes filled out by someone else if he is illiterate). When problems arise and firms start checking references, they are often found to be fictitious. Little attempt is normally made to verify references largely because of the difficulties involved in telephone communication, or the likelihood that a letter will go unanswered, and the fact that many companies do not maintain adequate records. Occasionally a new worker is assigned to an old one for a short period of time. In essence, he serves as an apprentice. However, the "master" usually has no input into the hiring or retention decision and the actual purpose of the apprenticeship is to give everyone a chance to "get to know" the new man.

INFORMAL INDIVIDUAL DEVELOPMENT

More informal, individual development took place at U.S. subsidiaries than at indigenous firms, largely because of the more highly motivated and ambitious individuals that U.S. subsidiaries attracted to their managerial, technical, and staff specialist jobs. On the other hand, and perhaps ironically, not many U.S. firms have made a conscious attempt to encourage informal development of their managerial cadres or other employees. Most of that which has occurred has been due to the self-motivation and initiative of employees, although the reward systems of the subsidiaries often indirectly encourage this.

Few of the American companies provided any help with the purchase of books, the payment of tuition (apart from certain formal management-development programs), or the provision of scholarships to employees. Literacy or other general educational programs were rarely furnished. The provision of scholarships and the sponsoring of educational programs for employees were more common at indigenous firms.

Company libraries were rare, but were found in both U.S. and indigenous firms. Employees of the former tended to make greater use of such facilities. The libraries at indigenous firms were less adequate in terms of managerial development literature. Where employees were encouraged to further their development, it was almost always in technical areas.

A number of Indian firms had established schools for employees' children. This accomplished two purposes. In the long range, it provided a pool of better educated employees, and in an indirect manner, it often upgraded the educational levels of existing employees. Illiterate parents were drawn into PTA activities, and many, in an effort to keep up with their children, learned to read and write by taking advantage of special night courses offered for this purpose. Such programs were not compulsory, but because the Indian parent desired to have his child acquire an education, they were often used to stimulate his own educational development. Such situations were not found in the U.S. subsidiaries examined. Reasons given included: "schools are the responsibility of the government" and, "if we set up schools, the first time the workers had a grievance, they'd wreck the place and probably stone the teacher."

An exception was a small U.S. firm managed by an Indian. During a difficult period where sales were cut back, the managing director, believing that better times were ahead, decided not to lay off his employees. Instead, he restructured jobs so that time not spent in direct productive work was devoted to housekeeping functions or to classroom attendance in a special school he established to teach reading and writing skills. Subsequently when business picked up, he had one of the few companies in India with an almost totally literate work force. He has since indicated that this has been a great help in introducing new projects and in maintaining a high esprit de corps, even though years have passed since this action was taken. Here, however, he pursued an Indian, not an American pattern.

Few companies studied in India attempted an identifiable strategy to provide on-the-job development in the managerial area. The firm that performed the best in this regard adopted a policy which was an extension of the U.S. top man's personal philosophy. Most of his key managers had been educated and had worked in the United States. Consequently, it was easy to communicate the basic foundation of his philosophy — that no subordinate would be permitted to bring a problem to his superior without also presenting alternative solutions and a recommendation. Throughout the organization, any manager who brought problems to his boss without alternatives and recommendations was asked to go back and think it over himself. Although many of the top-level managers saw what this philosophy was accomplishing, a number did not, and performed the ritual only because Mr. X demanded it. But its effect was startling. During the period encompassing the first two years after this practice was initiated, there was an appreciable upgrading of decision-making ability throughout the organization, permitting reorganizations which decentralized decision making down to levels far below those found in any other company in the industry.

LEVELS OF COMPENSATION AND FRINGE BENEFITS

The salaries paid foreign employees in U.S. subsidiaries are higher than those paid to nationals working at the same level, often by several hundred percent. The rationale behind this pattern is simple. Most U.S. managers come to India for short periods of time and the U.S. environment is taken as the base to which their working careers relate. In the case of Indian managers, the working sphere is India and compensation is tied to Indian standards.

British firms often set compensation levels about halfway between the local and the home country's standards. Many view managerial assignments to countries such as India on a considerably longer-term basis than do U.S. companies. The expatriate American executive can plan to spend somewhere between one and five years in India for his company, with an average term of three years. The expatriate Britisher is often there for five to ten years, or even longer.

U.S. subsidiaries pay higher basic salaries and wages than indigenous firms. On the other hand, the larger indigenous companies, of both progressive and traditional nature, tend to provide more in the way of perquisites and fringe benefits.

On the whole, the U.S. subsidiaries surveyed spend substantially more for each employee, taking into account both pay and fringe benefits. However, because the Indian tax structure favors fringe benefits as opposed to basic salaries, the differential in net personnel compensation (basic pay plus fringe benefits) between U.S. and Indian companies has been reduced somewhat. Consequently, many U.S. subsidiaries have recently increased their fringe benefits significantly.

Salary differentials for similar managerial and technical positions were usually at least 20 percent more at the U.S. subsidiaries surveyed than at their indigenous counterparts and it was not uncommon to find differentials of more than 100 percent. Even Western-trained nationals at Indian companies received significantly lower salaries than their counterparts in U.S. subsidiaries.

The same basic salary patterns were also found for clerical staffs, secretaries, and menial help (such as peons). Pay differentials for such jobs usually ranged from about 10 percent to well over 100 percent. The smallest differentials in relation to U.S. subsidiaries occurred at large and progressive Indian companies.

The U.S. subsidiaries paid at least one-third to one-half more than indigenous firms for new management, staff specialist, and technical trainees. Top starting pay usually went to individuals with graduate degrees from the United States, followed by graduates from schools in other advanced countries, graduates from the Indian institutes of management and a few other leading educational institutions in India, and accountants (particularly cost accountants).

For new salesmen, U.S. subsidiaries generally paid at least one-third more than their indigenous counterparts, although the differential was only about 10 percent at a few progressive Indian companies. Many also pay substantial commissions and bonuses to their salesmen — in many cases amounting to several months basic pay. Few other foreign drug firms or indigenous companies pay commissions or bonuses in such large amounts and very few pay both.

At the plant-worker level, there is little doubt that American companies take a lead in raising wage scales in many developing countries. They find themselves in this role for several reasons, not all of which are of their own doing. First, many American companies are more particular about the caliber of workers they require. They often utilize higher technology and more automated equipment in their production processes than do their indigenous counterparts. Consequently, they need workers more highly skilled and reliable than the average. By paying more, they attract the better workers. Second, labor costs are comparatively insignificant in developing nations vis-a-vis U.S. cost structures. In India, it is not unusual to find that less than 10 percent of the total manufacturing cost is contributed by direct labor, whereas in the United States the labor component usually runs at least several times higher. For this reason, many U.S. managers have a pre-conditioned attitude which justifies their paying more than the going rate because even larger percentage raises affect the total cost structure so slightly.

In some cases, U.S. companies pay more in an attempt to upgrade the living conditions and educational opportunities of the work force. But such altruistic aims are relatively rare. In most cases, the objective of obtaining good workers far outweighs the goal of improving the living conditions of the workers. However, the net effect often is the same.

U.S. companies are also subject to outside pressures which force them to take the lead in raising wage rates. Government policies aimed at upgrading worker conditions directly or indirectly exert pressure on U.S. companies to make the first moves. In countries where industries depend upon government licenses to manufacture new products or to import needed raw materials, government pressures can be exerted very subtly and effectively and foreign firms are often more vulnerable to such pressures than local companies. In other cases, countries may enact laws which explicitly discriminate against the foreign company and force it to pay higher wages and hire more people than it would do otherwise.

Union activities also push up the wage rates of U.S. companies. In developing nations unions recognize the vulnerability of U.S. companies to charges of exploitation.

The foreigner is suspect. Exploitation is a charge that can be built into a hot political issue. Consequently, recognizing management's vulnerability and its relatively lenient attitude towards increasing minor components of manufacturing costs, unions often attack U.S. firms first, in an effort to raise total industry wage levels. U.S. companies are, therefore, in the vanguard of those firms subject to great pressure from unions to initiate wage increases. As the wage rates of U.S. companies rise and labor shortages in skilled categories become acute, more individuals are drawn away from indigenous firms. These companies must then raise their wage scales to attract or retain good people, and the unions have achieved their purpose.

Some of the problems surrounding worker compensation in developing nations arise from patterns accepted within the legal framework. In many countries, direct wages provide only a fraction (frequently less than half) of total compensation. In India, for example, compensation includes a dearness allowance regulated by the government and based on a cost-of-living factor. This often exceeds basic wage payments. In recent years, companies in India have been required to pay all permanent workers bonuses related to basic pay as well as profits.

Fringe benefits can create serious problems for U.S. subsidiaries, especially in developing countries like India. This is somewhat ironical, since parent companies often spend just as much or more on fringe benefits and employee welfare in ralation to total payroll in their domestic operations as their subsidiaries spend. The problem arises, however, because the kinds of fringe benefits demanded are often quite different than those normally provided in the United States. They can include such things as free or subsidized housing (including utilities and furnishings), servants, meals, company transportation, social club memberships, entertainment allowances, company-run health plans (which may include the employee's family), schools and personal education, medical facilities, longer paid-leaves and more travel and vacation expenses, and free or low-cost loans for personal cars and housing. U.S. managers and firms often fight the introduction of benefits asked for by both workers and the government on the grounds that these benefits are not the kind which should be provided by business firms (i.e., they are not provided in the familiar U.S. environment). This gives rise to conflict as managements resist worker demands and both sides feel their positions are justified. Consequently, the important area of compensation patterns gives rise to many problems.

The U.S. firm which goes abroad should be willing to entertain proposals which it normally would not countenance in the United States. The only effective way of making such decisions is for top management to look closely at what it must do to achieve its goals and objectives and then do it, rather than operate by rules which may have been derived from a culture very different in value structure and economic needs. The same is true at all organizational levels, and not just with regard to workers.

U.S. firms have not gone as far as indigenous firms in extending various job perquisites down the managerial and specialist hierarchy. This can frequently be done at a relatively small cost to the firm, but with a highly positive impact on employee morale and productivity. Status is frequently a potent motivating force for Indian managers — including many who are relatively Westernized in their outlooks. Many of them may strongly desire a promotion not for the raise in salary but because of the perquisites — for instance, they may then be entitled to company-provided automobile transportation, if not a personal car.

PERSONNEL DISMISSALS, LAYOFFS, AND TURNOVER

In India and other developing nations, the problems surrounding layoff and dismissal are severe. This is a major problem area for management, since an elaborate series of laws exists to protect job security and increase employment levels in most of these countries. Employees caught blatantly violating the rules of the company — in the act of theft, or malicious mischief — often are not dismissed because it is too expensive to go through dismissal procedures and because the probability of success is slight. Many such proceedings drag out in the courts for years and result in the reinstatement of the employee with full back-pay for the entire period.

As a protective measure, companies resort to the practice of keeping large numbers of their work force on temporary status. The protection of the law usually applies only to the permanent worker who has completed a probationary period. The probationary period varies among nations and often among states and industries within countries, but typically runs from three months to a year. In many firms, both U.S. and indigenous, it is not uncommon for an employee to be maintained on the payroll until the day before his probationary period ends. Since at this point he lacks the protection of the law, he can be dismissed and in most countries no reason need be given. He can then be re-hired a day later and start a new probationary period. In this manner companies retain the flexibility to expand and reduce their work force according to economic conditions. This method of hiring and laying off was used to a greater extent by the Indian firms studied than by U.S. subsidiaries. In many cases, more than 50 percent of the work force was held in this status. However, it was not that uncommon even in the U.S. firms to find as much as 30 to 40 percent of the work force on temporary status. Nevertheless, political vulnerability imposed some practical limitations on the use of this practice by foreign firms.

In Bengal in particular, there has been a strong crackdown on the employment of temporary and casual workers since the coalition Leftist United Front government first took over in that state in 1967. There was a freeze on the dismissal of such personnel, and firms were pressured to give them permanent status. Some companies have circumvented such pressures through the use of personal influence and bribery, especially where non-Bengali workers have been involved, but in general, it has become more difficult to maintain large members of nonpermanent employees. This has reduced operating flexibility and increased concern over high absenteeism at numerous firms.

In other parts of the country firms surveyed expressed concern that unions and political leaders as well might move in the same direction as Bengal with regard to temporary and casual work. Some of these companies, primarily U.S. firms, have recently taken steps to improve their manpower planning, reduce the number of non-permanent employees, and cut down absenteeism.

The situation is usually somewhat different at the managerial level. The manager does not receive the same protection accorded to the worker, but the attitudes held by present and prospective employees often limit the freedom management has to fire or lay off workers at any level. In developing nations, the employee acquires a status akin to "family membership" within the firm. Laying him off in hard times would be considered analogous to giving away a child when a family's income is reduced. For reasons previously discussed at length, firing is a little-used managerial function and in most cases, an incompetent is placed where he can do little harm to the enterprise, although he is no longer a productive asset. This practice results in the accumulation of managerial deadwood, but this must be balanced against the possible alternatives of low morale, shaken confidence, and personnel unrest which may result from dismissal actions.

Problems associated with workers and managers can often be dealt with more effectively through the use of training and management-development activities. Where it is difficult to discharge poor workers, management can take special pains to ensure that workers confirmed as permanent employees meet certain standards — and do this prior to the time of confirmation. This would require the installation of training programs and rating and review procedures as well as a supervisory program to prepare first-line supervisory personnel to assume these responsibilities.

At the managerial level, various kinds of development activities may be useful to the manager who is having difficulty handling his current job. They may also pave the way for a move into a position which will suit him better. The explanation of why this often fails to happen is due to lack of requisite training skills, or because top leadership has neither the interest, the time, nor the ability to provide or stimulate these skills.

Generally speaking, constraints imposed by national legal structures have precluded the formulation of specific policies relating to layoffs and dismissal, and these measures are usually resorted to only under extreme conditions. However, throughout the country, growing pressures to improve efficiency and profits have increased the willingness of many foreign and indigenous firms to resort to layoff and firing practices.

In spite of an image to the contrary, the firms in India which have fired the largest proportions of permanent personnel in recent years — including workers, managers and other employees — have been indigenous companies. U.S. firms have released very few employees, although a few companies had major layoffs some years back.

Several years ago a large Indian engineering firm, badly hit by the recent economic recession, dismissed a sizeable number of employees, primarily staff. A number of British firms have done the same, and some U.S. firms which had been reluctant to fire at any level have recently dismissed some managers and white-collar workers. Paradoxically, the firms studied which have continued to be most reluctant to dismiss their employees are the most traditional and paternalistic indigenous companies whose losses have been most acute, and whose labor problems have been greatest.

Several U.S. subsidiaries surveyed have experienced significantly higher personnel turnover rates than their more traditional Indian counterparts. A major reason for this is that they have done a better job of recruiting and training personnel, and competitors have enticed staff personnel and skilled workers away with better jobs, more pay, and greater fringe benefits. In general, the operations of U.S.-based drug and chemical parent firms had considerably higher turnover rates than their Indian subsidiaries. For example, a relatively well-managed U.S. subsidiary had an average turnover rate for permanent employees of 5 percent per year during the 1960s. Its greater turnover involved lower-level managers and supervisors, technical specialists, and salesmen, while blue collar turnover averaged under 1.5 percent. The turnover rate for workers in the domestic operations of its parent company has averaged about 10 percent, and for all other personnel, about 9 percent.

Another leading U.S. drug subsidiary which has been paying wages and salaries well above the industry average has had a worker turnover rate in the vicinity of only 1 percent, but a significant number of managers have left.

The overall personnel turnover rate at a large semi-traditional Indian drug and chemical company has been in the range of 7 to 9 percent. In the managerial ranks it has been about 2 to 4 percent annually; in other white collar areas, between 5 and 10 percent (although it hit 15 percent one year); and among the work force, about 8 to 10 percent.

The overall turnover rate at a large Indian engineering firm has been close to 10 percent in recent years. In 1965-66, turnover was higher among workers than staff, but by 1969 the situation was reversed. Since 1965 the turnover rate among staff has averaged about 8 percent, and among workers about 11 percent. About one out of every five managerial and staff people who have left the company have been fired. The proportion has been smaller for workers, but it has been growing. At one of its Calcutta plants, nine out of twelve of the higher-level and departmental managers have left the company in the last several years. Quite a few of its foreign-trained personnel have left, as well as four recent graduates recruited from the Indian Institute of Management at Calcutta. In most of these latter cases there seemed to be a poor fit between the organization and the relatively dynamic and progressive individuals it hired.

CONCLUDING REMARKS

One of the most critical ingredients for success in the long-range operation of U.S. subsidiaries in developing nations lies in the upgrading and developing of personnel within the organization. It is people who make the decisions that make the organization run and who carry out the day-to-day activities of the firm. The success of the company is a direct function of the capability of its management. Perhaps the most critical area in terms of payoff to the U.S. firm, therefore, is the selection of top-level leadership which can encourage this developmental process. This is an area where U.S. firms often fail.

Too frequently, a gap exists between the capabilities top management expects from supporting managerial levels and the actual abilities that exist there. In many cases, top management's preconceptions of what things should be influences their behavior and obscures the actual picture until major problems have developed. The top manager of a subsidiary in a developing nation usually needs to be a generalist — the kind of person who has wide-ranging interests and a broad base of experience. He must be interested in working with the development of people as individuals and as managers. He cannot rely on the local environment to provide the requisite skills because the local culture is usually not compatible with the processes necessary to carry out industrial activity. Since he is not likely to find well-established communication channels to carry a steady flow of managerial techniques from the United States down into his lower organization levels, he must be prepared to develop them, and for a time to serve himself as the channel of communication.

Many managerial practices commonly applied in U.S.-based organizations could be effectively employed in developing nations if they were transferred — in some cases intact, and in many others with only minor degrees of modification. By increasing the flow and application of managerial know-how, the company is likely to increase the efficiency of its performance substantially, and pave the way for more stable and satisfying relationships with the host environment.

CHAPTER 15
DIRECTION,
LEADERSHIP,
AND MOTIVATION

A key to top management success lies in effectively directing, leading, and motivating personnel throughout the organization to perform their tasks most efficiently. This entails personal communication, man-to-man relationships, and the use of incentives and penalties to motivate employees in desired directions. It is the heart of getting things done with and through people, and putting the organization in gear to achieve its objectives.

Foreign firms and managers frequently place inordinate confidence on "rules of thumb" concerning human nature. An assumption that people are basically alike ignores the fact that much of human thought and behavior is actually learned and is therefore, in large part, a product of the local environment. Consequently, leadership styles, approaches to direction, and motivational techniques transferred from one environment to another may not achieve their desired effects.

LEADERSHIP STYLES AND APPROACHES TO DIRECTION

A basic tenet of management taught in most U.S. business schools today is that a broad base of participation in the formation of organizational goals — not only overall goals, but also objectives at the various levels of the firm — is likely to motivate managers, as well as other employees, by increasing their commitment to goal achievement. Such a view of participation is relatively rare in most developing countries, and it tends to be much more difficult and time-consuming to implement participative management effectively as compared to the United States. However, it may well be worth the efforts entailed, especially for foreign subsidiaries.

A fairly broad base of participation in goal setting is often more critical for foreign firms in developing countries because there is greater likelihood that an imposed set of objectives may not be consistent with the local value system or other environmental conditions. Within U.S. domestic operations, similar cultural backgrounds tend to create ties which link almost everyone from the lowest rungs of the organization to the highest paid managers. However, within U.S. subsidiaries in developing countries, foreign top managers, who have few links with the rest of the employees, often apply sets of objectives which have been selected by parent headquarters.

To make this type of firm (i.e., one which has its goals specified in terms of Westernized, economic targets) work effectively, management has to make a special effort to recruit and hire the relatively rare individuals from the local society who think in terms most compatible with Westernized patterns. If they are not able to find enough of these individuals they may be in serious trouble, since it is almost impossible to work solely with traditionally oriented indigenous managers. This is one of the reasons why in India, for example, "success" was so highly correlated with the number of U.S.-educated or trained managers in the firm.

In India, the Indian top executive is more likely to voluntarily include objectives which advance the country's overall economic and social development. His motivation may not be altruistic, but he will consider many non-economic goals. We have already discussed examples relating to the establishment of schools, the provision of local transportation, greater welfare benefits, etc., which testify to this willingness. Consequently, the Indian firm is often seen as a more responsible corporate citizen than is its foreign counterpart.

By failing to provide for participation of its indigenous employees in the goal-setting process, the U.S. subsidiary often appears to take an anti-social attitude towards the needs of its host country. Plans are drawn up without the benefit of the prolonged emotional commitment to the local milieu that nationals can provide. To counter this problem, it has been suggested that U.S. firms might structure overseas subsidiaries with a local national in the key policy-making position and then supply him with U.S. specialists to install the managerial techniques and practices needed to achieve company goals. Another alternative would be the two-man team at the top — one from the U.S. and the other from the host nation.

Effective personnel development efforts are frequently lacking in U.S. subsidiaries — and even much more so in most indigenous firms in developing countries. Few top executives feel it to be their responsibility to impress upon lower levels of management the need for effective supervision and the importance of training. They are typically unable to motivate their management cadres either through training, or by structuring the reward system (in both monetary and non-monetary terms) so as to recognize positive contributions to achieving company goals.

Another major set of problems confronting many U.S. subsidiaries relates to the relative impermanence of top-level subsidiary managers and the insecurity and frustration the ensuing changes entail. For example, one U.S. subsidiary studied has had four different managing directors in less than ten years. An American managing director who had broad experience in a variety of areas, who stressed participative management and decentralization, and who was generally an effective leader, was followed by an Indian who had a much narrower background, a different leadership style, and some basic differences in values and attitudes. The Indian was followed by two Australians, each of whom had a completely different style and set of interests from any of the others, and from one another in many respects. Similarly, another U.S. firm had a fairly effective American managing director who was a relatively strong and visible leader, involved in many areas of the organization. He was followed by a Britisher who was not nearly as strong a leader, but who was fairly effective in the areas of personnel management, human relations, and public relations. Another American followed him, a forceful but not very visible leader, whose experience in the United States was primarily in marketing. He devoted considerably less time to human or public relations, and emphasized improving operating efficiency.

Indian managers — especially the more traditional ones — working for U.S. subsidiaries frequently felt uncomfortable about the lack of strong personal bonds which exist in indigenous companies. Very little social interaction took place between U.S. and Indian personnel, either during or after working hours. The foreign manager usually interacted primarily with his immediate subordinates and was seldom accessible to lower-level managers or to the workers — quite the opposite of the typical Indian top manager. In many cases, this was done consciously in an attempt to avoid paternalism and to develop lower-level managers by forcing them to interact more directly with their subordinates. But it created great discomfort, even for many of the most Westernized of the Indians.

SUPERVISORY TECHNIQUES

One of the weakest links in the U.S. subsidiaries examined was found at the lowest levels of supervision. The situation tended to be considerably worse in the indigenous firms where the lower levels of supervision were not viewed as part of management but served primarily as communication channels. U.S. subsidiaries do a better staffing job on the whole at this level, and ideas and concepts practiced higher up in the organization slowly filter down through the middle and lower levels; nevertheless, although first-line supervisors are typically expected to take greater managerial responsibility than in indigenous firms, many do not know what is expected of them.

Unlike the situation in the United States, where it is quite common for the supervisor to be promoted directly from the ranks, class separation in developing nations usually results in supervisory personnel coming from distinctly different socioeconomic strata than the workers. Consequently, the supervisor tends to be distant from his men. He is more paternalistic and less "one of the boys," and has little social interaction with his men once the work day has ended. Frequently, the task of the supervisor — especially in traditional Indian firms — is seen as being largely concerned with paperwork, and the average supervisor stays very close to his desk.

One of the difficulties in training the work force arises from the fact that most first-line supervisors have neither the skills nor the desire to involve themselves directly in training activities. In a country where manual labor is the only livelihood for the majority, the individual who obtains an education that permits him to break away from menial chores tends to jealously guard his increased status. Consequently, he avoids any association with manual types of activity. In contrast to the U.S. ideal, he will not roll up his sleeves and pitch in, nor will he walk out into a machine shop to demonstrate the proper way to do the job. Not only may the dirt bother him, but he may not have much experience with machinery. Although U.S. subsidiary managers are more likely to pitch right in and become engrossed in training activities, they usually cannot afford the time; in many cases, they assume that their supervisors are already doing the job and consequently they never get involved.

It is surprising to note how frequently U.S. managers voiced complaints to the authors about their operations which showed total unfamiliarity with the way functions were being carried out at lower levels in their own organizations. Many did not recognize the need to look for themselves. Instead, they just assumed that subordinates were as capable in the subsidiaries as they would be in U.S. domestic operations, often overlooking cultural gaps and communications problems.

COMMUNICATION

One of the most important components of an effective organization is a well-functioning communications network. As objectives are being formulated, and decisions are being made, it is important that all levels of the firm be aware of what is going on. This is true regardless of whether the communications channels are used to convey decisions downward or to elicit participation.

It takes a special effort on the part of top management to make sure that good communications channels are open. It's easy to be misled; the support and enthusiasm of the few subordinates can lead a top manager into believing that similar attitudes exist throughout the organization when this may not be so.

This need is not peculiar only to developing nations; however, special care must be taken by the top executive in such environments, since there is a higher probability that value systems will differ throughout the organization. Even when the top man is convinced that he has established rapport with his middle management, he may find that middle management is out of tune with lower-level management and that a similar situation exists with respect to the workers. The sharp class distinctions within developing nations create wide gulfs.

Normal communications channels may not be sufficient. A company newspaper or posted announcements may be almost useless, since workers may be illiterate or unaccustomed to reading company bulletins. Instead, communications often have to take place on a more personal basis, so that it is necessary to make a conscientious effort to develop the communications abilities of the managerial cadre. Few companies have done this. Most of the U.S. firms studied had house organs but their only function was usually that of a morale builder (e.g., from the excitement over seeing a picture of oneself or one's fellow workers) and not as a broader communications medium.

Another difference in a developing nation is that many people within an organization, from workers on up, think of genuine communications in terms of direct personal contact with the man at the top — the father. This places a heavy burden on the top executive as he must spend more time with his people and less doing the kinds of tasks to which he is accustomed. He may also be disturbed by the need for close contact shown by his subordinates, equating such behavior with lack of decisiveness or initiative on their parts. He may feel that direct contact with managers and workers at lower levels will encourage individuals to circumvent supervisory levels, and therefore discourage effective middle-management development. Yet often a firm base of support is required to build the confidence necessary for the development of effective decision-making abilities. Somehow the top executive has to achieve a balance between his own needs and those of his people.

Although written forms of communication often prove ineffective in U.S. industry, they tend to be even less so in developing countries. Ironically, they also tend to be used much more for many matters that would be handled orally or involve no communication at all in the United States. For example, at one U.S. drug subsidiary in India a conflict arose between someone in the warehouse and a member of the accounting staff regarding an invoice. About eight or nine memos were sent between these two parties over a period of several months — often with copies going to other company personnel — but nothing was done. Nobody made an attempt to deal with the matter in person, or even to pick up the telephone to try to resolve the problem. The memos got more and more emotional; eventually other personnel were drawn into the conflict, and they, too, began to send memos. These came from the superiors of the two original correspondents, people in production, sales, and quality control, etc. Coalitions were formed, and the matter was finally resolved only when the British managing director and American production head stepped into the picture and began to communicate in person.

Top management could avoid many such problems by stressing the effectiveness of personal contact and oral communication and, particularly, by developing an atmosphere of trust and cooperation within the organization.

TRUST AND COOPERATION

One individual's trust in another is a function of several variables, the most important involving the following conditions: He must be sure that the individual to be trusted has good intentions; he must have faith in the person's ability to perform in whatever manner is required; and he must not feel that his own security, needs, or personal interests are being seriously threatened. Trust can usually form when these conditions exist and this in turn can become a building block for cooperation.

Communications channels are vital to determine what management's intentions really are, and to reassure workers who fear their personal security is being threatened. The worker or other employee who feels that he is being exploited, whether or not it is true, is not likely to give management his full support. The same applies to the relationship between communications and the concept of fairness. Often actions taken by superiors are seen as arbitrary and unjust by subordinates only because effective communication of objectives and limitations has not taken place.

It is interesting to note a paradox which exists in India with respect to trust and cooperation. Within the Indian firm, the concept of trust seems to have two very distinct components: The Indian owner-manager will usually trust no one with financial and other critical operating data and his employees accept this as a fact of life; yet the employees generally trust management completely with respect to the maintenance of working conditions and job security and show much loyalty to their employers. In essence, they do not feel any diminution in their loyalty because the trust relationship in the downward direction is not correspondingly complete. Consequently, the cooperative spirit tends to be high along vertical lines, although it is not specifically directed toward economic gain. On the other hand, the lack of trust and cooperation along horizontal lines often results in serious conflicts, problems, and inefficiencies. Different parts of the organization tend to act like "islands unto themselves."

In the U.S. subsidiary, on the other hand, operating data is usually handled in a much more open fashion, although certain kinds of cost and other information may still be guarded closely. Delegation of authority and participative management are much more common, and horizontal communication and interaction more prevalent; however, this does not necessarily substitute for the traditional bonds of personal relationship and establish the type of trust that it might in a U.S. setting.

In developing nations, U.S. top management often fails in respect to the "ability" underpinning of trust relationships. In the local environment, strong leadership is often synonymous with authoritarian management. The top manager who must continuously refer to his head office to get approval for his decisions or to add a cleaning man to the payroll once his budget has been established projects as a weak individual. His ability to produce results becomes suspect, since he may not be able to perform his "fatherly" role.

Numerous incidents were encountered in U.S. firms where communications breakdowns had resulted in unhappiness and unrest within the organization, for example, the following:

> One of the most promising young Indian managers was about to resign from a U.S. subsidiary only a week before a major promotion was to be announced. His reason for deciding to resign was that the company "does not recognize my abilities and there seems to be no future for me here." His boss had made a number of decisions which he felt were arbitrary. He had protested, and had been slapped down. No one at higher levels seemed to be listening to him.
>
> In actuality, top management was aware of the situation (mainly the ineptitude of his boss), had aired his complaints and suggestions carefully, and after evaluating the situation, had decided to move him up into his boss's slot and move his boss into a staff position which would utilize the man's great technical competence. These discussions extended over a period of three months, and yet at no time in this process did the soon-to-be-promoted man receive any feedback. The fact that he was under increasingly severe attacks from his boss had led him to conclude that top management was going along with the boss and had discounted his inputs.

It might seem extremely difficult to establish the degrees of trust and cooperation required when different value systems are involved. In practice, the foreign firm often has an advantage in this regard because employees are attracted to it just because it is different, and, therefore, they will accept deviant action more readily than they might in an indigenous firm. In other words, the foreign firm may have wider latitude to violate local taboos without arousing suspicion and distrust on the part of its employees; however, this must be handled carefully and with an understanding of the attitudes and values involved.

MOTIVATING MANAGERIAL PERSONNEL

Few of the Indian firms studied had any conscious plans for motivating their managerial and technical personnel. In many cases, the manager's entire career was mapped out for him by virtue of his education and his relationship with the owners. His salary and position at any given point in his career had been predetermined. The rewards he received were largely a function of his presence in the company, and were augmented little if at all for good performance. Motivation, as such, came from being regarded as a member of the "company family." Under such a system, the penalties for nonconformity or risk taking which ended in failure could be severe while the rewards for positive contributions were usually small. Motivation toward achievement tended, therefore, to be discouraged.

U.S. subsidiaries typically employed a different motivational system. The chief rewards were money, authority and responsibility, a chance to be creative and take initiative, and a generally challenging and satisfying job. As noted earlier, their reward systems were much more closely tied to merit.

However, few of the U.S. subsidiaries used bonuses, profit-sharing plans, or other rewards which were tied to performance. None of the subsidiaries surveyed had stock option plans. (Although a few indigenous firms had various kinds of stock plans, they were not tied to merit, but were aimed at developing company loyalty and providing greater benefits to employees over time.)

In addition to money and responsibility, several factors of lesser importance played a role in motivating managers in most of the U.S. firms. First, a major foreign company usually carries an aura of prestige. Its products are well-known and highly regarded. Its image in the eyes of the general public is usually higher than that of local competitors, and just the novelty of things foreign (unavailability, snob appeal, strange sounding names, etc.) helps to raise the image of the foreign subsidiary in local eyes as a good place to work. Second, there is always a possibility of foreign travel — to take advantage of the training program in the parent country or to attend an international meeting. In a nation like India, where the opportunities for travel and living abroad are very limited, this is often a major competitive factor with respect to attracting and retaining dynamic young managerial talent. The overseas possibilities also provide an incentive for performance, as the manager who is working his way up the ladder will have increasing opportunity to go abroad for short periods of time.

It is evident, however, that the types of motivational stimuli used by many U.S. firms are not those that would typically appeal to local personnel. They are designed largely for executives with American values, and consequently, they tend primarily to both attract and stimulate only the relatively young, Western-oriented manager. This has both advantages and disadvantages. Since the firm's orientation is usually Western, the major advantage comes from the fact that it preselects individuals who are more prone to accept the value system prevailing within the top management or parent company ranks. On the negative side, however, are two very important factors.

First, no matter how Westernized the local manager may be, his "Westernization" is only an overlay. He is still an Indian or a Colombian or a Nigerian, and many local values will still be meaningful to him. Consequently, in even the most Westernized of the U.S. subsidiaries studied, many of the most dynamic and rising young managers missed some of the social and psychic rewards they might have obtained from following more traditional patterns. In India, such managers complained about the lack of close supportive relationships and of frustration experienced at times as a result of what they thought was an overemphasis on economic efficiencies. Many found the organizations to be cold, impersonal, and uncommunicative, and some felt that their companies should provide more of the status symbols (such as company clubs) that Indian firms had. Similar complaints about aloofness of U.S. top management and machine-like daily operations were voiced by several Central American executives who were interviewed. For most of these people, however, the advantages of the

Westernized working environment outweighed the negative aspects. However, some twinges of regret were expressed by almost all — not that they worked in a U.S. company, but that the U.S. company couldn't adapt a little more to their "human needs."

The second negative factor, which is more critical, is the difficulty in staffing an organization completely with people who have the desired Western outlook. Consequently, many of the executive positions within U.S. subsidiaries are filled by persons holding more traditional views. These people find the motivational schemes much less desirable, especially since they are not likely to be among the group which is reaping the maximum benefits. Many such individuals were identified in the course of company interviews. Most were continuously tense and frustrated, and there is little doubt that their contributions fell far short of their capabilities. Several indicated that, if it were not for the high salaries and the vagaries of the job market, they would leave and try to find employment in a local company.

In essence, many U.S. subsidiaries ignore the needs of a large number of their managers by failing to incorporate in the reward system elements which will motivate the more traditionally-minded employee. U.S. managers often assume that Western types of stimuli will work. Moreover, the problem is compounded because these managers tend to become isolated from their more traditionally-oriented subordinates and seek greater contact with the more Westernized ones — the people they feel most comfortable with. This contact serves to reenforce their faith in the efficacy of the reward system and to remove them even further from the more traditional managers.

Delegation of authority in the U.S. subsidiaries often presented problems, especially when Indians were not yet ready to assume the full burden of responsibility. Many, even the most confident, at times felt the need for a more supportive relationship. This was especially true of junior managers in cases where delegation was not preceded by adequate training or communication. This situation could make them extremely uncomfortable, since they did not know how much of the authority they received could or should actually be exercised, and in some cases, they believed that top management was actually failing in its responsibilities by not making decisions. Delegation was, at times, seen as lack of decisiveness at the top.

In the long term, it was apparent that such decentralization and delegation strategies nurtured better decision makers within the company. However, in many instances it was clear that closer communication was needed throughout all organizational levels to clarify the purposes of such practices. Contrary to prevailing beliefs at the top, decentralization was not always seen in a positive light, even by the individuals who acquired greater freedom of action as a result. In many cases, it was necessary to pave the way.

Many of the more traditional managers were disturbed by decentralization, especially when decisions affecting them were made at lower than top levels. They were willing to accept almost any decision within reason if it came from the top but were suspicious if it did not. Here again, there seemed to be a strong need for some type of adaptive process, at least initially, to achieve a better blend between authoritarian and participative management structures.

Finally, it is worth emphasizing that status tends to be even more important to managers in most developing countries than in the United States and, perhaps even more important, status is often perceived in quite different ways; for example:

> The U.S. manager of a Latin American subsidiary decided to automate a number of accounting and computational procedures. A computer was purchased in the United States and shipped down. The Latin American manager (the chief accountant) who would operate the new computer center was told what was to happen and how the new computer would save costs and reduce delays. At the time the installation was made, the manager and his staff were given extensive training in the use and the capabilities of the equipment; yet a year after installation, nothing was running smoothly. The company was ready to abandon the project when it was discovered what had actually happened. Top management had assumed that the local manager would regard the change as one which gave him added status and prestige — supervising a modern, highly automated, fully air-conditioned computer center. However, they discounted the fact that this reduced the number of employees reporting to him which, in his eyes, considerably lowered his status. Instead of seeing this as a promotion, he saw it as tantamount to a demotion, as did many of the employees working within his area.

MOTIVATING NONMANAGERIAL PERSONNEL

Differences in the approaches of U.S., other foreign, and indigenous firms with regard to motivating nonmanagerial personnel (especially blue-collar workers) were not as clear-cut as they were with respect to managerial personnel. One reason is probably that there were fewer variations in attitudes and values among Indian workers than among Indian managers at the different firms studied. The ponderous legal structures relating to labor laws, as well as union constraints, were also responsible for this similarity, since they restricted the kinds of motivational alternatives which management could pursue.

A few American firms which initially experimented in India with worker incentives as part of base pay schemes were forced to give them up by court decisions which ruled in favor of fixed wages. The courts continually rule on both amounts and forms of payment. Consequently, companies stop experimenting and the reward system for the workers tends to be largely determined by legislation. The legislative influence is so strong that many companies (and unions) no longer even make an attempt to negotiate such matters: they just leave the issues to the courts. However, ways can be found in spite of legislative restrictions (e.g., the court usually establishes minimum patterns and companies may experiment over and above the minimum) but it takes considerable knowledge and dedication to persevere in spite of the obstacles.

Exceptions that were found occurred mostly in small companies (many of which were not subject to the same labor laws which affect large firms), where innovative Indian manager-owners tried to experiment. The most effective of these tended to use social relationships and to incorporate them in the motivational scheme.

> A small Indian foundry which was having difficulty achieving the productivity levels it management desired started contracting work to its non-permanent unskilled and semi-skilled workers. Prior to this time, workers received a monthly wage. Both absenteeism and turnover was very high. Under the new arrangement, management negotiated a price on a job — a price typically lower than the cost of doing the work on the former fixed-wage basis. The task (e.g., clean two tons of castings) was then contracted to the workers for a lump sum. Deadlines were established.
>
> Management was amazed with the results. Absenteeism dropped substantially, the workers earnings increased dramatically and capacity skyrocketed. Jobs were completed in a fraction of the time they had taken formerly.

> The above contrasts sharply with a U.S. company which, in an attempt to decrease absenteeism, raised wage rates and offered attendance bonuses. It discovered that absenteeism increased almost proportionately to the increase in pay and that the bonuses for attendance had little effect.

In the two cases described above, motivational stimuli, each interacting with local value patterns, gave rise to opposite but predictable results. In the first case, the worker who shirked his duty or failed to show up for the job was not hurting an impersonal employer. It was his own work group that he was letting down. Social mechanisms emanating from the close-knit relationships among the workers (many of whom were from the same caste) were turned into powerful motivating stimuli. These people were now self-employed, in their own "family" firm, and group loyalty became the motivating factor. In the second situation, no such mechanism was employed. Consequently, given the limited aspirations of many of the workers, they ceased working as soon as they had satisfied their immediate cash needs. Since the higher wage rate allowed them to reach this point more quickly, absenteeism rose. There were no counterbalancing mechanisms and consequently management's action had an effect opposite to what was intended.

A few Indian and British companies surveyed, as well as some U.S. subsidiaries, had introduced effective worker-incentive programs. One U.S. subsidiary used piece rates in several of its plants. In most cases standards were rather loose, although the company has tightened many of them recently with the support of its union. For several years, management had tried to introduce various kinds of productivity-sharing programs, but the union demanded greater fixed bonuses in addition. Recently, a 50-50 productivity-sharing plan was established and it has been quite effective. Many of the jobs on piece rates have become from two to four times more productive than they were on fixed wage payments.

The company has experienced much greater resistance to piece rates at its newer plants, primarily because it has established tighter standards to go along with newer and more productive equipment it installed. It has begun to experiment with various kinds of group incentives linked to group or departmental output, and various bonuses linked to total plant performance for indirect production personnel. However, the basic trend has been toward more fixed hourly wages. The problem is augmented by high "Dearness" (cost of living) allowances that must be paid to workers. Since these often exceed basic pay, piece rate systems used have not generally provided an adequate incentive to raise productivity.

A unique — for India at least — cost reduction program has been in effect at the above U.S. subsidiary since the early 1960s, patterned after the program used in the parent company's domestic operations. The program is enterprise-wide and involves improvement suggestions from all levels of personnel. It was introduced after considerable training and preparation.

The stress is on challenge, satisfaction, recognition, praise, and the possibility of merit increases and promotions. Bonuses are not given for suggestions. However, cost reduction committees in the different plants and at different levels of the firm select a limited number of the best proposals implemented each period, and their initiators and key collaborators are awarded prizes which range from 25 rupees to a maximum of 500 rupees each (500 rupees is roughly equivalent to the monthly pay of a highly skilled worker). Higher levels of management and technical personnel are not entitled to such prizes, since striving for continuous improvement in operations is felt to be part of their jobs. Production workers do not receive monetary rewards either, because of union and other problems, but they are encouraged to make suggestions; only white collar workers can actually receive prizes.

During the 1960s the net savings achieved with this program for the subsidiary as a whole ranged from about 25 to nearly 50 percent of the firm's after tax net profits each year. Foreign exchange savings alone accounted for about 15 to 30 percent of the net profitability of the program each year. They reached their peak during the 1965-67 period. Reinforcement and pressure from higher management has had to be applied to maintain the program's momentum. It has clearly had a positive motivational impact on many personnel, not only at the firm's plants, but also in its offices.

It is interesting to make some comparisons between the results of this program at the subsidiary and in the comparable domestic operations of the parent company. In the United States one out of every three or four suggestions have been implemented. At the subsidiary, one out of every 2.5 to 3.5 have been put into effect. Net savings in relation to total plant costs have typically ranged between 2.5 and 5 percent at both the domestic and Indian plants. However, the net profitability per implemented proposal has averaged about $4500 to $5500 annually in U.S. operations and only $1500 to $3500 (at the official exchange rate) at the subsidiary. The larger scale of operations in the United States probably accounts for much of this difference, along with much higher labor costs.

A large and diversified British firm, which produces consumer goods and agro-industry products, has had considerable success with the incentive systems it has been using in its plants. Good union relations have been very important in this regard. About 4,000 of its 5,000 plant workers have been on incentive programs, most of them involving group rates and bonuses based largely on performance and productivity. Many auxiliary employees, such as maintenance personnel, share in these incentives.

Most of the U.S. drug and chemical plants surveyed in India were making little or no use of piece rates, with the notable exception of packaging work in some cases. Several of their parents company's drug plants — but few of their chemical plants — in the United States have made considerable use of piece rates, chiefly for relatively unskilled and manual jobs. Only a few of the indigenous drug and/or chemical firms have tried piece rates or other worker incentives tied to job performance, and in most cases they have turned out to be ineffective and have been dropped.

In India's engineering and heavy industry sectors relatively little use is made of worker incentives as compared to these sectors in the United States. Of those firms surveyed which have been using such incentives, the foreign companies and collaborations have generally been more successful in relating them to performance. Most of the indigenous firms have had no industrial engineering staff to set job standards, although some of them have talked about doing this for years. Typical in this regard was one large, multiplant, Indian engineering company. Although 70 percent of its workers at one plant have been on piece rates, and from 25 to 50 percent at some of its other plants, very little serious attention has been given to the standards which have been used, how they have been determined, or how and when they should be revised.

In addition to its regular Provident Fund, an indigenous flashlight company started a Welfare Trust where the equivalent of one month's pay for each employee is deposited by the firm each year. A worker who joined the firm at 100 rupees per month, for example, and retired 30 years later at a salary of 300 rupees per month would receive shares having a face value of 15,000 to 18,000 rupees. The dividend return being about 20 percent (on face value), he would be assured of an after retirement income equal to the amount he was earning at retirement. It is not compulsory for the employee to take the stock. If he prefers cash for any reason, he can get a lump sum payment, which would be approximately 20,000 rupees in the example above. In addition to this stock retirement program, the firm has recently begun to give stock options to its personnel, including the workers. Although these stock programs are not really based on merit or individual performance, they have a major impact on employee loyalty or morale, if not on productivity. The company's turnover has been very low, its absenteeism rate relatively low for India, and it has generally had very good union relations.

Another fertile approach to motivating the work force indirectly is through union-management relations. However, in most cases, major U.S., other foreign, and Indian companies saw the unions as adversaries, to be fought and even subverted at every turn. Much of this was due to the political activities of the unions which often strained internal relationships over matters which did not directly involve the companies; however, with a few exceptions, little attempt was made to establish constructive relationships with the unions and to use these relationships to achieve higher productivity and closer ties with the work force.

RESTRICTIVE WORK PRACTICES

No distinct patterns emerged with regard to the amount of productive effort wasted as a result of restrictive work practices, with the exception of problems arising from union-management conflicts during the course of labor negotiations, in which U.S. firms suffered more.

Workers in both Indian and U.S. firms have definite ideas concerning the amount of effort they are willing to devote to their tasks. In the absence of effective motivating forces to change this pattern, the Indian worker's "fair days output" tends to be much lower than that of the U.S. worker. Often it is because he does not know how to think his way to greater output, although he may actually work harder in a physical sense. Not only does this lack of productivity manifest itself in his work pace but it also shows up in terms of "featherbedding" — nonproductive assistants, etc. Although U.S. firms generally tended to resist the establishment of such positions, most yielded, at least to some extent, because the skilled workers insisted, and it was necessary to employ helpers if one wished to hire or retain skilled men.

ABSENTEEISM

Absenteeism (net of holidays) generally runs considerably higher in developing countries than in the United States. There are many external and internal reasons for this. Various sociological-cultural and educational constraints relating to human motivation and behavior which have already been discussed contribute greatly to absenteeism. Legal and union constraints, which make it very difficult to dismiss employees or to discipline them effectively, also play major roles. Political unrest is also a major factor, as is the relatively poor health and stamina of workers. Poor local transportation is another contributing factor.

However, even firms in the poorest countries can reduce absenteeism considerably if they have the know-how and desire to do so. They can make a concentrated effort to recruit and hire personnel whose backgrounds make it less likely that they will be absent frequently. They can upgrade the health of their labor force and provide transportation for them. They can experiment with motivational techniques and supervisory practices which build employee loyalty, increase job satisfaction, and lead to lower absenteeism.

In all but one case studied, overall absenteeism rates were significantly higher at the U.S. subsidiaries during the 1960s than at their parent companies' U.S.-based operations. In most cases, absenteeism has been at least two to three times higher at the subsidiaries. In both the United States and India, worker absenteeism has generally been considerably higher than that of other kinds of employees especially managerial personnel.

Absenteeism in Indian industry typically averages between 12 and 20 percent, and runs as high as 40 percent or more during the marriage, festival, and harvest seasons, and immediately following payday. It is common for firms to experience average absenteeism rates of more than 20 percent, and this has been the case in recent years, at all of the smaller indigenous firms surveyed. A 20 percent level has been acceptable to most of them. Even larger Indian companies seem to believe that a 12 to 15 percent annual rate is normal and acceptable, and most are not as concerned about high absenteeism as the U.S. subsidiaries studied.

Absenteeism has been, on the whole, somewhat lower at U.S. subsidiaries surveyed than at indigenous companies in the same geographic area, and to a somewhat lesser extent in the same industry. Firms or plants which have had greater union problems have generally had higher absenteeism rates. with a few notable exceptions. In general, absenteeism has been higher in Bengal, particularly in the Calcutta area, in recent years than in most other parts of India. This has been due primarily to political problems, civil unrest, and union agitation. Absenteeism at firms in the Calcutta area reached a peak around the time of the 1967 elections, dropped slightly shortly thereafter, and then began to rise again.

Many U.S. and British subsidiaries, and a few of the indigenous firms, have tried various incentives and bonus schemes to cut down on absenteeism, including double pay for not taking casual or sick leave. However such incentives have not had a very significant effect on reducing absenteeism, and in most cases, substantial reductions achieved in absenteeism have been short-lived.

For example, when an American production manager came to an Indian-controlled heavy engineering company several years ago, he succeeded in cutting plant absenteeism from 26 to 16 percent. He required that all existing and new employees be immunized against tuberculosis, cholera, and other diseases. He tried to recruit workers who seemed to be relatively healthy and strong. He hired a nutrition specialist to determine the kinds of meals to serve employees (although the workers revolted against the serving of more wheat and less rice). He provided free company bus service, offered extra pay for lower absenteeism, and generally did much to improve the work environment and morale in the plant. However, within six months, absenteeism increased again to over 20 percent, and in less than a year it was up to about 25 percent. Interference by the Indian managing director was largely responsible for this. The American manager eventually left, and absenteeism soon skyrocketed to about 30 percent.

A large diversified U.S. subsidiary had overall average absenteeism rates in the range of 8 to 9 percent in the early and mid-1960s, with peak rates hitting 20 to 25 percent. It averaged between 10 and 11 percent during the 1967-69 period, with peaks of 25 to 30 percent. The highest rates of absenteeism, 12 to 14 percent, were experienced at its Calcutta plants. The average rates at its plants in Lucknow and Madras have been around 10 percent, but in its Bombay chemical plant they were only 7 percent. During the early start-up period of its Hyderabad plant, it was only 3 percent, primarily because most of the workers were on probation, but the rate reached 6 percent soon thereafter.

The overall absenteeism rate in recent years at one of this company's major competitors (in Bombay) has been in the range of 12 to 13 percent. Another competitor, in Allahabad, has had average absenteeism rates in the vicinity of 6 to 8 percent. This company has had an employee stock plan, as well as many other benefits. It is Muslim-owned and employs many Muslims.

The major indigenous drug and chemical companies surveyed which are located in Bengal have had average absenteeism rates of 16 to 20 percent and over in recent years. The overall rate at a large, multiplant, Indian engineering firm has been about 16 percent, with rates of 18 to 20 percent at its plants in the Calcutta area in the late 1960s. A diversified multiplant British company had an overall rate of about 12 to 13 percent in recent years, and 13 to 14 percent at its Bengal operations.

The U.S. subsidiary studied which had the lowest absenteeism rates was a drug firm in the Bombay area. Its rate ran in the vicinity of 5 percent in the early and mid-1960s, and only 3 to 4 percent in more recent years. This is the only U.S. subsidiary surveyed that had lower plant absenteeism than its parent company's domestic operations, and an overall rate nearly as low. Although the subsidiary became unionized only a few years ago, it has had excellent union relations. It was one of the very few firms surveyed that showed a noticeable decline in absenteeism in recent years.

Another major U.S. drug subsidiary headquartered in Bombay had an average absenteeism of about 17 or 18 percent in 1969, down from 24 percent in 1968. Transportation and labor problems revolving largely around the firm's new plant (which is quite a distance away from the Bombay metropolitan area) have been the chief reasons. Bus service to the new plant was finally begun in the summer of 1969. At the firm's old plant in the heart of the city, absenteeism averaged only 11 to 12 percent, and in some periods when the firm had good union and labor relations it was as low as 5 percent.

Absenteeism rates at other U.S. drug and chemical firms surveyed in the Bombay area in recent years have ranged from about 7 to 13 percent. For Indian firms of these types in this region the range has been from 9 to 15 percent.

A new large chemical company in the Bombay area (a joint venture with European interests) had the lowest absenteeism rate encountered: 2 percent. Management credits this to the fact that the company pays employees exceptionally well, provides many benefits, employs no illiterates (almost all personnel have at least secondary education), and has had very good personnel and union relations.

A large indigenous drug and chemical firm in Gujarat had overall average absenteeism rates of 7 to 8 percent in the first half of the 1960s, with higher rates for staff than workers. There was considerable staff turnover around the mid-60s and staff absenteeism then dropped substantially. During the 1966-68 period absenteeism averaged 5 to 6 percent, with worker absenteeism being higher than that of staff. The company was anticipating a significant increase in absenteeism when the Employee State Insurance and related sickness benefit average was increased by law in this region in March 1969, bringing the extended benefits more in line with the ones provided in other parts of the country, including Bombay, Calcutta, and Delhi. Absenteeism averaged about 7 percent between March and July of 1969 and around 8 percent in the second half of that year.

SUMMARY AND CONCLUDING REMARKS

Many top-level U.S. subsidiary managers accept low productivity and high absenteeism as facts of life. They often attempt to compensate by eliminating the labor content of tasks through automation and mechanization. Relatively few tackle the problems directly and effectively. Yet the Indian employee, including the worker, when properly motivated, directed, and trained, often proves to be as productive as his U.S. counterpart. For example:

> Mr. V. was considered to be so effective by Indian textile mill owners that they purchased textile equipment from the U.S. company he worked for only on the condition that Mr. V. would personally supervise the installation. Most of the Indian managers did not know why he was effective — they just knew that he could install the new equipment, train the workforce, and get the entire operation up to peak efficiency in less than half the time anyone else could.
>
> In talking to Mr. V., it became apparent that the main reason for his success was a very sharp deviation from normal practices. Upon his arrival at a job site, he would put the area off limits to all personnel not directly involved. He would then talk with the company's supervisors and on the basis of these discussions, he would very carefully select his work crew. Once he had assembled his work crew, he began extensive briefing sessions for the workers (almost unheard of in India), explaining the tasks that lay ahead, helping them with the actual installation, and teaching them personally how to run the equipment. He had no hesitation in rolling up his sleeves and getting grease all over his hands. Contrary to the common belief that by lowering himself to the status of the workers he would lose their respect, Mr. V. soon developed an extremely dedicated workforce. His workers showed great personal loyalty to him and to each other, his absenteeism rates were low and his productivity, he claimed, was as high as that of any similar installation process conducted in the United States. In a well documented case, a competitor took seven months to do a job that Mr. V. did in three, and upon completion of the installation had only brought his workforce up to 70 percent of the efficiency levels attained by Mr. V.

> In a follow-up study of one of the machine rooms installed by Mr. V. (after he had left) it was discovered that productivity had fallen off sharply and absenteeism increased substantially, although in both cases the figures were still significantly better than those found in other departments within the same company. The shift can largely be attributed to the transition back to more traditional Indian supervision and motivational patterns.

Although there are wide variations in cultural values and attitudes among people in different societies and of different social backgrounds, there are still characteristics which appear to be basic to human nature. Most people like to feel reasonably secure in their life and work. They like to feel that they belong to a group, and that they are respected or at least accepted by their superiors and subordinates, as well as by their peers. They like to feel that their tasks are meaningful, and to know what they are doing, and why. The establishment of such conditions can do much to improve relations and motivate personnel to higher productivity and better overall performance. Much too often, these basic needs are overlooked: the typical Indian worker learns only "how" to do something — and frequently not even that very well. He rarely learns "why." In this area, U.S. practices and techniques could make very positive contributions to the efficiency of operations.

A classic case has been written about a Ceylonese worker who was hired to maintain pressure in a boiler.[1] When he was placed on the job, all he was told was that when the needle on the gauge dropped below a certain point he was to add fuel to the furnace. When the needle rose above the point he was to stop. In this manner, the proper pressure needed to provide the steam supply for the plant would be maintained. No explanation was given other than that. One day, the company was surprised to discover that the pressure had fallen off and upon investigation they found the employee fast asleep in the boiler room with a pair of pliers jamming the needle to the desired position on the gauge.

The worker could easily have been an Indian, and the situation is unusual for a poor and developing country only in that it showed a fair amount of initiative on the part of the worker. This kind of an introduction to a new job is quite common. The assumption prevails that the worker knows nothing and cares less. Consequently, he is given only the simplest and most rudimentary information necessary to perform the tasks under "normal" circumstances. Top management which leaves the direction, leadership, training, and motivational processes strictly to lower-level supervisory personnel is likely to discover — if it ever investigates — that such activities are typified by the above example.

It is the responsibility of top executives to develop skills and to impress upon middle and lower management the need for effective direction, supervision, motivation and leadership, as well as the importance of training. This can usually only be done effectively by higher-level example.

CHAPTER 15   FOOTNOTE

1. "Ceylon Plywood Company," a case copyrighted in 1962 by the Board of Trustees of Leland Stanford Junior University (ICH 8G40).

CHAPTER 16
UNION-MANAGEMENT
RELATIONS

INTRODUCTION

The growth of trade unionism in developing countries presents special problems for the management of overseas subsidiaries of U.S. and other foreign firms. These problems differ from those experienced in the parent countries for three basic reasons. First, the union movement is relatively new in developing countries, in most cases having gained momentum in the post-World War II period. The newness of the concept of unionism, the low educational and skill levels of membership, and the crusading zeal of many union leaders resulted in an instability and a lack of maturity which was characteristic of U.S. unionism perhaps sixty years ago. Second, most of the unions are political in nature, strongly affiliated as they are with major political parties. Consequently, their interaction with any particular firm may be affected by factors outside the direct relationships between management and workers. Finally the vulnerability of foreign companies to political and social pressures makes them prime targets for union efforts to introduce changes in the employment scene.

The problems of dealing with unionism in developing nations are often acerbated by the personal sensitivities of the manager, if he is foreign to the local environment. The days when the foreigner was boss have, like colonialism, been relegated to the history books. Today, more often than not, the foreign firm finds itself in a symbiotic relationship with a host who can, at least politically, call the final shots. Where local governments are subject to strong countervailing forces, the foreign company may find itself in many disquieting situations — constantly under threat of political attack, and occasionally under siege. The individual manager is likely to take "anti-foreign" attacks in a personal manner and to conclude that unions are destructive forces, to be avoided if possible and to be treated as hostile parties.

NEWNESS OF THE LABOR MOVEMENT

In most developing nations, the labor movement is for all practical purposes very new. Only with the growth in industrialization and the move towards larger, more impersonal organizational structures, has the union movement become necessary or practical. Whereas managers who contemplate developing a new industry usually have access to industrial and managerial processes developed elsewhere in the world (and in many cases, may have been trained abroad), labor union leaders have little opportunity to learn from the history and experience of labor movements in other parts of the world; this is because the union movement springs from local sources. In its early stages, like business management, unionism is not seen as a professional movement, which could benefit from and requires specific managerial skills.

The result is that labor movements in developing countries today closely parallel the development stages of unions in more developed nations many years ago. Similar issues, similar methods for dealing with them, and the same kind of emotional atmosphere which surrounded the labor movement in the United States at the turn of the century typify the Indian labor scene today.

There are several important distinctions, however, to be made between current labor movements in developing nations and the early labor movement in the United States. One such difference is in the educational backgrounds of the workers.[1] In most developing nations, union members are illiterate, or poorly educated; moreover, they are frequently working away from home, and have few recreational outlets. Consequently, the worker can be an extremely volatile quantity in the hands of a skillful manipulator. Rumors can be fanned into major emotional issues very rapidly. The worker, unused to the restraints of city life, (usually because he has only recently left the farm), can be incited to violence much more easily than his U.S. counterpart. In many situations, it appears that industrial disputes may even serve as a welcome relief from the monotony of day-to-day drudgery.

Both the U.S. and the local manager are frequently faced with difficult problems in dealing with the labor movement. However, the local manager is usually more aware of the nature and volatility of the worker and more likely to accept conditions for what they are and act accordingly. The foreign manager is often misled, either because he tends to ignore differences, or because he overreacts to situations when they occur.

The nature and volatility of the relatively new labor movement in India can be illustrated by the example of a labor dispute which occurred in a South Indian company. This dispute, although certainly not typical, is illustrative of the type of thing that can happen.

The Gopal Machinery Company[2] was a medium sized company located in a large Indian city. The company's workers were organized by two labor unions, only one of which (affiliated with the political party in power) was recognized. The second union represented only a small number of workers and was affiliated with an opposition party. It had been trying to gain ascendency and had been involved in a number of serious (and occasionally violent) disputes with company officials and officers of the rival union. The situation steadily worsened, finally culminating in a show-down strike. The second union was determined to keep the company closed until both management and the work force acceded to its demands to supplant the other union. Consequently, approximately 30 strong-arm men were hired to obstruct the gates of the plant and to support the union's picketers by physically prohibiting entry into the premises. On the morning of the strike the group of hired "enforcers" left the union office to take their posts at the plant gate.

Located along the route from the union office to the plant of Gopal Machinery Company was Gopal Equipments Manufacturing Company, a totally unrelated firm which manufactured farm implements. It was a smaller company, not unionized and had excellent management-labor relations.

Somehow, the group got its instructions mixed, and upon seeing the sign for Gopal Equipments Manufacturing Company, thought that it had arrived at the destination. Pickets were immediately established, and several workers who attempted to enter the plant were beaten. The owner's car was stoned when he drove through the compound gate, although he was allowed to pass. Those workers who had not been completely intimidated remained in the street outside of the plant.

Shortly thereafter, the union officers, having discovered the mistake, arrived on the scene. However, when they realized that Gopal Equipments was not unionized, they only dispatched two-thirds of the pickets to Gopal Machinery, retaining approximately ten at the gates of Gopal Equipments. They then proceeded to coerce and organize the employees of Gopal Equipments.

The owner of Gopal Equipments was shocked by the way his employees were caught up in the emotional pitch of matters at the time the incident was precipitated. The subject of a union had never come up within the plant, and yet the workers were convinced within one day that they had been deprived of many of the benefits of their labor because they were not unionized. The initial demand to management for the establishment of the union was accompanied by an ultimatum demanding more than a 100 percent increase in wage rates. When the owner refused to accede to the wage rate demand, the union pointed to this as proof of the company's reluctance to allow the workers a decent livelihood. Some of the firm's loyal workers who objected were threatened and two were beaten. The emotional pitch reached such a point, that several workers went on hunger strikes outside the plant gates.

The dispute was finally ended by the courts almost four months later and resulted in the establishment of a union (although not the same union which had initiated the strike). Many important workers and customers had been lost, and the company was close to bankruptcy. The court decision required no change in the wage structure, although a bonus plan was instituted which was to commence only once the company had regained its former financial health.

The above example illustrates the unusual developments which can occur where unions in less developed nations are involved. The foreign manager and firm must anticipate the unexpected, and, even more important, be willing to deal with it. In many cases, the situations may seem so absurd that he may refuse to take them seriously, and only after a strike ensues and begins to drag out interminably does he discover that the matter cannot be treated lightly. By that time, emotions may run so high and the positions of the protagonists have become so set that many formerly viable and mutually satisfactory solutions are no longer feasible.

NATURE OF UNIONS

The typical worker in the developing nation has neither the organizational skills nor the interest required to establish a union; he is uneducated, relatively unambitious, and unknowing in the ways of the modern world. In many cases, he has left his family on the farm and come to the city to earn money. His motivation is neither to better himself nor to seek adventure. It is simply survival. The joint family system eventually overtaxes the land which a family owns to the point where it is incapable of sustaining the number of mouths it must feed. Each succeeding generation further dilutes productive resources. Eventually, the young, able-bodied males are literally driven off the farm and into the city.

Unfortunately, the union practices reminiscent of the early days of the industrial revolution are matched by local management practices which are often just as atavistic. Low pay scales, long working hours, poor working conditions, and other practices which have long since been legislated out of existence (at least in theory, and largely in practice) in the industrially advanced world are commonplace. Initially, few of the workers feel that they are being exploited. They have never known anything better, and have nothing to use as a standard for comparison. In fact, in many cases, the city with its distractions and its conveniences is a great improvement in their lives. It is only when the pace of industrialization begins to quicken, or when outsiders start exerting their influence that the worker starts to recognize the possibility of something better.

The major thrust towards industrialization in less-developed nations usually comes from the entry of foreign firms. Much of the spurt in the industrial activity is either directly attributable to foreign companies or is generated indirectly by foreign competition and/or example. As firms grow, the close "family" relationships begin to loosen and operations become more impersonal. The worker's feelings of loyalty begin to weaken as personal contact with the "family head" starts to diminish and rewards become less personal (e.g., more economic) in nature. Essentially, the atmosphere created in the industrial enterprise starts to deviate from his expectations of the "natural" pattern of things. As a result of these changes, several things happen.

First, the worker becomes more vulnerable to outside influences. He no longer has many of the restraints and behavioral mores imposed by the extended or joint family system, and, as various managerial levels intercede between himself and the owner, he starts to lose his close identity with ownership. He is also a free agent in the city, with few daily family ties since his family is likely to be many miles distant. His main source of interaction and camaraderie is therefore among fellow workers, who are in a similar situation. This sets the stage for the outside organizer.

A second important factor is that worker "exploitation" is often regarded as an offshoot of Westernization. Since the process of industrialization largely derives from Western ideas, values, and organizations, the formation of an active union movement is often seen as a necessity to protect the working man from some of the evils of these foreign influences. This does not mean that the labor union will be anti-foreign. It does mean, however, that Western values (and therefore Western companies) play an important role in the thinking of people who organize the unions.

A third factor relates to the impetus toward union establishment. The initial impetus does not usually spring from the working class, but from the more educated and politically astute elements of society. This factor, coupled with the fact that unionism is often a result of reaction to Western values, increases the probability that anti-establishment, anti-Western individuals will be attracted to the union movement. In India, for example, many of the labor leaders are lawyers, among them leaders of opposition groups with strong anti-American sentiments. Besides being well educated, they know the local worker and his culture, and are familiar with the complex Indian legal structure. They see labor unions as a valuable weapon in the political arena.

Finally, since the union movement does not grow from within (i.e., it is organized by people outside of the laboring class), its objectives usually go beyond labor-management relationships within a given firm or industry. The initial stimulus often springs from the organizer's desires to attain political power or personal notoriety. It is for this reason that so many of the labor unions in developing nations are affiliated with political parties. In fact "affiliated" is too weak a description, since in many cases, the unions are major decision-making and action units of their parent organizations.

The significance of this situation may be great to a foreign company operating in a developing land. Such companies must deal not only with their workers, but also with the nation's politics. The U.S. executive can find it very frustrating to discover that his company is emersed in a political brouhaha which has not direct relevance to his primary purposes of operation, and which may focus on matters which, in the United States, would be handled on the floor of Congress. Often, two very distinct and separate issues become enmeshed into one and, in addition to facing problems relating to employment, morale, and productivity, the executive may also have to deal with outside matters which relate only very indirectly to his particular operations, but the outcome of which can have critical implications for his business.

Shortly after a new labor agreement for the coming year had been reached, the managing director of one U.S. subsidiary received a delegation from his labor union. The company had established good relations with the union, and although there were some tense moments prior to the settlement, everything seemed to be going smoothly. The settlement contained a no-strike agreement. The delegation apologetically informed the managing director that the work force was going on a one-day strike during the following week. They explained that they were giving advance notice at this time so that the company could prepare for the shutdown. The political party with which they were affiliated had decided to call a wildcat strike in an attempt to close down all industrial activities in that city on that particular day. The union leaders informed the managing director that "this would not affect the excellent relationships which had been established." They explained that they felt the company had treated them very fairly in the negotiations; however, they had to go out because it was necessary to achieve certain political ends. By bringing activities in the city to a halt, they hoped to intimidate the local government into acceding to some of their demands — for better municipal transport, lower fares, and other social changes.

The above incident is unusual only in that the company's union relations were good enough to make the officials feel compelled to give advance notice and to offer an explanation. However, unions frequently take action against a particular company or industry only because by so doing they can exert pressure on the economy which will force the government to take the political action they desire.

This process has another unfortunate consequence. In most developing nations, a small number of industries are vital to the country's economic wellbeing. These may be particular manufacturing, mining, or agricultural operations, or transportation or communications networks. To strengthen their political bases, unions often engage in bitter and incessant battles to gain control over the work force in these particular sectors. The purposes of these battles are strategic in nature and usually have little to do with the betterment of the workers. However, many companies have found themselves in the midst of fierce disputes between two or more unions battling for the prize. Since foreign interests are usually well represented and often dominant in these critical sectors, foreign firms may be right at the center of the battleground. Consequently, they bear the brunt of the skirmishes which pave the way for future political action, and will face the impact of the political activity once the base has been established.

SPECIAL POSITION OF THE FOREIGN COMPANY

In many cases, unions attack foreign companies not as an expression of anti-foreign sentiments but because it is the shortest path to the desired end result. Because the union has a better chance of coercing foreign companies into initiating changes in industry wage and benefit structures, these companies are often their first target.

The leader of an extremely militant union whose membership was concentrated in an industry dominated by foreign firms, many of them American, was described by the foreign managing directors of some of these firms as "paranoid," "jingoistic," "bitterly anti-American," and "suffering from severe megalomania." They unanimously agreed that he was waging a personal vendetta against foreign companies, and U.S. companies in particular. Many of the indigenous managing directors denied this. They saw him as a shrewd operator, a little prone to the dramatic, but effective at making the most of opportunities to achieve his goals.

In the course of an interview, this leader gave evidence of just the opposite of the anti-foreign feeling attributed to him. He recognized the fact that U.S. companies were among the best paying in the industry, and that without them, much less progress would have been made in labor relations. He felt that, at least with respect to wages, they examined demands in a reasonable fashion, and he admired the fact that they dealt above the table and honored their agreements. However, he indicated that they did not know how to bargain, that they were "easy touches," and that, consequently, his union was able to use them very effectively. His comments contained no personal animosity; to the contrary, he expressed admiration for the managerial skills of foreign firms and for the positive contributions they were making to the country, and wished that more indigenous firms would follow their lead. Nevertheless, his gratitude for what the Indian labor movement had been able to accomplish through them would probably not have been regarded as a great compliment by those firms' managing directors.

LEGAL BASIS OF UNIONISM

In many developing nations, the legal framework tends to encourage unionism. In an effort to foster the wellbeing of the worker, the law often facilitates the formation of trade unions. On the other hand, the legal structure frequently details the nature of the relationship between managements and workers to such an extent that both parties are left with little freedom to negotiate. It is useful to examine a few of these legal constraints and to observe the effect that they have on industrial operations.

The Indian Trades Union Act of 1926 provided that a trade union may be registered by any seven or more individuals. Once the union has been registered, it is entitled to all of the rights accorded to a union under the law. Although this figure has since been modified, the number of individuals required to establish a recognized union remains very small. Consequently, as disputes arise within a particular company, splinter groups often form and establish their own unions, and political parties are likely to saturate firms with their unions. In India, it is not unusual for a group of workers (e.g., the skilled machinists) to be represented by three or more unions. Political parties may themselves splinter quickly; for example, when the Indian Communist party split between pro-Moscow and pro-Peking factions, this gave rise to a number of new unions. The consequences of this may be serious, since a company may find itself buffeted by forces which change at every political turn. As they vie for power, unions will often resort to tactics to make their competitors look bad, among them violence and industrial sabotage. Frequently, a company becomes a major battleground for opposing political factions.

One of the problems which arises from this proliferation of unions relates to the question of recognition. A company is required to recognize only one union, and the law requires it to do so only when that union controls more than 50 percent of the work force. Consequently, there are many situations where no union has a sufficient number of members to force recognition. Under these circumstances, the company may bargain with whomsoever it chooses (or with nobody for that matter). When a company recognizes one union, the other unions are free to challenge the recognition in the courts.

A company may enter into an agreement with a recognized or nonrecognized union. When the agreement is concluded, the provisions of the agreement are supplied to the authorities. Within a specified period of time, any of the unions which were not party to the agreement may raise their objections. The courts will consider the issues, decide on the validity of the objections, and settle the matter. Once settled, the agreement is technically binding on all parties. Consequently, the proliferation of unions, even when one of them is clearly recognized, can result in lengthy court battles before a final decision is concluded.

> A large Indian public sector firm received a set of demands from a union in early 1961. The matter first went to conciliation, which failed. By mid-1962, it went to arbitration. The award was made in 1964. Management obtained an order staying the award while it appealed the case. The courts heard the appeal in 1965. The workers, at this point, threatened a strike in spite of a court order prohibiting a strike during the legal proceedings. Consequently, an interim settlement (granting what management thought was fair) was made, and was retroactive to 1961. The matter was not finally settled until early 1966.

Although court procedures are supposed to be binding on all parties, aggrieved minority unions often ignore the legalities. The net result can be a long history of labor unrest and disruption.

> The workers of a large Indian company were represented by two unions. Seventy-five percent belonged to the larger of the two, with 15 to 20 percent enrolled in the smaller. During the course of labor negotiations, an issue arose concerning the amount of bonus which would be paid. Although no strike ensued, the dispute dragged on for eight months during which time the company was plagued by minor and major work slowdowns. The issue was finally settled between the company and the recognized union. The courts overruled the objections raised by the minority union and upheld the settlement as just and fair. Shortly thereafter, the minority union went out on strike. The strike lasted several months and involved a great deal of violence. Management indicated that it took more than three months after operations resumed to attain the levels of productivity which had existed prior to the strike.

Although the rules concerning the formation of a union are strictly applied, the laws relating to the honoring of agreements can often be enforced only against management because of the physical and political problems of enforcing union compliance (although, in some countries ruled by military regimes, very severe measures are taken against labor leaders who cause disruption). The net effect is that the bases of honoring agreements rest on 1) the establishment of reasonably good relationships between management and the workers and 2) the stability of the political situation.

Management, although relatively powerless in the second area, can do much to establish the types of relationships which will pave the way to trust and cooperation.

Because of the difficulty in holding the unions to their part of the agreement, many managements take a very strong anti-union stance. This is true of both foreign and indigenous firms. However, on the whole, indigenous firms seem to be more flexible and less emotional in their dealings, and do not seem to require the degree of finality that the foreign firms seek. This is probably attributable to the fact that they have never known the relatively stable labor conditions that many foreign firms experienced at home.

MANAGEMENT ATTITUDES TOWARDS UNIONS

It is probably safe to say that few managements in developing nations look happily on the prospect of unionism within their companies. There seems to be a basic difference, however, between the approaches taken by local and foreign companies, although the major goal of both is usually to thwart union activities.

First, local managements are more complacent and less sensitive to union threats. They do not fear charges of exploitation with the same emotionalism as the foreign firms do. They cannot be accused of "drawing out the country's life's blood." They are part of the local power structure and have a power base from which to operate. Consequently, they often tolerate much less harrassment and disturbance from the unions than their foreign counterparts will accept. They resort to lockouts more frequently, challenge the courts more openly, and may even hire their own strong-arm men to counteract those provided by the unions. They are much more likely to take direct and forceful action, while the foreign firm pursues a more low-key approach to direct dealings and spends more of its efforts in seeking legal remedies.

The second area where considerable differences arise is in the means used to combat the formation of unionism. Often indigenous firms will attempt to form company unions once they see the evidence of outside union organizers at work. The foreign company is less likely to pursue this avenue. The reasons are probably largely attributable to self-confidence in dealing with the local environment. The indigenous firm often believes that, through a company union, it can convince the workers that they can obtain all of the benefits of unionism without outside influence, and management has confidence in its own ability to control this type of situation. The U.S. firms are likely to feel that the formation of a company union is tantamount to clutching a viper to one's breast. "This just makes it easier for an outside organizer to come in and take over." Unfortunately, in India, such sentiments were frequently supported by fact. Here again, knowledge of the local environment was probably a great advantage to the Indian manager — a knowledge which the foreign manager did not possess, thus making the take-overs more likely.

The Indian personnel director of a U.S. company which had recently experienced a great improvement in its union relations stated the following:

> Mr. X [the managing director] no longer gets involved in our industrial relations, so ours have become more stable than most of our competitors'. He leaves things to the Indian managers. As a result, our labor relations are better than in other foreign companies. We know how to deal with the workers and the union leaders.
>
> Before, when these matters were handled by the managing director, local managers were not taken into confidence, and consequently they sat on the fence in labor problems, even though they knew what the union was going to do. They had no way to communicate their knowledge to top management and had to sit by while one mistake after another was made. One of the big problems was the foreign managers were too soft. There were too many changes and they weren't here long enough. Each man looks at things from a short-term viewpoint. He doesn't want to have his ratings marred by a labor problem or a plant shutdown. He must maintain production. When this function was turned over to the Indian managers, they were able to use what they knew, and short-range considerations were no longer important.

There is an area where U.S. and Indian companies are agreed on the objective, but not on the methodology to be employed to reach it. Managers of both nationalities express the thought that "workers will not pay dues to a union if they get nothing in return." Consequently, they often fight unionism by making offers which the union can not better through negotiating. To U.S. executives, this frequently means carefully assessing the minimum settlement that will be approved by the courts, offering that package to the union (or the work force) by the end of the negotiations, and then refusing to budge. If the union then strikes, or causes any major disruption, management can turn to the workers, after a court decision has vindicated their position as fair and equitable, and thereby demonstrate that the union has only created hardships for all concerned. This approach, although rational by U.S. standards, invariably evokes only greater bitterness between management and workers.

On the other hand, Indian firms which pursue a "nothing for your dues" strategy often offer very generous settlements to the workers prior to formal negotiations. During negotiations, their offers are much less generous, although still within limits they think acceptable to the courts. In some cases, the offers to the work force are so planned that, should they be contested in court, the courts may actually reduce the amounts. In such a situation, the union has a difficult time coming out ahead.

> One large Indian company faced what seemed to be very difficult labor negotiations. Two major outside unions and a small internal union (recently formed with the covert urging of management) were involved. None was recognized. Management opened negotiations with the smallest of the three — the internal union — and after a reasonable negotiation period, offered the union a five-year settlement on very generous terms. Simultaneously, it fought the demands of the other unions. It was quite evident that the settlement was more generous than the unions could obtain through court procedures. When the outside unions began to use violence as a tactic, the work force rebelled and several union leaders were roughed up. The company, although it still did not recognize the internal union, put the

settlement into effect for all members of the internal union plus any individual workers who would sign the agreement. Within a week the company was able to convince approximately 90 percent of its workers that there was no point in paying dues to outside unions which could not improve on things and only created violence and disruption — and that the five-year settlement would "guarantee" peace and harmony for the future. A few months later, almost 100 percent of the work force had signed the five-year agreement and, for all practical purposes, the two outside unions no longer existed within the plant.

Another difference in attitude towards unions is evident in reactions towards union organizers. The U.S. subsidiaries typically show the greatest concern over the activities of union organizers in the work force, and are likely to take stronger action to counteract their influence than their indigenous counterparts.

The management of one U.S. company suddenly discovered that a first line supervisor[3] was attempting to organize the work force. They immediately began an investigation and learned that he had a record of union-organizing activities (unknown at the time he had been employed). However, in the course of the investigation, they also discovered that his employment application listed educational qualifications which he did not actually possess. At about this time, he also got into a dispute with one of the company's officers for failing to complete a task which was assigned to him, but which he claimed was not within his job category. He was immediately charged with falsification of his employment application and with failure to obey orders. However, rather than take the issue to court (where uncertainty would prevail) management moved him to another position, equivalent in pay and responsibility, but one which the worker considered to be undesirable. He finally quit and that postponed unionization attempts for approximately a year and a half.

A final difference in the attitudes of U.S. and Indian managers concerns the use of the courts. In most companies in India, labor disputes are finally settled in the courts. However, many of the disputes involving indigenous firms are, in reality, resolved prior to the court decisions. The U.S. firm is more likely to use the courts to settle the disputed issues, whereas the Indian company is more likely to use the courts only to put a legal stamp on the agreement.

ISSUES IN UNION MANAGEMENT RELATIONS

One of the factors which inhibits the establishment of good union-management relations is the broad scope of data regarded as proprietary and the cloak of secrecy in which management in developing nations envelops such information. Both U.S. and Indian managers were extremely reluctant to provide any information which might be useful either to government licensing and taxing authorities or to competitors. Consequently many activities were surrounded by security measures worthy of the best spy novels. Top management was often fearful that, should unions (or employees, including officers) obtain data relating to productivity, cost structure, market share, output, etc., the data would leak to the outside world. Since the unions had special motives for using such information, communications barriers were invariably constructed around them and their members. This heightened the degree of suspicion and mistrust between the two groups.

> In one U.S. company, the accounting tasks were divided among clerical personnel in such a manner that no individual could see a complete cost picture. To prevent leakage, no cost data was provided to production personnel. The managing director and the chief accountant personally collected the various accounting data to try to gain a comprehensive picture of operations. However, prior to entering the bargaining session, the union assembled all of the clerks and was usually able to put together a more accurate picture of the company's cost structure than top management had. This information was then used both to justify wage demands and as a form of blackmail, since, by introducing such cost information before a labor tribunal, the union could make it part of the public record. The union was able to gain certain concessions through this process.

The procedure outlined above was used as a standard strategy by many unions. It worked much more successfully against the U.S. companies, primarily because they seemed to be more sensitive about the possibility of disclosure and because many of the Indian firms did not collect accurate data in the first place.

Relationships between managements and unions in developing lands seem to be characterized by mutual distrust. Bargaining in good faith has not yet become a firmly established practice. Consequently, the courts can become the major issue raisers and dispute settlers. There is a legitimate "chicken-and-egg" question here, however — has the preponderant role played by the law given rise to an atmosphere of distrust, or have other factors inherent in the culture fostered situations which require a great deal of court intervention?

It is interesting to note that labor relations are no better in the public sector industries, and in many cases they are worse. Some of the most violent labor disputes which occurred in India during the period of this study took place in public sector firms, and top managers of these firms were very unhappy with the union situation. The comments of the managing director of one such company reveal a major source of contention:

> We have too many wage disputes. The unions force the foreign companies up; they bring the entire industry up; and this puts pressure on the public sector. They [the unions] don't realize that they have to compare us with other government enterprises and not with the private sector.

ISSUES FOR BARGAINING

Many of the issues that are treated in union-management negotiations in developing nations differ from those considered in the United States. Although hours and wages are key issues for negotiation universally, more attention is usually devoted in underdeveloped nations to fringe benefits, and less to managerial matters (e.g., questions concerning methods improvement). In addition, certain issues are excluded from the bargaining process because they are proscribed by law (e.g., grievance procedures). Moreover, many issues which arise in the United States from the administration of incentive systems are absent from the Indian labor scene because fixed wage structures tend to dominate compensation patterns.

A representative labor settlement between an Indian union and management might contain the following types of issues:

1. Classification of workers: this is an area of extreme complexity in India. Only recently have companies started to move towards grouping workers into broad job classifications such as skilled, semi-skilled, and unskilled (with perhaps two or three subclassifications within each unit). In the past, almost every job had a different classification and a different pay scale. In many companies, the work force is divided into 40 or more individual job categories, necessitating an enormous amount of paperwork and creating numerous issues for bargaining purposes.

2. Scales of basic wages and salaries: the nature of the wage scales used in India adds another layer of complexity to union-management relations. Each job category is associated with an extremely detailed pay scale, and each of these is a subject for negotiation. For example, the following scale is used for clerk-typists in one particular firm: 50-5-70-7 ½-160-EB-10-220. This means that the employee will be hired at a rate of 50 rupees a month. Each year, thereafter, he will receive an increment of 5 rupees until he reaches a salary of 70 per month. Thenceforth, his yearly increments will come at the rate of 7½ rupees until he reaches a maximum of 160 per month. At that point he encounters an "efficiency bar." If his performance is considered to be outstanding, his salary continues to grow each year at the rate of 10 rupees per month until he reaches the absolute maximum wage of 220 rupees per month. Thus a man's total wage-earning career is completely mapped out for him with little weight given to merit except for the efficiency bar, which, in this case, comes only after 16 years of employment.

3. Dearness allowance: this is a cost-of-living allowance which often forms a larger portion of total remuneration than the basic salary. Several patterns have been permitted by the courts, and unions often spend a great deal of time negotiating the way in which the dearness allowance will be calculated. The base figures used, the particular indices applied, etc., become important issues.

4. Leave benefits: typically, three types of leave are given — sick leave, casual leave (which is leave which can be taken for various personal purposes), and privileged leave (vacation). Who is eligible and when, and how much time is due are basic issues. These benefits vary according to both length of employment and job category.

5. Various types of allowances: e.g., for house rent, uniforms, etc.

6. Gratuity: this is a sum which accumulates to the workman's account on the basis of the number of years he has been employed. It serves as a retirement plan and is paid to the employee either upon retirement or on termination after long service.

It also accrues to his family in the event of his death. Terms relating to both amount and eligibility are issues for debate.

7. Holidays: India has many holidays. Many of these have been instituted, it would seem, primarily to break up the monotony and tedium of daily life. Each religious group or sect has its own series of holidays. It is not unusual to find 20 to 30 holidays involved in negotiations. The trend is towards reducing these to no more than a dozen, but they are still issues for bargaining. In many cases, holidays are observed on a nonpaid basis.

8. Medical aid: these are provisions concerning operation of the company dispensary, availability of drugs, etc.

9. Incentive schemes: should a company have some type of incentive plan, this is usually a subject for negotiation.

10. Bonuses: the bonus system was originally initiated to stimulate productivity and reward workers for extra effort, and in many nations, it has become a fixed part of the payment scheme. In India, it was introduced during World War II as a way to get around wage ceilings; bonus issues are usually settled there by tribunals. However, negotiation takes place over the amounts, eligibility, base rate, etc.

An agreement will usually have some sort of statement concerning an industrial truce which signifies the good faith of the parties to abide by the settlement.

The following is a partial listing of benefits achieved by the workers of one large Indian public sector firm, and can serve as an example of the kind of benefits usually provided:

1. Subsidized housing
2. Uniforms and their laundering
3. A nursery for small children
4. Two canteens for workers (one for men and one for women) and several snack areas
5. Subsidized lunches and snacks
6. Two fifteen-minute tea breaks
7. Locker rooms
8. Two full-time doctors (a man and a woman)
9. An ambulance room in the plant, an ambulance, and a small hospital in the housing colony
10. Free medical aid to workers and dependents
11. Sixteen days of sick leave
12. Seven additional days of sick leave for family reasons
13. Ten days of casual leave (three days at a time)
14. Thirty days of earned leave (vacation)
15. Twelve holidays for plant personnel
16. Sixteen holidays for office personnel

17. Free school for all children of employees who live in the company's housing colony

18. A consumer cooperation store which handles food items for all employees

19. A recreation center and outdoor movie for workers

20. Subsidized transport service to and from the housing colony and to and from the nearby city

21. In addition to the above, the normal provisions relating to pension funds, life insurance, etc.

MANAGERIAL REACTIONS TOWARDS UNIONS

The three most significant differences between the way U.S. and Indian managers react towards unions relate to intimidation by the unions, insensitivity to local values, and the use of the courts to settle labor disputes. Each one of these is exemplified through the following incidents which occurred in U.S. firms.

The fear of possible repercussions from charges of exploitation, coupled with the desire to keep production going, leads many U.S. companies to take steps in dealing with local unions that they would not countenance at home.

> In one U.S. subsidiary the entire work force maintained a sit-down strike for six weeks. During much of this period, several hundred workmen squatted in the foyer of the managing director's office. Each morning the workers would appear at the gates, enter the plant, and proceed directly to the managing director's office or to their various departments, at which point they would sit down. In spite of advice from local police and government officials that he should forcibly eject the sit-ins from the plant, or at least lock them out, the managing director refused to take action in order "to avoid violence which might give the company a bad name." The company continued to serve its workers free tea and coffee at the regular break times and subsidized lunches in the company cafeteria. This was done to reduce the possibility of violence.

In contrast to this, an Indian public sector company which experienced a sit-down strike locked its employees out the very next day.

Indian companies take a stronger position against disruption both because they feel more secure, and because they know how far they can go without tearing the fabric of social acceptability. As an example, the plant manager of an established Indian firm related the following story:

> A few years ago we realized that our wage standards were far out of line. Many were 20 years old and workers were earning 200 percent and more of their base rates. We decided to change the standards but we couldn't reduce the pay of our old workers. Fortunately, many are near retirement. We decided to reduce the standards for all new workers we hired. Each supervisor was given approximate starting rates for each of the job classifications in his area and was told to change the standards for new men so that they would earn their base rate if they kept up with the older employees.

> This does create dissatisfaction, since a new man and an old man may be working side by side on the same job, each working just as hard as the other, and one is getting 100 percent of his base rate while the other is getting 250 percent. But we have to change the standards, and jobs in our locality are very scarce. The new workers really don't have any choice. By the time the job market tightens, we'll have brought all our standards into line. That won't happen for at least another 10 years.

In this particular case, the company had correctly assessed the job market and in spite of serious threats from the union and the possibility of social pressures, had gone ahead with its plan and implemented it successfully. It is doubtful whether a U.S. firm could have done the same even if it wished, since the union, realizing the company's vulnerability, would probably not have given in so readily.

Numerous incidents can be found to illustrate the insensitivity of U.S. managers to the needs of their employees. For example, the following incident precipitated a major labor dispute:

> A U.S. company established an infirmary on the plant premises. Based on the number of people who would use the facility, it was determined that a part-time doctor would more than meet normal needs. However, to have someone available at all times in case of an emergency, the company decided to employ a doctor on a full-time basis. The doctor was a male. In India, women do not go to male doctors, and approximately one-third of the work force was female. Upon receipt of the women's requests for a female doctor, the managing director emphatically stated that the company was too small to maintain even one doctor, let alone two, that the women would just have to use the male doctor, and that they should be grateful just to have a doctor available.

In the above example, the women believed that they were being cheated out of the medical treatment that was available to all male workers. The alternative which management had indicated — that they see the male doctor — was a "non-option" to them. This aversion to the use of male doctors by women is deeply ingrained in India (to the extent that some women would die rather than see a male doctor) and it was unrealistic of management to believe that they could change the pattern by fiat just because the hiring of a single doctor seemed to make economic sense.

> In the early sixties, one of the U.S. companies included in this study moved its plant from the center of a major Indian city to the outskirts. The company's employees, most of whom lived in the heart of the city, immediately discovered that there was no public transportation to the plant, since the bus line did not run near the new site. The union immediately approached management and asked that the company provide transportation free of charge from a central location in the city. The managing director flatly refused, indicating that "public transportation is the responsibility of the local government, not of private industry." The union leaders were told to take the matter up with the municipal authorities.

In all likelihood, the union would have settled for a jointly subsidized transportation arrangement, and probably one which could be phased out over a period of time. It was totally unrealistic, given the situation in the municipality, to expect the local authorities to provide buses for these employees. The company, however, did not see its responsibility as extending beyond the plant gates. How the worker got there and what he did once he left was his own problem. By contract, many of the Indian firms provided such service to their employees. This kind of insensitivity gives rise to many disputes and even where it doesn't precipitate a strike or slowdown, it adds heat to any issues that may be simmering below the surface.

POSITIVE APPROACHES TO UNION-MANAGEMENT RELATIONS

The major factor inhibiting good management-union relations is lack of trust. Managers are distrustful of unions because they never know what is motivating any particular action, especially since outside political considerations play such a dominant role in the activities of unionism. Consequently, the union is seen as an enemy and treated as such. This, in turn, evokes hostility on the part of the union and an unending cycle ensues, unless someone takes the first step to break it. The someone must be management, but few managers are willing to take the risk that trust involves.

One of the most potentially productive approaches to building constructive relationships between workers and managers is through union leadership. However, in almost all cases studied, union leaders were regarded with hostile suspicion and dealings with them were limited to those essential to keep operations going. Minimal contact was maintained and minimal information provided. Virtually no type of consultation occurred prior to major management or union decisions.

There were, however, several examples where companies (mostly Indian, but a few U.S.) tried to establish more constructive relationships, in most cases, with positive results.

The managing director of a small Indian firm was faced with a serious problem. About one year earlier, he had purchased a new piece of equipment which required a very skilled operator and it had taken him more than three months to find the man. About three months later, a serious illness occurred in the operator's family, and he needed a substantial sum of money to cover medical costs. The managing director had established a policy of loaning money to employees only after they had worked for the company for one year and had attained permanent status. He was, of course, concerned that the operator would leave if he did not receive the loan he required; on the other hand, granting the loan would set a precedent which would apply to many other nonpermanent employees and experience had indicated that many of these people just vanished after obtaining loans. The managing director finally decided to offer to establish a union fund which the union could loan to the work force. The fund would contain all outstanding loans plus an additional sum which he would provide, and no more. The union could establish loan policies and make loan decisions within a broad set of objectives that it would establish jointly with management. (An under-the-table part of this agreement was that the union would honor the operator's request.)

The above situation benefited the company in a number of very positive ways. One was that the union management was flattered that the managing director would give them this authority, and union relations (which were only fair prior to this time) improved dramatically. Another was that the union was able to police the loans more carefully than management had been able to and the number of bad debts began to decrease.

The following quotation is taken from an interview with a top-level Indian manager of a U.S. subsidiary. The firm had improved its labor relations sharply:

> In the past, we have forced every issue into the courts. The unions have always hit us with unreasonable demands. Unlike other companies which make unreasonable offers and hope for a splitting of the difference, we try to bargain in good faith. Since the unions would not accept our terms, every issue went to court. Almost invariably, we were upheld and the unions were then forced to honor the agreements. In fact, one issue was withdrawn when the court told the union it thought management had been too generous, and the award would probably be lower.
>
> About a year ago, we sent Mr. Y [the top manager responsible for negotiations with the union] to a management development course in the United States for a year. When he returned, one of the first things he did was to recognize the union and sit down with them to talk things over. Our relations have been excellent ever since. We have learned to understand and communicate with them.

This company has made great strides in establishing good relationships with its unions. What is surprising about this situation is the very rapid shift in the relationship. Prior to the new policy, the company's record in this area had been very poor. It had been the target of many industrial sabotage attempts, suffered a number of walkouts and strikes, and experienced a great deal of bitterness between labor and management. However, in a very short period, by dealing directly and honestly with the union leadership, a dramatic change had taken place. Subsequently, this company was able to conclude a long-term agreement with the union and eventually, the improvement in labor relations was one of the factors which led to an early Indianization of top management.

It is disappointing to see how few U.S. subsidiary managers are willing to take the risk of negotiating openly and honestly with the unions.

In spite of union hostility, U.S. managers must make an effort to learn more about the local environment and, specifically, about what motivates the labor movement, so that they will be able to assess correctly the significance of issues and actions. Only through knowledge and a willingness to innovate can a positive climate for labor relations be established, a climate which would be favorable both to higher productivity and to greater employee satisfaction.

RECENT UNION-MANAGEMENT RELATIONS IN INDIA – FINDINGS AND ANALYSIS

Most of the U.S. subsidiaries surveyed in India had at least some acute union and labor problems (including strikes) in the 1960s. U.S. drug, chemical, and oil companies in particular have been major union targets for pushing up wages and benefits. However, even in these industries a few U.S. firms have been able to maintain good union and labor relations. In recent years, more of the U.S. firms have been applying consistent policies to their dealings with the labor unions, and many have improved the effectiveness of their management negotiations (often by putting Indians in charge).

Indigenous firms in India, particularly those with relatively diversified multiplant operations or those belonging to the larger business empires, have generally been the toughest and most successful in union dealings and labor relations. On the other hand, many of the traditional but paternalistic Indian firms which have had no strategy for dealing with unions have recently been faced with serious labor problems, particularly in West Bengal. Some of the British subsidiaries surveyed — including a few with Indian top managers — have found an effective balance between toughness and fairness in union relations.

U.S. subsidiaries have generally been much more reluctant to use third-party arbitration and tribunals than indigenous firms, or even British companies. This is in line with management thinking in American industry where outside arbitration is often viewed as a managerial failure. However, in many cases U.S. firms in India might have avoided serious problems and obtained reasonable settlements by using arbitration. Those U.S. companies surveyed which did resort to arbitration usually obtained settlements which approximated their offers on basic wages and working conditions; in some cases, however, they were required to provide more fringe benefits.

The case of West Bengal

Union and labor problems have been far worse in West Bengal, particularly in the Calcutta region, than anywhere else in India since 1967. In that year's elections, the Centrist and Left political parties gained power in the form of a coalition called the United Front government. The Communists and allied factions became the dominant force in this coalition, although there was much political infighting and conflict among them. It was at that time the "Gherao" really came into prominence. A Gherao is a lockin or lockout of company management by the workers.

The courts first denounced Gheraos emphatically, but it was not until late September 1967, that the state's highest court declared them illegal. Between March and October of 1967 there were 1300 reported Gheraos in over 800 establishments, mostly industrial and business enterprises. However, there were not very many official strikes per se. The new law, along with the emergence of Presidential rule and the dismissal of the coalition government in Bengal in November 1967, led immediately to a sharp drop in Gheraos, but strikes — which were and still are legal — were reported at about 400 establishments. The total number of reported man-days lost because of both strikes and Gheraos in Bengal was 6.1 million in 1967 and 6.7 million in 1968.

Presidential rule ended when the coalition United Front government was returned to power again in Bengal by the electorage in February 1969. Between late February and mid-July of 1969, in the Calcutta region, there were nearly 300 reported Gheraos, 52 violent clashes at plants, and 78 inter-party political clashes leading to 265 serious injuries and 8 deaths. In early 1970, Presidential Rule was once again reinstated in Bengal, and the number of both Gheraos and strikes dropped sharply.

During the 1967-69 period, well over 10 percent of all the industrial establishments in West Bengal, and almost all of the major companies were directly affected by Gheraos and/or strikes. The engineering sector was hit hardest, followed by chemical, drug, and allied industries, textiles, tea plantations, public utilities, coal mines, city government offices, and educational institutions.

A recent study indicates that those firms in Bengal which were not affected by Gheraos tended to be those which had a history of relatively healthy and constructive collective bargaining. Neither their blue collar nor white collar employees — who tend to be highly politicized, as well as actively unionized at major firms — participated in the Gherao movement. Conversely, the intensity rate of Gherao — measured in terms of frequency and duration — was highest in those establishments where labor relations had been consistently bad. Adverse economic conditions have also served as major catalysts. A recent study indicates that more Gheraos have failed to achieve even their immediate aims or demands — where these have been identifiable — than have been successful in so doing.

Corporate examples

The companies studied in India which had the least union and labor troubles during the 1960s were of varying nationalities. One was a U.S. drug company in Bombay which has had a consistent policy of being fair but firm. The company has only been unionized since late 1967, and it has an independent in-plant union, although for a short period it had a communist union. It has never had a strike, and it recently entered into a "reasonable" 3½-year contract with the union. It provides relatively good pay, fringe benefits, and working conditions. This company has had an Indian managing director since 1968.

A large family-owned Indian drug and chemical company in Gujarat also had a relatively good record of union and labor relations. It has a Congress Party Union (INTUC) not only for its plant workers but also for its white collar personnel who earn less than 500 rupees per month. Its wage scales are comparable to other major indigenous firms in the industry and its benefits somewhat higher. The company has not entered into contracts with the union, preferring third-party arbitration, where tribunals mediate disputes. Either management or the labor union can initiate a change in conditions at any time; but this has usually occurred only every four or five years. Both management and employees at this company have evidently been content with the tribunal arrangement. Management feels that the workers have been less inclined to think that they could have obtained more, if only they had pressed harder, and the company has not had a strike for many years. Grievances have been rare.

A new, large, non-U.S., joint venture in Bombay also had relatively good relations with its labor force and its independent company union. The top administrative managers have all been Indians, and the top technical managers have been foreign. Cordial relations no doubt result from the high pay, lucrative benefits, and excellent working conditions provided by the company. The union has apparently not yet found anything worth complaining about. In 1969 a Communist union was trying to gain control.

Another company which has had good labor and union relations is a large, diversified, multiplant British company. This company has been fully Indianized in terms of personnel for several years, and its last two managing directors have been Indians. This company's policy regarding labor relations has been similar to that of the U.S. drug firm discussed above, but with one major difference: the British firm has been much more willing to use arbitration in arriving at settlements. This was the only company surveyed which had operations in Bengal and that had not experienced serious labor problems. It has not had a strike for over 15 years and it has been signing five-year labor agreements.

A large, diversified American subsidiary has had an erratic record of union and labor relations. The company recently adopted a firmer policy regarding labor relations aimed at eliminating small and continuous compromises and concessions, and management seems more willing to face major showdowns and confrontations if necessary. Although it has since been faced with many threats, continuous agitation, and constant bickering, it had had no major confrontations, although its major Calcutta plant recently had to switch from five-year to three-year labor contracts — the union originally sought even shorter-term contracts.

One U.S. company had very good relations with the plant's Communist union (AITUC) through the first half of the 1960s. At that time the plant was headed by an effective Indian manager holding an MBA from Harvard. There were no strikes under him, and not one grievance got beyond the plant. He dealt fairly and openly with the union and created an atmosphere of mutual trust. He treated the union leaders with dignity, and had tea with them at the same table in meetings — which is quite rare in India. The fact that he was a Southern Indian, and a Christian whose ancestry was from the lower castes, may also have been an asset. He felt that it was often easier to deal with unions and labor in India than in the United States because in India there were fewer job opportunities, fewer unemployment benefits, and very few financial resources at the union's disposal.

An Englishman then became manager of the plant and many serious labor problems emerged. When he went on extended leave and was replaced by another Indian, labor relations improved considerably. On his return, relations again deteriorated and a strike resulted. In the last few years, an Indian has again been placed in charge.

A U.S. subsidiary's flashlight plant last had a strike of several month's duration in 1967, but since then has maintained reasonably good labor relations. It has had five-year labor contracts, the last one being signed in 1966.

The same company's Bombay chemical plant has never had a strike, but labor problems have increased somewhat in recent years. Prior to 1969 the plant had a moderate socialist union headed by a strong and effective leader, who became a member of Parliament in Delhi. Since then a more militant independent in-plant union has taken over, but many of the workers have not been paying dues. Recent disputes have revolved around such things as "high" canteen prices. The plant has had only one tribunal case — involving bonuses and merit rating — and it lost. It also has had five-year labor contracts.

The leading indigenous battery company, with its plant in Bombay, had very acute labor and union problems during the 1965-68 period when it experienced major strikes, slowdowns, and almost continuous conflict. Management claims that the last major strike was settled on its terms, with the union getting no concession. Since 1968, there have been several short unofficial strikes, slowdowns, and persistent pressure of various kinds by the firm's Communist union, but no major confrontations. Management's philosophy has been to be tough with the union and to rely largely on discipline for motivating the work force. However, the company has recently increased wages and employee benefits.

A large, traditional Indian drug and chemical company in Calcutta, which historically has been paternalistic and has had relatively good labor relations, was hard hit by labor problems during the 1967-69 period. Two of its plants were idle most of the time and its third plant operated at only about 70 percent of capacity. Management was at a loss as to how to cope with the situation. In reaction to frequent Gheraos, management conceded substantial bonus payments and did not lay off a single employee, continuing to pay all personnel their regular wages.

A large, multiplant, indigenous engineering company has had many critical labor problems, particularly at its Calcutta plants. It had two major strikes in 1967, and a three-month strike at one of its plants in 1969. In February 1969, right after the election in West Bengal, management closed one of its Bengal plants for several months because of union agitation and labor problems, even though the union had not made any specific demands. The plant was finally reopened on management's terms and the company was praised in the moderate press and the business community for the tough stand it took against political and union agitation. Even under more normal conditions, it generally initiated more disciplinary actions against employees than any of the U.S. subsidiaries. However, productivity was not very impressive and employee morale did not seem high.

The largest U.S. drug subsidiary in India has had serious labor problems during a good part of the 1960s, even though it has been a leader with regard to pay scales and various benefits. It has experienced some major strikes, many slowdowns, some recent Gheraos, and various other conflicts revolving around wages, benefits, bonuses, hours of work, company services, etc. It has been signing three- or four-year labor contracts which have often been violated, generally by the union and labor. Until recently, management has had no consistent or clear strategy for dealing with the union or with labor problems.

Union and labor problems last became acute during and after the parent company president's visit to India for the opening of a new plant in 1968. A union election was coming up at the time. There was agitation and conflict over the lack of company transportation to and from the new plant, the addition of a second shift, overtime work, no-strike clauses in contracts, special "fancy" meals served to visitors, and various other issues. Management stated that it would not negotiate with the union unless all agitation was called off. The company began to deduct pay from and discipline employees involved in Gheraos or similar activities during working hours. It was finally decided to provide bus service, but the union would not let the buses operate because management would not agree to all of the pickup points sought. This was eventually worked out, largely on management's terms, and the bus service started in August 1969. Management also added a partial second shift at the plant around that time, chiefly to show the union that it must stick to the labor contract. Although issues continued to simmer below the surface, the company experienced no serious labor problems during the remainder of 1969 or in early 1970.

CHAPTER 16   FOOTNOTES

1. The nature of union leadership and the strength of political ties are probably the two other major differences. These are discussed later in the chapter.

2. Names have been disguised.

3. In India the foremen may be treated either as officers or as workers, depending on the terms of employment. This man was categorized as a worker.

CHAPTER 17
GOVERNMENT
RELATIONS

INTRODUCTION

The maintenance of sound government-corporate relations assumes greater importance in most developing countries than in the United States. In the United States, except for large corporations which flirt with anti-trust actions or supply substantial amounts of defense items, government-company relations tend to be impersonal. Although one cannot deny the benefits of personal contacts, interaction defined by a series of well-regulated legal relationships generally gives rise to impartial decision-making processes. This is not so in the developing country, especially in those where discretionary control is a way of life.

First, the government typically plays a much greater role in directing the nation's activity in underdeveloped countries. Whereas in the United States the government is seen as the vehicle for implementing the desires of the people, the governments of many developing nations function as prime movers who determine the needs of the people. Consequently, the government becomes a partner of virtually every business enterprise.

Second, greater discretionary government control in developing countries tends to increase the importance of personal relationships in influencing decision making.

BUSINESS-GOVERNMENT RELATIONS IN INDIA: HUMAN RELATIONSHIPS

Indian companies cultivate government officials at both national and local levels. A great deal of social interaction takes place, and a lesser amount of direct business negotiation. Most large indigenous firms, and many smaller ones, maintain offices in New Delhi especially for this purpose. An individual, usually one high up in the managerial hierarchy, is responsible for maintaining relationships with government personnel. When the firm requires some type of interaction with government officials, he serves as the contact man, and the friendship patterns which he has established are often of considerable value in any ensuing negotiations — even though he might not be directly involved in the discussions. Such social contacts often provide the avenue for establishing the most meaningful relationships between people not related by blood, and are usually initiated long before there is any specific need to use them.

Few of the U.S. subsidiaries studied engaged in the same type of activity. Few had special offices or officers assigned to government relations, although an increasing number of the U.S. companies have moved in this direction in recent years. One large U.S. firm moved its head office to Delhi, largely for this purpose. In most cases U.S. subsidiaries initiated contact with government officials when a specific issue arose, and the principal operating officer concerned usually pursued the matter. This meant that in one situation the purchasing manager would follow up, in another the marketing manager, and so forth. The managing director usually handled matters which involved top-level national officials. At times personnel from the parent company would also become involved in government negotiations.

Actual contact between representatives of U.S. firms and government officials — especially in the case of American executives — tended to be strictly on a business level. When a U.S. firm desired government approval, or wished to respond to a government action, the concerned company representative would usually obtain an appointment with the proper government official and visit him to discuss the subject. Meetings tended to be short and to the point, with little more than the normal, U.S.—style amenities before turning to the subject matter under discussion.

The Indian firms used a different approach. The appointment was usually established through the personal relationships which already existed. Furthermore, the position of the company would have been discussed earlier with the government official, and each party would be already aware of the desires and position of the other. Unlike the U.S. firms, the discussion did not start "cold"; talks tended to be less formal, less confined to the issues, and more vague with respect to specific decision outcomes.

Reactions of government officials varied considerably. The relatively traditional officials often saw the U.S. executives as cold, uninterested in anything but economic issues, and insensitive to local cultural and economic facts of life. The brevity and formality of the meetings led many to believe that they were being treated as socially inferior. (British managers, and even Western-trained Indian managers of British companies were regarded as more patient, open-minded, and even-tempered.) Indian officials frequently felt that they were being used in their dealings with U.S. companies — a feeling which, in the United States, might have been much more likely to have arisen from the approach used by the Indian companies.

On the positive side, many of the relatively Westernized and younger Indian government officials expressed admiration for the forthrightness and honesty of the U.S. firms. (However, such officials constitute only a relatively small, though growing minority in India, and few of them are in high positions.) They experienced no difficulty in determining where the U.S. firms stood on most issues, and although they resented the frequency of complaints voiced by these firms, they believed that their word was good. When a U.S. executive said he would do something, he generally did it; and when a law was passed, despite complaints, the firm would usually comply. On the other hand, many government officials resented involvement and interference of U.S. parent companies in the affairs of their subsidiaries.

The approach of the Indian companies was seen as more warm and "human." The personal relationships established by these firms did help open doors and it is likely that such firms received the benefit of the doubt with respect to unclear or marginal issues. Government officials did not feel that they were being used in these situations because relationships were well-understood, and controllable. Furthermore, officials felt comfortable in this pattern of interaction.

On the negative side, the relationships tended to be less direct with respect to business matters. Often, ambiguities were purposely left undefined. Whereas the U.S. firms were relatively direct and precise with respect to their plans and actions, the Indian companies were more oblique. This was especially troubling to some of the more aggressive, less traditional government officials who were trying to bring about change.

In general, a moderate approach, somewhere in between the U.S. and the Indian patterns seemed to be the most effective. It is difficult for a U.S. manager to assume the traditional Indian pattern because it does not come naturally to him and goes against the training and habits of many years. Unfortunately, many U.S. executives made value judgements as to what was "intrinsically correct" behavior (i.e., that expected in the United States) and failed to consider other alternatives. By so doing, they often missed opportunities to advance their firm's economic interests. Some of the progressive British companies seemed to have achieved the best blend between Western and traditional Indian approaches in their government relations.

A number of U.S. companies have begun to involve more of their U.S.-educated Indian managers in this process. However, in most cases, top-level government relations among the firms studied were still handled by U.S. personnel only. It is surprising that so many U.S. companies recognize the importance of good government relations when they establish foreign subsidiaries — one of the reasons why more of them have been seeking joint ventures — and that relatively few remember it during the course of operations.

The two most effective government-relations officers at U.S. subsidiaries seemed to be those at a diversified firm and a pharmaceutical company. The first was a middle-aged Indian with an MBA from the United States as well as considerable business experience in that country. He had been in his job for about eight years, and previously had experience in purchasing and auditing work in both the United States and India. He had a flexible personality and seemed to bridge the gap between the traditional Indian and modern American worlds easily and effectively. He had excellent government contacts and could arrange appointments with virtually anyone — including top Cabinet members and even the Prime Minister — on relatively short notice. His record for getting things done for his firm was impressive.

The other individual was a Western-educated Anglo-Indian who had been a high-level and widely respected member of the prestigious Indian Civil Service. He was appointed managing director around the time the subsidiary was formed in the second half of the 1950s.

OTHER IMPORTANT CONSIDERATIONS

Although good personal relations can reduce the problems of firms in their dealings with the government, other factors are equally important. For example, favorable treatment has often been given those companies willing to serve India's needs by offering local equity participation before government pressure had to be brought to bear. This is also frequently accomplished by placing Indians in most, if not all, key managerial and technical jobs, by engaging in substantial import substitution, and by various other means.

On the average, U.S. firms have employed bribery and other corrupt practices less often than most of their Indian counterparts. There are certainly many indigenous companies with a high degree of integrity and honesty who are willing to fight battles with the government on the merits of a specific case. However, there are also numerous Indian firms that function without considering the national interest by resorting to unethical or illegal activities. This is most often true among the smaller Indian firms, and in companies controlled by the more traditional managing agencies.

There is a strong tendency for firms in India, regardless of nationality, to blame many of their own deficiencies on the government. For example, in Indian industry delays involved in obtaining government approvals are often due to internal company problems; firms may not provide the government with proper or adequate information; they may fill out required forms and documents incorrectly and cause delays through their own poor planning and control; they may send the wrong people, too many people, or people without adequate authority to negotiate with the government; and they may persistently try to get around existing policies and regulations and to press for special concessions. In the case of foreign subsidiaries, many delays are compounded by factors introduced by the parent companies, such as final approval authority retained abroad or the desire to maintain uniform worldwide procedures.

SOME SPECIFIC EXAMPLES OF THE RECENT GOVERNMENT FREEZE ON INDUSTRIAL LICENSING

During the second half of 1969 and the first half of 1970, it became almost impossible for firms to get approval for new ventures, regardless of their nature, the type of firm involved, or its nationality. As a result, many firms became extremely pessimistic about the future.

One of India's largest indigenous companies engaged in the manufacture of drugs and chemicals had two large projects, several smaller ones, and an expansion application pending. Because of the political climate, management gave up trying to push these applications through. One major project involving insecticides was tabled after more than three years of haggling; the other, after more than four years of effort.

A large, progressive British company had its letter of intent for a new chemical project recalled by the government in 1969, a letter which had taken about three years to get in the first place. Two other foreign firms desiring to set up similar projects had their letters recalled at the same time. In their place a letter of intent was granted to an Indian firm which had high-level political connections. The plant was to be built in the Prime Minister's political constituency although the location of this plant in relation to raw materials sources (Gujarat) and markets (Bombay) made it an impractical choice.

A large American battery manufacturer also failed to get project or expansion approvals in 1969. (It was in a sensitive position since the Monopoly Inquiry Commission labelled it a monopoly. This company was trying to get a letter of intent for a new battery plant, but was told that it must export all the new plant's output if construction was to be seriously considered. (If it did this, large losses would result.) Between March and May of 1969, just before the freeze, letters of intent for establishment of new or expansion of existing battery plants were issued to ten Indian companies, several of which involved foreign collaborations. However, many of these Indian ventures were subsequently unable to get the required licenses.

The situation seems generally to have improved since Indira Gandhi's impressive victory at the polls in 1971. However, these examples present dramatic illustrations of the importance of maintaining good government relations and the impact which government can have on business operations in developing countries.

CHAPTER 18
PRODUCTION

INTRODUCTION

We found production to be one of the most neglected managerial areas in India. Even though U.S. subsidiaries performed significantly better in this sphere than their indigenous counterparts, production management was not one of the strong areas in U.S. subsidiaries.

However, since the mid-1960s both foreign and indigenous firms have become increasingly concerned with improving production management and operating efficiency. The decline of strong sellers' markets coupled with greater competition, excess capacity, import restrictions, and serious profit squeezes have been the reasons for this change in emphasis.

Our research indicates that a great deal of effort is usually devoted to the manufacturing function during the establishment of a new U.S. subsidiary plant; once it has been set up, however, the emphasis usually switches to marketing. Good market prospects trigger the plant's establishment in the first place, and this is where the focus is directed. During the early operating stage, bad habits and neglect characterize the production area. This situation is compounded by the fact that many of the individuals hired (from workmen to higher managers) have not previously worked in an industrial setting and therefore lack the attitudes or technical reference frame normally found in people from advanced industrial societies. Eventually, as environmental pressures which hinder profitability arise, greater attention is directed toward improving internal manufacturing efficiency. However, by this time the task is difficult because of already-established operating practices.

It is unfortunate that the production sector receives so little attention until serious adversity confronts the firm, since this is one of the areas where U.S. methods are most easily transferable. The technical aspects of many production processes provide a common base, many of the quantitative techniques which can be applied are universal, and the one additional requirement may be the direction of knowledgeable and adequately motivated people to the task.

One of the most effective approaches to this problem, employed extensively by the most successful of the U.S. companies, was to send key Indian manufacturing personnel to the United States (and, to a lesser extent, to send competent foreign experts to India) to train subsidiary production personnel. However, until quite recently, the focus of such training has been almost entirely on the technical aspects of production.

In the last few years increasing attention has been given to training with respect to the managerial aspects of production. Unfortunately, in many cases little improvement has resulted because the broad operating environment of the firm is created largely by the managing director. If he does not perceive production to be of major importance, it does not receive the necessary attention.

In developing nations it is important that production management be emphasized from the time a plant starts operating, since industrial enterprises are likely to be confronted with union and government pressures to reduce imports, expand exports, provide jobs and opportunities for unskilled workers and other personnel, and keep prices as low as possible.

Often the foreign firm finds its inclinations in direct conflict with government aims and policies when it attempts to limit the exposure of its capital to the local economy, and concentrates on those elements near the end of the production-marketing cycle which yield the greatest short-term profits. In contrast to government emphasis on the creation of jobs and the training of unskilled and illiterate labor, the foreign firm often moves toward automation both because it is accustomed to running automated facilities and because, by so doing, it may be able to reduce employment levels and, correspondingly, the related problems.

It should be noted that good records and accurate data were lacking in the manufacturing area more frequently than in any other basic enterprise function at firms surveyed in India. Consequently, in many instances the efficiency indicators presented in this chapter were based on estimates — some quite crude — rather than on detailed factual data. In fact, in several cases, various kinds of record-keeping and reporting systems were established within the firms we studied as a result of the gaps which became evident in the course of our attempts to obtain data.

OVERVIEW OF PRODUCTION MANAGEMENT

U.S. subsidiaries had more of the trappings associated with a high level of manufacturing efficiency in the United States — e.g., manuals, charts, check lists — than their indigenous counterparts, but much of this had little bearing on the way things were really done. Indian managers and production personnel often viewed anything systematized or relatively sophisticated as a U.S. "fetish" and inapplicable to India, and top management often made little effort to overcome such resistance.

At several U.S.-Indian joint ventures examined, American executives eventually gave up trying to implement modern production management skills and permitted the Indian managers to run the show. In fact, this was even the case at a few joint ventures where the U.S. firm had an equal or a majority equity position, for example, at an engineering enterprise which produces internal combustion engines.

On the other hand, many U.S. subsidiaries were over-Americanized in various parts of the production area and failed to adapt to local environmental conditions. More often than not this was due to constraints imposed on them by their parent companies. This was most common with regard to product quality and design, material and equipment standards, various manufacturing processes, and factor input choices.

For example, where the abundance of unskilled and semi-skilled labor justified more labor-intensive and semi-manual operations, U.S. subsidiaries often overemployed automated equipment. Where the lack of adequate skilled manpower and technical expertise called for a greater emphasis on basic work simplification, several U.S. firms were applying complex and sophisticated approaches. Many U.S. firms confronted with low-quality materials were unyielding — or else their parent companies were — about compromising on their high material input and related finished-product standards, even though this would probably not have affected their local or international reputations. (As an alternative, they could have marketed products under different brand names, but still have the product associated with their company.)

Several U.S. firms were adamant about modifying the technology and production processes they employed, in spite of the high costs and maintenance problems which resulted. In several instances, shortages of power, water, and fuel would not have been nearly as damaging if U.S. plants had had less automated operations; and, in several cases, plants would not have had as much excess capacity if they had greater flexibility in their prescribed production processes, made more use of labor-intensive operations, or had more smaller-scale multipurpose equipment.

PRODUCTION ORGANIZATION AND KEY RELATED ACTIVITIES

The production organizations of U.S. subsidiaries tended to be smaller for a given volume of output than those of their indigenous counterparts, broader in that they encompassed more functions, and better designed to give the production or plant manager control over his operations. With only a few exceptions, the U.S. subsidiaries also provided for more effective coordination between production, maintenance, engineering, marketing, purchasing, finance, and other closely-related functions.

In analyzing the organization of the production function, some closely-related functional areas were examined. These included warehousing, labor-relations, purchasing, industrial engineering, development engineering, equipment maintenance, plant engineering and maintenance, and quality control. These functions were compared, from firm to firm, with respect to their organizational positions and the tasks they encompassed. The major differences between U.S. and Indian firms were found in the areas of maintenance and quality control. Because of this, and also because of the importance of these two functions, they are treated separately in sections immediately following this one.

There seemed to be few clear distinctions between U.S. and indigenous firms with regard to the classification of either warehousing or labor relations. In both groups, there were cases where these activities were and were not included under the manufacturing function. However, more of the U.S. firms had both a central labor relations staff and one at the plant level, with the former typically exerting considerable functional authority over the latter.

Most of the companies studied had a manager specifically in charge of purchasing. The exceptions were smaller indigenous firms where the managing director or some other high-level executive handled purchasing along with various other functions. In nearly all cases, the purchasing function of major Indian firms was placed outside of production, usually in a parallel structure. Occasionally, their production or engineering personnel purchased equipment, components, or spare parts, but these activities were usually a minor portion of the total procurement effort. A majority of U.S. firms surveyed also had an independent purchasing function, but many also had small purchasing units at the plant level. In a few, most of the purchasing was done at the plant. Occasionally, the executive in charge of overall purchasing at U.S. firms reported to a higher authority in the organization, but in almost all cases he had more authority — e.g., to sign requisitions and make independent choices — than his counterpart in indigenous firms.

Only a small number of Indian firms, all large ones, had separate functions identified as "industrial engineering." Most of the rest had no industrial engineers anywhere in the company. Usually industrial engineering groups reported outside of production. However, in the most effective of these efforts purchasing was placed within the production function.

The majority of U.S. firms surveyed did not have industrial engineering groups. Those who did usually placed it under production. Others refused to establish industrial engineering functions because top management believed that such functions should be handled by the production personnel themselves.

According to the managing director of one U.S. subsidiary, who was basically a marketing man, "that's what the production people are getting paid for." However, there is little question that the press of day-to-day activities prevented many analyses which would have been valuable to cost-reduction efforts.

Some U.S. plants had industrial engineers reporting to the heads of each of their major manufacturing departments (which were usually organized along product lines). Such individuals were responsible for conducting studies, training personnel, and assisting production managers in whatever tasks they felt necessary. The most successful U.S. drug subsidiary maintained such an arrangement until the late 1960s when it formed a separate industrial engineering group under the head of the plant. A few large U.S. firms had both centralized and department-level industrial engineering groups.

Since relatively few firms studied in India were engaged in new product development, development or design engineering groups were rare. Those U.S. subsidiaries that did have them usually placed them under manufacturing. It was more common for Indian companies to have such groups and they were usually independent of the production organization. Where no separate development engineering unit had been established, individuals doing this kind of work reported to a variety of different managers, and no clear organizational patterns were discernable. However, the U.S. firms seemed to do a better job of integrating their engineering development efforts with their production programs than the indigenous companies.

MAINTENANCE

In all but a few indigenous firms, equipment maintenance was a separate function, divorced from the control of the top production executive and placed under engineering, machinery repair, or some other independent department or division. In the U.S. subsidiaries, the opposite was true, with few exceptions. A similar pattern applied to plant engineering and its related maintenance activities.

In most cases, the U.S. plants had a higher proportion of their personnel on full-time and direct maintenance and repair work than similar kinds of indigenous plants. The highest proportions were typically found at those plants which had the best preventive maintenance programs. At U.S. subsidiaries direct maintenance personnel of all types accounted for 4 to 7 percent of the work force. The figure for indigenous firms fell between 1 and 4 percent.

Many indigenous firms had no separate and distinct maintenance groups, and few if any individuals were assigned to full-time maintenance work. If one looks at the number of personnel engaged from time to time in some aspect of maintenance or repair work, the proportion involved in maintenance activities would be much larger than in U.S. subsidiaries in most cases. For example, maintenance was the responsibility of the engineering department in many indigenous firms, and such units often performed diverse functions; in addition to maintenance of plant and equipment, many also did heavy construction work and outside contracting. Some even manufactured machinery, components, small tools, spare parts, and other items for the company. Since functions and duties were not clearly separated, it was difficult to relate maintenance efforts to inputs. In terms of numbers, the work forces designated as "maintenance" within many indigenous firms were roughly double those of their U.S. counterparts, measured as a percentage of total factory employment. Nevertheless, the figures presented earlier, which reflect full-time maintenance personnel, are generally a better reflection of the effectiveness of the maintenance effort.

Nearly all of the firms surveyed in India which had reasonably effective preventive maintenance programs were U.S. subsidiaries. But even these firms introduced their programs only during the middle or late 1960s, and in most cases the programs have been less effective than those of their parent companies' domestic operations. For example, fewer standards have been developed and programs have met with greater resistance. However, there have been substantial improvements in planning and meeting regular maintenance schedules, and in repairing breakdowns more promptly.

A majority of the U.S. subsidiaries had no preventive maintenance programs at the start of the 1970s, although some were considering establishing them. In several cases, maintenance experts were sent from the United States to set up and help operate the subsidiary's maintenance program. Such experts usually stayed for at least a few months; in a few cases they stayed for more than a year.

Some U.S. subsidiaries developed their own programs with little or no direct help from the parent company. They typically employed U.S.-trained local nationals. (In some cases, Americans working at the subsidiary set up and ran their own programs.)

The preventive maintenance programs at the few Indian companies which had them were mostly set up by U.S.-trained personnel. In some cases, firms which had technical collaboration or licensing agreements with foreign companies were assisted by specialists sent from abroad or by their own personnel who were sent to the foreign collaborator for training. However, none of the indigenous firms studied had programs as effective as the better maintenance programs within the U.S. subsidiaries.

It has been more difficult to introduce the concept of maintenance, preventive or otherwise, at indigenous firms than at U.S. subsidiaries. For example, it took one leading Indian drug company about six years to introduce a maintenance program in its operations, and even then, no real preventive maintenance was being performed. Top management estimated that the existing breakdown maintenance program was no more than 60 percent successful. Only in 1969 did this firm really begin to implement an effective preventive maintenance program, when it shifted most of its maintenance effort from engineering to production.

Maintenance personnel invariably voiced complaints that production and sales personnel were so concerned with meeting rush production deadlines that they would not give up equipment so that preventive — or other kinds — of maintenance could be performed efficiently. The possibility of saving down-time in the longer run was subordinate to the pressures for meeting current output requirements. Much of this conflict could have been resolved by better integrated planning and control. Because of the production-maintenance conflict and the lack of preventive maintenance programs, the act of placing maintenance outside of the production function, or in an independent slot of its own actually helped to deemphasize maintenance in the Indian firms. To a lesser extent, the same was true of plant engineering.

In many cases — particularly in indigenous companies — the lack of preventive maintenance was the result of ignorance or lack of motivation on the part of maintenance personnel as well as of upper management. Some did not know how to initiate such programs while others were unaware of their value. Most of the maintenance managers interviewed complained that their functions were accorded low status, and that they were understaffed. One chief engineer indicated that his opinion was totally disregarded whenever it conflicted with the production manager's. Furthermore, when production personnel refused to give him machine time for preventive maintenance during regular shifts, he suggested that it be performed on weekends, but could not get top management to pay the overtime premiums that this would entail. His frustration was typical of that expressed by most of the maintenance personnel.

Detailed records were rare. Only a few companies had begun to collect data, but nearly all complained that their efforts were hindered by lack of clerical personnel.

Several maintenance departments, particularly in Indian firms, ran tools and spare parts stores. In most firms there was friction between maintenance and purchasing personnel over the question of equipment and spare parts purchases and inventories. In a few companies, mostly American, maintenance personnel were consulted at the time of new equipment purchases, but in most cases purchases were handled directly by the plant or purchasing people, and maintenance came into the picture only after the equipment was operating. In cases where maintenance and plant engineering were combined, the first contact of these personnel with new equipment was, typically, at the time of installation. Where they were separate functions, maintenance personnel were not involved, in many firms, until the first problem arose. In these firms complaints were commonly voiced that maintenance criteria were not factored into the original purchase decisions.

QUALITY CONTROL

Considerable differences were found in quality control patterns when U.S. subsidiaries were compared to their indigenous counterparts. With few exceptions the quality control function was separate from production in Indian companies; those involved with it generally reported directly to top management. On the other hand, at all but a few U.S. firms, quality control was located within the production function.

Two factors primarily account for the difference. First, the natural suspicion of strangers which is part of the Indian culture, combined with a strong desire for checks and balances, probably oriented thinking towards organizational separation in the Indian firms. In contrast, the U.S. subsidiaries were willing to place greater emphasis on the responsibility of the individual (i.e., the production managers). Second, in many cases the U.S. subsidiaries employed their top technical specialist (often imported from the United States or Europe) in the production manager slot, and felt safer if he were supervising the quality control operation.

The attitudes which developed differed greatly from those one might expect to find in the United States, where the main question involved in quality control would be: "Is production really doing what it is supposed to?" Unfortunately, but understandably, in developing nations, this question was often subsumed by another: "Are the local nationals doing what they are supposed to?"

It is difficult to make a comparison between the size of quality control organizations in relation to total factory or company employment in U.S. subsidiaries and their Indian counterparts. Many Indian firms used large numbers of production and other personnel to perform inspection operations along with their other duties. Several combined quality control with activities such as maintenance, new product development, and the handling of customer complaints.

Most of the U.S. subsidiaries had more full-time quality control personnel working directly on incoming goods, in-process items, finished products, and other inspection activities, in relation to total factory employment. The proportion ranged from 3 to nearly 10 percent, whereas only one major indigenous plant had more than 3 percent in full-time quality control work.

In most cases there were no significant differences between the proportions of quality control personnel responsible for checking on finished products in U.S. subsidiaries and the more reputable Indian firms. The major differences involved the inspection and testing of incoming goods and in-process inspection.

Many indigenous firms checked only major incoming materials, and often even this was done inadequately. They did little careful testing of incoming equipment, small tools, components, spare parts, minor materials, packaging items, labels, and so forth. Some of them relied on in-process inspectors to pick up discrepancies, but many of them had poor quality control at this stage as well.

U.S. subsidiaries were generally more effective than their indigenous counterparts but not as effective as their parent company's domestic operations, in the area of in-process quality control.

Most firms confined quality control effort to the identification of substandard goods. Where in-process inspections were made, the emphasis was more on detection than prevention; this was true even of U.S. subsidiaries whose parent firms subscribed to a "total quality control" concept, in which the effort began with the selection of equipment, processes, materials and suppliers, and was carried through the manufacturing process to the marketing effort. Only two subsidiaries surveyed had implemented such an approach. Here was another area in which a transfer of applicable U.S. practices had not occurred.

The U.S. subsidiaries typically transmitted quality control reports to those with the authority to take corrective action faster than did indigenous firms. This was especially critical where in-process inspection was performed, since delays in obtaining a report would hold up the production process and lessen the value of the report with regard to preventive action.

The U.S. subsidiaries usually handled quality checks more quickly with regard to finished products. For example, using similar products as the reference standard at major drug firms studied, it was discovered that the U.S. subsidiaries' average of one week for clearance was extended to about two weeks in the Indian firms. In the case of incoming raw materials and other supplies, it appeared that approval was faster in the U.S. firms; however, the data was inconclusive, since so many items were handled on a rush basis that it was difficult to identify "normal" patterns.

STABILIZATION OF PRODUCTION OPERATIONS

A classic trade-off in production management involves balancing inventory and production levels. On the one hand, production can be stabilized, relying upon fluctuating inventory levels to absorb changes in demand. On the other hand, inventory levels can be stabilized, utilizing changes in production levels to satisfy the ups and downs of demand. Each approach gives rise to a series of associated costs, such as those arising from inventory-carrying charges, training new employees, and product obsolescence.

Only a few companies studied — mostly U.S. subsidiaries — devoted a major effort to the analysis of the production-inventory relationship. Many of the U.S. firms had low employment-level policies and tried to confine most operations to one shift. It was especially important for such companies to maintain stable production. The Indian firms used more temporary personnel and favored multiple-shift operations.

It is interesting to compare the one-shift approach, used by the U.S. firms with the multiple-shift approach favored by Indian firms in the pharmaceutical sector. One would be led to conclude that the U.S. firms were building-in increased flexibility for an upward-bound market, while the Indian companies were providing themselves a cushion for a trend reversal. Assuming raw materials were available, labor was the only ingredient U.S. firms required to double or triple output, since they had all the necessary equipment, which was presently geared to a one-shift operation. In a downtrend, however, much of their capacity might become idle. On the other hand, the Indian firms could cut back without leaving portions of their plants idle, since only the labor levels would be affected. They would experience more difficulty in an upward trend, however, since they would require additional equipment. The situation probably also reflected attitudes towards foreign-exchange utilization.

In addition to the use of multiple shifts by Indian drug firms, two other methods were used to provide flexibility and to smooth the impact of market changes on company operating levels — the use of overtime, and the use of temporary employees.

Overtime was used by both the U.S and Indian firms; but more by the latter. In many cases, this was due to poorer planning and control. Usually overtime was used to take up temporary surges in demand, and was primarily given to skilled employees. Extra hour requirements for less-skilled jobs were generally filled by straight-time temporary people. In a few firms, the overtime had become institutionalized, as a "surge" in demand turned out to be permanent, and firms either hesitated to add new employees or were unable to find them.

As noted in earlier chapters, the use of temporary workers was more prevalent among Indian than U.S. firms, especially in the pharmaceutical and chemical sectors. This was one of the primary means by which indigenous companies obtained flexibility, while ensuring stability for their permanent workers. Essentially, their efforts were directed more towards building a stable employment base for long-term employees, than toward reaching a stable production level.

The U.S. subsidiaries made less use of temporary employees than the Indian companies for several reasons. First, they were not comfortable with the practice. Second, many U.S. company managers felt that temporary workers who were not familiar with operations or policies would probably be more trouble than they were worth. Finally, since in most cases U.S. plants were more automated and therefore less dependent upon manual labor than Indian plants, it was more difficult for them to make use of the type of unskilled labor generally available on a temporary basis. The higher dependence upon manual workers in the Indian companies provided them with greater flexibility in this area.

Finally, U.S. firms were often reluctant to employ temporary workers for fear of adverse public reaction. As foreign companies, they were always under scrutiny. Although Indian labor law and practice seemed to be aimed at providing a high degree of employment security — also the chief objective of the labor movement — protection did not extend to temporary workers. This seemed to be of little concern to the Indian companies, who felt free to hire and fire temporary workers as the need arose. The U.S. subsidiaries, on the other hand, were afraid that such manipulation of workers would be taken as evidence of callous attitudes towards the labor force and they therefore tended to shy away from it. There were some exceptions, but not in the drug or chemical sectors.

With few exceptions, the results of efforts toward stabilizing production were not impressive. Supply bottlenecks, market changes, poor forecasting, and internal managerial deficiencies led to frequent changes in production schedules and levels. Significant stability was achieved only in those operations working at or near 100 percent of capacity — only because stability is inherent in such a situation. Little analysis had been done, and except for the Indian firms' attempts to provide stable employment levels for their permanent workers, little conscious effort had been made in this area.

SIZE OF PRODUCTION RUNS

Within the pharmaceutical companies, production was generally carried out either in continuous or batch operations, and the nature of the product determined the size and timing of production runs. In almost all cases involving foreign ventures, batch sizes had been prepared by the parent or foreign collaborating firm. Even when these were tailored to match local equipment capacities, batch sizes were usually identical to those in the U.S. parent company, since equipment selection was often influenced or specified by that company.

The major differences found among the drug and chemical firms studied was the way in which they scheduled batch operations. The more traditional Indian firms scheduled on a first-come-first-serve basis. The most progressive Indian firm assigned its operations research staff to devise a plan whereby successive batches of different chemicals which shared common manufacturing equipment could be run through in a sequence which would minimize cleaning time. Most of the U.S. firms had made some sort of approximation of this kind, although few had actually experimented with an optimal schedule.

In discrete manufacturing operations, recognition of the economies of scale from large production runs and crude analysis of the trade-offs between large runs and inventory carrying costs were most common in U.S. subsidiaries. Many Indian firms, especially the smaller companies, seemed totally unaware of the benefits which could be realized from an increase in production run size. For example: one indigenous firm manufacturing optical equipment had originally begun producing an item for which demand was twelve units a month. At that time, they decided to schedule monthly production in two batches of six. Although demand had increased many times in the three years following, they were still scheduling in lot sizes of six. In fact, a customer's order for twelve units would be scheduled in two separate batches.

Market conditions also played an important role in determining production run size. Where demand strongly outpaced supply, the emphasis was placed on producing as much as possible as quickly as possible. Lot sizes could be expanded with no concern for inventory build-ups, since the market could absorb output as fast as it was generated. However this often generated severe problems for the reason that strong demand was frequently experienced for several products which had to compete for the same limited manufacturing facilities. In such cases, the production-inventory equation changes. Here the savings from long production runs of product X must be balanced not against the cost of carrying units of product X in inventory, but against the costs of stocking-out of product Y.

This area was just beginning to receive attention in the pharmaceutical industry. Once again, the U.S. firms had the know-how acquired from U.S. experience; but most of them did not have trained personnel who could recognize the value of such analyses and properly assign priorities to this type of work.

LABOR UTILIZATION

Most firms in India did a very poor job with respect to labor utilization. Perhaps it was because labor was so plentiful that top management tended to discount its value, or perhaps because of the relatively small portion of manufacturing cost accounted for by wages. For whatever reason, the benefits from more efficient utilization of labor were generally neglected. Even in the companies which had industrial engineering functions, the focus was generally directed towards improved layout and better utilization of equipment, and not the more efficient use of manpower.

Few firms applied detailed job descriptions to production tasks, and the exceptions were all encountered at U.S. subsidiaries. Some U.S. firms had such descriptions, but did not use them; others, both U.S. and Indian, had begun to prepare descriptions, but none had completed the task, and several had abandoned the project in midstream. As a result, job assignments were often unclear. Lower-level production managers used their less skilled workers in diverse manners, frequently moving them from task to task which inhibited the development of specific job-oriented skills.

The concept of efficiency through specialization and division of labor was de-emphasized, except in the case of skilled workers. Supervisory personnel in the production area were vague about their responsibilities and authority. The lack of well-defined job statements also inhibited the installation of effective performance review procedures.

Most companies seemed to assume that production workers brought to the job all the skills they required at the time they were hired. This was surprising, in view of the strong emphasis placed on training higher-level non-managerial employees (such as the medical representatives) in many of these same companies.

Not many companies extended their training and development activities beyond the technical aspects of the job. In this regard, one or two progressive Indian firms studied were doing a more effective job than any of the U.S. subsidiaries. As the managing director of one progressive Indian firm indicated, "we have to educate the workers to new patterns of thinking which are compatible with industrial activity."

A specific example related to an effort to work with the employees on a bottle-washing machine. The workers on this machine were in the lowest semi-skilled category. Their function was to stack bottles in the machine, make sure that temperature and other parameters were correct, stop the equipment if any problems came up, and unload and inspect the bottles as they came out. Occasionally, a bottle would break in the machine or in the course of handling, and scatter chips of glass into other bottles or into the machine mechanism. When this happened, everything stopped and the area, the machine, and the bottles in process had to be thoroughly cleaned before the operation resumed. The company conducted a major program to educate these employees to report broken glass. Before the program was initiated the fear of punitive action, coupled with the employees' lack of awareness of the consequences arising from glass chips, resulted in a number of unreported and potentially dangerous incidents.

Such efforts to train new employees in job skills and to provide a set of values which related to industrial life (e.g., the importance of attendance for assembly line workers) were recognized as helpful in increasing worker productivity. However, few firms took the time to do this, especially with respect to the attitude and value area.

Only one company studied — a diversified U.S. subsidiary — had a functioning suggestion plan of any consequence. This was a major area in which both U.S. and Indian firms failed to utilize the skills of their workers. In several other U.S. firms, plans had been introduced, but on the assumption that the workers would know what to do with them. U.S. management frequently failed to recognize the need to educate the work force, even in such simple matters as this, and to emphasize the importance of such programs. Whenever U.S. management practices or techniques relied upon patterns not indigenous to the local environment, there was a need to educate — one that was too often overlooked.

INVENTORY LEVELS

The techniques of inventory planning and control were in a rudimentary stage at most of the firms surveyed in India. The few valuable inventory management systems which were found had all been installed within recent years.

A quantitative analysis of inventory levels by category for different firms in India often is not meaningful because of significant differences in degrees of vertical integration, product mixes, locations, and various other factors. However, some distinct differences emerged between U.S. and Indian companies, particularly in the pharmaceutical sector.

For the 1960s as a whole, U.S. drug subsidiaries tended to have substantially bigger raw materials inventories in terms of number of days or weeks sales represented by the monetary value of inventory. This was largely due to their greater dependency on imported raw materials. Because of government licensing procedures and procurement delays, they maintained large stocks and usually imported their materials in large quantities and at infrequent intervals. However, the pattern has not been clear in the last few years. The fact that many U.S. subsidiaries have reduced their imports, usually under government pressure, is the chief reason for this.

A second difference was that U.S. subsidiaries tended to have larger goods-in-process inventories than their indigenous counterparts because of a greater emphasis on advance planning which allowed them to schedule production earlier and more efficiently. They were also more conscious of the benefits of economies of scale (e.g., chemicals would be prepared in bulk, later to be tableted or packaged as powders, whereas the Indian firms tended to produce what they needed to fulfill a particular moment's requirements). Another reason for the difference in goods-in-process inventories was that the Indian firms often operated on a hand-to-mouth production basis, with less than a few weeks worth of sales in process at any time. Although in the

United States such situations are frequently associated with meticulous planning, quite the contrary was true in India. In most of these situations, it was strictly a question of continuous operations on a crash basis.

Relatively few firms maintained regular or accurate figures on stockouts, and most of those who did were U.S. subsidiaries. Because inventories of finished goods were small, these stockouts typically gave rise to emergency requests for production. These were frequent enough to keep production planning in a continuous state of disruption. Lack of inventory control also caused production costs to skyrocket — although few firms collected data which would reflect the actual amounts involved.

Lack of systematic attention to inventory levels created many problems for the companies studied. Only a handful attempted to set levels by anything more sophisticated than guess work. In addition, poor coordination between sales, production, and purchasing, was the rule, especially at the more traditional Indian firms. In one case, a U.S. subsidiary overestimated the demand for a new product. Because communications were slow, a four month shut-down of one production line was required to bring finished goods inventories down to a reasonable level. During the early part of this period, raw materials inventory continued to expand, since no one had bothered to inform the purchasing department.

AUTOMATION AND CAPITAL INTENSITY

With few exceptions the U.S. subsidiaries surveyed relied more heavily on automated and mechanized equipment, and had more capital-intensive operations than their indigenous counterparts. During the 1960s, average fixed assets per employee at the five major U.S. drug subsidiaries studied in India ranged from about 14,000 to nearly 30,000 rupees. The range for the five private Indian drug firms was between 4,400 and about 16,000 rupees. A public sector Indian drug firm averaged about 18,500 rupees, and two British drug firms surveyed averaged slightly over 17,500 rupees.

Internal consequences

Within a developing nation such as India, automation usually has several major consequences, some beneficial and some detrimental. The changes incurred through automation basically affect three areas: product quality, productivity, and personnel.

One of the most beneficial results of automation in the pharmaceutical industry, as well as many other sectors, concerns quality of output. Once an automated piece of equipment has been set up (assuming reasonably good maintenance), its output is uniform. This tends to eliminate the discrepancies which result from less-consistent human performance and, especially where the labor force requires a great deal of training and development, usually provides a better product. Such has been the experience of many companies in India which have replaced manual operations with more mechanized processes.

However, there are two important caveats which should accompany the use of automation to improve quality. The first involves raw materials supply, and the second the crucial question of maintenance.

Many U.S. companies which automated ran into problems they had not anticipated. Their basic knowledge of automation had been transferred from the United States. However, a critical factor was present in the Indian setting which would not normally be a problem in the United States: the quality of raw materials was not consistent. Automated machinery often does not have the range of flexibility of a human being on the input side; although it may do a job better and more quickly, it is frequently designed to handle a limited range of inputs and to provide an even more limited range of outputs. Consequently, variations in the uniformity of inputs can create great problems. The case of a rubber-stoppering machine, in which the stoppers clogged the feeder mechanisms because manufacturers did not hold needed tolerances, is an example. The insertion of these stoppers by hand was no problem, however, because a worker with a mallet has greater flexibility of operation.

The introduction of automatic equipment should be accompanied by the recognition that greater emphasis has to be placed on securing reliable sources of supply. In most companies, this fact was not recognized until after the equipment had been installed and operations had commenced. Typically, firms scurried around for many months trying to correct the situation, either by obtaining the inputs they required or by modifying the machines. U.S. companies were usually the first to search out better sources of supply. When they found a source which could meet their specifications they often "locked in" on it, to the exclusion of any other vendors. Indian firms often chose the alternative of becoming their own source of supply.

A second factor was the need for better maintenance capability, which included the availability of spare parts and the skills of the maintenance force.

The spare parts situation often raised critical problems. Normally, along with importation of a piece of equipment, a number of spare parts were also purchased. However, these purchases were usually based on suggestions from the U.S. manufacturer or the U.S. parent company. Local operating conditions, the way the labor force handled the machines, and the quality of raw materials frequently created different wear and breakdown patterns, and the imported spare parts which were based on U.S. requirements were not always sufficient to meet maintenance needs. Furthermore, since many precision parts could not be obtained in India, companies often found themselves involved in complex importation procedures. Delays and disruption of production schedules resulted.

Keeping up high output standards is dependent upon the operating condition of equipment. This places a premium on maintenance. Many companies had difficulty finding competent personnel to deal with the mechanical and electrical problems involved in maintaining automated equipment. Such personnel were not readily available in the labor market, and few training facilities existed. As a result, many pieces of automated equipment functioned in a less than optimum manner.

Automation had both positive and negative consequences for productivity. On the positive side, the machinery often functioned at high speed, which increased output. One man, operating one or more automated pieces of machinery, could produce much more than many men using less automated processes. However, this situation also presented problems.

First, because the number of manufacturing channels (e.g., one machine versus eight men) were fewer, their continuous operation was more critical. When a man in an eight-man team was absent, only one-eighth of production was lost. When the machine malfunctioned, the entire production process might cease. This placed a premium on attendance, as well as on preventive maintenance and rapid repair capability. Unfortunately, few firms had developed effective preventive maintenance programs, and repair services ranged from poor to barely adequate, with few exceptions.

The use of automated equipment also limited the ability of the U.S. firms to adapt to changing conditions. When a machine broke down, they did not have readily available pools of trained workers who could switch to manual methods while the firm waited for a replacement part. (There were incidents where expensive pieces of equipment sat idle for months at a time.) In addition, as market conditions changed, Indian firms could reduce or increase production of particular items by shifting workers from one product to another, while U.S. firms found that they had to let a worker stand idle most of the day while he operated his machine on a limited schedule.

Other unanticipated factors were power, fuel and water shortages. Such shortages, endemic in India and in much of the developing world, frequently curtailed the operation of automatic equipment. Consequently, production was disrupted, sometimes for fairly long periods, and frequently for short but annoying periods of time.

One of the important objectives of automation as seen by many U.S. subsidiaries was the reduction of labor problems through the reduction of the number of people directly involved in production. However, there was little evidence that this strategy paid significant dividends. While it reduced the number of persons who might be potential trouble markers it increased the importance of each one who remained. But, more important, labor problems in India were less likely to result from employee discontent than they were from internal union struggles, or from outside political and economic issues.

A related problem came from finding workers capable of operating the equipment. In many cases, the number of workers who had experience in operating modern or sophisticated machinery was small, and no readily available supply of such individuals existed. The alternatives were few. Workers might be hired away from competitors; new men might be hired and put on the job in the hope that controls were simple enough to be operated through common sense; or workers might be trained for the new tasks. Because India does not have an industrial tradition, the second alternative was fraught with dangers. Nevertheless few firms had developed effective training programs.

In most companies, training for production workers consisted of letting the new employee watch an old hand operate an identical or similar machine before putting him to work. However, this did not prepare the new man for unusual situations that might arise. He generally learned "what to do," but not "why he did it." As a result, many of these workers were unable to anticipate problems as they developed and before they became critical. This contributed to substantially higher breakdown rates than would be found in the United States, according to production managers interviewed.

A final problem which affected the use of automated equipment related to government control of imports. Most companies in India have been feeling the squeeze of tightened import policies. Most of the U.S. firms are relatively new, and when they initially established plants, they often built in more capacity than they required. However, as time passed and their markets increased, capacity in certain areas became strained. When these companies applied for licenses to import additional equipment, they found that regulations had changed and they were no longer permitted to import the equipment they had originally purchased or that imports had been stopped completely and they had to turn to other sources. This increased the complexity of the production operation, since some of the new equipment was not compatible with what they already had. It also intensified problems with spare parts, since inventories had to be increased to service the various makes of machines.

A number of the more traditional Indian firms took the other extreme, feeling that they would automate as Indian industry developed the capability to service their needs. This did eliminate some of the problems faced by companies that were among the first to automate, but the price they paid in terms of lost advantages in productivity, quality, and cost probably more than offset their gains. Some of the more progressive Indian firms took an approach somewhere between the extremes. This often seemed to be the best course.

External consequences

Outside the firm, the impacts of automation were also significant. On the positive side, productivity often increased sharply, and the use of automated equipment provided examples for the nation's future industrial development. It also encouraged the development of higher-quality sources of supply for both equipment and raw materials. Furthermore, the application of automated equipment was equated in the mind of the average consumer with a high-quality image.

However, automated equipment presented problems with both union and government groups who were concerned with building up employment opportunities. Many of these organizations saw automation as a direct threat to increased employment and therefore as "immoral" in the Indian situation. This attitude was particularly evident in the case of major government construction projects, where manual labor was used in place of mechanization, even where it delayed the completion of the project by years. A controversy has been raging for some time as to whether the temporary employment gains are worth the loss in long-range progress incurred by not having the projects completed sooner. U.S. firms, because of their relatively high reliance on automation, were often accused of introducing their own values and trampling on the needs of their host nation. Little action was being taken to effectively counter this argument.

The other major area of conflict related to the use of foreign exchange. The importation of equipment requires foreign exchange. Consequently, each request for a piece of equipment or an imported spare part agitated certain individuals in the government hierarchy. Indian firms generally showed a greater tendency to purchase less sophisticated, locally manufactured equipment, or to make it themselves.

FACILITIES

The quality of production facilities in India varied in almost direct proportion to the age of the firm and the proportion of U.S.-trained employees. At U.S. companies the manufacturing facilities (both plant and equipment) were newer and many were set up as showcases. Attractive grounds, efficiently laid-out manufacturing areas, bright new machines, and spotless cleanliness characterized such enterprises.

The Indian companies ranged from modern, pleasant plants comparable to those in the United States, to archaic and unattractive-looking facilities. In general, the Indian companies' facilities were much older. Most had begun manufacturing while the U.S. firms were still in the exporting and importing stage, and others were functioning before the U.S. parent companies had even thought about establishing Indian subsidiaries.

The Indian firms which were most progressive and had the highest number of U.S. trained employees were, without question, the firms with the most modern facilities and equipment. Even some of the older plants, dating back 30 or more years, had been renovated and re-organized for smooth production flows. One such firm had devoted the largest portion of its industrial engineering effort to such tasks.

The emphasis on cleanliness in these plants was much closer to U.S. standards than to local ones. Not only were the manufacturing operation areas kept clean, but the aisles, offices, and grounds also received a considerable attention. Efforts were devoted to presenting an overall image of neatness, precision, and efficiency — three characteristics that are associated primarily with Western culture.

The more traditional Indian firms were less concerned about appearances, and in many cases, there was evidence that they cut corners in terms of attention to the manufacturing area. In general, they tried to make do with old equipment — many having developed their own maintenance and engineering departments to accomplish this task. In some firms such departments were both effective and innovative. At others they had become very large and had begun to manufacture many of their own products, and in a few cases to take on outside work as well.

Probably an extreme example of poor facilities was one traditional Indian firm in which manufacturing facilities were located in more than 100 separate buildings, scattered over a large plant area. Although manufacturing officials continuously complained of the problems this arrangement presented with respect to production flow, top management was reluctant to spend the money to construct new facilities as long as the old buildings were considered structurally sound.

SAFETY

Few firms in India maintained regular or detailed safety records or prepared any type of safety index. Most that did were U.S. subsidiaries.

From the limited data available, the U.S. subsidiaries generally had better safety performance records than indigenous firms in terms of accidents and related lost time per man-year worked. Accident rates, though not high, were not as low as in the United States. It was somewhat surprising that there were not more accidents in many of the plants visited in India, particularly in the older plants of the more traditional firms.

Much less attention was paid to safety precautions than in U.S. industry — for example, enforcement of the wearing of goggles and protective clothing was lax. U.S. subsidiaries emphasized safety much more than indigenous firms, and some had intensive safety programs, requiring all employees to wear appropriate safety equipment in the plant, and even providing fire-fighting training to the workers.

UTILIZATION OF PLANT CAPACITY

One of the most important measures of manufacturing efficiency is capacity utilization. This is an indication not only of the efficient utilization of real capital, but also of the ability of production management to obtain maximum output from its resources. Unfortunately, few of the companies surveyed in India regularly collected or analyzed data in this respect. Most of the U.S. firms and some indigenous companies did make estimates, but these were subject to substantial margins of error and usually lacked detail. In general, the U.S. firms had a better "feel" of their rates of capacity utilization than did most indigenous firms.

Nearly all the U.S. subsidiaries had made capacity estimates at the time they prepared their construction. Typically, these estimates had been supplied by the home office or by U.S. or other foreign equipment producers, and were based on the physical capabilities of the machinery which was to be installed. However, in most cases these figures had to be discarded as unrealistic, due to differences in raw materials, differences in skill levels of the work force, changed climatic conditions, different maintenance and spare parts availability conditions, and the fact that processing line configurations often had to be altered (and often equipment had to be substituted for one reason or another).

A few U.S. firms had actually established clear capacity utilization targets. But in most cases these were based not on a careful analysis of data but on off-the-top-of the-head estimates supplied by production personnel. Capacity figures were often presented in terms of product potential, rather than true machine capacity. However, where equipment was used to manufacture only one product (or a limited number of products), this measure was of some value.

There was one significant difference between the base commonly used to estimate capacity utilization in U.S. and Indian drug firms. In nearly all cases, figures were related to the number of shifts operated. In most basic chemical processes, three shift operations were normally the rule. But in pharmaceutical operations (e.g., formulations), one shift was most common in the U.S. firms, while two (and occasionally three) were more prevalent among the Indian companies. (It is interesting to note that most of the domestic drug operations of the U.S. parent companies were working multiple shifts.)

Invariably U.S. subsidiaries indicated that they would prefer two-shift operations (in order to minimize investment), but that the labor situation was such that it was impossible to find enough qualified workers, and especially supervisors, to work on second or third shifts. Many of the managers in the Indian firms claimed that this was patently absurd. They indicated that, first, the U.S. managers wanted to be on the scene while the plant was in operation and did not want to work on a second or third shift; second, that the managers of U.S. subsidiaries were not as investment-conscious as they would have been if they were using their own money, since they were working with the funds of their parent companies; and third, that the U.S. companies used the labor problem as an excuse for increasing their imports of foreign equipment (i.e., quoting higher capacity utilization figures to justify additional needs), thereby increasing their capacity and flexibility for the future when it might not be possible to obtain imports. None of these explanations seemed entirely convincing, but neither did the labor-problem argument of the U.S. firms.

In addition to the problem of relating output (either actual or theoretical) to the number of shifts worked, there were other problems involved in making capacity utilization comparisons in Indian industry. Many managers in India thought that capacity should be a reflection of past performance. Others thought it should represent the maximum possible output of a piece of equipment, assuming that it operated at top speed without stop during the period of reference. And still others had different views about the subject.

Moreover, at most firms subject to government licensing in India there is a difference — at times great — between the licensed and designed or installed capacity. A given firm may be producing below or above licensed capacity during a particular period, either within allowed limits and with the tacit approval of the government, or illegally.

Because of the limited amount of factual data on capacity utilization provided by the firms surveyed, it was necessary to estimate actual utilization of plant capacity in order to make comparisons. Unless otherwise noted, the figures presented below pertain to licensed capacity on the firms' major day shifts.

Nearly all the U.S. drug subsidiaries operated close to or above 80 percent of licensed capacity during the 1960s, with regard to overall pharmaceutical production — leaving aside occasional strikes and acute power and water shortages, and new plant start-up periods. However, for many specific drug items the figures deviated sharply — going as low as 5 percent.

Only one major indigenous drug firm surveyed — the most successful one — consistently operated around the 80 percent level with regard to its pharmaceutical operations during the 1960s. Two others avaraged roughly 65 to 75 percent, and the two most traditional averaged well under 65 percent. Several of these firms intentionally maintained some idle capacity in order to keep "safety" reserves. Chemical operations in all firms (foreign and indigenous) ran closer to 100 percent.

The most traditional of the major Indian drug firms studied has had severe plant utilization problems in recent years. This firm has a large pharmaceutical plant that normally operates one shift in some departments and multiple shifts in others. It also has two chemical plants that normally operate on a three-shift basis. During 1968 and 1969 the chemical plants operated well under 50 percent capacity — possibly under 30 percent — and the drug plant in the range of 40 to 60 percent. Labor problems were the biggest constraint. The lack of managerial and technical know-how was also a serious limitation. Other causes of idle capacity included a lack of demand for some of the firm's products, its inability to export, inadequate imports of raw materials and spare parts, and serious floods at the plants which could have been offset, at least partly, by better managerial and technical know-how.

Two small indigenous firms which manufacture drugs and chemicals — one having a licensing agreement with a U.S. firm — were operating at only 20 to 30 percent of capacity. The same major constraints described above applied to both of them.

While internal managerial and technical deficiencies have also seriously hindered capacity utilization at several major U.S. drug subsidiaries, external and largely uncontrollable factors have tended to be even more constraining. Such environmental constraints have included supply problems (both import restrictions and indigenous deficiencies), power and water shortages, and (particularly in more recnet years) the lack of demand for various products which, in several cases, was not predictable. Several drug firms (including non-American ones), as well as various firms in other capital-intensive sectors in India, have set up their own stand-by power and water reserves and water reclamation facilities in order to alleviate capacity utilization and equipment down-time problems. Labor problems, including major strikes, have also hindered capacity utilization at several U.S. drug firms from time to time. In some cases, these problems could have been avoided through more effective management, but in others they were probably inevitable, or at least largely uncontrollable.

A large and diversified U.S. subsidiary operated the polyethylene department of its chemicals and plastics plant close to full capacity during the first half of the 1960s, excluding the initial start-up year. During most of 1967 and 1968 it operated at roughly 55 to 60 percent of capacity, and it had to overproduce substantially for inventory in order to achieve this level. The inventory glut of finished polyethylene output was removed around April, 1969, and the plant achieved a 75 percent utilization rate shortly thereafter. The principal reason for this excess capacity was that large imports of polyethylene were made by the Indian government in 1967-68. Somebody convinced the Ministry of Foreign Trade that there was a large and growing supply gap involving this product and, as a result, this turned out to be the case. A large British producer of polyethylene in India had even greater excess capacity in this area than the U.S. firm. A major constraint on the U.S. plant's polyethylene capacity in 1969 was its inability to get government permission to import critically needed spare parts. If this constraint had not existed, management estimated that capacity utilization could have been increased by 15 to 20 percent with a similar resulting increase in sales and profits. As it was, in 1969 the company was still exporting polyethylene at a sizeable loss to maintain capacity utilization.

The same U.S. plant was operating close to full licensed capacity in 1969 with regard to its other overall chemical operations. However, for a few individual items it had considerable excess capacity. Its greatest excess capacity in the chemicals area occurred around 1966, when the utilization rate was only about 50 percent. At that time it could have profitably marketed everything it produced. The firm also had some serious internal technical problems, and U.S. experts were sent over to iron them out. This plant has dealt with the chronic water shortages in Bombay by setting up its own reserve and reclamation systems.

One of India's largest and newest chemical companies — a British-Dutch-Indian equity collaboration — put its fourth and final licensed plant into operation in the Bombay area in 1969. The plants were operating at an overall average capacity utilization rate of about 70 percent in 1969. Power, and to a lesser extent, water shortages have been major constraints on capacity utilization. For example, in April and early May of 1968 the plants experienced seven serious power failures. During the January-July period of 1969 there were about 80 shutdowns, some lasting a few days, largely because of power failures and water problems. The firm recently put in its own costly stand-by power generators. The government had promised the firm two power lines but only provided one. Lack of demand for some of the company's products has also contributed to excess capacity, as has the improper design of some large imported German turbines.

All three of the battery plants of a U.S. company operated at a minimum of 90 percent capacity during 1969, alternating between a two- and three-shift operation. During the 1960s average plant capacity utilization never fell below 70 percent in any one year, and in most it exceeded 80 or 85 percent. Labor problems and major strikes hindered capacity utilization during some periods, and in a few months and quarters it fell below 50 percent. Imported spare parts and the unavailability of suitable indigenous supplies have been the other serious constraints with regard to capacity utilization.

This U.S. firm's major indigenous competitor operated its plant at roughly 85 to 90 percent capacity in 1969 on a 2½-shift basis. However, its capacity utilization rates were much more erratic during the 1960s than at any of the U.S. firm's battery plants. For example, during the 1964-66 period the utilization rate ran roughly between 40 and 50 percent. Major strikes, import and other supply problems, and serious conflicts with the government were factors in this regard. However, internal managerial and technical problems have also presented constraints.

In general, firms in India's drug, chemical, and battery sectors (as well as various other consumer goods) have fared better with regard to capacity utilization than heavy industry and engineering firms. There has also been greater installed new capacity in the former sectors in recent years. There was, however, significant improvement in capacity utilization in heavy industry in the late 1960s. This was largely due to sub-stantial increases in exports and domestic economic recovery.

A large, multi-plant Indian firm in the electrical engineering sector was producing electric meters and motors above 90 percent capacity in 1969, compared to 70 to 75 percent during the height of India's recession in 1967-68. However, there were only 6 firms producing meters in India in 1969, compared to 14 in 1966. This firm managed to increase its capacity utilization for transformer production to 50 percent in 1969, com-pared to 35 or 40 percent during 1967-68. However, there were 19 firms producing transformers in 1966, and only 9 in 1969. Switchgear capacity utilized also increased to nearly 50 percent in 1969, compared to only 30 or 35 percent a few years earlier. On the other hand, the firm steadily increased its capacity utilization in connection with elevators, and was producing at almost full capacity in 1969. The big increases in elevator and transformer exports toward the end of the 1960s contributed signifi-cantly to the high capacity utilization in these areas.

Import restrictions (especially those involving copper and certain kinds of electrical steel), as well as lack of local demand were major constraints on capacity utiliza-tion in the transformer area. Lack of domestic demand and the inability to export were constraints with regard to switchgear, as well as electric motors and meters in earlier periods. With greater technical and managerial know-how, this company could be in a better competitive position both at home and abroad, and thus increase its capacity utilization especially with regard to these items. Both a British firm and a U.S.-Indian venture (with 50 percent U.S. equity) have had higher capacity utilization rates in the last several years than the above Indian company in connection with similar types of goods produced.

Capacity utilization as well as exports increased in India's steel sector in the late 1960s. In 1969, the industry was producing at about 85 percent capa-city, while a public sector steel corporation was producing at about 80 percent.

The lack of demand for various of its products, labor problems, internal spare parts inventory and maintenance problems, and internal managerial and technical deficiencies have been the major constraints on capacity utilization in this firm. Foreign exchange and imports have not been serious problems.

UNANTICIPATED EQUIPMENT DOWN-TIME

An important measure of production efficiency related to capacity utilization is unanticipated machine down-time due to breakdowns and repair. This is also a measure of the effectiveness of the maintenance function.

Few firms surveyed in India kept accurate records on equipment down-time, and many did not make realistic estimates in this area. U.S. subsidiaries did a better job than their Indian competitors, but one which was inadequate by U.S. standards.

Concern about production stoppages due to equipment down-time were expressed more frequently in interviews with managers of U.S. subsidiaries even though they had less lost time than indigenous firms. This apparent inconsistency can be explained by the greater pressure to maintain output placed on production managers in the U.S. companies. Although these managers usually were not held responsible for down-time, their weekly or monthly production reports were closely scrutinized. The production managers of Indian firms — especially the more traditional ones — were more inclined to accept down-time as an unfortunate but unavoidable fact of industrial life, and many expended little or no effort to eliminate or reduce it.

The lack of adequate spare parts and critical components, poor maintenance practices, and power, fuel, and water shortages have been the chief cause for unanticipated equipment stoppages. At U.S. pharmaceutical subsidiaries in India unanticipated equipment down-time in relation to total operating time has usually been between 5 and 7 percent in recent years. The best U.S. subsidiary plants studied had roughly 4 or 5 percent rates with regard to their pharmaceutical operations, and about 2 to 3 percent in their basic chemical operations. None of their parent companies' domestic plants have had rates averaging more than about 1 percent.

The drug plants of U.S. subsidiaries in India have generally had lower rates than British or other foreign drug plants surveyed. The latter have rates ranging from slightly over 5 percent to an estimated 10 or 11 percent, with all but one of these plants having a rate exceeding 7 percent. The Indian drug companies ran rates of 10 percent or more. Most had rates of at least 15 to 20 percent, and one traditional drug firm had a rate above 20 percent.

An American chemicals and plastics plant experienced between 10 and 15 percent average unanticipated down-time rates in its basic chemical operations during the second half of the 1960s, several times higher than the rates of domestic plants of its parent firm. Power and water shortages were chiefly responsible for this high down-time, although internal managerial and technical problems resulting from a major expansion and conversion program, also played a part. The same plant experienced unanticipated down-time of 20 to 30 percent in its polyethylene production.

One U.S. subsidiary conducted detailed studies of the causes of down-time at two of its battery plants. These studies revealed that spare parts and component problems accounted for 40 to 50 percent, maintenance and repair deficiencies about 10 to 20 percent, labor problems (mainly absenteeism) about 5 to 10 percent, raw and in-process material problems roughly 13 to 18 percent, power failures 4 to 7 percent, and other unspecified factors 10 to 15 percent. All of the domestic plants of this firm's parent company had much lower unanticipated down-time rates.

The oldest battery plant of this subsidiary had an unanticipated equipment down-time rate of about 15 percent in the mid-1960s, and around 12 percent in the late 1960s. One of its newer plants had rates of 15 to 20 percent during some periods before 1967, but had reduced the rate to 4 percent by 1969. The firm's newest battery plant had rates of about 8 percent at first, but brought the rate down to 2 percent by 1969.

India's leading indigenous battery producer — whose plant is comparable to the oldest U.S. subsidiary — has had an average unanticipated down-time rate of at least 15 to 20 percent in recent years, has sometimes gone as high as 25 to 30 percent.

The recently-modernized flashlight factory of the above U.S. subsidiary had down-time rates of 7 to 9 percent in the past. It began to keep better down-time records in 1966, and since 1968 has reduced its rate to 1 to 3 percent. This is higher than the rate at its parent's domestic plant, but lower than that of its major indigenous competitor.

The various plants of an Indian electrical engineering company recorded down-time losses on a number of specific days. Losses exceeded 20 percent on many days, and exceeded 7 percent in nearly every case. Internal managerial and technical deficiencies rather than external constraints have been the causes.

The equipment failure rate at a large indigenous tool plant was roughly 13 to 16 percent during the second half of the 1960s, even though it is a relatively modern plant.

From the limited data and estimates obtained from U.S. and other foreign firms — with at least 50 percent equity in the case of joint ventures — in India's engineering sector, these firms seem to have had less unanticipated down-time than the indigenous companies examined.

Equipment stoppages at the plants of India's huge public sector steel corporation averaged more than 20 percent of operating time in recent years. Gross deficiencies in the supply of critical spare parts and components, as well as poor management, have contributed to this situation.

EQUIPMENT PRODUCTIVITY

U.S. plants in India have made more productive use of equipment than indigenous ones, as evidenced by higher rates of output per unit of operating time. Production lines were more efficiently balanced and machines were run at higher speeds, even though labor problems and strong union resistance often kept equipment productivity below the levels desired by management. In comparison to parent company operations, their records were substandard.

A typical example of this was seen in an engineering plant in India which was 50 percent U.S.-owned. The plant was designed to produce less than 3 percent of the physical output of the parent company's domestic plant (in terms of value added) but required more than 8 percent of the gross plant investment of the U.S.-based plant. Although it was only about one-tenth the size of the U.S.-based plant, it required a tool ship equipped with twice the facilities and staffed with three times the labor. The Indian plant has required more than twice the number of machine hours per unit of output than the plant in the United States. And, although the Indian factory's wages have averaged only 7 or 8 percent of the U.S. rate, the total labor cost per unit has averaged between 50 and 65 percent of the U.S. standard costs.

LABOR PRODUCTIVITY

It is not surprising to find that in virtually every sector labor productivity in the United States is higher than in India. For example, according to data obtained primarily from official government sources, average levels of labor productivity for specific products in the U.S. chemical and pharmaceutical industries (as measured in terms of both physical and monetary output per man-hour) have ranged, during the 1960s, from about three to over thirty times higher than in India. In steel and other metal products, U.S. labor productivity ranged, on the average, from about four to ten times higher; it was five to twenty-five times higher in engineering products, two to ten times higher for similar types of batteries and flashlights, and two to fifteen times higher for textiles, shoes, other types of consumer goods, and paper.

In virtually every case, U.S. subsidiaries studied in India had lower labor productivity than comparable domestic parent operations. However, with very few exceptions, they had significantly higher labor productivity than their indigenous counterparts.

The question of raising labor productivity in India seems to be a particularly complex one with no clear-cut or ready answers. Specific practices that prove effective for one firm, or even for one of its plants, often fail when applied to another firm or plant. U.S. subsidiaries have been more willing to experiment with new practices, incentives, and techniques aimed at increasing labor productivity than have their indigenous counterparts. Incentives and other approaches that work well in American industry have not always been effective in India — in some cases productivity actually declined as a result, while in others it showed an increase.

There is a widespread tendency in Indian industry to assume that raising labor productivity is not an important objective because labor is cheap and abundant. However, the situation can be very deceiving, as illustrated by a comparison of three plants that manufacture chemicals and drugs. One plant is Indian-owned but has a licensing agreement with an American company. The second is the U.S.-based plant of the same licensor, and the third is the Argentine subsidiary of the U.S. company. All three plants are comparable in terms of size, product lines, and technology.

Physical units produced per man-hour during the last few years have been six to seven times greater at the U.S.-based plant and nearly five times greater at the Argentine plant than at the Indian firm. The average wage rate per man-hour (at official exchange rates) of the U.S. plant has been over $4.00, compared to $2.00 at the Argentine plant, and 60¢ at the Indian factory. The average total labor cost per unit of output has been about 13¢ at the U.S. factory, 10.5¢ at the Argentine plant, and 15¢ at the Indian plant.

Generally, those companies in India which have had the highest labor productivity in their industries have most, if not all, of the following characteristics: 1) managements are committed to increasing productivity; 2) the firms have a relatively high level of managerial, technical, and worker skills; 3) they do a good job of recruiting competent personnel and training them; 4) they try to keep personnel motivated, often using some kind of worker incentives; and 5) they maintain good labor relations.

U.S. subsidiaries ranked higher on the whole on the first three characteristics than their Indian counterparts, but they often had poor records in the area of motivation.

It was not clear whether U.S. or indigenous firms dealt with unions more effectively in connection with raising labor productivity; both good and bad records were found in both types of firms. Some British firms seemed to have better union relations than either their U.S. or indigenous counterparts, but they ranked lower on the first three characteristics than the U.S. subsidiaries.

Some U.S. firms surveyed maintained detailed records of labor productivity, especially for recent years. However, most company records ranged from crude to virtually non-existent.

Labor productivity was clearly higher at the major U.S. drug firms studied in India tha at their indigenous counterparts, with only one exception. This held true whether produc tivity calculations were based on physical output or sales value. For example, output per factory employee in rupees ranged from roughly 67,000 to over 155,000 at the U.S. subsidiaries, with the average being over 100,000 rupees. At the indigenous pharmaceutical companies the range was from 16,000 to nearly 70,000 rupees, with an average of 40,000.

Physical output per employee at the U.S. battery subsidiary was more than double that of its major indigenous competitor. If factory employment is used as the base, it was nearly triple. Labor productivity differentials, expressed in terms of output value, were even greater than the physical output indicators. Labor productivity in connection with the flashlight production of the U.S. subsidiary was approximately three time higher than at the major indigenous battery firm.

MATERIAL WASTAGE, REJECT RATES, AND SCRAP LEVELS

A number of environmental conditions have a bearing on the level of material waste, product rejects, and scrap. These include the skill levels of available personnel; their attitudes and motivation; the availability of suitable materials and other critical supply inputs (imports or indigenous); and the technology and production processes employed.

Even when the environmental conditions listed above are negative a firm can do much to reduce their impact. It can make a strong effort to recruit the most competent people available, and train and motivate them. It can seek out and develop better sources of supply. It can engage in related research and development work. It can do a better job of planning and control, and organize its activities more efficiently so as to keep wastage to a minimum.

In general, material wastage is more costly in Indian industry than in the United States because of the higher prices paid for most materials. Yet, with few exceptions, overall material wastage as well as in-process quality rejects were significantly higher at U.S. subsidiaries studied than at the domestic operations of their parent companies. Usually, less effective management, as well as technological or environmental constraints, contributed to this. However, several U.S. subsidiaries had lower finished-product scrap rates than their parents' domestic operations, primarily because low labor rates made it economical to reprocess faulty output.

With few exceptions, U.S. subsidiaries had lower material wastage and quality reject and scrap rates than their indigenous counterparts. Better management seemed to account for much of the difference.

Product yield is a common measure of material wastage in the drug and chemical industries. A 100 percent yield in the production of a particular item indicates no wastage. None of the U.S. drug plants studied in India had product yields of less than about 85 percent. Recently, some of their yields have been brought up to the 90 percent level, often with the help of experts from their parent firms.

Only one indigenous drug company had product yields (on similar products) comparable to those at U.S. subsidiaries. A second Indian firm had increased its yields to approximately 82 to 85 percent, but the others still had yields of under 80 percent.

In-process quality reject rates were generally higher at the U.S. drug subsidiaries than at their parents' U.S. domestic operations, based on the same quality standards. On the other hand, they were significantly lower than those of indigenous drug firms, many of which applied lower standards. The average rates at most of the U.S. subsidiaries ranged from about 1 to 5 percent in recent years, while for similar kinds of products and processes they averaged well over 5 percent at Indian firms, reaching 20 percent in some instances. British and other foreign drug subsidiaries examined have had product yields somewhere between the average yields of U.S. and indigenous companies.

The rejection rates for finished products in the U.S. pharmaceutical subsidiaries was almost nil, due primarily to careful in-process inspection. Only one U.S. firm reported a final rejection rate as high as 1 percent. The Indian firms which had good in-process inspection reported rejection rates averaging between 1 and 3 percent. Those which conducted little or no in-process inspection reported final reject figures of between 5 and 10 percent.

In general, U.S. chemical producers in India have also had less material wastage, higher yields, and lower reject and scrap rate on similar products, compared to indigenous firms. For example, the product yield achieved by one U.S. plant has averaged around 91 percent compared to 85 percent at a similar Indian firm. Another U.S. plant had yields in the range of 85 to 93 percent, compared to 73 to 80 percent at a similar indigenous plant.

In India's battery industry, an old U.S. plant experienced rising material waste, reject, and scrap rates during the second half of the 1960s. This was due primarily to raw material and other supply deficiencies and fewer imports. However, labor problems and other managerial factors have also contributed. Until recently the subsidiary's parent company has been applying the identical quality standards in India as in its U.S.-based operations. A basic policy has been to maintain 25 percent product quality superiority over indigenous battery competitors. However, on several battery types, quality standards have recently been cut by 5 to 10 percent.

Total material wastage at this U.S. plant increased from about 11 percent in 1966 to 13 percent in 1968, and 17 percent in early 1969. In 1969, a major effort was made to reduce material wastage, and indications were that it was successful. Material overuse above prescribed standards of this plant was 2.5 percent in 1964, 1.8 percent in 1965, 2.2 percent in 1966, 2.6 percent in mid-1968, and 2.07 percent in June, 1969. Final scrap figures ranged between 0.6 and 1 percent during the 1964-69 period — compared to 1 to 3 percent at its parent company's battery plants in the United States.

At another of the U.S. subsidiary's battery plants total material wastage increased from about 12 percent in 1966 to 16 percent in early 1969, but seemed to be decreasing by mid-1969. Its rejection and final scarp rates have been lower than those of the older plant. This firm's newest battery plant has had a total material wastage rate of 10 to 11 percent, which it expected to reduce to 8 percent in 1970. (This would bring it close to the parent company's international standards.) At the end of the 1960s the plant also had lower reject and scrap rates than the subsidiary's other battery plants.

From estimates as well as the limited data available, there is no doubt that the material wastage, reject and scrap rates at the two major indigenous battery plants have been higher than at even the lowest ranked of the three U.S. plants in India. Moreover, the lowest ranked U.S. plant has been producing a wider and more complex range of higher-quality products. Superior management and technological skill at this plant have been largely responsible for its better performance in this area.

The above U.S. subsidiary's flashlight plant has also had more efficient material utilization, and lower reject and scrap rates than the major indigenous flashlight plant. Moreover, its performance has improved in recent years, partly with the help of experts sent over by its parent company.

Material wastage, reject, and scrap rates have been higher at indigenous engineering firms surveyed than at U.S. and British subsidiaries, and at joint ventures where the Indian partners have not had over 50 percent equity. Moreover, the latter have typically been doing more to improve their performance in this area in recent years. However, there have been conflicts regarding quality at some U.S.-Indian joint ventures examined. For example, in one such firm the Indian partners wanted to maintain only about 75 percent of the quality levels desired by the U.S. collaborator. However, its U.S. partner has insisted that outputs in every country in which the firm operates conform to its international standards, since this would be beneficial with regard to interchangeable parts and components, and would also protect the company's reputation.

MANUFACTURING COSTS

Manufacturing cost proved to be a difficult measure to deal with, both because of the diversity of products and the variations in definitions, particularly with regard to overheads and direct labor. However, an examination of the relative percentages of total manufacturing cost attributable to materials, labor, and overhead did reveal several interesting patterns.

In general, the unit costs of most products in India were higher than in the United States. This was the case for example, for various drugs, chemicals, engineering goods, and batteries. Higher material and supply costs were largely responsible. Economies of scale, differences in technology and productivity levels, managerial factors were also significant in this regard.

A greater percentage of manufacturing cost was attributable to materials in the U.S. subsidiaries than at their indigenous counterparts. (Notable exceptions involved Indian firms which purchased materials at a premium in the "open" or black market.) For example, the average for major U.S. drug firms approximated 65 to 70 percent during the 1960s, whereas it was closer to 55 to 60 percent for major indigenous firms. This was due to the U.S. firms' use of more expensive ingredients (including imports), and smaller labor and overhead components. Essentially, the Indian firms used more labor per unit of output, total manufacturing cost was higher, and material accounted for a smaller percentage of total cost.

The percentage of manufacturing cost attributable to direct labor averaged 10 percent for U.S. drug firms as compared to 18 percent for indigenous companies. However, some Indian firms included supervisory wages in their calculations, while U.S. firms treated them as "indirect" and therefore incorporated them in manufacturing overhead.

Overhead figures showed a wide variation among many firms in the same sector. For example in the pharmaceutical sector, although total overhead costs averaged roughly the same for U.S. and indigenous companies, they ranged from about 10 to 35 percent within the U.S. subsidiaries and from 12 to 40 percent at the the Indian firms.

It was evident that standard definitions of overheads were lacking. In general, however, factory overhead percentages seemed to be slightly higher at U.S. plants than at their indigenous counterparts. This reflected their more costly staff support and service functions, as well as significantly higher depreciation charges.

The percentage of manufacturing cost to selling price was considerably lower in most U.S. subsidiaries, indicating that these firms also had higher gross-profit margins, largely as a result of the more effective management practices which had been transferred from their domestic operations.

CHAPTER 19
PROCUREMENT
AND IMPORTS

INTRODUCTION

Procurement is one of the most critical and at the same time one of the most ineffi-
ciently-performed enterprise functions in developing countries. It is surprising to discover how little of management's attention is directed towards this area and, in the
case of U.S. subsidiaries, how little transference of applicable practices and techniques
occurs.

Many of the purchasing problems found in industrialized nations are intensified
when the focus of operations shifts to a developing economy. New dimensions and
levels of complexity are frequently added, and consequently, the manager in charge
of procurement of the foreign subsidiary requires greater resourcefulness than his U.S.
counterpart if he is to be effective. He must have a broad knowledge of the local
environment, and must develop familiarity with applicable laws, the structure of
supplying industries, the economic infrastructure (especially communications and
transportation), the personalities of government officials and supplier representatives
with whom he will have contact, local patterns of doing business, any long-range
industrial plans of the government, and current political trends.

A detailed knowledge of the total environment is more critical in the developing nation than in the highly industrial country for several reasons. First, there are many sectors of industry where dependable sources of supply are limited and, therefore, frequently unable to meet demand. The purchasing executive must be able to locate these sources and satisfy his company's needs.

Second, personal relationships become more important. Often the large, impersonal marketplaces found in industrialized nations are replaced in the underdeveloped nations by a narrow market in which the establishment of a good purchaser-vendor relationship is an outgrowth of good *personal* relationships between contracting parties. The same may apply with respect to negotiations with government personnel over allocation procedures or import licenses. This puts a premium on the ability of the purchasing executive to understand and operate within the local culture.

Personal relationships may also be important with respect to maintaining quality. In many societies, written contracts are only as meaningful as the personal ties and understandings which bind together the people who have drawn up the document.

Often, sellers' markets exist, not only for end products, but also for the materials and components necessary to manufacture them. As a result, procurement managers need all their skills and resourcefulness to obtain steady supplies of the desired quality at reasonable cost. U.S. subsidiaries often make great concessions with regard to cost so as to increase the likelihood that they will obtain the necessary quantity and quality.

The importance of the human factor is exemplified by the experience of one supplier which was selling to a buyer's market:

> The manager of this Indian company, which produced spare parts for textile equipment, indicated that his reject rate from customers was entirely dependent upon his relationship with mill managers. When the relationships were good, the mills would accept even defective parts, and he would be paid promptly. When relationships turned sour, his rejections would rise, and payments would lag. He estimated that 40 percent of his work was defective, and that only 25 percent was being returned.

The purchasing manager must also be able to assess the future supply situation accurately. He must be able to judge when he should reject items which fail to meet standards; when he should recommend reprocessing within his own firm; and when he should charge the vendor for the cost of such processing. He can afford to be tough if he foresees a surplus, but may want to go easy if the supply situation is going to be tight.

The government planning area must also be watched closely. What will happen to import quotas in the future? Will items presently being imported be available? Should foreign goods be stocked or should local sources of supply be developed?

The purchasing manager must also be conscious of the country's economic position with respect to balance of payments and the availability of foreign exchange, since this will make it possible for him to anticipate future market conditions.

He must also watch government plans outside of his direct sphere of interest. For example, will a new emphasis on building up domestic capacity in certain industrial sectors shift favorable treatment away from his own? Will the government establish industries which will compete for the resources he is now obtaining?

We have discussed in an earlier chapter the case of the Indian pharmaceutical industry, which found itself in difficulty with regard to supplies of alcohol. A synthetic rubber plant was established and became operational before government approval for increased capacity was granted to alcohol producers. This placed the pharmaceutical industry in a severe bind regarding the manufacture of spiritous products, since the rubber plant siphoned off large quantities of the alcohol upon which it had depended.

The procurement executive must sometimes be able to outguess his own marketing and production people. Frequently the procurement cycle is so long that it is impossible to respond to rush marketing requests if purchases are made according to market forecasts. The purchasing manager must develop a sixth sense which allows him to anticipate future requirements, and then to act accordingly.

In many companies, the ordering cycle began with a market forecast which was sent to production personnel, who would then place orders with purchasing. In some plants, production personnel would request more than double the quantity indicated by market forecasts for key items, in an effort to adjust for the marketing department's habitual under-forecasts. Purchasing might then redouble the figures in an effort to forestall the usual emergency purchase requests which occurred when even the raised production targets fell short of demand.

Throughout India, U.S. companies failed to apply purchasing practices developed and commonly used within the United States. In the United States, the steady application of many of these practices has eliminated the need to emphasize them today. Except in the case of new items or rare instances of shortages, the techniques are either no longer necessary or are taken for granted — techniques relative to supplier development, in-plant inspection of vendors, and so forth. Consequently, they are often overlooked when assessing the managerial needs of subsidiaries.

AN OVERVIEW OF PURCHASING MANAGEMENT AT FIRMS STUDIED

Most firms surveyed in India rely on a variety of practices to deal with procurement problems. The use of personal influence, small "gifts" and outright bribes, and the placing of import orders with foreign suppliers before the necessary import entitlements were obtained from the government (in order to cut down delivery times), are examples. Although these practices often contribute significantly to more stable operations and higher efficiency, they occasionally create great embarrassment. For example, in 1966 one U.S. subsidiary did not get an anticipated import permit to cover 100,000 rupees worth of material it had ordered. Fortunately for the subsidiary, its parent company was able to straighten the matter out.

Many firms in India over-order local items or place multiple orders involving several suppliers for the same item to ensure that enough goods will be available when needed. This action is usually based on the assumption that any surpluses can be easily disposed of — perhaps at premium prices for items in short supply. However, as strong sellers' markets have been disappearing, many firms have been left with excess supplies. U.S. and other foreign subsidiaries also sell, barter, and lend goods in short supply to each other and to their parent firms.

Procurement planning

Even though procurement lead times in India frequently require more than a year — 18 to 24 months is not uncommon for imports — surprisingly few firms have engaged in meaningful procurement planning. Only in recent years has there been change in this area, notably in the U.S. subsidiaries.

Traditional indigenous firms typically have short time horizons, do virtually no systematized procurement planning, and generally handle purchasing in a crisis-ridden way. They have also been the most inclined to buy unsuitable items and to skimp on price. As a group, they have been characterized by poorly coordinated action between procurement, production, marketing, and finance. Much of this is a legacy from the past, since it was possible to make sizeable profits in black marketing activities on almost any supplies prior to 1967.

Only a few U.S. subsidiaries and progressive Indian companies have effectively integrated procurement planning and control with related company functions. Few have analyzed trends relating to the ordering and receipt of commodities so that lead times could be better predicted. For example, in the case of controlled items such as various kinds of steel, reasonable predictions of order, delivery, and receipt times could often be made by examining work order notifications, production plans, and programs for steel suppliers. (India's steel companies generally make only one type of steel during a given period and do not produce it again for many months.)

Similarly, little serious attempt has been made to balance inventories. It was common to find less than one week's supply of some items and several years' stock of others, all of which were components of the same end product.

Only a limited number of companies — again mostly U.S. subsidiaries — had coordinating committees composed of purchasing, production, and sales or financial managers. Very few companies have done value analysis or substitution studies, and make-versus-buy and vertical integration decisions have usually been made on the basis of "need," without detailed cost-benefit analysis.

Until quite recently, only one company studied had attempted to use a "materials-management" approach. Surprisingly this was an indigenous company, a successful and relatively progressive pharmaceutical firm.

This company appeared to be effectively coordinating all of the critical elements involved, in a comprehensive and integrated system. This involved coordinating the functions of procurement, production, sales, and finance. Analysis of stocks on hand, in-process and finished goods inventories, as well as related scheduling, dispatching, and expediting activities were a function directed by top management. Procurement planning was updated every three months in conjunction with sales forecasts for each of the following three months. Detailed inventory data was received weekly from all distribution points throughout the country, usually two to three days after each weekend. This was tied in with a streamlined distribution system of trucks, parcel post, and air freight. The system's objective was to balance and optimize raw materials and other critical supplies and reduce finished goods inventories.

Poor coordination, planning, control, feedback, follow-up, and staffing with regard to procurement have been serious and pervasive problems in Indian industry. In spite of external constraints in connection with the procurement function, there is much that firms of all types and nationalities could do to improve in the procurement area.

The purchasing function was generally more decentralized within U.S. subsidiaries than in indigenous firms; however, it was considerably less decentralized at the plant level than in the U.S.-based plants of parent companies. For example, a U.S.-based flashlight plant purchased 75 to 80 percent of all of its supplies, while an Indian subsidiary purchased less than 25 percent until 1966, and roughly 50 to 55 percent by 1969. The subsidiary's central purchasing staff continued to purchase imports and other restricted supplies.

Indian companies which have had the most effective purchasing management have usually had proportionately larger and better-qualified staffs working full-time than those firms with relatively poor purchasing performance. In fact, several U.S. subsidiaries had larger procurement staffs in relation to total employment than the comparable domestic operations of their U.S. parent companies.

In many of the firms, including most U.S. subsidiaries, purchasing functions were split between two sections, one of which handled local items and another which looked after imported materials. Some drug firms treated packaging materials as a separate category. Other firms, mostly Indian, organized their purchasing operations around the type of item being purchased: chemicals, non-chemical materials, equipment, and so forth; and a few divided their functions by point of purchase: e.g., their Bombay office handled all items purchased in that city, plus imports.

The most diverse patterns were found in machinery and spare parts procurement. Sometimes this area was handled by purchasing, sometimes by production, and occasionally, in the case of some U.S. subsidiaries, by the U.S. parent company. Maintenance or production personnel were involved in varying degrees at different firms.

MAKE-VERSUS-BUY DECISIONS AND VERTICAL INTEGRATION

Little attention was directed towards make-versus-buy decisions at most U.S. subsidiaries. However, this situation has changed as these companies have been confronted with more rigid import restrictions and indigenous supply problems. In the greater number of cases, the only question has been where to buy an item. The desire to minimize capital investment in India, and a narrowly defined concept of "acceptable" lines of business activity, have contributed to this purchasing predilection. Frequently, however, make-versus-buy decisions were not considered simply because it never occurred to purchasing managers to think in those terms.

Most companies studied in India had no mechanisms for effectively considering make-versus-buy decisions.

Production personnel usually lacked the cost information which might stimulate their thinking in this direction, while purchasing personnel typically knew little about manufacturing techniques or possibilities. Moreover, the procurement area did not usually have a sufficiently trained staff to perform the analysis required.

The top procurement executives in firms in India have usually been selected for reasons other than their technical knowledge of the field, or their managerial ability. Contacts have been a more important consideration, especially within indigenous firms. Some procurement organizations which were divided into sub-groups by type of item did force some degree of specialization and make possible the development of individuals with in-depth knowledge of various industrial supply sectors. However, this was the exception rather than the rule and, in traditional indigenous firms, a single man was usually responsible for purchasing virtually all supplies. Consequently, most procurement executives never became familiar with the products they were purchasing. This severely limited their capacity for considering make-versus-buy decisions.

In general, indigenous companies in India have tended to be willing to integrate their production vertically to a greater extent than U.S. subsidiaries. In the pharmaceutical sector, for example, nearly all the indigenous firms had been producing many of their basic materials for a long period of time. Many were making and printing their own packaging materials — including glass in a few cases — and fabricating their own machinery and components. Some had even established engineering groups to carry out construction and equipment installation projects.

The strategy followed by many U.S. drug subsidiaries has been to push for imports instead of integrating vertically. They have basically viewed themselves as pharmaceutical plants and antibiotic manufacturers. However, stringent import restrictions and other environmental pressures have forced many to move in the direction of vertical integration recently. Similar conditions have characterized India's chemical engineering and heavy industry sectors.

Even though U.S. subsidiaries in India have tended to be less integrated than their indigenous counterparts, they have engaged in more vertical integration than the domestic operations of their parent companies. For example, many U.S. subsidiaries produced from 25 percent to more than 100 percent more of the items required for production than did their domestic counterparts in the United States.

The U.S. battery producer in India made great strides toward vertical integration even before import restrictions became most stringent. It set up its own zinc rolling mill — its parent company does not have one in the United States — to support its battery operations. Its chemical plant made a large number of items for its battery plants, and various kinds of machinery, small tools, and components were manufactured in its shop. In some cases, the firm even diversified its product lines in order to make greater use of its vertically integrated facilities.

Although most U.S. subsidiaries preferred to buy rather than make needed items, it was not uncommon for them to make certain things that probably should have been bought. Inadequate analysis and fear concerning the reliability of local supplies were the reasons for this. For example, it took one plant about two years to make a certain kind of tool, although a local indigenous producer could have adequately supplied the firm's requirements within a year at significantly lower cost.

Decisions to manufacture a product were most often based upon the availability of supplies. Inadequate economic analysis was performed. Top management would decide the issue by asking the question, "Do we want to go into this business?", not, "Should we?".

Such questions were seldom considered solely in terms of producing for internal purposes. Instead, the focus was directed towards establishing a new product line, with the risk reduced by the assurance of an internal market. Consequently, such decisions were removed from the spheres of production and purchasing managers and were usually made by the managing director and board of directors. One of the few exceptions to this pattern was found in an Indian pharmaceutical company. Its industrial engineering group analyzed every request for equipment or a new material from a make-versus-buy standpoint. However, little was being done with respect to existing raw materials or components.

By virtue of their willingness to expand into new fields and to take risks, the Indian firms assured themselves of future sources of supply which could meet their needs with respect to quantity, quality, and dependability. Furthermore, within a planned and controlled economy, these decisions prohibited other firms from entry into the same areas. However, in some cases, considerable frustrations resulted. For example, one Indian firm established an operation to make a basic material which it required. Before granting a license, the government required the firm to agree to construct a plant with capacity in excess of its current needs and to sell a certain portion of its output to other competitive firms. The company's needs soon were greater than the amount which it could retain, and it was forced to go into the open market to repurchase materials which it had manufactured.

IMPORTS

Perhaps the best quantitative barometer of the severity of import problems at different points of time in Indian industry are the premiums paid for goods in the open or black market. Open market prices usually refer to legal transactions where one party is allowed to sell either import entitlements or actual imports to another. (The range of imports obtained in this way has been reduced considerably in recent years, as the government has banned many items from the open market.) Black marketing activity involves an illegal sale of import licenses or goods.

In general, U.S. subsidiaries have avoided using open and black market channels — particularly the latter-for purchasing imported commodities chiefly because more imports have generally been available to them than to their indigenous counterparts. Additionally, in sectors where import entitlements have been related to export performance, these subsidiaries have exported more than their indigenous counterparts and, thus, have been able to obtain imports in greater quantities. Better procurement management has also been a factor.

Premiums paid on most basic imported materials and components used in India's drug and chemical sectors reached their peak during the 1966 foreign exchange crisis. At that time they varied upwards of 200 percent, reaching as much as 400 percent for certain items, and as high as 1000 percent for a few special items. There was a downward trend after 1966, and the premiums paid for such goods in these sectors reached lows of 70 to 125 percent, during 1968. The premiums began to increase again in 1969 and in the second half of that year they ranged from about 120 to 160 percent.

The same pattern has existed in other sectors with regard to such items as imported copper, zinc, certain kinds of steel and other metals, components, and spare parts. Peak premiums paid on such basic imports in 1966 ranged from about 200 to 250 percent. They reached their lows, in the range of 30 to 50 percent, during 1968. By the summer of 1969 they ranged from about 40 to 75 percent.

Even in 1969, some of the indigenous firms surveyed were paying premiums in the range of 200 to 1000 percent for special and unique items, especially if they were smuggled goods. Such items included materials used in luxury goods (e.g., fancy perfuming chemicals), special kinds of components, instruments and tools.

Imported spare parts and components presented a more serious problem as did special-purpose equipment, and certain small tools and instruments, particularly the kinds used in R&D activity.

Officially, those firms in various sectors that export a certain portion of their output (e.g., 10 percent in the drug industry, 5 percent for batteries) are permitted to buy their imports from the cheapest source (also referred to as the preferred source). However, in 1969 even those firms surveyed which had achieved such export performance — and there were only a few — were not allowed to import from the cheapest source in most instances.

For many imported items, U.S. sources have been more expensive than Western European or Japanese sources, with no significant difference in quality. Import entitlements involving Communist countries are generally easier to get than those for hard currency areas, and sometimes the prices are also lower — along with the quality. There still seems to be some reluctance among private Indian drug and chemical companies — though to a lesser extent in engineering and heavy industry sectors — to import from Communist bloc countries. Many view imports from Eastern European countries with distrust, and feel that they are Soviet rejects.

In 1969 imported metals such as zinc and copper cost 50 to 100 percent more when purchased from non-preferred sources, including the United States, compared to the cheapest sources. Various types of steel were 25 percent higher if bought from U.S. sources rather than preferred Japanese vendors. However, indigenous prices have been running 50 percent to several hundred percent higher than world prices.

Imported spares, components, accessories, and instruments used by firms surveyed in 1969 were anywhere from 10 to 50 percent higher when they came from non-preferred sources, with Germany often offering the lowest prices. Indigenous prices have usually been at least double, and in a few cases as much as five to ten times higher than world prices.

U.S. subsidiaries in India usually import their materials and other goods primarily from the United States. Indigenous firms and other foreign companies have used a greater variety of sources. The total imports of U.S. subsidiaries tend to be higher as well. For example, during the 1960s, U.S. drug subsidiaries imported nearly half as much again of their raw materials — measured as a percentage of the total value of raw material requirements — as their Indian competitors.

The unreliability of imported materials has created problems for management. Indian licensing procedures required that items be imported in large quantities and at infrequent intervals, based on orders placed as much as a year before delivery. Great uncertainties existed with respect to market conditions for finished products at the time the raw materials were to arrive and as to future changes in government import policies. Furthermore, in cases where an entire lot had to be rejected upon receipt, long delays resulted before replacement could be made.

This situation was further complicated by customs clearance procedures. For example, when pharmaceutical materials were purchased domestically a company could accept sub-standard items and reprocess them. However, Government inspection was always required for imported goods. A lot which did not meet specifications was rejected by the government, and a long and drawn-out procedure was required to get it released for reprocessing and eventual use. In other cases the material would be returned. Sometimes it would be replaced, but frequently this was difficult, since the validity of the original import license might have expired before the transaction could be completed.

IMPORT SUBSTITUTION

Import substitution can be furthered either by a firm's vertical integration or through its development of other indigenous sources of supply. In India's pharmaceutical sector, U.S. subsidiaries have tended to choose the latter alternative and indigenous companies the former.

In 1954 more than 40 percent of the materials used in India's drug industry were imported. As of 1969, the proportion was less than 10 percent, and some government officials and managers have placed it as low as about 6 percent. By contrast, as of 1965, most U.S. firms were importing at least 50 percent of their materials (by value) while only one indigenous firm was importing more than 50 percent, and the others which were studied were importing from 10 to 50 percent.

By 1969, these same U.S. firms had made considerable progress in import substitution. For example, one of them cut its imported materials by more than 50 percent in the early 1960s and to 20 percent in 1969, in spite of the fact that the rupee was devalued from 4.75 to 7.50 per dollar in June 1966. Another cut its imports to 15 percent, and a third to 10 percent, by 1969. The indigenous drug firms surveyed showed similar reductions, as did firms of all nationalities in most other industries.

SUPPLIER DEVELOPMENT AND SELECTION

In the United States, many corporations send engineering and other personnel to the plants of vendors to help them begin production on a new item or to solve any problems which arise. This illustrates the principle that a supplier who knows your needs and can meet them can be invaluable in helping to avoid manufacturing problems in your own plant. In some cases, firms go so far as to supply capital, lend equipment, or assign their own personnel to a vendor's plant on a semi-permanent basis.

Since U.S. subsidiaries in India were reluctant to consider make-versus-buy decisions or to vertically integrate they should move in the direction of supplier development, particularly when indigenous supply sources were poor. With relatively few exceptions, they did not, until the recent cutback on imports forced some type of action. As late as 1969, few U.S. subsidiaries were making a strong effort in this direction. Although some U.S. subsidiaries have recently undertaken supplier-development activities, and are sending their own purchasing, production, and other specialists to supplier plants, the more usual course has been to seek out new sources of supply when old ones become inadequate.

Indian companies have been less active with regard to supplier development than their U.S. subsidiary counterparts. There are a number of explanations for this. First, within the Indian cultural pattern, one does not offer help to a "stranger" — he, or competitors, may be able to use it to one's disadvantage. Second, few Indian purchasing personnel had been exposed to the supplier relations philosophy which prevails in the United States, nor had they mastered the skills necessary to enable them to be of assistance to their suppliers. Finally, specialists who could have rendered such assistance were overburdened with work and lacked the time to visit or offer assistance to suppliers.

U.S. subsidiaries have been more apt to provide their suppliers with good samples of the components, materials, tools, and other items that they require. However, neither U.S. nor Indian companies have given their suppliers detailed drawings to go along with the samples.

One of the most progressive firms studied in India with regard to supplier development, has been the U.S. subsidiary producing batteries, flashlights, chemicals, plastics, and various other products. It has done an impressive job in connection with various kinds of spare parts, components, tools, equipment, raw materials, packaging materials, cartons, labels, and so forth. It has even assigned company geologists to assist Indian mining interests in their exploration and development of mineral resources. It has also given a number of suppliers both financial and technical assistance. As a result, it has been able to enter into mutually beneficial long-term contracts with many of its vendors.

Several U.S. drug subsidiaries have also increased supplier development activities recently. One of the most successful has been providing free training and technical expertise to important suppliers, while its parent company has sent experts to help some of them.

With regard to indigenous supplier selection, U.S. subsidiaries have usually relied upon firms with whom they had previously done business, or who were already supplying other foreign companies. Indian companies were more likely to select vendors on the basis of personal relationships between managing directors or other top executives. They used these relationships to keep cost and quality considerations within reason, although most available data indicated that these relationships worked more to the benefit of the supplier than the purchaser. Often, personal relationships outweighed price considerations. This pattern also existed to a lesser extent in U.S. subsidiaries, since the purchasing managers were invariably Indian, usually stamped from a traditional mold.

Gifts, or bribes, frequently played important roles in the purchasing picture. In some cases these were small and of little significance, while in others they were of major size and impact. Bribes moved in both directions, depending upon the particular item and the market situation. It is interesting to note that most U.S. managing directors denied that their firms engaged in such practices, while their purchasing people and suppliers often indicated otherwise. In actual fact, the top man was too remote from the action to know what was going on.

From discussions with suppliers and other parties it seemed that less bribery occurred in U.S. subsidiaries, although it was not uncommon among these firms. Many suppliers indicated that trying to break into a U.S. subsidiary was always an awkward process, because they could never be sure whether an offer of special consideration would enhance or hurt their chances, whereas the situation was more clear-cut when dealing with Indian companies.

REJECTION RATES ON INCOMING SUPPLIES

Although U.S. firms generally had higher quality standards for incoming materials, they experienced lower rejection rates at receiving inspection. This was due to their more careful screening and selection of suppliers, as well as to more effective supplier development activities. In the pharmaceutical industry, for example, rejection rates for U.S. firms averaged between 2 and 3 percent for raw materials. The rejection rates for indigenous drug firms started at about 3 percent for raw materials and went up to 40 percent, with 5 to 10 percent as a modal range.

The rejection rates for U.S. subsidiaries in other sectors — e.g., batteries, flashlights, chemicals — were also substantially lower than those for their indigenous counterparts. However, at times they, too, had dramatically high rejection rates for various items. For example, several years ago a U.S. flashlight plant in India had rejection rates of 40 and 50 percent on brass tubes, chiefly because of surface deficiencies. During some periods, as much as 80 percent of certain types of components were substandard although the firm reworked many of them itself.

A U.S.-Indian joint venture in the engineering sector has often had rejection rates exceeding 50 percent on sample parts furnished on a bid basis by potential local suppliers. Reject rates on parts purchased in production lots have ranged from 10 to more than 20 percent (compared to only 3 or 4 percent in a similar plant in the United States). About half a batch of 50 small parts sent to the United States for reliability testing were rejected.

TIMING OF PROCUREMENT

The timing of procurement is critical for imported goods. The red tape and delays involved in government licensing and import clearance procedures were responsible for some of the greatest headaches for all kinds of firms in India.

Although U.S. subsidiaries planned and timed import procurement better than their indigenous counterparts, their performance could have been much better than it was. For example, in one U.S. subsidiary, construction of a new plant was delayed for nearly a year because no one had calculated lead times on certain pieces of equipment which had to be installed sequentially. When an item was ready to be installed, management would discover that the order for it had not yet been placed, or that it had been placed too late to assure on-time delivery.

Locally-produced goods presented a somewhat different picture. Depending on the item and the location of the sources of supply, many such items could be obtained in a matter of days or hours, through a telephone order. Many U.S. companies had contracted with certain suppliers to obtain their estimated needs of critical products for an entire year. They submitted rough schedules indicating the timing of their needs, and could then periodically contact their suppliers and obtain rapid delivery.

In other cases, where the plants and the suppliers were located at some distance from each other, the vagaries of the transportation system had to be taken into account. This often caused severe problems, especially for perishable items since there were no refrigerated railroad cars in India in the early 1960s and there is still an acute shortage of them today. Among the other difficulties encountered were damage, pilferage, and lost shipments. These constraints had to be factored into the timing of procurement, and most firms did not have qualified transportation specialists and traffic managers. This aspect of the procurement function has been one of the most neglected of all.

SUPPLY INVENTORIES

Inventory levels — in relation to both output and sales — were greater at U.S. subsidiaries in India than at comparable U.S.-based divisions and plants of their parent corporations. They were at least double, and often two and a half or three times greater during the 1960s. In the pharmaceutical sector, annual inventory turnover at U.S. subsidiaries ranged from about 135 to 250 days, with most falling between 175 and 225. At U.S.-based operations, the range has been from 35 to slightly over 100 days, with most falling between 45 and 90.

Raw materials and other supplies (rather than finished goods or even in-process inventories) accounted for most of this difference. For example, they accounted for from 115 to over 200 days of inventory at the U.S. drug subsidiaries. The main reason for the large inventories was the vastly greater uncertainty and unavailability of adequate supplies in India, together with the subsidiaries' heavy reliance on imports. Similar patterns existed between U.S. subsidiaries and their parents companys' domestic operations in other sectors examined.

In spite of the precarious supply situation, efficient management of inventories of materials, spare parts, components, and equipment was generally found to be lacking. Although U.S. subsidiaries had better inventory management than their indigenous counterparts, their systems were also quite rudimentary.

There were few clear-cut patterns differentiating supply inventory levels at U.S. subsidiaries compared to indigenous firms in the same sector. In some cases, inventory turnover or levels were higher at U.S. firms, and in others they were lower. The absence of clear patterns can be explained by differences in degrees of vertical integration, the relative amount of imports used, and utilization of plant capacities, among other factors. However, available data indicated that U.S. subsidiaries had fewer stockout problems.

Some U.S. subsidiaries reduced their supply inventory levels during the second half of the 1960s without increasing production bottlenecks or stockouts. For example, one cut its inventories of imports from a five-month supply in 1965-66 to a three-month supply in 1969. It also cut inventories of indigenous supplies from three to two months, primarily through better management. Inventory levels involving indigenous supplies were roughly 50 to 100 percent higher during the 1960s at a major Indian competitor.

Few indigenous firms reduced supply inventory levels during this period, and most continued to experience more bottlenecks and stockouts than comparable U.S. firms. A number of firms even increased their levels. The largest public sector steel company estimated that nonproductive inventories — primarily spares and components — were equal to about 10 percent of sales (or about 300 million rupees) in 1969.

A major limitation to effective inventory management in Indian industry was that most purchasing personnel conceived their job to be one of finding sources of supply and negotiating contracts. Few had the competence to determine desirable stock levels or to control inventories. They lived by the rule, "Get what you can, when you can."

Although purchasing personnel received production reports in many cases, many were not provided with figures indicating additions or subtractions from inventories. Consequently, they were forced to guess about existing stock levels when placing orders. In many cases, they would make estimates on the basis of quantities on order minus quantities that were probably used to manufacture the production indicated, and their figures were often inaccurate. Procurement personnel sometimes waited for specific requests from production executives before they would place orders, since they lacked the information necessary to do it themselves. However, they often modified the amounts to provide a cushion against underestimates.

Few firms surveyed had collected or analyzed data on ordering costs, inventory-carrying charges, and the like. Most of them employed crude ordering procedures. In some cases, minimum quantities (based on experience) were used to trigger an order. One Indian firm ordered each locally produced item once a month. The purchasing manager decided on quantity, basing his order on usage during the preceding month. Another did the same, but only twice a year, ordering a six-month supply at a time.

U.S. subsidiaries tended to use rules of thumb to determine raw materials inventories, in contrast to the well-defined mathematical approaches of their parent firms. In most cases, inventory goals for domestic items were established for two- to three-month requirements, while those for imported items were set at four- to six-month levels. Most of the U.S. firms also seemed to lack a consistent pattern for determining a "month's requirement." One company indicated that it had no policy with respect to imports, but simply ordered what it could get. Another had established minimum order quantities, but the only guideline used by purchasing personnel was to "maintain large safety stocks" which they set "on the basis of experience."

Some early attempts at more sophisticated inventory planning and control were made by a few of the most progressive indigenous firms surveyed. For example, one drug company analyzed its raw materials needs and found that 15 percent of the items were used in more than 70 percent of its production. These items were then given special attention in planning inventory. More recently, a growing, although still limited number of U.S. subsidiaries surveyed have also begun to apply more sophisticated inventory-management techniques.

STORAGE

Storage facilities presented a problem to most of the firms studied in India. Moreover, the question of warehouse facilities and management was seen as unimportant, and scant attention was paid to it. At many firms, raw materials were stored in whatever space happened to be available at the time of arrival. Typically, storage areas were dark, disorderly, and inconveniently located. Frequently, storage areas were scattered around the plant site in small sheds, corners, and loading ramps. U.S. subsidiaries generally had better facilities than their Indian counterparts, but they, too, were quite inadequate.

Particular problems arose from the lack of effective warehouse management. In the pharmaceutical industry individual lots of the same item had to be kept separate so that if problems arose, the source of the difficulty could be discovered. Sloppy storage practices often necessitated hours of sorting to separate shipments which had become mixed. Often, shipments were temporarily lost, as new shipments were piled on top of old. When they were found, much unnecessary handling was required to extricate the lot.

Obsolescence and deterioration of stock also resulted from inadequate storage facilities. Most firms had adequately-equipped air-conditioned storage for items for which this was essential, but the other materials were usually stacked in piles on the floor. Breakage and spoilage rates were high. Because of inadequate records and physical control of inventories, pilferage was another serious problem.

Most storage space was poorly utilized, few companies having racks or shelves in their main storage areas. Consequently, items would be piled one on top of another until the piles started to become unstable. Typically, the eye of the stock handler would determine this point. Rooms with 12-foot ceilings were seldom used to a height greater than 5 feet. The problem was further complicated by lack of standardized shipping containers and materials handling equipment.

Shipments were received in containers of every type imaginable ranging from wooden crates to gunny sacks. (Only a few companies had begun to insist on standardized containers for shipments received from their vendors. The rest took what came.) This made stacking almost an impossibility. Boxes were of all sizes, materials, and strengths. Furthermore, only a few companies attempted to palatize their incoming shipments, since only a few had fork trucks or other equipment capable of moving or lifting heavy loads. Incoming shipments were usually moved and stacked by hand.

The warehousing area received so little attention primarily because of the low value the society placed on such concepts as space and human labor.

Some work was being done to improve warehousing management by companies located in the heart of the cities, and surrounded by buildings that restricted their chances to expand. However, the attention they were beginning to devote to storage facilities was prompted by pressures of space shortage rather than because warehousing, per se, was thought important.

The management of warehouse space was usually placed at a low level in the organization, and where it landed nearly always seemed to be an afterthought. In various firms, it was assigned to the managers of such functions as production, marketing, or procurement. Some firms had "administrative" or "commercial" managers who received the assignment. Occasionally it was the accountants responsibility, and in a few cases, the maintenance manager looked after it. Sometimes the responsibility was fractionated — the maintenance manager might look after spare parts storage, the commercial manager take care of packaging materials, and the production manager maintain stocks of chemical items — all of which were kept in the same facilities.

This is yet another area where U.S. practices were not transferred overseas. The explanation probably lies in the fact that it was typically far removed from the focus of attention (or the knowledge) of the managing director.

STANDARDIZATION

Much effort has been devoted in U.S. industry to the question of standardization of inputs. This does not obtain in India, probably because India has not developed the value system of an industrial society. The industrial revolution focused on the use of technology to achieve standardized (mass produced) output — which in turn required a certain uniformity of inputs. This emphasis on standardization has become incorporated into Western cultures.

This is not true in most developing countries. The concept of the traditional craftsman and his "one-of-a-kind" output prevails, and is honored. Standardization is a foreign idea, and consequently, without special guidance and training, the average Indian would be unlikely to consider it an important one. Once again, the lack of involvement of the U.S. personnel in subsidiary firms, coupled with the lack of training for purchasing executives, tended to favor the predominance of the Indian pattern and to inhibit the development of U.S. thinking.

Most of the companies studied — the exceptions again being U.S. firms and a few progressive Indian companies — had devoted little or no attention to standardization. As the need for a particular item arose, a production manager would submit a request, to his specifications, which procurement personnel attempted to satisfy.

> One Indian company carried 11 different brands of safety shoes. The managing director had insisted that every production worker in certain areas be equipped with safety shoes. Subsequently, each production department head placed an order for the brand he knew, and purchasing executed the orders.

Marketing decisions also influence the question of standardization of materials, especially with respect to packaging. In many companies marketing personnel designed containers for new products, and many of those designing were unfamiliar with the company's other products or the cost aspects of packaging materials. Drug companies often found (when they looked) that they were stocking dozens of different package and bottle sizes and shapes. Once a new packaging material had been introduced, any changing it was usually fought on the basis that illiterate consumers reordered by bringing in the empty container and asking for an exact replica.

> A U.S. drug company discovered that it stocked 30 different sizes of the same shape bottle. Only color and volume distinguished one from another. An analysis revealed that less than a dozen were actually needed. However, marketing personnel adamantly insisted that no changes be made.

Two of the more progressive Indian pharmaceutical firms (both companies with industrial engineering functions) had begun to consider standardization. One was approaching the subject in a random manner while the other had established a committee to work on standardization of incoming goods (including the shipping container study previously mentioned). These firms were hoping to obtain quantity discounts, to eliminate costly inventory control procedures, and to reduce problems of stockout by cutting down the number of individual items carried in inventory. In both cases, these efforts were spearheaded by U.S.-educated, Indian industrial engineers.

> One of the most dramatic changes was introduced in one of these Indian companies with respect to bottle stoppers. Previously, more than 70 were required to fit the specifications established by marketing personnel. Differently sized and shaped bottlenecks, and different colors and material requirements, were the cause of the difficulty. By standardizing, which involved a change in bottle design, the company was able to cut down to four basic stoppers. This eliminated one of their major production bottlenecks — stockouts due to late deliveries or poor quality in a particular type of stopper.

In a number of firms, initial orders for packaging material were placed by marketing personnel. In addition to designing the package, these personnel would find a vendor capable of meeting their specifications and would then obtain samples and place the first order. Only after the samples had been approved was the purchasing office brought into the picture. From that point on, they were expected to maintain the flow of supplies. This is a further indication of the low position accorded to purchasing management.

SUMMARY

In Indian industry, two key elements were lacking in the area of purchasing management: a mechanism for coordinating the purchasing function with the areas of marketing and production, and a cadre of trained purchasing managers.

The need for action in the procurement area was becoming more evident, as changing market conditions began to place greater emphasis on cost control. However, few facilities existed for training the personnel required, and purchasing executives were not selected or trained with the same care and attention devoted to marketing, finance, or production personnel. These factors had the effect of limiting the transfer of valuable U.S. know-how, much of which could have been transferred intact.

CHAPTER 20
RESEARCH AND
DEVELOPMENT

INTRODUCTION

Of all the activities associated with modern industry, the one that is probably weakest in developing nations is research and development (R & D). Many factors inhibit the growth of this function, some related to the nature of the environment, and others to the attitudes and skills of the companies involved.

Basic research is expensive. Although its long-range benefits may be substantial, the launching of even a small research effort requires a sizeable initial investment. Furthermore, research and development activities seldom have fixed timetables or guaranteed returns. Sometimes they are considered a luxury that the local economy cannot afford in view of other short-term and more pressing needs. More often, R & D is neglected because so many other opportunities exist to invest capital in relatively risk-free, short-run high-return ventures.

The developing nation frequently lacks the resources required for efficient R & D operations particularly in the case of basic research, for which equipment may be required which is not manufactured locally. Acquiring such equipment may lead to foreign exchange, delivery, and maintenance problems. Trained personnel may also be scarce. For instance, in countries which have no electronics industry, it is unlikely that universities will be turning out electronics engineers or solid-state physicists. It may also be difficult to find the legal talent needed to research patents, the technicians required to assist in operations, the engineers necessary for the design, construction, or installation of specialized facilities, and qualified managers to direct and coordinate R & D activity.

Market size is another factor which must be taken into account. Although local markets may be large in terms of population, they may be small in terms of buyers with purchasing power. Consequently, even if good products are developed, many years may elapse before R & D expenditures can be recouped through sales, unless substantial exports can be generated. Most firms have neither the organization nor the operating efficiency to develop such export markets and consequently, the rates of return do not look as attractive as they might in more developed nations.

Finally, company attitudes must be considered. Local firms typically adopt a risk-avoidance strategy. In R & D situations, the risks derive from investing in an effort that will not yield as good a return as other, more certain, activities. A foreign product that has already been developed and tested in the local market, and for which demand patterns indicate substantial growth potential is a much safer alternative. Consequently, the relatively sure bet is taken, and "research" tends to be oriented towards modifying such products to fit specialized local needs.

Foreign subsidiaries usually demonstrate the same type of thinking, but with two added factors. The first is that the subsidiary considers not only the risk of doing less well than it could with established products, but also the risks associated with increasing the investment of capital and know-how in the developing nation. Any investment in research facilities increases the firm's dependence on the local environment and power structure. In addition, the transfer of technical knowledge may increase a firm's vulnerability, as closely guarded trade secrets or expertise become more widely disseminated.

The second factor is that the foreign firm must often attempt to amortize the large sums it has probably expended for research and development in its home country. Frequently, the less developed nation is seen as a market place in which past R & D costs may be recovered. As a result, U.S. companies tend to introduce products which are already part of their product lines (in most cases in their U.S. forms), and shy away from the development of products for the local environment.

The attitudes of foreign firms can create tension with local governments. Government policy is likely to be directed towards encouraging the development of local technology and upgrading operations away from importation and toward the domestic creation and manufacture of new products. Yet, foreign companies often use their product and process technology as a club to obtain extra concessions from local governments, thus going against the trend and creating severe tensions. Furthermore, the lack of commitment to the local environment which this implies makes the motives of foreign companies somewhat suspect.

Another factor comes into play as the result of the attitudes of both U.S. and the indigenous firms. Because of limited research investment the local consumer is forced to buy a product that almost, but not quite suits his needs. In some cases, modifications must be made (e.g., where the U.S. formulation of a vitamin product will not maintain its potency under the local climatic conditions). But in other cases, the products can be used in their original form, although not as effectively as they might otherwise be (e.g., a motor vehicle in which the controls have been designed to accommodate individuals of greater size or physical strength).

THE CASE OF INDIA

Most U.S. subsidiaries studied have done little research and development work within India. New products and processes have usually been transferred to subsidiaries after they have been perfected and proven successful at home. Frequently, experts are sent out by the parent company to ease the transfer, requiring hard currency payments by the subsidiaries for their services. This kind of activity gives U.S. subsidiaries a competitive advantage over their indigenous counterparts.

To the extent that U.S. firms have engaged in R & D within India, they have stressed applied development work; primarily modification of products and processes to render them compatible with the local environment. An increasing number of subsidiaries have begun development involving import substitution, new material usage, and vertical integration; in general, the pace and extent of R & D by U.S. firms has increased in recent years. However, there are many instances where greater emphasis on R & D would be beneficial to individual companies and the country as a whole. Much more work in this area could be done within India by Indian personnel.

In many sectors — including pharmaceuticals — some of the larger indigenous companies have been conducting considerably more research and development activity than U.S. subsidiaries. Many of the smaller Indian firms have also been spending more in relation to their sales on R & D work than most U.S. subsidiaries. However, the total effort is still small.

In the Indian pharmaceutical industry, less than 1 percent of total sales volume has been spent on R & D, compared to roughly 10 percent in the United States. Most of the activity labelled R & D in India has been of an applied nature directed towards reformulation efforts. One large European drug company has established a substantial research facility. A public sector firm has also set up a research laboratory in which some basic research is conducted, although its R & D expenses have only been in the range of 1 to 1.5 percent of sales. However, it has produced a new drug product which has been licensed to foreign firms. Two private indigenous drug firms were also engaged in basic research, although their greatest expenditure was for applied research.

The leading U.S. drug subsidiary set up a separate R & D unit in 1969 primarily to work on import substitution and process development. The firm has done little product development work. Its R & D budget, which doubled in 1969, still only represented about 1 percent of sales. However, this was significantly more than any other U.S. drug subsidiary was spending.

Another U.S. drug firm has recently begun some development work on veterinary products which have not been produced by its parent company in the United States. Although this subsidiary has also increased its R & D expenditures significantly in recent years, as of 1969 it still had never amounted to as much as 1 percent of sales. By contrast, its parent company has been spending over 10 percent of sales on R & D in the United States, and employ 20 percent of its manpower in this area.

Rarely has a U.S. drug subsidiary considered developing or manufacturing a new product in India which has not been successfully marketed elsewhere. This has not been true at some Indian companies. However, most new and improved products developed by these firms have been based on extracts of ingredients from traditional Indian herbal preparations, and products of this type are no longer as profitable as they once were.

The leading private firm in India's pharmaceutical industry in terms of R & D is one of the oldest indigenous companies (firm D in Chapter 10). It employs a large number of U. S.- and other foreign-trained personnel.

Before 1950 the company engaged in relatively simple formulation research, but it has since increased its applied and development research and added a modest amount of basic research. It obtained two new patents in recent years, and has filed for two others. Some of these may have export potential. During the second half of the 1960s, the company introduced 15 new products and in 1969 it had several new projects awaiting government approval. In 1966 it initiated a modest 10-year research program involving amoebic dysentry. As of 1969, one new product had emerged from this program.

In 1969 the company also started a modest medical research program focusing on major indigenous diseases. It has also been doing some development work on import substitution and new material uses. For example, it introduced a program for substituting local cane sugar for imported lactose in certain products in 1963. The program was successfully completed in 1967. Since about 1966 it has increased its import substitution efforts significantly.

This firm spent between 1.3 and 2.2 percent of sales on research and development (including salaries) during the 1960-66 period, and has increased expenditures in this area since then. In 1969 it spent the equivalent of about 4 percent of sales on R & D. Its sales had increased substantially during the 1967-69 period. However, the accuracy of figures relating to R & D expenditures is questionable, since they tended to include some unrelated activities.

A few smaller Indian drug and chemical companies surveyed have also been expending greater efforts on R & D, usually with the help of outside consultants from the Indian Institutes of Technology or other organizations. However, they have not been as successful as they might be because of a lack of internal technical and managerial know-how.

Almost every drug firm examined in Indian contained a group labeled "R & D", but most were not functioning as such. In some firms this group was housed under quality control. In many, quality control was housed within R & D. In almost all cases, its primary function was quality control. And except for the examples noted above, no real basic research was being conducted.

For example, one U.S. drug firm had recently appointed a full-time R & D manager. His organization contained 17 people — the majority of whom were concerned with the design and selection of new equipment. A small number were supposedly concerned with new program development. In actuality, the equipment personnel spent most of their time drawing up detailed specifications and locating equipment requested by production. The new product people worked on formulations. The manager said that the organization was new, and that he did not know how it would develop. However, he indicated that basic research was too expensive and was not likely to yield results.

Almost all the drug companies had new product committees. However, their energies were directed toward keeping track of new products introduced by competitors, rather than development. It was rare to have a new product originate from an idea generated within the firm. In almost every case, "new ideas" were modifications of existing products or products introduced from abroad which were new to the local environment.

In the last several years many reports, investigations, and parliamentary debates have been initiated by Indian government officials who wish to reduce the life of pharmaceutical — and certain other — patents. India has had a 14-year patent law, compared to 17 in the United States. The most extreme dissidents want to do away with drug patents entirely. The more moderate advocates of patent reform would probably accept a 10-year patent life, and such a law may soon be passed. This has been an issue where foreign and indigenous drug companies in India have been at odds for obvious reasons.

Foreign drug firms have claimed that a change in patent laws would have a negative effect on the development and marketing of new products in India. There may be some truth in such claims, but they do seem to be exaggerated.

A few non-pharmaceutical U.S. subsidiaries and joint ventures in the battery, flashlight, and chemical sectors have been spending more on R & D and new product development — in both relative and absolute terms — and have also been doing a more effective job than their indigenous counterparts. For example, in 1958, a U.S. company produced only two varieties of flashlights and only one basic model. By 1963 it was producing fewer than ten types, but still of the one basic model. However, by the late 1960s it was manufacturing 35 varieties of several basic models for domestic consumption, and 10 varieties under a different brand name for export. It has been producing a broader and more complex range of flashlights than its major indigenous competitor, has been diversifying into new plastic and steel materials, as well as more brass and aluminum types, and has obtained only a limited amount of direction or assistance from its parent company. Since 1966, R & D expenditures at its flashlight plant have been in the range of 2.5 to 3.5 percent of sales, 3 to 4.5 percent of production costs, and 20 to 30 percent of profits. (The parent company's plant in the United States has been spending about 5 to 6 percent on R & D in relation to total production costs.)

Largely because of competition from this U.S. producer, the major indigenous battery company has entered into a collaboration agreement with a British firm which has been providing some direct assistance. The Indian firm has also sent some of its people to the United Kingdom for training.

The leading indigenous battery firm entered into a technical collaboration agreement with a French company several years ago. Since then it has expanded its product line significantly, improved the quality and appearance of its products and packaging, and has been producing some complex batteries for India's defense needs. In the last several years of the 1960s, this firm increased its R & D expenditures about 15 to 20 percent annually — a more impressive figure than that of its major U.S. competitor.

A full-time R & D staff was established in 1967 to work on import substitution and process improvements at the chemical and plastics plant of a large U.S. subsidiary. In 1969, the staff became a separate department, consisting of several very competent local nationals educated mostly in the United States. Considerable progress has been made on such items as gaskets, valves, and components. The plant had a traget of 15 to 20 percent more import substitution in 1970.

CONCLUDING REMARKS

In India, strong environmental pressures rather than potential opportunities or voluntary action have been leading to increased research and development activity at many U.S. subsidiaries. The same has been true with regard to other foreign companies as well as indigenous firms, although many of these have increased their R & D in a more voluntary and opportunity-seeking manner than their U.S. counterparts. Among the most important environmental pressures have been stringent import restrictions, pressures to increase exports, increasing domestic competition, excess capacity, and declining profitability.

Changes are also taking place in many smaller developing countries where the size of the market is more of an inhibiting factor than in India. The formation of common markets and free trade associations may do much to foster research activities. However, the basic question is still the willingness of the firms with the knowledge and the capital to commit themselves to the local environment, together with the creation of environmental conditions more conducive to research and development.

CHAPTER 21
MARKETING
AND EXPORTS

INTRODUCTION

One of the major characteristics of U.S. business operations in developing nations is an aggressive and effective marketing effort. This is usually true in both an absolute and a relative sense. In comparison to their competition — both indigenous and foreign — U.S. firms usually conduct bold advertising and promotional campaigns and establish aggressive sales techniques. They have well-trained sales forces and broadly based distribution systems, and are adapt at projecting their corporate presence. In most cases, their emphasis on marketing reflects a transference of U.S. know-how and practices.

The aggressive marketing approaches of U.S. companies have positive and negative aspects. On the positive side, they generate respect, even from managers of competing local firms, for their dynamism and success. Consumers appreciate the availability of product information and the prestigious image projected by mass advertising — especially important in status-conscious countries.

On the negative side, however, four sets of counterreactions are generated by these aggressive marketing approaches. First, governments of many developing nations voice strong objections to what they consider the "unreasonable amount of promotional

620

expense" contained in the prices of certain products. In India, this was especially evident in the pharmaceutical industry, where several attempts were made to enact legislation which would totally eliminate advertising. In most of these situations (usually confined to products thought to be important to the national welfare), government reactions are based on a desire to keep costs as low as possible, combined with the feeling that promotional expenditures are "nonproductive" and add little for the consumer except higher cost. This approach neglects the realities of the economic process. For example, the price effects of advertising are seldom weighed against the benefits which accrue by virtue of the fact that products become known to many more potential users and more effective distribution of goods is facilitated.

Second, traditional indigenous firms often believe that the U.S. style of competition is unfair. There is seldom a rationale for this feeling, which is usually based on the notion that indigenous markets belong to indigenous firms — a kind of economic chauvinism. U.S. companies, by taking a disproportionate share of the market through use of nonindigenous practices, are seen as interlopers. The complainants are seldom able to substantiate charges of unethical or illegal practices to support their beliefs. Instead, the practices are seen as "unfair" because they violate traditional ground rules.

Third, other foreign companies often believe that U.S. techniques are unfair. In India, this situation existed primarily among some of the British firms, and to a lesser degree among companies from other European nations. For example, the British sales manager of one English pharmaceutical firm commented as follows:

> We do most of our promotional work through the use of well prepared brochures and descriptive materials which are mailed or delivered to doctors and chemists. The U.S. firms are much more aggressive. They don't sell their products primarily on the basis of their merits. Instead, they try to do it by high-pressure salesmanship. Their medical representatives are continuously calling on chemists and doctors. They have widespread advertising campaigns, many directed at the consuming public. They are continuously pushing their product in a very unsportsmanlike manner.

Finally, the marketing practices of U.S. firms make them conspicuous. Their "high profile" establishes them as good targets for nationalistic or anti-capitalistic movements within the host nation.

The aggressive market action of U.S. companies stems from many sources. First, historically most of these firms has had a marketing orientation. For example, in India in almost all cases, the U.S. subsidiaries were founded as importers and sellers of U.S.-made products. Only recently — since the mid or late 1950s — have they engaged in manufacturing activities on a large scale. The marketing emphasis is reflected in the pattern of manufacturing evolution, which began with assembly-type operations and then slowly integrated back to production of basic components or materials.

Second, a large proportion of the managing directors of the U.S. firms are selected for their marketing backgrounds and skills. In discussions with executives in U.S. international home offices it was revealed that personnel selection for overseas subsidiaries was often closely linked to the marketing needs of the operations. (A financial-accounting background was the second most commonly found.)

Finally, many U.S. companies imported marketing practices which virtually duplicated those they used in the United States. These practices had evolved in an atmosphere of intense competition. Consequently, they appeared, in contrast with lower-keyed indigenous sales patterns, to be extremely aggressive. The U.S. companies seemed to be applying a type of marketing "overkill," but with impressive sales results.

While U.S. firms studied in India and other developing countries have generally been more effective, aggressive, and sophisticated than their indigenous counterparts in the marketing area, they have also made serious mistakes. Undue complacency, a feeling that sellers' markets were stronger and more lasting than they really were, and preconceived ideas have created problems. For example:

A U.S. firm held 75 to 80 percent of India's total flashlight market during the 1950s. During the 1958-62 period it had continuous problems with faulty bulbs, many of which were supplied by a leading European company in India. Largely because it was operating in a seller's market, the company did not attempt to solve this problem for several years, in spite of the fact that many of the flashlights sold to consumers would not operate until the buyer replaced the defective bulb that came with the flashlight. Even the U.S. parent company was complacent about the situation.

In the early 1960s, the leading indigenous flashlight producer began the manufacture of bulky brass flashlights similar to those produced several decades earlier in the United States by the U.S. subsidiary's parent company. The subsidiary was producing much lighter, more compact, less expensive, and more attractive models, and it was assumed that the indigenous firm would get nowhere with its brass line. However, because of the bulb problem, coupled with several important cultural factors — a symbolic desire for brass, the association of weight and bulkiness with quality and durability — the indigenous product captured a large share of the market, particularly in India's rural areas. Some Indian managers at the subsidiary who anticipated such developments had been overruled because the parent company was confident that a brass flashlight, long obsolete in the United States, would not sell well anywhere.

During the 1961-64 period, the subsidiary's flashlight market share declined steadily from about 75 percent to 43 percent, while the local firm increased its share from about 20 to 45 percent. Around 1965, there were cutbacks in imports of the copper and zinc needed to make brass, and the price of brass doubled. By 1967 the U.S. firm had recaptured more than 65 percent of the market, but when the import situation eased, it began to produce a line of brass flashlights. However, labor problems, in conjunction with an aggressive recovery by the indigenous firm, reduced the subsidiary's market share to 60 percent.

Both firms have recently begun manufacturing other types of flashlights, with the U.S. subsidiary taking the lead and offering a greater variety. It is now in a position to cope with any new competition likely to be offered in the foreseeable future. Management has also worked out marketing plans designed to promote sales growth and to maintain at least 50 percent of the market under any foreseeable competitive conditions.

An important result of the situation outlined above is that the U.S. firm has improved its marketing management and sales efforts throughout the company. It is now in a better position to deal with increasing future competition as well as negative environmental constraints, not only in its flashlight business, but also in other areas.

RECENT PERFORMANCE AND TRENDS

In Chapter 10 it was noted that with few exceptions, U.S. subsidiaries surveyed in India have had higher sales growth, sales per employee, and sales in relation to total assets than their indigenous counterparts. They have also had significantly higher sales in relation to total wages in most cases, even though they usually pay employees higher wages than indigenous firms. Moreover, they have had a greater number of salesmen in relation to total employment, and more sales per salesman than their indigenous counterparts. Their patterns of sales growth have in most cases been less erratic than those of their indigenous counterparts, and actual sales have been closer to planned targets.

The generally superior performance of the U.S. firms in the above areas is, of course, due to many factors. These include their brand names and worldwide reputation, differences in product lines, degrees of automation and vertical integration, pricing policies, and distribution channels.

Those cases where indigenous companies have grown at a higher rate than their U.S. or other foreign counterparts have typically been due to their acquisition of more government licenses for expansion and diversification. In some cases price increases or recent foreign collaboration agreements (mostly technical in nature) have also been factors. In a limited number of cases better marketing management has been a major factor.

In the drug industry, a recent cost-price squeeze has hit U.S. firms harder than Indian companies. One American drug company that had an average annual rate of sales growth during most of the 1960s of about 20 percent managed to grow by only 3 percent in 1968, and by about 5 percent in 1969. However, this company's net profit in relation to sales has remained steady, in the vicinity of 10 percent. Another U.S. drug firm which had an average annual rate of sales growth during the 1960s of more than 20 percent, achieved only a 12 percent growth rate in 1968, and about 4 percent in 1969. However, its net profit in relation to sales has held at approximately 10 to 11 percent.

The firm which experienced the greatest sales growth in India's pharmaceutical industry in 1968-69 was an indigenous company (firm D in Chapter 10). It achieved an annual average sales growth rate of 18 percent during the 1960s, and expected to achieve a 20 percent increase in 1969. Expansion of capacity, product diversification, and some price increases were the main factors on which this expectation was based. However, net profit in relation to sales has continued to be under 5 percent.

Another indigenous drug firm studied (company A) has been more typical of traditional companies in terms of sales performance in recent years. Although its sales increased by about 1 percent in 1968 it experienced a sharp drop in profits. In 1969 sales dropped sharply and the company incurred a sizeable loss. While it has been plagued with severe problems in recent years — in particular, labor unrest and a lack of critical imports — ineffective marketing management has also contributed considerably to its difficulties.

Most firms in India's engineering and heavy industry sectors were particularly hard-hit with regard to sales during the second half of the 1960s. A typical case involves an indigenous electrical engineering firm. After a sharp drop in 1967, its sales grew by only 3.5 percent in 1968. Profits dropped by about 30 percent in 1968, and net profit in relation to sales was only 2.5 percent. With India's economic recovery following the 1966-68 recession, the firm's sales grew by about 12 percent in 1969 and profits by nearly 15 percent. During the 1966-69 period as a whole, the firm experienced a net decline of 8 percent in sales. A relatively progressive British competitor fared significantly better. Even though its sales were hurt by the recession, it managed to achieve a modest increase during the 1966-69 period.

PRODUCT LINES

There were several important differences in the characteristics of product lines of U.S. and Indian pharmaceutical companies surveyed. The product lines of indigenous firms were broader in virtually every sense — number of basic lines, individual varieties, package types, shapes, and sizes, and so forth. This is clearly reflected in Table 21-1.

This table indicates that the five major U.S. drug firms produced a smaller number of products than the five major private-sector Indian drug companies. The maximum number of products for any U.S. firm was 80, while the minimum number for any Indian company was 85. On the average, the Indian firms carried nearly five times as many products than the U.S. subsidiaries, the larger number reflecting both a larger variety of items within a particular product line, (e.g., a larger number of different kinds of vitamin capsules) as well as a greater diversity of product groups.

The difference between the U.S. and indigenous firms would be even more dramatically highlighted if nonpharmaceutical products were included. Several of the Indian companies had branched off into the manufacture of ancillary products including glass, packing materials, and even machinery. Furthermore, manufacture of such items as

TABLE 21-1   Product lines and packaging varieties: U.S. versus indigenous drug companies in India

	Five U.S. sub-sidiaries	Five private sector Indian companies
Range of products	20-80	85-400
Average number of products	55	255
Range of packaging varieties	35-130	210-1,000+
Average number of packaging varieties	90	605
Range packages/products	1.6-1.8	2.2-2.6
Average packages/products	1.7	2.4

basic chemicals not used in pharmaceutical production, medical supplies, and miscellaneous projects that had been undertaken over the years were more common in the Indian firms.

U.S. drug firms typically preferred to manufacture narrower product lines consisting of high quality, high price, and high profit-margin items. Generally they were more reluctant to expand through product diversification and vertical integration, although this situation has changed in recent years. The indigenous firms tended to dilute their marketing efforts and carry outdated and unprofitable items either out of habit or for sentimental reasons. (The fact that they were older than their U.S. competitors and had accumulated a backlog of obsolete items over the years contributed to this.) The more traditional companies often appeared unaware of the actual unit costs of different items.

Several U.S. firms had begun to prune their product lines — the result of economic studies of profitability — but most of them had not been functioning long enough to have accumulated enough slow-moving products or packages to require a major or continuous effort in this area.

The same pattern emerged with respect to package styles. Once again, the largest number of packages found in any U.S. firm was 130, while the smallest number at any Indian firm was 210. Each individual item was packaged, on the average, in 1.7 different types of packages at U.S. firms, while it appeared in an average of 2.4 different packages at Indian firms. On the average, Indian firms used more than six times as many package types than U.S. companies. A few British drug firms surveyed which have been in India for a long time carried more products than the U.S. firms, but their package-to-product ratios were similar. It is important to note that the most progressive and successful of the Indian pharmaceutical companies (company E) was the one with the smallest number of products and package styles. On the other hand, the two most traditional and least successful indigenous firms (A and B) had the greatest number.

The difference in package styles at some indigenous firms was partly a reflection of conscious thought about the preferences of the Indian consumer. In most cases, however, it was the result of an accumulation over the years of various packaging styles, shapes, and sizes.

Because many Indian consumers are illiterate, companies hesitated to change packages, believing that consumers make repeated purchases by asking for a package identical to the one previously purchased. However, virtually no marketing research had been done to prove or disprove this assumption. This premise was accepted more unquestioningly in traditional Indian firms, and usually the only changes in their product lines and packaging varieties were additions.

Many of the companies studied had begun to analyze their sales patterns. For example, one large U.S. company had recently completed an A-B-C breakdown of its products according to profitability. The study indicated that 21 percent of its products yielded more than 70 percent of its profits. Plans were being made to analyze the remaining 79 percent of the company's products to determine whether some could be eliminated. The company also decided to focus its sales efforts on the most profitable of the items.

One of the more traditional Indian firms had conducted a similar study. However, its analysis was based upon volume of sales. The firm hoped to cut some low-volume items from its line. No attempt had been made, however, to determine the profitability of various items. The firm had simply assumed that volume and profitability could be equated.

Only one Indian drug company, the most progressive and successful, had established meaningful goals relating to new products. Using a five-year planning horizon, it had established targets for the introduction of both products and package styles. Plans were proceeding with a reasonable relationship to goals.

Several of the U.S. companies talked about new-product targets — typically two to four a year. However, actual introductions took place in a more haphazard fashion. Usually, new product additions resulted from suggestions of the parent firm, a particular pet project of the sales manager or the managing director, or in response to the introduction of new products by competing firms. The targets were actually little used as guides to action.

In several sectors U.S. subsidiaries have been producing a greater range of items than indigenous firms because they have been able to obtain profitable or potentially profitable products from their parent companies either to fill major voids in the Indian market, or to provide better service by offering a wider line to customers. For example, one U.S. company produces from two to five times as many kinds of batteries as its indigenous competitors. It also manufactures more flashlight varieties than its chief indigenous competitor.

The U.S., British, and other chemical firms with foreign collaboration have also been producing a wider range of products than the indigenous companies surveyed in this sector. One U.S. plastics manufacturer has even been selling processing equipment on a commission basis. However, in general, the British and larger indigenous manufacturers were more likely to market items not directly related to basic product lines. Some have even been marketing and exporting entirely unrelated products for smaller firms which do not have their contacts or distribution channels.

Indian firms primarily emphasized the quantity rather than quality of output. Often, a large proportion of the products they marketed were defective. For example, a sample of plastic, two-prong, electrical plugs taken from the market showed that more than 30 percent were defective due to faulty molding techniques. Upon questioning, company officials believed this to be inherent in the process and therefore of minor consequence.

In most cases, the U.S. subsidiaries protected the reputations of their parent companies by producing only to the highest quality standards, often creating difficulties for themselves because the local market could not supply raw materials to satisfy their needs. As a result of these high standards, however, products manufactured by U.S. subsidiaries were more highly regarded than those of indigenous companies.

Several U.S. subsidiaries had major disagreements with their parent firms on the question of lowering quality standards to a degree which would have been insignificant and unnoticeable to customers. A few handled the quality problem by putting out lower-quality items — including some for export from India — under a different brand name, although the parent company's name still appeared somewhere on the product or package.

DISTRIBUTION CHANNELS AND CUSTOMERS

The major difference between the U.S. and indigenous drug firms surveyed in India with respect to distribution channels was the greater dependence of the latter firms upon outside organizations to distribute and market their output. The U.S. subsidiaries placed greater reliance on internal sales forces and their own distribution networks. This is not surprising, since an aggressive marketing approach in a basically non-aggressive atmosphere would tend to require a high degree of control throughout the entire marketing process. Similar differences were found in the other industrial sectors.

All but one of the U.S. drug firms generated the major part of their sales through internal channels, while the reverse was true for most of the indigenous firms studied. One U.S. subsidiary has used the distribution channels of its Indian collaborator, but plans to establish its own distribution network by 1972, at which time it hopes to have adequate sales volume to make this economically feasible.

In most cases, U.S. subsidiaries have relied on outside distributors only when their sales volumes were not large enough to warrant an internal setup. Several which started out using external distribution networks have since merged with or acquired them. Most of the rest have established their own organizations. Even among large indigenous firms, particularly in the drug sector, there has been a recent trend toward more internalized channels of distribution. For example, one Indian drug firm began to handle most of its own distribution in 1967, and more recently another indigenous firm has begun to move in this direction.

Few firms studied in India have attempted a thorough analysis of their distribution systems. A diversified U.S. subsidiary, a diversified British firm, and the most progressive Indian pharmaceutical firm have been the notable exceptions. The drug company has even established an operations research group which identifies and analyzes demand patterns by region, for each product. They combine these demand analyses with estimates of transit times (using various methods of transportation under varying weather conditions), seasonal product patterns, production times, and so forth, and are attempting to develop a model of an "ideal" distribution system. Plans have been made to include in the model the location of depots, ideal inventory levels, suggested transportation forms, order patterns at both the depot and the chemist level, obsolescence factors, and service channels. No other Indian firm studied has undertaken this type of research and planning activity. Two U.S. drug subsidiaries had assigned industrial engineers and other specialists to look into distribution patterns, but neither had achieved any significant degree of sophistication at the time of this study.

Two aspects of distribution tend to differ considerably in developing nations as compared to the United States. First, many channels or middlemen usually exist between the manufacturer and the ultimate consumer, particularly with regard to consumer goods sold in outlying rural areas. It is not uncommon to find five or more middlemen for some products in India, as compared to only three or four in the United States. For example, agricultural supplies often go from the manufacturer's salesmen to distributors, then to wholesalers, sub-wholesalers, large dealers, smaller dealers, stockists in rural areas, sub-stockists, retailers, and finally to the consumer. At times various points in the network may be bypassed, however, and it is not uncommon for the manufacturer's salesmen, especially those of U.S. subsidiaries, to deal directly with dealers or even retailers when large orders are involved.

The second major difference relates to the margins within which the different channels in the overall distribution network operate. In India, distribution margins are usually narrower than in the United States. And even though there tends to be a greater number of links in the system, the differential between manufacturer's prices and retail prices is generally much smaller than in the United States. On the other hand, the manufacturer's margin tends to be greater in India, largely because volume is smaller.

Because of India's lower standards of living, achievement motivation, and aspiration levels, Indian distributors and middlemen are satisfied to net the equivalent of a few dollars a day. Hence, India's distribution channels are characterized by low-volume, low-markup sales. For example, the prices of batteries and flashlights to consumers in India have been only about 30 to 40 percent higher than the factory prices of the U.S. subsidiary (20 to 30 percent for indigenous manufacturers), while in the United States they have been in the range of 250 to 280 percent higher.

Both U.S. subsidiaries and indigenous firms tend to concentrate their sales efforts in urban areas, although these comprise only about 25 percent of India's population. However, indigenous firms seem to place somewhat more emphasis on reaching rural markets than do U.S. subsidiaries.

In the case of many products, Indian customers differ greatly from customers in the United States. Small customers in India include subsistence-level farmers, owners of small garages and workshops, and tiny retailers (often with only outdoor locations). A few of the most progressive U.S. subsidiaries have taken the lead in developing such small customers by re-educating their thinking, demonstrating the advantages of the company's products (particularly new ones), and encouraging them in the direction of growth. Many small customers have grown as a result.

Serious transportation and warehousing constraints have a major impact on distribution in India. Large firms are more inclined to provide their own transporation — ranging from human carriers, rickshas and bullock carts to motorized vans — as well as their own warehouses and depots. Smaller companies are often forced to confine their sales efforts to the immediate area in which they are located because of transportation and warehousing difficulties. They tend to engage in direct sales, unless they can find an agent to handle their low-volume, low-markup items.

Many firms surveyed have been selling to the Indian government, primarily for national defense purposes. Profitability on such sales is considerably lower than on sales to the civilian market. For example, one U.S. subsidiary has been making less than half — in some cases only about 20 percent — of the profit it does on civilian sales. An indigenous competitor had serious problems with the government several years ago because it did not want to sell at the low profit margins entailed in defense sales.

When it has had a choice — as has frequently been the case with regard to pharmaceutical products — the Indian government has been inclined to favor indigenous firms over foreign firms in the awarding of defense contracts.

PRICING

Invariably, the products of U.S. firms were priced higher than similar kinds of products from indigenous companies. Most of the exceptions were products manufactured by indigenous firms under foreign licenses carrying foreign brand names. However, where certain goods were in short supply, it was not uncommon for indigenous firms to charge the same price for lower-quality products.

In areas for which buyer's rather than sellers' markets exist, price trends have been downward at both U.S. and indigenous firms. In some cases, there have been huge price cuts. Such markets include those for various drugs and chemicals, many engineering and heavy industry goods, and various textiles and consumer goods. The price fluctuations for many of these products have been extreme during the 1960s.

It has not been uncommon for U.S. parent companies to place on their subsidiaries pricing constraints which have turned out to be ill-advised. For example, the parent company of one subsidiary placed a price equivalent to 3½d a pound on a certain chemical, since this was basically in line with the domestic price. The subsidiary had to enter into a 10-year contract with a major customer at this price even though it could have obtained two to three times more without upsetting its relationship with the customer, who did not have any adequate alternatives.

Firms surveyed recently in India's pharmaceutical industry have been among the most concerned about price controls. In fact, in May, 1970, the Indian government announced price cuts for some 17 basic drugs, and fixed or froze the prices of several other bulk drug products not previously subject to stringent controls.[1] Government approval is required for increases in the price of these items. The government reserved the right to cut prices further, and plans to conduct periodic reviews (probably annual) of drug prices. Higher markups will be allowed for periods ranging from three to five years on new products which involve "appreciable" research and development.

Even before the official announcement, many drug firms had sharply reduced or eliminated their advertising in newspapers because of the impending price cuts and price freezes. They also announced their intention of discontinuing advertisements in cinemas and on radio once existing contracts expired. It was expected that drug firms would reduce their sales forces and discontinue their sales drives in rural areas.[2] The profits of both U.S. and indigenous drug firms — as well as of other foreign companies — will suffer substantially as a result of these new controls. However, in most cases, the U.S. firms are in better shape since they have higher profit margins and greater overall operating efficiency.

Pricing decisions for products not subject to control were based largely on demand, strength, and competition. In some indigenous firms, cost calculations hardly entered the picture. Typically, the U.S. subsidiaries had a reasonable idea of their product cost structures, but the market situation -- in some cases combined with possible government or public reaction — was usually the final determinant of price.

The following comments are typical of those made by marketing executives of Indian firms:

> Previously we used to price our products by matching the prices established by competition. Now we use two factors: what we think the customer will pay and whether or not we want to eliminate some of our competitors by underpricing them.
> We look at what our competition is doing and try to price at the same level or just a bit lower.

One of the Indian firms was attempting to price on the basis of cost plus 10 percent. Although it examined the prices of its competition, this traditional company was one of the few to reverse the "going rate" pattern. It would sell at cost plus 10 percent or the market price, whichever was lower, whereas the other firms would typically use the higher of the two. Very often, this company's products were priced much lower than those of its competitors. However, the internal accounting system of the firm was so poor, and the overhead allocation process so crude, that it was impossible to determine whether or not they were actually making or losing money on any item.

The U.S. firms, on the other hand, attempted to compile detailed cost data. Although they ran into similar problems with respect to allocation of overhead, only a few attempted to use a contribution concept in their analysis. Most of them were able to compare their estimated costs with the going market rates established by competition. Although the latter factor usually played the most important role in determining the actual price, the cost calculations did establish a lower price limit.

In the Indian pharmaceutical industry, an important element in pricing was the numerous discounts given to dealers and drug stores. The discounts used by the more progressive Indian firms and the American companies were usually viewed as promotional devices. In the more traditional Indian firms, discounts were treated primarily as price reductions. These generally tended to be fixed elements in the price structure as opposed to the sporadic introduction and withdrawal of price reductions usually associated with promotional efforts. However, in all companies, these discounts were so prevalent that it was difficult to separate the promotional and the price-change effects.

Almost all of the drug companies surveyed claimed that they used "deals" (special discounts) only to meet competitive pressures. However, in almost all cases the discount-pricing patterns (resulting in higher margins to distributors and chemists who would, hopefully, place greater emphasis on moving the products) seemed to be a regular way of life. In one company, all but a fraction of 1 percent of its sales were made on a discount basis. The company employed a "discount" rather than a price reduction because it felt that a discount could be withdrawn whereas a price reduction would lock it into an inflexible situation.

SALES PROMOTION

Personal selling by the firms' own sales forces was the most important form of sales promotion used by most of the companies surveyed. Many spent up to 90 percent of their promotional resources on the personal selling effort. In the pharmaceutical industry, for instance, the sales representative was a combination salesman-order taker-information source. He would call on druggists or chemists to check their stocks, on physicians to tell them about new products and to maintain a good company image, and on institutions to sell the products directly.

The proportion of salesmen in relation to total company employment was generally much higher at U.S. subsidiaries than at their indigenous counterparts, but lower than at the domestic operations of their U.S. parent companies. For example, the proportion at all but one of the U.S. drug subsidiaries studied was over 15 percent, with the highest being nearly 20 percent. The proportion of salesmen was under 10 percent at all but the most progressive indigenous firm, which had 15 percent. The figure for the U.S.-based drug divisions of parent companies was between 24 and 30 percent.

The same patterns also prevailed in other industries. For instance, U.S. chemical producers in India have expended more effort on direct sales promotion and market development activities and on the conduct of demonstrations and tests in rural areas than Indian firms. In the engineering sector, U.S. and British firms have provided better field service for the machinery and equipment they sell.

The difference in effectiveness of sales promotion is largely a result of better methods of recruiting, screening, training, and motivating sales representatives. Most U.S. firms had higher standards for evaluating the qualifications of applicants. They tended to attract and hire better educated and motivated salesmen. In addition, they usually had more intensive sales training programs, paid their sales personnel better, and made greater use of commissions or bonuses than indigenous companies.

The salesmen of U.S. subsidiaries were also more knowledgeable about individual products, and were supplied with more and better promotional material to support their sales pitches. They were also able to offer a variety of "deals" and promotional incentives. Moreover, the U.S. companies offered more upward mobility for their salesmen, and provided them with better information and communication flows. Their sales representatives were required to submit periodic reports, were occasionally involved in the forecasting process, and had more flexibility in scheduling their work days than their counterparts in Indian firms.

Less mass media advertising was done in India than in the United States, and subsidiary expenditures in this area both in relative and absolute terms were lower than those of their parents' U.S. domestic operations.

Widespread illiteracy limits the use and effectiveness of newspaper and magazine advertising in India. And although newspaper circulation figures in India understate readership, since many readers share the same paper, circulation is so low as to limit the effectiveness of this media for most promotional efforts. Trade and professional journal advertising and direct mail are used for a limited number of products aimed at relatively sophisticated customers — e.g., doctors and hospitals in the case of drugs, manufacturing firms in the case of machinery.

Billboard advertising — stressing pictures rather than words — was as common in many of India's major cities as it is in the United States — but because private "highway" traffic is limited, roadside billboards are not as numerous. Commercial radio advertising is virtually nonexistent since the government owns the networks and prohibits advertising, and there are no TV stations in India yet. (Radio Ceylon was occasionally used to beam ads into India.) Trade fairs and conventions are also less common in India than in the United States.

On the other hand, the use of short film advertisements in movie houses was extensive, and research studies done by advertising agencies indicated that it was more effective than press advertising. Many companies used vans or jeeps to display and demonstrate their products, carry promotional information, and even present films and other forms of entertainment in rural areas. (Often these resembled the medicine man show of bygone days in the United States.) Drugs, batteries, flashlights, sewing machines, radios, small tools, farm implements, and a wide variety of other items were prompted in this manner. Another promotional ploy used extensively was the forcing of distributors and dealers to over-stock items, thereby pressuring them to make sales. (This was sometimes coupled with a special discount.) This practice was more common among indigenous firms than U.S. subsidiaries.

There are advertising agencies in India, including a few affiliates of major U.S. advertising firms. U.S. subsidiaries made greater use of them than indigenous firms; however, as Indian firms have become more aggressive in sales promotion, this has been changing.

Promotional expenditures, especially advertising, have come under great pressure from the Indian government, particularly in the case of U.S. and other foreign firms producing essential items like drugs. As a result, U.S. subsidiaries have developed internal sources for handling advertising campaigns, largely to ensure secrecy about advertising expenditures and other promotional costs. Some firms bury these costs under such headings as "travel" and "miscellaneous expenses."

Cooperative advertising — where the manufacturer shares costs with distributors or dealers — has been less common in India than in the United States. The few firms which have used it have all been U.S. subsidiaries.

Relatively few firms surveyed had planned advertising efforts on the basis of clear-cut criteria or analysis -- and only a handful had made cost-effectiveness studies in this area.

A U.S. subsidiary was one of the most sophisticated in determining the level of its advertising efforts. It obtained expert opinions from both internal and external sources before finalizing its advertising and overall sales promotion budgets, and did not arbitrarily assign them a percentage of total sales. It also used controlled experiments involving matched territories in an effort to determine the effectiveness of both promotional activities and pricing strategies.

Few indigenous firms even went as far as relating advertising to a percentage of sales. In most cases, promotional decisions were made arbitrarily without clearly defined criteria. Some Indian firms established a percentage of sales as an upper limit for advertising expenditures, but they usually spent amounts so much lower than the limit that the figure became meaningless. One firm, although it had not established guidelines, was making great advertising efforts in order to capture a larger share of the market.

CUSTOMER RETURNS AND COMPLAINTS

U.S. subsidiaries seemed to have fewer returned items and fewer customer complaints in relation to sales volume than their indigenous counterparts. They also dealt with returns and complaints more promptly and effectively. Few U.S. firms surveyed received more than 1 percent returns or customer complaints in relation to sales in any given month or year during the 1960s, while many indigenous firms had returns and complaints exceeding 1 percent of sales in many periods. The highest rates were typically in engineering and heavy industry companies, with several indigenous engineering companies experiencing return rates exceeding 5 percent of sales, and customer complaint rates of 10 percent or more during some periods.

U.S. subsidiaries tended to be more responsive to the needs, interests, and problems of their customers. Many emphasized customer service even when there was no need to do so in terms of profitability.

FINISHED GOODS INVENTORIES, STOCK-OUTS, AND LATE DELIVERIES

Few companies surveyed in India had undertaken comprehensive planning or installed control systems for finished goods inventories. Only one U.S. subsidiary had a system approaching the effectiveness of the one employed in the domestic operations of its parent firm.

The firms with the best finished goods inventory systems in India had the smallest number of stock-outs, unfulfilled orders, or late deliveries. They analyzed a broader range of factors related to desirable inventory levels than the other firms surveyed. Some of them had even ABC'd their finished goods inventories based on sales volume, manufacturing time, and transit time. Stocks were controlled according to rules relating to the lead times required to produce and move finished products from the factory to the depots or customers. Safety stocks had been set for all the high value (A) items. Some of these firms applied formulas providing for detailed differentiation by type of product, depot or customer location, lead times, and so forth.

In the more traditional indigenous companies stock-outs were commonplace, inventory records were sparse, and late deliveries were the rule rather than the exception. In a few cases, as many as 20 percent of the orders received from depots and customers were delivered late (sometimes as much as several months). Management often appeared unconcerned about such problems.

Until recently, few firms have worried about excessive finished goods inventories because they functioned largely in sellers' markets and there were critical shortages of numerous products. Turnover of finished goods was generally more rapid at firms in India than in similar companies in the United States. However, more recently, gluts of finished goods inventories have become more common. In general, U.S. subsidiaries have had fewer finished goods inventory problems than their indigenous counterparts.

EXPORTS

The Indian government has been using both "carrots" and "sticks" in the last several years to stimulate an increase in exports. On the "carrot" side, export incentive schemes have been used which provide for subsidies, import entitlements, and duty drawbacks and refunds. Although these incentives have evidently had a favorable effect in the engineering industry, they have not been as significant in most other sectors.

For many industries, including drugs and batteries, the "stick" has been more important in spurring firms to export. In such sectors, government policy requires companies to export a prescribed minimum of production (typically 5 percent in terms of value) if they wish to receive foreign exchange for imports. However, the government has not enforced this policy rigorously, as long as firms made a genuine effort to increase exports.

Export incentives for the engineering sector have, on the average, provided for a cash subsidy of 25 percent of either value added or F.O.B. export value, a 25 percent import entitlement in relation to export value, and duty drawbacks and refund of about 5 percent. However, some types of firms have received substantially more, and there has been flexibility in negotiations with the government on large tenders. This has been true, for instance, with regard to railway wagons and certain electrical equipment where case subsidies for each tender have typically been a matter for negotiations. In general, incentives have substantially increased exports of such products as railway wagons, transformers. lifts, machine tools and equipment, and other heavy industry goods.

In the pharmaceutical industry, the cash subsidy has been 15 percent of F.O.B. export value if exports reach 5 percent of total sales, and 20 percent if they reach 10 percent or more. The import entitlement has been 20 percent of export value, and duty drawbacks and refunds have averaged about 7½ percent. However, because of the prevailing high domestic prices for drug products, export incentives have not been considered important by firms in this sector.

Delays and red tape have been associated with export incentives. Many government agencies must scrutinize applications, and in some cases companies have not bothered to go through the trouble involved to get duty drawbacks or refunds. Government procedures have been streamlined, however, and in 1969 it took firms three to four months to get import entitlement (slightly less than before), and three to six months for duty drawbacks and refunds (a month or two less than earlier).

U.S. subsidiaries usually have an advantage over Indian companies with regard to export marketing, since they are part of multinational corporations. They can often export to other subsidiaries or affiliates of the parent corporation, in the form of components or accessories (as is the case with flashlight switches exported by a U.S. subsidiary to its parent company's plant in the United States), or in the form of material processing, assembly, or finished products. The U.S. subsidiary also benefits from the contacts, distributors, brand names, reputation, and many other advantages associated with being part of a worldwide network.

Executives of some Indian firms were quite pessimistic about increasing their exports to any extent in view of the fact that the U.S. subsidiaries, in spite of the many advantages they enjoyed, had still not been able to increase *their* exports appreciably. The high cost of materials in India has been a critical constraint even for

U.S. subsidiaries. Furthermore, many of their exports have been assisted by "subsidies" given by parent corporations.

All but a few Indian firms have lacked the knowledge, contacts, and facilities, to engage in large scale export marketing. Many of them are unaware of the size of the losses — or profits — they have incurred on export orders, since they do not know their true unit costs. Many of them have calculated inaccurately the true value of applicable export incentives. For example, although they consider the value of direct cash subsidies, duty drawbacks, and rebates, many overlook the benefits of import entitlements. An import entitlement of 20 percent of F.O.B. export value, coupled with a 50 percent premium on related imports in the open market can provide for an additional net incentive of 10 percent (0.5×0.2).

Indian firms experienced more difficulty in acquiring reliable distributors in foreign markets than U.S. subsidiaries. They were also at the mercy of foreign customers regarding prices, since the customers usually knew that they were forced to export, and had no powerful international parent corporation to bail them out. The Indian firms' lack of an international reputation was a major disadvantage, and their reliability and product quality were often suspect even where there was no real justification for this.

Consider the case of a large Indian tool company which has been exporting for many years. This firm is part of a giant Indian managing agency which has many sales offices abroad, including the United States. It has been exporting a limited quantity to the United States and, in the last few years, has tried to increase U.S. exports.

Several contacts were made in an attempt to obtain a large American distributor. However, the firm's Indian representative in New York failed to follow up on leads, and the process of sending samples and detailed data to prospects was slow. Moreover, several samples given to prospects were substandard. Even though the company is one of Asia's largest tool manufacturers, interested parties in the United States were skeptical about the reliability and product quality, in most cases simply because it was an Indian company.

Since few Indian firms have this company's resources with regard to export marketing, one can see how difficult it is for them to make any substantial increase in exports.

The Indian government has recently provided greater amounts of foreign exchange to some firms for export promotion purposes. However, they have not made significant amounts of foreign exchange available for opening or operating offices abroad. Government organizations and ministries concerned with export promotion have provided little assistance to companies with the exception of several big tenders involving heavy industry goods. Even the industry export promotion councils set up under the Ministry of Foreign Trade have not had much impact. The Ministry of Industrial Development recently opened a small export promotion office in New York, but many of the reports compiled by this office have not reached potentially interested firms.

The Indian government could certainly do more than it has to help firms increase their exports. It could provide training and other assistance in the area of export marketing to small as well as larger companies. It could consider joint or cooperative export programs, and encourage more U.S. and other foreign companies to enter into export ventures with Indian firms.

In the drug sector, U.S. subsidiaries have been more active than their Indian counterparts in the export field. Only one firm in this sector, an American company, has been able to export 10 percent of its output (in terms of value). It has been exporting 10 percent since 1968, most of it to Egypt. This has been an unanticipated windfall for the company. The Egyptians stopped buying from the firm's U.S. parent company following the 1967 war with Israel, and began placing orders with the subsidiary in India. Before 1968 this subsidiary had never exported more than 1 percent of output. The company still did not have an export manager in 1969, and management admitted that it should be more active in developing new export markets. The firm has been making a profit on its exports if export incentives are taken into account. For a few items exported to Ceylon and the Philippines it has been getting higher prices than in India. Only one other major firm in India's drug industry — a U.S. subsidiary not studied — exported more than 5 percent prior to 1969.

Another U.S. drug firm exported 5 percent for the first time in 1969. It exported 2½ percent in 1968, and an average of about 1½ percent of production during the preceding five years. It has not been making a profit, but has covered its direct costs with the export incentives. Indian prices for most of its products have been two to three times higher than world prices.

A third U.S. drug subsidiary exported 3 to 3.5 percent of production in 1969. This represented a substantial increase over past performance. It hoped to export 10 percent in 1970. Most of this will be shipped to the company's Asian headquarters in Hong Kong for redistribution. The company has been making a small overall profit on its exports with the incentives, although it does not even cover direct costs on some items which sell for 75 to 80 percent less than Indian prices. A British drug company surveyed expected to export 5 percent for the first time in 1969.

None of the major Indian drug firms for which export data was available had exported 5 percent of output, and none of them felt that it would be possible to keep up this level within the next few years. The major exporter of these indigenous companies expected to export less than 2 percent in 1969, more than it has ever exported in the past. The company recently created the position of export manager, but still had no effective foreign distributors. It has been exporting at a loss, the magnitude of which is not known since management does not have adequate cost data. On some exported products it has not even covered material costs. Even with export incentives, the firm estimates that it has been exporting one product at 25 to 50 percent below production costs. The local price for this product has been at least three times the world price.

Only one major Indian drug producer surveyed has ever exported more than 1 percent of output. Most of its exports go to Africa and the Middle East. One firm has used a British subsidiary as an agent for some of its exports, and has been trying to get assistance from the State Trading Corporation.

The chemical division of a large U.S. company expected to export 10 percent of its polyethylene output by value -- about 25 percent by volume in 1969. It has been doing this at a loss, barely covering material costs, even with a 10 percent cash incentive. Its export prices have been about one-third of its domestic prices. Its exports, going to Southeast Asia, Africa, and the Mid-East, have been high because of a lack of demand in India.

Another large chemical company with British, Dutch, and Indian ownership expected to export slightly less than 1.5 percent in 1969. Exports have been covering direct costs and some fixed costs, even though export prices have been from one-third to one-half of domestic prices for most products. The company set an export goal of 10 percent in 1970, most of it to Europe. However, a major constraint on this firm's exports has been the lack of bulk storage and transportation facilities in the Bombay area. The company has been building its own at great cost.

A U.S. battery producer has increased its exports steadily since 1966. Before the foreign exchange crisis and devaluation in 1966, this firm planned only an 11 percent increase in battery exports for 1966. This target was revised in mid-year to more than a 100 percent increase, and the target was nearly achieved. However, exports comprised only a small percentage of output. The company reached the 5 percent export level in 1968, and expected to export 6 percent of battery output by value and 10 percent by volume in 1969. The government has been strongly pressing this company to export 10 percent of its battery output by value, but it does not expect to achieve this in the foreseeable future. Its main battery line has been exported at approximately 15 percent net loss, as export prices have averaged about 45 percent less than domestic prices. Most of its other batteries have been exported at prices ranging from one-third to one-half of domestic prices, and for a few items only about 25 percent of domestic prices.

An indigenous battery firm expected to export a new high of about 1 percent in 1969. Most of its exports have been going to Eastern Europe and Africa. Its unit costs are 30 to 50 percent higher on similar items than those of the U.S. battery producer described above, and it has not been able to get as high prices on most export orders. Its export prices have been averaging less than half of domestic prices, and it has been exporting at a considerable loss. The company entered the export market in earnest in 1967, and it recently created the position of export manager. The managing director took a two-month export promotion trip to Eastern Europe and Africa in 1969. The firm's French technical collaborator has been trying to help with regard to exports. Management set an export target of 5 percent for 1970, but apparently did not really expect to achieve it.

A diversified British company which produces agro-industry products and consumer goods has been exporting voluntarily, even though it has not been entitled to incentives or seriously threatened by critical cuts in imports. It expected to export about 2 percent in 1969. It has been making profits on some exported items and incurring losses on other (e.g., soap). On the whole it has been making a small net profit on its exports, although considerably less than on domestic sales.

A large Indian engineering firm exported about 10 percent of its output (by both value and volume) during its 1968-1969 fiscal year, and expected to export 13 to 14 percent in 1969-1970. Prior to 1968 the firm had never exported more than 1 percent. Almost all of its exports have been transformers or elevators. The former have gone primarily to Asia and the Middle East, and the latter to Egypt and Sudan. This firm has a servicing agreement with a large international firm in some of its foreign markets. Export prices have been averaging 60 percent of domestic prices, and the latter have been close to production costs. However, if export incentives are taken into account, export prices have been similar to domestic prices, and in some cases slightly higher. This company has been receiving a cash subsidy of 25 percent in relation to F.O.B. export value, import entitlements of 40 percent, and duty drawbacks of 5 percent. Premiums on imports of the kind used by this firm have been averaging about 50 percent in the open and black markets. If all of the above factors are taken into account, the firm has received slightly more from some of its exports than from domestic sales.

India's large public sector steel corporation never exported more than 1 percent before 1967. In 1969 it expected to export 15 percent of its output by value and 18 percent by volume. Some of its exports have even been going to the United States. Its 1969 exports were estimated at nearly 450 million rupees, and the company expected to increase exports steadily in the following three years. Domestic prices for its products, which management has been trying to raise, have not been much higher than export prices.

CONCLUDING REMARKS

Many U.S. subsidiaries in India have been operating more effectively in the marketing area than in other basic areas. Although over-Americanized marketing policies and practices led to a number of serious problems, this is where the primary focus of talent was located.

U.S. techniques relating to such areas as sales training and incentives, sales promotion, distribution, inventory management, and customer service were transferrable. Lack of adaptation in the marketing area presented the biggest problems with respect to product specifications, design and quality, and, to a lesser extent, pricing.

There is little question that marketing was one of the areas which received major emphasis from the U.S. parent corporations. In some firms, market share received more attention than did profitability. As a result, subsidiary managers quite often focused primarily on increasing sales value, even at the expense of an increase in profit per unit which might have been obtained through greater cost reductions. But as long as market conditions assured profits on sales, this did not present serious problems.

As conditions have been shifting away from sellers' markets to greater competition, most U.S. subsidiaries have improved their marketing effectiveness considerably and several have begun to apply more of the sophisticated techniques used in the United States (e.g., the use of marketing research techniques to pinpoint market segments). The few progressive indigenous firms which had already started this process have had major advantages over their indigenous competitors. However, they typically had to develop most of this modern marketing know-how themselves, whereas it was waiting for U.S. subsidiaries to pick up from their parent organizations and apply in India.

CHAPTER 21   FOOTNOTES

1. See *Times of India,* Bombay, May 16 and 17, 1970.
2. Ibid.

CHAPTER 22
FINANCE

INTRODUCTION

The availability of funds has not been a serious problem for most larger companies in India, and even many small firms have been able to secure the money necessary for new projects. Moreover, the cost of capital has not received as much attention there as it has in the United States since frequently, the availability of government licenses has been a greater constraint on the undertaking of new or expansionary activities. However, finance has assumed greater importance for Indian industry in the last few years, because of declining profit margins, rising costs, excess capacity, increasing competition, tighter money, and more stringent price controls.

FINANCIAL MANAGEMENT

The U.S. firms studied in India have generally functioned more capably in the area of financial management than indigenous companies. This is chiefly due to their recruitment and training of managers and specialists with skills in the financial area, many with MBA or accounting degrees from leading U.S. universities. It is also due to the influence of their parent firms in establishing financial policies, procedures, and controls. Although the finance function has been overcentralized by many parent organizations, the controls have enforced a rigor which has been beneficial. They have compelled subsidiary managers to give more serious thought to the financial aspects of their plans and performance. This was affirmed by the president of a large Indian engineering company who said:

> U.S. firms tend to finance things relatively extravagently and are not likely to be under-capitalized, but tend to manage their financial affairs quite tightly. Indian companies are more likely to be undercapitalized, but to manage their financial affairs considerably more loosely and inefficiently.

While the U.S. subsidiaries studied made a more careful analysis regarding investment decisions than their indigenous counterparts, many had no clear-cut investment criteria relating either to the amount of money to be designated for various investment purposes or to the return such funds were expected to yield. In some cases, discussion with executives at international headquarters revealed that such standards were also lacking there. According to one international regional manager:

> It's very difficult to evaluate investment opportunities of a country like India. There are too many unknowns. Each year we sit down with all of the proposals of our [overseas] sub-sidiaries and try to compare the various alternatives we have for investing the available funds. I would like to be able to say that we will accept an Indian project that brings a return on investment of X percent. However, an awful lot of intangibles get factored into the decision, and these intangibles will vary depending upon the opportunities that are available to us. It's impossible to set a target cutoff point, since the political situation and the economic conditions, not only in India but in all the countries we are looking at, will determine what investments in India will be approved in any given year.

Because most proposed subsidiary capital expenditure requests had to be approved by international offices, using decision-making processes like that described above, subsidiary managing directors were often unable to estimate how much money they would have for capital investment or whether or not a specific project would be approved by the parent firm.

Over several years, some subsidiary managers had formulated rules of thumb, based on empirical evidence gathered from decisions previously made at international headquarters, as well as on their personal knowledge of the man who had made the decision. However, few could pinpoint the specific standards that had been applied, in spite of the fact that U.S. parent companies required detailed investment, cost, and income projections for new projects under consideration.

Once capital expenditure budgets were approved, they became the ad hoc standards against which the coming year's activities would be measured. Often, rigid limitations were placed on the contractual or spending authority of the managing director to assure that the "standards" would not be altered.

In recent years, several U.S. subsidiaries have begun to define minimum cutoff rates, and set other guidelines for investment decisions. Most have been using the payback period concept, typically on three-to-five year figures. Only a few of them have used more sophisticated techniques like discounted cash flow.

A large and diversified U.S. subsidiary made greater use of modern techniques with regard to investment and other financial decisions than any of the other firms studied in India. In some respects, it went even further than the comparable domestic operations of its parent company. All capital investment proposals exceeding 25 dollars were processed by a project-planning group headed by an Indian manager who held an MBA in finance from an American university. A detailed discounted cash flow analysis covering a period of 15 years was prepared for all proposals over $250,000, using a discount rate of 10 percent. (This arbitrary figure exceeded the firm's average cost of capital by several percentage points.) Contingency estimates and alternative plans were also drawn up, an analysis of qualitative factors was made, and projects were rank ordered. For proposals of less than $250,000 an average rate of return was computed and a qualitative analysis prepared. Relatively minor projects were decided primarily on the basis of qualitative factors which were presented in a standard format. A computer was used to assist in analyzing investment data.

Few of the indigenous firms surveyed had minimum cutoff rates or clear-cut criteria for their investment decisions. Not many used the payback concept; where it was used, a two- or three-year payback was usually desired. Investment, and other financial decisions, were usually based on an intuitive or subjectively felt "need," rather than objective economic analysis. Prestige and status factors frequently were given much weight.

For example, one heavy engineering company invested in a huge and costly press merely because many of the leading firms in the industry had similar equipment (although most were using it well below full capacity). This company utilized only 10 to 25 percent of its capacity, and would have been vastly better off if work had been subcontracted or handled in a slower fashion by using several smaller presses.

Only one indigenous firm — a progressive and successful drug company — was attempting to formulate detailed investment standards based on long-term, discounted rates of return. However, its top managers indicated that they planned to use this approach initially only as an experiment, since they were not sure how far and how accurately they could predict the future. They had previously used a payback period approach, but felt that this was of little value, since Indian conditions were such that it was often necessary to initiate ventures whenever the opportunity arose. If a company did not move early while government licenses were still available, it locked itself out of ventures which in the long run proved to be profitable. However, it might take many years to develop such infant industries to the point where they were breaking even.

SPENDING LIMITS

Within most U.S. subsidiaries, finance was the most centralized function by far. However, financial decision making was even more centralized within most Indian firms, and, in the case of companies operating under holding-company setups (e.g., managing agencies) the top enterprise manager usually had even less financial autonomy than a U.S. subsidiary manager.

A large diversified U.S. subsidiary had the highest spending limits of all foreign firms surveyed in India. This firm's most recent managing director has also been the regional director in charge of India for the parent company's Asian corporation. He was allowed to spend up to $250,000 (or 1.75 million rupees) without specific parent approval, as long as the project had been authorized in the company's long-range plans. However, a local appropriation committee examined many of the projects falling between $5,000 and $250,000. Contingency funds and leeway to overspend capital and other budgets were reasonable in this firm. In most cases, allowable deviation ranged from 1 percent to more than 5 percent of the budget or approved project. However, nonbudgeted capital items required top management's approval at the subsidiary if they exceeded 25 dollars (although this limit was in the process of being increased in late 1969).

In general, managers throughout the hierarchy of this U.S. subsidiary had high capital and other spending limits compared to managers in other foreign firms in India. Deputy managing directors were allowed to independently spend up to $5,000; division general managers about $3,500; plant managers ranged from about $1,000 to $2,000; and assistant plant managers, from $250 to $750. However, the limits of all of the subsidiary's plant managers were much lower than those of the managers of similar kinds of plants in the United States. For example, the top manager of a U.S. domestic plant of this subsidiary's parent company — with several hundred fewer employees, and a total budget of roughly the same magnitude — was allowed to spend up to $25,000 on authorized capital projects, and also had a discretionary spending fund of about $25,000 a year.

The managing director of the U.S. drug subsidiary which had the greatest financial autonomy had a spending limit of $20,000. The limit for second-echelon managers was about $2,500 and for third-echelon executives several hundred dollars. None of the other U.S. drug firms had limits anywhere near these levels, although they have been increased in recent years in several cases. The spending limits for their managing directors ranged from about $500 to $5,000. All but one of those surveyed gave some spending authority to second-echelon executives, ranging from about $25 to $750. About half did not give any discretionary spending powers to third-level executives, and those that did permitted from $25 to $100.

In general, there was a close correlation between the spending autonomy at drug firms surveyed in India and their relative economic success. In several cases, however, spending autonomy did not correlate with firm size. The managing directors of a few large subsidiaries surveyed in other sectors had discretionary spending limits of only a few hundred dollars, and in one case, only $100.

The managing directors of the two largest and most successful Indian drug companies — in both cases they were major shareholders — approved capital and non-budgeted expenditures up to about $15,000 (100,000 rupees), without referring them to their boards of directors. However, they could spend more — up to $100,000 in one case and $70,000 in the other — without board approval if they wanted to. Officially, second-echelon executives at one of the companies had authority to spend up to about $3,300, but they rarely did so. In the other company, second-echelon executives have had spending discretion in the range of about $20 to $100.

At nearly all other indigenous firms, only the managing director had any real spending authority, especially where the companies were part of a holding company. For example, virtually all capital expenditures at an indigenous battery firm have required approval of the managing agency which controls the company. In turn, virtually all spending of any kind has had to be authorized by the firm's managing director.

TYPES OF FINANCING AND SOURCES AND USES OF FUNDS

In most cases, U.S. subsidiaries had lower debt in relation to total capital than their indigenous counterparts. On the other hand, they used debt financing to a greater extent than their parent corporations.

For example, most U.S. drug subsidiaries had a debt to total capital ratio of 20 percent or slightly less during the 1960s. None was greater than 30 percent. Only one of their parent companies had a ratio exceeding 10 percent. The indigenous drug firms all had debt ratios of over 20 percent. In a majority of cases it was at least 40 percent, and in several it exceeded 50 percent. A few foreign drug firms — mostly Swiss and German — also had debt ratios of 50 percent or more.

In other industrial sectors the same pattern was found. With few exceptions, indigenous engineering firms had debt ratios exceeding 50 percent, the highest being at those run by managing agencies.

The most notable exception to the above pattern was a large multiplant U.S. subsidiary. It had a debt to total capital ratio ranging from about 45 to 55 percent during most of the 1960s versus a consistent 40 percent at its parent company. The subsidiary's major indigenous competitors had lower debt to total capital ratios. However, most of the U.S. firm's debt had been related to one highly capital-intensive product line.

The reasons why Indian companies made greater use of long-term debt financing than U.S. subsidiaries are not clear. It is likely that many of the U.S. companies, being relatively new to India, preferred to limit outside influence on their operations. Moreover, during most of the 1960s — except during 1969-1970 when money was very tight and costly in the United States — debt financing in India was significantly more expensive than in the United States and many firms may have felt it wasteful to pay high local interest rates. Some were also concerned about the uncertainty of meeting large debt obligations, especially in the earlier phases of their new ventures.

In most cases, debt financing at U.S. firms surveyed involved hard currency loans bearing lower interest rates than local debt financing. The parent companies of U.S. subsidiaries relied more on reinvestment and internal financing for expansion and diversification than did indigenous firms. In most cases, the profits of U.S. subsidiaries were considerably greater, in both relative and absolute terms, than those of their Indian competitors. Moreover, until recently, U.S. subsidiaries were more reluctant to undertake new capital projects (especially those involving vertical integration) than many of their indigenous counterparts. Finally, political factors may have made U.S. companies reluctant to use Indian public financial institutions for debt financing.

Few U.S. subsidiaries of any kind in India have made use of preferred stocks. However, preferred issues were commonly used as a source of long-term capital financing by indigenous companies — although not as much as they are used in the United States. Preferred stocks generally paid higher dividends than dividends based on the market value of common stock, and in some firms, preferred dividends were higher than the interest rates they paid on long-term debt.

None of the firms studied had either convertible preferred stock or debentures convertible into common stocks. This was not surprising, given the strong desire of company owners in India to maintain absolute control.

Indian companies typically raised their common stock equity from family members, close friends, and other insiders, and their stock was tightly held. U.S. and other foreign companies were more inclined to sell some common stock to the Indian public but, in many cases, only under strong government pressure.

During the 1960s, few clear patterns seemed to exist in either foreign or indigenous firms surveyed in India with regard to retained earnings or their rates of new investment and reinvestment. There were certain periods when U.S. subsidiaries and indigenous firms all cut back on reinvestment in order to avoid the risks of devaluation, uncertain market conditions, or adverse political action, and others where they increased reinvestment. However, during any particular year some firms were investing, reinvesting, and expanding quite rapidly, while others were repatriating (or paying out in dividends) everything they could. For a given firm the most important consideration with regard to new investment, reinvestment, and expansion was, typically, whether or not it had been able to obtain required licenses to initiate new or expansionary projects.

Just before the bank nationalizations in 1969 none of the U.S. or other foreign firms surveyed dealt with more than three banks, and most used only one or two. On the other hand, only one Indian company studied was dealing with less than three banks, and a majority had business with at least six or seven. About half the U.S. and indigenous firms surveyed had accounts with foreign banks in India.

In recent years many indigenous companies began to take deposits from private parties which they used for their own financing. Most paid from 9 to 12 percent interest on such deposits. One prestigious company paid only 8½ percent in 1969, in spite of a bank rate for deposits of about 9 percent. This company had 8 million rupees on deposit in 1969, equivalent to about 20 percent of its total equity. The law requires that company deposits be made for a minimum of one year's duration. This process provided a haven for much black-market money, and largely for this reason the government passed more stringent disclosure regulations for such deposits. No U.S. firms surveyed had employed this type of financing.

U.S. subsidiaries usually paid their suppliers more promptly than indigenous firms. The latter made greater use of suppliers as a cheap source of financing. Many U.S. firms felt that better supplier relations and "fair play" (by their standards) were important and in many instances this kind of policy has paid off in terms of better and more reliable service from suppliers.

Cash sales to customers were more common in Indian industry than in the United States. To the extent that credit was provided, the U.S. subsidiaries studied generally were less likely to incur bad debts, or have long overdue accounts, than their indigenous counterparts. They were also more discriminating about extending credit terms, and showed greater willingness to extend credit to small accounts which had promise and growth potential than their indigenous counterparts. They also controlled and followed-up collections more effectively. Several also experimented with incentives — e.g., discounts ranging from 0.5 to 2 percent for payment within 30, 45, or 60 days — to encourage prompt payment. However, the incentive plan did not generally prove to be effective.

All kinds of companies in India experienced long delays in collecting overdue accounts on government sales. In the case of the National government, the chief difficulty lay in collecting the final 10 percent. This final payment was only made after the government had completed all of its inspections and audits. But the government's usual practice was to drag its feet endlessly, and some firms finally give up trying to collect. Instead, they frequently add a factor of 11 percent to their original price or bid to compensate.

Collecting from state and local governments was even more difficult and time consuming. For example, a British electrical company tried to collect a large outstanding bill from the government of West Bengal for several years without success.

U.S. subsidiaries were generally more effective in planning and controlling cash than indigenous companies. They seldom found themselves in serious liquidity crises, nor did they maintain excessive or unproductive funds — patterns which characterized many indigenous companies.

COST STRUCTURES AND PROFITS

In terms of overall cost structures, U.S. subsidiaries spent considerably more in relative terms than their domestic counterparts in the United States on materials, and less on payroll and labor. In most cases the U.S. domestic companies spent proportionately more on overall overheads, primarily because of their research and development efforts, and greater staff support functions. However, this did not occur to the same extent on plant overheads.

For example, in the pharamaceutical sector the U.S. based firms surveyed spent 30 to 55 percent of their total expenditure on materials and supplies, and 24 to 30 percent on salaries and wages. Their related subsidiaries in India spent 60 to more than 75 percent of expenditures for materials, and from 9 to 18 percent on manpower.

The same basic patterns existed — though the actual proportions differed — at subsidiaries producing chemicals, batteries, flashlights, engineering goods, and other products. For example, the domestic flashlight and battery plants of a U.S. multinational corporation spent about 40 to 50 percent on materials, 15 to 20 percent on labor, and 30 to 45 percent on overheads during the 1960s. Its subsidiary plants in India spent 70 to 80 percent on materials, 2.5 to 6 percent on labor, and about 20 to 25 percent on overheads. U.S.-based chemical plants surveyed all spent under 60 percent on materials and over 13 percent on labor, while subsidiary plants in India producing similar products all spent over 75 percent on materials and under 7 percent on labor. Similarly, all but one of the U.S.-based engineering and heavy industry firms surveyed spent under 50 percent on materials and all spent over 20 percent on labor, while none of the U.S. or other foreign firms of this type in India spent less than 55 percent on materials or more than 15 percent on labor.

Few clear-cut patterns emerged regarding the relative proportions of overall labor expenditures between U.S. subsidiaries and Indian companies in the same sectors. However, U.S. subsidiaries had lower materials costs and higher overhead costs than their indigenous counterparts in a majority of cases. This was largely to due their greater staff support and service functions.

Few firms in India had a formal policy of regularly donating some of their profits to charitable or civic causes — the usual practice of companies in the United States. However, more indigenous firms surveyed did so than U.S. subsidiaries or affiliates. A few had established trust funds — often bearing the owning family's name — for this purpose. (These companies usually donated about 5 percent of their net profits each year.)

INTEREST RATES, DIVIDENDS, AND STOCK PRICES

Interest rates came down slightly in India in 1969, but continued to be higher than they were several years earlier. In 1969 the Reserve Bank rate was in the 5 to 5½ percent range, and the prime commercial bank rate for companies was in the 8 to 8½ percent range. However, in mid-1970 the commercial banks were instructed to raise the interest rate on all loans by at least 0.5 percent and the Reserve Bnak ordered a general credit squeeze. It was too soon to tell what impact this would have on industrial firms or the economy as a whole, at the time of this writing.

During the 1960s interest rates paid on short-term bank loans and overdrafts were similar at the U.S. subsidiaries and most of the major Indian firms surveyed, running between 8½ and 9 percent in 1969. Other indigenous firms surveyed — including a few small ones — were paying 9½ to 10 percent interest on short-term bank financing, and several smaller Indian firms which had to resort to private money lenders paid monthly interest rates of 30 percent or more.

No difference was found in the rates for medium- and long-term rupee financing, although a few U.S. firms were able to get financing which was 1 or 2 percent cheaper. However, U.S. and other foreign companies and joint ventures were able to get lower rates on foreign exchange loans, largely because of the influence of their parent firms.

Major firms usually paid 8½ to 10 percent for medium- and long-term rupee financing during the last few years. U.S. subsidiaries which were able to obtain lower interest loans, paid 6 to 7½ percent on loans from AID and some other institutions. They usually paid about 7½ percent for foreign exchange loans, while indigenous firms paid 8½ to 9 percent. One large European firm recently obtained a 6 percent tax-free foreign currentcy loan with a three-year moratorium on payments from its international parent company.

Those firms surveyed which had preferred stock paid dividends on such stock ranging from 7.15 to 11.5 percent. In most cases, the yield exceeded 8.5 percent.

The common stock of U.S. subsidiaries usually paid somewhat lower dividend yields on market value — but higher on face value — than that of indigenous firms; and in most cases the stock of U.S. firms also sold at higher price-earnings ratios than that of their indigenous counterparts. Higher future expectations among investors, the greater prestige of the U.S. firms, their more stable and higher growth and earnings performance, and the more stable dividend records of many subsidiaries probably were the chief reasons for this.

Most successful U.S. and other foreign subsidiaries examined paid dividends of 5 to 6 percent based on the market value of their publicly-held common stock, and in excess of 20 percent on face value. The Indian companies with publicly-held common stock averaged dividend payments of 6 to 8 percent in relation to market value. Although some firms which had earned negligible profits or encountered losses continued to pay dividends to maintain continuity, several others suffered such large losses during some years that they failed to pay any dividends at all. Few of the Indian firms surveyed paid dividends which exceeded 20 percent of the face value of their stock.

Stock prices showed little difference between U.S. subsidiaries and indigenous firms with respect to market fluctuations. By contrast, however, their peaks and valleys in bull and bear markets were not as sharp as those of their U.S. parent companies. The only differences between U.S. and local firms was found in the depressed prices of those local companies which stopped dividend payments as a result of operating losses. U.S. firms tended to maintain their dividend payments through bad periods.

CHAPTER 23
CONCLUSION

When one looks ahead, it becomes increasingly apparent that the growth of international business and the thrust for accelerated economic development among the poorer nations are two of the major factors which will mold the world of the future. We have already reached the stage where U.S. industrial activity outside of the United States has become one of the dominant economic forces in the world. Through this effort the products and ideas of the United States have spread throughout the globe, and as a consequence its currency, technology, and even its language have been accepted as part of the commercial life style of many nations.

The intense international and multinational activity does not come solely from the United States. Japan, West Germany, the United Kingdom, Holland, many of other European nations, and to a lesser extent some of the Soviet bloc nations have similarly increased their international business activities. More and more, the trend is away from pure and simple trade, and toward the establishment of widespread global networks engaged in a variety of operations.

It is interesting to note that this process is taking place despite another trend which would seem to lessen the need for such geographic dispersion — the lowering, and even removal, of many barriers to foreign trade. However, the removal of trade impediments is only another manifestation of a new international awareness. This awareness, presently confined largely to economic matters, has not yet really reached political spheres but may be a portent of the future in all areas. Certainly, what is occuring in the economic sector facilitates a greater exchange of ideas, many of which overflow into political, social, and other areas of interaction.

The developing nations are beginning to realize that they must participate in this movement. No longer are they willing to serve as passive recipients of goods and services provided by their more highly industrialized neighbors. Many are starting to recognize that economic activity based solely on agricultural production or mineral extraction is not sufficient to guarantee the achievement of long-range goals and objectives. Increasingly, these countries are beginning to plan for the future, and are devoting considerable energy to the development of sound industrial bases. In many areas, where local markets are too small to sustain concentrated industrial activity, new alliances are emerging, designed to consolidate markets and permit the economies of scale necessary to sustain efficient industrial production.

These alliances, based on production and economic considerations, are also giving rise to new political and social institutions. This can be most dramatically seen in the European Economic Community, which, although it has not yet resulted in a united Europe, has altered much more than just the economic sphere among the participating nations. It has had great impact on European government and scientific institutions and has influenced living patterns and styles.

As companies continue to expand, and as countries press for continued economic development, the pressures for maximum utilization of resources will continue to mount. Individual companies will feel these pressures simultaneously with others generated by increasingly skilled and aggressive competition. They will have no choice but to make their multinational operations more efficient and more responsive to the environment. In some cases they may have to develop totally new philosophies and organizational concepts for conducting business on a multinational scale.

Similarly, governmental attitudes will continue to change at an accelerated pace. The governments of developing nations will experience greater pressure to achieve and maintain maximum rates of economic development and growth. The stresses which are building up are tremendous, as the populations of "have-not nations" become aware of the attainments of their more affluent neighbors. Aspirations are changing, and going beyond the traditional, static patterns as people who have been complacent with their lot begin to learn (via films, radio, and television and as well as through the examples provided by multinational corporations) what society is actually capable of providing. Slowly but surely the dominance of "fatalism" as the philosophy of underdevelopment is beginning to dissipate, and, more and more, nations are attempting to control their destinies.

The implications of this trend for both multinational companies and for developing nations are important. Not only will current pressures continue to mount, but the entire environment in which these companies operate and many of the assumptions under which they have conducted business in the past will continue to change.

Furthermore, the governments of the developed nations will be subjected to different kinds of pressures. People are becoming more aware of social problems and of the ecological aspects of daily life. Moreover, a world consciousness is developing in the United States: the problems of poverty in India, of tidal-waves in Pakistan, of earthquakes in Peru, of conflict in the Middle East, and of social injustice in South Africa are no longer relegated to a few sentences on the back page of the newspaper. Instead, they are major issues which affect the thinking, the conscience, and the actions of people around the world. Problems of environmental pollution, population control, and the exploration and exploitation of new worlds (e.g., the ocean bottom and the moon) are no longer confined within the boundaries of individual nations. Countries are beginning to recognize that we are truly living in a "spaceship earth" in which everything that happens is, in some manner, related to everything else.

The economically-advanced nations have developed a social consciousness which has lead them toward increased involvement in these problems. More and more one hears the feeling expressed that such nations have a responsibility to use their resources and technology to improve the lot of all mankind.

Since the impetus for awakening these perceptions has come, and will continue for many years to come from economic activity, it is here that the major focus of attention should be directed. The satisfaction of spiritual needs is closely linked to the satisfaction of material needs, and the latter are easier to change than the former. Consequently, it is essential to understand the factors influencing international economic activities so that such activities can be directed towards achieving desired goals in the most effective manner.

One of the best methods yet developed of studying the relationships between different national patterns and the economic forces which affect that interaction is that of comparative analysis. This study has attempted to undertake such an analysis. By looking at the interface between U.S. and Indian industrial activities, relating it to the industrial and social patterns of each country concerned, and analyzing the results, it is possible to determine what combination of actions and attitudes will be most likely to achieve a particular set of goals. The setting of these goals is in large part a function of value judgements — and the goals of the interacting parties may well be different. However, given an understanding of the environments (both on the local and international levels) and given the available resources (human, physical, and ideological), it is possible to determine the best-ways that these goals can be achieved.

This book has attempted to do just that by providing a conceptual framework for analysis, by examining and evaluating the relevant environmental factors, and finally, by looking at the specific experiences which companies have had in making the decisions and managing the activities they have selected to achieve their goals.

SOME GENERAL IMPLICATIONS FOR DEVELOPING COUNTRIES

In India, the greatest impetus for awakening and stimulating a social consciousness on the part of foreign firms and for hastening Indianization of the companies (both in terms of ownership and management) was pressure exerted by the government, the unions, and other outside forces. This experience would seem to suggest that companies have to be lured into the environment, and then entrapped there in such a manner that they will align their own goals and objectives more closely with those of the host nation.

This pattern, although fairly prevalent in the past, is beginning to change. As firms start to envision wider international operating environments, they are coming to recognize the value of creating and maintaining images as citizens of each of the countries in which they operate. A climate of cooperation is replacing one of suspicion, and the emphasis is shifting toward an interest in what governments of developing nations can do to stimulate their economies. Several areas are important in this context.

First, governments should provide as many opportunities as possible for young people who will be entering careers in business and industry to obtain exposure to those Western concepts and values which are related to business management. This includes encouraging scholarships for foreign study, establishing business education institutions patterned to a considerable extent on the Western style, and permitting and facilitating exchanges of personnel. It must be recognized that many elements necessary for industrial development are missing in developing nations, and must be sought in other cultures and other countries.

Similarly, there is a pressing need to develop a cadre of government leaders cognizant of the problems of industrial development. As was seen time and time again in India, the attempt to translate government idealism into actual social progress, often led to results which were diametrically opposed to the government's objectives. For example, the attempts to reduce consumer costs by eliminating advertising showed little understanding of the distribution process which is required to build up both the market and the capacity to deliver goods. Consequently, efforts have to be made to train officials (including potential future officials) to be aware of the balanced needs of society and industry.

Not only must government officials become familiar with the concept of industrial development, but they must also learn management techniques which can be utilized in administering those areas of activity which relate to industrial growth and development. This need for training was especially evident in the public-sector firms which were studied. Most top-level managerial personnel in these firms had little industrial experience. People with backgrounds in government had no way of mastering the requirements of running large corporations except on a trial and error basis. The same need for training applies to such activities as customs operations, industrial licensing, and the allocation of scarce resources.

Where resources are scarce, an effective planning process can facilitate the best possible use of what is available. Again, a thorough understanding of the processes of industrialization is required. Government planners must be aware of the impact that various elements of their plans have on the totality of the sectors they are dealing with. Techniques such as input-output analysis can do much to point out areas of interaction; but officials must understand not only the physical effects, also the psychological repercussions that government actions have on both the buying public and the managers of producing firms.

One important consideration which was not highlighted in this study because focus was largely directed toward a comparative analysis of private sector firms is the fact that public-sector firms appear to be less efficient in developing nations than their private-sector counterparts. There is a reason for this. Public-sector firms are usually managed by government officials, and run in a fashion consistent with the government bureaucracy. Moreover, this is an area least likely to undergo the change in value orientation that is required for effective industrial management. The private sector — even the indigenous private sector — is forced by competition to alter its perceptions with respect to ways of doing business. It does not have the relatively unlimited capital resources of the government or the power to create monopoly, and it cannot afford to remain uncompetitive for a long period of time. Consequently, it must continually seek to improve. With only a few exceptions, public-sector firms observed in developing nations were less efficient than private-sector companies.

Finally, "understanding" is a two-way street. Although the primary burden of adapting and accommodating to the local environment rests with the foreign subsidiary, the governments of developing nations must also learn about the methods and procedures used by foreign subsidiaries. They need these foreign inputs to develop their industrial capacity, their technology, and the skills of their work forces. The development of such knowledge would go far towards alleviating many of the misunderstandings which arise. Certain actions taken by foreign firms could be evaluated in the light of the motives which underlie these actions — motives which are often misinterpreted because of differing value orientations. An understanding of the value systems of foreign managers would often reveal that what might otherwise appear to be a sinister, exploitative, plot is nothing more than a misunderstanding arising out of different culturally-based ways of looking at issues. In many situations the local government might be able to find a way to work out differences in a manner which could be understood and accepted by the foreign firm — thereby preserving the good relationships which most parties would like to maintain.

SPECIFIC IMPLICATIONS FOR INDIA

Although she has experienced severe problems and major gaps still exist, India has managed to develop a broad industrial base and infrastructure. It would appear that a critical mass market has been developed, giving the nation has the potential to dramatically accelerate its economic growth. However, many government attempts to direct and control this process have actually retarded it. It is too massive and too complex a task for a government which has had little experience, and no tradition in industrialization. Many existent laws and procedures have served as leashes, holding back development in critical sectors.

The size and scope of the base which has been built is great enough so to allow the government to let market forces and competition play a greater role in regulating economic activity. The market itself is capable of generating better-directed and more intense pressures to encourage managerial efficiency. Controls on investment, foreign exchange, factor inputs and outputs, prices, and so forth, should be relaxed in a systematic manner. The country should consider moving toward a tariff-based import system and the application of multiple exchange rates. Less emphasis should be given to short-run balance of payments problems and highly rigid import substitution, and greater emphasis should be placed on increasing exports. Adequate foreign aid to fill critical gaps is also more likely to be available if the Indian government presents a sound and realistic overall development plan which has a good chance of increasing the nation's self-sufficiency more substantially in the not-too-distant future.

It is clear that India is not yet ready for unrestrained industrial competition. Some industries, types of firms, and specific products still require a considerable amount of government control in order to assure efficient resource utilization; however, their number is considerably smaller than the number of firms which are regulated at present. Government planning and control need to be more selective, more carefully conceived, more precisely stated and systematically integrated, and more effectively enforced than they have been to date. With fewer regulations and controls this should not be impossible to achieve. It seems likely that India would benefit by implementing many of the features of France's system of indicative economic planning.

A major problem in allowing greater competition (and exerting less government control) in India's economy involves the inefficient or marginal producers, which include thousands of small enterprises that might be forced out of business. But this is, in fact, what actually happened on a broad scale during the depression of 1966-1968. It is healthier for the economy in the long run for highly inefficient firms to go out of business because of healthy competition than for them to do so because of economic recession.

On the other hand, relatively inefficient firms still need some protection, particularly if there is a reasonable chance that they will become more viable in the future. Various kinds of assistance programs could be effective in this area. Foreign assistance programs, foreign experts and management contracts, and foreign technical licensing agreements could also assist this process. Foreign ownership need not be involved.

If marginal firms could be encouraged through various kinds of incentives and pressures, to merge or otherwise join together and concentrate on their more productive lines, the resultant economies of scale, increases in efficiency, and improvement of products would contribute greatly to the nation's growth.

SOME IMPLICATIONS FOR DEVELOPED NATIONS

The industrial activities of foreign nations, especially where they involve manufacturing operations which directly affect the lives of many people in the local population, serve to represent the lifestyle and philosophies of these foreign countries. The old adage, "actions speak louder than words" is applicable in such cases.

In most situations, the assumption that the activities of U.S. firms are direct extensions of U.S. foreign policy is fallacious. It is hard to argue, however, that in the aggregate their activities do not present an image reflective of U.S. values, though in most cases U.S. firms operate independently of the State Department.

Unfortunately, not only is this distinction unclear, but in many cases the U.S. government seems to prove the contrary proposition. In one situation after another — disputes in Ecuador over tuna boats, in Peru over oil interests, in Chile over copper, in the Middle East over oil — the U.S. government directly intervenes in the affairs of U.S. companies. To a lesser extent, this is true of governments of other developed nations. The appearance this gives cannot help but result in charges of exploitation, and of U.S. economic imperialism. It enforces the belief that the expansion of U.S. firms is a direct part of U.S. foreign policy.

Very few (in comparison to the total number) U.S. companies are engaged in practices which continuously violate social values in the local culture. From time to time, most firms are guilty of defying some norms, and a few firms are guilty of many infractions. Yet, in the few situations where companies have clearly transgressed what is considered to be proper, publicity is usually blown up out of proportion and similar practices are ascribed to all firms of that nationality.

Similarly, the United States government involves itself in the affairs of U.S. business firms in very few cases. But when it does happen, these affairs also receive widespread publicity. The net effect is that the United States government appears to be using a club "every time" one of its companies gets into serious trouble. Instead of the foreign subsidiary being perceived as a local citizen, working in the local environment in much the same manner as its indigenous counterparts, it is seen as an instrument for exploiting and extracting wealth from that country. Each intervention by the government makes life more difficult for the remaining firms — especially in situations where nationalistic feelings are strong.

Some regulations passed by the United States provide fuel to nourish these same misconceptions. The extension of U.S. anti-trust and tax laws to U.S. companies operating in developing nations provides one example. U.S. regulations relating to trade with Communist nations also create misunderstandings, especially when a U.S. subsidiary is operating in a nation which maintains relations with the Communist blocs, and an order is received for goods which would provide jobs and increased foreign exchange for the nation if the U.S. subsidiary were able to accept it.

In essence, the United States often appears to be talking about free enterprise, while actually interfering to protect the rights of its companies in a manner which seems anything but "free." (Such involvement also gives U.S. companies the added advantages which can be supplied by U.S. government leverage.)

In discussions with many executives of U.S. companies in Asia and Latin America, opinions varied as to the role that the U.S. government should play. However, the majority of managers of well-established firms which had made a good adjustment in a foreign country believed that the best course of action was a total "hands-off" policy by the government. Many of these men even went so far as to state that it would be worth giving up investment guarantees if that meant that U.S. intervention in other areas would cease. In most cases, these executives felt that the few of their colleagues who got into trouble received bad publicity, and created international incidents more than deserved the action taken by local governments. They resented the U.S. government's attempts to come to the rescue, especially since they blamed many of these situations on poor management. The U.S. government intervention often raised "non-directed" nationalistic outcries that affected their own operations.

Obviously, there are exceptions — situations where local governments have operated in an irresponsible manner. However, in a large number of situations in recent years, this has not been the case.

Many newer companies, and many U.S. companies considering overseas expansion, although they would also like to have the U.S. government stand clear, are not as willing to give up other government benefits such as loan programs and guarantees. This is understandable, since these programs reduce risk. However, one can raise the valid question of why foreign investment decisions should be considered different from domestic decisions to invest capital, technology, etc. All investment decisions involve risk. The degree of risk may vary, but this means only that a different set of numbers must be factored into the deliberations when a decision is being considered.

Many U.S. firms do not seem to have confidence in their managerial skills and technological know-how when they decide to enter a developing economy on an equal footing with companies that are already established there. The primary reason for this insecurity is the fact that they lack a thorough understanding of environmental conditions in the country concerned, the temperament of its political and social institutions, and the prevailing value systems. Where they are able to adapt to these patterns, their managerial skills give them a decided advantage — one which can help to assure stability and permanence of operation.

GENERAL CONCLUSIONS AND IMPLICATIONS — THE INDIVIDUAL FIRM

A number of general conclusions may be drawn from this study which can be useful to both foreign subsidiaries and indigenous firms. Here it is assumed that the firm's primary objective is to become effectively integrated with the local environment in a manner which will promote long-range economic growth, profitability, and the general wellbeing of the company. However, experience indicates that in the long run such aims will be successful only when they are coupled with strong attention to economic factors. A company must be strong and viable if it is to influence its environment positively. In essence, therefore, these conclusions and implications are framed in terms of the achievement of the long-range economic stability and prosperity of the firms and nations concerned.

Foreign subsidiaries

The findings of this study indicate that the three most important factors which affect the performance of U.S. subsidiaries in developing nations are: 1) their knowledge of local environments; 2) their familiarity with existing managerial techniques and practices; and 3) their ability to blend the first two factors into a meaningful whole. Each of these is crucial to the long-range success of operations.

As has been shown throughout this book, the environments of developing nations have characteristics which distinguish them in many ways from the environments of more economically advanced countries. It is critical that executives, not only in the foreign subsidiary but also in the headquarters of the parent company, understand the nature of these differences so that they can recognize the need for new approaches to deal with them.

For the international parent companies, probably the most significant contributions they can make, in terms of adaptation to the foreign environment are, first, the selection of the right people to operate the subsidiaries and, second, the establishment of control procedures to ensure that the subsidiary's goals relate to those of the total enterprise, but, at the same time give the subsidiaries the latitude they need to meet changing conditions. Too often, the procedures imposed upon subsidiaries by their parent companies are designed for the convenience of those companies and tend to restrict subsidiary management's flexibility and inhibit its ability to adapt to local conditions. Similarly, the view of the foreign subsidiary as a smaller, and therefore less sophisticated operation often influences the managerial selection processes to such an extent that many subsidiaries do not receive the kind of managerial attention and expertise they badly need.

Ideally, the U.S. executive who goes abroad should be intimately familiar with both local conditions and language. However, there are cases where this is not possible. In such situations, there is a second-best alternative. The executive who is familiar with the kinds of patterns found in developing nations, who knows what problems to look for and what he must learn during the early stages of his tenure, and who approaches the task with as few preconceptions as possible, is far along the road to achieving the kind of understanding that is required.

Although the sum total of problems facing India is unique to that nation, many of her more pressing needs are common to other developing countries. In addition, the problems faced by India (although they may manifest themselves in different forms) are often typical of those found in other developing nations, especially when compared to conditions in the more developed parts of the world. The U.S. executive must be prepared to deal with such an environment on its own terms, and to evaluate his own values and ways of operating in relation to it.

This kind of executive is needed not only in the subsidiary but also in the home office if maximum adaptation is to occur. There is little question that home offices need to develop their own awareness of the problems which face multinational operations. They must be willing to restructure their systems and procedures so as to provide for a greater degree of responsiveness to local needs and requirements.

Many companies, in an effort to make this kind of adjustment, are beginning to show a greater propensity for sharing ownership, and even managerial control. Joint ventures, licensing agreements, sales of securities to local parties, joint management efforts and the employment of foreign nationals in top-level subsidiary and headquarters positions can do much to help the adaptation process.

With respect to the application of managerial know-how, the key element rests in the selection of individuals. U.S. companies have generally done an excellent job of providing adequate physical resources and technological expertise for their overseas subsidiaries. They have been less effective, however, in transmitting managerial know-how.

In order to provide the managerial expertise necessary to operate subsidiaries most efficiently, personnel must be hired who can apply existing managerial technology and train others to do the same. These personnel must be thoroughly familiar with the whole range of managerial techniques developed in the United States, and must have the discrimination to know which ones are applicable to the local environment.

Throughout the study, it was startling to see the close correlation between company success and the employment of managers who had been exposed to both the local and the U.S. cultures. The companies which exhibited the highest degree of economic success were those in which upper-level Indian managers (bringing local environmental knowledge into the picture) had been educated or trained abroad (providing inputs of Western values and Western managerial techniques).

Several conditions must be met in selecting competent managerial personnel. U.S. executives who are sent abroad must be familiar with the environments of developing economies. They must have a broad base of knowledge related to the functional areas requiring the greatest amount of attention in such nations — i.e., those in which the needed managerial skills are most likely to differ from indigenous thought patterns. They must also have the skills necessary to select and train personnel for the subsidiary operations — and especially those needed to establish training programs at all organizational levels. Few of the executives encountered during this study who were selected for overseas positions were chosen according to these criteria.

Finally, it is necessary to achieve a blend between U.S. practices, values, and techniques, and those which characterize the local environment. The U.S.-educated Indian seems to be the most effective agent for achieving these results. This seems to imply that it is easier to acquire U.S. managerial techniques and an overlay of U.S. values than it is to acquire a detailed understanding of and commitment to a foreign environment.

During the period studied, encompassing almost a decade, a chronological pattern of development was observed in U.S. firms, a pattern which is discernible in many developing nations, and will probably be the direction of the future in all of them. Initially, upon entry into the developing economy, the U.S. firm was able to succeed on the basis of its products, technologies, and financial resources. Their success was helped by the fact that U.S. managerial practices are more conducive to a high degree of industrial activity than are traditional Indian patterns. Very often, during this stage, industrial enterprises became indifferent to the long-range trends in the surrounding environment, and complacent with respect to their operating practices, because of the large profits they were generating. This was also a time when these firms wielded substantial power vis-a-vis the local government because their activities were so essential to the growth and development of the economy. Considerable tensions arose because of the fact that many of these firms were committed to foreign operating patterns and unwilling to modify their positions unless forced to do so in bargaining situations. Where they had the upper hand, the degree to which they were willing to change was relatively small. This behavior characterized the operations of many U.S. companies in India through the first half of the 1960s.

However, conditions began to change in India as environmental pressures for greater efficiency increased, and as the more progressive indigenous firms became competitive. At the same time, the world situation began to change, and the government started to achieve some of its economic development objectives. A rapid transition took place beginning in the mid-1960s, which accelerated in the last half of the decade. The more progressive Indian companies began to learn and apply modern managerial techniques — partly as a result of competition with U.S. firms, partly because they hired executives away from U.S. subsidiaries, and partly because of a policy of hiring Indians who were trained in the United States and Europe, and understood these modern practices.

During the transition period, the need for efficient management within foreign subsidiaries increased. Simultaneously, the advantageous bargaining position of the U.S. subsidiaries began to decrease. For example, a foreign pharmaceutical firm, without whose products an important public health program could not have been carried out, suddenly found itself facing intense competition as indigenous firms developed the capacity to make products similar in quality and price. Suddenly the government was less tolerant and less yielding than before, as the focus of bargaining power began to shift. Furthermore, the company discovered that it had built up reservoirs of ill will which came back to haunt it.

For this reason it is important that the U.S. company recognize the need to adapt to the local environment as early as possible. Attitudes relating to the social consciousness of business in a developing country, to good corporate citizenship, and the like, may sometimes be labeled altruistic. However, in the long run, they make sound economic sense. The company which attempts to fit in — which has accepted its responsibilities as a local citizen — is the one most likely to flourish as its host nation moves toward greater economic growth and development. Also, it will probably have provided itself with the best possible protection against the waves of rising anti-foreign feelings which are so common in developing nations.

An examination of the changes which have taken place in India during the period under study, dramatically illustrates the trend we have just described. The move toward Indianization accelerated rapidly in the latter half of the 1960s. More Indians were given responsibility in business operations and greater flexibility was granted to subsidiaries by U.S. parent companies in response to competitive challenges which were nonexistent in the past. As profit margins started to decrease, U.S. companies turned their attention to increasing internal efficiency, keeping costs down, establishing maintenance programs, diversifying, and even relinquishing some ownership. In many cases, this required undoing much of what had been done in the past, since executives had permitted sloppy operating procedures to exist in many functional areas. U.S. firms were able to maintain their lead only because the same problems faced their Indian counterparts. These firms also began intensive reorientation of their value systems, organizational structures, and methods of operation.

This transformation is as yet far from complete. It is a continuing process, and one which will probably take place as long as we have nations at different levels of economic development. However, it would probably be safe to say that companies which have moved most rapidly to the maximum point on the adaptation spectrum are those which have experienced the greatest success during transition periods, and which have the greatest flexibility to adapt to change.

Local companies

The typical Indian firm can learn a great deal by studying the operating practices of its foreign counterparts. It is, however, important for it to know which of these practices are applicable. In many situations, local companies which are experiencing competitive difficulties vis-a-vis foreign operations attempt to reject their own methods of operation and adopt, in their entirety, the techniques of their foreign competitors. This can create many problems, because the local company may not know how to make those particular techniques work. Here again, it is necessary to stress the fact that any managerial system is closely linked to the values and culture — or sub-culture — of the society in which it originates.

Many Indian firms were partially successful in motivating their personnel, or at least satisfying their basic needs. They provided working environments which were more supportive of their employees than those of foreign firms. However, many were not able to call forth the kind of efforts and energies that were needed to compete with aggressive foreign enterprises. Many of their top managers did not understand what it took to operate in a modern industrial environment, rather than in the traditional Indian one.

The indigenous firms which were most successful in overcoming environmental constraints were those that made greatest use of U.S.-educated Indians in their management structures. Even in the more successful family-controlled firms, it was common to send key employees to study abroad.

The Indian companies had no difficulty in determining their degree of commitment to the local environment. Their resources were not spread around the globe, their opportunities were limited, and their stake in making their local operations (and the Indian economy) work was extremely high. Consequently, in many areas, they were willing to take greater risks with capital, new concepts, and new ventures than were their foreign counterparts. These strengths are important with regard to long-term development.

Because of the difference between the traditional environment and the conditions required in an industrial setting, the relatively progressive Indian firms often had another important advantage. Once they recognized and accepted the difference, change, although gradual, became a vital part of the operations. The more successful and progressive firms were continuously exploring their internal operations with a view to making them more efficient and successful. They were forced into this action by the dramatic impact of foreign firms on their economy, which made it apparent that they must change in order to survive. The foreign subsidiary, on the other hand, often entered the environment with a mode of operation that gave rise to immediate success. Consequently, little was done to change managerial approaches until changes in the market and the economic environment made re-evaluation a necessity. Consequently, the Indian firm was often more responsive to innovation than the U.S. company.

This pattern is clearly visible as one looks at India over the entire span of the 1960s. In the early stages, U.S. and other foreign firms held the advantage. Little internal innovation took place in these companies. However, a number of the more progressive Indian firms had begun to develop their internal resources. By the mid-1960s, the situation had reached a new stage, with the Indian firms closing the gap very rapidly, and exerting pressure on U.S. companies. By the end of the decade, many U.S. firms were shaken out of their lethargic state and were beginning to regain momentum. Meanwhile, those Indian firms which had reached comparable stages of internal development as a result of a long and sustained drive were still continuing to innovate at a rapid pace.

TRANSFERABILITY AND APPLICABILITY OF MODERN MANAGEMENT SKILL AND PRACTICE

In essence, this study has revealed that many of the managerial practices and techniques developed in the United States and other industrialized countries can be transferred and applied to developing nations. Some of them can be transferred intact, while others need modification. And of course, some must be discarded and replaced by totally new approaches.

The major factors inhibiting an effective transference appear to be lack of knowledge about the local environment (i.e., how practices must be modified, or what practices must be discarded in favor of new ones) and the lack of a vehicle to actually transfer such managerial techniques. Few executives at operating levels (especially at middle-management levels) have the substantive knowledge to introduce new techniques. The emphasis needs to be placed largely on training, and on the selection of individuals to carry out these functions.

There are ways to analyze such situations — and to do an effective job from the outset. A company does not have to spend ten or fifteen years acquiring experience before it discovers that it must blend into the local environment. By examining, as this book has tried to do, the various elements of the environment and relating them to the requirements for action and decision making in each of the managerial and productive functions of the business firm, a company can anticipate which managerial style is likely to prove most effective and what skills it will require.

This means that, prior to establishing a new venture, an intensive survey must be conducted, encompassing the physical, political, legal, economic, social, educational, and cultural factors within the operating milieu. The company must identify the resources it has available to work in such an environment — people, capital, technology, and management skills. Only then can it plan its operations, both physically and philosophically, so as to achieve maximum long-range benefits from its investment.

It is surprising to see how many companies will sink millions of dollars into an overseas venture, and then either abandon the project, or, through the trial and error process, learn that they must completely alter their style of operation if they are to survive. The relatively small amount which must be invested for research and analysis will yield substantial returns by ensuring that both new and existing ventures have the maximum likelihood of success.

A CONCLUDING COMMENT ON INTERNATIONAL BUSINESS AND THE MULTINATIONAL CORPORATION

In fairness to international corporations it should be stressed that both domestic and international constraints can inhibit them from emerging into genuinely multinational structures of the geocentric type. Such constraints inhibit and retard the international flow of capital, goods and services, people, expertise, and ideas.

What seems to be more and more urgently needed is a reasonably effective supernational world mechanism, or at the least some kind of world charter which would represent virtually all nations and deal more adequately with multinational corporations on a global scale. This would entail bypassing national boundaries; it would stimulate the further de-politicization of international business and reduce the disparities in national policies which vitally affect multinational corporations.

A world-wide mechanism of this type may well become less of a remote possibility as men, and their leaders, come to realize that the present order is too unstable to survive the arms race and the population explosion, or to alleviate the unfulfilled human wants and misery which exist today; moreover, this order is ill-equipped to solve the enormous ecological problems, or to cope with the awesome technological and social revolutions now taking place. It seems essential that public policy emphasize and encourage the expansion of multinational business, since it is one of the few operating structures we have today that can function effectively to strengthen world order.

INDEX

Absenteeism, 160, 197, 198, 287, 529, 532–535

Accounting, 457–459, 461, 462, 506, 548

Achievement and work, attitudes toward, 35, 59, 106–109, 144–152, 522

   class structure, individual mobility and, 146–150

   Communist, 146, 148

   of managers, 113–114, 144, 147, 151, 164, 165

   minority groups and, 147–150

   n-ach (need for achievement), 113, 114, 144–150

   religious values and, 145–146, 148, 149

   Spanish-American, 108–109

   training programs in, 148–149

Adaptation process, 98–99, 104, 111, 414–415, 491, 658–661

"Adaptation Spectrum," 18, 408–409, 412–429, 661

   stereotype firms at extremes of, 409–412

Adelman, A., 66

Advertising, 72, 297–298, 453, 503, 620, 621, 632–633

Agency for International Development (AID), 228, 273, 275, 351

   investment guarantee program, 331

Aid-India Consortium, 326, 346, 353

All India Management Association, 86, 87

Annual Surveys of Industry, 325

Astrology, 102, 163

Attitudes, socio-cultural: toward achievement and work, 35, 59, 106–109, 113–114, 144–152, 164, 165

   toward authority, responsibility, subordinates, 35, 120–133

Attitudes, socio-cultural: toward
    achievement and work:
  toward business management and
    business careers, 35, 111–114,
    118, 159
  toward change, 36, 59, 72, 107, 166–
    167, 445, 447–448
  toward foreigners and things foreign,
    38, 310, 313–315
  toward physical and manual labor,
    114, 115, 480–481, 495, 522
  toward public sector positions, 116
  religious views and values, 99, 102,
    104–108, 110–111, 145–146, 149,
    155, 163, 181, 282–283, 308–309
  toward risk taking, 36, 164–166
  toward scientific method, 36, 59,
    161–163
  toward wealth and material gain, 36,
    158–161
Authority:
  attitudes toward, 135, 102, 120–133
  foreign firm and, 130–133
  indigenous firm and, 128–130
  and organizational structures, 127–
    128, 130–131, 470
  spectrum (hypothetical) of opposite
    views, 121–126
  of Western managers, 130–132
  functional, 395–396, 483–484
Automation, 378, 566, 574, 578–582

Bacon, Francis, 162
Balance of payments, 39, 338–343, 349,
  364
Banking and monetary policy, 36, 254–
  261, 387–388
Birla's, 119, 150, 211, 241, 334
"Black money," 189, 257, 272
Blocs, political and economic, 38, 321–
  322

Calvin, John, 145
Capital markets, 37, 250, 271–277, 346–
  352, 387, 646–647
  (See also Banking and monetary policy;
    Financial institutions)
Capital spending, 393–394, 458, 642–645
Capitalism, 11–12, 145, 238–239
Caste system (see India)
Chandey, K. T., 231
Change, attitudes toward, 36, 59, 72, 107,
  166–167, 445, 447–448
Class structure and individual mobility,
  35, 152–158, 522
  and achievement motivation, 146–150
  and occupations, 89, 105–106, 153–155
  and recruitment of managers, 147
  and staffing decisions, 152–156
Colombo Plan, 319
Common markets, 321, 322, 387
Communication and information flows,
  67, 102, 396, 399, 433, 444, 522–525
  literacy problems, 66–73, 523
Communications systems, 295–298, 379–
  380
Communism and Communists, 11, 146,
  148
  economic system, 238–239, 253, 261
  Indian Communist Party, 135, 543, 555
  unions (AITUC) in India, 135, 136, 557,
    558
Communist nations, 79, 253, 261, 280,
  306, 319, 350, 352, 387, 603, 656
Compensation systems, 160–161, 190,
  388, 526, 548–552
  "dearness allowances," 160, 198, 199,
    514, 530, 549
  "efficiency bar," 549
  fixed-increment system, 198–199, 508,
    549
  fringe benefits, 199–200, 512, 514, 548
  incentive systems, 160–161, 528–531,
    549, 550

Compensation systems:
  legal aspects of, 196–200, 286, 528
  levels of, 512–515, 549, 551–552
Computers, 72, 93, 379, 441–442, 459,
  464, 509
Consulting services, 231–232, 299
Control, 41, 71–72
  as critical managerial element, 30
  financial, 393–395, 457–459, 461, 462,
    548
  information systems and, 460–463
  in international enterprise management,
    451–469
  as managerial function, 27–28
  marketing, 452–453
  in multinational corporation manage-
    ment, 380–383, 393–395, 472, 658
  procurement, 456–457
  production, 453–456
  standards, 452–459, 461, 464, 468
  techniques, 459–460
  tight versus loose systems of, 465–467
  timeliness of corrective action, 461,
    464–465
  unintended effects of, 467–469
  (*See also* Inventory control)
Cooley Funds, 352, 357*n.*
Cooperation as environmental factor, 35,
  58–59, 133–143
Copen, Melvyn, 13
Critical elements of management process
  (*see* Management process)

Defense of India Act, 192, 202
Delphi Technique, 54, 58
Desai, Moraji, 212
Direction, leadership, and motivation:
  absenteeism and, 529, 532–535
  communication, 522–525
  cooperation and trust, 524–525
  as critical managerial element, 31, 42

Direction, leadership, and motivation:
  in international enterprise management,
    519–536
  leadership styles, 519–521
  as managerial function, 29
  of managerial personnel, 397–398, 525–
    528
  in multinational corporation manage-
    ment, 399
  of nonmanagerial personnel, 528–532
  status symbols, 514–515, 526, 528
  supervisory techniques, 521–522
Distribution channels, 24, 192, 390,
  627–629
Dutt Report on Industrial Licensing
  Policy, 194, 245–248

Economic factors, 36–37, 39, 40, 234–
  299
  balance of payments, 338–343, 349,
    364
  banking system and monetary policy,
    36, 254–261, 387–388
  capital markets, 37, 250, 271–272, 346–
    352, 387, 646–647
  factors of production, 37, 277–288
  fiscal policy, 37, 261–267, 387
  foreign aid, 346–354
  in international environment, 39, 40,
    338–354
  international trade patterns, 343–346
  market size, 37, 288–290
  in multinational environment, 387–
    388
  price stability, 267–271
  social overhead capital, 37, 290–299
  type of economic system, 238–239
Economic success indicators, 417–419,
  423–426, 428, 429
Economic systems, types of, 11–12,
  239–251, 253

Economy (national), 238–253
key factors for efficiency of, 251–253
planning and resource allocation, 187–188, 218, 239, 243–245, 251–253, 655
type of economic system, 238–239
Educational environment, 35, 41–42, 58, 65–95, 383, 471
in India (*see* India)
Efficiency comparison study, 43–62
Efficiency indicators, 44–53, 417–419, 425–429
Employment agencies, 143, 505
Enterprise (productive) functions, 23–26, 31–32
Environmental constraints, 5–7, 10, 32–43
and critical managerial elements, 40–43
matrix of inter-relationships, 41–43
economic, 36–37, 39, 234–299
educational, 35, 65–95
international, 34, 37–39, 302–354
classification scheme, 38–39
multinational, 375–388
national, 33–37
classification scheme, 35–37
political-legal, 36, 38, 181–232
socio-cultural, 35–36, 38, 98–100
(*See also* specific constraints)
Equipment breakdowns, 55–62, 588–589
European Economic Community (EEC), 321, 651
Exploitation, 11, 112, 195, 540, 541
charged against U.S. operations abroad, 137, 365–366, 435, 513–514
Export-Import Bank, 273, 353
Export marketing, 329–331, 634–639
Exports (*see* Export marketing; Imports and exports; India)

Factors of production, 37, 277–288
Farmer, Richard, viii, 13, 111

Finance:
control, 393–395, 458
costs and cost control, 457–459, 461, 462, 548, 594–595, 647–648
as critical managerial element, 32, 42
as enterprise function, 25
financial institutions, 37, 39, 271–272, 346–350
interest rates, 468–649
in international enterprise management, 641–649
international financial organizations, 346–350
in multinational corporation management, 391
spending limits for subsidiaries, 644–645
stock dividends and prices, 649
types of financing and sources of funds, 645–647
(*See also* Banking and monetary policy; Capital markets)
Fiscal policy, 37, 261–267, 387
Food for Peace Program (PL 480), 351–352, 357n.
Foreign aid, 312–313, 343, 346–354
international financial organizations and, 346–349
U.S. programs, 350–352
Foreign exchange, 337–341, 387–388
controls, 38, 215, 224–227, 248, 324, 337–338
Foreign investment, 9, 370, 316, 331–335, 370–371
AID investment guarantee program, 331
Foreign policy, 10–12, 36, 59, 203–206
Foreign subsidiaries, 119–121, 130–133, 658–661
chronological pattern of development in, 660
management of (*see* International enterprise management)
Foreign trade, 343–346, 386–387

France:
  banking system, 260
  "Le Plan," 251–252, 655

General Agreement on Tariffs and Trade
  (GATT), 319–320
Gandhi, Indira, 92, 156, 209, 211–214,
  216, 231, 259–260, 564
Gandhi, Mohandas (Mahatma), 106, 207,
  308
Giri, V. V., 212, 259
Government regulation, 213–232
Government relations, 138–140, 435–436,
  560–564

Hall, Edward, 103
Hazari report, 247
Hinduism, 99, 102, 104–108, 110–111,
  125, 149, 282–283, 308
  and achievement and work motivation,
    145–146
  fatalism concept, 69, 102, 106–107,
    149, 163, 166, 432
Husain, Zakir, 155

Imperialism, 365, 656
Imports and exports, 9, 306, 310
  in India (see India)
  international trade patterns, 39, 343–
    346
  restrictions on, 38, 59, 205, 323–331,
    368
India:
  agriculture, 280–284, 286, 288
  attitudes and views (see socio-cultural
    attitudes below)
  balance of payments, 341–343
  banking system and monetary policy,
    255–261
  devaluation of rupee, 205, 224, 257

India:
  banking system and monetary policy:
    equity and "effective say" in loanee
      firms, 250, 261
    nationalization of banks, 188, 212,
      259–261, 276, 284
    black market activities, 159, 192, 244,
      257, 261, 326, 338, 599, 602–603
    bribery practices, 186, 191, 196, 218,
      256, 293, 563, 598, 606
    capital buildup, 287–288
    capital markets, 250, 272–277, 284–285
    development finance corporations
      (DFC's), 272–274
    foreign, 274–275
    interest rates, 255, 258–259, 274–
      275, 648–649
    private deposits, 258–259, 275, 646–
      649
    securities exchanges, 275–276
    (See also banking and monetary
      policy above)
  caste system, 89, 91, 125, 128, 184
    and achievement motivation, 149–150
    described, 105–107
    and discrimination in employment,
      153, 156, 157
    and occupations, 89, 105–106,
      153–155
    staffing and, 152–155
  class structure and individual mobility,
    152–158
  communications systems, 295–298,
    379, 380
  Congress Party, 204, 207–209, 211–
    212, 221, 236, 241
  Communist Party, 135, 543, 555
  consulting services, 299
  defense and military policy, 201–203
  devaluation of rupee, 205, 224, 257
  Directorate General for Technical
    Development (DGTD), 215, 222,
    225–228

India:

Dutt Report on Industrial Licensing
Policy, 194, 245-248
economic performance, overview of,
234-251, 253, 255-267, 269-277,
279-299
economic reforms proposed and under
way, 245-251
education, 68-95
attitudes toward, 68-69, 89-91
caste system and, 89, 154-155
company literacy programs, 71, 73,
511
company primary and secondary
schools, 70, 90, 511
cooperative work-study programs, 78,
80
higher education, 79-86
India Institutes of Management, 80,
83-84, 87, 90
India Institutes of Technology, 80,
82, 84, 90
literacy level, 66-73
management-development programs,
non-company, 86-88, 509
primary and secondary schools, 73-75
semiprofessional and vocational
training, 75-78
educational match with industry
requirements, 81-83, 91-95
misuse of high-talent manpower, 95
staffing problems, 70, 77, 93-94
unemployment and shortages, 92-93
employment data, 496, 497
factors of production, 277-288
family system, extended (joint), 105,
107, 125-127, 133, 282, 470, 540,
541
financial institutions (see banking system and monetary policy and
capital markets above)
fiscal policy, 262-267
fishing and forestry industries, 284-285

India:

foreign aid, 213-313, 343, 347, 350-354
foreign exchange controls, 215, 224-
227, 248, 337-338
foreign investments in, 307, 316, 332-
335
foreign policy, 203-206
foreign trade, 326-327, 344-346
Fourth (Five-Year) Plan, 237-238, 240,
264, 279-280, 283-285, 287, 291,
293-295, 316, 333, 342-343, 345,
354
government-industry relations, 118,
138-140, 159, 561-564
government regulation, 213-232
administrative problems, 218-221
national policies, goals, priorities,
216-218
political organization and regulatory
bureaucracy, 59, 213-216
recommendations for, 229-232,
654-655
government structure, 213-216
Hinduism, 99, 102, 104-108, 110-111,
125, 149, 282-283, 308
imports and exports, 224-227, 248,
257, 324-331, 344-346, 581, 587,
602-604, 607, 634-639
government trading corporations,
326-327, 330
new import policy, 326-328, 330
Industrial Cost and Prices Bureau, 250-
251
industrial enterprise management, 405-
664
(See also International enterprise
management; Multinational corporation management and specific
managerial elements)
industry: capacity utilization, 244-245,
269-270
New Industrial Policy, 246-250, 261
organization of, 239-242

India:

  information system, 165, 243, 444–
    445, 461–463
  international business trends and impli-
    cations, 654–655
  international organization memberships,
    319–322
  labor and population, 285–287
  labor movement (*see* union–manage-
    ment relations *below*)
  language problems, 67, 69, 102, 155,
    208–209, 207, 311
  legal environment, overview of, 183–
    186
    law enforcement deficiencies, 184–
      186, 196, 202
  legal regulation: of domestic flow of
    goods, 190–191
    Factories Act, 196, 240–242
    of foreign firms and personnel,
      200–201, 316–319
    of labor and personnel, 195–200,
      515–574
    of monopolies and restrictive trade,
      194–195, 247, 249–250, 330
    patent laws, 193–194, 319, 618
    of profit remissions, 335–337
    of quality controls, 187
    of securities exchanges, 275–276
    of supplier–customer relations, 191–
      192
    tax laws (*see* taxation *below*)
    of unions, 543–545
  licensing (industrial), 187–188, 191,
    194, 211, 214, 215, 218, 243–250,
    255, 267, 330–331, 564, 604
    decision procedures, 222–223
    Dutt Report on Industrial Licensing
      Policy, 194, 245–248
    government freeze on, 564
  literacy levels, 66–73
  managing agencies, 119, 240, 241, 249,
    476, 477, 484, 644

India:

  market size, 289–290
  mineral resources and mining industry,
    279–280
  Ministry of Foreign Trade, 215, 219,
    224, 225, 327, 330–331, 586, 636
  Ministry of Industrial Development,
    214, 215, 222, 225, 227, 228, 250,
    330, 636
  national economic planning, 187–188,
    218, 243–245
    [*See also* Fourth (Five-Year) Plan
      above]
  national ideology, 307–309
  nationalism, 311–313
  nationalization of banks, 188, 212,
    259–261, 276, 284
  nationalization of foreign trade, 326–
    327
  natural resources, 279–285
  New Industrial Policy, 246–250, 261
  oil concessions, 320–321
  political environment: current situation,
    210–213
    historical perspective, 207–210
    stability, 207–213, 308–309, 311–
      312, 316
    state-level problems, 221–222
  power and water supply, 291
  price controls, 192–193, 250–251
  price stability, 270–271
  research and development, 616–619
  social overhead capital, 290–299
  socio-cultural attitudes: toward achieve-
    ment and work, 106–107, 149–
    152
    toward authority, responsibility, and
      subordinates, 125–133
    toward business management and
      business careers, 113–114, 118
    toward change, 107–108, 166–167
    fatalism concept, 69, 102, 106–107,
      149, 163, 166, 432

India:
  socio-cultural attitudes:
    toward foreigners and things foreign,
      311, 314–315
    Hinduism (*see* Hinduism)
    passive resistance ("Ahimsa") philo-
      sophy, 308
    toward public sector positions, 116
    toward risk taking, 164–166
    toward scientific method, 163
    toward wealth and material gain,
      159–161
  socio-cultural environment, 102, 117–
    118, 125–130, 143, 149–150, 153–
    156
    cooperation, interorganizational and
      individual, 133–143
    evolutionary stages of management
      and, 115–117
    overview of, 104–111
    U.S.-Indian interface, case studies of,
      172–180
    (*See also* caste system *and* class
      structure and individual
      mobility *above*)
  stereotype of traditional firm, 409–411
  taxation, 139, 189–191, 213, 265–267
    of foreign firms and personnel, 317–
      319
    "Octroi" taxes, 191
  trade agreements, 319–321, 346
  transportation, 191, 292–295, 629
  union-management relations, 134–137,
    531–532, 539, 543–559
    bargaining issues, 548–551
    foreign company and, 542–543
    "Gheraos," 555–556, 558, 559
    labor courts, 198–200
    labor legislation, 195–200
    labor movement, 538–540
    legal basis of unionism, 543–545, 549
    management attitudes, 545–547, 551–
      553

India:
  union-management relations:
    politics and, 135–137, 210, 537–538,
      555–556
    recent findings, 554–556
    union federations, 135
    unions, nature of, 540–542
  Industrialization, 6–7, 653–657
    Western values and, 408, 413
  Information systems, 56, 165, 239, 243,
    252, 382, 396, 399, 444–445, 460–
    463
  International business:
    as agent of social change, 98–100, 103–
      104, 119–120, 157, 305, 363
    trends and implications, 650–662
  International corporations, types of, 362–
    363
  International enterprise management,
    405–664
    control, 451–469
    direction, leadership, and motivation,
      519–536
    finance, 641–649
    government relations, 560–564
    marketing and exports, 620–640
    organization, 470–493
    overview of, 405–429
    planning and innovation, 431–450
    procurement and imports, 596–613
    production, 565–595
    research and development, 614–619
    staffing and personnel, 494–518
    stereotype of highly Americanized
      firm, 411–412
    union-management relations, 537–559
  International environment, 34, 37–40,
    302–354
    balance of payments, 338–343
    blocs, political and economic, 321–322,
      387
    economic factors, 338–354
    foreign aid, 312–313, 343, 346–354

International environment:
  foreign exchange controls, 38, 215, 224–227, 248, 324, 337–338
  foreign firms and personnel, legal rules for, 316–319
  foreign investment, 9, 307, 316, 331–335, 370–371
  foreigners, attitudes toward, 310–315
  import-export regulations, 38, 323–331
  international organizations and agreements, 319–322, 346–350
  national ideology, 303–309, 313
  nationalism, 309–313
  political ideology, 315–316
  political-legal factors, 315–338
  profit remission restrictions, 335–337
  taxation of foreign firms and personnel, 317–319
  trade patterns, 343–346
  U.S. investment and capital export restrictions, 331
International environmental constraints, 34, 302–354
  classification of, 38–39
  inter-relationship with national factors, 39–40
International Monetary Fund (IMF), 320 341, 349–350
International organizations, 39
  financial, 346–350
  political and economic blocs, 38, 321–322
  trade and treaty groups, 319–321
International subsidiaries (see Foreign subsidiaries; International enterprise management)
Inventory control, 382, 612, 634
  procurement and, 399, 608–609
  production management and, 573, 575, 577–578
  standards for, 457, 468
Investment guarantees, 319, 331

Johnson, Lyndon B., 306, 331

Kapp, H. William, 105, 107
Kidder, D., 154

Labor movement (see Union-management relations)
Labor officers, 76
Lambert, Richard, 107
Language problems, 67, 102, 155, 208–209, 297, 311
Leadership (see Direction, leadership, and motivation)
"Le Plan," 252
Legal regulation, 36, 181–200
  contracts and documentation, 385, 386
  of foreign exchange, 337–338
  of foreign investment, 331–335
  of foreign trade, 386–387
  of imports and exports, 323–331
  international restrictions, 323–338
  and multinational operations, 385–387
  U.S. antitrust laws, 364, 386–387
Licensing, industrial, 187–188, 191, 194, 211, 214, 215, 218, 243–250, 255, 267, 330–331, 564, 604
  decision procedures, 222–223
  Dutt Report on Industrial Licensing Policy, 194, 245–248
  government freeze on, 564
  Monopolies and Restrictive Trade Practices Bill, 194, 247, 249–250
  New Industrial Policy on, 246–249
Linking operations, multinational, 375–383
  and degree of problem intensification, 381–382
  distance problems, 378–381
  parent-subsidiary relations and, 376–377

Literacy, 35, 612, 626
advertising and, 72, 297, 632
company programs to improve, 71, 73, 511
managerial implications of, 72-73
staffing problems, 70, 73, 494, 495
Litwin, George, 110
Lokanathan Committee, 248

McClelland, David, 144, 148, 149
Maintenance, 455-456
of automatic equipment, 579, 580
equipment down-time, unanticipated, 56-62, 588-589
preventive maintenance programs, 570-571, 580
production management and, 569-571
Make-or-buy decisions, 57, 600-602
Management, 21-22, 104
enterprise (productive) functions, 23-26, 31-32
evolutionary stages of, 114-120
of international subsidiaries (see International enterprise management)
"know-how," 4-7
managerial functions, 26-31
of multinational corporations (see Multinational corporation management)
socio-cultural views of, 111-114, 118
styles of, 121-126, 383
what and who it is, 21-23
Management transference process (see Transferability of management know-how)
Management development, 369, 508-512, 516-518, 520-521, 523, 525
Indian Institutes of Management, 80, 83-84, 87
non-company, 35, 86-88, 509
use of subsidiary for, 390, 393, 397, 498

Management process, critical elements of, 29-32, 40-43, 50-51, 53-62
classification of, 30-32
control, 30, 41
direction, leadership, motivation, 31, 42
enterprise (productive) functions of, 31-32
environmental constraints and, 32-44, 50-51
related to managerial effectiveness and productive efficiency, 44-62
finance, 32, 42
in international subsidiaries (see International enterprise management)
managerial functions of, 26-29
marketing, 31-42
in multinational corporations, 388-400
(See also Multinational corporation management)
and national ideology, 305
organization, 30, 41
planning and innovation, 30, 41
production and procurement, 31, 42
public relations, 32
research and development, 32, 42
staffing, 30-31, 41
(See also specific elements)
Managerial effectiveness, 43-62
comparative research model, 51
comparative study of matched firms, 49-52
control conditions for comparisons, 48
efficiency indicators, 44-53, 417-419, 425-429
equipment breakdown study, 55-62
objectives, evaluation of, 48-49
Managerial functions, 26-29
Managers:
achievement drive and effectiveness of, 113-114, 144, 147, 151, 164, 165

Managers:

attitudes of, toward authority, responsibility, and subordinates, 35, 120–
125

"father" view of, in Indian firms, 129–
131, 410, 523, 524

in foreign socio-cultural environment,
100–104

insensitivity of, to local values, 369,
552–553

motivation of, 397–398, 525–528

nationality of: as effectiveness factor,
131, 398, 416, 447–448, 495–496,
520, 659

    and recruitment, 368–369, 398, 499–
    505, 520

    and union relations, 137, 545–547,
    551–553

procurement, 596–598, 601, 606, 612–
613

of public sector enterprises, 116

recruitment of, 147, 151–152, 658–659

role conflicts of, 398

selection criteria for middle managers
and specialists, 499–500, 503

selection criteria for top executives,
151–152, 397, 398, 497–500, 502–
503, 658–659

socio-cultural attitudes toward management careers, 35, 111–114, 118, 159

turnover, short-term, 394, 397–398
497, 500, 521

Managing agencies, 119, 240, 241, 249,
476, 477, 484, 644

Market size, 37, 388–290, 615

Marketing, 24

control standards, 452–453

as critical managerial element, 31, 42

customers returns and complaints,
633–634

distribution channels, 192, 390, 627–
629

as enterprise (productive) function, 24

Marketing:

exports, 634–639

in international enterprise management,
620–640

in multinational corporation management, 390, 391

product lines, 395–396, 624–627

sales growth patterns and trends, 623–
624

sales promotion, 631–633

in India, 72, 621–640

packaging and, 611–612, 625–626

pricing and price policies, 24, 629–631

sales force performance, 452–453, 623–
624

Marx, Karl, 11

Mead, Margaret, 103, 108

Menon, Krishna, 201

Monopolies, 194–195, 247, 249–250

Mufatlal, 241

Multinational corporate system, elements
of, 375

Multinational corporation management,
375–400

communication and information flows,
399

controls, 380–383, 393–395, 472,
658

direction and leadership, 399

effects of parent firm on foreign operations, 388–389

finance, 391

marketing, 390, 391

multinational environment and, 375–
388

organization, 395–397

planning, 389–390

policies and problems, 390–393

production and procurement, 392

research and development, 392

short-term turnover of subsidiary
managers, 397–398

staffing, 392–393, 397–398

Multinational corporations, 361–373, 663–664
  benefits to host countries from, 370–372
  competitive advantages of, 372–373
  criticisms and charges against, 137, 365–366, 435, 513–514, 656
  differences between international and multinational firms, 389
    conceptual, 361–363
    structural, 377
  environmental factors and, 363–364
  ethonocentric, 50, 363–364, 367, 369, 376–378, 414, 415, 473, 484, 485
  geocentric, 362, 363, 473–474, 485, 663
  management of (see Multinational corporation management)
  multinational environment and, 375–388
  parent-subsidiary relations, 376–378, 380
  polycentric, 50, 363
  U.S. subsidiaries abroad, performance of, 658–661
Multinational environment, 375–388
  definition of, 376
  and degree of problem intensification, 381–382
  distance problems, 378–381
  economic factors, 387–388
  educational factors, 383
  legal factors, 385–387
  linking problems, 375–383
  and management process, 388–389
    (See also Multinational corporation management)
  political factors, 384–387
  and product characteristics, 384
  socio-cultural factors, 383–384

n-ach (achievement need), 113, 114, 144–150
Nair Kusum, 109

National economic planning, 239, 251–253
  in France, 251–252, 655
  in India, 187–188, 218, 243–245
National environmental constraints, 33–37
  classification of, 35–37
  as critical managerial element, 41–43
National ideology, 303–309, 313
Nationalism, 309–313
Nationalization, 386
  in France, 260
  in India, 188, 212, 259–261, 276, 284, 326–327
Natural resources, 278–279
Nehru, Jawaharlal, 207, 209

Oil concessions, 319–330
Organization:
  administration as, 21–22
  authority: functional, 483–484
    responsibility and superior-subordinate relationships, 127–133, 470
  committees, directors and group decision making, 484–488
  centralization versus decentralization, 472–476
  confusion and friction in, 488–490
  as critical managerial element, 30, 41
  departmentation and grouping of activities, 479–480
  "deputy" system in India, 477, 478, 502
  flexibility of, to meet change, 492–493
  informal, 490–492
  in international enterprise management, 470–493
  as managerial function, 28
  middle management, role of, 130–131
  in multinational corporation management, 395–397
  of multinational versus international company, 376–377

Organization:
  size, 471–472
  socio-cultural environment and patterns
    of, 127–133, 470–471, 488–489,
    493
  spans of control and organizational
    levles, 477–479
  staff services, use of, 482–483
  work specialization and division of
    labor, 480–482
Organizations, international, 39
    economic and political (blocs),
      321–322
    financial, 346–350
    trade and treaty, 319–321

Packaging, 379, 382, 625–626
  illiteracy and, 612, 626
  standardization, 610, 612
Parent-subsidiary relations, 376–378
  "appendage" view of foreign operations,
    376–377
  authority and, 472–476
  staff services and, 482–483
Patent protection, 193–194, 319, 618
Phatak, Arvind, 13
Planning and innovation, 432–450
  as critical managerial element, 30, 41
  employee participation in, 442–443
  flexibility of plans, 438–440
  goal-setting, 389–393, 431–434, 436,
    438
  information problems, 444–445
  and risk taking and change, 445–448
  in international enterprise management,
    431–450
  managerial approaches to, 443–444
  as managerial function, 27
  methods, tools, techniques, 440–442
  in multinational corporation manage-
    ment, 389–390
  multinational environment and, 382

Planning and innovation:
  performance, planned versus actual,
    448–450
  of procurement, 440–441, 599–600
  of products and product lines, 436–437,
    446
  sales forecasts and targest, 437–438,
    440–441
  and socio-cultural values, 432
  time horizons and types of plans, 434–
    438
Planning, national economic (see
    National economic planning)
Political factors, 36, 41–42, 181–183,
    201–213, 221–222, 384–385
  critical managerial elements and, 41–42
  defense and military policy, 201–203
  economic and power blocs, 321–322
  foreign policy, 203–206
  government regulation of industry (see
    Government regulation)
  ideology, 38, 146, 148, 315–316
  international organizations and treaty
    obligations, 319–321
  in multinational environment, 384–387
  stability, national, 206–213
  (See also Legal regulation)
Political ideology, 38, 146, 148, 315–316
Price controls, 192–193, 250–251, 269,
    630
Prices:
  of imports in open and black markets,
    602–604
  stability problems, 267–271
  transfer, 368, 385
Pricing and price policies, 24, 204,
    629–631
Procurement, 23, 58, 475, 606
  control standards, 456–457
  as critical managerial element, 31, 42
  import problems and, 602–605
  in international enterprise management,
    596–613

Procurement:
  inventory management and, 599, 608–609
  make-or-buy decisions, 57, 600–602
  manager, 596–598, 601, 606, 612–613
  in multinational corporation management, 392
  planning, 440–441, 599–600
  policies and problems in multinational firms, 392
  rejection rates on incoming supplies, 606–607
  standardization and, 611–612
  storage facilities and management, 610–611
  supplier development and selection, 605–606
  timing of, 607–608
  vertical integration and, 601–602
Product standardization, cultural factors in, 384
Production, 79
  automation, 578–582
  capacity utilization, 269–270, 583–588
  as critical managerial element, 31, 42
  as enterprise function, 23–24
  equipment down-time, 588–589
  equipment productivity, 589–590
  in international enterprise management, 565–595
  inventory levels and, 573–575, 577–578
  labor productivity, 455, 535–536, 590–591
  labor utilization, 573–574, 576–577
  maintenance, 569–571
  manufacturing costs, 594–595
  material wastage, reject rates and scrap levels, 591–594
  in multinational corporation management, 392
  organization of, 567–569
  plants and facilities, 582–583
  quality control, 571–573

Production:
  safety, 583
  size of runs, 575
  stabilization efforts, 573–574
  training, 566, 576–577, 580–581
Productive functions, 23–26, 31–32
Productivity:
  automation and, 580
  equipment, 589–590
  labor, 455, 535–536, 590–591
Profit remission restrictions, 38, 335–337
Public Law 480, 351–353, 357n.
Public relations, 25–26, 203, 306
  as critical managerial element, 32, 42
  as enterprise function, 25–26
  government relations, 560–564
  in international enterprise management, 560–564, 537–559
  union-management relations, 537–559
Public sector enterprises, 116, 200, 211
  in India, 240, 246
  views of managerial jobs in, 116
Purchasing (see Procurement)

Quality control, 187, 454
  automation and, 578–579
  production management and, 571–573
Quality standards, 191–192, 384, 567, 592–594, 627
  for incoming materials, 606–607

Religious and cultural views, 102, 163
  Buddhism, 99
  Calvanism and Protestantism, 99, 145, 146
  Catholicism, 99
  and discrimination in employment, 155
  fatalism concept, 69, 102, 106–107, 149, 163, 166
  Hinduism, 99, 102, 104–108, 110–111, 125, 145–146, 149, 282–283, 308–309

Research and development, 143
  centralization of, 367-368
  as critical managerial element, 32, 42
  as enterprise (productive) function,
    24-25
  in international enterprise management,
    614-619
  in multinational corporation manage-
    ment, 392
  staff members, 482, 483
Reserve Bank of India Bulletin, 223, 325
Richman, Barry M., 13
Risk taking, 445-446
  attitudes toward, 36, 164-166

Sales promotion, 631-633
Scientific method:
  attitudes toward, 36, 59, 161-163
  and risk taking, 164
Service fees, 367
Shastri, 209
Social overhead capital, 37, 290-299
Socio-cultural factors, 40-42, 98-180,
    303-315, 383-384
  achievement and work, attitudes toward,
    144-150
  authority, responsibility, and subordi-
    nates: attitudes toward, 120-121
  foreign firms and, 130-133
  framework for analysis of, 121-125
  in India and other developing coun-
    tries, 125-130
  business management and business
    careers, views of, 111-116, 118
  change, attitudes toward, 166-167
  class structure and individual mobility,
    152-158, 522
  cooperation, extent of, 58-59, 133-143
  and evolutionary overview of manage-
    ment, 114-116
  fatalism concept, 69, 102, 106-107,
    149, 163, 166, 432

Socio-cultural factors:
  foreigners and things foreign, attitudes
    toward, 310, 313-315
  Indian-U.S. interface, case studies of,
    172-180
  international business as agent of change
    in, 98-100, 103-104, 119-120, 157,
    305, 363
  in international environment, 38,
    303-315
  international executive, orientation of,
    100-104
  language, 67, 69, 102, 155, 208-209,
    297, 311
  and mobility of multinational personnel,
    383-384
  in multinational environment, 383-384
  national, 35-36, 98-180
  nationalism and national ideology,
    303-313
  physical and manual labor, views of,
    114, 115, 480-481, 495, 522
  and product characteristics, 384
  public sector management jobs, views
    of, 116
  religious views and values (*see* Religious
    and cultural views)
  risk taking, attitudes toward, 164-166
  scientific method, view of, 161-163
  wealth and material gain, view of,
    158-161
Staffing, 26, 28, 57, 382, 494-518
  appraisals, promotions, and raises,
    506-508
  caste system and, 91, 152-155
  civil service and government agencies,
    208, 214-216, 219-221
  class structure and, 152-158, 522
  compensation (*see* Compensation
    systems)
  as critical managerial element, 30-31, 41
  discrimination in hiring, 147, 153, 155-
    158

Staffing:
  dismissals, layoff, turnover, 197, 198,
    200, 286, 515–517
  employment data, 496–497
  foreign personnel, legal rules for, 316–
    318
  in international enterprise management,
    494–518
  job descriptions, 506, 507, 576
  labor officers, 76
  literacy problems, 70–73, 494, 495, 511
  as managerial function, 26, 28
  in multinational corporation manage-
    ment, 383–384, 392–393, 397–398
  and mobility of multinational personnel,
    383–384
  personnel records, 505–506
  recruitment and personnel selection,
    497–505
    local nationals, 501–505
    parent country nationals, 497–500
    third country nationals, 500–501
    selection criteria: for middle managers
      and specialists, 499–500, 503
    for skilled workers, 495, 505, 510
    for top (expatriate) managers, 151–
      152, 397, 398, 497–500, 502–
      503, 658–659
  temporary and casual employees, 197–
    198, 515–516, 574
  training, 508–512
    (See also Management development;
      Training, employee)
  turnover, management, continuity and
    succession problems, 397–398, 521
  unskilled workers, 494–495, 505
  women, 156, 196
Stereotypes of overseas enterprises:
  American, 411–412
  traditional Indian, 409–411
Storage facilities, 291, 292, 610–611, 629
Subsidiaries, management of (see International enterprise management)

Suggestions systems, 530, 577
Supervisory techniques, 521–522
Supplier relations, 58, 142, 605–606, 647

Tanden, P., 231
Tapline (Trans-Arabian Pipeline Com-
  pany), 305–306
Tariffs, 319, 320, 322–324
Tata Industries Ltd., 87, 90, 119, 130,
  150, 165, 240–241
Taxation, 139, 262, 364, 385
Time standards, 455, 456
Training:
  employee, 149, 510–511, 516, 522, 580
    apprenticeships, 73–74, 198, 495, 510
    cooperative work-study programs, 76,
      78, 80
    literacy programs, 71, 73, 511
    in skills, 566, 576–577, 580–581
  management (see Management develop-
    ment)
Training programs, achievement, 148–149
Transfer pricing, 368, 385
Transferability of management know-how,
  4–7, 11–12, 100–101, 104, 111, 405–
  406, 662–663
  adaptation spectrum, 408–409, 412–
    429
Transportation, 191, 291–295, 378–379,
  607–608, 629

Union–management relations, 134–137,
  513–514, 537–550
  in India (see India)
United Nations, 112, 319, 321
United States:
  capital exports restrictions, 306, 331
  charges against U.S. firms abroad, 365–
    369, 656
  foreign aid programs, 350–353
  foreign investment, 9, 331–333

United States:
  government role in international
    business, 656–657
  restrictions on trade with Communist
    nations, 306, 387, 656
  subsidiaries abroad, performance of,
    658–661
    chronological pattern of development
      in, 660

Wages (*see* Compensation systems)
Warehousing, 291, 292, 610–611, 629
Waste disposal, 298–299

Wealth and material gain, attitudes
  toward, 36, 158–161, 211, 272
Weber, Max, 145
Women, status of, 156, 196
Work, socio-cultural attitudes toward, 35,
  59, 108–109, 144–152
  physical labor and, 90, 480–481, 495,
    522
Work specialization and division of labor,
  57
  social taboos and, 153–154, 480–
    481
World Bank, 264, 273, 346–348, 350–
  352, 354

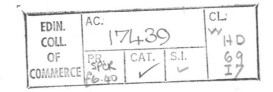